England's Islands in a Sea of Troubles

England's Islands in a Sea of Troubles

DAVID CRESSY

OXFORD

UNIVERSITY PRESS

OXFORD
UNIVERSITY PRESS

Great Clarendon Street, Oxford, OX2 6DP,
United Kingdom

Oxford University Press is a department of the University of Oxford.
It furthers the University's objective of excellence in research, scholarship,
and education by publishing worldwide. Oxford is a registered trade mark of
Oxford University Press in the UK and in certain other countries

© David Cressy 2020

The moral rights of the author have been asserted

First Edition published in 2020

Impression: 1

Published in the United States of America by Oxford University Press
198 Madison Avenue, New York, NY 10016, United States of America

British Library Cataloguing in Publication Data
Data available

Library of Congress Control Number: 2020937774

ISBN 978-0-19-885660-3

DOI: 10.1093/oso/9780198856603.001.0001

Printed and bound by
CPI Group (UK) Ltd, Croydon, CR0 4YY

Acknowledgements

My core concern as a historian has always been to explore relations between the centre and the periphery, the metropolis and the margins, elite and popular viewpoints, and official and unofficial religion. This curiosity now extends to England's island fringe. My research changed direction when Vanessa Wilkie, keeper of British manuscripts at the Huntington Library, showed me a recently acquired compendium, in different hands and languages, of protocols, precedents, and correspondence concerning the governance of Guernsey from the sixteenth to the eighteenth centuries. I have been puzzling about it ever since. Darryl Ogier, archivist to the States of Guernsey, helped me understand the context and significance of this volume, and has been generous in directing me to related island sources. Thanks are due too to the archivists and librarians at the Jersey Archives and the Lord Coutanche Library, St Helier. The award of a visiting fellowship at Christ Church, Oxford, enabled me to work on manuscript collections in the Bodleian Library and in London. Continuing access to the databases and resource sharing of the Ohio State University and Honnold Library of the Claremont Colleges allowed me to work at home.

As an early modern social historian, I have accumulated debts to specialists in legal, constitutional, imperial, and military history. Numerous scholars have contributed advice and information, including John Adamson, John Callow, David Farr, Lori Anne Ferrell, Paul Halliday, Tim Harris, Paulina Kewes, Steve Koblik, Jane Ohlmeyer, Jason Peacey, and Tim Thornton. Two anonymous readers for Oxford University Press pushed me to widen my horizons and sharpen my analysis. I am grateful, too, to audiences at the Pacific Coast Conference on British Studies and the North American Conference on British Studies for responding to my papers on island prisons. My greatest debt, as always, is to Valerie Cressy, who read draft chapters, and accompanied me to castles and coastlines in the Channel Islands, the Isles of Scilly, and the Isle of Wight.

Contents

List of Figures

Abbreviations

APC	*Acts of the Privy Council*
BL	British Library, London
Bod.	Bodleian Library, Oxford
Commons Journal	*Journal of the House of Commons*, 10 vols (1802)
CSPD	*Calendar of State Papers Domestic*
HCA	High Court of Admiralty (TNA)
HMC	Historical Manuscripts Commission
Lords Journal	*Journal of the House of Lords*, 10 vols (1802).
ODNB	*Oxford Dictionary of National Biography*
PC	Privy Council (TNA)
SP	State Papers (TNA)
TNA	The National Archives (Kew)

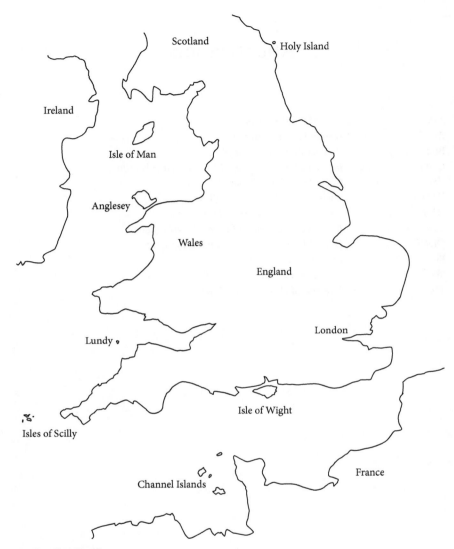

Scotland

Holy Island

Ireland

Isle of Man

Anglesey

Wales

England

London

Lundy

Isle of Wight

Isles of Scilly

Channel Islands

France

England's Islands

Introduction

Britons of the imperial era conceived their history as an 'island story' and spoke confidently of their 'island race'. H. E. Marshall, *Our Island Story: A Child's History of England* (1905), was reportedly formative reading of former British Prime Minister David Cameron. The title of Winston Churchill's *The Island Race* (1964) echoes that of the Victorian versifier Henry Newbolt, *The Island Race* (1898). Patriots of that time attributed English national identity to their offshore location on a moated isle, a homeland fastness from which to range the seas. They belonged to a tradition that attributed England's national character to her topographical and figurative insularity, and saw islands as places of robust distinction.[1] Like William Shakespeare, they imagined England as a 'sceptred isle...set in the silver sea', but they knew, as did most people, that their country occupied only half of the island of Britain. Early modern writers referred casually and boastfully to 'the island of England', sometimes rating it 'the most famous and plentiful island in all the earth'.[2] The trope of English insularity provided a geopolitical metaphor for a fictive national identity.[3]

English monarchs exercised dominion over a scatter of lesser islands, mostly to the west and south, that were difficult to administer, and sometimes prone to neglect. Yet their strategic positions gave them value and importance that far outweighed their size. Principal among them were the Channel Islands of Jersey, Guernsey, Alderney, and Sark; the Isle of Man in the Irish Sea; the Isles of Scilly beyond Cornwall; and the Isle of Wight across the Solent. Other parts of the archipelagic perimeter included Anglesey off Wales, Lundy in the Bristol Channel, St Nicholas Island outside Plymouth, and Holy Island on the coast of Northumberland. Edward Chamberlayne, the seventeenth-century compiler of *The Present State of England*, waxed lyrical about these and other 'ocean islands... scattered in the British sea like so many pearls to adorn the imperial diadem'.[4] Successive governments treated England's islands as troublesome outliers, or as manageable assets, but also as priceless jewels. Sharing some of the geology of Britain's highland zone, they bestrode the edge of the English world.

Relationships between the islands and the rest of the kingdom reflected their legacies of history, constitutional arrangements, opportunities of commerce, considerations of security, distance, and remoteness of location. Their economies tied into maritime, metropolitan, and international networks of commerce and communication. Dependent to varying degrees on the mainland, the islands cherished their exceptions to legal and administrative norms. Though London saw the

England's Islands in a Sea of Troubles. David Cressy, Oxford University Press (2020). © David Cressy 2020.
DOI: 10.1093/oso/9780198856603.001.0001

islands as appurtenances or dependencies of mother England, the islanders more often regarded their homes as privileged places with varying degrees of autonomy.

Each of the islands was fortified, and most had garrisons that served the state. Their harbours and roadsteads were places of strength, coveted by rivals and enemies. At times they were vulnerable to foreign incursion, and all faced threats from pirates or corsairs. They served as places of exile and havens of refuge, and sometimes housed political prisoners, especially in the central decades of the seventeenth century. In civil war they were divided and contested, fought over and occupied. Their civilian inhabitants engaged in lawful and profitable pursuits, such as agriculture, trade, and fishing, as well as less reputable privateering, smuggling, and the plundering of wrecks. Mostly they wanted to be left alone. In the Channel Islands, the Isle of Man, and parts of Anglesey and the Scillies, the common people did not even speak English. London's agents might be baffled by Jèrriais or Guernésiais French, Goidelic Manx, north Welsh, or west Cornish. Island religious culture, though primarily Protestant from the mid-sixteenth century, did not necessarily accord with the established Church of England. External authority was sometimes light of touch. Islanders often argued with each other and caused headaches for their officers and governors. Outsiders were puzzled by insular constitutional anomalies, peculiarities of law, and by claims made by islanders to unique rights and privileges.

This book treats England's islands as distinct locations with their own cultural patterns and political heritage, yet deeply involved in affairs of the nation. Exploring connections between the local archipelagic experience and the policies and problems of the early modern state, it places them in English and British history. By examining how governments dealt with difficulties and distractions at the maritime and insular margins, and how islanders coped with the centralizing demands of the state, it sheds light on the dynamics and application of power from the mid-sixteenth to the early-eighteenth centuries. My intention here is to show how national and insular concerns intermeshed, and to understand the complexity of these interactions. How the state handled outlying islands and anomalous jurisdictions may be as revealing as how it dealt with marginal peoples, at home and abroad.

Though well served by local scholars, the island experience rarely features in mainstream histories of England. The governance, politics, religious culture, military involvement, and maritime economy of England's islands appear only marginally, if at all, in the best-known studies of the period. The islands make only fleeting appearances in works on the early modern era and are hardly ever considered collectively. Yet they are rich in incident and episodes that expose significant threads and patterns in the tapestry of the British past. Taking their measure entails engagement with legal, social, political, constitutional, religious, military, maritime, and economic history. Their fortunes form part of the larger 'island story'.

The clerical author Peter Heylyn, who visited the Channel Islands in the 1620s, found them 'pleasant and delightsome, but yet so small in the extent and circuit' that they appeared 'an abridgement only of the greater works of nature'. Remarking on the diminutive scale of these islands, and the disproportionate attention being paid to them, he suggested that readers might wonder 'how I could say so much on so small a subject, if the great alterations which have happened there...had not occasioned these enlargements'.[5] My reactions as a historian are somewhat similar. Another seventeenth-century writer referred to the Channel Islands as 'a nook of the world', meaning an obscure and outlying corner, that nonetheless demanded national attention.[6] Islanders in the 1640s, speaking for the Isle of Wight as well as Guernsey and Jersey, recognized their homes as 'mere spots of earth in respect of the whole nation', which harboured momentous developments.[7] Similar claims could be made for the rest of the scattered archipelago, whose history was part of English history, no less for being offshore.

England has, of course, many more islands than the cluster considered here. A more comprehensive reckoning might include Flat Holm and Steep Holm in the Bristol Channel; Brownsea Island and Hayling Island on the south coast; Cocquet and Farne associated with Holy Island (Lindisfarne) in the North Sea; the Welsh islands of Bardsey, Caldy, Ramsey, and Skomer; the Kent and Essex islands of Canvey, Foulness, Mersea, Sheppey, Thanet, and the Isle of Dogs. There are also almost-islands such as Portland, Portsea, and Purbeck, and the inland or fenland islands such as Axholm and the Isle of Ely. Some of these were barren patches with ruined hermitages, but others supported industrious populations. Some were estuary islands or mud-fields separated by ditches and marshland. Others were lapped by currents and waves, though barely offshore. William Harrison mentioned most of them in his Elizabethan 'Description of Britaine', noting that not all islands were 'environed with the sea'.[8] His contemporary William Lambard reached Sheppey 'by water between the isle and the main land of the shire', and found Thanet 'sometime divorced from the continent by a water, but now is almost united again'.[9] William Camden recognized Purbeck in Dorset as 'only a demy island compassed round about with the sea, save only of the west side'.[10] These lesser islands were less contentious than those featured in this study, and readers seeking their history must search elsewhere. Ireland too, as always, is a different story.

The legal, political, administrative, religious, and military history of England's islands has yielded a surprisingly rich density of documentation. Channel Island sources are especially abundant, both in the islands and in the metropolis. Generations of governors, proprietors, petitioners, and litigants from all parts of the island fringe have left traces of their dealings with the central government. Reams of correspondence survive in major collections, illuminating the alarms and aspirations of their authors. Printed works too address the status and experience of islands and islanders, from ephemeral early modern pamphlets to more ambitious treatises. My notes and bibliography attempt to do these sources justice. All works cited were published in London, unless otherwise indicated. Early modern spelling and punctuation have been modernized except in the titles of printed sources. Dates are given 'old style', but the year is taken to begin on 1 January.

The phrase in my title is most associated with Hamlet's soliloquy, in which his boldest step would be 'to take arms against a sea of troubles, and by opposing end them'. But the phrase is not Shakespeare's invention. It was, rather, a common expression, used by dozens of Elizabethan writers from the literary entertainer William Painter to the martyrologist John Foxe. The Calvinist William Perkins wrote of 'a sea of troubles' to characterize the human condition, with more nautical imagery to advance his message: 'the sea is the world, the waves are calamities, the church is the ship, the anchor is hope, the sails are love, the saints are passengers, the haven is heaven, and Christ is our pilot.'[11] The puritan Henry Burton, who spent three years on Guernsey as a prisoner, saw himself and his country facing 'a sea of troubles' in the reign of Charles I.[12] My usage is both metaphorical and literal, invoking the crisis of 'England's troubles' and the maritime situation of England's most salient islands. Attentive to the language of contemporaries, and my own, I am offering a populated history, rich in incidents, personalities, and expressions. Within a narrative of continuity and change, *England's Islands* presents a sea of stories, dramas great and small, in multitudinous seas of trouble. The chapters are organized as follows.

Part One, Island Conditions, addresses the constitutional and jurisdictional peculiarities of England's offshore territories and dominions, and their material circumstances, primarily under Elizabeth I and the early Stuarts.

Chapter 1, 'Island Insularities', frames this study by reference to scholarship on regional variation, the British Atlantic archipelago, problems of overlapping and conflicting jurisdictions *within* early modern England, and the processes and personnel of state formation. Informed by interdisciplinary 'island studies', it considers the distinctiveness of offshore communities, including difficulties of access owing to maritime conditions.

Chapter 2, 'Lundy: An Island Story', serves as a micro-history of a little-known island and as a prologue to the main account. The questions of ownership and jurisdiction, defence and occupation, piracy, dependence and independence that troubled this small outpost in the Bristol Channel prefigured the problems of the rest of England's island fringe.

Chapter 3, 'English Islands in the Norman Sea', examines the legal and constitutional idiosyncrasies of the Channel Islands. As remnants of the Duchy of Normandy, Jersey, Guernsey, and their dependencies were outside of English law, and lay beyond the reach of courts and parliaments at Westminster. Yet they were subject to crown-appointed military governors and could be answerable to the monarch's Great Seal. Royal and papal charters assured their neutrality in times of war. This chapter explores the spectacle of London's attempt to impose its will on the islands, and the islanders' insistence on their customs, privileges, rights, and immunities. It shows how governors and captains of varying competence and rectitude sparred with bailiffs and jurats over authority, appointments, resources, and jurisdiction.

Chapter 4, 'Island Anomalies: The Isle of Man, Scilly, Wight, and Anglesey', considers the geographical conditions and jurisdictional arrangements that made English islands hard to govern. It examines the tension between concerns of central authority and insular assertions of privilege and exemption. The Isle of Man, with its Gaelic roots and Viking heritage, had claims to be an independent kingdom ruled by the earls of Derby. The Isles of Scilly were part of Cornwall, the Isle of Wight was politically attached to Hampshire, and Anglesey was a county of Wales, but each behaved as if it were partly autonomous.

Chapter 5, 'Island Economies: Bounties of the Land and Sea', reviews the material foundations of island life in agriculture, commerce, fishing, and foraging, amid the perils of offshore isolation. Island economies were predominantly maritime, yet every island featured farming, either for subsistence or for the market. Channel Islanders grew apples for cider and experimented with tobacco. On Scilly they were lucky to grow oats and run sheep. Inter-island trade linked the Irish Sea to the Channel, with extensions across northern Europe and the Atlantic. Among the goods traded were stockings knitted in Jersey and Guernsey, mainly from English wool. Piracy and smuggling were economic enterprises too, with volatile profits and high degrees of hazard. So too was the harvest of maritime wrecks, which provided windfall enrichment to coastal residents and island officials.

Part Two, Island Troubles, connects the local history of different islands to the stresses and struggles of English history under the Tudors and Stuarts. Successive chapters explore religious and military affairs, the crises of the civil war and interregnum, and the efforts of Restoration regimes to dominate the islands from London.

Chapter 6, 'God's Islands', examines the religious culture and ecclesiastical arrangements of various island communities, showing how devotional activities and godly discipline were affected by politics and custom. The Isle of Wight was part of the diocese of Winchester, with patterns of conformity and dissent similar to those of the mainland. Lundy was extra-parochial and seems to have been forgotten by the bishops of Exeter. The Scillies, too, belonged to the diocese of Exeter, but episcopal influence was almost invisible. The Isle of Man had a bishop of its own, but godly conformity was rarely attained. Religious radicals reached most islands in the decades of revolution and lingered or revived in the later seventeenth century. The Channel Islands, as ever, were anomalous, having adopted a Presbyterian discipline under Elizabeth I. Jersey was brought into conformity with England's prayer book and canons, at least officially, in the reign of James I, but Presbyterianism continued in Guernsey until the Restoration. Each island experienced conflicts in the later seventeenth century over worship, discipline, conformity, and dissent. The disputes of laity and clergy, deans and bailiffs, and governors and the godly formed an offshore drama against the continuing development of the national Church of England.

Chapter 7, 'Fortress Islands', traces the military history of England's islands from Elizabethan times to the civil war. It considers the vulnerability of the islands to foreign invasion and their utility as bases of English power. Fortifications were regularly strengthened in times of threat and suffered neglect in intervals of peace. Militarized islands had garrison economies, with substantial investment from London. This chapter examines the shifting deployment of ordnance and soldiery, the condition of castles and garrisons, and their role in England's wars. Some of the jurisdictional issues addressed in earlier chapters had implications for national security, as island governors marshalled forces and braced for attack.

Chapter 8, 'Refuge and Resistance in Times of Troubles', traces the military history and political allegiance of England's islands in the age of civil wars and revolution. When English loyalties fractured in the 1640s, the islands too became divided between king and parliament. Some changed hands several times in this often-overlooked theatre of operations. The Isle of Wight and Guernsey (except its castle) were swiftly secured for parliament, but Jersey, the Isles of Scilly, Anglesey, and the Isle of Man became royalist strongholds, until they eventually fell. Defeated cavaliers found refuge in the islands, before retreating to the Continent. The presence of Prince Charles on Scilly and then on Jersey in 1646, and his return to Jersey after the regicide as king-in-exile, made those islands places of national, dynastic, and diplomatic significance.

Chapter 9, 'Interregnum Assets', examines the garrison governments that managed most islands during the 1650s, following the parliamentary victory. Customary constitutional arrangements were overridden, and island culture became both anglicized and militarized, as the revolutionary state sought to incorporate the periphery into a national administration.

Chapter 10, 'Restoration Responsibilities', studies the exercise of royal authority from 1660 to 1700 on islands that were assets in international wars. Like its predecessors, the Restoration regime balanced political and strategic needs against local customary rights and privileges, though mostly to its own advantage. Though Charles II assured islanders that he recognized their traditions, immunities, liberties, and customs, the balance of power generally tilted in favour of the crown.

Part Three, Island Confinement, examines the use of the islands as holding pens for political prisoners by successive regimes from the 1630s to the 1690s, when the protections of *habeas corpus* had only limited application. The state took advantage of offshore insularity to isolate its most dangerous enemies during periods of tumultuous political change.

Chapter 11, 'Puritan Martyrs in Island Prisons', examines the material conditions and spiritual responses of the first victims of island incarceration in the reign of Charles I. When the state imprisoned the minister Henry Burton on Guernsey, the lawyer William Prynne on Jersey, and the physician John Bastwick in the Isles of Scilly for the crime of seditious libel, it raised their profile as 'puritan martyrs' and pioneered a new kind of political detention. Their experience shed new light on London's deployment of its island facilities.

Chapter 12, 'Charles I on the "Ile of Wait"', deals with the remarkable year-long imprisonment of King Charles himself on the Isle of Wight, after his defeat in the civil war. It examines the conditions of the king's confinement in Carisbrooke Castle, his relations with his captors, and his attempts to escape from the island that a contemporary cartoonist called 'the Ile of Wait'. The island became a centre of national attention during this fatal twilight of the Stuart regime.

Chapter 13, 'Island Prisoners of the English Republic', shows how the victors in the civil wars emulated the royalist regime by isolating enemies in island prisons. Victims of the Commonwealth and Protectorate included cavalier conspirators sent to the Isle of Wight and the Channel Islands, religious radicals held on the Isle of Wight and Scilly, and dissident army officers exiled to Jersey, Guernsey, and the Isle of Man. Revolutionary England supported a chain of offshore prisons, where inmates often likened themselves to the godly prisoners of Scripture.

Chapter 14, 'The Restoration Prison Archipelago', examines the offshore confinement of radical republicans and others who threatened the restored monarchy of Charles II. It shows how Cromwellian officers, reprieved regicides, and other adherents of the 'good old cause' were imprisoned in military facilities on Jersey, Guernsey, the Isles of Scilly, the Isle of Wight, Holy Island, and the small island of St. Nicholas in Plymouth Sound. This chapter views the archipelago of confinement through the dealings of prisoners and their families, keepers, and authorities, paying particular attention to the experience of Major General John Lambert, who endured twenty-two years of post-Restoration island captivity.

The concluding chapter, 'Islands in an Island Empire', returns to the problem of anomalous and competing jurisdictions in a world of quickening economy, expanding global ambition, and extended foreign wars. Looking forward through the eighteenth and nineteenth centuries towards the present, it considers the survival and mutation of distinctive offshore legal arrangements, amid the changing relationships of the archipelagic periphery, the metropolitan core, and the international order. Like other parts of the expanding British world, the islands gave allegiance to English authorities while maintaining their distinctive characters.

PART ONE
ISLAND CONDITIONS

1

Island Insularities

England's islands were problematic outliers of the early modern state. As marginal, distant, and sometimes isolated communities, they were hard to govern, and difficult to understand. Yet they played, as has been noted of the Channel Islands, a 'unique role at the interface between different societies and jurisdictions'. Islands, with multiple modes of insularity, were 'particular kinds of legal spaces', in tension with metropolitan authority. Geography and heritage made them different, though often in varied and surprising ways.[1] Relations between the archipelagic periphery and the central regime were often strained, as islanders, governors, and Privy Councillors clashed over protocols, privileges, and responsibilities. The needs of national security had to reckon with the cultural and constitutional peculiarities of particular offshore territories. Islanders clung to claims of identity, heritage, and law that might seem specious, outmoded, or inconvenient to administrators in London. Channel Islanders, like the rulers of the Isle of Man, never ceased reciting the rights, immunities, and exemptions accorded them by precedent and custom.[2]

This chapter introduces questions that recur throughout this book about the exercise of authority over offshore territories and dominions. It asks how England dealt with its island dependencies, and how successive regimes coped with the opportunities and problems they posed. Tackling these issues requires consideration of the common strains between the centre and the periphery, between the metropolis and English provinces, as well as peculiarities offshore. To what degree did the central government's dealings with the islands replicate or conform to relationships with other parts of the early modern kingdom? To what degree were difficulties with island communities different from strains on the mainland? How did regimes based in London impose their authority on places as close and familiar as the Isle of Wight, or as remote and peculiar as Jersey or the Isle of Man? How did they use that authority to advance a national religious policy or the military needs of a unified state? How were islands used, how did islanders respond, and to what degree were they integrated into the burgeoning power of the kingdom? How were England's islands implicated in the stresses and crises of the early modern era, with how much continuity, how much change, between the early years of Elizabeth I's reign and the later years of William III? What was special about islands, and why were they so hard to govern?

England's Islands in a Sea of Troubles. David Cressy, Oxford University Press (2020). © David Cressy 2020.
DOI: 10.1093/oso/9780198856603.001.0001

British Islands

These questions can be approached through several areas of current scholarship that may help to frame discussion. The history of England's islands has implications for the 'British Problem', which is usually taken to refer to the fractious interrelations of the three kingdoms of Ireland, Scotland, and England and Wales. London's dealings with the lesser archipelagos of the Channel Islands and the Scillies, and islands as different as the Isle of Anglesey and the Isle of Man, may also reflect problems of kingship, law, and administration within the larger Anglo-Britannic 'Atlantic Archipelago'. ('London', of course, is a synecdoche for the institutions, power, and authority of the central government that operated from Whitehall and Westminster, embracing the personnel and politicians of the City, the court, the Privy Council, and sometimes parliament.) The difficulties and variabilities associated with the islands may also be informed by reference to the vibrant historiography on 'centre and locality' in early modern England. The sometimes-puzzling pretensions and peculiarities of offshore communities can then be related to regional tensions and jurisdictional anomalies *within* mainland England, and to the phenomenon of legal pluralism. Finally, taking a cue from J. G. A. Pocock, who reminds us that 'islands and archipelagos can contain more histories than can be easily seen together, or explained away',[3] the special characteristics of England's islands may be illuminated through the interdisciplinary scholarship of 'island studies'. Such features as separateness, remoteness, and more than material insularity were exacerbated in jurisdictions surrounded by water.

Historians have responded energetically to Pocock's call for a new British history that embraces the greater islands of Ireland and Britain, and the diversity of their littorals. The 'British' or 'three-kingdoms' approach has transformed scholarship on the crises of the seventeenth century, and continues to generate research. A distinctive analytical paradigm now engages the braided and interactive histories of the principal British Atlantic islands, whose monarchs became entangled in archipelagic webs.[4] At the risk of perpetuating an Anglocentric focus, a crucial thread of this discussion has followed the efforts of governments in London to increase their cultural and political domination over adjacent polities.[5] It has been salutary for historians of England to attend to this wider range of territories, offshore from continental Europe and into the oceanic world. Yet the lesser islands are generally ignored in these treatments, despite Charles I being locked up for a year in the Isle of Wight, and his sons finding refuge in the Isles of Scilly and on Jersey. The islands and mainlands were all linked by commerce and politics, pirates, privateers, and military provisions, wherever the English crown claimed sovereignty. Several of the political and religious problems of seventeenth-century governance were solved, or at least managed, by employing the islands as special prisons. A richer picture emerges when the experiences of offshore communities are brought into view.

England's lesser islands are often rendered invisible. There are any number of histories of 'the British Isles' that mention the Channel Islands and the Isle of Man only glancingly, and the others not at all. Norman Davies's magisterial account of *The Isles* describes the Vikings 'island-hopping' from Ireland to Cornwall via the Isle of Man, Anglesey, and Lundy, and mentions medieval assemblies on Man and the Channel Islands. But his only other reference to the Channel Islands and the Isle of Man is as modern 'dependencies within the British Isles but outside the United Kingdom'.[6] Other historians of the British Isles have argued that coverage 'should include the Isle of Man, the Channel Islands', and the major islands of Britain and Ireland, without actually investigating them.[7] Pocock mentions that his mother came from the Channel Islands, and later moved to New Zealand, so more than one archipelago is involved, but the Isles of Scilly seem not to be on his radar.[8] The role of England's islands in the civil wars, and in the country's legal and constitutional history, is rarely mentioned. Yet Tudor and Stuart governments were concerned with the irregularities, vulnerabilities, and demands of the realm, including the insular periphery. Here, I hope, they get their due.

English Divisions

Though nominally integrated under one crown, one faith, and a body of common law, the English polity was riddled by differences. Working against the formation of a powerful centralized state were regional cultural traditions, including variations in dialect and language; the persistence of local loyalties of fealty, kindred, and custom; and attachment to factional and economic interests. As Jack Greene long ago noted, peripheries within England as well as British 'extended polities' overseas possessed their own 'peculiar socioeconomic, legal and political traditions' at variance with those of the core.[9] It was a challenge to successive regimes to cope with these internal divisions, and even more difficult in territories offshore. Religious and ideological differences compounded these problems on England's islands as well as in mainland provinces.

Early modern governments faced the task of ruling and directing a patchwork of territories and jurisdictions with varying traditions of separateness and autonomy. Steering a course between cajolement and discipline, the central government worked repeatedly to bring the localities into line. This applied as much to the reign of Elizabeth as to the revolutionary protectorate of the 1650s, except that Lord Burghley relied on his management skills while Oliver Cromwell had the backing of a politicized standing army.[10] Governments based in London attempted to marshal their regional resources, and to mobilize provincial assets, with increasing urgency and effect. The centre sought to sway the periphery, for purposes of policy and power. A similar dynamic applied to the islands, but was handicapped by problems of distance and isolation, as well as insular claims to privileges, liberties, and special consideration.

Medieval remnants such as the palatinates of Durham and Chester, and the duchies of Lancaster and Cornwall, still held courts of law, as did the Council of Wales and the Marches and the Council of the North until the reign of Charles II. Courts of Quarter Sessions, hundred courts, baronial courts, mayors' courts, and ecclesiastical courts contributed to the jurisdictional mosaic. Corporate towns and cities cherished their charters, and clung to their liberties and privileges. Lords of manors, governors of castles, coastal vice admirals, and the wardens and jurats of the Cinque Ports exercised a variety of ancient and customary rights that sometimes frustrated the wishes of the crown.[11] In this context, the bailiwicks of Guernsey and Jersey, the lordship of the Isle of Man, and the claims of proprietors of other islands did not necessarily look so odd, though they all created additional challenges for Whitehall and Westminster. In this regard, the jurisdictional anomalies of England's offshore dominions may be regarded as extreme examples of patterns that prevailed on the mainland that were not so readily subject to metropolitan control.

Relations within and between these varied communities can be considered as aspects of 'legal pluralism'. Legal scholars have developed this term to examine the jurisdictional politics of competing and interactive systems, especially with reference to colonial and neocolonial legal environments. Lauren Benton and Richard Ross refer neither to the Channel Islands nor to the Isle of Man in their work on 'empires and legal pluralism', but their discussion of 'overlapping or clashing royal, ecclesiastical, local and seigneurial jurisdictions' and 'layered legal arrangements within composite polities' is surely applicable to these and other offshore settings. Analysis of interactions between islanders and metropolitan officials in the early modern era may fruitfully inform this discussion as well as benefit from it.[12] It is well to be reminded that mainland England, as well as its island fringe, experienced the pluralities of customary law and legislated law, common law and civil law, martial law, admiralty law, ecclesiastical law, and divine law, as well as the local peculiarities of the Manx and Norman inheritance. It was part of the genius of the English state that it did not so much suppress these variations as absorb them into its structures of power.

The English provincial patchwork was material and economic as well as cultural and jurisdictional. Appreciation of this diversity has been at the heart of agrarian studies. Social and economic historians have long been familiar with the maps of farming regions depicted in *The Agrarian History of England and Wales*. The broad distinction between the highland zone of the north and west and the lowland zone of the south and east was made more complex by areas of pastoral or arable preponderance in wood–pasture or sheep–corn concentrations, overlain by varieties of animal husbandry, dairying, grain-growing, and mixed agricultural enterprise. The islands are mostly missing from these maps, though their social and cultural insularity may be similarly materially grounded.[13]

The suggestion has long been mooted that different kinds of farming, based on underlying conditions of geology, soil, and climate, gave rise to distinctive communities. While steering clear of material determinism, scholars have pointed to differences in population density, settlement patterns, and tenurial relations associated with economic activity. Local studies of contrasting communities in Cambridgeshire, and in the chalk and cheese lands of Somerset, Dorset, and Wiltshire, have indicated the possibility that religious culture and even political allegiance, as well as demography and social structure, might in some sense be rooted in the soil.[14] Localist readings of mid-Stuart England's troubles associate patterns of allegiance and neutrality in the civil wars with 'different constellations of social, political and cultural forces... in different geographical areas', though the robustness of such linkage remains controversial.[15]

Early modern England exhibited local and localist ideologies, as well as overlapping and conflicting jurisdictions. These could be seen in the risings and disturbances of the Tudor period, and in episodes of obstreperousness and recalcitrance under the Stuarts. Alan Everitt's classic account of *Change in the Provinces* drew attention to 'the insularity of local communities and the tenacity of local attachments'. 'Insularity', he argued, was a fundamental feature of provincial England, whose gentry were consumed by local administrative problems and grievances.[16] John Morrill observed that various counties, especially in the north and west, 'had established conventions and customs to meet local needs, many of which ignored or went against the provisions of statute... The government of Charles I had posed a threat to the integrity of such local customs, but it had not destroyed them.' Fractured regional attachments re-emerged in the 1630s, when disputes over money and politics 'reawakened dormant but profound jurisdictional conflicts'.[17] Other scholars have noticed how the efforts of the centralizing state to deal with regional diversity and administrative complexity 'infringed on local rights and liberties', to the extent that 'obstructionist resentment of central interference underlies the major developments in mid-seventeenth-century England'.[18] Provincial interests and localist ideologies shaped the course, if not the origins, of the English civil wars.

Geographical, cultural, and economic diversity has been a persistent feature of the English experience, but central authorities found ways to assert and extend their power. Recovering from regional rebellions in the sixteenth century, Tudor governments gained control, or at least traction, over areas with historical immunities, liberties, and privileges, and turned them into vehicles for administering royal policy. Despite divisive tendencies, England became one of the most integrated of early modern polities. The demands of citizenship and subjecthood were broadly understood, and applied as much in Shropshire as in Suffolk, in Nottinghamshire as in Surrey. The nobility occupied itself in service to the crown, at court, in Council, and the House of Lords, and harboured no alternative centres of power. (The Earl of Derby's fastness on the Isle of Man was the prime post-Elizabethan exception.) The gentry, despite localist rivalries, were mostly aligned with the national project until forced to choose sides in the civil war.

Stuart regimes were generally successful in securing obedience, until Charles I and James II overstepped the mark.

Notwithstanding the patchwork of the English agrarian landscape, its crops and commodities were tied into inter-regional and national systems of distribution. Drovers drove sheep and cattle overland to country fairs, while barges and wagons moved grains and other foods to markets. English roads, though sometimes muddy and treacherous, provided links across the land with very few tolls or tariffs. Carriers carted packages and parcels between London and major towns. An expanding system of postmasters and messengers sped official communications between the capital and the rest of the English mainland. Migrants and travellers, both local and long distance, met few barriers. Island traffic, by contrast, required crossing a sea, with all the extra costs and risks of maritime shipping. People arriving from England could not necessarily be understood in island communities where the dominant local language was French or Cornish, Manx or Welsh. There was little room for wayfaring on territories bounded by water.

English governments benefited from legal and logistical arrangements that served to unify the realm. Overlaying the agrarian and jurisdictional mosaic was a standard system of coinage and currency, general acceptance of the English common law, a national parliament, and a broadly comprehensible though locally inflected English language. The courts of Westminster—Chancery, Exchequer, Common Pleas, and King's Bench—had nationwide reach, while the High Court of Admiralty had jurisdiction over England's seas. Star Chamber, until its abolition, had authority throughout the land. Ecclesiastical law ran parallel with common law, in a country nominally uniform in religion. Social, civic, fiscal, and military obligations applied nationwide, with very few immunities or exceptions. Islands, however, were different, as if the sea eroded the chain of command.

State Formation

Recent scholarship on 'state formation' offers another framework for considering the central government's relations with England's islands. Despite making minimal mention of such territories, this literature provides another grid against which to examine offshore authorities and communities. Michael Braddick characterizes the state as 'a coordinated and territorially bounded network of agencies exercising political power', whose authority and capacity expanded across the seventeenth century. Transformed by exigencies of civil war, the early modern English state saw a greater military, fiscal, and administrative mobilization, which may be construed as 'modernization'.[19] More sensitized to the involvement of the 'middling sort', and less swayed by social theory, Steve Hindle represents the state as 'a matrix of institutions, personnel, political theory and culture, in which the law functions at both the centre and the periphery'. State authority, he finds, was 'comparatively fragile', as the government struggled to secure compliance with its demands. Yet Hindle and Braddick agree that Elizabethan and early Stuart England experienced an 'increase of governance' and an 'elaboration of the role of the state', which only grew in legitimacy, authority, and impact in the reigns that followed.[20]

Studies like these prompt challenging questions about the aims and apparatus of central government as it dealt with the island periphery. For what purpose, to what effect, through which instruments, and against what obstacles, did regimes based in London exercise their authority in England's islands? How did the leaders and managers of the state secure compliance with their legal, bureaucratic, military, and religious demands when island authorities claimed immunity or exemption, or when island subjects withheld cooperation? How did successive regimes cope with the opportunities and problems of offshore administration in times of peace, war, and revolution, and how were their difficulties compounded by the problems of distance, access, and insular isolation? How were they handicapped when so many of the instruments of state formation—the English courts of law, the meetings and statutes of parliament, the culture of the public sphere, even the commonality of the English language—either did not apply or had limited purchase in territories and dominions offshore?

Every island was different—in history, heritage, custom, population, economy, and law—yet all posed problems to governments with a centralizing or unifying agenda. These are matters to bear in mind when considering the strains between governors, bailiffs, and jurats in the Channel Islands, the refractoriness of the Stanley lords of the Isle of Man, the privileges of proprietors of the Isles of Scilly, and the challenges of security, provincialism, and local distinctiveness in such outposts as Lundy Island, Anglesey, and the Isle of Wight. The governance of the islands was constituted differently from the rest of the crown's dominions, but still demanded the attention of officials in London.

To fulfil its purposes in England, the Privy Council relied upon networks of appointed officials, lords lieutenant, county sheriffs, coroners, commissioners, messengers, justices of the peace, and judges of the assize and central courts. Omnicompetent and ever attentive, the Council operated as the central executive agency, the eyes and arms of the kingdom. It served as the conduit of correspondence, instructions, and memoranda, and could summon any subject to appear. Noble magnates were answerable to the Council's authority, and local magistrates acknowledged its demands. Westminster parliaments helped to bind the nation, and generally made the laws that central government required. Ties of kinship and interest, and flows of news and information, further served as cultural and political cement. Compared to many parts of early modern Europe, England's 'integrated' political system provided a 'high degree of cultural, legal, and administrative uniformity' that facilitated the processes of state formation.[21] Treasury officials and excise officers served a strengthening national administration in the decades after the Restoration, though their counterparts in the islands were less amenable to their fiscal and political demands.

Many of the resources of state building were limited or non-existent with regard to offshore dominions. English officials, magistrates, and dignitaries carried no weight. Neither common law nor parliamentary statute applied in the Channel Islands or the Isle of Man. The equity courts of Westminster had no purchase there, and even the authority of Star Chamber was contested. As remnants of the Duchy of Normandy, the Channel Islands had their own courts of law with proceedings in island French. The English royal governors of Guernsey and Jersey struggled against local bailiffs and jurats, and difficulties of communications reduced their effectiveness. The Isle of Man, with its heritage as a quasi-independent Viking kingdom, was governed by Keys and Deemsters, Tynwald and Sheadings, using the Goidelic language of Manx. The noble Lords of Man perennially restricted initiatives of the English crown. Commissions under the monarch's Broad Seal commanded respect and attention, but their value too was limited if the commissioners could not communicate locally. Outsiders were puzzled by insular constitutional anomalies and claims of protected status.

Islands closer to the mainland also exhibited degrees of political insularity. The Isles of Scilly were part of Cornwall, Lundy belonged to Devon, and the Isle of Wight was legally attached to Hampshire, yet each behaved as if it were partly autonomous. Cornwall's justices, coroners, and sheriffs had no business in the Isles of Scilly, and islanders had little truck with mainland jurisdictions. Scilly's lord proprietor controlled all island tenancies, and his informal court, called 'The Twelve', took none of its cues from London and kept no records. The small garrison on St Mary's answered to a military governor or captain, who was often a kinsman of the proprietor. The Isle of Wight also operated independently of much of county government. Residents of the island were generally exempt from service at the Winchester assizes or quarter sessions, unless the matter directly concerned them. The Isle of Wight also had governors or captains, whose autocratic behaviour occasioned complaints to the Privy Council. Anglesey was a county of Wales, and returned members to the parliament at Westminster, but its status as a frontier island allowed it exemption from military levies. Lundy, as the next chapter shows, was largely ignored.

Concerned with national security, the crown's resources, the kingdom's honour, and the well-being of subjects, the Privy Council made repeated demands on the islands, and eventually increased its grip on them. In a halting and idiosyncratic manner, the processes of state formation made headway in the periphery, though not without resistance. From the sixteenth century to the eighteenth, the legal and political correspondence of Privy Councillors is rich with complaint about obstruction and defiance, and frustration at the recalcitrance of island inhabitants.

Island Studies

Scholars in various disciplines, in diverse parts of the world, have converged in recent decades on the topic of 'island studies'. They have developed a vocabulary, and an expanding range of interests, to deal with 'elements of islandness', including spatial attributes, jurisdictional anomalies, and ambiguities of sovereignty. Several of their concerns have relevance to this study of England's islands in the early modern era. Though circumstances and contexts differ, conceptions of the 'phenomenology of islands', 'jurisdictional enclaves', and the 'limbo granted by peripherality' are pertinent to historical analysis. From the island point of view, in a small and bounded territory, it could be confining or comforting to know your limits.[22]

Recognition that seas were conduits as well as barriers, in multiple connections between islands and mainlands, confirms the often-used aphorism that 'no island is an island, entire unto itself'. It surely applied to England's offshore territories, which experienced pressures and attentions from anxious mainland administrators. Practitioners of 'island studies' recognize that insularity was constrained and compromised, that every island was different, and that 'the island experience' covers many variables, past and present. It is also useful to be reminded that the word 'mainland' itself may be politically charged, privileging one side of a relationship. Apartness and separation are relative concepts, and one person's 'edge' could be another person's centre. Islanders lived 'beyond seas', from the metropolitan perspective, no matter how close their ties to the homeland.[23] Comparable insights can be gained from 'the new coastal history', which attends to the 'liminal, amphibious spaces' of the environment of 'shorefolk'.[24]

A crucial insight of 'island studies' is that mainlands and offshore entities were locked into relationships. Their mutual awareness, needs, and interests brought them together, and energized their frictions. In the early modern era, the anomalies of island jurisdiction were more than curiosities or legal relics. They were, rather, zones of contention, with both local and national consequences. While preserving insular privileges, they prevented inhabitants from full participation in the benefits and responsibilities of Englishness. If English law did not apply, if its application was limited or constrained, the liberties of the subject could not be guaranteed. If the prerogative of the crown did not fully run, or if parliamentary statutes had scant effect, the power of the state was diminished. If the full force of mainland power was muted, then island distinctiveness could be negotiated and preserved. Historical actors—mainlanders as well as islanders—understood that the peculiarities of offshore arrangements carried opportunities and advantages, mutualities and divergent interests, as well as pitfalls and perils. They sometimes referred to the 'continent' of England, and spoke of their islands as 'foreign' parts.[25] Early modern troops and administrators sent from the mainland often thought the islands hardship postings, and were generally eager to leave.

Islands, large and small, had both appealing and threatening characteristics. They could be places of isolation and insulation, refuge or abandonment, desperation or delight. Generations of visitors have found England's islands engrossing, familiar yet different, detached yet connected, with lore and customs that set them apart.[26] Islands, past and present, have stirred meditative, historical, poetic, and epistolary endeavours. Work written on islands, work written about islands, and work written by islanders, constitute an engaging body of texts, with distinctive offshore perspectives. Authors from St John of Patmos to D. H. Lawrence have found island isolation inspiring. Little worlds surrounded by water could fire the imagination, though some islands proved confining, limiting, and too small. Island-bound authors had time enough for writing and reflection, though few with whom to share their work. Marooned by circumstances as stranded travellers, garrison officers, political prisoners, or refugees from conflict, they have reflected on problems of insularity, distance, estrangement, and connection that are recurrent themes in this book.

The Elizabethan army captain Thomas Blenerhasset, 'sitting on a rock in the sea...in Guernsey castle', composed poetic histories of English princes as respite from his 'despair'.[27] The puritan Henry Burton, locked for three years in the same Castle Cornet, wrote polemics against the bishops of Charles I, and mused that he would not have been so productive if not so isolated. William Prynne, a contemporary prisoner on Jersey, occupied himself by writing verse. The fifth monarchist John Rogers produced his own 'vison of the prison Patmos', filling folios by the hundred while confined to the Isle of Wight. Savouring an interlude of 'wonderful contentment' and productivity following defeat in the civil war, Sir Edward Hyde, Charles I's Chancellor of the Exchequer, wrote much of his 'History of the Rebellion' in Jersey's Castle Elizabeth. King Charles himself, imprisoned on the Isle of Wight, wrote close to a thousand letters during his confinement. After the revolution, the parliamentary grandee Lord Say and Sele, at odds with the regicides, retreated to lonely Lundy to write works of philosophy and romance. The restoration prisoner Robert Overton, immured on Jersey for almost eight years, wrote hundreds of pages of contemplative poetry. The islands made up in tranquillity what they lacked in literary resources, effectively focusing the mind and freeing the pen.[28] Such features have been noticed by practitioners of 'island studies', and promoted by organizers of modern writers' residencies and island workshops.[29]

Literary scholars and cultural critics write evocatively of 'island enchantment', 'island logic', 'the lure of islands', and 'the enthralment of the island' from Homer to Shakespeare to the present. Their islands, physical and metaphorical, real and imagined, could be places of fantasy and reinvention, utopia or terror, and are prominent in the so-called blue humanities that address the culture of the seas.[30] At least a dozen of Shakespeare's plays refer to islands, including the 'seceptr'd isle' of England and 'that nook-shotten isle of Albion'. 'The isle is full of noises, sounds and sweet airs, that give delight and hurt not,' assures Shakespeare's Prospero in his mysterious offshore fastness.[31] Discussions of such conceits have their place in 'island studies', alongside colonization, postcolonialism, globalization, ecocriticism, and postmodernity, though they may have limited application to the problems of the English archipelago in its early modern sea of troubles.

Rough Passages

'Environed with the ocean waves', in the words of the Elizabethan geographer William Harrison, England's 'many fair islands' experienced a moatedness that afforded both security and isolation.[32] With no means of arriving or leaving except by ship, they were estranged as well as connected by maritime conditions. It was their very remoteness and separateness that made islands suitable as political prisons, hard of access, and for many people out of mind.

The demands of sea travel created problems of a different order for island administrators, compared to governance on the mainland. Passengers, cargoes, and correspondence were subject to nature's caprices, and could not be guaranteed a safe or timely arrival. Island governors repeatedly complained about the time it took for supplies and instructions to reach their sea-girt fastnesses, while their masters in England fumed at the tardiness and patchiness of their dispatches. Routine maritime mishaps disrupted communications. Information, in both directions, was likely to be filtered, incomplete, late, or wrong.

Difficult journeys impeded traffic to the Channel Islands and the Isles of Scilly, though even crossings to inshore islands such as Anglesey and the Isle of Wight involved risk and uncertainty. Hidden rocks, cross tides, swirling currents, and impenetrable fog could frighten the hardiest mariner, while leaky vessels, fouled gear, and inattentive helmsmen added to the problem. Too many charts of coasts and rocks were 'strangely mistaken' (see Figure 1).[33] Travellers on England's muddy roads had it easy by comparison.

Landsmen had to trust their lives to the masters and crews of ships if they needed passage to an island. Voyages across the Channel, the Irish Sea, and the Solent may have passed without incident, but every journey was subject to delay and danger. Every mariner knew the peril of the deep. Pirates and other predators routinely molested traffic, and the sea, which gave the islands their being, could torment those who sailed on her. Island waters were especially hazardous, and created companies of casualties. Winter crossings were especially dangerous, though foul weather could erupt at any time. Early modern narratives are replete with accounts of travels interrupted, and of maritime adventures that ended ill.

Governors, soldiers, and administrators who needed passage to the Channel Islands had to find shipping from one of England's south coast ports, most commonly Southampton, Weymouth, or Plymouth. Island merchants and

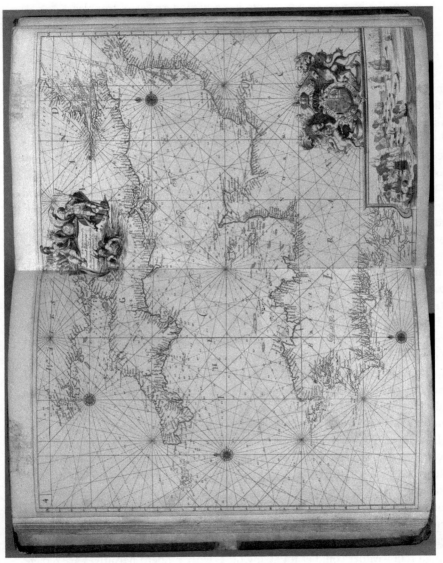

Figure 1. The Channel (Greenvile Collins, *Great Britain's Coasting Pilot*, 1693; Huntington Library)

petitioners needed reciprocal arrangements, unless they went via St Malo in France. The vessels they depended upon, even if furnished and available, had to wait for the wind. The passage was perilous without an experienced pilot, for island waters were notorious for their tidal churn, shifting shoals, and submerged reefs and ledges. The 'race' and the 'swinge' around the island of Alderney were especially challenging, with 'conflicting currents, and rocks, and storms, and perils of every description'. Darkness, mist, and unpredictable winds increased the navigational dangers, as mariners knew to their cost.[34] Seventeenth-century examples illustrate the range of difficulties, while indicating the richness of the sources.

Based on Jersey, where he sought the office of bailiff, Sir Philip Carteret apologized to the Privy Council in March 1621 that 'the bark in which my brother went miscarried, so that my letters have not come to your hands'.[35] The lieutenant governor of Guernsey lamented a few years later that 'it is a mischief to us here that the passage is so stopped that I can receive no comfort nor instructions'.[36] The *Anthony* of London 'happily arrived' in Guernsey in November 1628 'having lost in a storm the fleet, as also the main mast, the fore-mast much shattered, the ship much leaky, and many tackles spoiled'. Sailors judged the ship 'much crazy', and 'not in case to go to sea', but it completed its return to England.[37] The sea was relatively calm the following spring when Peter Heylyn sailed to the Channel Islands as chaplain to the Earl of Danby. But it still took three difficult days to make landfall in Jersey, the passengers troubled by the 'sickly and unpleasing motion' of the vessel. The return voyage was likewise uneventful, though delayed several days by 'the crossness of the winds and roughness of the water'.[38] Less fortunate was one of the king's ships, carrying another royal governor, that was cast away at Jersey at noon-tide on a fair day in August 1636, when the pilot ran against a hidden rock.[39] As knowledgeable commentators remarked, 'long experience is required to make one a good pilot upon these coasts'.[40]

The puritan activists William Prynne and Henry Burton, dispatched in 1637 to prisons on Jersey and Guernsey, each arrived safely, though only after a maritime ordeal. Setting out from North Wales, it took fourteen winter weeks in 'a bruised ship-wrecked vessel, full of leaks...through dangerous storms and seas', before Prynne's party reached the Channel Islands. Safety was not yet assured, for 'a very high wind arising, and contrary to our course', the ship was blown back towards Alderney or Sark, 'in very great peril and extremity' amidst 'abundance of rocks'.[41] Burton's voyage from Liverpool took six 'long, tedious, and perilous' weeks, limping and leaking through ports of call in Ireland, South Wales, and Devon, all the while 'tumbled and tossed' by storms. The only comfort was comparison to St Paul, who also suffered at sea while bearing witness to the gospel (see Chapter 11).[42]

Dozens of reports of passages to the Channel Islands relate similar difficulties and deliverances. Military supplies and reinforcements were frequently imperilled.[43] When Colonel Edward Popham's ships approached Guernsey in September 1649 one of them 'bulged upon the rock, and would not be got off', while the pilot of another was unwilling to adventure through the Race.[44] Captain Thomas Large's ship the *Lark* met extreme winds and 'much snow' on its way to Jersey in February 1658, which drove the vessel off course. Fearing for their lives, the crew cut the main mast and rigging, 'in regard of the extraordinary quantity of ice that was frozen to the ropes'. Severely disabled, 'their fingers and toes being almost mortified by the cold', they found shelter in Plymouth, victims of a winter storm at the peak of the 'little ice age'.[45] Successfully bringing soldiers and equipment to Jersey after the Restoration, Sir Herbert Lunsford, remarked that 'we had...been sacrificed to Neptune', but for 'the blessing of almighty God, and prudence of our captain'.[46]

The Isles of Scilly, barely 30 miles from Land's End, could be reached in a day of plain sailing, but still tested seamanship and endurance. Their uncharted islets, tidal shoals, and semi-submerged ledges snared 'poor travellers...that are not skillful of our roads and harbours'.[47] Even coming into St Mary's haven could be dangerous: 'It must not be attempted when the sea is agitated, or the atmosphere foggy, the channels that lead to it being very narrow and winding,' warned the cleric John Troutbeck.[48] 'Thick' or foggy weather compounded navigational problems, leading too many journeys to end in shipwreck.

Voyage accounts relate some of the difficulties of passage to the Scillies, although they may have exaggerated the dangers. The royalist John Grenville spent 'five days at sea in a continual storm, very likely to be cast way', before arriving at Scilly in February 1649.[49] The parliamentary garrison that replaced him grew short of pay, supplies, and medicine in October 1651, 'in regard the passage thither is very uncertain, especially this winter time'.[50] When the Commonwealth ship *Greyhound* carrying gunpowder for the Scilly garrison left Spithead in December 1658, she was twice forced back by the violence of the storms. More tempestuous weather scattered another flotilla attempting to leave the Isles of Scilly for Ireland, driving one vessel into the cliffs, and stripping another of her masts.[51] Nothing compared to the catastrophe of October 1707 when Sir Cloudesley Shovell's fleet, homebound from the Mediterranean, shattered on Scilly's western rocks, with the loss of four warships and as many as 1,600 lives.[52]

Even the short passage to the Isle of Wight could test a traveller's nerve and endurance. The complex double tides and currents of the Solent could be unforgiving. Captain Richard Plumleigh encountered 'an extreme gust of wind in the nature of a tornado' off the island in August 1631, and reported, 'by extremity of contrary winds it was seven days before I could get to the Isle of Wight'.[53] The ship-killing Needles, at the western tip of the island, reminded Peter Heylyn of Scylla and Charybdis.[54] Sir John Oglander, who knew the Solent well, experienced two near-shipwrecks in 1638 while travelling to his duties in Hampshire.[55] Other transits between the mainland and the island, both military and civilian, exposed passengers to 'distemper at sea', 'tempestuous weather', and risk of drowning. This was the fate of two young men from Oxford who were 'miserably cast away crossing in a boat... into the Isle of Wight' in September 1657.[56] A worse disaster occurred in June 1706 when thirty-five women and six children perished as the hoy transporting them from Cowes to Portsmouth foundered in a 'brisk' north-north-east wind.[57]

Traffic to the Isle of Man was similarly stressed by the challenges of the Irish Sea. The misery of the crossing was one reason the earls of Derby so rarely visited their domain. Another may have been the 'infernal spirit' said to inhabit rocks to the east of the island, whose 'hideous noises' caused 'such disturbance in the waters in the night time, that many ships were wrecked and many more in hazard'.[58] Letters from Lord Strange to his captain on the island were delayed for a month in March 1634, while the ship carrying them was windbound on the coast of Lancashire. Other vessels had too much wind, or wind of the wrong sort, and foundered on the island's coasts.[59] When parliamentary forces supplanted the Earl of Derby in 1650, their supplies and orders came almost a month too late, held back by contrary winds.[60] Even the island of Anglesey, close enough to the mainland for some inhabitants 'weekly to ferry over to the market at Carnarvon', could be cut off by bad weather. Passengers crossing the Menai Straits experienced 'great danger and frequent hazard of their lives and goods', while travellers around the north coast of Anglesey risked shipwreck.[61] Several hundred enlisted men from Cheshire drowned there in April 1625 'through the extremity of the foul weather in their passage'.[62] John Milton's friend Edward King (the subject of *Lycidas*) also drowned off Anglesey in August 1637, in an area of poorly charted reefs and dangerous tidal races.[63]

These incidents exemplify some of the perils of offshore travel and communication between the mainland and the islands. Not every voyage was dramatic, but stresses and delays were common. The Privy Council in London had to reckon with such difficulties every time it sent a letter, appointed an officer, commissioned an enquiry, or dispatched pay or equipment to an island garrison. Supplying and administering the islands, and responding to their challenges, entailed levels of frustration, expense, and effort of an order different from internal or domestic dealings. The task was worth the trouble, because the islands had enormous strategic and commercial value, and were jewels of the crown of England.

From London's point of view the islands were encumbrances as well as assets, requiring attention, intervention, and expenditure, as circumstances required. They were appendages or possessions at the end of lines of intermittent communication, in the hands of independent-minded islanders, corrupt and self-serving officials, and governors of varying probity and competence. One senses a sigh of frustration among Privy Councillors whenever island business arose: hence their reliance on lessee proprietors, appointed commissioners, and military commanders whenever possible. London was constantly relearning the histories, peculiarities, and provisions that made each island different.

Island inhabitants, with varying resources, needs, and interests, appealed to the Council when it suited them, and otherwise downplayed London's demands. They seem to have valued the benefits of protection and attachment, so long as their sense of heritage and identity was preserved. For much of the time they preferred to be left alone. Relations between England's central government and its offshore periphery entailed qualities of reciprocity and negotiation that were not always forthcoming. The islands were swept into the maelstrom of religious and international conflict, and were buffeted by the troubles of the British civil wars. The legal, constitutional, and managerial complexities of their experience, as well as their political, religious, and economic histories of insularity, are discussed in the chapters that follow.

2

Lundy

An Island Story

Many of the peculiarities of islands, including moated isolation, difficulty of access, and anomalous jurisdiction, applied to the small and often-forgotten island of Lundy. An outcrop in the Bristol Channel barely 3 miles long and half a mile wide, two dozen miles out from the Devonshire port of Ilfracombe, Lundy Island has a history of violence and dispute disproportionate to its scale. Lundy's experience in the early modern era illustrates many of the problems of geography, governance, security, and war that are treated more expansively elsewhere in this book. The following narrative introduces an island troubled by contested ownership, neglectful government, inadequate defences, and pirate predation. Like several other English islands, mid-Stuart Lundy saw a civil war in microcosm, as royalist and parliamentary forces vied for control.

Sitting amid sea lanes between south Wales and south-west England, Lundy could command maritime traffic linking Bristol, Bideford, and Cardiff to Ireland, the Atlantic, and beyond. It was important as a strategic asset, and worth possessing to deny it to potential enemies. 'Begirt about with dangerous unapproachable rocks', Lundy's steep cliffs and perilous entrance gave every advantage to armed defenders, so that 'ten men may repulse fifty'.[1] The Elizabethan William Harrison remarked that 'the inhabitants there with huge stones may keep off thousands of their enemies, because it is not possible for any adversaries to assail them, but only at one place, and that with a most dangerous entrance'.[2] The early Stuart geographer Tristram Risdon also described Lundy's 'inaccessible cliffs and rocks, on every side defending it', and deemed the island 'in manner impregnable'.[3] Lundy's defences would be challenged several times in the following century, and they did not always hold.

Lundy's relationship to mainland jurisdictions long remained uncertain. The Jacobean poet Michael Drayton imagined the island as 'a nymph to idle toys inclined', as Wales and England competed for her hand. It remained a matter of doubt 'to whether, Lundy doth belong', though the prize was hardly worth the struggle: 'Of traffic or return she never taketh care: I Not provident of pelf, as many islands are.'[4]

Lundy had fresh water, and was rich in rabbits, birds' eggs, and feathers, but offered little else of value besides its position. According to Risdon, 'horses, kine, sheep, seine [fishing], and goats it affordeth, with store of conies [rabbits]; but

England's Islands in a Sea of Troubles. David Cressy, Oxford University Press (2020). © David Cressy 2020.
DOI: 10.1093/oso/9780198856603.001.0001

their chief commodity is fowl [seabirds], whereof there is great abundance'.[5] Servicing sailors and pirates, and suffering the costs of isolation, the population of Lundy rarely reached the hundreds, and was sometimes barely in the dozens. Its few families of warreners, shepherds, samphire-gatherers, and tenants of absentee proprietors relied for supplies on passing ships or boats from Barnstable or Ilfracombe, the ports of departure for the modern tourist traffic (see Figure 2).

Though once a possession of Cleve Abbey, Somerset, and briefly granted to the Knights Templar, Lundy was extra-parochial, almost an orphan island, and never part of any mainland entity. The bishops of Exeter, whose diocese encompassed Devon and Cornwall, had no business there. At the dissolution of the monasteries, the meagre tithes of Lundy reverted to the crown, though they were leased to investors in 1583.[6] From the late Middle Ages to the early modern era, the island was held of the king by knight service, and passed through several families of aristocratic proprietors. Lundy was a spoil of feudal patronage and inheritance, but never a profitable asset. Later assertions that Lundy was 'free', and therefore exempt from mainland rules and taxation, were effectively true but had no basis in law.[7]

By mid-Tudor times the island was possessed by George St Leger and his heirs. The bankrupt John St Leger sold Lundy for £1,000 to his son-in-law Sir Richard Grenville in 1577. Grenville described 'his manor, territory or island commonly called or known by the name of the Isle of Lundy' in 1586 as being 'within the precinct or liberty of the county of Devon', but no Devonshire magistrate had jurisdiction there. Other contemporaries associated the island with Cornwall rather than Devon, measuring its distance from Bude Bay rather than Bideford. Disputes over Lundy would be aired in Chancery or before the Privy Council rather than at Exeter or Bodmin.[8]

The Grenville family's hold on Lundy persisted for several generations, but was often more nominal than effective. Other landowners and claimants litigated for rights to the island. At some time in the 1580s, John Hathersleigh of Hartland purchased an interest in 'a certain isle or island called Lundy', and found himself in dispute with creditors and sureties. By this time the island had a dozen or so inhabitants and a few cattle and sheep.[9] If there was any religion there, it was whatever accompanied the visitors and settlers. If there were defences, they were little more than the remnants of Marisco Castle, which dated from the reign of Henry III and had suffered centuries of neglect. Battered by winds and swirled by high tides, the approach to Lundy was perilous at the best of times. A typical encounter was that of the flotilla led by Sir Anthony Cooke, bound for the war in Ireland, which planned to put into Lundy in March 1599, but found themselves fouled and cast upon rocks, and lost six horses drowned.[10]

Around this time a kinsman of the Grenvilles, Sir Robert Bassett (1573–1641), a Devonshire man with Plantagenet ancestry, began to imagine the island as the springboard to a kingdom. Bassett had served the queen in Ireland, and seems to

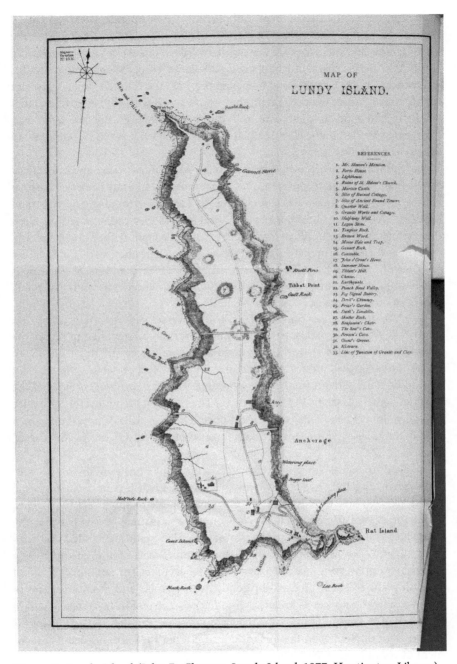

Figure 2. Lundy Island (John R. Chanter, *Lundy Island*, 1877; Huntington Library)

have been drawn towards Roman Catholicism. A correspondent warned Queen Elizabeth's chief justice Sir John Popham in 1600 that Bassett 'resolved to have the isle of Lundy, and there to place a malcontent fellow, one Ansley, a Somersetshire man'. After the accession of King James, Bassett fled abroad—one source cites his 'pretensions to the throne'—and in September 1603 the Council issued a warrant for his arrest. Bassett wrote to his brother from Paris, 'I wish with all my heart that I was at Lundy in as poor case as I came from thence', but the letter was intercepted at Plymouth. He remained in exile until 1611, when he withdrew to estates in north Devon.[11]

Early modern Lundy was infested by pirates, who gained 'a sure and safe refuge' on the island in the sixteenth century.[12] At various times Lundy became a base for corsair operations, and a place for pirates to forage for supplies and to strand captives. Neither naval authorities nor local proprietors could effectively keep them at bay. The rich traffic of the Bristol Channel brought Irish, British, Spanish, French, and Flemish predators to Lundy's waters, where they were joined in the seventeenth century by raiders from North Africa. The island itself was a poor prize, with scant resources, but it was used for several centuries as a pirate landfall, a lookout, and a place of occasional shelter.[13]

In 1534, the English captors of a Spanish vessel put the crew ashore on Lundy Isle, 'that they might perish of hunger'. French pirates tried to secure the island in 1543, but lost their ship to a company from Devonshire that landed with greater force. English pirates appeared to enjoy high-level protection, for in 1547, instead of routing them from Lundy, Admiral Thomas Seymour, brother of the Duke of Somerset, seemed to favour them. The Elizabethan pirates John Challice of Wales, John Piers of Padstow, and Robert Hicks of Saltash used Lundy as a base in the 1570s, and the Earl of Bath's forces captured 'divers rovers and pirates' there in 1587.[14]

Spanish strategists imagined Lundy as a potential prize in their war with Elizabethan England. A Spanish crew plucked an English gentleman from the island in 1594, and took him prisoner to Spain, perhaps to extract intelligence about the Bristol Channel. The Privy Council was justifiably worried that the Grenvilles had not done enough to protect the island, and demanded that they fortify Lundy, 'so as it might not be easily impeached of the enemy'.[15] The government grew even more alarmed when reports reached London in 1597 of Spanish plans to land 140 men on Lundy, with victuals and munitions, and to send forth light pinnaces as raiders.[16] Another obscure plot in 1600 seems to have been aimed at securing Lundy for the Catholic cause through the actions of Sir Robert Bassett. Neither of these plans bore fruit, but they reminded the government of continuing vulnerabilities.[17]

Lundy was sufficiently inviting, and its status sufficiently anomalous, for one of England's boldest pirates to seize one of England's smallest islands. In March 1610, Captain Thomas Salkeld (sometimes 'Sackwell') landed guns and provisions on the island, declared himself 'king of Lundy', and vowed 'to keep it from all men'. Testimony from seamen who managed to escape from the pirate, and from others who endured his regime, described a reign of terror. Salkeld demanded that his subjects abjure their loyalty to the crown. The naval captain Sir William Monson remarked: 'I have never known villain so desperately bent against their countrymen, compelling them to forswear their allegiance to his majesty.' He threatened captives with shooting or hanging, shaved their heads, and forced them at swordpoint to build a quay, erect a gun platform, and work on the neglected fortifications. At the height of his power this 'notorious and rebellious pirate' commanded 130 men 'and six or seven ships, besides small boats and others he takes daily'. Recruits arrived from Ireland, some 'against their will'. According to a dispatch from the Earl of Bath, 'he swears he will never leave the place till the king pardons his life, and gives him the island for his inheritance'. Salkeld was clearly delusional as well as ruthless, but the Jacobean navy seemed powerless to deal with the menace. The pirate's guns, however, depended on limited supplies of gunpowder, and were insufficient to withstand an uprising of prisoners armed with stones. One of his captives, the Bridgewater merchant George Eastcotte, described how they overcame Salkeld's guards by bombarding them with Lundy rocks. Within a month the occupation was over. The pirate king fled, with English naval forces in pursuit. Westerly winds impeded Salkeld's escape to Ireland, bottling him up instead at the mouth of the Severn, and by August he was reported dead.[18]

The domestic pirate menace may have abated after this dramatic episode, but ships still risked predation in nearby waters. Lundy was lightly settled, and still inadequately protected, when it was seized in August 1625 by three pirate ships from Algiers. The 'Turks', as they were called, held the island for several weeks, 'took away the people', and raided ships bound for the Irish Sea and the Atlantic. Three years later, when England and France were at war, Lundy fell briefly to four French ships, whose crews stripped the island of supplies. An attempt by Biscay pirates to land on Lundy in 1630 was less successful, as the inhabitants beat them back with boulders and stones, ammunition with which Lundy was infinitely endowed.[19]

Landings and losses raised questions about the ownership of Lundy, and whether the proprietors took care enough of defence. Successive possessors and tenants invested more in lawsuits than in fortifications. In 1622, the Devonshire gentleman John Stukely, a scion of the St Legers, claimed in Chancery that he was 'lawfully seized of and in the Isle of Lundy' in succession to his father Sir Lewes Stukely, the betrayer of Sir Walter Raleigh, who died 'a poor distracted beggar' there in 1620. Stukely alleged that, challenging his rights, a group of kinsmen led by Simon and Francis Weeks came over to Lundy and purloined 'divers deeds and writings' that documented his interest in the island. They also made off with various tools and implements, including a small brass cannon.[20]

In 1630, prospective purchasers thought that the Grenvilles might sell or lease their island, and Sir Henry Bouchier (later Earl of Bath) expressed interest.

Sir John Eliot, vice admiral of Devon but at that time a prisoner in the Tower, enquired whether Lundy's fortifications were sufficient, and who paid for them. Sir Bevil Grenville, Lundy's heir apparent, declared his love for the island, and claimed to see 'several ways how to make great profit by it ... I shall never call it to sell, or woo any man to buy it'. Thomas Arundell attempted to buy Lundy in 1636, but overlordship remained with the Grenville family until the death of Sir Bevil in battle in 1643.[21]

The notorious pirate Robert Nutt took prizes near Lundy in July 1632, while his vice admiral Smyth held the island as a base to attack shipping bound for Ireland. This time the government acted, sending Captain Richard Plumleigh to hunt the pirates, and to rout them from their 'den'. Finding that Smyth had abandoned Lundy, Plumleigh pursued the pirates into the Irish Sea, but Nutt escaped to fight another day.[22]

Lundy remained vulnerable, however, and suffered another invasion by Spaniards and Biscayners in July 1633. This was a violent assault by eighty armed attackers, who killed one resister and tied up the rest of the population. The invaders then systematically stripped the island of goods and provisions. According to one report, 'they burned our farms, took away young sheep and our daughters, and left us only old ewes and old women'. When the Lords of the Admiralty instructed Sir John Pennington to assist Captain Plumleigh in investigating the outrage, he replied that Lundy was outside his jurisdiction, and he was not responsible for acts committed there.[23]

Lundy under Charles I was more a nuisance than an asset to its proprietors, its slender profits stripped by predation. The central government seemed incapable of controlling this troublesome island, which an Admiralty report in 1634 identified as 'the chief rendezvous of pickaroons and pirates'. When the traveller Sir William Brereton passed by Lundy in July that year he remarked that the island was 'accustomed to be the pirates' harbour', and that 'Turks and men-of-war often commit spoil here'. Anglo-Irish pirates, French privateers, and Turkish corsairs all made landfalls, and ranged around Lundy's waters. Neither the Grenville proprietors nor Charles I's Ship Money fleet displayed sustained interest in routing them.[24]

Sir Bevil Grenville, to his credit, made repairs to Lundy's harbour, quay, and castle, and dreamed of raising horses on the island, but returns did not repay the effort. Short of funds in 1638, he appears to have mortgaged part of his estate to the family of Lord Saye and Sele, a transaction with profound consequence.[25] After the cavalier Sir Bevil had died in battle in Somerset early in July 1643, the parliamentarian Lord Saye and Sele (William Fiennes) gained title to Lundy. Civil war made the island a valuable but contested asset, and Saye and Sele began to stock it with goods (some said embezzled) from the besieged city of Bristol, where his son Nathaniel was commander. There was talk of moving royalist prisoners from Bristol 'to a place of more safety' on 'Lord Saye's isle of

Lundy', but, according to critics, 'the governor was unwilling to send any company to that place, whereby the mysteries of that island might be discovered, and observation made what was carried in and out there'.[26]

Prince Rupert's spectacular capture of Bristol later in July put an end to these efforts, and allowed the royalist mining entrepreneur Thomas Bushell to occupy Lundy for King Charles. Resisting parliamentary assaults in 1644 and 1646, Bushell told challengers he would 'die in the place, rather than yield without his majesty's consent'. Though not a prize of major significance, like the Channel Islands or the Isles of Scilly, Lundy served as a base for Stuart privateering, and provided a refuge that was hard to reduce. But so primitive were Lundy's facilities, so acute its isolation, that men based there might just as well have been prisoners. After Bristol changed hands again in September 1645, Bushell made Lundy into one of the last royalist strongholds, with a garrison of over a hundred men. They repaired the castle, built a chapel, and even operated an unofficial mint, as they braced for assault by Lord Saye and Sele, whose campaign had both personal and parliamentary motivations.[27] It was during this period that leading royalists considered Lundy as a possible place of confinement for their disgraced western commander Sir Richard Grenville, Sir Bevil's younger brother, before he escaped to France (see Chapter 8).[28]

Lundy had neither the facilities nor the resources to be more than a temporary royalist refuge, and would have made an especially miserable prison. As Bushell told friends in 1646, it was 'desolate and stormy, and hath nought to invite the inhabitant', except one who sought solitude. In other letters Bushell described the island as 'this remote rock', 'the naked promontory of Lundy', and 'useless, except in some advantages it may yield to me'. Besieged by parliamentary shipping, the island received few supplies. At the end, the depleted defenders were close to starving, and 'scarce drank a barrel of beer in two years'. In contrast to better-favoured islands, Lundy was no place for a cavalier to divert himself by reading and drinking.[29]

As early as January 1646 the Committee of Both Kingdoms discussed 'a proposition to be made to Captain Bushell about delivering up Lundy'.[30] Hoping that the island could be taken by agreement, rather than military assault, parliament opened negotiations with its royalist defenders. Several times they summoned Bushell to surrender, in January, April, and May 1646, but he said he could not yield without permission from the king. Finally, King Charles wrote from Newcastle on 14 July, permitting Bushell to use his discretion with regard to surrender, 'with this caution, that you do not take example from ourselves, and be not over-credulous of vain promises'. Similar messages would go to other declining outposts. Even with this authority in hand, Bushell would not budge. He shared his belief in September 1646 that those who rebelled against the king would be punished in the future, and he determined to maintain Lundy at any cost. It took another year of negotiation before terms could be agreed, and even longer for

Bushell to surrender. At issue, beside questions of honour, was Bushell's claim to mineral rights in Devon, and the matter of his debts, for which he was liable to arrest if he left his island fastness.[31] Lundy, for Bushell, was a bargaining chip, as well as a source of status as a cavalier.

Sensing an opportunity, Bushell's creditors attempted to serve him with a writ, 'but could not come to him, he being . . . in the isle of Lundy, where he stands upon his guard'.[32] Bushell demanded financial guarantees and legal protections before he would yield the island, and after many months of prevarication was ready to come to terms. It was agreed in principle in July 1647 'that upon delivery of the Isle of Lundy to Lord Saye and Sele, or his assigns, by Mr Thomas Bushell', the royalist's delinquency would be removed, his sequestration discharged, and his rights restored to mines in Cornwall, Devonshire, and Wales. It was further agreed 'that the men that were with him in the island, being not men of estate or quality, be pardoned, or freed from delinquency and sequestration'.[33]

The devil being in the details, Bushell agreed to come to London, with safe conduct, to treat with Saye and Sele 'about the surrender of the said island to the use of the parliament', and while there 'to be free from any arrests, suits, or molestations whatsoever'. But, notwithstanding this protection, Bushell was arrested in September 1647, and imprisoned at the suit of his creditors for a debt of £130. To complicate matters, the man who stood surety for Bushell's bail was also arrested, and the creditors blocked his release. Parliament's reduction of Lundy was stalled while lawyers, politicians, and leaders of the army debated Bushell's rights and obligations. Sea conditions caused further delays, as the delegation sent to accept the surrender of the island had to wait fifteen days in north Devon before it was safe to cross. The handover eventually took place on 24 February 1648, when Bushell's garrison surrendered with dignity, and twenty-two men accepted transfers to the mainland. Bushell returned to his earlier obsession of 'discovering mineral treasures' while attempting to restore his fortunes.[34] Six months later, had Bushell remained in control, the island might have become a royalist base in the second civil war. Instead, Lundy reverted to a point of navigational reference and a place of shelter for naval and commercial shipping, periodically harassed by Irish, Flemish, and Breton pirates, and by Prince Rupert's rovers.[35] The parliamentary admiral Robert Blake visited Lundy in June 1649 when 'strong weather' forced him to seek shelter there while pursing royalist privateers.[36]

The parliamentary grandee Lord Saye and Sele treated Lundy as a spoil of victory, as well as his by right, and used it as a place of retirement. Widowed in 1648, and estranged from the regicides at Westminster, Saye and Sele chose Lundy as a writing retreat, and a place to nurse his melancholy. He may have been joined in 1650 by the independent clergyman William Lampit, who claimed to have been 'minister and governor in Lundy island, and was never excepted against by the army . . . or the state'.[37] A royalist privateer who intercepted some of Saye and

Sele's provisions in 1651 referred scathingly to him as the 'petty prince' of 'that pretty island', where his isolation was near complete.[38] During three years on Lundy he is credited with writing a romance (now lost), and with honing the political theories of *Vindiciae Veritatis*, before returning to his war-damaged family home in Oxfordshire.[39]

Breton, French, and royalist raiders menaced the Bristol Channel during the 1650s, prompting the Commonwealth 'to secure the trade about Lundy', without much practical investment. Similar threats recurred after the Restoration, when Flemish, French, and Dutch ships preyed on local shipping, and occasionally landed on the island. In want of provisions, the captain of the *Grantham* called at Lundy in January 1659, but found himself in peril when a sudden storm arose. The ship escaped by cutting its cables and abandoning its anchors, and continued up the Bristol Channel in great distress.[40] There would have been scant welcome from Lundy's depleted and isolated settlement.

When Lundy was restored to the Grenvilles after the Restoration, Thomas Bushell also resurfaced, seeking to retrieve his estates and to retaliate against his enemies. He recited his version of 'the rendition of Lundy Isle' in a petition of May 1660, and in various printed remonstrances, cataloguing the services he had rendered and the affronts he had received in his majesty's service. Bushell did not return to live on Lundy, but used it rhetorically to memorialize his grievances.[41]

In subsequent decades the island featured more as a navigational feature or seamark than a place of inherent interest. Mariners warned of the vulnerability of Lundy in the Dutch wars of the 1660s, and cited the multiple threats to Severn shipping, but little was done to improve the island or attend to its defences. In the summer of 1667 several foreign seamen pilfered possessions from houses on Lundy, but were gone before authorities could react.[42] 'In the reign of William and Mary', a late-Georgian gazetteer reports, 'the French seized it by a stratagem, and maintained themselves in it a considerable time'.[43] A naval visitor to Lundy in 1704 found 'the ruins of a house or two, but no inhabitants, having been disturbed formerly by the French privateers, who often used here in the war'.[44] One of the island's most celebrated visitors in this period was the pirate captain William Kidd, who was brought from New England to Lundy in chains in April 1700, for transshipment towards his trial and execution in London.[45]

Eighteenth-century Lundy suffered long periods of neglect, interspersed by attempts at pasturage, and occasional raids by marauders. Bristol merchants in 1742 suggested that 'this island could be annexed to the crown, and a garrison of about forty men kept there' to prevent depredations by the French and other privateers. The government was unresponsive. The entrepreneur Thomas Benson obtained a lease of the island in 1748, and used it as a base for smuggling. Benson also had contracts to transport convicts to America, but dropped them instead at his private prison on Lundy. He argued that 'it mattered not' where they were sent, 'so long as they were out of the kingdom', encouraging the belief that Lundy was not part of England, and not beholden to the crown. Benson eventually overreached himself, and fled abroad after the failure of various schemes and scams.[46] The customs collector at Cardiff claimed that 'there never lived a man on Lundy who was not concerned in smuggling', and recommended that the crown should buy the island to forestall that menace. The government did not rise to this suggestion as it later did for the much more profitable Isle of Man.[47]

Later owners found little use for the island, beyond the establishment of a lighthouse. A scheme in 1786 to establish Lundy as 'a proper place for the receptacle of convicts' came to nothing.[48] Similarly fruitless were plans to develop the island as a granite quarry, a menagerie, or a holiday resort. Nineteenth-century owners took advantage of Lundy being 'unrecognized for the purposes of imperial taxation and local rating', and styled themselves 'sovereign lord of the island, with an independence far exceeding some of the minor foreign potentates'. The late-Victorian proprietor the Revd H. G. Heaven was known as 'king of Lundy island'. Boldest of all was the twentieth-century owner Martin Coles Harman, who issued his own coinage, the Lundy 'Puffin' (with his own image), and refused to acknowledge the jurisdiction of any mainland court. The island had value as a curiosity, remote and removed from the complex modern world. It was disputable in the 1950s whether residents of Lundy should vote in the electoral division of Torrington (Devon), and even whether Lundy should be part of England or Wales, as Michael Drayton had noted in 1612. Only in 1974 was it formally recognized as part of Devon.[49] The island was saved for the nation in 1969, and is now leased to the Landmark Trust as a nature reserve for ecological tourism. Followers of British weather may best be familiar with Lundy from the BBC shipping forecasts.

Lundy remains an English island, though little known and little visited. Its history of disputed ownership, anomalous jurisdiction, and general isolation echoes that of other islands in miniature. Though insular and eccentric, it was by no means untouched by mainland developments. Lundy in the early modern era had maritime value and strategic significance that brought it passing attention. The Grenvilles and their rivals, the pirates Salkeld and Nutt, and the mid-Stuart contestants Thomas Bushell and Lord Saye and Sele, invested energies in Lundy's primitive infrastructure. Its potential as a prison attracted several schemes. The Privy Council, parliament, and the navy took occasional note of its needs. The island was vulnerable to attack, and subject to neglect. Proprietors and occupiers made what they could of Lundy's scant resources, and enjoyed or endured it as a place of solitude. Lundy's story introduces many of the themes of England's islands in a sea of troubles.

3

English Islands in the Norman Sea

Sometimes fancifully imagined as the isles of 'the English Hesperides', the Channel Islands of Jersey, Guernsey, and Guernsey's dependencies of Alderney and Sark enjoyed an especially anomalous relationship with the English state. A 'Norman archipelago' within 'the Britannic ocean', 90–120 miles beyond Hampshire, they lay closer to France than to England. As dominions of the English crown, they extended the sovereignty of the seas almost to foreign shores and were constantly exposed to threats from abroad.[1]

This chapter examines the historical, constitutional, administrative, and political entanglements that bound the Channel Islands to the English crown, which made them both intractable and indispensable. Concerned primarily with the Elizabethan and early Stuart period, it explores the interaction of local and central authorities, the competing claims of islanders and royal officials, and the complexity of overlapping jurisdictions. Later developments are addressed in later chapters. Islanders generally went about their business without much outside interference, but occasionally sought assistance or relief from London. Royal governors and captains of varying competence and rectitude competed for authority with island bailiffs and jurats against a background of local rivalries, alliances, and ambitions.

Arguably the most remarkable of all English islands, the Channel Islands were certainly the best documented, thanks to the record-keeping propensities of the island courts, the hoarding by island families of papers and precedents that supported their property and privileges, and the perennial concerns of the Privy Council. Their circumstances, however, were not well known in early modern England (as may still be the case in some quarters today). The Elizabethan geographer William Harrison identified Jersey and Guernsey as a 'parcel of Hampshire', a claim that islanders would refute.[2] Clerks in Charles I's High Court of Admiralty made a similar erroneous assumption when they recorded the examination of the mariner Thomas Gilbert of 'Garneseye', Hampshire.[3] The persistence of this notion prompted one Restoration official to explain, with regard to Guernsey, that 'the people of that island, nor their estates, have never been under the jurisdiction of any of the courts of justice in England, nor has any writ out of any of those courts ever been in force there. Whoever will call it part of Hampshire grossly errs from the truth.'[4]

The metropolitan viewpoint was often tinged by ignorance and condescension. Describing an incident in the reign of Philip and Mary, the martyrologist John

England's Islands in a Sea of Troubles. David Cressy, Oxford University Press (2020). © David Cressy 2020.
DOI: 10.1093/oso/9780198856603.001.0001

Foxe described Guernsey as 'an obscure island, in such an outcorner of the realm, far off from the court, and practice of English laws'.[5] Commending reserved fellowships for Channel Island students at Oxford, an orator in the 1630s referred to them as 'tiny outlying sprinklings' of the king's dominions.[6] When the exiled Charles II took temporary refuge in Jersey in 1649, a supporter lamented his isolation in that 'nook of the world'.[7] Writing in the reign of William III, when the islands were a front line in the war with France, the Jerseyman Philip Falle still thought it necessary to dispel the 'lame and imperfect notions' of some English commentators, 'as if these islands had been situated, not as they are in the British Channel, but some degrees beyond the [equinoctial] line'. He later thought it helpful to represent the islands as *tabulae ex naufragio*, planks saved with much difficulty out of that terrible shipwreck in which all the rest of Normandy was lost to England', and to remind readers of their undying loyalty to the crown.[8]

Metropolitan and insular viewpoints clashed across the archipelagic periphery, but were especially fraught on Guernsey and Jersey. In the Channel Islands, as elsewhere, the art of governance centred on pleasing the crown without jeopardizing local stability or good order. From the point of view of the islanders, it involved the continuance of cherished customs and privileges, without domination by London. Royal governors, under orders from the Privy Council, were tasked with maintaining military strength and meeting the needs of the garrison, without alienating civilian officials and key community interests. Government officials exercised a variety of powers that could favour their friends and benefit their families, while coping with insular opinions, jealousies, and interests.

Proximity, language, trade, and ties of family sustained close connections between the Channel Islands and the ports of Normandy and Brittany. The novelist and Guernsey resident Victor Hugo aptly described them as 'portions of France which have fallen into the sea and been picked up by England'.[9] Islanders used French pistoles, livres tournois, sols, and deniers more often than English money. They traded more frequently with St Malo than with Southampton. Their ministers were more often trained in Huguenot seminaries than in colleges in England. The seigneurial and office-holding class were mostly bilingual, but most of the inhabitants spoke only dialects of Norman French. One Stuart observer remarked of the islanders that, 'by reason of their language, they are reputed by the vulgar in England for French, when in France they undergo all the disadvantages of English'.[10] Declaring their everlasting loyalty to the English crown, once again at war with France, the leaders of Jersey assured William and Mary in the early 1690s 'that though our tongues be French, our hearts and swords are truly English'.[11]

An example of the difficulties that could arise from difference of language was the confrontation on a Jersey beach in 1593, when an island farmer and an English garrison soldier fell to fisticuffs, 'upon occasion of speech falling out, though the one understood not the other'. When the soldier subsequently died, and the yeoman was imprisoned, it took the combined efforts of the governor, bailiff, jurats, and the English Privy Council to disentangle the complexities of military and civilian jurisdiction amid the 'the laws and privileges of that island'.[12]

It is often convenient to consider Guernsey and Jersey together as the 'Channel Islands', but they never constituted a single political unit (see Figure 3). Though

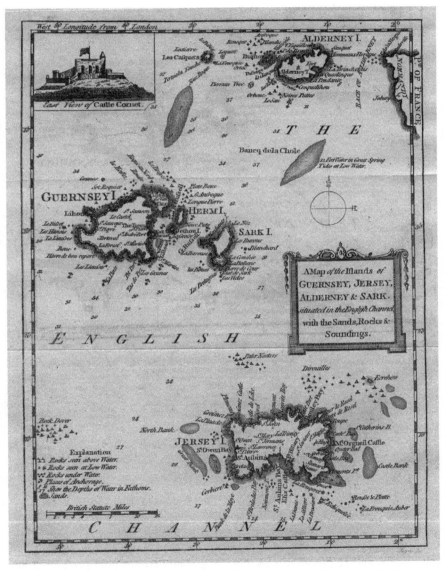

Figure 3. The Islands of Guernsey, Jersey, Alderney, & Sark (*Gentleman's Magazine*, 1779; author's copy)

they shared so much in common, their histories and cultural identities were distinct. Each community of islanders considered itself most special. Sir Peter Osborne referred in 1646 to 'the natural animosity between the islanders of Guernsey and Jersey', and other early modern visitors observed 'no great kindness between the two neighbouring rival islands'.[13] Though the jurats and bailiffs of each island were periodically at loggerheads with their governors, Jersey seemed, for the most part, less fractious, and more amenable to the needs of the crown. Guernsey sided with parliament throughout the civil war, and clung longer to its presbyterian heritage. Jersey, by contrast, was quicker to embrace the Church of England, and cleaved more wholeheartedly to the royalist cause. The dominance on Jersey of the Paulet family, and then the de Carterets, stifled opposition, whereas a wider range of families competed for office on Guernsey. The families of Lemprière and Dumaresq shared prominence in Jersey, while Guernsey's jurats were often named de Beauvoir, le Marchant, Carey, Andros, de Sausmarez, or Gosselin.

The Channel Islands were home to pastoralists, agriculturalists, fisherfolk, mariners, stocking manufacturers, and traders. One seventeenth-century visitor put their combined population at 50,000, though this was a gross overestimate. Jacobean Guernsey had a population of less than 9,000, perhaps rising towards10,000 by the Restoration. Figures for Jersey were higher, though not by much. A plausible estimate in 1685 was that that Jersey's population 'will hardly exceed 15,000'. When Lord Danby asked 'how such a span of earth could contain such multitudes', Sir John Peyton answered 'that the people married within themselves like conies in a burrow; and further, that for more than thirty years they never had been molested either with sword, pestilence, or famine'.[14]

Elizabethan Alderney had four score households, and could muster a hundred men for defence, according to a report of 1575.[15] By the 1620s, Alderney's population had grown to around 800, with 'well near an hundred families' in the main settlement of St Anne, according to the traveller Peter Heylyn.[16] Queen Elizabeth had granted the depopulated island of Sark to Philip de Carteret, 'to people and plant it', and the island had 'some forty households', perhaps 200 inhabitants, by the reign of Charles I.[17]

Medieval Islands and the Early Modern State

As relics of the medieval Duchy of Normandy, the Channel Islands enjoyed distinctive dealings with governments at Whitehall and Westminster. They were dominions of the crown, yet not fully part of the kingdom. The tangled history of the Plantagenet era produced a plethora of grants, charters, precepts, and promises, many of which were renewed or revised by subsequent monarchs. Guernsey alone received nineteen charters between 1341 and 1668, each of which acknowledged its exceptionalism.[18] The central government demanded the loyalty of the islands, as dynastic, commercial, and military assets, while islanders sought recognition of their rights and traditions. The crown's allowance of 'very large privileges or immunities to the people of those islands' made it 'their greatest interest to depend on England', especially when the alternative was domination by France. The English government secured strategic castles and harbours, and flows of foreign intelligence, while the islanders gained profit, protection, and the maintenance of their 'liberties'. A balance of mutualities sustained their relationship. Successive monarchs confirmed the 'rights, jurisdictions, privileges, immunities, liberties, and franchises' of the islands, even as some of their representatives undercut them.[19] While other parts of the English domain moved closer to integration, the Channel Islands remained odd and apart.

Early modern authors took pains to understand the laws and customs of Jersey and Guernsey because their governments had to deal with their administrative and political consequences. English visitors and island officials attempting to explain their peculiar constitutional arrangements invariably included a historical narrative, to tell how such conditions arose. Key developments included the conquest of England by William of Normandy in 1066, King John's loss of territories on the continent in 1204, and the military and diplomatic achievements and setbacks of other monarchs from Edward I to Henry VIII.[20]

Some antiquarians claimed that English rights to the Channel Islands had Saxon origins, predating and independent of the Normans. It was more usual, however, to claim unbroken title from the eleventh-century Duchy of Normandy, whose rulers became kings of England. It could then be argued, against the French, that continual English governance of the islands according to Norman law and custom kept alive the *de jure* rights of the crown to the rest of the Norman inheritance. English monarchs still claimed rights to the throne of France, and possession of the Norman islands helped to sustain that fantasy. Elizabethan and Stuart charters specifically located the islands 'within our Duchy of Normandy'.[21] It became a maxim, as 'Lord Coke says, that a seizin [legal possession] of the Channel Islands is a good seizin in law of the whole province'.[22] From the French point of view, by contrast, the islands were unredeemed territories that threatened their security and implicated their honour. Despite half a millennium of English possession, the islands were still claimed and coveted by France. As late as 1668, the French king warned Charles II that he had not forgotten his title to the Channel Islands, though 'in honour he was obliged not to attack them till he had given notice'.[23] It was a point of pride for some local patriots that their islands were never conquered by kings of England, but rather that England had been bested by Normandy.[24]

The most clearly iterated opinion, argued in Calvin's case before King's Bench in 1608 in a matter originally concerned with Scotland, recognized Guernsey and Jersey as 'parts and parcels of the dukedom of Normandy, yet remaining under the actual leigeance and obedience of the king'. They were 'no parcels of the realm of England, but several dominions, enjoyed by several titles, governed by several laws'. 'Realm and dominion differ', explained an Exchequer report, 'because a thing can be within the dominion of the king of England not within his realm'. Lord Chancellor Thomas Egerton insisted that the islands were dominions of King James, 'under his subjection and obedience' if not answerable to his laws. Subjects born in Guernsey or Jersey, like natives of Ireland, 'be no aliens, but capable of lands in England', yet were governed by their own 'ancient laws'.[25] Unpacking this constitutional conundrum would challenge multiple generations of administrators and lawyers, and today is barely resolved.

Most authoritative, and most often quoted, was the early Stuart jurist Sir Edward Coke, who recognized that the Channel Islands were not bound by English acts of parliament, unless specifically mentioned therein, and that 'the king's writ runneth not into these isles', except by commission of the Great Seal; and even then 'the commissioners must judge according to the laws and customs of these isles'. The jurats of Guernsey were not answerable before justices in England, and matters arising there could be determined only by 'the custom of the said island', though appeals to the Privy Council were still permitted.[26] The legal status of the islands remained ambiguous, though Coke's opinion allowed wide room for insular autonomy.

Holders of land by feudal tenure in the Channel Islands owed fealty to the monarch in his capacity as Duke of Normandy, and normally discharged that duty by attendance at the islands' Royal Courts. The island seigneurs venerated their ancestors and flexed their muscles, vying with each other for precedency and respect.[27] The seigneurial system lasted through the twentieth century, obliging crown tenants to attend the island Court of Chief Pleas. Personal performance of feudal loyalty had all but disappeared from Stuart England, but courtiers of Charles I witnessed an unusual spectacle in June 1637 when the Guernseyman Amice Andros, the feudal seigneur de Sausmarez de St Martin, did homage for his fief at Whitehall in person, on his knees, with his hands enclasped by the king, saying: 'sire, Je demure vostre homme a vous porter foy et homage contre tous.' Andros was honoured because he served the court as a Marshall of Ceremonies, a good foundation for a man who would later be bailiff of Guernsey, and whose son would hold high office on the island and in the English American colonies.[28]

Channel Islanders took no part in English parliaments, and were generally untouched by parliamentary legislation. Royal proclamations did not normally affect them. They could not be summoned before English courts, and were not answerable to Quarter Sessions or Assizes, or to the Westminster courts of Chancery, Common Pleas, Requests, the Exchequer, or King's Bench. Neither the prerogative court of Star Chamber nor the writ of *habeas corpus* had effect, despite occasional attempts to invoke them. Nor did commissions from England's High Court of Admiralty have effect in the Channel Islands, as demonstrated in the case of a ship abandoned off Sark in 1608, which was resolved by reference to lawyers at Rouen.[29]

The jurist Sir Matthew Hale (1609–76) wrote that the Channel Islands 'are annexed to the crown of England, and though not *infra regum*, yet they are *infra dominion regni Angliae*'.[30] Yet the English Common Law had no purchase in these parts of the king's dominion. The central government could not turn to the islands for troops or taxes, so that none of the subsidies, forced loans, Ship Money, or related fiscal instruments employed by the Stuarts reached their shores. Islanders looked instead to their own courts and assemblies, where they conducted their business by their own law, in their own French.[31] The ecclesiastical affairs of the islands were also Francophone and idiosyncratic. Though nominally subject to the bishop of Winchester (though outside his diocese), they were dominated by presbyterian colloquies under Elizabeth and the early Stuarts, and later by semi-autonomous anglican deans (see Chapter 10).

Visiting this strange society in 1629 as chaplain to the Earl of Danby, Peter Heylyn found the laws of the Channel Isles 'of no great affinity with the laws of England'. Instead, he believed, the islanders enjoyed distinctive 'privileges and immunities', and lived 'in *libera custodia*, in a kind of free subjection, not any acquainted with taxes, or with any levies either of men or money'. He was not the only visitor to remark that the islanders were 'never pressed, as in England, for the king's service', an exemption especially benefiting their maritime community.[32] They were under the English crown, but not controlled by the English state, as remains the case today. In governing the islands, successive monarchs renewed the 'privileges, jurisdictions, immunities, liberties, and franchises, which have been indulged, given, granted, and confirmed' by their predecessors, without necessarily understanding them. Charles I's Privy Council sought advice in 1633 'concerning the laws of the isles of Jersey and Guernsey', and thought it fit to ask whether 'subjects there are governed by the edicts of France', and whether 'their children may be bred in England'. They could have turned to Lord Chancellor Egerton's determination in the *post-nati* case a generation earlier, which answered no to the first question, and yes to the second.[33]

The legal antiquarian John Selden complicated matters, in his Latin treatise *Mare Clausum*, which first appeared in 1635 and was several times published in English as *The Right and Dominion of the Sea*. In contrast to Coke, Selden emphasized the crown's rights in the Channel Islands, and insisted that they belonged to the dominion of England, independent of their roots in the Duchy of Normandy. English kings, he asserted, were lords of the sea and 'the islands placed therein', so that Guernsey, Jersey, Alderney, 'and the sea lying about them, did...constitute one entire body of empire with the kingdom of England'. In support of this view, which favoured royal power over privileges claimed by islanders, Selden recalled that fourteenth-century monarchs sent justices errant or justices itinerant to the islands, to uphold the king of England's law, 'though the inhabitants did indeed exclaim, and sometimes preferred their petitions against this kind of jurisdiction'. Island patriots were still railing against Selden's views more than two hundred years later.[34]

Early modern Channel Islanders cleaved more to Coke than to Selden, and relished their 'singularities'.[35] They were adamant in preserving their unique constitutional status as independent bailiwicks, in which the lesser islands of Alderney and Sark were seigneurial dependencies of Guernsey. Jersey, its seventeenth-century historian Philip Falle observed, was 'properly a peculiar of the crown of England', and therefore of 'natural and necessary consequence' exempt from parliamentary taxation, and untouched by the courts of Westminster.[36] Islanders never tired of citing their liberties and immunities, which were often surprising to outsiders.

Neutrality as Far as Man Can See

One of the most jealously guarded privileges of the Channel Islands was their ability to continue trading with all parties during wartime. No mainland community had such rights. Enjoying a unique commercial advantage, traders from Jersey, Guernsey, Alderney, and Sark could conduct their business in Normandy and Brittany, even while England and France were at war, while 'merchants of all nations may come and resort to that isle with security in time of hostility'.[37] This right of neutrality extended offshore 'so far as the sight of man can reach from any of the islands'—an uncertain distance that varied with vantage point and weather conditions; on a fair day observers on Jersey could see the low cliffs of France's Cotentin peninsula. The privilege of neutrality dated from the reign of Edward IV, and was confirmed by a papal bull in 1481.[38] The Restoration protestant Jean Poingdestre believed, however, that Pope Sixtus IV merely ratified existing arrangements, which benefited all parties, so that the waters around the islands could be called *mare pacificum*. Tudor and Stuart monarchs up to the reign of James II confirmed that 'all merchants, as well enemies as friends, may come in time of war as in time of peace, within as far distance as a man can see from the island, without any restraint upon their bodies, ships, or goods, which privilege time out of mind they have enjoyed'. For several centuries the islands enjoyed 'a continual truce', which allowed 'Frenchmen and others, how hot soever the war be followed in other parts, to repair hither without danger, and here to trade in all security'.[39]

This island privilege of neutrality was tested in England's foreign wars, and, though sometimes challenged, was usually maintained until the reign of William III. The Elizabethan governor of Guernsey Sir Thomas Leighton was forced to release several French vessels he had seized in 1587, on the grounds that their cargoes belonged to England's enemy Spain, and he faced reprimand for acting 'contrary to the privilege of the island'.[40] Trading continued, despite hostilities, and the principle of commercial neutrality prevailed. Garrison officials sometimes worried that unregulated international traffic might deplete them of useful resources, and allow the intrusion of interlopers and foreign spies, but the principle was generally accepted that 'all merchants, as well enemies as friends, may freely trade thither without prejudice', be they English, Spanish, French, or Dutch.[41]

Charles I's war with France from 1627 to 1630 posed new challenges to Channel Island neutrality. Stocking-knitters on Jersey feared ruin, but Sir Philip Carteret (by now dropping the 'de') intervened to ensure that their trade should continue with France, 'with due cautions and limitations'. This privilege, he argued, was not only 'the policy of former ages', but also strategically advantageous, for an enemy was unlikely to invade a place with which they trafficked. Carteret also claimed that 'free intercourse' yielded intelligence advantages to England, as well as profits to island merchants, not least his own kinsmen. Blind eyes were turned to the illicit trade in gunpowder and munitions, in which islanders shipped contraband to England's enemies.[42] Traders throughout the islands feared that 'our times give no hope to presume further', but reasserted their claim of neutrality. The merchants of Alderney invoked 'certain charters and immunities obtained from the king of England, with the mutual consent of other princes, that they should in open war as well as in peace remain free places of traffic, and intercourse of all sorts of merchandize', and hoped for ratification. Charles I's government confirmed these rights, stressing their value in binding the islanders to the crown, without mentioning that one of those helpful 'other princes' was the pope.[43]

Practice did not always follow policy. One ship, the *Fern* of London, lading hides in Jersey for sale in St Malo, was prevented from sailing in September 1627 on the grounds that 'it was unfitting for the provision to be carried to our enemies, and whoever took that ship should do the king good service'. Other vessels, however, were unimpeded, carrying wine, soap, tallow, fish, and other commodities between the islands and ports in France.[44] In June 1628, when intelligence suggested that the enemy was imminently 'resolved to set upon these isles', Sir Philip Carteret proposed a blockade of French vessels approaching Jersey, and urged his counterpart in Guernsey to take similar action. But, despite some military nervousness, the international traffic continued.[45]

Governors, Bailiffs, and Jurats

Unlike the typical arrangement in English counties, with crown-appointed lieutenants, deputy lieutenants, sheriffs, and locally based justices of the peace, the islands of Guernsey and Jersey each had a military governor or captain, dispatched from London, and locally independent civilian bailiffs and jurats. (Officers in the

Cinque Ports on the coast of Kent and Sussex had similar titles, but fewer privileges.) The title 'governor' (sometimes 'governor general'), considered grander than 'captain', became fixed in Jersey in 1618.[46] Governors of Guernsey up to the civil war included Sir Francis Chamberlain (1561–70), Sir Thomas Leighton (1570–1609), George Carew, Earl of Totnes (1610–21), and Henry Danvers, Earl of Danby (1621–44). Jersey's governors in this period included Sir Hugh Paulet (1550–74), Sir Amias Paulet (1574–90), Anthony Paulet (1590–1600), Sir Walter Raleigh (1600–3), Sir John Peyton (1603–30), and Sir Thomas Jermyn (1631–43).

These Channel Island governors, like their counterparts on the Isle of Wight and in some of the New World colonies, were career administrators, aristocrats, and courtiers, independent of island society.[47] Though their office was honourable and profitable, it could sometimes appear as an irksome exile, a hardship posting, and a brake on higher ambitions. Preoccupied with estates, families, and obligations in England, many appointees chose not to reside in the islands, and governed instead through subordinates. They were often slow to take up their duties, and, after coming into residence, expressed frequent longing to return home. Sir Walter Raleigh, for example, spent just a few weeks on Jersey in the summer of 1602, during his three years as governor. The Earl of Danby presented his credentials on Guernsey soon after being appointed in 1621, but spent most of his twenty-three-year governorship in England. He expressed his unhappiness when Charles I ordered him back to Guernsey in 1627, at a time of war with France, saying, 'I think it not fit for his majesty's honour, nor suitable to my own reputation' to be shut up in an island castle. It was surely enough, he wrote from his estate in Oxfordshire, to be 'continually kept solicitous' of island affairs by his lieutenant Sir Peter Osborne, who was also his brother-in-law.[48] Having travelled dutifully but briefly to the Channel Islands in 1629, Danby had no eagerness to go there again, though he made a short visit in 1636. Ordered in September 1640 'to repair at once to your government of Guernsey, and defend the island against all assaults', he made repeated excuses, and never actually made the voyage.[49] Ambitions and duties at court in England likewise excused the Caroline governor of Jersey, Sir Thomas Jermyn, from ever visiting his island.[50]

Island governors and their deputies served the crown by commanding castles and garrisons, mustering the island militia, and maintaining public security. Their tasks, in addition to their military responsibilities, included correspondence with the Privy Council, hosting distinguished visitors, pursuing pirates, and sometimes keeping custody of English political prisoners. Governors controlled access to certain island offices, and enriched themselves through sinecures, perquisites, and fees. The Elizabethan governor of Guernsey Sir Thomas Leighton, for example, recovered for the crown the feudal dues of *champart*, a tithe on land and crops, and the queen rewarded him with the licence 'to make sale of it, to his best advantage', which he did accordingly.[51] Leighton also enriched himself from dues charged on merchandize imported by foreign vessels, though this was strictly against the privileges of the island. The governor also served *ex officio* as admiral, which meant that he shared the profit from prizes and wrecks.[52] Governors and their lieutenants also regulated the coming and staying of 'strangers' (foreigners and non-islanders), and distributed the wool that was imported for the islands' knitters, which were two more sources of influence and controversy. Dependent upon London, their remit was grander than that of any provincial official in England. All royal revenues, profits, and emoluments from the bailiwick passed through their hands.[53]

Whether their authority was superior to that of the bailiff and jurats, as some governors claimed, was a continuing bone of contention. Governors were supposed to assist the island officials 'in the execution of their judgements', but often behaved like independent satraps. The early Elizabethan Privy Council instructed the bailiff and jurats of Jersey to be 'obedient and conformable... unto all such things as [governor Sir Hugh Paulet] shall from time to time prescribe unto you for the good order, surety, and defence of that isle', and expressed surprise when the islanders pushed back. Channel Islanders repeatedly complained of being 'grossly oppressed, their laws infringed, and their constitutions violated', requiring intervention and redress by royal commission.[54] The Restoration lieutenant bailiff of Jersey Jean Poingdestre argued that the governors were not *domini* or overlords, but were merely the military representatives of the crown. Civil and criminal matters, he reminded his readers, belonged exclusively to the bailiff and jurats, notwithstanding the attempt by some governors to encroach on that authority.[55] Struggles between bailiffs and governors punctuated Channel Island history under the early Tudors, and continued into the nineteenth century.

The bailiff, like the governor, occupied a royal office 'granted immediately by the king's most noble ancestors', and was usually appointed for life. He was tasked with the contradictory and sometimes impossible responsibility of representing simultaneously the interests of the islanders and of the monarch. Having two crown officers on each island, one in the castle, the other in the Royal Court, was a potential source of trouble. While the captain or governor looked upward and outward, the bailiff turned locally and within. Unlike the outsider military governors, the bailiff was invariably a wealthy islander, and was expected to maintain residence. As Sir Philip Carteret recognized, when he solicited that office in Guernsey in 1621, any effective bailiff needed familiarity with 'the common country language of the isle, the terms of our laws, customs, and style of proceeding, hardly known to ourselves'.[56] He would be master of its mysteries, and adept at obfuscation. The bailiff presided over the island's Royal Court, which had 'cognizance in all pleas, suits, and actions, whether real [concerned with landed property], personal, mixed, or criminal arising with the island', except for matters of high concern like treason.[57] Special circumstances might require the summoning of the States, an occasional deliberative assembly of the bailiff and jurats, the rectors and constables of parishes, and the king's Attorney General.[58] Governors often advised and sometimes meddled in the appointment of the bailiff, and the two officers repeatedly struggled over their respective roles and precedence.

Channel Island jurats were 'chosen and elected' by the States, members having sounded the opinions of leading parishioners and local office-holders. Elections were sometimes influenced, it was alleged, 'by bribes, treats, promises and threatenings', though probably with no more corruption than in many an English county. Like that of the bailiff, their election was for life.[59] The jurats worked alongside an array of minor officials—douzeniers, vignteniers, and constables, as well as le Procureur du Roi, l'Avocat du Roi, and the Greffier or recorder. The sheriff or Prévôt (provost), another honourable and contestable position, was the executive officer of the States and the Royal Court. The islanders conducted their business in French in the Cour Royal, and in such customary courts as La Cour d'Héritage, La Cour de Catel, and La Cour du Billet on Jersey, and the courts of Chief Plaid, Namps, and Mobiliare on Guernsey, which outsiders found baffling. Nothing was more strange to English eyes than the Clameur de Haro, the feudal cry for restraint of a wrongdoer, which still has some efficacy today.[60]

Maintenance of the crown's interests required cooperation with island authorities, but governors, bailiffs, and jurats were often at odds. According to an order of 1568, they were supposed to 'join together in good friendship and concord, whereby they may, with more commodity, each of them attend their several charges'.[61] In practice, however, there was friction. The governor had 'sole and absolute power of the militia', as bailiff Sir Philip Carteret of Jersey acknowledged, but this was not without 'some opposition, and distractions of evil consequence'.[62] Though the governor had primary responsibility for the island's defence, charters dating back to Henry III authorized the bailiff and jurats to inspect all castles, and to make sure they were properly supplied, thereby encroaching on the governor's military domain. Islanders had obligations to serve in the militia, and owed labour for island defences, but this could be challenged and abused. They were obliged to defend their territory, but were exempt from levies or conscription for overseas service.[63] The stage was set for conflict between the castle and the island, between military governors and civilian officials, across the reigns of the Tudors and Stuarts.

Successive governors pitted their wits against island officials whose Greffiers kept registers of letters and warrants, and against local notables who accumulated their own archives of charters and precedents. Almost any initiative from London could be countered by invoking 'the ancient usage and custom of this isle' or 'the fundamental constitutions of the island'. Local officials appealed repeatedly to 'le coustume et constant pratique de temps immemorial en cette isle'. The Privy Council was understandably frustrated by 'controversies that have long time depended, and by the uncertain interpretation of those laws and customs are full of ambiguity and doubt'.[64] As late as 1700, the jurats of Guernsey could bring proceedings to a halt by citing the fourteenth-century Book of Extent and the fifteenth-century Precept of Assize.[65]

Friction between governors and bailiffs was recurrent, if not perennial. They clashed repeatedly over policies and procedures, overlapping cognizance, and questions of jurisdictional pre-eminence. Relationships became especially fraught under the governorship of Sir Thomas Leighton on late Elizabethan and early Jacobean Guernsey, and during the ascendancy of the Paulet family on Jersey during the same period. Among Leighton's high-handed actions, still smarting almost a century later, was his refusal to allow the islanders 'to go in foreign countries about their business without his leave, as if the said inhabitants were his domestical servants'.[66]

In an effort to diminish the authority of their governor, Elizabethan Guernseymen took to referring to Sir Thomas Leighton as 'the captain', a title with merely military connotations. Leading islanders asserted in 1587 that 'the captain is bound by oath to maintain the privilege of that isle, and to be reformed by the bailiff and jurats in case of ignorance, or other ways he should do or attempt anything contrary to the liberties and privileges of that isle'. Against executive decisions by the governor dealing with trade and shipping, they reminded London that the bailiff and jurats themselves had full jurisdiction in all criminal and civil matters, excepting only 'treason, false coiners of money, and laying violent hands on the bailiff or jurats exercising their office'. The governor, by this analysis, was merely the queen's martial representative, with minimal constitutional standing. Guernsey's bailiff and jurats even claimed the right to oversee the condition of Castle Cornet, 'and if they find occasion, to give straight commandment unto the captain in her majesty's name, to see the same forthwith furnished'. Leighton, of course, saw things differently, and attempted to rule as the queen's vicegerent. He had already governed Guernsey for seventeen years, and now that his country was at war with Spain he would do all in his power to advance her majesty's interests.[67]

As trouble continued, Leighton's deputy, Lord Edward Zouch, called on the jurats of Guernsey in August 1600 'to have copies of their privileges, that I may know what belongeth unto them and what unto me'. But all he gained was frustration. Zouch complained to Leighton a month later, that 'I have nothing but the copy of your patent, and such copies of privileges as Mr Bailiff will consent unto ... but whether I have all such writings as I should have, that I know not ... I find the whole world here are willing to keep me as ignorant as they may'. The jurats met privily, without informing the lieutenant governor, and seemed to disparage or disregard him. 'I know not my authority therein, neither what they themselves might do therein,' Zouch wrote plaintively in October. The best he could hope for was a royal commission 'to set down a certainty in all matters'. Zouch seemed vexed and perplexed by his posting among a 'froward' people in a 'backward' place, and was never able to govern with assurance.[68]

Matters of power and politics in the Channel Islands were framed by reference to history, law, and custom, and were sometimes religiously inflected in the period of presbyterian ascendancy. An impasse might lead to a commission of inquiry under the monarch's Great Seal, in which each side set forth its grievances. Successive commissions addressed relations between governors, bailiffs, jurats, and the rest of the propertied elite, but never resolved the underlying tension. Royal commissions on Guernsey in 1607 and on Jersey in 1617 attempted to reconcile the constitutional ambiguities of the islands, and to resolve charges against the governors, by reference to earlier precepts and precedents.[69] More problematic than the corruption or high-handedness of particular individuals was 'the confusion and undistinction of the authority of the public places and offices in the isle, the governor usurping upon the justices [jurats], and the justices upon the liberty of the people'.[70]

The common view in Jacobean London was that all positions of authority in the Channel Islands stemmed from the crown, and that the governor's power was paramount for reasons of state security. But the bailiff too was a royal appointee, with local claims to pre-eminence. Orders from London that they work in harmony gained only begrudging compliance. Intervening in island affairs, the Privy Council had to remind Sir Thomas Leighton that nomination of the bailiff was by the king, not by the governor. Captains of Jersey were similarly 'forbidden to intermeddle in any wise in the nomination of the baillie', but that did not stop them trying.[71] Struggling to perform his duties, governor Sir John Peyton of Jersey informed the Earl of Salisbury in January 1608 that 'touching his majesty's prerogative, and all other general causes concerning the government of this island, there is much misconstruction of the commissioners' orders ... Almost all things ... now grow into question.'[72]

Lord George Carew, Leighton's successor as governor of Guernsey, faced similar problems among a people he deemed 'proud', and an island ministry 'full of heat'. A veteran of the Irish wars, and a councillor of the colony of Virginia, Carew was no stranger to unconventional arrangements, but on Guernsey he was out of his depth. Shortly after arriving in July 1610, he wrote plaintively to Lord Salisbury that 'I use my best diligence to inform myself of the estate of this government, which in civil causes (as well as in the ecclesiastique) so far differs from the course held in England, as I find some difficulty to understand them'. Pursuing enquiries, he found 'the king's charter granted to the bailiff and jurats so much stood upon by them, as they are apt to encroach upon the governor'. Carew looked forward to returning to London as soon as possible to kiss the king's hand, when, he told Salisbury, 'I hope to be able to anatomise this government unto you'.[73] Sophisticated understanding was needed to govern well in the Channel Islands, but Lord Carew was little better equipped than Lord Zouch.

On Jersey the Jacobean governor Sir John Peyton and the controversial bailiff Jean Herault clashed over tithing and taxing, powers and precedence, judgments and appeals, but most of all over Peyton's insistence that the terms of his patent entitled him to appoint or remove any subordinate officer, including the bailiff. Herault complained to the Council that the governor and his lieutenant did 'all in their power to disgrace me and hinder me in my duties', while neglecting responsibilities of their own. Peyton protested that Herault had ascribed 'more power unto himself than ever was attempted or imagined by any precedent bailiff'. In Herault's view, the office of bailiff in Jersey had greater dignity than that of captain, with no person on the island his superior. Peyton, of course, disagreed, claiming that 'anciently the bailiffs there have been nominated and appointed by the governors'. Herault's allies argued that the governor had violated island customs to aggrandize his power, and, remarkably, in this instance, King James concurred. The king conceded that there had been a drafting error in Peyton's initial appointment, 'contrary to our royal intent and meaning'. By letters patent in August 1616 the crown reconfirmed Herault in his 'present and peaceable possession of the said office of bailiff', and ordered that no captain or governor of the island should 'intermeddle in any wise in the nomination, institution, and appointment of the said office'. This was a stunning victory for the islander, but it did not settle questions of duties and jurisdiction. Nor was it long lasting, for within four years renewed conflict led to Jean Herault's dismissal and imprisonment, followed by further oscillations in his career.[74]

The Privy Council sought to settle affairs through another royal commission, led by Sir Edward Conway and Sir William Bird, who arrived in Jersey in March 1617. Their task was to address 'disorders both in the martial and civil administration' of the island, and to adjudicate the dispute on precedency between the bailiff and the governor. The commissioners got off to a good start by reminding the islanders, in English, 'that you owe obedience to the most wise, most just, and most loving prince that ever subjects had'. In what was mostly a listening exercise, in a mostly Francophone island, the commissioners recognized that recent governors had usurped the power of appointing the bailiff and confirmed that none but the bailiff should preside at island assemblies. Bird's grasp of the situation was perhaps handicapped because, unlike his fellow commissioner, he had no 'use ... of the French tongue'.[75] The commissioners filled reams of paper, and cleared the air for a year or two, but did little more than stabilize the status quo.

Royal governors and their deputies under Charles I sometimes interpreted their responsibilities for island defence to extend to control of harbours and shipping. They assumed for themselves power over the movement of people and commerce that would have been unthinkable in any mainland county. Lieutenant Governor Nathaniel Darrell of Guernsey instructed in 1626 that none should leave the island without his permission, prompting the complaint from the bailiff and jurats that this violated their privileges. Darrell protested in turn that the jurats interfered with his musters, and undermined security in a time of war. To which the islanders responded that they were 'fatigued with watching, warding, and repairing the fortifications' and ought not to be 'constrained, as they are'.[76] Similar clashes occurred from time to time throughout the seventeenth century.

Governors of Jersey struggled similarly to compel contributions towards island security, including 'the providing of his majesty's castles with necessaries and victuals'. When islanders objected, citing their privileges and customs in 1627 at the time of an expected French invasion, the governor argued that their attachment to rights and immunities jeopardized his military preparation.[77] Jersey's lieutenant governor Francis Rainsford experienced further 'dissension' in 1628 when he tried to make islanders watch and ward in response to the pirate menace, and to provision the castles against attack. The bailiff and jurats insisted that defence of the island was entirely the governor's responsibility, not theirs, and that they would oppose any 'novelty' as a 'wrong' and 'an exaction upon the country'. Rainsford described the recalcitrants as 'stubborn and mutinous' and sought to imprison them for 'neglecting and slighting their duties', but the jurats insisted he had no such power. Speaking for the islanders, bailiff Sir Philip Carteret told Rainsford 'that if he did take upon himself by force to imprison the king's subjects, he must look to answer it'. Carteret concluded that the bailiff and the lieutenant governor 'hath authority enough to do the king service . . . without encroaching one upon another, but it will prove dangerous to the state here when a governor shall take upon him to punish or imprison as he pleaseth only with this motto, *sic volo, sic jubeo*' (as I wish, so I command—a quotation from the Roman satirist Juvenal).[78]

Seeking to clarify the matter, Charles I's Council of War requested papers, precedents, and certificates from the archives in 1632, 'to distinguish of the isles of Guernsey and Jersey, what is the king's, and what is the governor's'. Many of those documents also addressed the question of what belonged to the inhabitants, the bailiff, and the jurats, and what to military officers of the crown, in wartime and in peace.[79] These were unsettled questions that would reverberate for generations. They were raised in the late 1630s when the English state used Jersey and Guernsey for the arbitrary incarceration of prisoners of state. They came to the fore in the disturbed decades of England's troubles, when the islands took opposing sides, and remained in contention after the Restoration. Discussion of the sparring between governors and Channel Island officials across later decades of the seventeenth century, and the use of island prisons, is reserved for later chapters.

Appeals and Doléances

As contentious as the competition between bailiffs and governors was the matter of appeal beyond the island courts. The Royal Courts of Guernsey and Jersey claimed complete jurisdiction in all criminal and civil matters, except for treason, coining, and violence against the bailiffs and jurats in the execution of their office. Island authorities had the power to expel offenders from their territory. Anyone caught wandering or begging was liable to be sent packing on the next boat, a sanction not available to mainland magistrates (although English constables were known to have shunted offenders across parish and county boundaries). The practice of removal caused another rift between London and the islands later in the seventeenth century, when sheep-stealers condemned to 'perpetual banishment' by the bailiff and jurats of Jersey obtained royal pardons in England, and the Privy Council insisted that they be allowed to return.[80]

Island criminal jurisdiction was normally unchallenged, and civil matters concerning title, inheritance, rents, leases, debts, arrears, and the like were usually locally determined. Everything had to be settled according to the customs and procedures of the islands, derived from the laws of Normandy, of which the bailiffs and jurats were the principal interpreters. There could be no appeal to Chancery or the Court of Requests, but dissatisfied parties in civil causes could still appeal to the crown. Such interventions were costly and complicated, involving time and sea travel. The cost of preparing documents and carrying them to England could outweigh the financial sums involved.[81] Appeals to the Privy Council for determination under the monarch's Great Seal could be protracted and inconclusive, as contending parties cited competing precedents and sought to sabotage their opponent's case. It was nonetheless a privilege and potential benefit for Channels Islanders to invoke the authority of the crown, one of the mutualities of interdependence. Depending upon their investment in the case, however, island officials could represent outside appeals as 'great slander to the bailiff and justices there' and an attack on their laws and privileges.[82] Responding to appeals from the Channel Islands, Privy Councillors grew irritated by the 'underhand dealings' and delays of island officials and became frustrated when their orders were ignored. Demands from London 'to give execution accordingly' to the Council's instructions routinely faced procedural hurdles. Island lawyers and litigants proved skilled in obfuscation, while island courts treated instructions from England with suspicion or indifference.[83]

Privy Councillors, government commissioners, and island authorities all discouraged appeals that aggravated divisions and increased their workload. They attempted to limit the time in which appeals could be lodged, to restrict them to cases of a minimum value, and to require the posting of bail for costs and a deposit to be forfeit if the appeal did not succeed.[84] But wealthy island litigants were undeterred, and repeatedly sought favour from London. It remains an open question whether islanders were more litigious than their English counterparts, but their small confined world was fertile of contention. One English visitor to the Channel Islands remarked on 'the quarrelsome temper of the inhabitants', who went to law over 'trivial and inconsiderable' matters, and appealed their case as high as they could.[85] Another commented on the islanders' litigiousness, making 'frivolous lawsuits about every petty matter'.[86] Successive English administrators were exhausted by bickering in and out of the islands' courts, which continued throughout the seventeenth century.[87]

Appeals addressed the merits of a cause at law, whereas, doléances, unknown to English jurisprudence, were complaints of unjust proceedings or errors. Channel Island doléances may have done much the same work as the English writs of *mandamus* and *certiori*, correcting and directing decisions of the court. Early Stuart Councils usually referred appeals and doléances back to the island for rehearing or review, but some cases went on for years, or even decades. Islanders resisted arbitration as contrary to their 'ancient charters and customs'.[88] Administrators on Restoration Jersey sought once again to short-cut litigation, 'doléances being of an odious nature, as intended principally against the judges, whose honour is to be maintained for the sake of justice'.[89] But islanders, who with one breath asserted their separateness from England, were just as likely to lobby the Privy Council if they sensed the possibility of advantage, using every instrument at their disposal.

Two cases from Elizabethan Jersey illustrate some of the difficulties. Thwarted in a suit before the island's Royal Court in 1586, Hilary Paine determined to appeal to the Council in England, on grounds that the sentence against him was in error. Jersey's bailiff George Paulet set out to thwart him, telling Secretary Walsingham that 'I have used all good means to compound the matter here, to the end your honours might be no further troubled therewith, and had not Paine's willful obstinacy been too too great, the matter had been once ended'. While Paine took his case to England, to make 'difficulty by sinister means', one of the jurats was assigned to follow him, as soon as 'passage and wind will permit'. Paulet used his power to have the appellant arrested, and Paine protested that he was 'unjustly vexed and imprisoned' in Mont Orgeuil Castle. His only hope lay in further appeals to London to free him from confinement and to have his case heard, a course of action that his adversaries persistently blocked.[90]

Even more tangled was the appeal of Jean de Carteret and others in 1588, stemming from proposals to remove an ancient island church. When the bailiff and jurats of Jersey ruled against him, de Carteret, a jurat himself, collected hands to a petition 'without the privity of the governor's lieutenant or bailiff', and went over to England to appeal directly to the queen in Council. De Carteret claimed that the sentence against him was wrong, and had been obtained by the corrupt influence of bailiff Paulet's faction. He went so far as to demand 'the extirping of the court in that isle called the Court Extraordinary', where he had been worsted, as well as reversal of its judgment. Countering this, Paulet's agents told Attorney General Sir John Popham that the island's Extraordinary Court was valuable and venerable, handling 'obligations, contracts, and promises betwixt party and party', and that its suppression would deprive the bailiff of his customary 'fees and commodities'. De Carteret's proceedings, his enemies alleged, were 'factious and dangerous to the state and government' of Jersey, deserving of imprisonment, and the English Privy Council agreed. Rejecting de Carteret's appeal, they consigned him to London's Marshalsea prison until he acknowledged his fault, with the comment that 'he and his confederates do rather deserve some sharp reprehension for their proceedings'. The jurat spent several months behind bars in England 1588, appealing for another hearing and reflecting on the perils of petitioning.[91]

Appeals from early Stuart Guernsey also exposed constitutional stresses within the island and difficult dealings with London. A slow flow of petitions and responses passed between the Royal Court and the Privy Council, with appellants seeking the highest authority. Bailiffs and jurats complained that any appeal against their decisions impinged upon their liberties.[92] Adjudication by royal commissioners did not necessarily resolve the matter, for suits that went back several generations could continue in succeeding reigns.[93]

An ordinary dispute about debts and acquittances that began in 1622 acquired larger constitutional significance when the Guernsey merchant John Blanche invoked the power of Star Chamber against his enemy John de Quetteville, and de Quetteville counter-sued in the same court. Appeals and petitions in this case went back and forth between Guernsey and London for the next eighteen years, until Star Chamber itself was dissolved. Lawyers in 1625 prepared four pages of 'reasons for which the inhabitants of the Isle of Guernsey are not subject to writs of subpoena issuing out of Star Chamber in cases between party and party'. These included the practical difficulties of distance and isolation, shipping and sea conditions, and the cultural problem that most of the islanders spoke only Norman French. A chain of charters and precedents supported the island's 'unquestioned privilege' of exemption from English courts, including Star Chamber. Most telling of all was the assertion that 'it is not in the memory of any man living, or extant in any record, that any writ of subpoena hath been issued out of the said court, upon any of the said inhabitants, in the space of three or four hundred years'.[94] Nevertheless, island litigants sought judgment from English jurisdictions when they thought it useful, and English courts and Councils chose occasionally to hear their appeals.[95]

Blanche's case could have been settled by island jurats, but de Quetteville was one of those jurats himself, and subsequently bailiff, and Blanche believed he was wronged. Repeated appeals to London produced little effect, besides further harassment for the appellant, as the island authorities 'contemptuously refused' to execute the Privy Council's orders.[96] By 1636, John Blanche was in prison on a commission of rebellion out of Star Chamber, facing a suit for £500 by de Quetteville. His petition in 1637, seeking damages for unjust imprisonment and loss of reputation, gained traction in London but not on the island. Blanche was still imprisoned on Guernsey in 1638 when the Privy Council peremptorily demanded his release, and ordered the jurats to allow damages. Their response to this and similar directives from London was to remind the Privy Council that 'the jurats of the island by their ancient charters and customs ought to determine all matters of justice and controversies', and to repeat their claim of exemption from writs of Star Chamber.[97]

Taking advantage of a revolutionary moment, Blanche appealed to parliament in December 1640, 'forasmuch as the said orders of the Council have been so often disobeyed, your petitioner having no hope to obtain redress for his great oppressions and grievances . . . unless he may be relieved by your lordships'. But there was little anyone could do, on or off the island, if the government in Guernsey chose not to cooperate with external authorities. The jurats who cocked a snoot at the king's Privy Council were even less likely to countenance the authority of an upstart English parliament.[98]

In another long-simmering case, appealed from Guernsey and sent back to the island, Lieutenant Governor Peter Osborne complained to King Charles in 1636 about the 'slow and refractory proceedings' of the bailiff and jurats and the 'dangerous consequence of this public and presumptuous contempt' for his majesty's commands. Progress, apparently, was impossible without bribes to the bailiff's faction. Complaining that the jurat John Bonamy 'hath demeaned himself very disobediently in this business', Secretary Francis Windebank wrote a stiff letter in December 1638 discharging him from his office, but it went against custom for a king to dismiss a jurat. Amice Andros of Guernsey warned the Privy Council in 1639 'how much it will derogate from their lordships' power and authority', if their letters continued to be slighted, adding that the stand-off 'will cause multiplicity of evils and debate in the isle'.[99]

The exigencies of civil war made it difficult to pursue appeals, but in April 1648, when the war seemed to be over, the Guernseyman John Perchard referred his dispute about inheritance on the island to Westminster. Perchard claimed to have been judged in Guernsey's court 'contrary to the laws and customs there used', and sought reversal of the decision of the bailiff and jurats. He had attempted to appeal to King Charles, but, owing to England's troubles, found that form of remedy 'not now in use'. Arguing that the High Court of Parliament formed 'the only and proper judges of appeal', Perchard asked for 'the whole process, pleas, defence, depositions, and examinations' (most of them in French) to be transmitted to England. The court in Guernsey accepted his 'pledges for cost and charges, in case he fail in his appeal', parliament appeared willing to take up the matter, and Perchard crossed over to England to make his case in person. But, unfortunately for the appellant, 'the present distractions at sea, and specially about the isle', made it difficult to send documents from Guernsey, even if the jurats were willing to release them. Crucial writings were lost or delayed amid the naval uprising of the second civil war, while the parliamentary timetable grew crowded with their lordships' 'more weighty affairs'. Perchard was still petitioning for relief in November 1648, when the quickening revolutionary crisis put all other matters in the shade.[100] It should have been clear to all concerned that English and Norman law were poorly aligned, and that the protocols and privileges of the Channel Islands had limited purchase in London.

Life went on quietly enough in the environs of St Helier and St Peter Port, but the cultural problem of a 'froward' people in a 'backward' place, compounded by the constitutional challenges of contested jurisdiction and the complexities of heritage, distance, and insularity, made England's governance of the Channel Islands a headache if not a distemper.

4

Island Anomalies

The Isle of Man, Scilly, Wight, and Anglesey

Every island was different, and their degrees of difference variable, but each posed problems of governance and control. There were always strains between mainland and offshore perspectives, and these were exacerbated by the legacies of distinctive local histories, cultural complexions, and legal peculiarities. Outsiders were puzzled by constitutional anomalies, and by claims to special status. The correspondence between Privy Councillors and island officials is thick with complaint about obstruction and defiance, and marked by frustration at insular recalcitrance. Difficulties varied with distance from the mainland and exposure to foreign enemies and altered with changing political environments. This chapter explores the tension between London's attempt to regulate the islands, and islanders' attempts to live their own lives.

The Atlantic Isles of Scilly were part of Cornwall, Lundy in the Bristol Channel belonged to Devon, and the Isle of Wight across the Solent was politically attached to Hampshire, yet each behaved as if it were partly autonomous. Anglesey was a county of Wales, and returned members to the parliament at Westminster, but its status as a frontier island, across the Menai Straits, allowed it exemption from military levies. Even Holy Island off Northumberland, a dependency of the garrison at Berwick, and St Nicholas in Devon, attached to Plymouth, had their own petty captains and customs. The Isle of Man, like the Norman Channel Islands, lay beyond the reach of English courts and parliaments, but could be answerable to the crown's Great Seal. Its Manx language and constitution, its heritage as a quasi-independent Viking kingdom, and its domination by the earls of Derby, made it especially hard to comprehend and manage (see Figure 4).

The Isle of Man

Several parts of England's island periphery displayed insular intransigence, but none was so resistant to intervention from London as the Isle of Man. A substantial territory halfway across the Irish Sea, supported by farming, fishing, and trade, the Isle of Man had a seventeenth-century population approaching 10,000. Cultural and economic influences came as much from the north and west as from England to the east, and as many as 90 per cent of the islanders spoke

England's Islands in a Sea of Troubles. David Cressy, Oxford University Press (2020). © David Cressy 2020.
DOI: 10.1093/oso/9780198856603.001.0001

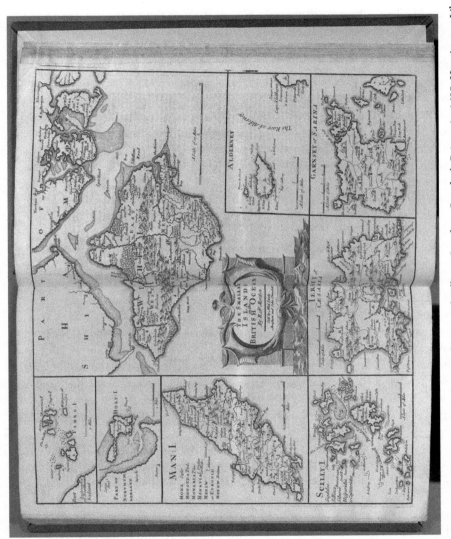

Figure 4. Smaller Islands in the British Ocean (William Camden, *Camden's Britannia*, 1695; Huntington Library)

Manx Gaelic rather than English.[1] One contemporary observer remarked that 'the wealthiest sort, and such as hold the fairest possessions, do imitate the people of Lancashire', while 'the common sort of people, both in their language and manners, come nighest unto the Irish, although they somewhat relish and savour of the qualities of the Norwegians'.[2] Another noted that those in the north of the island had an 'affinity with the Scotch', and those in the south 'with the Irish'.[3] William Sacheverell, who published a valuable *Account of the Isle of Man* in 1702, remarked that, while 'the common sort speak their native language, the gentry [speak] better English than in the north of England'.[4]

Though one of the dominions of the English kings, 'in homage and subjection' to the English crown, the island was never part of the kingdom of England.[5] Its Gaelic ancestry and medieval Scandinavian heritage conditioned a distinctive political culture, outside of English governance and law. From the point of view of London, the island appeared strange, separate, and perversely independent. Its unique constitutional arrangements of Lordship, Deemsters, Keys, and the assembly of the Tynwald were baffling to outsiders, defying expectations of how English territories should behave. The island had its own 'laws and constitutions ... customary practices and precedents', and its own 'course of the common law'.[6] The Isle of Man was honoured with its own coat of arms (the three-legged triskele), which, according to the seventeenth-century visitor William Blundell, 'was never permitted either to the Isle of Anglesey, Wight, Guernsey, Jersey, or any other island subject to the monarchy of Great Britain, Ireland only excepted'.[7] (Blundell was wrong, for both Guernsey and Jersey had arms featuring three lions passant.)

Though often harassed by pirates, the Isle of Man was not directly threatened by England's foreign enemies, and was less of a strategic headache for London than other offshore dominions. The Stanleys maintained the island castles, garrison, and militia, relieving the crown of that burden. Unlike the islands further south, Man had not been known to the Greeks or Romans, as if 'concealed by magical arts with mists and vapours' like some of the islands of romance (see Figure 5).[8]

Though owing fealty to the crown of England, the early modern Isle of Man was a semi-independent fiefdom of the Stanley earls of Derby, who were Lords of Man and were sometimes styled its kings. The earls themselves dropped that usage early in the sixteenth century, but their medieval title, *Rex Manniae et Insularum*, was used in island documents until the end of the seventeenth century.[9] Peter Heylyn's *Help to English History*, which went through multiple editions, listed the Stanley earls as 'kings and lords of Man'.[10] The late-Stuart traveller Thomas Denton also identified the ninth Earl of Derby as 'king of Man'.[11] Guy Miege in *The New State of England*, published in 1691, reputed the earl 'Lord of Man, though a king in effect', with 'all kind of civil power and jurisdiction over the inhabitants'.[12] Commenting on this part of the king of England's dominions, the

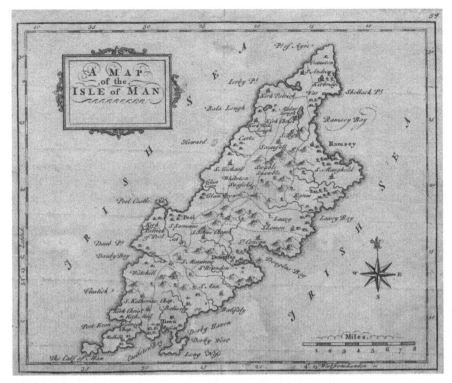

Figure 5. Isle of Man, 1748 (Alamy Images)

jurist Sir Matthew Hale dryly noted that Derby's descendants 'have long enjoyed it by the reputed name of king of Man'. No other English noble had such prerogatives and power.[13]

The Stanley family claimed ancient title to the Isle of Man, confirmed by grant of Henry IV 'with all regal authority and power thereunto belonging'.[14] Inheritors included Ferdinando, the fifth earl (1559–94), William, the sixth earl (1584–1642), James, the seventh earl (1607–51), Charles, the eighth earl (1628–72), and William, the ninth earl (1655–1702). The seventh earl declared appreciatively that 'to be a great lord is a more honourable title than a petty king'.[15] A succession of powerful women became countesses of Derby, including Margaret Clifford (1540–96), Alice Spencer (1559–1637), Elizabeth de Vere (1575–1627), and Charlotte de Trémoille (1599–1664). Several of them took an active interest in island affairs.

The death of the fifth earl, Lord Ferdinando Stanley, in 1594 threw title to the island into doubt when his heirs general (his three daughters) disputed the inheritance with his heir male (his brother William, who became the sixth earl). It took sixteen years of legal wrangling before the matter was resolved, during which time the crown took the Lordship of Man under its protection. The suit had extraordinary complexity, as Barry Coward explains, owing to 'the vexed question of whether the Isle of Man was part of the dominion of England or not'.[16] Concerned lest enemies should choose this moment to attack, while the war with Spain dragged on, the Privy Council appointed the soldier Sir Thomas Gerard to be the Isle of Man's captain 'for the security of the place'. The oath Gerard swore in August 1595 confirmed his allegiance to her majesty, with no mention of the Earl of Derby. He served, with some gaps, until 1608, when another royal appointee, John Ireland, filled the post. Only when the inheritance dispute was settled did the Stanleys regain their customary authority and independence.[17] This hiatus allowed London to exert unusual influence on the Isle of Man, but none of its constitutional apparatus was changed. The crown explicitly promised not to 'disturb or innovate the civil government' of the island, nor to 'wrest their usual constitutions proper and belonging to the same'.[18] With a royal appointee in charge, however, answering to a sympathetic English government, the moment was ripe for appeals to King James. In one such case involving episcopal leases the bishop of Man complained against islanders who sought relief from the Privy Council in London, while holding its authority in contempt in the Isle. They petition 'to keep their ancient laws afoot and in force', alleged bishop John Phillips in 1606, 'yet themselves are the first that seek to infringe the same, and to bring them under foot'.[19]

By 1612 the sixth Earl of Derby was fully possessed of the lordship of Man, with 'all its royalties, regalities, privileges, etcetera'. The 'etcetera' left a lot to be argued, but the Stanleys claimed it gave them absolute dominion, without possibility of appeal.[20] All land on the island was theirs, the inhabitants simply tenants. The island's lieutenant or governor, receiver, comptroller, attorney general, and water bailiff were all clients and appointees of the Earl of Derby, and served at his will and pleasure. Island institutions—the Tynwald, the Keys, Deemsters, Sheadings, and other courts—all did their business in the earl's name, with no appeal outside the Isle of Man.[21] Remarkably, the sixth earl deputed his wife, Countess Elizabeth (née de Vere, daughter of the Earl of Oxford) to deal with island matters. There is no evidence that she ever visited the territory, but until her death in 1627 she was effectively Lord of Man, busying herself in island affairs, and efficiently extracting its rents and revenues.[22]

In the early seventeenth century the Isle of Man was worth £2,000 a year to its noble proprietors, who jealously guarded their privileges.[23] An account from the reign of Charles I recognized the island as the inheritance of the Earl of Derby and Lord Strange (the junior title of the Stanley earldom), 'and they are admirals thereof. And they have the regal power to make and execute all laws and statutes in the same at their wills and pleasures.' They could punish and pardon as they pleased. It was their 'undoubted' right to nominate to the bishopric of Sodor and

Man, to appoint subordinate officers, and to treat their tenants as subjects.[24] The island was virtually an independent kingdom, and the earls of Derby its monarchs.

It suited the Stanleys for everyone to believe that the Isle of Man was 'a distinct dominion, and no part of the realm of England...The king's writs do not run there'. As one of their later Stuart lawyers explained,

> the Isle of Man is an ancient kingdom, and while it remained in the hands of the crown was not subject to the laws of England; for which reason no writ of error or appeal lay to any of the king's courts; but in case of injuries or wrongs the king granted a commission to certain persons to determine controversies according to the laws of the island; so that it appears that the jurisdiction of the kings of England in the Isle of Man... was exercised in another manner than the government of England.

The case of the Isle of Man bore no comparison with colonial plantations, where the king acted through deputies or governors, nor with Guernsey and Jersey, where, despite the particularity of their laws, 'an appeal lies to the king, because he is still lord and proprietor of the islands'. The earls of Derby, by contrast, were absolute in the Isle of Man, with *jura regalia*, exclusive royal rights, 'without any interposition from the king of England'. The Privy Council had no voice in the island, so the Stanleys insisted, and its residents lacked all rights of appeal. The island lay outside the jurisdiction of English courts, beyond the reach of Chancery, and was untouched by the legislation of English parliaments, unless a statute specifically named and addressed it.[25]

The very stridency and vigour of the Stanleys' repeated assertions suggest that their claims could be contested. Recitation of the constitutional uniqueness of the Isle of Man sustained the power of the earls against any centralizing monarch, and against any upstart islander who might dare to seek justice beyond them. Challengers could invoke alternative sets of precedents, proofs, transcripts, and histories, but were thwarted by the Stanleys and their agents.

The peculiarities of Isle of Man jurisdiction had complex practical consequences. In October 1624, for example, when Sir Henry Marten, the judge of England's Admiralty Court, attempted to resolve the matter of the *Cardinal* of Rouen, a vessel brought into the Isle of Man by Dutch pirates, the case foundered on the exemptions and privileges that the Earl of Derby claimed as his right. Marten called on the king and Council for assistance, because 'the Earl of Derby is not likely to relinquish any privileges which by custom he could hold'. The only way forward was a direct appeal to the Countess, since the formal jurisdictional protocols were too tangled.[26] The Isle of Man handled criminal offenders in its own idiosyncratic manner, and exercised the option of banishing sheep stealers to Ireland or England.[27] It was an insular advantage, shared with Jersey and Guernsey, to remove unwanted elements from their shores.

When civil war came, the Earl of Derby sided with King Charles, making the Isle of Man a royalist base and refuge. Its military history is discussed in Chapters 7 and 8. Progressive elements proposed changes in the system of government, only to be charged with subversion of 'the fundamental laws of this island'. Any attempt to conform island practice to the customs of the mainland would be crushed as sedition. When Edward Christian, a former official under the Stanleys, proposed replacing the twenty-four Keys, who had life-time appointments and were sworn to their lord, with men chosen by the parishes for three-year terms 'for the general good of the isle and the people thereof', his agitation cost him his liberty, and six years confinement in Peel Castle.[28] Later in the seventeenth century, when the government of Charles II put legal, fiscal, and political pressure on the Isle of Man, the Earl of Derby pushed back, insisting all the more vigorously on his independence. These post-Restoration developments are discussed in Chapter 10.

Scilly

The Isles of Scilly, anciently known as the Sorlings, a sprinkle of rocks and *terra firma* 28 miles and more south-west of Land's End, were a detached part of the county of Cornwall. They were only lightly integrated into the governance of England. The Crown, the Duchy of Cornwall, the Admiralty, the bishop of Exeter, the county lieutenancy, the coroner, the sheriff, and the magistrates of Cornwall all had interests in Scilly, but because of distance and neglect their authority effectively lapsed. Pre-Reformation abbots of Tavistock had religious cells in the Scillies, and a claim on island tithes, but the anchorites disappeared with the Reformation, and all rights reverted to the crown. The Duchy of Cornwall acquired the lordship of Scilly in 1540, after the attainder of the Marquis of Exeter, Hugh Courtney, but it later became ambiguous to what degree the Scillies 'appertained' to the Duchy. Little immediate benefit accrued from the annexation of these islands, described by a Tudor Francis Godolphin as no more than a 'bushment of briars and a refuge for ... pirates'. The Duchy remained in the background, with residual rather than active rights. The Arundell family leased the tithes in 1546, but saw little profit.[29] The Godolphin family became proprietors in the reign of Elizabeth I, and held the lordship for several centuries of 'his majesty's isles, islands, territories, and rocks commonly called the Isles of Scilly'.[30] The later Stuart traveller Daniel Defoe referred dismissively to the Scillies as 'excrescences' of the island of Britain, though a Georgian Admiralty surveyor recognized them as 'an appendage of the crown of England'.[31]

The Isles of Scilly served the realm as a strategic stronghold, a place to safeguard shipping, and an outpost against foreign enemies. Watchers on the islands kept track of approaching fleets, and warned of potential foes. Friendly vessels found refuge from the dangers of pirates, rocks, and storms. A few tenants farmed, fished, foraged, and served the impoverished military establishment. Edward VI's mid-Tudor government bolstered Scilly's defences, and later regimes expanded and repaired them, but the military commitment wavered whenever peace was restored (see Figure 6).

The Isles of Scilly were essentially ungoverned when Sir William Godolphin first acquired his lease in 1558.[32] Successive generations of Godolphins received the royal 'command to employ their servants, tenants, and tinners, for defence of the said island upon all occasions'.[33] In exchange, the proprietors enjoyed full

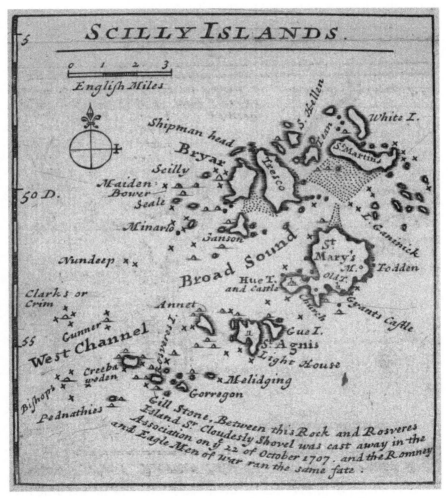

Figure 6. Scilly Islands (Herman Moll, *A Set of Fifty New and Complete Maps*, 1739; Huntington Library)

delegation of civil power, rights, and appurtenances, including 'all liberties, customs, and wrecks of sea'. These were mutually beneficial arrangements, accruing status and profit for the proprietors, and frontier protection for the crown. Medieval proprietors had paid their rent in puffins (fifty puffins a year under Edward I), but the Godolphins made cash bargains. After renewing their lease in 1570 they owed the crown £10 a year, increasing to £20 a year from 1604, and £40 a year from 1636, 'for fifty years in reversion of all the time yet in being'.[34] It was during this period in the autumn of 1623 that the future Charles I, as Prince of Wales, spent a few days in the Scillies on his way home from his courtship debacle in Spain. The royal party found food and fresh water, and an opportunity to stretch their legs, but no resident governor to greet them.[35]

The early modern population of the Scillies numbered in the hundreds, and rarely reached a thousand. Island residents mostly spoke Cornish—a form of Brythonic Celtic—at least until the seventeenth century, though the elite among them knew English. The military garrison housed a few dozen soldiers—mostly from the mainland—whose numbers might expand to a hundred or more in times of crisis.[36] A parliamentary survey in 1652 survey listed 180 tenants, implying a population of around eight hundred.[37] The 176 signatories to the Association Oath (to defend William III) in 1696 suggests a similar total.[38] A detailed island by island survey in 1715 found only a slight expansion to 822, with 477 Scillonians clustered on St Mary's.[39]

The Godolphin proprietors rarely set foot in Scilly, leaving its management to lieutenants, deputies, stewards, and junior kin. The islands provided them with prestige, rents, and occasional windfall profits from shipping and shipwrecks. The terms of their proprietorship required the governors to defend the islands, and this became urgent and expensive in time of war. The Elizabethan Sir Francis Godolphin 'bettered his plot and allowance' by erecting Star Castle on St Mary's Island in 1593, a fortress that would serve for several centuries. Scilly's new castle was built with the governor's 'invention and plight', and much of his own money, but its manning relied on the crown, whose attention and funding were inconstant. Sir Francis envisaged a summertime garrison of at least eighty men, but pay was often late and numbers chronically fell short.[40]

Godolphin after Godolphin succeeded to the governorship of Scilly, 'with all wages, fees, profits, commodities, emoluments, and advantages thereunto'.[41] Their government was seigneurial and authoritarian, allowing little intrusion from the mainland. As one anonymous contemporary remarked, 'the inaccountable sovereignty which the Governor enjoys in those islands' could be 'a consideration of great moment to an ambitious man who hath, as it were, *imperium in imperio* [an empire within an empire] in that microcosm'.[42] No wonder that Sir Francis Godolphin declared in 1597 that 'he would rather adventure his son there than place in the government one that can neither be so well beloved, nor so well to be trusted'.[43] When a later Sir Francis Godolphin died in 1640, his nephew, yet another Francis Godolphin, became 'Captain of the Isles of Scilly and the new fort and garrison there'. By this time the 'total improved value' of the islands, including rents and tithes, approached £1,000 a year, a handsome return on the family's investment.[44]

No written precepts or protocols governed arrangements on Scilly, apart from the proprietor's lease and the governor's instructions. There were no local gentry to provide leadership, and few men of education, besides officers of the garrison and captains of passing ships. Neither lawyers nor schoolmasters took up residence before the eighteenth century. The only clergy in these dark corners of the land were occasional curates and chaplains of the Godolphins. Nobody could live on Scilly, or leave the islands, without the proprietor's permission. Nobody enjoyed freehold. As tenants and dependents, the inhabitants lived under 'a distinct jurisdiction...under the direction of a Lord Proprietor', with neither the benefits nor the duties of parish or national citizenship. By tradition, if not by law, they could not 'be sued in any of the courts of Westminster, for any matter or cause arising within' the islands. *Habeas corpus* applied in principle everywhere in England, but island distance and insular intransigence barred its path. Neither chancellors nor sheriffs, assizes nor quarter sessions, impinged on Scillonians' lives. It had not been forgotten that a medieval coroner of Cornwall who ventured to investigate a slaying on Scilly was denied all assistance, was ill-used and imprisoned, and was reminded of the limits of his power. The ecclesiastical courts of the diocese of Exeter made no appearance in the Scillies, and exercised no cognizance. Instead islanders looked to the authority of 'The Twelve', a customary court convened by the proprietor, which had no formal status and kept no records. Here were determined 'all matters of debt, trespass or property', as well as offences 'in language or morality'. Serious criminals might be shipped to the mainland, but minor anti-social behaviour could be corrected by 'the ducking chair at the quay head' or by whipping. In its day-to-day affairs the community governed itself, under the eye of Godolphin's steward and the garrison commander. 'The islands have but the shadow of government,' declared the Cornish antiquary William Borlase.[45] English state formation made little headway here.

Generations of Godolphins monopolized island offices, but differences developed between the garrison and the town, between the concerns of the castle captain and the interests of the lord's steward. These were mostly petty affairs, relating to land use and boundaries, or shares of particular perquisites, but they also implicated national defence, and affected the profits of the proprietor.[46] As always, on every island, questions of jurisdiction, precedent, and practicalities gave ways to the changing needs of peace and war. Star Castle above St Mary's acquired new utility as a political prison in the late 1630s. The Isles of Scilly were thrust into fresh prominence in the 1640s, first as a royalist stronghold, then as a refuge for the fleeing Prince of Wales, and as scenes of sieges by parliamentary forces. The drama of developments in these islands in the course of the civil war is reserved for Chapter 8. Scilly's state prisoners are discussed in Chapters 11, 13, and 14.

The Isle of Wight

Historically part of the county of Hampshire, barely 2 miles across the Solent at its narrowest point, the Isle of Wight was closely associated with mainland England. Nevertheless, as 'a considerable frontier of the kingdom', the island experienced military burdens and administrative strictures that underscored its difference. Though the islanders revelled in their Englishness, they were, in the words of one early commentator, 'discriminated by peculiar circumstances'. The island seemed a 'world by itself, so it differs from Hampshire in many things', declared another.[47] 'Thou little world, divided from the great, I Where pleasure sports, and plenty rule in state,' trilled an eighteenth-century enthusiast for the island.[48] Andrew Coleby, the modern historian of Stuart Hampshire, finds the Isle of Wight 'a distinct community on its own', an extreme example of the patchwork of difference in early modern England.[49]

Chains of authority linked the island to London, Winchester, and Southampton, though its effective centre of power was Carisbrooke Castle, above Newport. The crown's principal representatives were termed wardens, captains, or more commonly governors. Early historians recalled that Henry VI invested Henry Beauchamp, Duke of Warwick, as 'king of Wight', though that title soon expired, and meant little more than honorary captain or governor. As one eighteenth-century memorialist reports, 'this dignity, as to the royal part of it, died with its first and only possessor'.[50]

The Isle of Wight guarded the kingdom's southern flank, and was potentially exposed to foreign invasion. Suspected enemy shipping frequently hovered offshore. The island's governors, based at Carisbrooke if they deigned to take up residency, were usually military men of aristocratic rank. In the early modern era they included Sir Edward Horsey (1565–1583), Sir George Carey, Baron Hunsdon (1583–1603), Henry Wriothesley, Earl of Southampton (1603–24), Lord Edward Conway (1625–31), Lord Richard Weston (1631–4), Jerome Weston, Earl of Portland (1634–2), and Philip Herbert, Earl of Pembroke (1642–7). Often engaged in national affairs of state, these men generally left routine island matters in the hands of deputies or lieutenants. Like other early modern administrators, the governors pocketed sinecures and perquisites, including the vice-admiralty, which gave them profitable jurisdiction over prizes and wrecks. They held their own court, the Knighten Court, which handled all civil matters under 40s. (raised to £20 in 1626) and exercised considerable patronage and influence. Control of additional offices of coroner, constable, steward, surveyor, receiver, bailiff, and warden of the forest of Parkhurst augmented the governors' power, and fattened their purses, to a degree unthinkable among mainland county lieutenants.[51]

The governors had primary responsibility for the island's defences—castles, forts, and artillery sconces, with their garrisons and staff—as well as the civilian-trained bands or militia. In times of war, or threat of war, several hundred more soldiers might be sent to the Isle of Wight, with equipment for military installations (discussed in Chapter 7). A system of beacons warned of imminent attack. Elizabethan governors were obliged to 'array the whole people of the isle, as shall seem meetest for defence'.[52] Like the Channel Islands, the Isle of Wight readied regiments of militia, and maintained its parochial artillery. Islanders took part in musters and training, with no greater enthusiasm though perhaps a greater likelihood of deployment than in inland counties. Militia numbers under Charles I were close to 2,000, a level maintained for most of the seventeenth century. Wartime preparations in 1626 included the recommendation that the Captain keep residence on the island, 'to set and keep the country in readiness' in the face of expected attack.[53]

As an island close to the mainland, well-integrated politically with the rest of the kingdom, the Isle of Wight had a social structure and economy similar to that of southern England (see Figure 7). Populous and prosperous, it was described in 1626 as 'a fertile island able to nourish twenty or thirty thousand souls'. Actual population numbers are unknown, but are unlikely to have been much higher than 12,000.[54] The entire range of rank and status was represented, with knights, esquires, and gentlemen, professionals, merchants, yeomen, husbandmen, artisans, and labourers. The Oglanders of Nunwell, near Brading, were predominant among a score of gentlemen freeholders who served as officers and justices, and who were notorious for their disputes over precedence.[55] The island's three parliamentary boroughs—Newport, Newtown, and Yarmouth—each sent two members to Westminster, though rarely without the governor's influence.

Island status conferred several privileges. A concession in 1561, confirmed in 1626, exempted residents of the Isle of Wight from serving as jurymen or witnesses at mainland assizes and quarter sessions, unless the matter directly concerned them. They paid no rates for Hampshire's house of correction, nor for support of its maimed soldiers, instead handling such matters themselves.[56] The islanders considered themselves exempt from purveyance (mandatory royal provisioning), and pleaded in 1609 to 'deliver us from this fear, and suffer not more to be imposed on us now than has been in former times'.[57] Isle of Wight mariners and ships were supposedly free from impressment, 'so as they may be ready upon all occasions for the service and safety of the island'.[58] Confidence in this exemption may have encouraged some English sailors to hide on the island in the 1620s to evade naval service.[59] Island status did not free inhabitants from the state's fiscal demands, though they contributed only sluggishly to Charles I's forced loan and Ship Money, and offered resistance to Charles II's Hearth Tax and Excise.[60]

Governors of the Isle of Wight from Sir George Carey onwards had the discretionary power to intercept writs and mandates from mainland courts, so that inhabitants 'may not be molested by the sheriff or any other minister outside the island'.[61] In 1625, the island's lieutenant governor went so far as to send

Figure 7. Isle of Wight, 1591 (Alamy Images)

'a constable with a warrant, as for a felon' to thwart an officer from Whitehall who was chasing local pirates. Captain Burley of Yarmouth Castle, a subordinate of the governor (and later a champion of Charles I), told London's emissary Anthony Ersfield that he 'will not suffer me or any of mine (as with foul speeches he sendeth me word) to meddle there, and saith he careth not a surreverence for me or my deputation'.[62]

The Isle of Wight was the only one of England's major islands to be visited by reigning monarchs. James I and Prince Henry came to hunt in 1609, in pursuit of a stag that had swum across from Hampshire, and stayed for dinner at Carisbrooke Castle. The king crossed over to the island for similar exercise in 1611. Prince Charles, as Prince of Wales, called at Cowes in August 1618 to review some military exercises, and made similar ceremonial visits as king in 1627 and 1628.[63] Later, of course, Charles I grew intimately acquainted with the Isle of Wight in the exceptional circumstances of 1648. Charles II enjoyed a day trip to the Isle of Wight in July 1671, finding time to have dinner with the governor at Newport, and made another brief visit in July 1675.[64] Newsletters in September 1683 reported King Charles's intentions to visit the Isle of Wight again after reviewing his naval forces at Portsmouth.[65]

War made exceptional demands on frontier islands. Lord Hunsdon's administrative excesses were justified by emergencies in the Elizabethan war with Spain. In 1627, when Charles I was fighting both Spain and France, his government needed ships, men, horses, carts, and money and, in violation of custom, requisitioned every boat on the Isle of Wight to transport soldiers. Some owners waited more than a year for payment after their vessels had been pressed into service in campaigns against the Isle of Rhé and Cadiz.[66] Island householders bore the burden of billeting. Among troops awaiting deployment on the Isle of Wight in 1627 were 1,500 hungry and disorderly Scots, who left 'at least seventy bastards' in their wake.[67] When King Charles visited the island in 1628, Sir John Oglander asked for recompense for billeting and defences, but the king offered only half-promises. 'In Queen Elizabeth's time...the state was well ordered,' mused Oglander in his commonplace book, but now the Isle of Wight was depressed, 'insula fortunata, now infortunata'.[68]

With interests and ambitions common to their class, the island gentry sometimes clashed with the military administration. The problems of precedence, authority, and jurisdiction that troubled other militarized islands also arose on the Isle of Wight. Islanders cherished their privileges, however slight, and, in the words of their eighteenth-century historian, 'discovered a proper spirit of freedom whenever any encroachments on their liberties were attempted'.[69] Their cooperation with authorities at Carisbrooke and Westminster became tangled with matters of patronage, profit, and principle, as the central state augmented its power.

Sir Edward Horsey, the virtuous Elizabethan who preceded Lord Hunsdon, may have been the last Isle of Wight captain who 'lived in perfect harmony with the gentlemen there'. Hunsdon served at the time of the Armada crisis, and prioritized 'the strength of the country' over the rights of its inhabitants. He preferred the title 'Governor' to 'Captain' because it implied a greater reserve of authority. He interfered in the island's commerce, demanded licences for traffic and markets, and even prohibited 'free passage over the water into the mainland' without his permission, rather like his contemporary Sir Thomas Leighton on Guernsey. Gentlemen who protested against the governor's arbitrary rule were rebuffed, and one of them, Robert Dillington, was committed to the Fleet prison for his agitation 'for the liberty of the isle in a dangerous time'. Hunsdon rejected the petitioners' complaints as 'frivolous', and deemed anyone who crossed him 'a papist or a misliker of the present state'. Not for the last time, island residents learned that their liberties grew leaner in times of national emergency.[70]

The Jacobean governor the Earl of Southampton was renowned for 'his just, affable, and obliging deportment', at least in the eyes of Sir John Oglander, who thrived under his regime. Southampton's immediate successors, Lord Conway and Lord Weston, pleased the local gentry even more by not visiting the island. Slack administration under the early Stuarts maintained the peace, while some gentlemen enriched themselves, and the island's military posture was neglected. When the second Lord Weston, Earl of Portland, arrived as governor in 1639, his aristocratic entourage drank healths 'till they were scarce *compos mentis*', and used up £300 worth of gunpowder in celebratory shots, 'never so much powder fired, except against an enemy'.[71] Portland established his household at Carisbrooke Castle, with his Roman Catholic countess, but was removed by parliament on the eve of the civil war, and replaced by the Earl of Pembroke (see Chapter 8).

Wight islanders endured military government in the years of civil war, but do not seem to have been greatly inconvenienced. Royalists like Oglander grieved for their losses, but the island was generally quiet. A principal inducement for the parliamentarian Colonel Robert Hammond to accept the post of governor was the relative tranquillity of the Isle of Wight, a tranquillity that was rudely disturbed. Everything changed when Charles I arrived unexpectedly in November 1647, and spent more than a year at Carisbrooke as a prisoner (see Chapter 12). The king's detention brought the national political crisis into the local community, and imprinted the Isle of Wight on the larger public sphere. Parliament's military presence expanded, and the island gained national attention, as soldiers, diplomats, politicians, spies, and would-be courtiers flocked to Newport and Carisbrooke, until the king was removed to the mainland, to his death.

Anglesey

Anglesey, the largest and most integrated of islands, was not even English, being a county of Wales. The Elizabethan William Harrison was wrong in claiming that 'for temporal regiment it appertaineth to the county of Caernarvon'.[72] Henry VIII's Acts of Union (1536–43) had merged Wales with England, preserving Anglesey as a county with members of parliament and justices of the peace.[73] According to the Elizabethan traveller Thomas Phaer, 'the isle of Anglesey is in length direct 22 miles, and 14 broad'. Its chief town Beaumaris possessed 'a strong castle . . . a goodly haven, and a road for all ships'. A short ferry ride from the mainland, the island was on three sides 'beaten upon with the surging and troublous Irish Sea', and bordered on the fourth by the Menai Straits.[74] The waterway served both as conduit and as moat, and was sometimes considered impassable. Residents could normally cross in their own small boats or take the Menai ferry, which in the seventeenth century consisted of 'little round sea boats, holding no more than three horses at a time'.[75] The Jacobean John Speed thought Anglesey 'very well peopled', no less than the Isle of Man, and its the population may have exceeded 10,000 by the end of the seventeenth century (see Figure 8).[76]

Most of the islanders spoke only Welsh, though elites spoke English and were assimilated into the dominant Anglo-British polity.[77] Indeed, with its anglicized gentry, and its representation at Westminster, Anglesey more closely resembled the Isle of Wight than any other offshore community. The island's public life was dominated by the Bulkeley family (ennobled with an Irish peerage in 1644), who served as magistrates, crown officers, and members of parliament. Anglesey's isolation, though significant, was alleviated by its position on the main route from London to Dublin, through the transit port of Holyhead.[78]

Anglesey's farms and fields were vulnerable to external attack, but the island's frontier situation conferred certain privileges as well as dangers. Elizabethan precedents exempted Anglesey from contributing to military levies, so that the men could stay home to combat foreign enemies or pirates. This did not prevent demands from the state for manpower for service in Ireland—forty-six men in 1595, and fifty in 1624—which were duly challenged.[79] The deputy lieutenants of Anglesey claimed exemption from national military recruiting in 1624, arguing that, because 'the said isle lies open to the sea, and is subject to great danger if it should be attempted by invasion', it should be 'specifically forborne' from contributing troops. To support this claim they submitted a 'remembrance' from 1586, to the effect that there should be 'no levies in Anglesey'. Left with their own 'men and furniture', they were better able to defend their island.[80] In 1625, when Charles I went to war with Spain, the Privy Council excused Anglesey from army levies, in light of feared attacks by Irish catholics. They accepted the claim that the men of Anglesey were better enabled 'to defend the said isle by exempting them from the public services wherein other counties were charged'.[81] Leading gentlemen of Anglesey evoked the same privilege in 1643 when they asked King Charles 'to follow the example of his royal predecessors' to 'exempt this island from any press of men at this time' of civil war.[82] The island was not, however, excused contributions to parliamentary subsidies or the prerogative obligation of Ship

Figure 8. Anglesey and North Wales, 1579 (Alamy Images)

Money. Nor was there any immunity from demands of the courts of Westminster.[83] Towards the end of the civil war Anglesey provided a refuge for retreating royalists, until parliamentary victory absorbed it into the revolutionary state (see Chapters 8 and 9). That island pride survived the Restoration is shown by petitioners to Charles II who asked that the English garrison at Beaumaris Castle should be removed and replaced with 'native' Anglesey men.[84]

Lesser islands lacked the clout of the Channel Islands or the Isle of Man, but stood from time to time on their particular privileges. Each had noteworthy individuality. Simply being offshore put them at a remove. Most of the distinctive constitutional features of England's islands accrued from their history as dynastic possessions, feudal grants, military governorships, or seigneurial proprietorships. The maintenance of insular exemptions and immunities depended upon a watchful cadre of inheritors, office-holders, and elite islanders with sufficient legal, linguistic, and archival skills to resist encroachments from London. The Stanleys were most diligent in upholding their rights and preserving the Lordship of Man. The Godolphins, on a much smaller scale, kept their grip on the Isles of Scilly. The Channel Islands, with their local legal structure derived from the Norman inheritance, were best prepared to lock horns with the Privy Council. English civil society was more deeply entrenched on Anglesey and the Isle of Wight, though even on those inshore islands a sense of difference and distance prevailed, along with a willingness to challenge Whitehall. The Oglanders and the Bulkeleys behaved like provincial English gentlemen, but they too were sensitive to the perils and opportunities of insularity.

5

Island Economies

Bounties of the Land and Sea

Discussing England's 'many fair islands...environed with the ocean waves', the Elizabethan geographer William Harrison observed that they varied in the resources and comforts they afforded, but all contributed to the wealth of the kingdom. 'Some are fruitful in wood, corn, wildfowl, and pasture ground for cattle, albeit that many of them be accounted barren, because they are only replenished with conies...without either man or woman otherwise inhabiting them.' Others were 'so enriched with commodities, that they have pleasant havens, fresh springs, great store of fish, and plenty of cattle, whereby the inhabitants do reap no small advantage'.[1] This chapter builds on Harrison's comments to address the varied economic assets, activities, and problems along the archipelagic edge.

The defining feature of island economies was the sea. Islands not only possessed a coastline, like a score of English counties, but were ringed by coastline. The sea enfolded them, energized them, and sometimes brought torments. With no means of coming or going except by water, their experience was shaped by marine conditions. The characteristics and contradictions of insularity marked the economic life of England's islands as well as their political culture. As theorists of 'island studies' well recognize, they were isolated yet connected, separate yet engaged, and different from each other and the mainland.[2] The prime value of the islands to the state was strategic, but money could be gained there too.

Islanders made what they could of their available resources, terrestrial as well as maritime, but their mainstay, from fish and lobsters, to seaweed, coastal trade, and the accidents of shipwrecks, was the bounty of the sea. International streams of commerce touched island shores, while freebooters and smugglers frequented their headlands, beaches, and coves. Coastal traders brought supplies back and forth. The crown's strategic necessities—the infrastructure of defence and deployment of garrisons—also underwrote island economies, channelling resources from the centre to the periphery. Fishing, farming, shipping, and military services provided the material basis for their engagement with the rest of the English world.

England's Islands in a Sea of Troubles. David Cressy, Oxford University Press (2020). © David Cressy 2020.
DOI: 10.1093/oso/9780198856603.001.0001

Work of the Soil

Every island had *terra firma*, with land that could be cultivated, as well as generous miles of coastline. Even tiny Lundy had acres that could be cropped; even St Nicholas had room for a garden. Island fields provided grains for subsistence, and pasture for cattle and sheep. The quality of the ground varied, from rocky salt-sprayed barrens to soil described approvingly as 'fat'. Harrison described the soil of the Isle of Wight as 'very fruitful, for notwithstanding that the shore of itself be very full of rocks and craggy cliffs, yet there wanteth no plenty of cattle, corn, pasture, meadow ground, wild fowl, fish, fresh rivers, and pleasant woods, whereby the inhabitants may live in ease and welfare'.[3] The Jacobean writer John Speed similarly commended the Isle of Wight as 'plenteously stored with cattle and grain', and found it 'pleasant for meadow, pasturage, and parks, so that nothing is wanting that may suffice man'.[4] Later authors remarked on the 'almost proverbial' fertility of the island's soil, its rich yields of wheat and wool, and the varied abundance of its fish. The downlands of the Isle of Wight were comparable to those of southern England, with deer parks, sheep folds, and rabbit warrens.[5] The island supplied markets in Portsmouth and Southampton with 'wheat, flesh, cheese, and butter', and raised sheep with 'so fine a fleece, that the wool hereof has the precedency of that of the Cotswold in Gloucestershire'.[6] Island farmers prospered as suppliers of grain to the southern mainland, and as exporters of malt to Cornish and Devon ports, in partnership with island shippers. The seventeenth-century population may have been 12,000 or more.[7]

Anglesey too was well favoured, as generally fertile lowland beyond the uplands of North Wales. The island was rich in pasture and tillage, abundant in corn and cattle, supporting 'good trade of merchandise and many gentlemen'. Its fields were larger and more open than most of mainland Wales, yielding 'barley most plenteously'. Like the Isle of Wight, Anglesey exported malt to brewers in England. Anglesey cattle and dairy products went to Chester and Liverpool. Other commodities came and went to Ireland through the small port of Holyhead. Everything had to go by boat. With approximately 10,000 people in the Elizabethan era, Anglesey was considered 'meetly well inhabited', or 'very well peopled', and enjoyed 'continual abundance'.[8]

The Isles of Scilly, by contrast, comprised a scatter of rocky islands, with thin and unpromising soils. Their number, by some counts, made 'one hundred and forty-seven, each of them bearing grass', but no more than half a dozen were permanently inhabited. At best, William Harrison reported, the islands 'yielded a short grass, meet for sheep and cattle', with 'wild swans, puffins, gulls, cranes, and other kinds of fowl in great abundance'. Tenants grazed a few animals, dug a few fields, and harvested a little grain, while a small force served the garrison or laboured in Scilly's unprosperous tin mines. Fishing and maritime services were the mainstay, under the eye of the proprietor's steward. The Isles of Scilly are omitted from maps and discussion in *The Agrarian History of England and Wales*, but could be regarded as an especially windswept and wave-lashed outlier of western Cornwall. The land that was dismissed in the sixteenth century as nothing more than 'a bushment of briars' was made more serviceable by manuring with burnt seaweed, a practice that may have been learned from the Channel Islands.[9]

A parliamentary survey in 1652 listed tenements on Scilly, island by island, recording their acreage, dwellings, and rentable value. The total population was barely 800. Few holdings had more than 20 acres, and many less than three. Only 5 of 180 named tenants were described as 'Mr', which sometimes denotes a gentleman but here seems to indicate men with larger holdings who might elsewhere be ranked as husbandmen. Their parcels of 'poor barren heathy ground' were mixed with pasture and arable, with occasional gardens and orchards. Recent civil-war 'troubles' had damaged the islands, leaving cony burrows (rabbit warrens) 'destroyed by the soldiers and others', houses and enclosures 'now fallen down and ruined since the taking of the Scillies from the enemy', and boats and fishing tackle 'much impoverished and wasted'. The survey took note of a tin mine on St Mary's, 'of no value, or not of value to answer the charge' in working it. The annual 'profits of the harbour' were estimated at £6 13s. 4d., and the proprietor gained a like amount from wrecks. The 'total improved value' of the islands approached £1,000, which is why the Godolphins were eager to get them back after their losses in the king's service.[10]

The seventeenth-century Isle of Man has been described as 'geographically marginal, culturally isolated, and economically backward', though it had many more resources than the Scillies.[11] With an economy based on grazing and grain-growing, as well as fishing, shipping, and smuggling, the Lords of Man commanded considerable assets, including almost 10,000 subjects. Early modern observers remarked on the Isle of Man's 'thin soil, and unfruitful blasts from the sea', its 'cold and sharp' air, and its 'extraordinary high winds'. Yet the island was 'reasonable fruitful for cattle, fish, and corn', though 'two parts of three are mountains'. There was land enough for the harvesting of oats, wheat, and barley, and the grazing of hardy cattle and sheep, though more desirable comestibles had to be imported from Ireland or England.[12] 'The sheep of this country are exceeding huge, well woolled', Harrison remarked, 'their hogs are in manner monstrous'. A later writer modified this to observe that the Isle of Man had 'good flocks of sheep and herds of cattle, but none of the biggest size'. Boats with calves and cattle from the Isle of Man supplied ports in Lancashire and Cumberland. Like the Scillies, the Isle of Man had 'abundance of puffins ... chiefly used for their feathers, and oil made of them. But their flesh being pickled or salted, as it has fish-like taste, so it comes little short of anchovies.'[13] A somewhat jaundiced eighteenth-century commentator observed that the island 'is said to labour under some natural misfortunes, occasioned by a thin unfertile soil, which requires more experience, labour, and manure, than the inhabitants in general are qualified to bestow upon it'.[14]

Commentators on the Channel Islands remarked on their many advantages. The Jacobean geographer John Speed counted only blessings on Guernsey, with summer fields 'so naturally garnished with flowers of all sorts, that a man, being there, might conceit himself to be in a pleasant artificial garden'. Jersey too he rated 'a very delightsome and healthful island', a view shared by generations of residents and visitors. Jersey's soil, he wrote, 'is very fertile, bringing forth store of corn and cattle'.[15] This contrasted with the Jacobean military assessment, 'that considering the barrenness of those islands, that in the plentiful years can do little more than sustain themselves', they could not produce enough to feed a garrison.[16] Another seventeenth-century observer wrote of Jersey, 'the whole island seems but a rock, covered over with earth, some places more, and some less'. The Jersey cleric Philip Falle reported that 'the higher grounds are gritty and gravelly, some stony and rocky, but others of a fine and sweet mould. The lower are deep, heavy, and rich', encouraging productive agriculture. Everyone agreed that Jersey's waters yielded 'great store of fish, but principally conger and lobster, the greatest and fattest upon the coast of England'. The Restoration Jerseyman Jean Poingdestre devoted three pages to describing his island's 'infinite store' of fish.[17] By this time islanders also had a century of experience of fishing the banks of Newfoundland. Writing in 1685, Philippe Dumaresq, thought that too many of Jersey's youth were drawn to Newfoundland fishing or the western plantations, to 'the general neglect of husbandry'.[18] Jersey's population by this time approached 14,000, Guernsey's perhaps 10,000, with another thousand in the dependencies of Alderney and Sark.

The English cleric Peter Heylyn, who toured the Channel Islands in 1629, found them 'pleasant and delightsome, but yet so small in the extent and circuit' that they appeared 'an abridgement only of the greater works of nature'. He saw 'pretty hillocks', 'pleasant valleys', and 'dainty rills or riverets' watering a soil that was 'sufficiently fertile in itself, but most curiously manured' (a reference to the application of seaweed or *vraic*). The islanders, he noted, grew 'several sorts of apples, out of which they make a pleasing kind of cider, which is their ordinary drink'.[19] Other productive fruit trees included pears, plums, cherries, and apricots.[20]

Comparing the two islands, Heylyn found the people of Guernsey to be 'much more sociable and generous', with greater wealth and openness owing to 'continual converse with strangers in their own haven, and by travelling abroad' in trade. Those of Jersey, by contrast, were 'more poor, and therefore more destitute of humanity'. Heylyn saw beggars on Jersey, but none on Guernsey. He deemed the Jerseymen 'very painful [i.e. painstaking] and laborious, but by reason of their continual toil and labour, not a little affected to a kind of melancholy surliness incident to ploughmen'. Their problems were compounded, he thought, by partible inheritance 'by the name of gavelkind', whereby lands were equally 'divided amongst the sons of every father, and those parcels also to be subdivided even *ad infinitum*'.[21]

The later Stuart traveller Charles Trumbull considered Jersey more fertile than Guernsey, although the islanders, he recorded, 'usually think the contrary themselves'. He found Guernsey 'destitute almost of wood and trees, and of gentry to promote and further their growth', whereas on Jersey 'the whole island is now almost become one great orchard'.[22] For fuel, the island relied on local seaweed, and firewood imported from France. If castles or seigneurial homes wanted coal—known as sea-coal in the early modern period—it too had to be brought in by ship. Later analysts deemed almost two-thirds of Guernsey's land—a little more than 10,000 acres—'fit for cultivation'.[23] Islanders grew wheat, barley, rye, flax, and hemp, along with cider apples.[24] Entrepreneurs hatched schemes in 1691 to develop the manufacture of linen and paper on Jersey and Guernsey, the ground being 'very proper for sowing and raising hemp, and the people qualified for such work'.[25] Some also made money by quarrying island rock. Governor Hatton of Guernsey offered Lord Clarendon a shipment of building stone as a gesture of friendship. More than 200 tons of Guernsey stone reached London in 1698, with much more to follow in the eighteenth century.[26] The islands had small runs of sheep and cattle, but not yet the famous Jersey cows, which were a product of Victorian dairying and animal breeding.[27]

Channel Islanders made productive use of another of nature's gifts, the abundant seaweed that festooned their shores. Seaweed, commonly bladder wrack or oarweed (*fucus vesiculosus* or *laminaricae*), known in the Norman islands as *vraic*, was used as fertilizer, fuel, and as a supplement to animal fodder. Organized gathering of *vraic venant*, the drifting seaweed that piled up on the foreshore, occurred in February and March. The better-yielding *vraic scié* was cut from coastal rocks in the summer. Repeated applications of *vraic* improved the yields of the islands' cultivable land. Channel Islanders may have taught this use of seaweed to their Isles of Scilly cousins.[28]

Pioneers of tobacco plantation introduced the addictive weed from America. To protect the Virginia colonists, who had little else to sustain them, a royal proclamation in December 1619 prohibited the growing of tobacco 'within this our realm of England, or dominion of Wales'. Channel Island planters claimed exemption, because English laws did not touch them, and the proclamation made no specific mention of Guernsey or Jersey.[29] Charles I's proclamations in April 1625 and August 1627 expanded the restriction, banning tobacco cultivation in England, Ireland, Wales, or 'any isles or places thereunto belonging', but the orders were widely ignored.[30] Channel Islanders continued to cultivate tobacco, claiming that, 'by their privileges, as belonging to the Duchy of Normandy, [they] are not within the restraint of a proclamation against the plantation of tobacco', and therefore could grow what they pleased. Sir Peter

Osborne of Guernsey worried that tobacco might prove so rewarding a crop that islanders 'would convert their ground to that use, which might more profitably for the country be employed in tillage'.[31]

Further instructions from London in September 1628 to destroy all tobacco plants in Guernsey and Jersey were generally disregarded, and illicit cultivation continued, despite a similar command in March 1631. Only in 1638 did 'a proclamation concerning tobacco' specifically restrict planting in 'our islands of Jersey and Guernsey, or either of them, or within our Isle of Man', but this only dampened the nascent tobacco enterprise.[32] Large amounts of American tobacco passed through the Isle of Man, for re-export to Ireland, Scotland, and England, and that island proved ideal for smuggling though unsuitable for cultivation.[33]

Island Knitting

A principal by-employment and major source of income for many Channel Islanders was the knitting of woollen stockings, primarily for export to France. The English historian of the industry describes stocking knitting as 'a peasant handicraft that was successfully commercialised'. The work could be done year round by men, women, and children, and even by mariners at sea.[34] An observer on seventeenth-century Sark described a barn full of men, women, and children singing while working on stockings, gloves, caps, and waistcoats.[35] An English visitor to later Stuart Guernsey similarly described the evening *veille* or watch-meeting of female knitters who, 'wearied with work and discourse, set themselves to singing'. Always free with his opinions, Charles Trumbull criticized the Jerseymen engaged in 'a constant course of lazy and effeminate knitting, who should be forced to undertake some more laborious and manly profession'.[36]

Depending on supplies of wool from England, and a network of distributors in France, the islanders produced 'waistcoats, stockings, and other manufactures made of wool, wherein they are exceeding cunning'. The knitted worsteds of the Channel Island, sometimes known as jerseys, used finely spun thread, and achieved a better shape and tighter fit than most of their competitors. The wool was imported by the tod, in bundles weighing 28–32 pounds, each tod sufficient for some sixty pairs of stockings. Finished stockings came in a great variety of styles and colours, intended more for the male fashion market than for women. They sold from 2s. to 5s. a pair, English money, or 18 to 38 *livres tournois* per dozen, with luxury items costing more than twice that sum. Charles Trumbull rated Guernsey stockings 'generally of a finer sort than those of Jersey, some of them so curiously knit and so fine that they may be drawn through a ring, and worth 20 shillings or 30 shillings'. One Guernsey dealer of that decade offered thirty-three varieties of styles, sizes, and decorations to his agents in northern France.[37]

Though island sheep produced 'wool very fine and white', there was never enough for the knitters.[38] Jacobean legislation restricted the export of wool from England, but the islanders operated under licence. Their privilege of free trade did not cover this crucial commodity, so periodic renegotiation was necessary. Guernseymen petitioned James I in March 1621 for continued licence to import wool, free of customs, 'for setting the people on work, who are chiefly employed in converting wool into stockings and other knitwear'. The agreed amount was 5 tons a year, to be shipped from London or Southampton, enough for more than 20,000 pairs of stockings.[39] Island leaders repeatedly petitioned for continuance, restoration, or expansion of their privileges in this regard. The centrality of stocking knitting to the Channel Island economy, and its reliance on raw material shipped from the mainland, encouraged cooperation with the English state.

Island knitting boomed in the seventeenth century, but was susceptible to slumps, changing fashion, foreign competition, and the vicissitudes of war. Hostilities with France in 1627 interrupted the stocking trade, despite the privilege of neutrality, when islanders faced ruin, so they said, without other means of support.[40] The English civil war also interrupted supplies of wool to the islands, with different consequences for parliamentarian Guernsey and royalist Jersey. Guernseymen thanked the Earl of Warwick in July 1643 for ensuring a supply of wool to the island, to be employed by the poorer sort in making stockings.[41] In August 1645, they reminded the Committee at Derby House that 'the making of stockings is the only trade that the people have to get their livelihood', and that 'the retarding of the transportation of wool for the isle will deprive the people of their daily food'. This posed a security threat as well as an economic problem, since parliament's control of the island required an orderly population. A delegation of Guernseymen appealed for a frigate to guard their waters against 'obstruction' in the import of wool.[42]

While English wool reached Guernsey throughout the 1640s, imports into Jersey were severely limited until royalist control came to an end.[43] The quality of Jersey worsted stockings deteriorated as the war cut off supplies. Sir George Carteret attempted to sustain the industry by regulating the length and mesh of Jersey knitted stockings, while Sir Edward Hyde, taking refuge in Jersey, used his influence with the Earl of Ormonde to obtain wool from Ireland 'for the supporting the manufactures here'. He also sought means to bring English wool to Jersey, as 'a sure way to compose all fears and apprehensions here'.[44] Recognizing that 'the trade of worsted stockings' was 'the chief commodity which that our isle doth yield', and that 'many thousands of our subjects there...subsist by that only manufacture', the exiled Charles II instructed the bailiff and jurats of Jersey in August 1649 to prevent ruinous competition among the merchants, who 'circumvent each other therein' to the prejudice of the common good.[45] After their victory, England's republican government licensed the shipment of more wool to Jersey, 'to advantage the inhabitants, by setting them to work'.[46] But an unknown amount of this wool was re-exported, for the benefit of corrupt officials.[47]

Protectionist legislation proposed at the Restoration restricted the export of wool, yarn, and fuller's earth 'out of this realm of England', but a hastily scribbled amendment allowed the transportation to the Channel Islands of 2,000 tods of wool per year for knitters in Jersey, 1,000 tods for Guernsey, 200 tods to Alderney, and 100 tods to Sark.[48] Petitioners in 1660 described these amounts as 'the least quantity they have need of', and asked for guarantees of future supply. Parliamentary legislation met this minimal demand.[49] The merchant John Barcroft petitioned in March 1666 to import 1,000 tods of wool ('half combed, and half uncombed'), and a quantity of leather and lead into the islands of Jersey and Guernsey, remarking that 'the great support of those islands consists in their knitting and making of woollen stockings with English wool...which now in this time of war they cannot so easily obtain'.[50] The stocking-knitters also had to cope with the vicissitudes of embargoes and the apparent capriciousness of French import tariffs.[51] Wool was so scarce and poverty so severe in September 1666, at the height of the Anglo-Dutch war, that some islanders recommended 'transplantation' to Ireland or America.[52]

Dependent as it was on English wool, the Channel Island knitting industry was subject to both political and commercial pressures. Importers either ignored the official limits or sought permission to bring in more.[53] Control of this traffic was yet another perquisite of office for island governors, providing an opportunity to seek favours from London while also lining their pockets. Sir Thomas Morgan of Jersey issued licences, and imported 500 tods each year for his own use, which he disposed of 'to advantage'.[54] His successor allocated the like amount to garrison officers, 'which they sold to the inhabitants at a dear rate'.[55] Governor Christopher Hatton of Guernsey exercised similar power in May 1681 when he allocated the island's quota to the knitters.[56] When trade between the islands and Normandy was suspended in 1682 over money due to the stocking merchants, Governor John Lanier of Jersey intervened, because, he said, the island 'subsists for the most part by the vent of their stockings to the French'.[57] It did not help that a lieutenant governor on Jersey was exploiting shortages by exacting 5d. per tod on wool imported from England, without any authority to do so.[58] Around this time Jean Poingdestre estimated that Jersey knitters could produce 10,000 pairs a week, an output that seems somewhat exaggerated.[59]

Petitioners to parliament at the beginning of James II's reign in 1685 asked that the statutory limits on wool shipments to the Channel Islands be doubled and that exports be allowed from other ports than Southampton. On Jersey alone, they said, some 6,000 knitters consumed 100 tods of uncombed English wool a week, nearly 5,000 tods a year, some of which they obtained illicitly in France. Knitting was vital to the subsistence and security of the islanders and therefore 'beneficial to the kingdom of England in general', for without the sale of stockings they would be 'poor miserable creatures unable to defend themselves'.[60] Surveying the people and commodities of Jersey that year, Phillip Dumaresq estimated that 'half at least depend upon the manufacture of stockings', producing some 6,000 pairs per week.[61] The new allocation, confirmed in 1687, would allow 4,000 tods of uncombed wool for Jersey, 2,000 for Guernsey, 400 for Alderney, and 200 for Sark.[62]

Stocking-knitters and their distributors lost their primary market in 1689 when William III ended the commercial neutrality of the Channel Islands.[63] Island exports to enemy France were prohibited, though some got through to St Malo clandestinely. When the Peace of Ryswick restored relations in 1697, lobbyists from Jersey pressed the English government to include special protection for the island's stocking trade.[64] In 1699, diversifying the market, 2,930 dozen pairs of Guernsey stockings were exported to England, along with 3,172 knitted waistcoats.[65]

The Life Blood of Trade

The sea connected islands to each other and to mainland havens, Neptune permitting, so that ships, goods, people, and news could reach all shores. Major waterways were 'liquid borders', which facilitated as well as inhibited contact. The Channel in particular was an international seaway, linking the economies of the North Sea and Baltic with those of the Irish Sea, the Atlantic, and the Mediterranean. It did not merely separate England and France.[66] Maritime traffic gave the islands especial valance as hubs, nodes, and destinations, as well as suppliers of ships and men.

The observation that 'the livelihood of the merchant is the life of the common-wealth' applied especially to commercially active islands.[67] The Isle of Wight, for example, was a stopping point for vessels of London or Dover on their way to the New World, and a common port of call on their return. Newport merchants had interests along and across the Channel, and much further afield. Coastal and international shipping made frequent calls in Isle of Wight havens. Commercial exchanges, and sometimes wrecks, brought oils, wines, and other products of the south to island shores, allowing gentry like the Oglanders to furnish their homes and tables with cosmopolitan fare. Island mariners benefited from expanding English trade, but overzealous customs officials at Southampton had to be reminded in 1675 that 'the Isle of Wight is not the open sea' when they attempted to collect duties on items from across the Solent. Vigorous commerce fuelled the dispute over the island's 'market trade to the neighbouring towns on the main'. Customs commissioners took note in 1686 that 'the Isle of Wight is of late years become a very considerable place of trade', especially with the American plantations.[68]

The Isles of Scilly were similarly visited by local and long-distance mariners, both English and foreign. Shipping between the English Channel and the Irish Sea, and between the Bay of Biscay and the Bristol Channel, took shelter in Scilly's havens. Grateful mariners paid cash or in kind for the governor's hospitality, and for 'preserving from spoil and pirates'.[69] The boatmen of the Isles of Scilly provided pilotage through treacherous waters, while shore dwellers supplied labour for haulage and shipwreck recovery. Many home-bound vessels from across the Atlantic made Scilly their first English landfall, unloading part of their cargo, though one such mariner declared, 'Scilly is but a melancholy station for foul ships', not much more than a seamark and a rendezvous.[70]

As in the Isle of Wight, Scilly islanders profited from supplying sailors and servicing vessels. Breton linen, French wine, and New World commodities passed through the islands on their way to richer markets. The commercial success of the Channel Island merchants inspired the proprietors of the Scillies in the 1630s to propose that they too should become a privileged entrepôt, a status they never achieved.[71] While forces loyal to the Stuarts held the islands in the 1640s, their royalist frigates plied a trade that linked the Isles of Scilly to the cavalier diaspora in Jersey, Ireland, the Isle of Man, Spain, and France. Expanded commercial shipping after the Restoration brought more goods and men to the thinly populated Scillies. Increased traffic later in the seventeenth century made it worthwhile for the government to install customs officers in Scilly, though they met with local obstruction.[72]

Anglesey's participation in the international economy is illuminated by William Harrison's observation in the 1580s that wine was as 'plentiful and good cheap there most commonly as in London, through the great recourse of merchants from France, Spain, and Italy unto the aforesaid island'.[73] Further indications appear in the diaries and account books of Anglesey notables like the Bulkeleys, whose housekeeping included such imported luxuries as tobacco, sugar, raisins, and pepper.[74] Shipping often sheltered in the roads of Beaumaris, and much of the traffic between England and Ireland made Holyhead its hub.

The trade of the Isle of Man, according to one seventeenth-century commentator, 'hardly deserveth a chapter', but this was too dismissive. Dickinson's modern discussion of the commercial economy of the early modern Isle of Man extends over a hundred pages. The island's strategic position between England and Ireland guaranteed a flow of military and commercial traffic, though generally modest in scale. The island exported hides and skins, with some fish and corn; imports were everything else, including wood, iron, and finished goods that the island lacked.[75] The Earl of Derby's water bailiff supposedly had 'cognizance' of all goods entering or leaving the island. Efforts by London to impose dues on the island's commerce proved predictably unrewarding.[76]

Every island depended on trade, but none so much as the Channel Islands. Sir Edward Conway, who had served as James I's commissioner in 1617, observed that Jersey 'is happily situated for traffic, and having not many growing commodities, nor indeed sufficient to maintain themselves, they must be enabled by trade to increase their people, and by the produce of that trade be enabled to fortify and arm themselves'.[77] Island merchants took full advantage of their favourable commercial location, and of English naval and diplomatic protection.

Channel Island traders were especially active in the French ports of St Malo and Morlaix, and in the southern English ports of Poole and Southampton. Merchants and mariners from Guernsey and Jersey ranged far afield, from the Bay of Biscay to the Baltic, and joined in trade to the Caribbean, New England, and the North Atlantic fishing grounds.[78] Island traders thrived on their privilege of neutrality, enjoying an advantage over mainland competitors. The busy commercial shipping that connected Jersey and Guernsey to Normandy, Brittany, and the rest of northern France, and to Spain, Portugal, and the Americas as far as Newfoundland, continued in times of war as well as peace.

Reports of wrecks, as well as manifests and port books, indicate the continental and even global reach of island shipping. Commodities of all sorts changed hands, with English cloth, tin, and wax among principal exports, and linen, canvas, wine, and brandy among wares imported from France. Petitioners from Jersey claimed in 1679 that the balance of trade was uneven, 'the islanders carrying in their vessels only stockings... which is but of small bulk though of great value, and the French bring in corn, salt., etc., which are of great bulk yet of small value comparatively'.[79] By this time Jersey maintained a commercial fleet of 'thirty or forty ships of some burden which pass over into France and England', while Guernsey's ships, according to Charles Trumbull, were fewer but bigger.[80]

Ancient custom allowed the Channel Islanders free traffic in goods and wares to and from England 'without paying any customs, subsidies, or duties'. Commerce between Guernsey or Jersey and the mainland was supposed to be as unencumbered as trade between Hampshire and Dorset, though their importation of wool was strictly regulated.[81] These freedoms were challenged in the reign of Charles II, when excise officers in London attempted to impose tariffs on Jersey cider. In this instance the shippers reminded the Privy Council that the 'ancient charters, privileges, and immunities' of the island permitted their free trade with 'all ports and places of his majesty's kingdom of England and dominion of Wales', without any charge of 'custom, excise, or other duties and imposition', and the Council reluctantly agreed.[82]

Jerseys' Restoration governors took to taxing French imports to the island, 'five shillings per ton burthen', while revenue officers exacted duty on goods brought to the islands from England 'as if they had been intended to export or transport the same to any foreign parts'. Jerseymen challenged these violations of their privileges, and in May 1679 obtained an order from the king inhibiting both practices. Governor Sir John Lanier protested, saying he had not been consulted, and six months later the Lords of the Council reversed themselves. Five shillings per ton would still be collected on French vessels trading with the island, but henceforth the money would go to 'the public occasions and benefit of the island', including repair of the castle, rather than to 'the private advantage of the governor or any other person'.[83] Channel Islanders complained that trade dried up when neutrality ended after 1689, although an illicit traffic continued that authorities were powerless to prevent.[84]

Trade and peculation always went hand-in-hand, but reports of fraud, false documents, forged licenses, bribery, and evasion were especially common after the Restoration.[85] Virginia tobacco was unloaded directly in Guernsey to avoid paying duties in England.[86] French ships evaded the terms of the Navigation Act by trading under Jersey or Guernsey papers.[87] The islands developed a lucrative entrepôt trade, re-exporting items brought duty free from England, and distributing food and drink from Spain and France. Alluding to underhand dealings, Sir Christopher Hatton in 1664 called Guernsey 'the magazine of all contraband goods from England'. Whole cargoes of uncombed wool from England and Ireland passed through Guernsey to France and Holland, 'in despite of the brand of felony the statute imposeth upon it'.[88] Islanders themselves acknowledged that some trade went in 'in the night and by stealth', thereby evading registration.[89] The establishment of London's Board of Customs in 1671 acted as an accelerant to extra-legal activity.[90] Appointing a new commissioner for customs for Jersey in 1687, James II remarked that 'great art and industry is used to defraud us thereof'.[91]

The Channel Islands became the hub of an international smuggling network, linking Devon and Cornwall, Normandy and Brittany, exploiting what Renaud Morieux has called 'the dubious boundaries of sovereignty'. The islanders insisted on trade without frontiers, sending English wool and American tobacco to northern France, and French wine and spirits to southern England, regardless of the state of hostilities or the efforts of excise men.[92] War may even have quickened, rather than inhibited, the illicit traffic in luxury goods and arms. The islets of Les Écréhous, midway between Jersey and France, served as a rendezvous for the exchange of French brandy and English gunpowder, even while the nations were at war.[93] The Scilly Isles too were notorious smugglers' havens, made apparent in the 1680s by their landing of goods 'in greater quantities than those islands can consume'.[94]

Smuggling was also endemic on the Isle of Man, facilitated by the island 'being not subject to the laws of any of the three kingdoms'. Several generations of smugglers frequented the island's coasts. Almost equidistant from England, Scotland, and Ireland, yet outside their jurisdiction, the Isle of Man was ideally situated as 'a receptacle and refuge to goods that are intended clandestinely to be conveyed...in small parcels...as are not easily to be discovered or prevented'. Shipments of tobacco, silks, silver, and gold lace, and other fine goods were smuggled into Ireland in the 1670s by way of the Isle of Man. It was widely known that the smugglers lodged their goods in warehouses on the island, 'till they can see the coast clear to land them in open boats in some of the northern creeks, where are persons ready to receive and convey them in small portmanteaux to the respective places of sale without paying any duty on the same'. Customs commissioners in Dublin demanded in 1683 that the Earl of Derby crack down on the traffic, but with little hope of remedial action. The earl insisted that he and his agents, indeed his whole island, enjoyed exemption from duties of any kind, and this gave cover to his multiple clients and allies.[95] It was a source of local satisfaction, though frustrating to London, that they were 'no way clogged nor burdened with taxes, customs, or other grievous impositions'.[96] Like residents of the Channel Islands, and to a lesser extent the Isles of Scilly, Manxmen exploited the benefits of insularity that accrued from ambiguities and anomalies. They would seek advantage wherever opportunity and profit beckoned, and their smuggling would only develop further in the decades that followed.[97]

Pirates and Privateers

Pirates posed a perennial problem to island authorities. They lurked in coastal waters, waiting for prey around the Isles of Scilly, the Channel Islands, the Isle of Wight, the Irish Sea, and the Bristol Channel. Some were occasional scavengers, others determined freebooters, 'the worst sort of seafarers', according to the Cornishman Richard Carew.[98] Spoiling ships and taking prizes, ruining some traders and inhibiting others, the pirates were a persistent feature of the maritime economy and a distressing drain upon it. Marauders took their toll of island shipping, but some of them also traded with shore communities, selling their booty and purchasing supplies. Some even enjoyed unofficial patronage and protection. They posed a challenge to the authority of the state, which struggled to suppress their predation.

Privateers were, in principle, more reputable than pirates because they operated under letters of marque, which specified their authority and targets. In practice the distinction could blur, as privateers lapsed into piracy, and pirates claimed to be privateers. Some of them conducted a maritime guerilla war, raiding the commerce of enemies and rivals. The corsairs of North Africa, generally known as 'Turks', were feared more than the European Dunkirkers or Biscayners, because they hunted for slaves rather than material cargo.

The archipelago of the Scillies, remote and thinly populated, yet relatively rich in traffic, always attracted pirates. Though the islands were poor, their vulnerability made them easy pickings for marauders in search of supplies. The early Tudor traveller John Leland reported that 'few men be glad to inhabit these islets', fearing French and Spanish 'robbers of the sea . . . that take their cattle by force'.[99] In 1547, the Scillies experienced the depredations of the corsair Thomessin, 'the greatest pirate in the world', who took refuge in a ruined castle on one of the smaller islands until an English fleet flushed him out.[100]

The Channel Islands too were pirate refuges. The governor of Guernsey reported in 1564 that 'the coasts are much haunted by piratical Englishmen, by whom many murders and outrages are committed'.[101] One of those marauders, guilty of 'that most horrible and detestable life', was the pirate Richard Hitchins, who committed 'divers and sundry piracies, namely upon Flemish fishers and other merchants, as well upon the coast of England as upon the coast of Spain', before his luck ran out in 1566. Most of Hitchins's crew managed to escape when their ship, *John of Sandwich*, wrecked on the coast of Alderney, only to be arrested by Guernsey authorities and held in Castle Cornet. Elizabeth I's government determined that two or three 'most culpable and fittest for example' should face immediate execution, and the rest sent to England to sue for their pardons. Hitchins, 'whose past life showed him wholly given to piracy', was 'hanged and strangled until dead' at the low-water mark near St Martin's point, where his body was left in chains.[102] Such treatment did nothing to deter the pirate captain Gisborne, who terrorized shipping around the Isle of Wight until his capture in 1581.[103]

The pirate problem may have become more acute in the reign of James I, as Elizabethan warships were decommissioned, and sailors departed from military service.[104] Hardly a year went by without reference to pirates, picaroons, or sea rovers around island and mainland shores. They thrived especially in periods of disruption, and in uncertain, marginal, and little-policed jurisdictions. English officials complained in 1609 that 'the islands are full of French pirates', while their French counterparts protested about English pirates like Thomas Pin. Thomas Salkeld's exploits around Jacobean Lundy formed an outrageous but short-lived episode of pirate brutality and excess (see Chapter 2).[105] Another 'arch-pirate', John Ward, took ships off the Isles of Scilly and in the Irish Sea. Officials claimed in 1611 that as many as forty pirate vessels, crewed by 2,000 desperate men, were molesting Scilly's waters.[106] More swarms of pirates molested the Channel Islands in the early 1620s.[107]

Corsair raids in the reign of Charles I redounded 'to the great dishonour of his majesty, and damage to his subjects'.[108] As many as sixty pirate vessels, 'thought to be Turks', were sighted in the Isles of Scilly in 1625, the same year that three pirate ships from Algiers seized the island of Lundy.[109] Reports of pirates in the Channel were so common that the Isle of Wight became known as 'another Algiers'.[110] 'Turkish' pirates from North Africa who took captives from the Isle of Wight in September 1625 allegedly said that 'they liked English women so well that before they departed they would have every man one'.[111]

French and Biscayne raiders plied the waters between Scilly and the coast of France, 'taking and sinking all of our nation that comes athwart them'. The governor of Plymouth complained in 1627 that, 'if it be not prevented in time, there will be no trading as much as from port to port, much less into foreign parts'.[112] 'Loose and desperate' pirates threatened Jersey in the early years of

Charles I's reign, 'so as the trade and commerce unto other his majesty's dominions is for the most part quite cut off.'[113].

In March 1628, Sir Philip Carteret, lieutenant governor of Jersey, was himself captured by privateers, and held to ransom. Carteret and his party were returning from England on board the *Diana* of Portsmouth, escorted by the pinnace *Mary*, when they were overpowered at night by five Dunkirkers off the Isle of Wight. Among their losses were money and munitions intended for Jersey's garrisons, and papers containing instructions for the island's defence. Carteret and others were held prisoner in Flanders for several months until ransoms could be negotiated. It was a blow to English honour, and an intelligence windfall for the French, to whom some Dunkirk pirates reported.[114] Relating this episode, the Venetian ambassador in London observed that the Dunkirk pirates 'are doing great mischief on these coasts, and meet with no resistance, so that English ships themselves dare not pass from one place to another, causing great inconvenience and scarcity of everything'.[115] It was a reminder of the perils of insularity, and the problem of servicing offshore establishments.

No part of the island periphery was spared. Residents of Anglesey petitioned for relief in May 1629 from the 'piratical prejudice' that afflicted their island, as 'trade is already grown to an infinite decay in those parts'. An English pirate ship of 100 tons, with a well-armed crew of eighty men, had recently taken two barques on the coast of Anglesey, stripping 'sundry passengers of quality' of all they had.[116]

'Egypt was never more infested with caterpillars than the Lands's End with Biscayners,' wrote Captain Richard Plumleigh in June 1630. Despite the navy's efforts, nimble shallow-draught pirate vessels 'graze the shores and run in amongst the rocks where we cannot follow them', some finding refuge in the Isles of Scilly.[117] Pirates around Alderney and Sark similarly used small boats in shoal water to evade capture in the Channel Islands.[118] Elie Brevint of Sark describes English pirates coasting the isles, rustling cattle and taking prisoners, before being captured and executed in Brittany. Sark was also menaced by Breton pirates, who stripped travellers of their clothes and purses.[119] More marauders, 'pataches of war, men of several nations, having no commission but living by piracy', operated from the French island of Chausey, between Jersey and St Malo.[120] Others ranged the Irish Sea, pillaging shipping around the Isle of Man, taking prisoners, killing fishermen, and making off with booty of linen and wine.[121] English authorities were helpless when officials on the Isle of Man gave shelter to Irish pirates, rather than arresting them.[122] Untouched by English justice, the island was long known as a place where privateers could bring prizes, sell cargoes, and refit vessels.[123]

Scilly islanders gained an unusual close view of a Spanish pirate vessel in January 1631 when one was cast ashore, and some of its goods entered the Scilly economy.[124] More raids by so-called Turks occurred throughout the 1630s, so that Scilly, like Lundy and Wight, was termed 'another Algiers'.[125] The damage caused by Turkish and other pirates was one of the justifications for Charles I's Ship Money, to build up the navy and assert the sovereignty of the seas.

Naval and privateering actions in the years of England's mid-seventeenth-century troubles distracted from the pirate menace but did not entirely eclipse it. Privateers from Stuart bases in Jersey, the Isle of Scilly, and the Isle of Man kept up a campaign against the parliamentary 'rebels'. 'Pirates' from royalist Jersey captured a parliamentary supply ship bound for Ireland in March 1647, and disposed of its cargo of drapery, clothing, and ammunition in St Malo.[126] In April 1649, the republican government complained of 'pirates ... sheltering themselves in the Isle of Man', who offended the coast of Cumberland; and a few months later they remarked on the 'mischief' done 'by pirates now about the Isle of Scilly'. Just as bad were 'persons dangerous and disaffected to this commonwealth' who traded with the enemy in plundered and smuggled goods.[127] Privateers periodically brought prizes into Channel Island ports to register claims and to dispose of captured cargoes.[128]

A parliamentary news writer complained in March 1651 of the 'many pranks ... upon our vessels' by raiders and privateers. His report illuminates perceptions of the pirate menace and of the political economy of the pirate world:

The pirates issue daily forth of Scilly and Jersey, in shallops and small vessels, that rove abroad at catch, for an advantage, and then when they have robbed, they run into every small creek for shelter, where no ship can follow them. Besides, they are protected by a squadron of their own confederacy, which lie at the Land's End; and with them all is fish that comes to the net. What they get is apportioned out to every man among them, according to his rank, and a surplusage is reserved into a common stock, for the maintenance of their designs, the trimming of their vessels, and other extraordinary occasions: so that you see, a commonwealth even of rogues cannot stand without law and policy. We hope some course will be taken with them.[129]

After royalist Jersey had fallen to Admiral Blake in 1651, a pair of parliamentary frigates stood guard against 'pirates and pickaroons that daily rove about the said island'.[130] In May 1654, the military governor of Jersey mobilized forces against a French pirate 'passing rashly in sight of the island'. An armed merchant ship joined the pursuit, but, 'instead of taking the pirate, had himself taken by the same'. English naval vessels opened fire and forced the pirate to wreck on the coast of Normandy.[131] Other naval forces exchanged fire with pirates off the Isle of Wight several times in 1656,[132] and campaigned in the Irish Sea that year to 'endeavour the restraining of one Bradshaw, an old papist Isle of Man pirate, from committing any more insolencies'.[133]

Pirates followed the money, and privateers of all nations pursued prizes and reprisals, in the increased maritime traffic following the Restoration. 'Algerine' or

'Turkish' corsairs continued to range the Channel, taking men and ships from the Scillies and the Isle of Wight.[134] The losses suffered by merchants and coastal communities were only partially offset by the flow of prize goods and booty that found its way into island and mainland markets.[135] Merchants of Jersey complained to their governor in December 1675 about the 'picaroons, Ostenders, or Biscayners, which are everywhere about us, so this it seems almost impossible to avoid them'.[136] One such offender, Jean Brooke, the notorious captain of an Ostend caper, was captured in 1676 and held prisoner in Jersey. But, to the embarrassment of the authorities, he escaped by a rope over the walls of Mont Orgeuil one night in December 1677, and was thought to be 'lurking in the country'.[137] Another Ostend privateer came boldly into the harbour at Guernsey in March 1683, and had to be restrained from taking prizes, though for prizes legitimately taken the governor would demand his share.[138] Obscure constitutional arrangements were as useful as obscured coastlines in giving the pirates cover.

Shipwrecks and the Bounty of the Sea

A little-remarked element in the economy of England's islands was the booty that accrued from shipwrecks. English merchant shipping expanded from 50,000 tons in 1572, to 115,000 tons in 1629, and 323,000 tons by 1702. The tonnage of foreign shipping grew even greater, led by the Dutch with approximately 175,000 tons of merchant shipping in 1567, and 500,000 tons by 1636.[139] A significant proportion of this traffic came through island waters, especially around the Isle of Wight, the Isles of Scilly, and the Channel Islands, and an unknown amount was cast away. Reliable statistics are wanting, but as many as one in thirty voyages may have gone amiss.[140]

In lay language, a wreck indicated the violent end of a maritime venture. The word conjures images of ships in distress, bulged on rocks, dashed against cliffs, or stranded on sands. In law, however, a 'wreck' designated a particular set of conditions, with regulated consequences for the owners, the cargo, and the people on board and on land. It was not just the foundering that designated 'wreck', but the circumstances of its casting-away. The foreshore became a zone of contention, where officials, claimants, and coastal inhabitants competed for goods that could be salvaged or retrieved.

In principle, under Norman and English law, the crown was entitled to shipwrecked goods within the king's domains. Procedures in the Channel Islands 'to the point of wreck' (*varech* in Norman French) were said to be 'altogether the same with those of England', though not subject to English Admiralty intervention or parliamentary legislation. Wrecked goods became crown property if nobody came forth to claim them, but island custom determined the shares of governors or captains, bailiffs and jurats, landowners, and local inhabitants.[141]

A statute of Edward I complicated the matter by declaring that 'where a man, a dog, or a cat escape quick out the ship', neither that ship, nor anything on it, should be judged wreck, but should be saved for restoration to its legal owners.[142] An equally potent statute of Edward III provided that those who 'saved and kept' shipwrecked goods should be paid 'convenient for their travail', while any who misappropriated them should be sanctioned.[143] Lawyers would have to determine whether material coming ashore was technically 'wreck', which claimant's rights should be respected, and whether unauthorized scavenging was punishable or permissible.[144]

Islands, being rich in coastlines, were especially rich in wrecks that introduced materials to the economy of makeshift and redistributed gear and commodities in unpredictable ways. Seigneurial lords argued with crown officials, and each other, about their rights or 'droits', while coastal residents sought benefit for themselves. Bolts of silk, pipes of wine, barrels of oranges, and pieces of eight found their way into island homes and economies, along with ships' furnishings and timbers.

Wreck harvest, by its nature, defied quantification. So much was hidden, under-reported, and undervalued, as claimants and salvors jostled for advantage. Flotsam and jetsam arrived unpredictably, at the mercy of waves and weather. Yet coastal inhabitants and the lords of coastal manors treated wreckage as wealth. In some seasons the sea might yield raisins and lemons, in another it cast up Spanish treasure. Successful retrieval might produce a temporary local glut of fruit or olive oil, and a useful supply of cables, clothing, furnishings, and anchors. Wreck salvage offered work and rewards, and piecemeal augmentation of the island economy. It made a change from farming, fishing, and knitting. Recipients could give thanks to a providential but capricious deity who cast godsends of 'droits' and booty on their shores.

Charges against the Elizabethan governor of Guernsey, Sir Thomas Leighton, included misuse of his authority over wrecks. Islanders complained that the governor had given them only £150 'for taking pains in saving of the said goods', when the recovered value exceeded £2,000, though Leighton claimed he was only following the Book of Extents. Their charge in 1580, that 'oftentimes ships and barks cast upon the coast of Guernsey by force of weather are taken for wrecks, notwithstanding that men escape out of them alive', testifies to knowledge of the law of wreck, and its violation.[145]

A court case in 1593 involved a tussle between island salvors and local sei-gneurs. When Barnaby Godfrey found a butt of wine in the sea off Jersey, he claimed it by law, 'que toutes chose trouvées au bal de la mer appartiennent a l'inventeur' (as everything found bobbing on the sea belonged to the discoverer). The Seigneur of Saumares, however, on whose land the wine came ashore, claimed by ancient records that half was due to him as wreck, and the island court upheld his claim. A similar case in 1620 allowed the seigneur 'half of goods so found and landed, and the finders the other', though disputants appealed to England's Privy

Council.[146] Island records reveal contest over wreck between rival seigneurial families, while also detailing the harvest of ships' ladings and fittings that came ashore.[147] When a Dutch vessel laden with 'pepper, logwood, and other rich commodities' foundered on Alderney in February 1654, the islanders 'pilfered and shared most of her lading', prompting inquiry into how much was 'embezzled, sold, or conveyed away'.[148] Later seventeenth-century cases involved cargoes of wine and brandy, fruits of the Mediterranean, spices, cloth, and 'merchandize, tackle and apparel' that went into local hands.[149] Opportunistic plunder was unstoppable, as one of Governor Hatton's correspondents remarked of wrecks as well as of piracy, 'all being fish that comes to the net'.[150]

On the Earl of Derby's domain of the Isle of Man, his lordship's water bailiff served as admiral, and took charge of all wrecks, 'that they might be disposed of for the lord's profit'. The earl's officials examined wreckage found afloat or ashore, so that all 'dues and forfeitures' accrued to the lord.[151] On the Welsh island of Anglesey, the sheriffs supervised searches of castaway goods, 'to cause all that may be found to be inventoried . . . to be disposed to such to whom that same shall be due and appertain'.[152] The island magistrate Robert Bulkeley made three trips to supervise recovery after a ship foundered on Anglesey in a 'most horrible storm of wind and rain' in September 1631 and enriched himself with four barrels from the cargo as his share of the spoils.[153]

So too on the Isle of Wight, magistrates and lord of manors worked alongside agents of the governor, who often had the additional office of vice admiral. The Earl of Portland under Charles I was especially insistent on his 'droits' from wrecks, noting that 'the Isle of Wight . . . is a place apt enough to be fruitful of such perquisites'.[154] When a Portuguese ship split in pieces on the Isle of Wight in August 1633, islanders made 'spoil upon those parcels of goods which the sea cast upon the shore'. 'A multitude of inhabitants' helped themselves to the wreckage until the captain of Cowes Castle ordered them 'to desist from such outrages, and withal to depart'.[155] Islanders and officials competed similarly for Spanish money that spilled into the surf after a Hamburg merchantman was cast away in October 1635. Determined digging and grappling recovered much of the treasure, but 'small parcels and driblets [were] taken up by the country people', and long remained 'in the hands of many people of the island'.[156] Shipwrecked wine and weapons disappeared into island farmsteads after more shipwrecks in 1636, when the people took 'what goods they could . . . notwithstanding they were commanded the contrary in the king's name'.[157] Similarly, when the *Thomas* of London, laden with Irish butter, beef, and pork, wrecked on the Isle of Wight in January 1655, the governor of Carisbrooke Castle supervised salvage in his capacity of deputy vice admiral, but most of the cargo went missing.[158] Incidents abounded in which pipes of wine and bars of silver were appropriated from wrecks by islanders engaged in 'robbing and spoiling'.[159]

The 'benefit of shipwreck' was one of the 'contingent profits accruing to the government of Scilly' and a valuable part of the proprietor's revenue.[160] Sir Francis Godolphin expressed disappointment with this income in 1578, because 'travellers are now more acquainted with the place, and better experienced in their navigation', though expanding traffic increased maritime casualties.[161] A century later another Godolphin complained 'of his losing the benefit of wrecks, which had its consideration in the rent he pays for the island', when the brethren of Trinity House proposed building a lighthouse on the outer island of St Agnes.[162] Wrecks continued in abundance, because the Scillies were dangerous and ill-charted, with the proprietors demanding 'a fifth part, over and above the king's part', of all wreck riches from their islands.[163] Islanders earned wages or reward for assisting in salvage, or helped themselves to whatever they could find.[164] Local dwellings in the Isles of Scilly were reinforced by recovered ships' timbers, and islanders were said to be 'clothed and supplied by wrecks sent in by the sea'.[165]

A Restoration-era observer remarked that the rocks of the Scillies caused 'more shipwrecks than happen perhaps in all the other seas of Europe together', which was bad news for mariners but potential profit for Scillonians.[166] Flotsam washing in the waves alerted residents to mishaps in their western approaches. A survivor of one wreck in December 1667 complained 'of the cruelty of the islanders, who left him upon a rock a day or two', because they were more interested in 'the saving of the goods and money than his life'.[167] Such remarks fuelled Daniel Defoe's overblown charge that the islanders of Scilly were 'so greedy, and eager for the prey, that they are charged with strange, bloody, and cruel dealings' and that seamen 'find the rocks themselves not more merciless than the people who range about them'.[168] Legend claimed that the shipwrecked admiral Sir Cloudesley Shovell was murdered for his clothing and jewels, but his body was dead long before beachcombers at Porth Hellick Cove gave it their attention. The disaster of October 1707, with the loss of four warships and as many as 1,600 lives, brought rich reward to Scilly scavengers, while the nation mourned and began serious investigation of the means of calculating longitude.[169] It was, as the proverb maintained, an ill wind that blew nobody any good.

No island was entirely self-sufficient. All were connected, in varying degrees, to the commerce and consumption of the mainland and the larger maritime world. Island economies were shaped by their insularity, but each was affected in different ways by local geology, geography, and social structure. Producing crops, conducting trade, and exploiting opportunities also depended upon political arrangements and constitutional constraints. The examples cited here show many of the ways in which the wealth and welfare of island communities were entwined with the pulses of politics and war.

PART TWO
ISLAND TROUBLES

PART TWO

ISLAND PROVERBS

6

God's Islands

The post-Reformation maxim of *cuis regio, eius religio*—that the religion of the people should match the religion of their ruler—applied as much in principle in Britain as in the Holy Roman Empire, and as much in the islands as the mainland. The English were Protestants because their rulers made them so, though the Scots were Presbyterian, and the Irish mostly Catholic. Under Tudor rule in the sixteenth century, the authority of the pope was extinguished, worship was in the vernacular, and the structures, discipline, and theology of the Church of England were supposed to prevail. English monarchs headed an episcopal church, which hewed to the beliefs of the Thirty-Nine Articles and the services of the Book of Common Prayer. Acts of Uniformity gave statutory muscle to these spiritual provisions, which the church did its best to enforce. The ecclesiastical canons of 1604, supported by episcopal visitation, regulated large swathes of devotional and parochial life.

Successive regimes sought religious conformity, with varying degrees of laxity and rigour. All pressed for uniformity and order, but were limited by counter-vailing factors. Elizabethan administrators prioritized the establishment of a national Protestant church, with power to discipline its members, but variations of inertia, intransigence, and custom sustained diversity at the local level. James I demanded conformity and obedience, but in practice was willing to wink at many things. His son Charles, in harness with hard-line bishops, promoted *jure divino* authority and the beauty of holiness, but faced, and may have aggravated, a growing puritan threat. Revolution fractured and temporarily extinguished the Church of England, and spawned a flourishing of spiritual experiments and sects. Restoration Anglicans imposed another Act of Uniformity, with a revised Book of Common Prayer, and sought to consolidate their success. But later Stuart church-men high and low disagreed on liturgical practice, religious dissenters gained degrees of toleration, and all were girded against the resurgence of popery. Historians may have exaggerated the degree to which religious contention less-ened and spiritual passions cooled in the later decades of the seventeenth century, but despite irritants the established church became comfortably complacent and secure.[1]

As subjects of the crown, denizens of their majesties' dominions, the inhabit-ants of England's islands were expected to conform to the official religion of the kingdom. English religious culture was supposed to be seamless, by land and by sea, though expectations of uniformity were never fully realized. Local historical

England's Islands in a Sea of Troubles. David Cressy, Oxford University Press (2020). © David Cressy 2020.
DOI: 10.1093/oso/9780198856603.001.0001

factors challenged this design, and the islands were especially at risk. Their religious life was shaped by insular traditions, the preferences of governors and garrisons, and even the presence of religious exiles and prisoners, as well as pressure from Lambeth and London. This chapter examines the organization and performance of religion in island communities, and their degree of conformity to the policies and aspirations of the mainland. It shows how anomalies and irregularities allowed some divergence, which lessened as the official religion of the centre achieved overall dominance.

Lundy, Wight, and Anglesey

Lundy, we have seen, was generally unchurched, with no resident minister to serve its people, and no episcopal administration offering oversight. The devout could emulate St Francis and preach to the birds. Bishops of Exeter ignored Lundy, and the island's proprietors made no religious provision. No parish claimed its people. The royalist Thomas Bushell built a chapel on Lundy in the 1640s, dedicated to St Anne in honour of his late wife, and his parliamentary successor Lord Saye and Sele lived there for a while in godly isolation. Otherwise, the island lay outside of ecclesiastical history. Catholic, Protestant, and Moorish raiders left little cultural trace.

The Isle of Wight, by contrast, was fully integrated into the Church of England. William Harrison's Elizabethan survey listed 'twenty-seven parish churches, of which fifteen or sixteen have parsons [rectors], the rest either poor vicars or curates, as the livings left are able to sustain...In spiritual cases it yieldeth obedience to the see of Winchester, of which it is a deanery.'[2] John Speed, a generation later, counted thirty-six churches on the island.[3] The market town of Newport had no parish church, only a chapel attached to Carisbrooke, though subscribers provided a new font and pulpit, and established a weekly lecture there in the 1630s. For several years the mayor and burgesses of Newport had been trying to have their chapel of St Thomas upgraded to a parish church, but without success.[4]

The clergy of the Isle of Wight were generally as well educated as their colleagues elsewhere in England, and shared their range of diligence and devotion. Among those serving Charles I were the royal chaplain and controversialist Alexander Ross, vicar of Carisbrooke; John Hooke, vicar of Freshwater, and father of the natural philosopher Robert Hooke; and Richard Fawkener, rector of Yarmouth since 1615, who was ejected in 1643 for senile debility and insufficiency, yet restored at the Restoration. The island was generally quiet and conformist, with neither puritans nor Arminians making much stir. Only in 1641 was there much reaction to reports of a Catholic cell at Carisbrooke Castle, during the governorship of the Earl of Portland (1633–42), 'whose wife and divers of his sisters and servants were papists'.[5]

The revolution, however, brought controversy and sequestrations. The expanded army garrison proved a breeding ground for religious radicalism, which made some way among parishioners. Godly islanders sought a more vigorous religious provision, and parliament gave 'countenance and encouragement' to the ministers it sent forth. In the purges of the 1640s, more than a quarter of the island's Church of England clergy were replaced by Presbyterians and Independents.[6]

Radical religion was impossible to quarantine, though island authorities had some ability to expel agitators and inhibit their landing, an exclusionary tactic less available on the mainland. The Anabaptist John Chandler of Chichester was quickly sent packing in 1646 after he began preaching at Newport, and was bound at the Winchester assizes not to return. Nine months later, however, Chandler and two disciples tried again to preach the holy spirit on the Isle of Wight, 'to persuade the people that the ministers of England are no true ministers of Christ but of Antichrist'. Chandler's companions were Bartholomew Bulkley, a mercer of Lymington, Hampshire, and Mark Dewy, a butcher of Wimborne, Dorset, who had come over privily by boat. They claimed to be empowered by God to 'endeavour reformation' and to baptize believers, and spent noisy evenings disturbing 'the peace of this island'. Chandler even preached at Carisbrooke, though in the house of a widow, not at the castle. Mayor John Clark of Newport had the troublemakers arrested in May 1647 and wrote to the island's governor, the Earl of Pembroke, to seek their expulsion.[7]

Within a month of the Anabaptist agitation Newport officials petitioned again to 'settle convenient means for the maintenance of a godly preaching minister in the town', reminding Westminster that they had '4,000 souls and no minister yet settled'. If necessary, with parliamentary permission, they would assess the inhabitants, to a maximum of £2, to provide for religious services and instruction.[8] Yet Newport remained a curacy within the ancient parish of Carisbrooke, from which the royalist Alexander Ross was ejected.

Carisbrooke Castle had no resident chaplain when King Charles arrived there in 1647, and for most of his period of imprisonment he had no access to the sacraments. The parliamentary garrison followed the Directory of Public Worship, which his majesty refused to countenance. Several clerics served the king during the Newport treaty negotiations in November 1648, though none with local roots. Prominent among island Presbyterians was Robert Dingley, newly installed rector of Brightstone, who urged the parliamentary governor in 1653 to counter 'atheism, profaneness, and heresy' and to promote the Lord's glory.[9]

Oliver Cromwell's regime in the 1650s punished leading Fifth Monarchists by imprisoning them on the Isle of Wight. Though confined, for the most part, to Carisbrooke Castle, they managed to make some converts among islanders and in the army. Christopher Feake and John Rogers, in particular, revelled in their godly suffering, and identified the Isle of Wight with Patmos, the Aegean island of St John's *Revelation* (see Chapter 13).

Quakers also made inroads on the Isle of Wight, as they did elsewhere in Interregnum England, declaiming against 'steeple houses', withholding tithes, and refusing to swear oaths. Island authorities responded by expelling Quaker agitators and trying to prevent them from coming ashore. Removed from the island and imprisoned at Winchester, the militant Quaker Daniel Baker campaigned in print against the 'hireling priests' of the Isle of Wight for their financial exactions and 'sinful' preaching.[10] If any of those priests preached in the church at Carisbrooke, they could have stood in the fine new pulpit, dated 1658.[11]

The Restoration restored the Church of England, and the Act of Uniformity of 1662 purged nonconformist ministers. When the new bishop of Winchester George Morley visited the Isle of Wight in August 1662, a thousand people, including most of the gentry, presented themselves for confirmation.[12] Pockets of dissent remained, but the veteran royalist Walter Slingsby, deputy governor under Lord Culpeper, devoted considerable energy to rooting out nonconformists, even on one occasion sending a Koran (in English) to imprisoned Quakers in the hope of discrediting them.[13] Baptist and Quaker conventicles were reported on the island in the 1660s, and a few Presbyterian ministers gained limited toleration in 1672. Thirty-three dissenters were cited at Newport in 1673 for absenting themselves from church, but they formed a very small minority in a broadly conformist population.[14] In general, the religious complexion of the later-Stuart Isle of Wight matched that of the rest of rural southern England, with an unreflective and dutiful Anglicanism.

The Isle of Anglesey, with its seventy-four parishes, formed an archdeaconry within the diocese of Bangor, in the archiepiscopal province of Canterbury. Though legally integrated with the Church of England, it was culturally separate, since most Anglesey parishioners spoke only Welsh. The pastoral mission of the largely bilingual clergy was assisted by the publication of the New Testament and Psalms in Welsh in 1567, a Welsh translation of the Bible in 1588, and a Welsh version of the Book of Common Prayer in 1599.[15] The anglicized gentry, who formed a protestant cultural elite, had generally conservative religious inclinations, and cleaved to 'the true protestant religion as by law established'. Few had truck with puritanism. Their clerical cousins were renowned only for their 'somnolent apathy' and 'relaxed morality'. Mid-Stuart Anglesey exhibited few signs of religious disturbance, though interregnum radicals considered it one of the 'dark corners of the land'. Religious radicalism accompanied the parliamentary army but put down shallow roots. The island gentry resisted 'godly' government in the 1650s and helped the Church of England to survive. The few ministers intruded by the Commissioners for the Propagation of the Gospel (1650–3) and the Commissioners for the Approbation of Public Preachers (1654–7) proved lacklustre and ineffective, and those who survived the Restoration proved pliable conformists. Later Stuart Anglesey became another bastion of Anglican complacency, not to be disturbed until the Methodist revival in the eighteenth century.[16]

The Isles of Scilly

The Isles of Scilly, remote and thinly populated, were further from God than parts of far west Cornwall. Though formally within the diocese of Exeter, they drew no episcopal attention and had no parochial structure. Islanders lived and prayed without religious discipline or regular resort to the sacraments. The inhabitants were not entirely unprovided, having a small old church on St Mary's, the remains of another on St Martin's, and storehouses serving as chapels on other islands. But there was no resident minister before the 1650s. As on ships and similar outposts, laymen could lead worship without performing other clerical functions. Garrison chaplains met some spiritual needs, though preachers were not always part of the military establishment.[17] Superstitions flourished, amid a casual folkloric Christianity, but the religious culture of pre-civil-war Scilly mostly remains a blank. The puritan John Bastwick, who spent three years there as a prisoner of Charles I, found the islands utterly benighted. The unitarian heretic John Biddle, who was imprisoned there under Oliver Cromwell, probably thought the same.

The revolution brought religious controversy to the Isles of Scilly. A few Church of England divines sheltered with other royalists in St Mary's Castle and several more arrived with Prince Charles's entourage in the spring of 1646. The Irish friar Hugh Bourke sensed opportunities in the Scillies to 'give a startling lesson to the English', in hopes of spreading Roman Catholicism.[18] Anglican clerics were among those promised safe passage later that year when the garrison surrendered to parliament. One or two returned to the Scillies when royalists regained control of the islands between 1648 and 1651.[19]

Godly army chaplains accompanied the parliamentary occupiers and provided services between the civil wars and under the Commonwealth. The religious proclivities of the soldiers are undocumented, but they may have included sectaries and radicals. When the parliamentary commander Colonel Anthony Buller was arrested at church in September 1648, the presiding minister most likely followed the Directory of Public Worship rather than the Book of Common Prayer.[20] The royalists who ousted Buller promised to reinstate 'the protestant religion according as it was professed and exercised in the times of its greatest purity, and uninfected with the common contagions and licentiousness of England'. There would be no 'Gangraena' in the Scillies, so far as orthodox churchmen were concerned.[21]

The first named clergyman associated with the Isles of Scilly was Edward Wolley, misnamed Wolby in the pamphlet that printed his intercepted letter.

Wolley had served as rector of Adderley, Shropshire, in the reign of Charles I, was deprived and sequestered at the beginning of the civil war, and accompanied retreating royalists into exile. By April 1649, he was in the Scillies, calling God's blessings on 'his majesty's service', and arranging for the import of supplies. Writing to Edward Ball, Prince Rupert's agent in Ireland, Wolley assured him

> that the Church of England is practised here according to the pattern at the king's chapel as near as possible, and as established by law; and that the governor is so careful of God's honour, that though papists or sectaries may land or trade, or live here, yet none shall dare defame or disturb the catholic service of God.[22]

Parliament's recovery of the Scillies in May 1651 brought this Anglican interlude to an end and put 'sectaries' in charge of God's worship. None of their names is known. The army surgeon Christopher Salter, who served the Scilly garrison, wrote in 1653 of his spiritual journey in this 'place far remote'. Having earlier been 'counted a puritan', he 'turned to the Presbyterian, after that to the Anabaptist, then to the Seeker', and finally, with the assistance of John Goodwin's *Redemption Redeemed* (1651), was 'led by the Spirit once more to the Scriptures'. Salter's case was not uncommon, in these turbulent times, but he found the Scillies a lonely place for a questing Christian, with 'but two or three in all these west parts likeminded in this point', the rest being 'bewitched with tradition'.[23] Once again, the garrison and the populace seem to have been worlds apart.

The Restoration brought Scilly closer to mainstream conformity. The Godolphin proprietors repaired and expanded the town church and brought in a series of resident chaplains, who even began to keep registers. Among the first was Edmund Hughes, who had been ordained at Exeter in 1639, served in Cornish parishes under Charles I, and was buried at St Mary's in 1669. Around this time, a visitor judged the islanders to be 'very zealous observers of the genuine Anglican religion, and the most loyal subjects which the king has in his kingdom', although this foreigner's comment may have applied more to the officers than to the population at large. A later cleric remarked that, though residents of Scilly were 'members of the established Church of England . . . some are addicted to superstitious notions'. They had no schoolmaster, and most of the islanders were illiterate.[24] By the 1670s, there were churchwardens at St Mary's, who gathered collections for the poor, though there was still no rector or vicar. Nicholas Phillips, the garrison chaplain in 1677, published one of his sermons on 'faith's triumph over all worldly pomp and glory'—godly cheer in a grim environment—but it seems not to have earned him preferment.[25]

Bishops of Exeter continued to ignore their most distant charges on Scilly, conducting neither institutions nor visitations. John Troutbeck, who served as chaplain to an eighteenth-century proprietor, lamented that diocesan jurisdiction in Scilly was 'quite laid aside' and attributed 'the causes of the entire neglect of the spiritual authority there' to 'the separation of these islands from their neighbour-ing country by a very rough sea'.[26] When the Society for Promoting Christian Knowledge reorganized their mission to the islands in 1796, they treated the Scillies as 'overseas', in the same category as Canada or Pitcairn Island in Polynesia.[27] The islands were renowned for their spiritual darkness, which few on the mainland cared to rectify.

The Isle of Man

Just as much separated by sea, but with greater cultural depth and self-sufficiency, the Isle of Man was formally part of the English episcopal establishment. Its seventeen parishes broadly followed the principles of English Protestantism and paid tithes to the Earl of Derby's Receiver-General.[28] The episcopal see of Sodor and Man had ancient origins and belonged to the province of York. The arch-bishop, however, had very little to do with it. The diocese was poorly resourced and was dominated by the secular Lords of Man. The bishopric was valued at a mere £140 a year (almost poverty by English episcopal standards), and there was no cathedral dean and chapter.[29] According to William Harrison, writing in the 1580s, the incumbent was 'but a bishop's shadow, for albeit he bears the name of bishop of Man, yet have the Earls of Derby, as it is supposed, the chief profit of his see'. The appointment was in the gift of the Stanley earls, who firmly controlled its income.[30] Being 'no lord of parliament', as one seventeenth-century survey explained, the island's bishop did not sit in the House of Lords, 'none being admitted to that honour, but such as hold immediately of the king himself'.[31] Successive bishops of Sodor and Man were men of mean distinction, thwarted of greater preferment, who often held other livings in Lancashire, Cheshire, or North Wales.

The reformer John Phillips, appointed to Sodor and Man in 1604, wrote plaintively in June 1610 that he had spent 100 marks on his 'ruinous bishopric', and yet the Earl of Derby's lieutenant denied him a pass to come over to England. Philips spent decades translating the Book of Common Prayer and the Bible into Manx, the language of common parlance, and died on the island in 1633. William Sacheverell, writing late in the Stuart era, credited Phillips for his work on the prayer book, but noted that his Bible translation was 'now not extant'.[32] Renewed efforts led to the appearance of the New Testament in Manx in 1767 and an Old Testament translation in 1772, a century later than similar productions in Wales.

Isle of Man church services followed the Book of Common Prayer, in some places in English, but elsewhere in 'the tongue of the natives they call Manx'. The clergy were poorly prepared, mostly of local provenance, and included 'two or three illiterate men brought up in the island in secular professions'. ('Illiterate' here means lacking Latin, rather than unable to read and write.) The archdeacon, who held court alongside the bishop and his two vicars-general, was described in 1634 as 'a man altogether illiterate, brought up in the island except in the English tongue'. In answer to enquiries that year by the newly appointed bishop William Forster, 'whether the minister read publicly in the church the Constitutions and Canons Ecclesiastical', he learned from most parishes 'that we have no such books, that the minister may read them'.[33]

The shallow reach of orthodox religion is suggested by reports of Manx superstition. William Harrison reported that the islanders

> were much given to witchcraft and sorcery (which they learned of the Scots, a nation greatly bent to that horrible practice) insomuch that their women would oftentimes sell wind to the mariners, enclosed under certain knots of thread, with this injunction, that they which bought the same should for a great gale undo many, and for the less a fewer or smaller number.[34]

Recent scholarship has documented early modern Manx beliefs in charms, witchcraft, malignant fairies, and the efficacy of cursing, which were elements of a widespread folk religion.[35]

The leaders of the English commonwealth, who gained control of the Isle of Man in the 1650s, considered it one of the dark corners of the land. English administrators would be needed to bring about 'the reformation of the manners of that people' and to instruct them in 'the knowledge of God'. The laws against drunkenness, swearing, profanation of the Lord's Day, adultery, and fornication needed enforcement and a programme set up to bring the islanders 'to as near a conformity to the English as may be', in laws, language, habits, and 'all laudable customs'.[36] Reformed religion would be a tool for national integration. Though episcopacy was now abolished, church tithes were still collected, 'for the better encouragement and support of ministers of the gospel, and for the promoting of learning'. Presbyterians, Independents, Baptists, and other Protestant sectaries gained footing on the island in this period of English military rule. Quakers also appeared on the Isle of Man, as elsewhere, and the authorities did their best to have them summarily ejected.[37]

When the eighth Earl of Derby regained control of his island in 1660, he sought 'the settling of religion and all ecclesiastical affairs as they were in my late father's time'.[38] Stanley's Anglican chaplain Samuel Rutter became bishop of Sodor and Man, and undertook the task of restoring the Church of England. His successors Isaac Barrow (1663–71) and Henry Bridgeman (1671–82) consolidated the work. Efforts to improve the quality of the Isle of Man clergy continued, with the crown establishing a fund of £100 a year towards the maintenance of orthodox and disciplined ministers. There were, however, differences between the Earl of Derby and the Treasury in London about how that money should be raised and applied.[39]

Religious authorities on the Isle of Man had one weapon that was not available on the mainland: they could banish offenders, as well as imprison them. This was the fate of several families of Quakers who troubled the island in the 1660s, precipitating yet another constitutional conflict. At the instigation of the ministers Robert Parr and John Harrison, Isle of Man officials imprisoned and then banished the Quakers William Callow and Evan Christian, and their wives and children. Uniformity would be maintained by shipping dissenters overseas, though this involved yet another jurisdictional contest between the Stanleys and Charles II. Callow said that he and fellow Quakers had 'often laid our sufferings before the Earl of Derby, but could have no relief of him', which is why they petitioned the king and Council. Jane Christian was one of the Quakers banished into Ireland, but the Dublin authorities immediately 'caused the shipmaster to take her and the rest of her friends back again into the island ... because they had been banished out of the king's territory, into the king's dominion'. Ridding the Isle of Man of troublemakers who served God 'according to their consciences' would require pastoral, legal, administrative, and logistical efforts, which were not always successful.[40]

Dissent never disappeared, but later-seventeenth-century observers found the islanders 'ready to entertain the form of the English church, there being no room for any persons popishly affected, Quakers, or other sectaries'.[41] William Sacheverell, publishing in 1702, praised the Isle of Man for its 'perfect unanimity in matters of religion, strictly conformable to the doctrine and discipline of the Church of England'. 'Without vanity', he boasted, 'in its uniformity it outdoes any branch of the reformed churches'.[42] It was a uniformity obtained by not pressing too hard for true understanding of the faith.

God's Channel Islands

If God brought the Channel Islands timely rain, fair harvests, prosperous voyages, and good returns, the devotion of most islanders was untroubled. They weathered the transition from Roman Catholicism to Genevan Presbyterianism, and thence to Anglican conformity, with little drama and no great haste. The clergy performed their duty, and the laity behaved as expected.

The relative isolation of the Channel Islands hindered attempts to regulate them from the English mainland. Their proximity to France exposed them as much to continental religious currents as to those emanating from Lambeth, Whitehall, or Westminster. By orders dating back to the reign of Henry VII, renewed by successive monarchs, foreigners, including Normans and Frenchmen, were forbidden to reside on Jersey, except to engage in licensed trade. But these rules were rarely observed. Huguenots and Catholics came at will. According to Sir Philip Carteret, writing in 1642, many inhabitants took Norman maids and menservants, and harboured papists and strangers, without the governor's knowledge.[43]

The general population of the islands was Francophone—by one estimate not one in forty knew English—so vernacular services and sermons were in French. Many of their ministers had trained in continental Huguenot seminaries. A French version of the Book of Common Prayer was published 'pour les Isles de sa magesté' at the end of Edward VI's reign and was printed again with the queen's Injunctions after the accession of Elizabeth.[44] Sir Francis Walsingham asked his agents to obtain a copy in Guernsey in the 1570s, to give to 'Monsieur', the Duke of Alençon, a possible husband to Queen Elizabeth, to instruct him in English Protestantism.[45] Later, when Jersey became a royalist stronghold after the English civil war, islanders used a French version of the catechism, services, and litany 'pour l'usage de cette partie de l'eglise Anglicane', with prayers for the royal family. After the Restoration, another French translation of the Book of Common Prayer was ordered for the parish churches of the Channel Islands, as soon as it could be printed.[46]

While most of the inhabitants spoke French, the island's governor and garrison were English, and used English prayers, though they did not always have a chaplain or resident clergyman. Linguistic difference heightened a cultural estrangement between the islanders and the military establishment, which also appeared in clashes over jurisdiction.

The Channels Islands had no bishops of their own but fell under the authority of the diocese of Winchester. Until early Tudor times, they were subject to the Norman bishop of Coutances, within his archdeaconry of Bauptois. A papal bull in 1496 transferred authority to the diocese of Salisbury, and another in 1500 purportedly gave jurisdiction to Winchester, but these high-level rearrangements had little immediate consequence. Island churches continued to look to France for clergy and direction beyond the reign of Henry VIII, and the bishop of Coutances asserted his authority for as long as possible. An Elizabethan order of 1568, confirmed in 1569, brought the islands more firmly under English ecclesiastical authority, making them 'perpetually united' to Winchester, though not strictly incorporated within the diocese.[47]

Not all clerics on the islands recognized this distant English authority. Nor were episcopal officials at Lambeth or Winchester particularly interested in their charges across the Channel. The bishop of Winchester from 1560 to 1580 was the Protestant reformer Robert Horne, a former Marian exile, who treated the islands with benign indifference. Horne attempted to exert his authority in 1569 by commissioning the dean of Guernsey John After to undertake a visitation of the Channel Islands. The intention was to ensure their compliance with the Book of Common Prayer, even if necessarily in French.[48] But it was already too late, since Presbyterianism was firmly entrenched, and episcopal injunctions were ignored. Traditionalists claimed that the actions of island leaders tended 'rather to maintain factious tumults than any reformation of their wonted evils', but by 1571 the position of dean was effectively abolished.[49] In 1575, the churches of Guernsey reminded the bishop of their 'respectful attachment', as well as their system of synods, when they sought his 'helping hand' against the troublemaker Elias Bonamy. Horne, in reply, made pious noises and referred the matter to the governor Sir Thomas Leighton.[50]

Protestantism spread to the Channels Islands not from England but from France. Lutheran influences had reached Jersey and Guernsey in the 1530s and 1540s, followed by Calvinist Huguenot émigrés in the reign of Edward VI. Furthering reform, the Royal Court of Jersey moved in 1549 against 'maintainers of the superstitions of the Bishop of Rome'. But many of those 'superstitions' remained strong and were reinforced by the Marian counter-reformation. The grotesque public burning of the 'heretics' Catherine Cauchés, Guillemine Gilbert, and Perotine Massey and her baby at St Peter Port in July 1556 was imprinted in local memory, as well as in the pages of John Foxe's *Actes and Monuments*.[51] Several islanders, including William de Beauvoir of Guernsey, sought refuge in Geneva during Mary's reign, and brought back Calvinist ideas and contacts when it was safe to return.[52]

Huguenots from France guided the establishment of Presbyterian ecclesiastical arrangements in the Elizabethan Channel Islands. Jersey's governor Sir Hugh Paulet asserted in 1560 that 'most of the inhabitants much misliked these devices in matters of religion set forth under the private fantasies or a few, chiefly Frenchmen'. But the islands proved hospitable to travelling Calvinists, whose teachings gained popular and official acceptance. An inter-island synod in 1564, the first of its kind, laid foundations for the development of Presbyterian discipline. But traditionalists claimed that the actions of island leaders tended 'rather to maintain factious tumults than any reformation of their wonted evils'.[53] The suggestion in 1567 that most of the bells in Guernsey's parish churches should be sold, and the money applied to fortifications, was not considered outrageous in a Calvinist religious culture averse to excessive bell-ringing.[54] Godly magistrates passed ordinances against dissolute singing and dancing, though the need to repeat those orders casts doubt on their effectiveness.[55]

More Huguenot refugees settled in the English islands after the St Bartholomew's Day massacre in France in 1572 and the resurgence of the Catholic League in 1585.[56] English religious radicals were also drawn to the Channel Islands as places of refuge and preferment. The Presbyterian Arthur Wake, deprived of his rectory in Northamptonshire, found safety as chaplain to the governor of Jersey in 1573. He was joined in 1575 by Percival Wiburn, another prominent Presbyterian, who assisted in the codification of 'classical' or Genevan discipline.[57]

The warrior Sir Thomas Leighton, Queen Elizabeth's governor of Guernsey, was sympathetic to Protestant reform. He and his counterparts at Jersey (Sir Amias Paulet, followed by Anthony Paulet) gave approval, if not support, to the developing Presbyterian programme. An inter-island synod in June 1576, attended by both governors, formally adopted the Calvinist *Police et Discipline Ecclésiastique*, which set forth the rules of church government. United hand in hand, island magistrates had 'charge and direction of the bodies and goods' of parishioners, while ministers took charge of their consciences and souls. Blasphemy, idolatry, and superstition were to be avoided or punished.[58] Adherence to these rules was made apparent on Guernsey in 1594 when governor Leighton appointed a day for the 'consecration' of new fortifications at Castle Cornet, and the presiding Presbyterian M. Milhommau would only offer prayers for God's protection.[59]

Presbyterian discipline was further consolidated by the arrival of the puritan leaders Edmund Snape and Thomas Cartwright, who came to the islands in 1595 after suffering deprivation, degradation, and imprisonment in England. Snape became chaplain at Mont Orgeuil, Jersey, and Cartwright took a similar post at Castle Cornet, Guernsey. They helped to reconcile the divided churches in the islands, and gave guidance to the synod on Guernsey in October 1597 that confirmed their 'consistorian practices'.[60] Jacobean critics of 'the affairs ecclesiastical in the Isles of Guernsey and Jersey' described this Book of Discipline as a 'usurpation', containing 'many strange and dangerous things', but it established the framework for several generations of island religious culture.[61] English gentlewomen who came to Guernsey to learn French also acquired instruction in 'their Geneva discipline', according to the godly Lucy Hutchinson, the daughter of one such island visitor.[62]

Protestantism may have triumphed, but unofficial folk beliefs and remnants of traditional Roman Catholicism coexisted with the reformed religion, as they did in parts of England, with varying degrees of acceptance and toleration. On Guernsey, for example, calendar customs and night-time revels with gadding and disguising continued well into the seventeenth century.[63] The Presbyterian pastor of Sark, Elie Brevint, noted the observance of Christmas, Lent, the midsummer feast of St John, and the autumn feast of St Michael. Expectant mothers prayed for the help of St Margaret. Superstitious mariners feared the May-tide season of Sts Simon and Jude, and appealed to the holy maid of Walsingham when in danger of shipwreck. Islanders believed that devils among them were made manifest through witchcraft and sorcery.[64]

Comfortable in his Presbyterian certainty, Brevint seemed to marvel at religious practices elsewhere. He had heard that at Padua, in Italy, if caught in the street at the time of the curfew bell, you were supposed to doff your hat and say an *Ave Maria*, or else you would be hauled before the Inquisition; and that on feast days, unless you could attest to having gone to mass, you would be denied lodging and dinner. On entering Rome, he noted, you were asked your religion, and, if you were Huguenot, your stay was limited to three days; and entering Roman churches, you had to uncover your head and sprinkle yourself with holy water.

He noted the English saying, popularized under James I: 'No ceremonies, no bishop; no bishop, no king.' The sectarian Brownists, he had heard, held both women and goods in common. His own views were guided by confidence in the goodness of God and the surety of heaven. He believed, with fellow Presbyterians, that their government of the church was by divine right and was disturbed to hear of English secularists *de droict humain*. Observations of this sort appear in Brevint's notebooks, and may have featured in his conversation and sermons.[65]

The Laudian conformist Peter Heylyn, who visited Guernsey and Jersey in 1629, summarized the history of the 'bringing in and working out of the Genevan discipline' in England's 'adjoining islands...the better to lay open the novelty, absurdity, and ill consequents of it'.[66] It galled him that during Queen Elizabeth's reign the authorities in the Channel Islands, and the queen's advisers in London, had acceded to these distortions. Heylyn judged toleration of Presbyterianism to be 'improvident', because it 'opened that gap unto the brethren [puritans], by which they had almost made entrance unto mere confusion in this state and kingdom'. Although he knew of the early Huguenot influence, Heylyn opposed 'the whole body of the Genevian discipline obtruded on both islands by Snape and Cartwright', perhaps giving too much credit to those Elizabethan nonconformists. His report to Archbishop Laud, and his subsequent publication, disparaged Channel Island irregularities that detracted from 'the honour due to God and his church'.[67]

Congruent with the practice of other Calvinist confessions, ministers and elders of the island consistories met in *Colloques* quarterly, and sometimes monthly, to regulate both the spiritual status and the social discipline of the inhabitants. Attended sometimes by governors, deputy-governors, and bailiffs, these church assemblies were akin to Scottish Kirk Sessions.[68] The secular authorities provided muscle for enforcing sabbath duties and church attendance, with constables to sanction neighbours caught gossiping in churchyards or drinking in taverns. Ministers and civil magistrates were supposed to 'sustain and defend each other', as one put it, 'subject to the sceptre of Christ'.[69]

Surviving registers of *Colloques* on the island of Jersey from 1577 to 1614, and Guernsey from 1585 to 1619, reveal their involvement in a wide range of matters, from payments and appointments to domestic scandals and blasphemy. With support from the bailiff, and toleration by the governor, the Presbyterian parishes governed themselves, and counselled each other, without the need for a dean or bishop. They also corresponded with their 'brothers' on neighbouring islands on matters of doctrine and discipline, connected to international Calvinism. An inter-island synod in 1597, advised by Snape and Cartwright, expanded the role of the *Colloque* in nominating and appointing ministers.[70] The result was a reformed church more radical, more Calvinist, in complexion than anything elsewhere in the queen's dominions. English authorities accorded these arrangements begrudging toleration, and the bishop of Winchester kept his distance.

Pressure to Conform

In England, the Elizabethan regime cracked down on the Presbyterian movement and imprisoned some of its proponents; but it allowed this deviation to flourish in the Channel Islands. The government did this because it feared a worse alternative: it was better that the islands should fall into Protestant error than that England's Catholic enemies should gain a foothold in such important strategic outposts; religion was vital for good order, and Genevan discipline was preferable to popish confusion; and, so long as Presbyterianism was contained on the islands, it had little chance of infecting mainland England. Insularity limited orthodoxy, but kept heterodoxy at bay.[71]

This logic still applied in the seventeenth century, but was not unchallenged. When James Stuart became king in 1603, the Channel Islands were the only parts of his English dominions where Presbyterians held sway. King James, who had grown up in Presbyterian Scotland, confirmed, or at least acknowledged, these arrangements in August 1603, but his government later sought to roll back Presbyterian autonomy and to reclaim the island churches for the Church of England. It was always his policy, his advisers believed, 'to order some course for the redress of those things which are loose and unsettled there, and to reduce them to some such conformity as might answer the uniformity of government in other parts of his dominions'.[72]

Conformists had more success on Jersey than on Guernsey, especially after the appointment of the anti-puritan Sir John Peyton as governor later in 1603. Facing a ministry that he saw as over-mighty as well as distasteful, on an island that he poorly understood, Peyton sought to reduce clerical power by advancing the claims of civil magistracy. He used his understanding of Jersey's constitution to refer ecclesiastical as well as civil jurisdiction to the bailiff and jurats, and asserted his own right to nominate to vacant benefices. Eroding the ascendancy of the *Colloque,* Peyton advised island ministers in 1609 to 'walk humble before your lay brethren, and bestow two parts of your time in study of divine things, and them to preach and write so as you may be reverenced in the present and memorable in the future times'.[73] He encouraged his allies to petition for the restoration of a dean and a book of common prayer. Peyton furthered his campaign by appointing an English-ordained cleric as chaplain at Mont Orgueil Castle, in defiance of the presbyteries, and in 1613 he precipitated a crisis by appointing another Church of England minister, the Oxford-trained islander Elias Messervy, to a vacant Jersey living. Despite Presbyterian objections, Messervy was admitted to his Jersey benefice, 'quietly to exercise the form used in the Church of England', and served as rector of St Peter's until his death in 1627.[74]

The Calvinist ascendancy on Jersey was crumbling under anti-Presbyterian pressure from Mont Orgueil, and it was further reduced by directives from

London. In November 1613, the Privy Council informed the governors of the Channel Islands that their nonconformity should cease. Details would be negotiable, and progress would be slow, as centralizing forces clashed with Presbyterian self-confidence and with the islanders' many claims to privilege and exemption. Remarkably, though wanting 'conformity according to the government of the Church of England', the government intimated that it might be willing 'otherwise to dispense there withal, and to tolerate another form', if a broad consensus could be agreed. King James desired 'the quiet and peaceable government' of all his dominions, and aimed for 'the establishment of true religion and ecclesiastical discipline, in one uniform order and course throughout all [his] realms', but recognized that peace and uniformity might not always be compatible.[75] It would take the best part of two decades to make Jersey conformable to the Church of England, while the religious submission of Guernsey would have to wait until the Restoration.

The design to bring Jersey closer to English religious arrangements progressed in May 1617 when Sir Edward Conway and Sir William Bird arrived to investigate the island's governance, after Governor Peyton's bruising contest with the bailiff Jean Herault. Though primarily concerned with military and civil matters, the commissioners also commented on irregularities in religious administration, noting that, 'since there hath ceased to be a dean, the most of causes have been ordered by the bailiff and justices, and the presentations by the governor'. Further to their thankless task of reconciling the island's constitutional complexities, the commissioners proposed undoing 'the last forty years of novelty in the ecclesiastical jurisdiction' by ending Presbyterianism. This would be accomplished by restoring the office of the dean, who would have power to 'censure all spiritual and scandalous offence committed against the honour of God and church discipline', comparable to the authority of English bishops and archdeacons. 'Nominated only by the king's majesty,' the new dean would deal with cases of 'blasphemy, apostacy, heresy, schism, incest, adultery, fornication, drunkenness, profanation of the sabbath, [and] abuse or profanation of the church and churchyards', which were currently handled by the Presbyterian 'Consistory and Colloquies', or by the secular authorities. He would also regulate testamentary and matrimonial matters deemed to be of ecclesiastical cognizance, which were currently 'administered if not with partiality, with ignorance'.[76]

Conway and Bird claimed that the re-establishment of a dean 'will stand with the desires of the ministers, the liking of the people, [and] the honour and use of the church discipline'. But many island interests resisted the plan, and even the bishop of Winchester was jealous lest his rights be infringed. The bailiff, jurats, and ministers of Jersey all raised objections and sought to limit the power of the dean, 'that the authority heretofore possessed by the Court be not diminished'. In March 1619, however, the States agreed that a dean should be appointed, without specifying the extent of his powers.[77]

The first incumbent, the Swiss-born island minister David Bandinell, was not able to take up his appointment as dean until April 1620. While trying to impose 'Anglican' worship and discipline, he faced obstacles and frustrations over such matters as the appointment of churchwardens and the allocation of tithes. His enemies accused him of favouring witchcraft and sorcery, and of reintroducing the mass, which was patently untrue. Sir Philip Carteret, returning to Jersey in June 1620, found 'great discontent in many of the people, and much dissension' between the dean and bailiff, a tension that long continued.[78]

The revival of the office of the dean only added to Jersey's jurisdictional tangle and created new opportunities for infighting. The introduction of a new official with powers like those of an English suffragan bishop added complexity to an already contested insular political environment. The authority of the dean extended to

> all matters which concern the service of God, the preaching of the word, administration of the sacraments, matrimonial causes, the examination and censure of all papists, recusants, heretics, idolaters and schismatics, persons perjured in causes ecclesiastical, blasphemers such as have recourse to wizards, incestuous persons, adulterers, fornicators, common drunkards, and public profaners of the Lord's Day.

He also had authority over the entry and probate of wills, and the registration of inventories, as well as the subtraction of tithes—all areas of potential friction with the jurats as well as ordinary parishioners.[79]

Backed by the crown, and with initial support from the governor, Dean Bandinell devised disciplinary canons for the island to operate 'as near as conveniently might be' to the practices of the Church of England. No minister was to be admitted without episcopal ordination. All services had to follow the approved form of prayer. The dean's court replaced Consistories and *Colloques*, and churchwardens replaced elders and deacons.[80] Predictably, there were objections from the bailiff, the jurats, and many ministers, but a committee of English bishops reviewed Jersey's canons, and King James ratified them in June 1623.[81] The last recorded *Colloque* in Jersey's surviving register was in November 1614, though informal gatherings may have continued. Any such Presbyterian assembly would henceforth be condemned as an unauthorized and disorderly conventicle.[82] The continuing *Colloques* on Guernsey periodically sent out feelers in the hope of returning their sister island to fraternal Calvinist discipline, a prospect that seemed possible in the fractious circumstances of the 1640s.[83]

On Jersey, the dean's task was to make anglicized arrangements work, in an island accustomed to Presbyterian worship, where Huguenot refugees continued to receive hospitality, and where the Carteret family was used to the exercise of power.[84] Friction grew between secular and ecclesiastical authorities, especially over the dean's suspension of Calvinist ministers and his excommunication of troublesome parishioners. Sir Philip Carteret protested against Bandinell's lust for tithes and fees, 'whereby the garrison and the king's revenue are diminished', and asked for another commission under the king's Great Seal to examine the dean's 'oppressions'. These struggles were mostly about money and authority, though simmering beneath them were strains in religious culture. Disputes about glebe land and tithes further exacerbated tension between the dean and the island gentry.[85] The accusation in October 1626 that the dean's son James (or Jacques), himself an island minister, scandalously described England's present government as worse than that of Queen Mary may have been designed to smear him.[86] The establishment of three fellowships at Oxford for clerical candidates from the Channel Islands was designed to wean the rising generation from Presbyterianism and to institute an English-leaning learned ministry.[87]

Bandinell's efforts persuaded English episcopal authorities that Jersey was 'settled for church business in some reasonable conformity with the Church of England',[88] but the absence of harmony was revealed by the open hostility between the dean's faction and the Carterets. When Sir Philip Carteret declared for King Charles in the second year of civil war, the dean took the opposite course, more out of spite than conviction, and he and his son were accused of raising and fomenting rebellion. They spent a year imprisoned in Mont Orgueil Castle until February 1645, when Dean Bandinell fell while attempting to escape and died of his injuries. Nobody filled his place until the Restoration.[89] Sir George Carteret supported liturgical conformity, which was reinforced by the arrival of clergy accompanying exiled cavaliers. The presence in Jersey of Prince Charles Stuart from April to June 1646, and again as 'king' from September 1649 to February 1650, made the island the de facto centre of the Church of England. An account of the royal party at communion in the parish church of St Helier in May 1646 records them receiving the bread and the wine devoutly on their knees at their places at the table, rather than at altar rails, as in Laudian England.[90]

*

The conformist success in Jersey could not be matched in Guernsey, where the Presbyterian system was strongly established, with both political and popular support. Governor Lord George Carew, who spent little time on the island and was indifferent to matters of ecclesiology, observed in 1610 that 'the people are proud, and the ministry full of heat. I do not think I shall find any of either quality inclinable to the Church of England, so far is the reformed discipline rooted in their hearts.' Carew believed that 'the church discipline aims at superlative power' over both the governor and the bailiff, but he had no desire to stand in its way.[91]

Reinforcing their partnership with the Calvinist island ministry, the bailiff and jurats of Guernsey published articles in April 1611 elaborating Christian duties. The secular courts would punish swearers, blasphemers, and drunkards, and anyone persistent in idolatry and superstition who clung to the pope and the mass. The Sunday sabbath would be reserved for exercises of piety, with strict prohibition on labour or trade. Dancing was strictly forbidden, along with the singing of impudent or dissolute songs. These were strictures in accord with the programme for the reformation of manners, which was especially favoured by Jacobean puritans. They were not uniquely Presbyterian, nor fully enforceable, but they signalled the interlock of morality, church, and state.[92]

When London applied pressure to make Guernsey conform, islanders sent their talented minister Jean de la Marche to England to plead for 'the continuation of our ecclesiastical government'. De la Marche proved effective in face-to-face interviews with King James, and won his majesty's personal assurance in November 1616 that Guernsey's unique status could continue. Not for the last time, James proved willing to wink at practices that his church officially disapproved, so long as essentials were maintained.[93] The Estates of Guernsey skilfully deflected attentions from Lambeth and 'l'eveque de Winchester', and endorsed proceedings according to the island's 'discipline ecclesiastique'.[94]

Charles I's government was much more demanding of conformity for its own sake, though distant insular irregularities were not high on the Laudian agenda. Caroline Privy Councillors wanted Guernsey restored to its 'ancient ecclesiastical jurisdiction', under episcopacy, but had no immediate capacity to make that happen. The clerical author Peter Heylyn reminded his masters how recently 'Jersey was made conformable in point of discipline and doctrine to the Church of England' and urged similar reformation for the neighbouring island. When Heylyn visited Guernsey in 1629 as Lord Danby's chaplain, he was denied permission to read the liturgy or administer the sacrament in Samuel de la Place's parish church and had to use the great hall in the castle instead. Heylyn's account of his visit was not published until 1656, but it circulated in manuscript in the 1630s. In his opinion, the continuing irregularity of Guernsey disgraced the honour of the king and the integrity of the Church of England. As a first step, he recommended 'the restitution of the dean', with powers similar to those of the dean in Jersey. The Guernsey ministers to whom Heylyn broached this suggestion responded that it was 'physic worse than the disease'.[95] One of them, the firebrand Jean de la Marche, was removed from his benefice and imprisoned in the castle in 1633 after preaching against hierarchy and episcopacy.[96]

Noting the apparent achievement of conformity in Jersey, King Charles asked in 1636 why 'the like [was] not done for the island of Guernsey...either at that time or since', especially in light of the island's 'greater consequence to this kingdom'. He instructed governor Henry Danvers, the Earl of Danby, to 'take this business into your present consideration, that both islands may go alike'.[97] Danby, a Jacobean pragmatist, set forth reasons in writing 'why the discipline ecclesiastical in the Isle of Guernsey should not be made conformable to the Church of England'. This was a reasoned rejoinder to Caroline policy, invoking neither the claims of honour nor the name of God. Reporting in April 1637, Danby argued that strategic and intelligence considerations outweighed the desire for religious uniformity. Guernsey's close 'correspondence and association' with Calvinists in France served English interests, because 'those of the French church' gave the islanders 'notice of all practices and designs against them'. Huguenot refugees, including 'persons of great quality', naturally gravitated to places where 'the discipline agreed with their practice', and it was surely better for such people to be entertained in Guernsey 'than admit them hither' into England. Though distasteful to Laudian conformists, the strictness of the island's reformed Protestants served to keep papists at bay. Most powerful of all was the argument that 'it may well be thought dangerous to give a general discontent unto the inhabitants . . . by altering the form of their discipline so affected by them and long enjoyed'. King Charles's predecessors, Elizabeth and James, had tolerated the quirk of Guernsey Presbyterianism because the goodwill of 'the natives' was vital for the island's defence. In any case, Danby concluded, 'there can no prejudice come to the present government of our church, as no man is suffered to speak against it, and the English come to the castle where service and sacraments are celebrated after the English manner'.[98]

King Charles and Archbishop Laud were not used to hearing such practical wisdom, which grated against their proclivities, but had little choice but to follow it. One wonders whether their regime would have ended so catastrophically had they taken similar counsel with regard to Presbyterian Scotland, which erupted in revolt later in 1637, when London tried to impose its ceremonial form of worship.

Presbyterian 'prophesyings' or study sessions continued to flourish on Guernsey in the late 1630s, along with consistories and *Colloques*, at the time when the English puritan Henry Burton was a prisoner in Castle Cornet (see Chapter 11). Among local activists was Burton's friend and admirer the minister Jean de la Marche, who followed him to England and was later appointed to the Westminster Assembly of Divines. Also sympathetic to Burton was the Presbyterian pastor of Sark, Elie Brevint, who expressed disquiet when Burton later sided with the Independents, 'the Jesuits of our religion'. News of religious affairs in England and Scotland reached Guernsey in the years of the 'bishops' wars', to be interpreted in terms of prophetic scripture.[99]

Religion in Troubled Times

Religious controversy gripped the Channel Islands in the decades of civil war and revolution. The House of Commons committee on scandalous ministers discussed the religious discipline of the Channel Islands in May 1641 and asked for a report on 'the matter of Guernsey'. Later that summer they read a petition from de la Marche relating 'the great disturbance' caused by recent attempts to promote episcopacy in the islands and asking 'that they might be restored to the practice of their ancient church discipline again', meaning Presbyterianism. Far from being suppressed, the Calvinist discipline of Guernsey seemed in the 1640s to offer a model for the rest of England. As far as de la Marche was concerned, they shared a common struggle against 'the Harlot' and 'the Beast' of Rome. The translation and publication in London in 1642 of *The Orders for Ecclesiasticall Discipline... of the Iles of Garnsey, Gersey, Spark, and Alderny* (the articles of 1597) were explicit encouragement to English reformers.[100] Activists seeking to reshape the Church of England are generally thought to have sought guidance from Presbyterian Scotland or congregational New England, but the Channel Island way suggested kindred possibilities.

When parliament selected Jean de la Marche and his colleague Samuel de la Place for participation in the Westminster Assembly of Divines, the lieutenant governor of Guernsey Sir Peter Osborne, by no means a friend to reformed religion, petitioned that the two be excused, lest their parishes suffer loss of lectures and sermons, 'which the islanders can ill spare'. Guernseymen, Osborne continued, 'being well content with the discipline of France so long enjoyed, have not the curiosity to intermeddle in the government of other churches'. If the islands were to send ministers to Westminster, he suggested, only one should come from Guernsey and the other from Jersey.[101] When de la Place nonetheless joined the Assembly of Divines in December 1643, along with de la Marche, the minister petitioned parliament that his French-trained son might replace him in his island parish, 'according to the usual custom and order established in that place'.[102]

The troubles of the 1640s added to the stresses of island religious culture. 'Take heed', Sir Peter Osborne warned the people of Guernsey in December 1644, 'that many Anabaptists, Brownists, and other sectaries, agreeing neither in form of government nor confession of faith with any orthodox church... are come over in troops to settle their residences in your said island, the sooner to make themselves master of it'.[103] Among the interlopers was Thomas Collier, a self-declared minister of obscure social origins, who brought to Guernsey his heady brew of Anabaptism, Arminianism, and separatist Antinomianism. In 1646, 'he and many more of his followers whom he had seduced' were 'banished out of Guernsey... for their heresies and turbulent behaviour', to the satisfaction of local orthodoxy.[104]

Royalist petitioners on Jersey claimed in March 1646 that their settled religion was 'sans heresie, et sans schisms', and that they wanted only to be left in peace, with the authority of their laws and the favour of their prince.[105] Their tranquillity was tested by Laudian high churchmen, who arrived with the royalist diaspora, and insisted on ceremonial practices that went against the local grain.[106] Sir Edward Hyde, perhaps too optimistically, described an island 'in full submission and reverence to the doctrine and episcopal government of the Church of

England, and where the liturgy is universally used'.[107] But, notwithstanding the conformist ascendancy, Jersey by 1647 was divided between supporters of Anglican orthodoxy and enemies they described as 'a company of anabaptists' and 'malignants'.[108] Men of moderation were shocked when Charles de la Marche denounced the family of Stuarts, soon after the regicide, and preached in the town church of Guernsey to the effect that the late King Charles was among 'the most wicked that ever lived, and as if he had been cast in the deepest pit of hell'.[109]

Reformed religion in the Channel Islands faced other threats, not least from popular traditionalism. Reformers had long complained that Sundays on Jersey occasioned 'dancing and frequenting of taverns' and playing of violins, as they did in backward mainland parishes.[110] Accusations of witchcraft still occasionally erupted.[111] A parliamentary committee in 1643 claimed that Guernsey was rife with 'Romish superstitions', without specifying them.[112] The proximity of France, and the traffic of mariners, exposed the islands to Catholic influences. Authorities reacted with a frisson of horror when such popish trinkets as an *agnus dei* were brought to the island by Breton or Irish seamen.[113] They may have been equally horrified by reports of sacrilege 'at the reducing of Jersey' in December 1651, when a sectarian 'eased himself upon the communion table, and in the pulpits of a church or two in the island'.[114]

Parliament's grip on Guernsey, and its reduction of Jersey in 1651, brought both islands under the control of the English commonwealth. Army chaplains, some of them religious radicals, ministered to the occupying garrisons.[115] Island clergy participated in meetings of the States, 'a deliberative voice... about temporal affairs', but, bailiff Michael Lemprière reported, 'their turbulency and *brouilleries* have made themselves unworthy of that assembly'. Presbyterian *Colloques* continued on Guernsey into the 1650s, becoming 'fasheux et ennuyeux' (vexing and wearisome) according to the pastor of Sark Elie Brevint.[116]

The religious complexion of the Channel Islands in the 1650s was determined as much by force as by persuasion and tradition. As in other 'dark corners of the land', the government attempted to reform religious culture by sponsoring a puritan preaching ministry. The parliamentary military governor of Jersey James Heane proposed to Oliver Cromwell in 1653 'that none shall be admitted preachers, but such as will preach once a month in English'. This prompted island petitioners to point out that such a move 'would be to keep the poor inhabitants in darkness and ignorance', since their 'vulgar tongue' was French.[117] In line with the spirit of the times, Pierre de la Place, the new rector of the parish of St Ouen, Jersey, was instituted in January 1653, not by a dean or bishop, but by other Presbyterian ministers who gave him the 'hand of friendship'. De la Place served as pastor until he was suspended by conformists in 1663.[118]

The years of military conflict, and the confusions of Commonwealth rule, left a legacy of religious turmoil. The fracturing of religious culture that destabilized interregnum England also occurred in the Channel Islands. The old divisions between reformers and traditionalists, puritans and conformists, were exacerbated by splits among Presbyterians and Independents, Seekers, Quakers, and Anabaptists. The English garrison troops tended to be more radical in religion, or else more vehemently secular, than many of the island inhabitants.

On Jersey, the army chaplain Thomas Ashton, a congregational Independent who had been favoured by Oliver Cromwell, fell out with John Mason (governor 1659–60), who had time only for Anabaptists. There was chaos in Jersey's castles, so Ashton claimed, as the governor and his favourites advanced their 'arbitrary, bloody, and tyrannical proceedings'.[119]

A contemporary witness to these developments was the American-born, Harvard-educated, New England puritan Increase Mather, who served as a chaplain on neighbouring Guernsey. Mather regarded Ashton as 'a naughty and malicious person', who undercut fellow ministers and ingratiated himself with army grandees. Visiting England in 1658, after picking up a degree at Trinity College, Dublin, Mather accepted the position of chaplain to the garrison at Castle Cornet, with a salary of £120 a year. He lived there from April to December 1659, preaching in English every Sunday in the castle and the town. Mather found 'the sabbath to be much profaned in that island', but was pleased that the Lord blessed his endeavours, 'so as to cause considerable external reformation'. His conversation with the island's francophone Calvinists is unrecorded. After spending the first few months of 1660 in England, Mather was back in Guernsey by May 1660, when Charles II was proclaimed. He 'did out of conscience openly refuse' to drink the king's health, which put him at odds with Restoration temporizers. He stayed in post, however, until March 1661, to secure his arrears of salary, and was increasingly troubled by restored Anglican ceremonies. After quitting the island, he moved in godly circles in England, before sailing back to America in June 1661.[120]

Restoration Deans and Discipline

The Restoration involved not just the reassertion and expansion of monarchical power throughout the British realms, but also determination by church leaders to bring all the king's dominions into religious conformity. The kingdom's recent troubles showed the dangers of religious diversity, demonstrating that uniformity was a matter of safety as well as devotion. Though broadly successful, the religious standardization project of the Restoration met pockets of resistance, especially on Guernsey, where Presbyterian forms were deeply rooted. Mainland authorities lacked understanding of island culture, governors were at odds with bailiffs and jurats, while laity and clergy had competing interests. Charles II declared his 'chief care to cement the unhappy discomposures we found at our restoration, by a decent settlement of the church, according to divine truth, and the ancient laws of our kingdoms', but it proved an uphill struggle in the Channel Islands.[121]

The island historian Richard Hocart correctly observes that 'the imposition of the Anglican order in Guernsey has not yet been studied in detail', so the discussion here must be regarded as preliminary.[122] Of necessity, it is based more on English sources than island archives. The salient historiography of the later Stuart church, though extensive, makes no mention of the Channel Islands.[123]

Guernsey, which had not had a dean in a hundred years, was pushed towards conformity by the Restoration revival of that office. The first appointed was Philip le Couteur, rector of St Martin's parish, followed by the installation in the summer of 1662 of John (or Jean) de Sausmarez, as dean for life. The new dean, island born, was a staunch royalist and a zealous Anglican, a canon of Windsor, rector of Great Haseley, Oxfordshire, and minister of several island parishes. It would be his mission 'to extirpate the brood of unconformity' and to turn the neglected churches into 'comely places for holy assemblies'.[124] He sparred repeatedly with Guernsey's governors, sometimes sheltered under their authority, and lived until 1697.

In partnership with the Restoration governor Lord Christopher Hatton, who had not yet taken up residence on Guernsey, the dean undertook to enforce the Act of Uniformity, to prevent the islanders from 'relapsing into their former distempers'. He assured the governor's son Christopher Hatton Jr that he would do everything in his power 'which tends to the glory of God, and the peace of the church and kingdom', which included the restoration of church rents and tithes, and the ornamenting of churches 'in a fit and decent manner'.[125] Not surprisingly, the dean's pursuit of order, and his demand for money, stirred up antagonism among his Presbyterian neighbours. It was a relief to some that he continued to hold preferments in England, sometimes 'requiring residence there.'[126] The dean's periodic absences weakened his local influence, but strengthened his ties with the English episcopal elite. He was assisted by his wife, Rachel (née Briard), described by Hatton as a woman 'of so violent and imperious tongue, hands, and spirit, that what was by him enacted at London was by her repealed at Guernsey'.[127]

When Dean de Sausmarez explained his commission to the assembled ministers of Guernsey in 1662, all but one refused to conform. The most outspoken, Thomas le Marchant, the minister of the Vale and St Samson, 'publicly inveighed against the church liturgy, saying that he would rather turn Turk than submit unto it, that the Book of Common Prayer was the mass and worse, that he would not turn priest after he had been a minister upon twenty years, and that he would be a thorn in the dean's side as long as he lives.' Le Marchant and his fellow Presbyterians decided 'to quit their cures rather than submit' and exhorted their parishioners 'to remain constant in their former way'. Mainland ministers had similar choices to make after the 1662 Act of Uniformity. Rumour spread among the island populace 'that the dean intended to seize upon all their bibles, to set up images in their churches, and entrance and establish popery'. De Sausmarez was determined 'to introduce all at once the liturgy in its complete dress', including 'the people kneeling at the table set altarwise' for communion, but was willing to compromise on ministers wearing a surplice.[128]

Nathaniel Darrell, the deputy governor of Guernsey, reported in August 1662 that the dean needed an escort of soldiers as he went about his business, because many on the island were 'much startled' at 'the change of discipline in the church government'. Darrell loyally declared the Church of England to be 'the best church in the world', and promised all in his power to see it 'settled here, and the king obeyed'; but controversial liturgical changes, 'and chiefly using the sign of the cross at baptism, hath much distasted the common people here, which I cannot attribute but to their ignorance and simplicity'. Only this morning, Darrell wrote on 13 August, 'I sent a woman to the dungeon for seditious words against this discipline'.[129]

The newly appointed Governor Hatton, before he arrived in the island, assured Dean de Sausmarez in September 1662 that 'the Act of Uniformity now in force and made rule there in Guernsey by his majesty's letters' would not be relaxed, allowing room for 'neither conscience nor toleration nor dispensation'. Though advocates for 'the Presbyterian way' continued to make 'a great noise', London saw their opposition as no more than 'a nine days' wonder'. With church and state in unison, the authorities believed, the islanders 'will all come into one fold in the outward profession as to the discipline, as they agree with us in the doctrine'.[130] A company of 100 English soldiers arrived on Guernsey late in September, to add muscle to the remaking of island religious culture.[131]

Gradually, de Sausmarez reported, Guernsey came into line. The bishop of Winchester instituted ministers out of England to the parishes vacated by the Presbyterians, and the people became 'sufficiently disposed to comply with all reasonable injunctions from their superiors'. Le Marchant was prosecuted and imprisoned as 'a great disturber of the common peace', then withdrew into France before returning to cause more trouble as a dissenter.[132]

The dean's continuing difficulty with recalcitrant parishioners appeared in his report to the Privy Council in April 1663 that, 'having exceedingly laboured to reconcile them to uniformity', he still struggled with 'troublesome and unquiet spirits'. God so blessed his labours, however, that at Christmas 1662 'there was 200 orthodox communicants' in one of le Marchant's former parishes, though under that minister's 'seducements' the number fell to 48 the following Easter.[133]

Worse for de Sausmarez, it appeared that le Marchant gained the ear of the incoming governor, who was much more pragmatic than zealous in his religious inclinations. Word spread, no doubt misreported, 'that the governor obligeth no man to conform, that all men may live at their pleasure as they did before in point of church discipline'.[134] Sir Christopher Hatton surely intended no such thing, which would have put him at odds with his masters in London, but he may have tried to restrain the dean's bull-headed Anglicanism. He also tried to moderate de Sausmarez's demand for tithes and his replacement of parish elders with churchwardens.

Relationships between the dean and the governor deteriorated after Hatton had arrived on the island in April 1664. Each sent damaging reports to London, and each accused the other of undermining his authority. Whereas de Sausmarez demanded conformity to church discipline, and stood on his dignity to achieve it, the governor urged more subtle measures. When the dean accused him of being led by nonconformists, Hatton replied that his policies of modest accommodation did more for the church than the dean's hard line. I 'have served the church with a true and conscientious duty, and more advantage than my accusers', he assured the Earl of Clarendon. Under attack from Dean de Sausmarez, and from his own lieutenant governor, Hatton explained in May 1664 that 'I have carried myself with all indulgence to men's conscience here, and do conceive his majesty's service here is so concerned in it, and the condition of this place doth so require it'. Hatton acknowledged that he 'made use of lay nonconformists in civil affairs', where their knowledge of local laws and customs was of service to the state, but protested that his zeal for the Church of England was unabated. 'In the choice of men for employment either in civil or military affairs, I do absolutely choose the most able, most peaceable, most sober, most ready to serve his majesty, without having regard to their conformity or not conformity, which I humbly conceive appertains not to me to take notice of.' Perhaps, like King Charles himself, the governor was willing to ignore minor religious irregularities for the sake of the greater political good.[135] But, unlike Charles II, he did this without the wit and charisma of the crown.

Dean de Sausmarez visited England in the summer of 1664 to shore up support from religious and political leaders. He seeded 'whisper... of my lord Hatton's remissness', to the effect that the governor protected and even cherished 'notorious nonconformists and enemies' of the Church of England. Influenced by this, Clarendon wrote in August that, unless Hatton supplied proof of his 'unquestionable fidelity and affection to the church', the king would have to 'awaken him out of this drowsiness, and require him to take the business of the church more to heart'. London saw the dean as 'a very sober man, and full of duty', whereas Hatton regarded him as an 'impertinent' martinet who spread 'abominable falsities'. Hatton valued le Marchant for 'his great reading and dexterity in the affairs of this island', whereas the dean knew the former minister to be a dangerous nonconformist. Clarendon agreed that the reformation of religion in Guernsey 'must be introduced with all sweetness and affability, and not with severity and roughness', but thought de Sausmarez the man for the job.[136]

The dean and the governor of Guernsey were clearly incompatible, and in the struggle between them it was Hatton who lost. Complaints against him, spread by de Sausmarez, included offences against ecclesiastical finances, personnel, liturgy, and discipline. Hatton, by this account, was at best indifferent to religion, at worst a crypto-Presbyterian, who had seized 'small revenues that belong to the fabric of the church, to apply them to the mounting of the guns of the castle, and to other profane purposes'; who dissuaded parishioners from paying their tithes, and 'imprisoned those churchwardens who refused to advance money to his purposes'; who 'did upbraid the dean, telling him he had put the church in confusion, because he had put down presbytery'. Furthermore, de Sausmarez claimed, Hatton publicly 'mocked the censures of the church, asking the people whether any excommunicated person was the worse for being excommunicated, bidding them not to care for it'. And, 'to put all things in a greater confusion, his lordship caused the communion tables, which before were altarwise, to be changed and to be placed after the Presbyterian manner'. All this, de Sausmarez alleged, was to thwart the dean and bring down his 'faction', and 'to make himself the more popular and to improve thereby his estate'. The governor even attempted to prevent de Sausmarez from travelling to England to make his report, so his adversary claimed.[137]

Unable to ignore these allegations, Clarendon lost confidence in Governor Hatton, telling him in December 1664 that 'your carriage in and towards the church hath done you much harm, and will be examined in all strictness'. Hatton replied in despair, with appropriate maritime imagery, 'we were beginning to settle here in peace and quietness, and thought we were got into a safe harbour, but we are beat out again to sea, and have no compass to guide and direct us but your lordship's goodness'.[138] Island factionalism had got the better of him. The Council recalled Hatton to London, though he used every excuse to delay his departure. A visitor to Guernsey at this time found 'the honest part of the clergy were disgusted...the generality of the people in high discontent'. Christian forbearance was as short of supply as castle provisions.[139]

The dean's drive for conformity and compliance was thwarted, not just by the governor but by recalcitrant ministers, who 'made the people subscribe a covenant not to return to our church', but to compose instead 'a church according to the word of God'. Writing to the king in July 1665, de Sausmarez complained of illicit and 'seditious' Presbyterian assemblies, so disruptive that the substitute governor was forced to intervene.[140] This was Sir Jonathan Atkins, under whose regime (1665–70) 'the church did enjoy much peace and did recover what it had lost'.[141] Charles II aided the project by ordering the bailiff and jurats of Guernsey to give every assistance to the dean, 'conducive to the advancement of God's worship'.[142] The work was facilitated by John Durel's translation of the Book of Common Prayer, as *La Liturgie. C'est à dire, le formulaire des prieres publiques, de l'administration des sacramens; et des autres ceremonies & coûtumes de l'eglise, selon l'usage de l'eglise anglicane* (1667), which gave an official francophone voice to Anglican orthodoxy.[143]

The anglicanization of Guernsey continued apace under the second Lord Hatton, who held the reversion to the office and succeeded as governor in 1670. Presbyterianism was reduced to a sub-stream of dissent, though its adherents gained support from French Huguenot refugees and from co-religionists in

England. The project of uniformity was still plagued by 'scandalous and open despisers of both church and government', so the dean protested in 1671. He enjoined the bailiff and jurats to assist him in identifying and punishing any minister who 'shall presume in his sermons and prayers to meddle with civil and secular affairs (which by dreadful experience has been found to be matter of dangerous consequence), or to add anything of his own to the known and public liturgy of the church'.[144]

While following the worship of the Church of England, Restoration Guernsey still gave extraordinary attention to the singing of psalms in French, and its ministers still favoured the French habit of cloaks and closely buttoned cassocks rather than surplices.[145] Communicants gathered 'about' the table, rather than before an altar rail, and were seen to 'clap on their hats at sermons … according to the French mode'.[146] Baptisms might still omit the sign of the cross. By some reports, no doubt false, Governor Hatton showed 'favour' to the island's 'fanatics and sectaries', though he was scrupulous in his public duties.[147]

Charles II's Declaration of Indulgence in 1672 gave comfort to Guernsey dissenters, and encouraged some islanders, including de la Marche and le Marchant, to 'set up conventicles, and establish presbytery and Calvin's liturgy'. Church officials reacted with displeasure.[148] Dean de Sausmarez urged Governor Hatton in July 1672 to show 'zeal for the peace of our church, on which doth depend that of the whole island … by taking care of God's worship'. It was the governor's duty, the dean insisted, to enjoin strict reading of evening and morning prayers, at canonical hours, according to the rubrics of the Church of England, and to root out conventicles: 'you are the great wheel, to whose motions the small ones will conform.' It was the obligation of state authorities, he repeated, 'to be aiding and assisting to the dean and his deputy upon all occasions, wherein they shall have need of it towards the maintaining of the discipline of the church and the liturgy thereof'. As for the king's proclamation (the Declaration of Indulgence), 'we are neither named nor intended in it', so the toleration could not apply to Guernsey.[149] Setting forth these positions again in 1677, the dean viewed the state as an instrument of religious discipline, which should be his ally rather than his adversary in the quest for uniformity.[150]

Endorsing this view, the Privy Council stood up for the ecclesiastical administration, and instructed the governor, bailiff, and jurats to give it full support. Every officer under the crown was obliged to assist the dean 'in the maintenance of the discipline of the church and the liturgy thereof'. If churchwardens assessed parishioners for the repair of decayed churches, the state was to 'take care that the same be duly levied'. If the dean's court 'proceeds as far as excommunication against contumacious persons', the civil magistrates should be employed to bring such persons to obedience. Recognizing that dissent remained a problem, the Council insisted that orders for suppressing conventicles be 'duly executed'.[151] Dean de Sausmarez acquired even more authority when he acquired the office of

Judge Delegate and acting bailiff, with influence over the places of Greffier, King's Sergeant, and island Advocates.[152]

The dean needed every weapon in his arsenal to combat the continuance of religious insubordination. One of his allies, Elias des Hayes, rector of the Vale and St Samson (Thomas le Marchant's former parish), alleged in September 1677 that a less steadfast colleague, John Martin, rector of St Andrew, had declared that, although Charles II was rightly titled Defender of the Faith, 'it was the faith of his concubines, and savoured strongly of their papistry, and that he was led by the king of France as he pleased'. Another accuser reported Martin saying that, when his majesty was in France, 'qu'il alloit frequemmant de la Messe au bordel, et du bordel à la Messe'. These were scandalous words that demanded examination, a sign of a ministry lacking discipline.[153] Governor Hatton, however, noted Martin's reputation for 'discretion and sober carriage', and the licentiousness and violent passions of his accusers, and advised London to take the matter no further.[154] The spat between Martin and des Hayes was *ad hominem* as well as *ad clerum*, a sign of a rift in churchmanship as well as personalities. The governor's handling of it earned him no credit with the dean.

Another glimpse of religious culture in Restoration Guernsey is afforded by the observation that one of the island's leading nonconformists, the learned Charles de la Marche, was 'so extremely devoted to mystical numbers' that some considered him 'mad with doting upon that subject'. His numerological gauging of the end of the world in 1666 had proved false, but he may have found firmer ground with his prediction, recorded in 1677, 'concerning the Prince of Orange, of his advancement to be head of the united protestants'.[155] Only a dozen years later the Prince of Orange became England's William III, leading an alliance against the Catholic Louis XIV.

In 1699, when the bishop of Winchester proposed ecclesiastical canons for Guernsey modelled on the Jacobean canons of Jersey, island ministers deemed them superfluous, since, they said, they already observed the canons of the Church of England.[156] When the bishop pressed ahead and proposed fifty-six new canons for the ecclesiastical government of Guernsey, Sark, and Alderney, they proved predictably controversial. Several ministers and parishioners objected, though more on financial and jurisdictional than liturgical grounds. The States politely asked that the canons be amended 'in conformity with the laws of this isle', and Governor Hatton urged 'a stop put to this whole proceeding till all parties may more coolly and temperately dispose themselves'.[157] Guernsey's conformity worked best if it was not overexamined, which, some would say, was the recipe for success elsewhere in later Stuart England. 'Dissenters they have none,' wrote Thomas Dicey in the eighteenth century, though he allowed that six out of ten Guernsey ministers still evidenced Presbyterian inclinations.[158]

*

Jersey was traditionally more compliant, though here too were signs of backsliding in the later seventeenth century. Jersey's Presbyterian heritage was more remote, and several generations of conformity had been capped by a decade of cavalier royalism. Charles II instructed that only men of known loyalty and good affections, and of 'orthodox principles' relating to the Church of England, should serve as jurats on Jersey, and such men were not hard to find.[159] Evidence suggests, however, that religious orthodoxy in this island too was more contingent than devout. A report from the early 1670s indicated that the islanders made only 'a show of conformity with the Church of England, for the ministers themselves do read our liturgy only *par maniere d'acquit*' (in a negligent or perfunctory manner). Charles Trumbull, visiting Jersey from Oxford, remarked on the use of the prayer book in French, 'but in many places rather slubbered over than reverently read, not in that decent order as with us, but piecemeal and the order frequently inverted'. Island preaching, also in French, he found 'frequently vehement, after the Huguenot mode'. Accustomed to Anglican altars, Trumbull was disquieted to find the communion tables unrailed, 'in the midst of the church without cover and unregarded, and any way rather than north and south'. Another disorderly practice he sniffed at was the islanders 'seldom suffering their children to be baptized with the sign of the cross'.[160]

The Restoration deans of Jersey (Philip le Couteur 1661–71, followed by his brother Clement le Couteur 1672–1714) had constant trouble with difficult parishioners. Dean Clement le Couteur informed the archbishop of Canterbury's chaplain in 1680 that

> heresy makes but small disturbance amongst us; but which is as bad and as intolerable, profanation gets daily new credit with us. A character of piety and honesty, or an ecclesiastical employment here, are sufficient to beget the odium and the contempt of the most part upon the owner, so that no ecclesiastical laws nor Christian remonstrances are regarded at all.

Anticlericalism and secularism were rampant, if the dean is to be believed, and the canons and rulings of the church were ignored.[161] Le Couteur complained again in 1682 that 'certain officers, who have jurisdiction only regarding civil affairs', intruded into ecclesiastical matters, especially regarding 'the treasure of our churches'.[162] Anglican discipline did not necessarily extend to the payment of tithes. Clerical incomes were 'mean and inconsiderable', according to the Jersey minister Philip Falle, who spent much of his energy angling for preferment in England. 'Dissenters we have none of any sort', wrote Falle in the 1690s, though, like Sacheverell in the Isle of Man, he was probably not looking very hard. Secure against the heresies of Catholic France, protected by the crown of England, Jersey, in Falle's estimation, enjoyed 'the best religion' in communion with 'the best reformed church in the Christian world'.[163]

Relations between deans and governors of Jersey were less fraught than on Guernsey, but the laity in the parishes were not necessarily more religious. On both islands the hegemony of the established church was challenged by the arrival of refugee French Protestants, both before and after Louis XIV's revocation of the Edict of Nantes in 1685. Anglo-Norman networks on the Continent aided the escape of Huguenots to Jersey and Guernsey.[164] Roman Catholics also flexed their muscles during the reign of James II, when the king imposed a popish priest and garrison commander on the island.[165]

Jurisdictional issues continued to cause more problems than matters of ecclesiology or belief. Appeals from the dean's court to higher ecclesiastical officials in England could be as troublesome as appeals from the island's Royal Court to the Privy Council, and just as tortuous. A seemingly routine case of incest in Jersey in 1679 spiralled past the bishop of Winchester and the archbishop of Canterbury, raising questions whether an appeal to the Court of Arches 'would there be respected or confirmed'. 'There' meant on the island where the case originated. It would be up to the lawyers to determine whether Jersey was subject to English ecclesiastical law, and a matter for the islanders whether they accepted it. George Morley, the bishop Winchester, who had nominal spiritual oversight of the Channel Islands, but who recognized his limits, declared despairingly, 'in such a case as this, I dare not rely upon mine own judgement only'.[166]

A variety of ecclesiastical disputes in the reign of William III spilled over from the dean's court in Jersey to the court of the bishop of Winchester, and then became the concern of higher authorities. Some concerned observance of the Lord's Day, or wine for Holy Communion, but matrimonial matters could be especially contentious.[167] One such case turned on whether the Jersey yeoman John Bichard had promised matrimony to Anne le Bas before they had sex, and whether he was now obliged to marry her, and to own the child she was carrying. The island court 'adjudged' the matter in June 1699, and 'condemned' John to marry Anne, 'to his very great surprise and amazement'. Bichard appealed to Winchester, and a year later the bishop's court confirmed the sentence. He then appealed to the king in council, and the matter was referred in April 1701 to the Committee for the Affairs of Jersey and Guernsey. This committee redirected the appeal to the Dean of Arches, the principal legal official of the archbishop of Canterbury, who declared his jurisdiction to be inadequate.

By this time Bichard had bigger problems, for, in May 1701, in consequence of his case, he was excommunicated for remaining 'obstinate in his sin' as a contumacious offender and the putative father of a bastard child. Endorsing the decision of the dean, the Royal Court of Jersey ratified the sentence, forbidding 'all except his domestics ... to have any dealings or society with him'. Bichard, resourceful and persistent as ever, requested a commission under the Great Seal of England for judges delegate to resolve his problem. The Privy Council agreed to this request, but it took them another two years, until March 1703, to order that 'the sentence of Jersey should be suspended, till the said delegates had determined the cause'. The Court of Delegates met in July, but advocates for Anne le Bas persuaded them 'that the mainland judges had no jurisdiction, their commission being founded on the statute of king Henry VIII for appeals, and that the Isle of Jersey was not within that statute'. Island exceptionalism once again prevailed. Bichard's only remaining recourse was to ask for a Royal Commission of Appeal, an exceptional measure for so small a matter, on the grounds that he, 'being a Jersey man, had no right to claim the benefit intended to our subjects of England by the ordinary course of appeals upon the statutes of this our realm'. Bichard's case went forward, with great expense and frustration, demonstrating yet again the array of opinions on religious jurisdictional issues.[168]

By the end of the Stuart era, the religious culture of island communities was less deviant than it had been a century earlier. Travellers from the English mainland would find less that seemed strange. The Anglican ecclesiastical polity generally prevailed, if somewhat bruised and subdued after decades of war and revolution. Parish churches everywhere followed the Book of Common Prayer, or its local language equivalent, while nonconformists gained toleration. Confessional contention dwindled, while folk practices and superstitions continued. Though the Isle of Wight, Scilly, Man, and the Channel Islands had different religious histories, they shared in the protections of the Declaration of Rights, the comforts of the Church of England, and the care of a benign but distant monarch. They also shared memories of violence, division, betrayal, and invasion, which they generally sought to suppress. Though not fully compliant with the official religion of the mainland, they were less likely to be considered 'dark corners of the land'.

7

Fortress Islands

Island isolation allowed inhabitants a measure of security, but also exposed them to danger. Responsible English governments fortified their islands against external threats, and developed them as outliers of dynastic and national power. Frontier islands served the state as bastions and bases, protecting the homeland and its periphery of force. Island harbours and roadsteads sheltered commercial shipping and served as springboards for naval operations. Their castles, garrisons, and munitions represented the kingdom's honour as well as its strength. Part of their task was to deny such facilities to England's enemies as the international situation unfolded. Islanders had to acknowledge their place in the imperial dynastic project, though their local view was less strategic than the wider concerns of London. This chapter examines the never-ending effort of councillors, captains, and governors to maintain readiness in islands at risk of attack. It recognizes the difficulties of access, as well as the urgency of supply, that affected both defence and communication from Elizabethan times to the English civil war. Insular martial and material arrangements formed the local face of grand strategy and foreign relations.

The natural fortifications of many islands gave comfort to military planners. 'Firm against the Gallick inroads', their cliffs, rocks, and waters inhibited enemy attack. The western part of the Isle of Wight, for example, was 'fenced about with steep and craggy rocks', and 'southward, where it looks to France, it is inaccessible', though other parts were more exposed.[1] Guernsey was likewise 'encompassed around with a pale of rocks, being very defensible...from the attempting invasion of enemies'.[2] Other islands similarly took advantage of their natural mottes and moats. 'Being divided from all other countries by the ocean', as one seventeenth-century commentator observed, they were 'not subject to those incursions that contiguous countries are'.[3] There seemed little likelihood of islanders facing foreign cavalry. By the same token, most islands lay beyond the speedy reach of reinforcement. Their situation, as defenders of the Scillies and the Channel Islands understood, was 'so remote as it cannot be seasonably seconded from the main'.[4]

Military architecture, military hardware, and military leadership stood between the islands and their enemies. The authorities had responsibility for infrastructure, weaponry, manpower, and supplies, as well as intelligence and training. The insular terrain generally gave advantage to defenders. Any intending invader faced the hazard of tides and currents, cliffs and shoals, as well as the prospect

England's Islands in a Sea of Troubles. David Cressy, Oxford University Press (2020). © David Cressy 2020.
DOI: 10.1093/oso/9780198856603.001.0001

of landing under fire. Even the smallest of islands had defensive breastworks and platforms, sconces and walls, with musketry, cannon, and forces to man them. Although island militias, in a pinch, could mount some resistance, it took professional soldiers to operate heavy ordnance and to perform the duties of garrisons. Every island governor wanted culverins and gunpowder, as well as well-paid and well-victualled soldiers. Sometimes the politicians contributed more by lobbying in London than by resident service in the locality. When governor Danby of Guernsey sought reinforcements in 1627, he advised the Privy Council that his garrison was 'subject to divers delays and casualties of weather, both to be brought and sent for', though he himself had little interest in crossing the Channel to join them.[5]

Available weaponry ranged from demi-cannons, which could fire a six-inch shot over half a mile, down to hand pieces and bows and arrows. Defenders on Lundy threw stones. The most commonly deployed ordnance in garrisoned island castles were demi-culverins, ten to twelve feet in length, with a bore of four and a half inches, firing a ten-pound ball; sakers or quarter-culverins, around eight-foot long, with a three-inch bore, firing six-pound shot; minions, slightly smaller, firing three-to-four-pound balls; and six-foot falconets, with a two-inch bore for one-and-a-half-pound bullets.[6] 'Brass' ordnance (actually bronze) was preferable to iron guns, which were cheaper to make but rust-prone and brittle. All relied on gunpowder brought from mainland stores, which was subject to deterioration (although there were some local efforts to make saltpetre).

Artillery and its ancillary equipment needed regular maintenance and skilful handling, neither of which could be guaranteed in remote offshore facilities. Experienced gunners knew that 'it chanceth many times through the negligence or fault of the founders, that some pieces are not truly bored' and that such weapons were 'very dangerous to shoot for fear of breaking'.[7] Oxidization and neglect had similar consequences. It was hardly surprising, therefore, that an armourer on Guernsey was 'like to have been slain, the piece breaking in divers pieces', when he tested one of the castle guns in 1600.[8]

Foreign Threats

Every war, and every rumour of war, signalled danger. The islands were the first places to be menaced when hostilities broke out. Their defences needed to be hardened, their readiness tested, especially in 'stirring and troublesome times'. (The phrase is from Sir John Peyton, governor of Jersey in 1621, but could apply to most of the early modern era.[9]) Island forces braced time and again for invasion, remembering earlier threats. Even the Channel Islands, with their privilege of neutrality, could not let down their guard. During periods of peace, the island fortresses were often neglected, their guns dismounted, their garrisons run down.

When trouble approached, there was catch-up work to do. Fishermen, mariners, and watchers on shore provided warnings of suspected enemy intentions. Island governors characteristically blamed their predecessors for deficiencies of preparation.

French pressure on the Channel Islands was perdurable, their medieval ambitions not forgotten. French kings still nourished claims to the Norman inheritance and coveted island ports that were better than their own. The close proximity of the Channel Islands to France made them especially vulnerable. Some of their French-speaking inhabitants were believed to harbour infiltrators and spies, who might betray the islands to the enemy.

Previous episodes of aggression cast long shadows over English military planning. History advised preparation. There had been damaging French landings on Jersey in the fourteenth century. Guernsey was in French hands from 1339 to 1341, and, as William Harrison reminded Elizabethan readers, was again 'sore spoiled by the French' in 1371.[10] Weakness and treachery in the fifteenth century allowed the French to hold Jersey from 1461 to 1468. Henry VIII's French wars put the islands under further pressure, which intensified in the reigns of Edward VI and Mary I. French troops who landed on Jersey's north coast in 1549 moved several miles inland before being turned back. Though Sark was 'every way so inaccessible that it might be held against the Great Turk', that island fell in 1549 to French invaders, who held it for half a dozen years. Alderney changed hands several times during these conflicts, while Guernsey was feared to be in peril.[11] News reached London in the first year of Elizabeth's reign that a French resident of Normandy, a Monsieur Glatigni, had planned to surprise the castle in Jersey, as a prelude to renewal of war.[12] More reports circulated in 1563 of a French fleet 'threatening to do some exploit in the islands of Guernsey and Jersey'.[13] Precautionary initiatives were imperative, as governors and captains looked to their bastions and walls.

Every island was at risk. The French invasion of the Isle of Wight in 1340, with the burning of villages and a siege of Carisbrooke Castle, was still remembered three centuries later in local Shrovetide cudgel plays.[14] Who could tell when the enemy might come again? They came in July 1545, when French galleys landed on the eastern tip of the Isle of Wight and set up camp.[15] Henry VIII's great battleship the *Mary Rose*, refitted to fight the French, sank just off the Isle of Wight that month in the course of that campaign. The Isles of Scilly too, though rough and remote, were menaced by France in the 1540s. Like every other island, they attracted corsairs and pirates as well as foreign forces.

Elizabeth I's Spanish war, which lasted from 1585 to 1603, brought the threat of invasion to all of England as well as to the island fringe. The Spanish Armada of 1588 had contingency plans to seize the Isle of Wight, as a prelude to the conquest of England. King Philip II instructed Medina Sidonia, the Armada commander, that, should he miss his rendezvous with the Duke of Parma, 'you will see whether you are able to capture the Isle of Wight, which is not so strongly defended as to appear able to resist you'. Spain would then have 'a secure port in which the Armada may take shelter, and which, being a place of importance, would open the way for further action by you'.[16] In the event, of course, the Armada scattered into the North Sea, and England was spared. The government may not have known of Philip's secret instructions, but they understood the military importance of the Isle of Wight.

The Channel Islands were similarly vulnerable. Writing from Jersey in May 1591, Sir John Norris advised Lord Burghley to urge Queen Elizabeth to 'have some greater care of these islands, which no doubt the Spaniard will have a great eye upon as fit means to make these parts of Brittany subject to him'.[17] Similar concerns emerged in 1593 that the Spanish 'may surprise the Isle of Man, as a place very commodious for their victualling and watering'. The government in London worried that the island 'forces are but meanly provided, either of necessaries or soldiers of any experience to defend it', and introduced a veteran captain 'for the resisting of any sudden attempt'.[18] Spanish warships hovering off the Scillies ventured such an attack in 1591, and in April 1595 were expected again 'to burn and spoil' those islands.[19] Thinking primarily of Scilly, but with wider application, Sir Francis Godolphin remarked in 1595 that 'the gathering of these Spaniards seemeth as a cloud that is like to fall shortly in some part of her majesty's dominions'.[20] In 1597, it was learned, the Spanish had eyes on anchorages near Beaumaris on the Isle of Anglesey, as well as on Lundy in the Bristol Channel, further imperilling the island perimeter.[21] The islander Thomas Marchant, who spent five years as a Spanish prisoner, later revealed that 'during this time he was often solicited by the Admiral of Spain to engineer the betrayal of Guernsey castle', which was more likely to fall from treachery than assault.[22]

Foreign threats should have abated during the peaceable reign of James I. But rumour kept defenders worried. There was talk of plots in Jersey or Guernsey in the first year of James's reign, 'to deliver one of the said isles' to the king of France in exchange for 2,000 crowns.[23] The governor of Guernsey sought support to strengthen his castles in October 1621, as Louis XIII assumed the reins of power, warning that 'peradventure the young French king will have the same ambition to recover those rags of Normandy that his predecessors showed in the repossessing of Calais'.[24]

As the Jacobean peace began to fray in the early 1620s, authorities on land and at sea became alert to 'the suspicion and danger of sudden attempts'.[25] Fortunately the 200 Spanish ships seen approaching the Scillies in March 1624 turned out to be Newfoundland fishermen, bent on their lawful business.[26] The invading army said to have landed on the Isle of Wight in May 1624 was simply the crew of a Hamburg vessel that had been accidentally driven ashore. The emergency beacons were fired, amid reports of 500 enemy marching, a number that soon doubled to 1,000. The island magistrate Sir John Oglander sagely observed 'how fear will make men say and avow that to be true on their own view which they never saw'.[27]

Worries grew more substantial when Charles I took England into European war. Residents of the Isle of Wight panicked in June 1627 when they mistook a peaceable Dutch flotilla for a Spanish fleet making for their shores.[28] In 1629, when England was fighting France as well as Spain, Oglander himself feared invasion and moved his children from the island to a house on the English mainland.[29] Nerves frayed again in May 1639, when two Spanish warships with 360 men aboard took refuge in the Isle of Wight after being attacked at sea by the Dutch.[30]

Channel Islanders shared these anxieties, despite their hedge of commercial neutrality. Nathaniel Darrell, lieutenant governor of Guernsey, warned in August 1626 that the French had 6,000 troops and 60 sail of Biscayners ready for an attempt against 'these isles' and had acquired the services of an English papist who was an experienced pilot in local waters. There was talk in Normandy of 'the benefit it would bring' if Guernsey could be 'annexed to France, and that without it the French would always be annoyed'.[31] Some islanders feared in 1627 that Louis XIII's Cardinal Richelieu 'may do some exploit worthy of his new office of Admiralty, his wings being too short to fly as far as England, and his meditations too low to reach to so high a pitch'. Jersey or Guernsey appeared to be his most immediate target.[32] The French king, it was reported in 1628, was 'resolved to set upon these isles', and had already granted Jersey and Guernsey to their future governor, a Monsieur Thorax, who was amassing troops in Normandy.[33] Invasion fears were fanned by sightings of French fleets, news of armed preparations, and reports that the islands 'may be suddenly attempted'.[34] Treachery might prove as effective as frontal invasion. In January 1630, Charles I's government learned that the French 'had gained one Fullerton, a Scotchman, a prisoner in the Bastille, to betray and deliver to them the isle of Guernsey and Castle Cornet, and they had sent one Porsier to view the island'.[35] Not a decade went by without report of an impending foreign invasion or suspected betrayal.

Defending the Islands

Watchfulness, training, repair, and investment would be needed to keep the islands safe from enemies who 'have long had an envious eye' on them.[36] Walls and culverins would be needed, as well as intelligence and prayer. Materials and equipment would have to be brought from the mainland, with providential assistance from heaven. The Privy Council in London pressed endlessly to have its local representatives furnish and refurbish their military facilities.

The strategic importance of the Isles of Scilly was well understood. As the guard and gateway of England's western approaches, they commanded the sea lanes between Ireland and the Channel Islands, linking Spain to Bristol, the Channel to the Irish Sea. As one early modern analyst observed, whoever 'could gather strength enough to hold the place...would gain command of the navigation of England, France, and Holland'. Once an enemy found 'a resting place', it would be hard to drive them out.[37] If the Scillies fell to foreigners, warned another commentator, 'the Channel trade from Ireland, Liverpool, and Bristol to London and the south of England, could not subsist'. It was unthinkable that Scilly's forts and harbours should fall to any enemy, who 'might much molest and trouble the trade of these parts of Christendom'.[38]

The Isles of Scilly were always vulnerable, especially in times of war. In the sixteenth century they were 'often robbed by the Frenchmen and Spaniards'.[39] 'Turkish' raiders and foreign fleets plied Scilly's waters, as did pirates and privateers of all nations. As lessees of the crown, the proprietors were obliged to defend the islands,[40] but modern castles and garrisons required investment by the state. Naval patrols attempted to keep predators in check, assisted by forts and batteries on shore.

The medieval castle of Ennor, on the main island of St Mary's, was unserviceable by the early sixteenth century, and most of Scilly's medieval fortifications had fallen into decay. A new site and a new facility were needed. When Edward VI's Lord Admiral Seymour examined western defences in 1547, he planned to 'make the fort in our Lady's isle of Scilly upon the little hill betwixt fresh water and St Mary's road'. In 1549, its summer garrison was increased by a hundred. By 1553, the island had 150 troops, commanded by Captain Thomas Godolphin, though neither the fort nor the force was maintained in following years.[41]

Queen Elizabeth's long Spanish war put new pressure on the Scillies, which became acute in 1591, when news reached London of a Spanish plan to capture the islands. Sir Walter Raleigh was sent 'to save Scilly, if it be not taken', and the proprietor stirred himself against 'the late attempts of the enemy in those parts'. A serviceable fort would need at least eighty men, it was believed, and six or eight demi-culverins and sakers to fend off potential invaders.[42]

To this end Sir Francis Godolphin began work on Star Castle on St Mary's in 1593, using 'his invention and purse' to reduce the island 'to a more defensible plight'. Named for its shape, Scilly's new fortress offered 'a sure hold, and a commodious dwelling', inspired by the *trace Italienne*, though not necessarily the most effective of military facilities. Six years later, the fort was still 'half naked'.[43] The addition of garrison walls and outer bastions about 1600 remedied earlier defects, and created a fortified compound on the western peninsula of the island. A critic in 1637 declared the castle 'uncapable to lodge and accommodate a garrison of twenty soldiers, and so ill contrived in the fortification that the least assault of an enemy could easily carry it'.[44] Star Castle had changed little when parliamentary surveyors described it in 1652:

The castle is built in the form of an acute octagon fort with a good stone rampart of the same, but very low and little, consisting of a hall or new room, buttery and two cellars, with a kitchen, pastry, and larder below stairs, with a dining room and four chambers in the second story, and seven little rooms over them, and four little turrets upon the leads.

More rooms around the ramparts served for gunners, guards, and stores.[45] Today it serves as a hotel.

The military readiness of the Scillies followed familiar cycles of urgency and neglect. The islands received money and attention when England fought with France or Spain, but were allowed to run down when threats receded. In 1600, the garrison strength on St Mary's was only fifty men in summer, and twenty-five in winter.[46] Under James I, the castle at Tresco was virtually abandoned and other establishments poorly maintained.[47] Nonetheless, government accounts for 1612 show £554 4s. 2d. spent on St Mary's 'in Scilly Isle', more than twice the amount spent on the castle at Dover. In addition to manpower, the state pledged the meagre amount of twenty-four barrels of gunpowder each year.[48]

Charles I's foreign wars brought more alarms to the islands. A report from Scilly in June 1628 related renewed fear of invasion, 'which causes the women and unserviceable people daily to quit the place'. Male islanders were prevented from leaving only by Sir Francis Godolphin forcibly restraining them. There were plans to expand the garrison to 500, though there were rarely more than 125 soldiers in residence.[49] Scilly's garrison strength was still 125 in 1634, when Godolphin proposed raising it to 300.[50] Yet, by September 1637, there were only twenty-five soldiers in the castle, the rest scattered in island billets.[51] At the outbreak of civil war in 1642, the garrison counted 160 soldiers and a dozen officers, including a surgeon but no chaplain. There were thirty-six pieces of ordnance to hand (no more than on some of the king's warships), but at least sixteen of these were deemed 'unserviceable'.[52] Both men and munitions would see action in the 1640s, until parliament secured the islands in 1651 (see Chapter 8).

*

Much closer to the rich but nervous mainland, the Isle of Wight guarded the naval base at Portsmouth and the commercial port of Southampton, and commanded the vital shipping of the Solent and the western Channel. Islanders understood that they inhabited 'a considerable frontier of this kingdom ... of manifest consequence to the whole realm', and that their island's southern shore was 'the first place accessible to land from France'.[53] The government acknowledged that, 'by reason of the nearness, and fitness for incursions and attempts into the adjoining counties', any enemy occupation of the island would be 'more dangerous and offensive to this our kingdom ... than any place whatsoever in the main'.[54]

'Nearness' meant that the Isle of Wight lay close enough to the rest of England to be reinforced in times of emergency. A long-established system of beacons and guard-poles relayed signals from point to point across the island, and over the water into Hampshire. A single flaming beacon warned of an approaching enemy, two beacons authorized mainland forces to fire their beacons and to march to their rendezvous, while three beacons indicated an 'alarm unto all England in token the enemy is so strongly invaded' that island forces could not resist them.[55]

Commenting on fortifications in the Isle of Wight, the seventeenth-century writer Guy Miege observed that 'there are more castles in this spot of ground than there is in any the like spot in England'.[56] Principal among them was the medieval motte and bailey stronghold of Carisbrooke Castle, on high ground above Newport. Carisbrooke served as garrison quarters, home to the resident governor or captain, and a potential refuge for islanders in the event of invasion. But it was not on the coast, and was powerless against ships. In the 1570s, the castle had eight pieces of ordnance, of varying size and antiquity.[57] Queen Elizabeth spent lavishly to modernize Carisbrooke between 1587 and 1601, but military facilities on the Isle of Wight were neglected under James I. The artillery platforms and coastal forts that Henry VIII built at Cowes, Sandham, and Yarmouth fell into varying states of disrepair. Yarmouth had four brass demi-culverins in 1623, but Cowes and Sandham each had but one demi-culverin and one brass falconet.[58]

Charles I's wars with France and Spain in the late 1620s revived the island's military significance. Planners took note that Carisbrooke Castle and the coastal forts were dilapidated and poorly defended, with none served by more than a captain and three gunners. Sandham Castle, which protected the island's vital southern shore, was at risk of falling into the sea.[59] When Charles visited the Isle of Wight in June 1627, as a wartime monarch, he promised repairs to Sandham and other facilities, but the money was slow to arrive.[60] Leading islanders complained in January 1629 that 'our castles and forts were either demolished or so unserviceable as not able to defend us'. The government pledged £3,000 towards island defences, promising new demi-culverins for Sandham, though it took many years for gun platforms to be equipped.[61] All of this investment went into coastal installations, leaving the inland fortress at Carisbrooke much as it was in 1603. Ten pieces of ordnance destined for Sandham Castle were still at the Tower awaiting shipment in June 1636.[62] Island officials were still complaining in 1640 that their forts were out of repair and their munitions under-supplied.[63]

Part of the government's strategy for the Isle of Wight was to have the island 'well peopled, and the inhabitants constantly resident, well armed, and ordered for defence'.[64] Close to 2,000 volunteer militiamen could be mobilized at the beginning of Charles I's reign, but they had the usual defects of inaptitude, ill equipment, and lack of training.[65] Sir Edward Conway in 1626 thought at least 200 soldiers necessary for the defence of the Isle of Wight, rather than the few dozen professionals currently deployed.[66]

Huge numbers of troops arrived on the island in the build-up to the expedition to the Isle of Rhé in western France. Sir John Oglander scathingly described some of their swaggering captains as 'such young men as never saw sword drawn—fitter for a May game than to manage an army'.[67] As many as 3,000 troops were billeted on the island by the end of 1627, including the Scottish 'redshanks', who disgraced themselves by rapes and robberies and poaching the king's deer.[68] Further disturbances were caused by mariners avoiding impressment, and runaway sailors, who hid in the island's woods and secret places.[69] Though islanders themselves were not normally pressed or levied for the king's forces, the military presence put strains on the Isle of Wight's civilian culture.

*

Other islands made minor contributions to England's maritime shield. Elizabethan St Nicholas Island, offshore from Plymouth, had facilities for four resident gunners in peacetime, and twelve in time of war. St Nicholas was further fortified in the 1590s, when as many as forty men were sent to guard it from Spain. In 1601, the island claimed seventeen pieces of brass and iron ordnance, mostly demi-culverins and sakers, though almost half of them were deemed 'unserviceable'. Neglected under James I, the installations on St Nicholas were repaired from time to time under Charles I, but played little part in the nation's affairs. In 1627, they were used as a staging post for impressed soldiers on their way to the Channel Islands, and later saw service as a state prison. The St Nicholas garrison in 1638 comprised fifteen men, who spent some of their time recovering shipwrecks.[70]

Holy Island, also known as Lindisfarne, a fortified dependency of the Berwick garrison off the coast of Northumberland, was among the minor outposts of the Stuart realm. Barely 2,250 paces east to west, and 1,250 paces north to south, it was an island only at high tide. Rocky, 'unpeopled, and unprofitable', according to John Speed, with soil unfit for tillage and poor for grazing, Holy Island nonetheless had an ancient church, a small fort, and 'a commodious haven'.[71] Its military significance lay in its location. The English government fortified Holy Island during its sixteenth-century wars with Scotland, and neglected it when the northern threat abated. The island had been demilitarized under James I, but Charles I's Secretary of State Sir Henry Vane recognized it as 'a place of too great importance to let fall through neglect', which acquired 'wonderfully great consequence' in England's renewed Scottish wars at the end of the 1630s.[72]

The Welsh island of Anglesey faced perennial perils, being vulnerable to attacks from the sea. The pirate problem was unabated. The bishop of Bangor warned Charles I in December 1625 that Irish Catholics and their local co-religionists might be plotting an invasion. 'These parts are very weak and unfurnished,' he wrote, detailing the decrepitude of the island's military equipment. Arms were old and unserviceable, and the gunpowder 'through age and worse keeping turned to dirt'. Defences were inadequate, despite the presence of medieval Beaumaris Castle, Lewis Bayly continued, for 'one hundred armed men would surprise the Isle of Anglesey', which, once lost, 'God forbid, cannot so easily be recovered'.[73] This claim would be tested several times in the decades that followed.

No such pessimism afflicted the Isle of Man, which was a world unto itself, under its feudal overlords. Fortunately for the Stanley earls, and for their English monarchs, the Isle was rarely a target of foreign predation. Though potentially of value to England's enemies, Man lay too far north to be hotly involved in European wars. The last French and Scottish raids were in the fourteenth century, though Spain threatened more in the 1590s. The pirate menace was, however, perdurable, and the island gained the attention of freebooters, smugglers, and privateers. Its defensive capability was enhanced by being 'situated in a very boisterous sea, encompassed on all sides with high cliffs of stone, or precipices of sand'. 'The island stands like a man in triumph upon the sea, exalting its head on high', affirmed one seventeenth-century traveller. The two medieval castles, Peel on St Patrick's Isle to the west, and Castle Rushen on the south, were maintained by the earls of Derby, with neither oversight nor investment from London. Castle Rushen was especially 'well-fortified', and 'planted with drakes, field pieces, and cannon of several sizes'.[74]

Channel Island Castles

A recurrent fear of English strategists was that the French might attack the Channel Islands. With no great port of their own between Brittany and Calais, the French, it was believed, wanted only opportunity to strike at England's islands.[75] Even in peacetime their intentions could not be trusted. Island security depended upon the advantages of geography, investment in military infrastructure, manpower, leadership, and munitions. Only the efforts of government kept them 'free from surprise, spoil, invasion or conquest'.[76] Only divine favour brought these efforts success.

The islanders themselves could not be expected to put up much resistance. The inhabitants, according to an assessment of Guernsey in 1567, were 'without armour, inexperienced, and not to be trusted for courage'.[77] Another report two decades later found the Channel Islands 'inhabited of poor labourers and fishermen unexpert of the wars, in respect of the puissance of Brittany and Normandy bordering near upon them'. The soldier Sir John Norris scorned Jerseymen in 1591 as 'a fearful people, that take the alarm...upon sight of every ship that is seen, and would run out of the island if they had a back door'. Another report in 1607 judged the inhabitants 'not to be relied upon, seeing they make not profession of arms, though in truth their hearts are well-affected to his majesty'.[78]

Guernsey, 'a place of great consequence, lying in the very heart of the Channel', was credited with possessing a natural harbour 'able to contain the greatest navy that ever sailed upon the ocean'.[79] It was, declared a visitor in the 1640s, 'the best harbour that the wit of man...could not devise to plan it better for that purpose'.[80] Guarding this asset, on a rocky islet outside St Peter Port, accessible only by boat or tidal causeway, was the medieval fortress of Castle Cornet. Though obviously outmoded, Guernsey's castle was still considered 'the key and guard of all these poor Norman relics'.[81] Established in the thirteenth century, and period-ically upgraded and expanded, Castle Cornet was in 'extreme ruin and decay' when commissioners examined it in 1567. They found its crumbling walls 'ill-fashioned and disorderly' and its inner wards 'so decayed that some part falls yearly'. Much of the iron ordnance was outdated and rusted by salt sea air. Though the castle might provide some defence against pirates, commissioners thought it would be no match for the French, who 'have lately practiced to invade these isles'.[82] There began a century-long process of refurbishment, often inter-rupted, that sought to make Castle Cornet an efficient centre of power. Incoming governors repeatedly complained about the sad state of the castle and the neglect by their predecessors of the island's fortifications.

Nearly all the lime, lead, and timber needed for this and other Channel Island castles had to be shipped from England, which was also the source of funding. Sir Thomas Leighton, who became governor of Guernsey in 1570, secured money from London, oak from Hampshire, and lime from Dorset to repair Castle Cornet. He asked for brass culverins, to replace unserviceable weapons, and attempted to make the fortress battle-ready.[83] Castle Cornet was further fortified against the Spanish threat in the 1590s but was never put to the test. Leighton wanted a garrison of three hundred soldiers, but the normal wartime establishment was only twenty-eight men (reduced to fourteen in peacetime).[84] When Henry Danvers became governor in 1621, he argued for a Guernsey garrison of a hundred men, but soon adjusted his request to the more manageable level of fifty. In July 1624, however, towards the end of the long Jacobean peace, Castle Cornet still had only a single gunner and fourteen warders.[85] On occasions when a chaplain could be found, Castle Cornet was the only place in Presbyterian Guernsey to use the prayer book services of the Church of England.[86]

The renewal of war in the later 1620s justified doubling the Guernsey garrison to one hundred, then doubling it again between 1627 and 1629.[87] Every increase of English soldiers on the island strained relations with the civilian population, tested understanding of the constitution, and posed new challenges to governors and bailiffs. 'And the better to conform some perverse spirits amongst that people, who conceive themselves little less than a free state, and are rather peevish in their opinions than sensible of their own dangers,' the governor of Guernsey and his lieutenant were empowered to impose martial law. This apparent over-throw of custom so 'startled the people' that the government was forced to declare in September 1628 that, despite the previous announcement, martial law was intended 'only for the better regulating and governing of the 200 soldiers'. King Charles, through his Council, reassured the islanders that he intended nothing 'to diminish or abrogate the ancient liberties and privileges you have enjoyed in the times of his royal progenitors'.[88] Similar reassurance would be required in subsequent periods of crisis as the state exercised its power.

Guns were always a problem, subject to neglect and damage, and the decay of their wooden carriages. Salt spray and hard weather made a poor environment, in which iron rusted and wood rotted. Ordnance accounts during the Jacobean peace show Castle Cornet equipped with only thirteen pieces of mounted brass artillery, and eighteen of iron, several of them sadly 'unfit'. The armoury included hand-guns, muskets, pikes, halberds, and bows and arrows, with just three lasts of gunpowder in store.[89] It was enough to ward off occasional pirates, but unlikely to withstand a determined assault. Warships and East Indiamen were better armed and equipped.

A build-up of weaponry accompanied the lurch to war, though reports of the number and condition of ordnance depended on who was doing the counting. One account in 1624 reported forty great guns at Castle Cornet, while another later in the year noted forty-seven pieces, all with new field carriages.[90] The Earl of Danby reported 'forty-seven pieces of great ordnance' within the circuit of Castle Cornet in 1627, while his chaplain Peter Heylyn two years later found 'almost an hundred pieces of ordnance, whereof about sixty are of brass'.[91]

Guernsey's dependent islands Alderney and Sark were even less well provided. Though ravaged by pirates and threatened by the French, Elizabethan Alderney had just two sakers, four minons, and two falcons to face the foe. Officials rated it very vulnerable if 'any breach of amity should fall out between the realms of England and France'.[92] Fortunately for the islanders, when the French did mount an expedition against Alderney in April 1628, a great tempest 'prevented their designs'.[93] Efforts to fortify these outpost islands for Charles I's wars had limited success, though Sark had six pieces of ordnance by 1638. William Essex, the elderly and cash-strapped lieutenant of under-resourced Alderney, blamed the island's troubles on 'the imbecility of my deputy, and the great want of all necessaries for defence'.[94]

*

Jersey, too, was 'a frontier place', 'farthest remote from the rest of [the king's] dominions... being thereby most exposed to danger of invasion or incursion of foreign enemies'.[95] The coast of France could easily be seen from Jersey's eastern shores. Nature aided the island's defence, for 'the strength of Jersey does chiefly consist in its situation', surrounded by water and rocks. But that still left 'many places open for an invader to land in'.[96] It would take investment, art, and effort to make the island safe. Paced by the pulse of peace and war, Jersey's castles, like those elsewhere, experienced phases of neglect followed by urgent upgrade and repair. Its garrison of English soldiers had a long history of friction with local Francophone inhabitants, who complained of their offences against 'right and the laws and good customs of the said isle'.[97] Jersey could muster as many as 2,700 men with arms, but how they might fare against an invading army was open to question.[98] In 1628, the island parishes had thirty small field pieces between them, but no great skill in artillery, and 'great want of powder and ammunition'.[99]

Jersey's traditional stronghold was the medieval fortress of Mont Orgueil, a proud place indeed, sometimes called Gorey Castle after the nearby community. 'Strongly built and stately', it stood on a rocky promontory, joined to the main island by a narrow isthmus, and had been expanded and improved to meet centuries of danger. Like Guernsey's Castle Cornet, it dated from the thirteenth century, and was modified for the gunpowder age. By Elizabethan times, however, Mont Orgeuil Castle was seriously out of date, bypassed by developments in warfare and munitions. Sir John Norris in 1591 deemed it 'of very little account'. A seventeenth-century commentator observed that Mont Orgeuil 'was undoubtedly strong in times of bows and arrows', but was now much decayed.[100] Though apparently formidable and imposing, 'a lofty pile' in William Prynne's phrase, Mont Orgueil was overlooked by nearby Mont St Nicolas, 'which being possessed by an enemy, the castle could not long endure the fury of the cannon'.[101]

Elizabethan engineers designed a new fort, named for the queen, that was more modern and better protected. The building of Castle Elizabeth was contemporary with Star Castle on Scilly, and construction took just as long. Situated on an islet near St Helier, Castle Elizabeth was 'compassed about with the sea six hours each flowing of the tide'. Comparing the facilities, one author generously described the old castle as superior 'in stateliness ... though not in strength'.[102] Another judged Castle Elizabeth 'the key of the island' and rated it almost impregnable but by famine'.[103] A smaller Tudor gun platform in St Aubin's bay, west of Castle Elizabeth, was reinforced in 1643 and was known as St Aubin's fort.

Captains of Jersey repeatedly declared that, though 'the castle is sufficiently furnished of munitions to pass over some little time of peace and quietness', more dangerous circumstances left it 'less than sufficient to defend ... against the enemy'.[104] Governor Sir John Peyton found Mont Orgeuil in 1607 'in much decay', while 'the new castle called Elizabeth' was 'unfinished'. Much of the ordnance was too dangerous to be serviceable, even if there had been powder and shot to fire it. Peyton justified expanded expenditure on Jersey's defence by telling the Earl of Salisbury in May 1610 that 'in every hundred crowns bestowing I save from ruin that which would in short time cost five hundred'.[105] Both castles needed to be strengthened, he argued, even though England was at peace (see Figure 9).

Jersey's castles were still considered 'disfurnished' in 1615, when Peyton requested more armaments from the Tower of London. The Master of the Ordnance begrudgingly authorized the transfer of two minions and two falconets to Mont Orgeuil, field carriages for other heavy guns, and new platforms for the guns at Castle Elizabeth.[106] An inventory in May 1617 listed sixteen pieces of ordnance at Mont Orgeuil, and eighteen at Castle Elizabeth, few of them more potent than sakers.[107]

Hastily equipped and braced for attack in 1628, Castle Elizabeth mustered thirty-seven pieces of ordnance, with a hundred barrels of gunpowder in store,

Figure 9. Mont Orgeuil, 1783 (Alamy Images)

though insufficient victuals to withstand a siege.[108] Another spurt of refurbishment in 1634 fixed the roofs, mended the locks, and swept the chimneys of Jersey's two castles, without much altering their military effectiveness.[109] Castle Elizabeth in April 1635 had eleven brass pieces and thirteen of iron, including two culverins and five demi-culverins. Mont Orgeuil was more sparingly defended, being valued more as government offices than a military bastion. The governor's chaplain was based at the old castle, which also served as a prison.[110] The lawyer William Prynne, who spent three years incarcerated in Jersey, mentioned just 'fifteen cast pieces of artillery' in Mont Orgeuil,

> With sundry murdering chambers, planted so,
> As best may fence itself, and hurt a foe
> ... strong enough till war begins to thunder.[111]

Castle Elizabeth was supposed to have thirty soldiers, plus a porter and a master gunner, and Mont Orgeuil was supposed to have twenty men, but both were under strength. A remarkable list of Jersey's soldiers in 1617 gives the name, age, marital status, and place of birth of each man on the establishment, and whether they resided in the castle or on the island. Most hailed from the mainland (principally Somerset, Hampshire, and Dorset); their average age was 45, and several were in their sixties; almost two-thirds were married, and most of the men with wives lived outside the castle. Another list from Mont Orgeuil in 1626 includes the soldier William Harbin, aged 76. Jersey, it appears, was garrisoned by ageing veterans, rather than by fighting men in their prime.[112] Since it was the governor's responsibility to maintain the garrison, it was not surprising that he was skimping on expense.[113] A chronic problem, only occasionally documented, was governors keeping garrisons below strength and pocketing the difference in pay. Successive governors asked for more men and munitions, but money for reinforcements was slow in coming, stores remained unfurnished, and deliveries were unfulfilled.[114] Rivalries between governors and bailiffs reduced efficiency and hindered the collaboration required for construction and training.

War with France and Spain mandated an expanded garrison, and the Council authorized the sending of two hundred more men to Jersey in July 1627. Many of these soldiers proved 'incorrigible and inefficient' and had to be replaced.[115] Billeted on Jersey, they had little to do besides quarrel with each other and with the islanders, and, when orders came to redeploy to Holland in July 1629, after England and France had made peace, an embarrassing number went missing. Some hid among the rocks on the island, and a few English soldiers even fled to France.[116]

The security of England's islands depended upon the blessings of providence, and the inactivity of aggressors, as well as the provision of fortresses and weapons. Their status was little changed between 1560 and 1640, though their defensive capability was hardened. Their provision and repair caused recurrent friction between military and civilian authorities. Early Stuart governors and captains could not have imagined that when their islands were actually put to the test the challengers would be fellow countrymen, even fellow islanders, in the catastrophe of civil war. The crisis of the British kingdoms, which led to the downfall of Charles I, saw islanders shooting at each other. The emergency was internal, local, within the archipelago, and between the mainland and its islands. The guns of Castle Cornet, intended to defy the French, were trained instead in the 1640s on civilians in St Peter Port. Jersey's ordnance was likewise ranged against English shipping. Other islands experienced political division and military challenge. The only invasion fleets successfully to subdue a fortified island were parliament's navy at Scilly in 1646 and 1651, and at Jersey and the Isle of Man in 1651. Island fortresses fell when their external support evaporated, and when they were attacked rather than defended by forces based in London. As developments in the revolutionary era demonstrated, it would take patience, strong preparation, overwhelming naval superiority, and relatively calm conditions to bring an island to submission.

8

Refuge and Resistance
in Times of Troubles

The British civil wars of the seventeenth century—sometimes called 'the wars of
the three kingdoms', and more narrowly and euphemistically 'England's
troubles'—began in Scotland in 1638 and ended with the Cromwellian conquest
of Ireland in 1652. The central phase of the conflict pitting the Stuart crown
against the Westminster parliament was fought in the island periphery as well as
the English heartland. Indeed, the struggle could not be resolved until offshore
resistance was overcome. One might not recognize this from the lack of attention
accorded to the islands in standard histories of the conflict. Although this period is
one of the most intensively researched and most hotly debated in British history,
its offshore aspects are rarely explored.[1]

The catastrophe of civil war and revolution exacerbated strains and rifts in
England's island communities. When English loyalties fractured in the 1640s, the
islands too became divided between king and parliament. Government and
faction became more than ever contested. Island armaments and defences—
more neglected than nurtured in previous decades—acquired unexpected importance and were subject to fierce competition. This chapter examines the island
episodes in a complex internecine conflict that extended across the British Isles
and beyond. The archipelagic focus offered here allows a decentred view of the
times of troubles, a fresh perspective on a familiar story. Insularity insulated the
islands from the most destructive campaigns of the civil war, until turns of
circumstance brought the conflict to their shores.

Island communities exhibited every variant of partisanship and neutrality, but
their governors generally determined their path of allegiance. The Isle of Wight, so
close to the mainland, was swiftly secured for parliament. The Isle of Man,
controlled by the Earl of Derby, remained wholeheartedly for the king. So too
did Anglesey, despite some factional division. The thinly populated Scillies, under
the royalist Godolphins, were solid for King Charles. Lundy also remained a
royalist asset. Parliament would have to claim them by force.

The situation of the Channel Islands was more complicated, as England's
revolutionary crisis exposed and tested their constitutional peculiarities. The
local squabbles of governors, bailiffs, and jurats continued, but were overshadowed by the emergencies of the kingdom. Riven by 'intestine discord and

England's Islands in a Sea of Troubles. David Cressy, Oxford University Press (2020). © David Cressy 2020.
DOI: 10.1093/oso/9780198856603.001.0001

party feuds ... bitter disputes, recriminations, and impeachments',[2] the islands became divided between supporters of the parliament and loyalists to the crown. A goodly number wished simply to be left alone. Parliamentary supporters secured the island of Guernsey, but lieutenant governor Sir Peter Osborne held the fortress of Castle Cornet for the king. Jersey affected allegiance to both king and parliament until bailiff Sir Philip Carteret declared Jersey for the crown in 1643, and occupied Castle Elizabeth and Mont Orgeuil. The king to whom the islanders looked for protection became locked in conflict with half his subjects. The parliament, in which islanders took no part, and whose laws they did not recognize, sent forth fleets and armies for their subjugation. The eventual defeat of the royalists in every mainland theatre of operations drove some of them to seek refuge offshore.[3]

England's islands served as stepping stones to France or Ireland, and also as bases for a possible Stuart restoration. Arms, news, papers, and people found transport across a sea of troubles, from St George's Channel to the Gulf of St Malo. Jersey and the Scillies, in particular, were links in cross-channel networks of supply and communication, and served as havens for royalist privateers.[4] Prince Charles's sojourn in Jersey in 1646, and his return there as king-in-exile in 1649, made that island a centre of royalist resistance, before it too succumbed to the revolutionary state. Parliament's mastery of Guernsey, and eventual control of Jersey, subjected both islands to military exigencies, skirmishes, and sieges. The history can be related from a variety of sources, not least the testimony and observations of island residents. The journals and notebooks of the Guernsey schoolmaster Pierre le Roy,[5] the Jersey landowner Jean Chevalier,[6] and the minister of Sark Elie Brevint[7] add detail and texture to this mid-Stuart drama. Few English historians have acknowledged their witness, no doubt because they wrote in archaic French from relatively remote spheres of endeavour, but their testimony is remarkable for its freshness and immediacy.

Island strongholds generally maintained resistance longer than outposts in England because their fastnesses were too remote and too well fortified to be easily besieged or stormed. The defenders enjoyed the advantages of island isolation. Parliament briefly regained the Scillies in 1648, but royalists were not finally rousted from those isles until June 1651. Parliamentary victory at the battle of Worcester in September 1651 ended the civil wars on the mainland, but royalist diehards in England's islands maintained their defiance for several months longer. Anglesey was in parliamentary hands by 1 October, and the Isle of Man capitulated a month later. Resistance on Jersey, and at Castle Cornet on Guernsey, continued into the winter. Mont Orgeuil and Castle Elizabeth held out for Charles II until mid-December, and the subsequent surrender of Castle Cornet a few days later cemented commonwealth victory. By the end of 1651, all of England's islands were in parliamentary hands.

The Isle of Wight

Like gentlemen and office-holders elsewhere in England, the principal inhabitants of the Isle of Wight abhorred the prospect of civil war. As 'tumults' approached in August 1642, they pledged to defend 'the true protestant religion established in the Church of England, against all papists or other ill affected persons' and to 'join the utmost of our endeavours for the peace of this island'. Their loyalty was pledged to the king 'and to his parliament', with no desire to choose between them. In another declaration, the islanders promised to prevent 'the incoming of any foreign forces', on behalf of both king and parliament, though the tendency of their allegiance was signalled by their allowance to the Earl of Warwick of 'what supplies of fresh victual he should be pleased to accept of' for the incipient parliamentary army.[8]

Parliament moved efficiently to secure the island's castles and to quarantine royalist zealots. Captain Barnaby Burley brandished his weapons on the battlements of Yarmouth Castle, swearing that he would never 'obey an ordinance of parliament without his majesty's consent' and 'that before he would lose his honour he would die a thousand deaths'. He was carried away under guard. Cowes Castle was put in safe hands, and Sandham was secured, according to the officer in charge, 'to the great rejoicing of the inhabitants of the island'.[9] The only remaining threat was the castle at Carisbrooke, the island's principal fortress.

Parliament stripped the popishly inclined Jerome Weston, Earl of Portland, of his governorship of the Isle of Wight, and replaced him with the much more reliable Philip Herbert, Earl of Pembroke. But, even after Portland's arrest in August 1642, his countess clung to Carisbrooke, hoping to hold it for the king. It took an act of vigilante action to bring about her capitulation. Moses Read, the mayor of Newport, secured the assistance of captains of ships in the River Medina, and marched the Newport militia, with four hundred naval auxiliaries, against the castle. With less than two dozen defenders, and barely three days' provisions, the castle was disadvantaged, but the countess, a daughter of the Earl of Lennox, 'went to the platform with a match in her hand, vowing she would fire the first cannon herself ... unless honourable terms were granted'. After making this Amazon display, she allowed the castle to surrender. Though short of provisions, Carisbrooke Castle was found to have sixty barrels of gunpowder, and arms for 1,500 men.[10]

Having secured the Isle of Wight without bloodshed, parliament held it throughout the civil war, replacing cavalier administrators with army officers. Although royalist elements had pockets of strength, they never won the island back for King Charles. The king's supporters had little chance of shaking London's military grip, though the abundance of creeks and havens, and the short boat ride to the mainland, offered opportunities for people to slip in or out of the island unobserved. Governor Pembroke's task was to safeguard the Isle of Wight 'in these times of imminent danger', against 'foreign forces as well as home-bred designs', by expanding the island's garrisons and hardening its defences.[11] Military shipments to the island in August 1643 included 300 bandoliers, 500 swords, a ton of bullets, and 100 barrels of gunpowder; in September, 10 culverins and 20 sakers; and, in December, 600 more soldiers.[12] Parliament maintained this level of force for most of the civil war and poured additional resources into the Isle of Wight after the king became a prisoner there in 1647.

None of this weaponry was deployed in anger. The Isle of Wight was never invaded, nor did 'malignants' rise up in revolt, except for the hot-headed Captain Burley. Perhaps the greatest excitement was caused by the arrival in April 1645 of the glamourous French intriguer Marie de Rohan, the Duchess of Chevreuse, a confidante of the French royal family. English naval forces had intercepted two vessels carrying Madame Chevreuse and her company, along with 'papers and bills of exchange' for 'great sums of money', and brought them to Newport on the Isle of Wight for safe keeping. The purpose of her mission was obscure, but the presence of an exotic and voluptuous aristocrat in a small island town caused excitement, as well as speculation that she intended some service for Charles I and his queen. She was held on the island for two months until shipping could be arranged to take her to Dunkirk.[13]

Most extraordinary of all was the arrival of King Charles himself, in flight from his captors in November 1647. The king's year-long presence on the Isle of Wight made this somewhat sleepy backwater a hub of national and international attention. The imprisoned Charles I became the focus of mutinous mariners in the second civil war, who planned to attack the Isle of Wight in July 1648 in the hope of freeing their sovereign. Parliamentary commissioners crowded island hostelries that autumn to arrange a treaty that would free the kingdom. A further influx of parliamentary soldiers carried the king away to his end (see Chapter 12).

Anglesey

The island of Anglesey, a musket shot away from the mainland, had strategic significance as 'the nearest point of England or Wales to Dublin'. Its medieval castle at Beaumaris commanded the Menai Straits, and its coastline breasted the Irish Sea. Petitioners early in the civil war described Anglesey as 'an island situate between Ireland and Lancashire, lying open and subject to invasion on all parts, being daily robbed on our coast by the rebels of Ireland and parliament ships, which are many in number at this time in Liverpool'.[14] The region held for the king during most of the civil war, and the island was the last place in Wales to surrender to Westminster. Sir Thomas Bulkeley reported Anglesey 'in a very sheepish posture' in January 1643, when parliamentary armies approached, and considered moving his family to Ireland; but he remained to stiffen royalist resistance and spent heavily on Beaumaris Castle.[15]

When royalist forces collapsed in the summer of 1645, counsellors about Charles I considered where best to convey 'the king's person' away from danger. Charles was attempting to regroup 'his broken troops', when Lord Digby wrote to Prince Rupert from Raglan Castle on 13 July that the king intended to make a stand in Wales. 'It is unanimously understood here to be the safest and most effectual course for his majesty to cherish these parts with his presence.'[16] With his military options shrinking, the king moved north through the Brecon mountains, reaching Brecknock late on 4 August. Thoughts of flight and refuge were heavy on his mind when he wrote next day to Prince Charles that 'it is very fit for me now to prepare for the worst'. The king instructed his 15-year-old son and heir 'that my pleasure is, whensoever you find yourself in apparent danger of falling into the rebels' hands, that you convey yourself into France, and there to be under your mother's care, who is to have the absolute full power of your education, in all things except religion'.[17] These would be powerful considerations for Prince Charles's handlers as they retreated further west, and during the prince's sojourns on the Isles of Scilly and Jersey.

September brought news of further disasters: the fall of Bristol, Montrose's defeat at Philiphaugh, and the debacle at Rowton Heath. As the royal party considered 'whither to go', and where to position the king, some advisers recommended Anglesey as 'a place of safety, and an island fruitful enough to support his forces, which would defend itself against any winter attempt, and from whence he might be easily transported into Ireland or Scotland'. Rejecting this advice, the king decided to move from Denbigh to Worcester, and thence back to Oxford. Anglesey remained an option, as a refuge or part of an escape route, but divisions and jealousies within the island diminished its attraction.[18] 'You may see how near the lees we are drawn,' wrote the cavalier John Ashburnham in December 1645. Losses and misfortunes compounded each other, leaving 'no more hopes of determining this quarrel in the field'. One royalist contingency plan involved getting the Duke of York to Anglesey, to the temporary shelter of Beaumaris, and thence to Ireland, 'there to stay in case the peace be made, if not to go from thence into France'.[19]

Divided and demoralized, yet clinging to status and privilege, the royalist defenders of North Wales braced for defeat. John Williams, the Welsh archbishop of York who had retreated to Conway Castle, found only 'treachery among false friends, and disagreement among true ones'. Williams thought it 'prudence to preserve the Bulkeleys, that great family of Anglesey, in the vice-admiralty of those seas', in hopes they could command the loyalty of lieutenants, gentry, and landlords, but other men of ambition stirred 'mutinies and high threats' in this year of darkness and gloom.[20]

Anglesey eventually fell to military and political pressures amid the general royalist collapse. While parliamentary forces besieged Caernarvon Castle in May 1646, they offered bribes of £2,000 for the surrender of Anglesey 'to draw the inhabitants from their allegiance'. Pressure mounted in June, as parliamentary frigates appeared off Beaumaris, blocking resupply and inhibiting retreat. Caernarvon capitulated on 4 June, but Anglesey held out ten days longer, its surrender effectively ending the civil war in Wales. The island was now under parliamentary protection, though by no means solid in its allegiance.[21] Anglesey men petitioned their new masters 'to have the garrison as much decreased as may be, the island being in the nature of a garrison in itself, able to defend itself against any ordinary invasion'.[22]

Royalist hopes revived two years later when Sir John Owen led a revolt in North Wales that sparked the second civil war. Parliament learned early in July 1648 that 'the king's party' was 'still very active' on Anglesey, and resolved 'to keep the island for the king', who was at this time a prisoner in the Isle of Wight. This threat became explicit on 14 July, when the self-declared 'chief inhabitants' of Anglesey rose in arms against the parliament, intending 'to govern themselves according to the Commission of Array'. More than three dozen gentlemen, led by Thomas and Richard Bulkeley, pledged in writing 'to preserve the said island ... in due obedience to his sacred majesty', for the 'reinstating of our gracious sovereign (who hath long endured the tyranny and oppression of his barbarous and bloody enemies) to his rights, dominions, and dignity'. Westminster officials observed that without the Bulkeleys 'there had been no revolt in Anglesey', notwithstanding their 'promises of fidelity ... upon the first reducement of it to the parliament'.[23] Once more in royalist hands, the island offered a base and refuge for the cavaliers, connected by sea to their other offshore outposts of Jersey, the Isle of Man, and Ireland.[24] No one could predict that they would inevitably be dislodged.

Anglesey in 1648 was by no means solid for the king. A rival faction announcing itself as 'the well-affected of the commonalty of the isle and county of Anglesey' invited parliament to send troops to crush the royalist revolt. Parliament mobilized ships and men for the reduction of Anglesey, while royalists also dispatched ships 'to fortify the courage of those islanders'.[25] A civil war in miniature played out about the Menai Straits. Owen Wood of Rhosmeirch, who served as high sheriff under the Bulkeleys, later tried to persuade parliament that he opposed the island's revolt 'to the uttermost of his power'.[26]

An account prepared by the royalist Sir John Byron related how, 'through the endeavours of Colonel Robinson, the isle of Anglesey declared for the king', and the mutinous parliamentary commander of Beaumaris 'joined with them in it'. Their force of 100 horse and 300 musketeers was augmented by a scatter of royalists from north-west England, especially following their defeat at Preston in August. Byron managed to swim his horse across to Anglesey from Abermenai, west of Caernarvon, but was shocked 'instead of a welcome to receive a repulse'.

Royalists on the island were factionalized and bitterly divided. Byron blamed archbishop Williams for thwarting his plans and aspirations. He was also upset to be overruled by the son of the prominent Lord Bulkeley, 'an ignorant and wilful young man'. Byron believed that Anglesey could be defended for several months, and could be reinforced with soldiers from Ireland, but Williams and other defeatists declared that enemy forces were irresistible, and that expectation of relief was vain. Byron, with hindsight, declared 'it had been very easy to defend the island from a far greater force, had any man of care and judgement [such as himself] had the ordering of the business'. But ignorance and negligence allowed a night-time landing of the enemy with 'as many men as nine boats would carry', who easily surprised the guard. Anglesey fell with little resistance after a skirmish on 1 October. Byron managed to escape to the Isle of Man, and thence to Holland and France, while other leading defenders accepted exile or sought reconciliation. Parliament congratulated Colonel John Jones and other commanders on successfully 'gathering forces, boats, and other provisions for reducing the Isle of Anglesey' with so little loss in deploying them. The island was again under parliamentary control and could serve for transshipment of troops for the reduction of Ireland.[27]

Holy Island

Holy Island, small and neglected, was drawn into the nation's troubles when England and Scotland went to war. In September 1640, when the Scottish Covenanters appeared ascendant, Captain Robert Rugg of Holy Island assured his masters in London: 'I have sworn all my men sacramentally never to yield, without famine enforced.' Rugg had twenty-two men under his command, but they were short of munitions, candles, victuals, and pay.[28] As civil war loomed, Sir John Brook replaced Rugg as keeper and captain of Holy Island and Ferne Island, with orders for 'one gunner, a gunner's mate, and nine soldiers to be always resident'. Restocked with arms and ammunition, Holy Island would help to secure the seaways between Berwick and London.[29]

The conflict mostly bypassed Holy Island, its fortunes fluctuating with those of nearby Northumbria. It ended as it began, as a minor parliamentary asset. When King Charles fled to the Scots in May 1646, the kingdom's northern resources acquired greater importance. The House of Commons decided that Holy Island should be reinforced again, to prevent it being 'surprised by a foreign power or possessed by any not well affected to the parliament'.[30] The island's vulnerability was tested again in the second civil war, which jangled nerves everywhere. Captain Robert Batten reported in July 1648 on his 'besieged condition' at Holy Island, the cavaliers being 'masters of all the country hereabouts'.[31] Parliament responded by ordering as many as a hundred men to expand the garrison, but they would have little to do except to scan the sea for pirates and privateers.[32]

The Isles of Scilly

The Isles of Scilly were a seigneurial backwater until they were drawn into streams of larger significance by the exigencies of civil war. They were even a source of humorous though not very subtle punning on its people as 'silly'.[33] The Scillies gained importance as a royalist stronghold after 1642, and later as a refuge for retreating cavaliers.

Obliged by their grant to defend the islands 'upon all occasions', the Godolphin family of proprietors remained determinedly loyal. The latest Sir Francis Godolphin had been 'Captain of the Isles of Scilly and the new fort and garrison there' since March 1640 and maintained his allegiance to the crown.[34] He funded his operations from the estates of west-country 'delinquents', as well as from maritime prizes.[35] In September 1642, when a ship from London with supplies for Protestants in Ireland took shelter in Scilly, mistakenly believing 'the inhabitants to be well-affected to the parliament', the governor seized the cargo and converted the vessel into a royalist man of war.[36]

Parliamentary ships kept watch on the Scillies throughout the period of conflict, but made no serious effort to attack them. The islands grew in significance after the parliamentary victories of 1646, when defeated royalists sought refuge further west, and the Scillies became bases for privateering. The brief presence of Prince Charles and his entourage on Scilly in the spring of that year made the islands a centre of national attention.

Captured parliamentarians grew familiar with civil-war Scilly, while awaiting ransom or exchange. Mainland royalists also considered St Mary's Castle as a suitable prison for high-ranking detainees. In August 1645, King Charles instructed Governor Godolphin 'to receive and detain in your custody the body of James Duke Hamilton...for safeguarding and keeping' on Scilly, after the disgraced nobleman was moved from Pendennis.[37] By November, however, Hamilton had been moved to St Michael's Mount in Cornwall, where he remained until parliamentary forces arrived the following April.[38] The mutinous royalist commander Sir Richard Grenville, who was imprisoned at Launceston Castle and then at the Mount after feuding with fellow officers, was also ordered early in 1646 'to be conveyed speedily to the islands of Scilly, to be there kept as close prisoner'. Subsequent directives countermanded this order, with instructions to transfer Grenville to Jersey or Lundy, to be held at the king's pleasure. In the event, Grenville went to none of these islands, at least as a prisoner, and escaped to France during the confusion of the royalist collapse.[39]

As King Charles's prospects in the west disintegrated, the primitive royalist outpost on Scilly was prepared for the reception of a prince. The beleaguered royalist garrison at Exeter came close to mutiny for fear of being abandoned. Rumour circulated within the army that Prince Charles's handlers were taking him to France. A petition circulating in Cornwall in December 1645 urged the prince to declare that 'no adverse fortune should compel him to depart the kingdom'. Royalists in England still hoped to rally around a royal person, but among exiled courtiers in France 'the prince's coming was hourly expected'. Some members of the prince's Council smelled defeat, and already imagined the delights of Paris. Resisting this, Sir Edward Hyde, the Chancellor of the Exchequer, thought it best for the prince to remain within the king's dominions, telling Sir Henry Jermyn that, if 'the season shall require it, we may be able to steal to Scilly or Jersey, where we may safely take any new resolutions shall be thought fit'. Some of the prince's advisers, Hyde perhaps among them, 'who were very faithful, and tender of his safety, would rather wish him in the hands of the enemy' than under the control of the French.[40] The question of where best to seat the Stuart heir, and where he should keep his court, remained unresolved and controversial for most of the next five years.

Royalist forces in Devon and Cornwall crumbled in the face of the parliamentary advance, making the disposition of the prince most urgent. When Sir Thomas Fairfax's army reached Bodmin on 2 March 1646, Prince Charles's advisers decided it was time to escape 'a very Cornish mousetrap'. Most of the king's forces in the west surrendered on 12 March, though Exeter held out for another month. Pendennis Castle, the last royal stronghold in the west, capitulated on 17 August, and some of its defenders scattered to Jersey and the Scillies. Royalists everywhere were in disarray. King Charles himself fled to the Scots in May, and his wartime capital of Oxford surrendered in July. It was *sauve qui peut* for the king's supporters.[41]

Some of Prince Charles's closest advisers remained undecided where to take him, even as they abandoned Pendennis Castle in 'haste and disorder'. They joined a panicked and bedraggled group aboard the *Phoenix* on the night of 3 March, uncertain of their destination. As Sir Edward Hyde later recalled, 'the public resolution was for Scilly', but the option remained open 'when they were at sea to go for Jersey, if the wind was fair for one and cross to the other'. On this occasion, wind and weather took them west rather than south. Their rescue was facilitated by Dunkirk-built frigates supplied by the Marquis of Antrim.[42]

One of the retreating aristocrats, Lady Ann Fanshawe, the wife of a royal counsellor, recalled the discomfort of the journey, when the seamen 'broke open one of our trunks, and took out a bag of sixty pounds and a quantity of gold lace, with our best clothes and linen, and all my combs, gloves, and ribbons'. Safe but impoverished, and in her case heavy with child, she joined the prince's party, 'set ashore almost dead in the island of Scilly'.[43]

Prince Charles and his followers arrived at Scilly on 4 March 1646 and set up court in cramped quarters in St Mary's Castle, which was commanded by the brusque cavalier Sir Thomas Bassett.[44] As many as 300 soldiers, courtiers, clerks, and dependants augmented the island garrison, enduring 'the ill diet and ill accommodation of Scilly'.[45] Lady Fanshawe found herself in 'a bed, which was so vile, that my footman lay in a better ... we were destitute of clothes, and meat and fuel ... and truly we begged our daily bread of God, for we thought every meal our last'.[46] The prince's accommodation was not much better. Supplies of food and ammunition came occasionally from Ireland, Jersey, and St Malo, but never enough for a royal household or to support an extended siege. Neither news nor provisions arrived when needed, 'the wind having been contrary so long'.[47] Back on the mainland, Sir Ralph Hopton, lieutenant-general of the king's western army, did not even know that the prince had departed.[48]

Retreating royalists had imagined Scilly as 'a place of unquestionable strength' but upon inspection found 'the strength of the place in no degree answering their expectation or the fame of it'.[49] Almost immediately an advance party visited Jersey to inspect facilities and prepare them for Prince Charles.[50] John Osborne, the son of the captain of Guernsey's Castle Cornet, was among those who preceded the prince in evacuating Scilly, 'where victuals are extremely scarce'. He assumed that Prince Charles would remain there only 'till such times as the islands of Guernsey and Jersey may be secured for him'. Hearing that the prince was in Scilly, royalists elsewhere assumed, or feared, 'that he will be transported into France'.[51] The prince himself complained that he 'had not heard from the main in above a month' and was perpetually short of provisions since coming to Scilly.[52] His agents had already set out for the Channel Islands, by way of St Malo, to make them ready for 'his majesty's service'.[53]

A stream of letters from Henrietta Maria begged Prince Charles to move to a place of greater safety, ideally close to her bosom. Courtiers about the queen wrote urgently on 6 April for the prince to quit Scilly 'instantly' for Jersey or 'any port in France'. The obsequious Sir Henry Jermyn told Sir Edward Hyde that 'your stay in Scilly may have been necessary, but it hath been unfortunate, in that it is no abiding place, and a new venture must be run to find one'.[54]

Hearing that Prince Charles had reached Scilly, parliament dispatched a letter inviting him to London. The Speaker's letter was 'delivered by trumpet' under temporary truce on 11 April, demanding surrender and offering terms. The same ship brought the retreating royalist commanders Sir Ralph Hopton and Lord Arthur Capel to Scilly, where Hopton presented his 'Relation of the Proceedings in the West of England'. Unfortunately, according to Hopton, Prince Charles had no trumpeter of his own, but asked for a pass for his letter-carrier to go to London, 'and to return him to the Isle of Jersey', and also for passes for the prince's tutor, the Bishop of Salisbury, with his family and servants, 'to come to him in Jersey'. Prince Charles's letter did not reach Westminster until 26 April, by which time the royal entourage had already relocated across the Channel.[55] The appearance of a parliamentary fleet in Scilly waters exposed the vulnerability of the islands, and the prince's Council 'thought it high time to remove from that unsecure place' to the stronger refuge of Jersey.[56]

On 16 April 1646, Prince Charles and his company set sail for Jersey aboard *The Proud Black Eagle*, a twenty-four-gun frigate, whose commander Baldwin

Wake would be knighted for his service. By one account the prince was allowed to help with the steering. Others followed in the *Doggerbank* and a small gun-boat, packed with followers and gear. Ann Fanshawe described their arrival, 'the pilot, not knowing his way, sailed over the rocks . . . but God be praised, his highness and all of us came safe ashore through so great a danger'.[57] The governor of the Scillies, Sir Francis Godolphin, was among those sailing to Jersey, but he headed back to St Mary's in June to resume his office, and to trade in firearms and tin.[58]

Most cavalier notables left the Scillies with Prince Charles, but more retreating royalists soon replaced them. Some arrived after the fall of Mount St Michael, and more landed in the islands after the capitulation of Pendennis. A force of 300 men from Ireland arrived at Scilly in May 1646, too late to be of use to the prince, and Sir Thomas Bassett sent most of them back. They may have thought their mission had been to escort Prince Charles to Ireland.[59] Royalists across the maritime arc linking Jersey, France, and Ireland kept the Scillies supplied, but the parliamentary grip on the islands was tightening. The Scillies remained a strategic prize, though their political significance faded when the prince and his court moved away.

Having subdued all other royalist outposts in the west of England, parliamentary forces invested the Isles of Scilly, by sea and by land, and forced their capitulation. They demonstrated the inadequacy of Scilly's guns against a well-mounted operation. Vice Admiral William Batten accepted the surrender on 25 August 1646, and supervised the transfer of all 'ordnance, ammunition, and furniture of war' to parliament's control. Following convention, the victors took pains to preserve the honour of the defeated defenders. The soldiers of St Mary's garrison were obliged to hand over their weapons, but leading officers were allowed to keep their horses, arms, and goods. 'Old soldiers' who had become 'farmers and inhabitants of those islands' were allowed to stay, and the rest were offered passage to Cornwall or France. Sir Francis Godolphin and the royalist major Christopher Grosse remained behind as hostages for the due performance of these articles, while Colonel Anthony Buller assumed command at Star Castle.[60] Control of the civilian population became easier when they were disabused of the notion that parliament 'intended to put out the old inhabitants, and make a new plantation'.[61]

After winning Scilly, parliamentary authorities were lax in its maintenance. The islands slipped from their attention. Soldiers went unpaid, and supplies were not renewed. By May 1647, the naval commander Sir George Ayscue was using his own money to import food from Plymouth and entered questionable agreements with Bristol merchants. By June, the Scillies were in 'very great distress', with islanders and soldiers 'reduced to an allowance but of one half pound of bread a day, and scarce any other provision'. The promotion of Colonel Buller to be governor only began to address the problem.[62]

Conditions worsened, and neglect continued during 1648, while London was preoccupied with the second civil war. Warnings about the weakness of Scilly were ignored, until news broke in September that 'the garrison of the Isle of Scilly is revolted from the obedience of the parliament'. One report had it that 'a party from France' had seized the islands, and that the invaders declared 'that they will keep the said castle, forts, and island for his highness the Prince of Wales'. More reliable information described how conspirators within the garrison seized the castle while Governor Buller was at church, and made the leading officers their prisoners. Resistance among the islanders was half-hearted and easily quelled. The Scillies changed hands this time through internal betrayal rather than by dint of external assault.[63]

Defiant royalists rejected parliamentary addresses, saying, 'we are resolved with the hazard of our dearest blood to maintain and defend his majesty's absolute ["power" crossed out] property in these isles...as also the protestant religion according as it was professed and exercised in the times of greatest purity, and uninfected with the common contagion and licentiousness of England'.[64] The coup was a propaganda victory for the royalists, while King Charles himself remained locked up on the Isle of Wight. The Earl of Ormonde wrote dismissively to Lord Jermyn on 30 September that 'the Scilly business seems to be but a tumultuary rising of the common soldiers, and I fear will come to nothing'. He was wrong. Prince Charles reinstated Sir John Grenville as governor, although by the time he returned to the islands England had become a republic, and Charles was an emigré king.[65]

*

The royalist recapture of Scilly in September 1648 came too late to affect the outcome of the second civil war, but it gave the king's supporters a valuable base, connected by sea to Ireland, Jersey, the Isle of Man, and France. Weapons, supplies, troops, news, and instructions passed back and forth between the royalist island strongholds, as Prince Rupert offered to make Scilly 'a second Venice', a place of 'security and benefit' for the king.[66] Parliament scrambled to raise ships and men to retake this place 'of so great concernment', but failed to dislodge the 'malignants', who used Scilly to prey on coastal shipping.[67] By the time of the regicide, the royalists on Scilly had had a year to consolidate their position, though they remained deficient in money, provisions, and discipline.

Sir John Grenville, who had returned from Jersey to take command of the Isles of Scilly, observed in February 1649: 'the necessity and ill condition this place was in by reason of disorder, mutinies, and war.' He found his garrison distracted, supplies short, and too many commodities embezzled or lost. To restore vigour to the islands would take tireless leadership, and money. Grenville reported to Charles Stuart's advisers:

> I have with great industry endeavoured to regulate these people into some better condition and order, and have already brought them a little more conformable to the advancement of his majesty's service; and I hope every day they will know

more duty and obedience ... doubt not by God's blessing to give his majesty good account of this place.[68]

A first order of business was to recognize the Stuart succession, in defiance of the republicans in London. Bringing news of 'the most horrid murder and treason committed on the person of his most sacred majesty', Grenville declared 'a day of mourning and humiliation for our most fatal and incomparable loss'. Then on 22 February he proclaimed 'his majesty, now king', Charles II, 'with as much joy and cheerfulness as possibly could be expected after so sad news'.[69] In no other place in England was such a public proclamation possible.

Grenville's networks distributed clothing and victuals to besieged and distressed royalists in the Isles of Scilly, the Channel Islands, St Malo, Ireland, and south-west England.[70] The arrival of more officers and divines brought him useful 'additions of strength'. Among those trading in Scilly was Edward Wolley, a chaplain to the exiled Stuarts, who brought 'salt, powder, and corn', as well as coal, timber, hemp (to make ropes), and books from associates in Ireland.[71] Grenville's Scilly was among few remaining places where the services of the Church of England could be openly performed.

Though determined to extinguish royalist enclaves, the government in London did not act with the forcefulness that its rhetoric implied. Members of a parliamentary delegation sent to Scilly in March 1649, 'to know the state of the place, and to see if there might be any hope of recovery of it', were promptly taken prisoners and sent to Jersey. The Council of State responded by ordering naval commanders to seize equivalent 'persons at sea by whom you may make their exchange'. The task of dislodging the royalists from the islands was temporarily overshadowed by problems of prisoner redemption. The government was still trying to arrange 'exchanges for such of our men as are prisoners at Scilly' eight months later, and considered sending excess royalist prisoners to Barbados, 'if any merchants will take them'.[72] Parliamentary naval patrols could not prevent Scilly-based predators from adding to their tally of prizes. Nor could they stop 'disaffected persons' in western coastal communities from trafficking with island privateers and 'malignants', who sold plunder and purchased supplies with apparent impunity.[73]

So many prizes and prisoners were taken at sea that travellers called Scilly a second Algiers.[74] Royalists reported with satisfaction that 'Scilly is very rich by reason of several prizes and good wrecks ... which will better enable the governor to increase the number and fortification of that garrison'. Among the ships brought to Scilly in 1649 were a Virginia trader laden with tobacco and beaver, Flemings freighted with shoes, and a merchantman ferrying English troops and supplies to Ireland. This glut of prizes brought Scilly to 'a very flourishing condition'. Surplus ships were sent to Morlaix in Brittany for disposal.[75] Further profits accrued from the redemption and exchange of prisoners. In April 1650, the

Council of State exchanged Richard Thornbury, a royalist held at Pendennis, for 'one Gold, prisoner in Scillies'.[76] On another occasion the Council authorized retaliation against Sir John Grenville's kindred on the mainland in hopes of speeding the release of prisoners from the islands.[77]

Despite its successes, royalist Scilly was neither happy nor united. Edward Wolley mentioned 'giddy discontented islanders' and soldiers 'apt to mutiny'.[78] News broke in April 1650 that some of the officers and soldiers of the Irish regiment there, bribed by the parliament, 'had a conspiracy to have murdered Sir John Grenville ... to have seized it, and delivered it to the rebels'. The intended plot mirrored the royalist takeover of Scilly in September 1648, but this time the governor acted quickly and had five or six mutinous officers executed.[79] Demoralized royalists elsewhere found comfort in the news that some of the 'best heads and stoutest hearts ... in the adjacent [sic] islands of Scilly and Jersey' were 'waiting for an opportunity to get footing in England, where they hope to find many friends'.[80] Among those brokering the traffic in men and material between Ireland, the Continent, and Scilly was Henry Leslie, the bishop of Down, several of whose letters from St Mary's survive.[81]

Another year passed before parliamentary plans for the reduction of the Scillies were ready. By this time there were believed to be 2,000 royalist soldiers at Scilly, '400 whereof have formerly been officers'.[82] They would not be easy to dislodge. As English naval forces approached the islands in the spring of 1651, they learned that a Dutch fleet under Admiral Van Tromp was also nearby, ostensibly retaliating against Grenville's privateers but possibly with predatory intentions. The Council ordered Admiral Blake to monitor the Dutch, and if necessary to prevent them landing.[83] At the same time, the government in London reminded its counterpart at the Hague that 'the islands of Scilly or Sorling are and have been anciently a part of the lands and territories belonging to the commonwealth of England, and were in possession of the parliament, and kept for them by a garrison paid by them', which was only partially true.[84]

Blake's forces reached the islands by mid-April, intending to land on Tresco. But, owing to confused orders, difficult conditions, and 'timorous or treacherous pilots', they found themselves under fire among 'craggy and inaccessible' rocks. A second attempt met 'stout resistance', but, thanks to 'the manifest providence and power of God', in Joseph Leveck's account, the attackers achieved dominance. Blake prepared to take St Mary's by battery and assault, and eventually persuaded the Scilly garrison to yield.[85] Each island could be seen from the next, so the defenders knew the odds against them.

Sir John Grenville accepted articles of surrender on 23 May 1651, for implementation by 2 June, 'wind and weather permitting'. Parliament took immediate possession of all territories and facilities in the Scillies, including all serviceable weaponry, powder, and shot. Civilians would enjoy all liberty, privileges, and immunities, 'they submitting themselves for the future to all acts of parliament'. Merchants would be free to stay or go, secure in their money and goods. Servants, the sick, and the wounded could also leave or remain 'without any prejudice, reproof, or abuse'. Grenville's garrison of officers, soldiers, gentlemen, and clergy were allowed to march out 'with beat of drums, sound of trumpets, colours displayed, and matches lighted at both ends', as a salve to their honour, and to take with them their horses, arms, money, and plate. Even the Irish were allowed to go free. Parliament offered Grenville and his followers safe passage, provided they withdrew from combat. These were generous terms for 'malignants' who had suffered total defeat. Grenville expressed a desire 'to go unto the Isle of Man and join with the Earl of Derby', but this was rejected because parliament's soldiers 'have a commission as soon as they are done here to go against that place'. Royalist options in the islands were rapidly shrinking. Grenville would be permitted to go either to Ireland or the Continent, providing he pledged his honour to engage no more against the parliament.[86] Some of the royalists who left the Isles of Scilly fought again for Charles II, and were further routed at Worcester in September 1651. Among several captured cavaliers, 'formerly of Scilly', the Council recommended that the Earl of Cleveland, Lord Grandison, Colonels Thomas Blague and John Butler, and Major Edward Broughton should be tried as traitors.[87]

After this success, parliament's strategic planners congratulated themselves on their control of the islands, so that now

> the Barbados ships are at liberty to go about their design, and the parliament
> ships to go to hinder the importation of soldiers . . . by the Duke of Lorrain or any
> other foreign state; and it may perhaps occasion the Dutch to think the Isle of
> Scilly may be an ill neighbour unto them, if they be so weak as not to agree with
> us at present.

The reduction of Scilly advertised the new reach of English power to the world.[88] Commenting on the fall of Scilly in June 1651, a London merchant advised a colleague: 'those that relate to trade rejoice at it; the next place you will hear of [will be] the Island of Man, which I hope will prove less difficult.'[89]

The Isle of Man

Held tenaciously by its feudal suzerain James Stanley, the seventh Earl of Derby, the Isle of Man remained a royalist stronghold throughout the civil war. Rumours that the Scots intended to attack the island persuaded the earl to move there in June 1643. In addition to strengthening strongholds at Castle Peel and Castle Rushen, Derby's men fortified Fort Royal at Ramsey and Derby Fort on St Michael's Isle to the south. Local stirrings on behalf of the parliament were easily put down.[90]

The Earl of Derby kept residence on the Isle of Man between 1643 and 1651, except for intervals fighting on the mainland, when his formidable countess took charge. The earl's household gave hospitality to aristocratic cavaliers and entertained them with masques and feasts. Castle Rushen was palatially appointed with luxuries found on no other island fastness, nor in many castles under siege. Derby himself gave thanks for 'this island, which hath been to me a very blessed and happy retreat from the storms and inconveniences of the war'.[91] Parliamentary prisoners had very different experiences, some enduring threats by the countess to drown them in the sea.[92] A refuge for some, a prison for others, the island justified its reputation as a near-impregnable stronghold.

Royalist Isle of Man proved an essential link to resources in Ireland, a base for transshipment of troops, and a platform for raids against parliamentary shipping. It also became a fallback position for mainland cavaliers on the run, many of whom moved thence to Ireland or the Continent. A small wave of royalists and their dependants retreated to the island after their defeat at Philiphaugh in September 1645, with more following later in the autumn after the collapse of the Northern Horse at Carlisle Sands. Sir Marmaduke Langdale and Lord George Digby were lucky to find a cock-boat to take them to the Isle of Man. They reached the island 'with forty more, being all that was left of 1,500', according John Ashburnham's demoralized report.[93] Another fleeing royalist, Colonel John Robinson, also escaped to the island 'in the disguise of a labourer' after the fall of Anglesey.[94]

The Earl of Derby's retainers on the Isle of Man achieved fame for 'their hospitality to strangers, as great numbers of English in the late civil wars'.[95] Among those receiving 'entertainment and means' from the earl was Major Walter Whitford, the assassin of the parliamentary diplomat Isaac Dorislaus, who presented the very dagger he used to Lord Stanley.[96] Lord Digby recalled 'great civilities from my lord of Derby and . . . his noble lady' during his month of residence.[97]

Others sheltering on Man were said to include 'great store of English papists . . . who have licence to go to mass there'. One of them, the Lancashire gentleman William Blundell, hoped to find in the Isle of Man 'a place . . . freed from our fears and troubles'. The island was also a haven for royalist privateers, who ravaged the coastlands of the Irish Sea, and kept the Stanley cellars full of delicacies and wine.[98]

Following the regicide in January 1649, England's Council of State set out to crush all remaining pockets of royalist resistance. Commissary General Henry Ireton invited Derby to surrender the Isle of Man, but the earl replied that he would keep it, 'with the utmost of my power, to your destruction'. The island would continue to be a 'general rendezvous and safe harbour' for supporters of the Stuart cause. Sir Marmaduke Langdale and Sir Lewis Dives backed him, promising to hold the Isle of Man 'for his majesty's best advantage', in defiance of 'the tedious temptations and importunate solicitations' of Westminster.[99] As royalist prospects brightened in the following year, it was not unreasonable to think that their forces, backed by the Irish and the Scots, might launch a third civil war and use the Isle of Man to stage landings in England.

In March 1651, parliament prepared forces under Major General Thomas Harrison to attend to the Isle of Man, 'to prevent the mischief designed'.[100] A mark of concern that August was parliament's warning to the governor of Beaumaris Castle to keep a watchful eye on the Isle of Anglesey, 'lest any attempt should come from the Isle of Man'.[101] By this time Charles Stuart had been crowned in Scotland and was moving his army south.

On 12 August 1651, the Earl of Derby left the Isle of Man with 300 men to join Charles II's forces, leaving his French-born countess Charlotte de Trémoille in charge. Within a month all was ashes, as the royalist cause collapsed at the battle of Worcester, and disorders broke out on the island. Taken prisoner after the battle, the earl became a parliamentary asset and was willing to come to terms. Recognizing the 'deplorable estate' of his family and the 'sad condition' of the island, Derby informed parliament on 29 September 1651 that he was willing to surrender the Isle of Man if trusted intermediaries could arrange a settlement. He wrote again on 11 October, offering the island for his life. The countess also considered yielding the Isle of Man to secure her husband's release, but, before terms could be agreed, the earl was executed at Bolton on 15 October 1651. Island 'malcontents' took advantage of these developments to stage a revolt. Led by the militia captain William Christian, a former Stanley official, the rebels assisted parliamentary forces in subduing the island. Facing a parliamentary fleet and three regiments of soldiers, the countess and her allies had little choice but to surrender, finally yielding on 1 November.[102] The Stanleys had governed regally for generations, but their rule gave way to military discipline for the next nine years, as London took control.

Guernsey

The Channel Islands were divided and contested in the 1640s, more stressed than ever in their early modern history. Parliament controlled Guernsey throughout the civil war, except for Castle Cornet, which held out for the king. The island's Presbyterian heritage inclined many of its inhabitants towards Westminster, but the parliamentary Committee of Government suspected that several of the island's gentry and jurats were closet royalists, 'who, as fire in ashes, do not show themselves but wait an opportunity to express their virulent disposition'.[103] The Earl of Danby formally remained governor until his death in 1644, but his authority had vanished. Parliament gave the position to Robert Rich, Earl of Warwick, but royalists acknowledged only Danby's deputy and kinsman Sir Peter Osborne, ensconced in Castle Cornet.

England's war constituted a constitutional crisis as well as a military emergency, in which islanders of opposing persuasions upheld their customs, rights, and liberties. Parliamentary supporters on Guernsey invoked their island's unique character and its 'unspotted fidelity to the crown of England, ever since the Conquest', as they sought Westminster's assistance against royalist malignants.[104] Brandishing history for opposite purposes, the royalists under Osborne rejected parliamentary authority, insisting that 'these islands, reserved by all princes to their own peculiar, and governed by the laws of Normandy, of which they are a part, have never had to do with parliaments, whose ordinances and commands not to extend hither hath been ever accepted one of their chiefest freedoms'.[105] The constitutional ambiguity of island allegiance had violent repercussions on the ground.

Jersey's declaration for King Charles in February 1643 increased Guernsey's vulnerability, but made it all the more vital for parliament to maintain its grip. Sir Peter Osborne blamed the jurats of Guernsey for bringing miseries to the island by their 'causeless interesting yourselves in the troubles of England' and their 'stupidity and blindness not to foresee that inundation of calamities you will then wilfully suffer'. Castle Cornet would never yield without signed instructions from the king, he repeated, 'these islands being no ways subordinate to other jurisdiction, but to his majesty alone as part of his most ancient patrimony'.[106] The jurats in turn registered grievances against Osborne, charging the lieutenant governor with violating the island's laws and privileges and stirring up turmoils and divisions.[107]

The French watched warily, making manoeuvres that islanders thought threatening. A letter from Guernsey to the House of Commons in January 1642 warned of '12,000 men at St Malo and 4,000 more looked for', whose intentions appeared hostile. More reports followed of 'French troops making ready near, and upon the coast bordering upon the island', who might be planning an invasion.[108] Charles I's French queen had kinsmen and supporters in Paris, and royalists were already gravitating to the court of St Germain. Another report circulated in 1644 'of an army in Brittany ready to invade' the Channel Islands, either to assist the Stuarts or to secure advantage for the French, whose agents supported royalist enclaves, emigrés, and intrigues.[109]

The year 1643 was especially dangerous for Guernsey parliamentarians. Some feared for their security and worried that royalists on Jersey and in Cornwall were preparing 'to come against this island'.[110] Many subscribed to a 'vow and protestation' (in French) pledging to defend Guernsey's islands for parliament against any forces directed against them.[111] Sir Peter Osborne's outpost at Castle Cornet maintained its defiance, and threatened the rest of the community. Supplied by sea from Jersey and France, the castle lay within musket shot of the town and periodically turned its heavy guns in that direction. Osborne's batteries fired on St Peter Port for three days in March 1643, sending more than 200 cannon balls among residents. This particular barrage occasioned no loss of life, though later bombardments caused injuries and death.[112] Before the siege ended, Pierre le Roy reports, some 30,000 cannon shots fell on the town.[113] Islanders petitioned Westminster for money to repair the houses damaged by Osborne's artillery, and parliament replied that the sums could be paid from Sir Peter's confiscated estates. Osborne denounced the 'seditious and desperate persons' who opposed him, and characterized the islanders as 'a people disorderly and divided, hating those that rule them, and yet not knowing what to do of themselves'. The struggle, in his view, was between divinely constituted authority and upstart populism, and between the Church of England and rampant Presbyterianism.[114]

As the siege dragged on, the royalist defenders of Castle Cornet despaired that they would starve. Risky landings on moonless nights brought in dribbles of food and fuel from Jersey and France. At times the garrison lived on biscuits and porridge, water and fish. Sir Peter Osborne sent his own apparel and linen to St Malo for sale or pawn to buy provisions and complained that Sir George Carteret on Jersey was not doing enough to help. Soldiers sickened and went short of medicine and clothes. The garrison burned its housing and carriages for fuel. At least one soldier deserted to the enemy, betraying the extent of the castle's privation, and another who attempted to escape was shot.[115]

The siege of Castle Cornet was suspended from time to time for the exchange of news, messages, and prisoners. The castle served as a royalist prison and housed several parliamentary captives and hostages. Late in 1643, the Guernseymen Peter de Beauvoir des Granges, Peter Carey, and James de Haviland were imprisoned in Castle Cornet, while on a mission of parley, but managed a dramatic escape under gunfire after a month and a half of confinement.[116] Less fortunate was the parliamentary captain Thomas Seppens, who was held for ten months in Castle Cornet as a prisoner in the castle ward. During this time, 'neither hearing from his friends, nor any hope at all of his releasement', he was persuaded to write a letter urging the parliamentary commander Colonel Russell 'to deliver up the isle of Guernsey' to the royalists. From a parliamentary point of view this was treason, and, when Seppens eventually gained release, he was condemned by court martial, although the sentence was later respited.[117] Other prisoners in Castle Cornet included mariners captured by royalist privateers, such as Joseph Bransby, commander of the *Scout Frigatt*, who languished for several months in 1645 while waiting to be exchanged.[118] Both sides taunted each other and periodically traded prisoners taken by sea or by land.

As parliament consolidated its successes in England, it gave more attention to the royalist-held islands and castles. In December 1645 and January 1646, the besieging forces of the Earl of Warwick exchanged letters with the defenders of Castle Cornet about 'giving up the castle of Guernsey to the parliament'. Warwick, as admiral and nominal parliamentary governor of the Channel Islands, invited the royalists to make an honourable surrender, but Sir Peter Osborne insisted that he could not violate his oath to his majesty, 'for the shame that would follow me living and accuse me dead'. Osborne again played the jurisdictional card, arguing that parliaments never held sway in the Channel Island, so their commanders lacked all authority.[119] He was buoyed by relief from royalist forces in Jersey—'our principal stay'—who claimed to be 'very forward' in plans to tackle Guernsey, but also took account of 'the natural animosity between the islands', which might make Guernseymen 'resist to the utmost if any of Jersey shall endeavour to reduce them'.[120]

Rumour circulated again in April 1646 that Cornish, Irish, or French troops were ready to invade Guernsey, supported by hostile warships. Prince Rupert was said to be readying a thousand men for that campaign. Three heavily armed frigates were spotted at St Malo, 'to be employed in the design against us', and more royalist men-of-war were daily expected to join the attack.[121] Guernsey seemed all the more vulnerable now that Prince Charles and his court were based in Jersey. Parliament sent 400 men in October, 'for the preservation of the isles of Guernsey, Alderney, and Sark, from present danger', but there was little for them to do besides exercise and prepare.[122]

As royalist Jersey gained ascendancy, it seemed likely that Guernsey would fall, though in fact the opposite happened. Short-term successes in England's second civil war in 1648 encouraged some royalists to hope that their navy might win back Guernsey for the king. Queen Henrietta Maria's agent Stephen Goffe proposed recruiting 900 French mercenaries for this task, though the scheme was quietly abandoned.[123] Guernsey's social fabric was in fact quite fragile at this time, showing signs of discontent and distress. Divisions between factions mirrored those in England, aggravated by island animosities. Allies of the bailiff, jurats, and lieutenant governor accused each other of malignancy and oppression.[124] The civil war produced economic dislocation and an abnormally large number of actions for debt.[125] Though Guernsey was under parliamentary control, administrators feared there were traitors in their midst.[126]

Sir Baldwin Wake, who replaced the exhausted Osborne as lieutenant governor at Castle Cornet in May 1646 and took over management of the siege, declared perpetual allegiance to his majesty and swore that he would never surrender. Commanders on Guernsey invited the royalist garrison 'to throw themselves into the harbour of the parliament's protection', but few responded to the offer. There may have been sixty to eighty defenders still behind the castle's walls.[127] By April 1647, however, the stress of the siege began to tell, for royalists reported that Sir Baldwin, 'by some distemper and indisposition of body, had contracted a distemper of brain', and had to be locked in his chamber. Shortages of food and fuel induced sickness, including symptoms of scurvy.[128]

Wake may not have been mad, but he was certainly sickly, choleric, and unstable. Hyde had doubts about his sobriety. At a royalist meeting in September 1648, Wake called his ally Sir George Carteret 'a presbyterian', and deemed the islanders no better than 'French dogs'.[129] After the news of the regicide reached Castle Cornet, Wake proclaimed Charles II 'in the hearing of the town', but the islanders at Peter Port persisted in their 'villainy'.[130]

The republican Council of State tackled the problem of Channel Island governance in the summer and autumn of 1649, proposing a commission to examine 'the distempers and factions' that threatened 'the whole state of the island' of Guernsey. The governor, bailiff, and jurats were expected to support the commissioners' efforts to 'settle the island in safety', but little could be done until military affairs were resolved.[131] Parliamentary forces under Colonel Alban Coxe arrived in Guernsey in October 1649, to command 'all the castles, forts, towers, and places of defence' and to conduct courts martial under the laws of war (which overrode the laws of the island). Transport ships brought troops from Portsmouth and Weymouth.[132] This may have persuaded Wake to abandon Guernsey, to pursue his private commercial and privateering interests, but royalist resistance at Castle Cornet continued until the fall of Jersey. Short of food and medicines, its defenders starved and sick, Castle Cornet held out for the Stuarts until 19 December 1651, the last outpost anywhere to surrender. Fifty-five men walked out. The siege had lasted eight and three-quarter years, 3,190 days.[133]

Jersey

The customary rights, privileges, and immunities of the Channel Islands fared poorly in these troubled times, though not for want of invocation. In the juggling for ascendancy in the spring of 1642, when civil war seemed likely, Jersey's bailiff and lieutenant governor Sir Philip Carteret claimed that 'the king's rights and revenues' in the island were threatened by 'factious persons pretending to be against the liberties of the people'. Seeking support in London, he asked both the king and parliament to confirm the island's privileges. Opponents petitioned that he not be allowed to come home.[134] Maintaining power against all opponents, the Carteret faction rode roughshod over some of the liberties they claimed to protect.

Critics protested that Sir Philip Carteret himself, by his exercise of arbitrary power, had gone 'against the liberties and charters of the isles'. 'His violent carriage and sundry considerable oppressions', they charged, had 'withdrawn the affections of the people from him...being absolute in that island, so far remote from the eyes of the state'. Since he combined the offices of bailiff, lieutenant governor, and farmer of the king's revenues—'incompatible in one person'—and also served as judge in the island court and captain of the militia, it was not surprising that Carteret had enemies.[135] More than a century of infighting among leading families and interests lay behind these charges, which had as much to do with the control of appointments, licences, imposts, and port dues as with principles of island governance. The language of island exceptionalism became blended with factional struggle and the discourse of ideological conflict.

When Sir Philip Carteret eventually declared Jersey for the king in February 1643, parliament responded by ordering his arrest. They declared Carteret's administration illegitimate, and his conduct 'exorbitant and tyrannical', but could do little besides bluster.[136] The island was 'full of distempers', each side accusing the other of 'usurpation', close to a local civil war. There were shots and skirmishes between the town and the castles, between the militia and the cavaliers, as Sir Philip occupied Castle Elizabeth, and his wife withdrew to Mont Orgeuil.[137] Both strongholds were well provided with ordnance, powder, firewood, cider, and stores of basic food. Both could be resupplied by sea from St Malo with all necessities.[138] Having used 'his own means and fortunes' to repair Castle Elizabeth, Carteret had no intention of giving it up.[139]

William Prynne, who had spent three years on Jersey as a prisoner, enjoying Carteret hospitality, judged the island's castles to be 'so strongly situated and fortified, that they must have an army by land and a fleet by sea to block them up; that an hundred men in each would maintain the castles against all the force the island could make, and three times more', so that, even if invaders managed to land, they would face a hard task in reducing the forts. Both Castle Elizabeth and Mont Orgeuil, he declared, were 'well furnished with ordnance and ammunition, for two or three years siege', and both could receive 'fresh supplies, victuals, men, and whatever they wanted' by water.[140] Advice of this nature made parliamentary strategists pause before proposing an assault, though some thought it excessively cautious. Prynne's critics claimed that, 'if the parliament rightly knew the full consequence of those islands, they would esteem them more, and speedily secure them from the enemy'.[141]

The absentee Sir Thomas Jermyn continued as governor of Jersey until his death in 1644, and was succeeded by his son Sir Henry Jermyn, Earl of St Albans. Parliament assigned that office to the Earl of Warwick in June 1643, but the forces in the castles were unmoved. Carteret and his allies consolidated control by removing rival jurats 'for siding with the authors of the late rebellion', and by confiscating the goods of delinquents.[142] A royal proclamation in July 1643 pardoned inhabitants of Jersey for their brief lapse of loyalty, excepting five named 'traitors', including Dean David Bandinell and his son Jacques, who were accused of supplying intelligence to the rebels.[143] Parish minsters denounced each other for spreading disaffection. Sir Philip Carteret remained dominant until his death in August 1643, though 'seditious spirits' and 'factious ministers' (from the royalist point of view) still had strength in St Helier.[144]

Within days of Sir Philip Carteret's death, parliamentary forces under Major Leonard Lydcott, acting for the Earl of Warwick, landed in Jersey, gained control of most of the island, and installed their ally Michael Lemprière as bailiff.[145] Lydcott came with 300 men and a train of artillery, which he set up to annoy the castles. The royalists in turn fired back with more persistence, through no greater precision. The Jersey chronicler Jean Chevalier counted 335 cannon shots rained on the town of St Helier between August and November 1643, greatly exceeding the number the castles received in return.[146] On 11 October, the States of Jersey appointed a public fast to divert the wrath of God from the distractions of the kingdom, with no discernible effect.[147]

Captain George Carteret, the late bailiff's nephew, operated a maritime supply chain to Jersey's besieged castles and brought in reinforcements as well as victuals and munitions. The newcomers included English, Irish, Cornish, and even French soldiers, many of them said to be 'papists'. The military balance shifted when George Carteret himself took up residence in Mont Orgeuil Castle on 17 November, displaying the king's commission. He also exhibited instructions from the king to arrest known traitors, including Lemprière and the Bandinells, father and son.[148] Carteret quickly rallied resistance and forced Lydcott's indolent forces to withdraw. Some of parliament's soldiers even defected to the castles. Carteret quickly won ratification from the States as lieutenant governor and bailiff, and by late November made Jersey a beacon and refuge for supporters of the crown.[149] Dean Bandinell tried to make his peace with the Carterets, but, as Jean Chevalier observed, it was too late. The dean and his son were imprisoned in Mont Orgeuil with other alleged fomenters of rebellion. Their ill-considered attempt at escape in February 1645 ended disastrously, when the elder Bandinell died after falling from a rope to the rocks. Jacques Bandinell was returned to imprisonment in Mont Orgeuil and died there a year later.[150]

Strongly entrenched in Jersey's castles, with command of the whole island, the royalists secured an important maritime outpost for the king. Enemies were denounced, uncooperative officers were removed, and the property of delinquents confiscated. Jurats were normally appointed for life, but four of them who had supported parliament were removed from office and replaced.[151] Justifying their continuing defiance of Westminster, the Royal Court of Jersey invoked their ancient constitution. 'Tout le monde scait', declared their manifesto of March 1646, that the island was a relic of the Duchy of Normandy, that the present king's ancestors possessed it from antiquity, and that it had never been considered part of the kingdom of England. Indeed, they were subjects of the Duke of Normandy long before they saw the English. While bound in duty to the Stuart crown, the islanders had no obligations to England's parliament, where they had no representation. They wanted only to be left in peace, they said, under 'l'authorité de nos loix et la faveur de nostre prince'. Subscribed by islanders from every parish, the manifesto's constitutional nicety provided cover for a Carteret autocracy.[152]

Jersey's declaration credited Sir George Carteret with saving the island from the calamities, combustions, and ruin that afflicted their brethren in England. The lieutenant governor proved an energetic administrator, who made Jersey a haven for wandering royalists. One of them, Dr Henry Janson, who had been with the king at Oxford, and then with the queen in France, had arrived in Jersey in November 1645 'with a commission from his majesty for the settlement of the peace of this island'. Jersey, he reported, was 'as yet in very good condition' and had raised above £20,000 for the king. If neighbouring Guernsey could be 'reduced into the same condition ... this association of islands would be able to defy all the rebels' power'. Mirroring parliamentary thinking on Guernsey, Janson recognized 'the huge importance of that island to the security of this, and how impossible it is for this to subsist long ... if that near neighbour be utterly lost'.[153] Forces on each island eyed each other warily, each anticipating imminent attack. Each threatened retaliation against adherents of the other. Parliament mandated 'a speedy course for the reduction of Jersey', but preparations were slow, and resources were repeatedly directed elsewhere.[154] Carteret's vessels harassed parliamentary shipping in the western Channel, carried men and materials between France, Scilly, and Ireland, and ferried supplies by night to their allies at Guernsey.[155] Periodic parlays and exchanges of prisoners kept open communication between the opposing sides.[156]

Prince Charles's Island

After four years of civil war, in which royalist forces sometimes seemed ascendant, the king's armies on the mainland fell apart in the summer of 1645. Parliamentary victory at Naseby in June crushed royalist hopes in the Midlands. The defeat of the Marquis of Montrose at Philiphaugh in September sealed the Stuart fate in Scotland. The king's Northern Horse were routed at Carlisle Sands in October, leading to a scattered exodus of cavaliers.[157] The most agile of them headed for the islands, a process that accelerated after losses in the west and at Oxford in 1646. Even before this catastrophe King Charles had urged his exiled queen, Henrietta Maria, 'I recommend to thee the care of Jersey and Guernsey, it being impossible for us here to do much ... being weak at sea'.[158]

Royalist defeat on the mainland did not end hostilities in the Channel Islands. Jersey continued to hold firm for King Charles and provided a base of operations for his son. Royalists frequently mentioned the island as a place of refuge, and dozens of the king's 'faithful and loyal subjects' moved to Jersey after mainland strongholds had fallen. The courtier Sir Thomas Fanshawe was among those scouting a refuge for his friends and family. Some held out hope of using the island as a springboard to reduce the 'neighbour rebels' in Guernsey.[159]

Prince Charles and his entourage reached Jersey late on 17 April 1646, after fleeing the Isles of Scilly. He would stay on the island for sixty-nine days, until departing for France on 25 June. Setting up court at Castle Elizabeth, the prince arrived with 'not twenty pounds in the world', needing loans from islanders 'for his support and expence'.[160] The royal retinue included two earls, three lords, five divines, six knights, a physician, and scores of gentlemen, servants, pages, grooms, and military officers. They brought with them four fine horses for the prince's use and a collection of liturgical furnishings. Many of the refugees were destitute, and several were wounded or sick. More cavaliers were expected to join them daily. Jersey suddenly had three hundred or more extra mouths to feed, and persons of quality seeking accommodation.[161] Ann Fanshawe, who was seven months pregnant, was pleased to see 'many gentlemen's houses' on the island, but her group was lodged 'at a widow's house in the market place, Madame de Pommes, a stocking merchant'. Oh, the indignity! When her daughter was born in June, she was cared for by Lady Carteret, who was herself big with child.[162] Other lodgings bulged with cavalier gentlefolk and their servants. Some shared facilities with prisoners at Mont Orgeuil, where 'the narrowness and want of room' put further pressure on resources.[163] Visitors included the royalist poet Abraham Cowley, who lamented that 'verse does not in this island grow'.[164]

The arrival of Prince Charles made Jersey a focus of royalist hopes and intrigue at a time when the Stuart cause elsewhere was in ruins. Islanders, for the most part, were energized and roused by the prince's presence. Complaints were muted when lieutenant governor Carteret commandeered the island's food supplies, imposed an oath of loyalty, and forbade anyone to leave without his permission.[165] Though transitory, and suffering short shrift, the prince's court on Jersey offered a richer range of services than his father's confinement on the Isle of Wight. Makeshift royal protocols ruled a regime of improvised ceremony and honour, with formal dinners, services, and processions, in which Sir George Carteret was made a baronet. The prince and his party took communion in the parish church of St Helier, at a table furnished with silver jugs and platters brought from the Isles of Scilly. Celebrations in all twelve parishes marked the prince's arrival, and his sixteenth birthday on 29 May was marked by cannonades, musket volleys, and an extravagance of bonfires that went on until midnight.[166] In more sombre moments, many of the wandering royalists were wondering where to flee to next.

The geography of royalist retreat was as complicated and contentious as its politics. Royalists of the bedchamber and royalists of the battlefield had different experiences and concerns. Sir Edward Hyde and other councillors stood firm for maintaining the king's cause from within the king's dominions, while courtiers of the queen's faction urged Prince Charles to join his mother at St Germain, outside Paris. Hyde maintained an active correspondence across the cavalier diaspora, coping with declining hopes and dwindling resources. The survival of Hyde's papers makes him appear central to this network, and perhaps over-privileges his point of view. Sir John Culpeper and Sir Henry Jermyn urged Hyde to join them in France. Others suggested that he move to Ireland, Denmark, or the Netherlands. Courtiers around Henrietta Maria were adamant that the islands were 'no abiding place' and pressed Hyde to relocate Prince Charles to France. They promoted

Paris as 'the pleasantest and most glorious city' with 'a noble enlargement of conversation', but they did not want it overrun with impecunious cavaliers. Jermyn urged Hyde to come with 'the fewest you can charge yourself of inferior persons', who in multitudes will be 'of intolerable burden'. Others in Paris wanted the prince's train reduced, 'especially of the inferior people, whereof many will be of no use at all to the prince when he is here'.[167] A hundred troops from Ireland landed at Jersey in May 1646 to augment the prince's forces, but feeding them, paying them, and disciplining them posed additional problems.[168]

Parrying entreaties and invitations from the circle around the exiled queen, Hyde extolled the advantages of staying in Jersey. It was 'as pleasant and as strong an island as can be imagined', he wrote in one letter in May, 'the pleasantest place I ever saw, and by the grace of God of unquestionable security', he wrote in another. 'We can defend the island from any force the parliament can bring against it, and when that is lost here are two castles impregnable,' he wrote to Secretary Nicholas.[169] Prince Charles apparently liked Jersey too, having 'no more thought of leaving that island than of going to Virginia'. Should the situation deteriorate, it was 'always in his power in four hours to go into France, whither nothing but an undeniable danger of falling into the enemy's hands can draw him'.[170]

The question of where the heir to the throne should reside, posed earlier in 1646 in Cornwall, took on additional significance when King Charles himself became a prisoner. Sir Edward Hyde drew up a register of 'the advantages and disadvantages that are naturally like to attend this most important resolution'. At stake were not only the safety of the prince, and the happiness of his mother, but also the fate of the English crown and church. Against the promise of French hospitality, and the uncertain prospect of French military assistance, lay the political danger of over-reliance on a foreign Catholic power. It was far better, thought Hyde, that the prince should remain within his father's dominions, to be seen daily at worship in the Church of England, than to be seen 'at mass with the queen; so that the question is not, whether the prince be like to be corrupted in his religion by going into France, but whether generally the people of England will be persuaded to believe that he is so. And then what a fatal consequence is like to be.' Knowing Prince Charles, Hyde worried that he was more likely to contract an unfit marriage than to join a false religion, but both nightmare prospects were reduced by keeping him in Jersey. 'God be thanked, we are yet in the king's dominions,' Hyde declared on 1 June 1646.[171] His concern that exiles might fall for the allurements of popery would become increasingly acute in the decade ahead, as cavalier courtiers, and even members of the royal family, embraced the church of Rome.

The question of location came to a head three weeks later when leading royalists from France and Jersey met together at Castle Elizabeth to decide the prince's disposition. Urgency required them to confer face to face, since ciphered letters took up to six weeks to pass between Paris and Jersey. Over two days of hot discussion on 20 and 21 June, with breaks for walks and worship, royalist émigré grandees addressed this 'matter of great importance, on which the fate of three kingdoms might depend'. Meanwhile, over 150 miles away in England, the parliament was drafting the Newcastle Propositions, to bring a conquered monarch to heel.[172]

Items for discussion at Castle Elizabeth included the run-up of the prince's debts on Jersey, prospects for relieving the garrison at Scilly, and the circumstances of friends in Ireland, but these paled beside larger strategic and constitutional considerations. Hyde argued, as before, for the 'very many benefits and conveniences in his highness staying in the king's dominions', in a place of proven security. But this position crumbled against insistence that 'the prince should obey his father and mother, who had positively commanded his repair into France'. A 'sudden reservedness and strangeness... grew between those who advised the going, and those who were for staying'. Pragmatic constitutional royalists were forced to defer to claims of absolutism and blood. The prince himself, three weeks past his sixteenth birthday, agreed to leave, but the island's 'baffling' weather prevented departure: 'the wind was so high that no man durst put to sea.'[173] This led some on Jersey to hope that the prince would change his mind, but to no avail. As soon as conditions improved, Prince Charles thanked the islanders for their 'good affections', and by 25 June he and his handlers were in France.[174]

Several senior royalists, including Capel, Hopton, and Hyde, chose 'to wait a seasonable opportunity' in Jersey rather than decamp to the Continent. Their growing community included such refugees from the fall of Pendennis as Lionel Gatford, the garrison chaplain, and Joseph Jane, the member of parliament for Liskeard. Hyde's friend Sir Henry Killigrew also set out for Jersey in August 1646 but died of his wounds at St Malo. His body was brought for burial on the island.[175] Cavalier refugees from Cornwall continued to trickle into Jersey in the autumn, some of them arriving by way of Brittany and St Malo.[176]

Hyde's anxiety about the Francophile royalists, who now controlled the prince in Paris, was raised to alarm in October 1646, when news reached Jersey that their absentee governor, Lord Jermyn, perhaps already a Catholic convert, was negotiating to transfer the island to the French in exchange for a dukedom and 200,000 pistoles (worth roughly £160,000). 'It is publicly talked of in Paris that both the islands [Jersey and Guernsey] are to be delivered to the French, and my Lord Jermyn is to be made Duke of France,' reported John Osborne from Rouen. Horrified by this betrayal, which 'cannot consist with the duty and fidelity of an Englishman', Carteret, Capel, Hopton, and Hyde engaged with each other to thwart 'so infamous a transaction, which we are confident his majesty will abhor'. Permitting Jermyn's plan to proceed, they remonstrated, would violate 'our personal allegiance and relation to his majesty and the crown of England, our duty and affection to our native country, the protestant religion, and the laws and liberties of the English nation'. It would be 'an irreconcilable blemish' on the royalist cause, which would yield mastery of the Channel to the French and advance French plans 'to make the king of England their tributary'. The Channel Islands, Hyde reminded King Charles, were 'a principle foundation of your sovereignty in the narrow sea', and their loss would be 'unspeakable'.[177]

Recriminations against Jermyn's 'treachery and infidelity' went on for months, while Charles I remained a prisoner of the Scots, the prince was in France, and royalists across the diaspora expressed concern that the islands might be 'severing themselves from their obedience to the English nation'. But, fortunately for the Channel Islands, and for England, Jermyn's transaction never came to pass. 'I do more fear a French army than the Presbyterians and Independents,' Hyde later wrote, though, should foreigners make an attempt on Jersey, he was confident they would 'receive a very sour welcome'.[178]

Hyde recognized that his decision not to follow the prince was 'heartily censured by some, and too much controverted by others'. He salved his honour by believing that he served his king best by living in island retirement and writing the history of the rebellion. 'I think myself much fitter for contemplation than action,' Hyde wrote to King Charles, 'and I flatter myself with the opinion that I am doing your majesty some service in this excellent island, whilst I am preparing the story of your suffering, that posterity may tremble at the reading of what the present age blushes not to excuse'. Island seclusion gave flight to his muse. By November 1646, Hyde had filled sixty sheets of writings and requested more paper by every messenger. By August 1647, the number of sheets completed in 'this blessed isle' approached 300. 'Besides meat', he observed, 'my greatest expence will be paper and ink . . . I write with all fidelity and freedom, of all I know, of princes and kings, and the oversights and opinions of both sides'.[179]

Comfortably settled in Castle Elizabeth, after the departure of the prince, Hyde found 'wonderful contentment' in Jersey and could not say enough about the kindness and 'civility' of Sir George Carteret and his lady. He had arrived on the island with less than £6 but profited from a share in a small ship involved in trade and privateering. There was never a shortage of good company, or French or Malaga wine. The works of Cicero, Livy, Tacitus, and Seneca were readily available as well, at some delay, as 'the London prints'. 'We are a handful of very honest fellows, who love one another heartily,' Hyde wrote to Lord Cottington in November. 'We make one very good meal a day, and go to church Wednesdays and Fridays, and have a good sermon on Sundays, for we have two or three very honest English clergymen with us,' he reported to Secretary Nicholas. In letter after letter, Hyde proclaimed the 'unquestionable security and advantage' of life on Jersey and justified his decision to remain. He recommended the island to anyone seeking 'thrift and repose . . . where they may make their cloaks into suits, and their boots into shoes', in relative if temporary calm. He worked three hours a day on his History and enjoyed the leisure and utility of gardening. In his memoirs, Hyde recalled 'the greatest tranquillity of mind imaginable' in this period of his life, with the words of Ovid inscribed above his door '*Bene vixit, qui bene latuit*' (he lives well who lives concealed).[180]

Students of the psychology of exile mention the sense of dislocation and dispossession that can accompany shelter in an alien environment. The scattered royalists had lost the war and lost a kingdom, suffering loss of status, wealth, and even identity in island isolation amid 'a sea of foreignness'.[181] Hyde, like others, experienced bouts of melancholy, but he found comfort, like others, in the Bible as well as the classics. Hyde's book of choice was the Psalms, rather than Revelation, for he saw there 'many lively descriptions of ourselves and our condition'. The Psalms revealed 'the inevitable judgements pronounced upon prosperous wickedness, pride, and oppression, and the protection and exaltation promised to those who suffer unjustly'. Though 'a lying and flattering generation…endeavoured to bury our fame in the bottomless pit of their reproach', Hyde, like King David, and like his master King Charles, found in God's providence 'a strength that could not fail him'. Hyde's daily programme included meditation on the Psalms, as well as work on his History.[182]

The cavalier presence on Jersey shrank when Lord Arthur Capel left the island in November 1646, and Sir Ralph Hopton departed early the following year. In a letter most likely written in March 1647, Hyde reports that he had left the castle only once since Hopton's departure; he missed his wife and friends but found satisfaction in an excellent French chef. Work on the island's defences continues, he reports, 'the guns are already in, and the ditch almost digged'.[183] Jersey royalists lost confidence after the departure of Prince Charles and increasingly felt themselves abandoned.[184]

Fortification became a pressing necessity in 1647, since islanders knew by early March that Sir Hardress Waller had 20 ships and 3,000 men ready to attack Jersey. Parliamentary plans for the reduction of the island had been repeatedly postponed, as other military exigencies intervened, but by the spring of 1647 a new campaign was in preparation. Defenders thought that, supplied with food and ammunition from Ireland and France, the island might hold for six months or more, but Hyde made his will on 3 April, expecting the worst.[185]

Parliament's Colonel Rainsborough was poised in May 'for reducing of the isle of Jersey', but mutinies within the army in England distracted this effort. Hyde informed Nicholas that parliamentary ships anchored within cannon shot of the castle, under protection of a white flag, had sent messengers with trumpets with letters to the commander demanding submission. He was pleased to report that the seamen who accompanied the envoy 'were well entertained with wine from the castle', and 'they all spoke with more duty and good manners of the king than their betters have used to do'. Prospects for a royal recovery looked promising, and the defiant jollity of Castle Elizabeth was allowed to continue.[186]

November 1647 brought the extraordinary news that King Charles had escaped from Hampton Court and had landed on the Isle of Wight. His supporters in the

Channel Islands did all they could to help, including preparing a ship to transport the king to Jersey, if he was free to travel. Had events unfolded differently, his majesty might have reached safety among friends, instead of languishing at Carisbrooke. 'I see nothing goes on towards a settlement, but all things make haste towards confusion,' Hyde wrote despairingly on 9 December. Only Jersey offered contentment.[187]

Royalists on Jersey celebrated the anniversary of King Charles's accession in 1648 with gun salutes and banquets, and on 1 May they erected a maypole. Their hopes rose with news of risings in Wales, north-west England, Kent, and Essex, and a revolt of the fleet that redrew the strategic map in their favour. The Duke of York managed to escape captivity in St James's Palace, and it seemed possible that King Charles too might soon be free. These developments were uncoordinated, and news of the second civil war reached Jersey slowly. Sensing possibilities, Prince Charles detached himself from his mother's skirts and gathered cavalier supporters in the Netherlands, where Sir Edward Hyde agreed to join him. Ignoring calls to come to Paris, Hyde left his comfortable island on 24 June and braved perils by land and by sea to reach the Netherlands.[188] He served the Stuart cause for the rest of his life, but never saw Jersey again.

Royalist successes in the second civil war were illusory and fleeting and left their hopes in confusion. The revolt of Scilly for the king in September raised their morale but could not offset parliamentary victories elsewhere. The island of Jersey, and Guernsey's Castle Cornet, still held out, as did Ireland and the Isle of Man, but the king himself, on the Isle of Wight, was approaching the end of his road. Supporters of the Stuarts found 'very great divisions in the councils' of the diaspora, with disagreements whether they and their princes should live in Holland, Ireland, Scotland, or France, or return to their island strongholds.[189]

Channel Island Endgame

The execution of King Charles on 30 January 1649 had little immediate effect on the Channel Islands. Unofficial news of the regicide reached Jersey on 7 February and was confirmed a few days later. Charles II was proclaimed on Jersey on 17 February 1649, and at Castle Cornet soon after, although he was not officially recognized elsewhere on Guernsey until the Restoration.[190] The new king's plans were uncertain, even to himself, but some expected him to return to Jersey, if only on his way to Ireland.[191] A royal letter early in 1649 referred to Jersey as 'that important place of our residence... where we may again for our conveniency choose to spend some time'. Sir Edward Hyde understood the island as 'a convenient place to retire to in order to consider what was next to be done, yet it was not a place to reside in, nor would be longer safe than whilst the parliament had so much else to do that it could not spare the wherewithal to reduce it'.[192]

Meanwhile the struggle would continue. Writing from The Hague on 1 May 1649, Charles II authorized his government on Jersey to punish 'all crimes, misdemeanours, and offences whatsoever, according to the law martial and customs of war, be it by death, banishment, imprisonment, fine, or otherwise' and to 'execute all other acts and things whatsoever that shall be necessary for our service', regardless of island tradition.[193]

The republican government in London understood that its victory was incomplete so long as diehard emigrés and cavaliers held sway offshore. Prince Rupert's fleet of royalist privateers operated out of Jersey and maintained connections between Ireland, the Continent, and coastal Britain.[194] Stuart loyalists still posed danger to the revolutionary state and, though defeated in two civil wars, might still hope for success in a third. It is no wonder that a most pressing priority of the Council of State, within weeks of the execution of Charles I, was to 'oppose and suppress' all who would 'set up or maintain the pretended title of Charles Stuart, eldest son of the late king, and 'to use all good ways and means for the reducing of Ireland, the Isle of Jersey, Guernsey, Scilly, and the Isle of Man'.[195]

After wandering in the Low Countries and France, in the months following the regicide, the young Charles II returned to Jersey on 17 September 1649, intending, so everyone expected, 'to transport himself so soon as it should be seasonable into Ireland'. He announced his intention of reconciling factions within the island, so long as all returned to their duty. He arrived with a heavily armed escort, once more in his own dominions, determined to advance his cause.[196]

Parliamentary grandees were 'hotly alarmed' at news of the landing of 'Mr Charles Stuart', but their frigates could do no more than 'hover' off Jersey's shores. 'Michaelmas storms' gave the island defenders an extra measure of protection.[197] The young king brought with him his train of some three hundred courtiers and officials, plus a royal mistress, with their horses and carriages, but very little money. The teenage Duke of York joined the royal party in Jersey, passed his time 'very merrily in that island, and in continual exercise', and received the courtesy title of governor. The king (as we may now call him) spent the next few months engaged in royal pursuits, hunting, banqueting, and conducting the diplomacy of a government in exile in relatively primitive conditions. A new riding suit replaced clothes 'so spotted and soiled that they are not to be seen out of this island'.[198] Taxes on the inhabitants, based on the value of rents, helped pay for this regime.[199] Service books for use in this outpost of 'l'eglise Anglicane' included prayers for 'nostre tres-sacré souverain seigneur le roy Charles' and his brother, 'le duc d'York', and for deliverance from their enemies. The Jersey chronicler Jean Chevalier wrote of golden rays of sunrise dispelling the shadows of gloom.[200]

The king-in-exile exercised his judicial function by hearing appeals from Jersey's Royal Court and his ceremonial function by touching for 'the king's evil' and handing out honours. When Charles bestowed the Order of the Garter on the Duke of Buckingham in September, he apologized for not being able to mount the normal ceremony at Windsor. In October, he invited the gentry of Devon and Cornwall to rise upon his behalf, to 'free our faithful subjects from the grievous tyranny and oppression they groan under'. They declined, though subscriptions from royalists in England helped to subsidize the court in Jersey. Islanders subscribed a new Oath of Allegiance in November, forswearing all communication with rebels. The Council of State in London took these posturings seriously and responded by mobilizing naval resources to inhibit further landings from France and to prevent royalist designs against south-west England. Colonel Edward Popham's orders were to 'face them at Jersey with your fleet, and hover thereabout for some time, whereby you may annoy them at Jersey, and trouble their counsels, and retard their executions of what they shall resolve'. Commonwealth ships coasted the islands, and sought intelligence from local fishermen, but still mounted no major offensive.[201]

Hard-headed strategists recognized that Charles's island interlude was just a stopgap. 'The truth is, the king's condition in this place is so uneasy, so inconvenient, and so out of the way of his affairs, that he hath just causes to desire to make as little stay here as he can,' Secretary Long wrote to the Earl of Ormonde on 12 October. Lord Byron, writing the same day, was more forthright in recommending that Charles should move to Ireland, 'whilst he has something left to fight for, and not to be taken here in a nook of the world, with his hands in his pockets, as he is sure to be, if he continue here till the season of the year permit the rebels to attempt it'. 'Our remove is uncertain,' wrote another of the king's followers in Jersey. Ireland, Scotland, even Fronde-stricken France offered better long-term prospects than this 'nook of the world'.[202]

Despite the indecision, post-regicide Jersey was filling up with royalists, because that was where the king held court. There may have been five hundred or more cavaliers on the island by the end of 1649, their numbers boosted by refugees from campaigns in Ireland. More trickled in from St Malo and other parts of France. Sir Edward Hyde was not among them, having accepted the king's embassy to Madrid, but Sir Edward Nicholas reached Jersey in October. Money and food grew short, as the court consumed resources and began to operate on reduced rations. Courtiers considered relocating once again, though parliamentary successes rendered Ireland an increasingly unsuitable destination. Charles II meanwhile engaged with commissioners from Covenanter Scotland, who were offering him a throne and a kingdom in exchange for supporting their cause.[203]

One of Charles's last acts before leaving Jersey was to award a patent in colonial America to Sir George Carteret, calling the territory New Jersey. This venture, on an island in northern Virginia, soon failed, though the name would be attached to a more successful colony in the 1660s.[204]

Charles and his court left Jersey for France on 13 February 1650, after 149 days on the island.[205] Within a month they were at Breda in the Netherlands, continuing negotiations with the Scots. Prince James, the Duke of York, remained on Jersey for another six months, nominally serving as governor but directed by Sir George Carteret. 'The want of money' restricted the duke's options, keeping him 'under some straits at Jersey', but the welcome gift of £600 from Sir Richard Grenville allowed him to follow his brother.[206]

Royalist morale on Jersey eroded after the second departure of the court, though some still hoped for the reduction of Guernsey and full command of the Channel Islands. The young King Charles was said to have remarked of nearby Guernsey that, 'next London, it is the place most to be desired'.[207] Desiring was short of accomplishing, however, and Guernsey, except for Castle Cornet, remained in parliamentary hands. Pressure on Jersey mounted, as parliament built up its forces by sea and by land. Intelligence reached London that spring to the effect that 'a panic fear hath seized upon the malignants there, to the transporting their goods to St Malo'. By April there were estimated less than 250 royalist 'strangers' on Jersey, 'men of note as well as private soldiers', their numbers rapidly depleting.[208] Sir George Carteret drew up contingency plans to respond to an attack, amid infighting among disgruntled defenders.[209]

In June 1650, King Charles took passage to Scotland and subscribed the Covenant that his father had fought to reject. On 1 January 1651, with an army now as well as a court, he was crowned king in Scotland. Stuart hopes rose and fell over the following months but were finally crushed on 3 September at the battle of Worcester. News of the defeat reached Jersey on 21 September and was kept secret for as long as possible, but was revealed by celebrations on Guernsey.[210] Retreat to an island now proved untenable, and royalists had few options besides exile in France or impoverishment in England.

By the autumn of 1651, after several false starts, and with resistance elsewhere virtually extinct, parliament was ready to undertake the forcible reduction of Jersey. A well-equipped fleet of more than seventy ships set sail from Weymouth.[211] With Admiral Blake in command of naval operations, Colonel James Heane leading the soldiery, and officers with local knowledge attached to the general staff, the landing on Jersey on the night of 23 October proved relatively easy. The spirits of the islanders were reportedly 'miserably broken', and most of the trained bands folded without a fight. The two castles maintained stiff resistance, but Mont Orgueil capitulated on 27 October. Explosive bombs lobbed into Castle Elizabeth did massive damage, destroying the garrison chapel and the powder magazine in its vault. Exhausted defenders finally yielded on 15 December.[212]

Kimpton Hilliard, a parliamentary officer who took part in the assault on Mont Orgueil, expressed amazement that 'such a stronghold' should fall, since it was, in his judgement, 'neither stormable or to be injured by mortar pieces'. Hilliard judged Castle Elizabeth 'a most invincible place, but the Lord is able to overcome them'.[213] When the victors finally gained possession of Castle Elizabeth, they inventoried fifty-three pieces of ordnance (seventeen of brass and thirty-six of iron), plus stores of small arms, ammunition, food, and wine. Mont Orgeuil had already turned over eighteen heavy guns (seven of brass) and enough provisions for seventy men for a month.[214]

The defenders of Castle Elizabeth were allowed 'all the honours of war': to march out with their colours flying and drums beating, the soldiers keeping their swords, and the officers their swords, pistols, and horses. All were indemnified for actions during the troubles, with permission to depart for England or France. Amice Andros, the courtier Seigneur de Sausmarez, was allowed to leave with 'one servant, one horse, two swords, two case of pistols, one suit of arms, one carabin, one chest, one trunk, one small box, and one portmanteau containing his clothes, books, papers, and other necessaries'.[215] Sir George Carteret obtained full indemnity, full possession of his property without composition, and the use of a vessel to take him and his dependants into exile. Carteret moved to Brittany, taking with him the island's seal, inscribed *Sigillum Insulae de Jersey*, and a quantity of deeds and documents. There he continued to hatch plans to retake the Channel Islands, perhaps with the assistance of the French or the Dutch.[216]

Reports of further plotting prompted parliament to renege on the terms of surrender and to confiscate the 'lands of inheritance, rents, and other revenues' of 'George Carteret, formerly called Sir George'. Among the Carteret family's losses was the island of Sark, which henceforth was to be 'safely kept and preserved for the use and benefit of the commonwealth'. Three dozen more Jersey cavaliers, 'notorious and capital enemies of the commonwealth', lost their lands for aiding and assisting the late king and Charles Stuart his son, 'ever since the beginning of the wars of England to 1651'.[217]

The royalist stronghold on Guernsey held out fractionally longer than its counterparts on Jersey. Roger Burgess, who had succeeded Sir Baldwin Wake as commander at Castle Cornet, repeatedly declared his 'absolute resolution' to keep the castle for his majesty, 'to whom it rightly belongs...against all power whatsoever that shall oppose it'.[218] Though parliament gleaned intelligence that Castle Cornet was 'in great straits', and that its defenders were now 'very few and inconsiderable, being put to great exigence and want of food', replenishment of provisions from Jersey enabled the garrison to endure the siege.[219] When parliamentary forces launched an assault in March 1651, they were repulsed and lost several prisoners. London blamed 'the disaster that befell our forces at the storm of the castle in Guernsey' on 'the perfidy of some people in the island combining with the enemy', rather than the ferocity of the defenders or inadequacies in the plan of attack.[220] The siege continued, and Castle Cornet fell only on 19 December 1651, after Jersey had capitulated and all hope of external support had been extinguished.[221]

Some of the men who served the royalist cause had seen service in a succession of island locations, linking England, Ireland, the Channel Islands, Scilly, the Isle of Man, the Isle of Wight, and France. One such was Thomas Brookes, a mariner of

Jersey, who told his story in 1661 in the hope of recognition and relief. When civil war broke out in the Channel Islands, Brookes was attached to Sir George Carteret's forces on Jersey, engaged in supplying the beleaguered royalists at Castle Cornet on Guernsey. He was captured during one night-time operation and was held a prisoner of war, 'in a loathsome dungeon with thirty-nine pounds of iron upon his legs for the space of eleven months', until he was released. By 1648, he was serving the imprisoned King Charles, transporting private packets from the Isle of Wight to the queen in France, 'and never was discovered'. He later served Charles Stuart on Scilly and, after the islands had fallen to parliamentary forces, escaped on a frigate to the Isle of Man. From there he went to England to fight again for the Stuart cause. He was wounded and captured at the battle of Worcester and endured seven more years' imprisonment 'for his loyalty to his majesty'. He was indignant at the Restoration, not only that his sacrifice was unrecognized, but that some of the late king's tormenters were the ones reaping rewards.[222]

Others asking for places at the Restoration included Richard Long, who had served as an officer at Jersey and in the Isles of Scilly under Sir George Carteret, had undertaken missions to Ireland and France, then returned to be present at the fall of Scilly and the surrender of Jersey, before being taken as prisoner to Plymouth. Equally deserving, in his own eyes, was William Noye, who had suffered long imprisonment after parliament took Scilly, escaped to Jersey, and served there until that island also fell to parliament.[223] These were veterans with multi-theatre experience across the English archipelago, but as losers they rarely had their due. Island residents, with less mobility and fewer options, mostly stayed to face the interregnum regime.

The decade of civil war brought the islands struggle and conflict, and in some cases sieges, assaults, and violent changes of fortune. Drawn into the nation's conflict, they commanded national attention. London could not ignore them, nor could they hide from the storm. With this stage of England's troubles behind them, the islands remained garrisoned for decades to come, on the maritime frontier of a burgeoning imperial power.

9

Interregnum Assets

By the end of 1651, all English territories were in parliamentary hands. The winners had friends to favour, and foes to sanction, as they consolidated power. The revolt in Ireland continued, but otherwise the Commonwealth of England, Scotland, and 'the dominions thereunto belonging' were under unitary military authority. For the first time ever the London government controlled the entirety of the British mainland and the English islands, with hopes of integrating fringe territories into a centralized republican regime (see Figure 10).[1]

The unprecedented reach and power of the revolutionary state posed challenges to the island periphery. Local polities and communities that cherished their traditions of autonomy faced a government not afraid of innovation. This chapter examines island experiences during the republican military ascendancy, with special regard to the problem of state integration.

The new regime faced dangers at home and abroad. Popular loyalties were unpredictable, royalist conspirators remained active, and foreign foes clouded the horizon. Forces favouring a Stuart restoration could still put ships to sea from the shelter of continental ports. The French, Spanish, and Dutch all had quarrels with the British republic, and posed threats to outlying islands. The Council of State had intelligence in August 1652 'that the Dutch have some design upon the Isle of Wight, for the surprise thereof', with similar reports in the years that followed.[2] French designs on the Channel Islands had never abated, nor had maritime marauders abandoned their attacks. State security required the maintenance of every asset, on the mainland and offshore.

While giving lip service to local traditions of law and governance, the republican regime appointed English army officers to rule the islands. The parliamentary colonel Robert Hammond, who had governed the Isle of Wight during King Charles's imprisonment, was replaced there by the harder-nosed Colonel William Sydenham, who governed from 1648 to 1659. Colonel Charles Fleetwood shared responsibilities on the Isle of Wight until his promotion to commander in Ireland.[3] The Isles of Scilly were governed by Lieutenant Colonel Joseph Hunkin from 1651 to 1660, in charge of an expanded garrison. The former parliamentary general Lord Thomas Fairfax became 'Lord of Man and the Isles' and ruled through a military deputy governor and captain. The centralizing state tried to treat this part of the periphery as 'a part of England', though they left Manx social structures and institutions mostly intact.[4]

England's Islands in a Sea of Troubles. David Cressy, Oxford University Press (2020). © David Cressy 2020.
DOI: 10.1093/oso/9780198856603.001.0001

Figure 10. Great Seal of England, 1651 (Alamy Images)

Local bailiffs and jurats still held office in the Channel Islands, but there too military power was dominant. A series of army colonels served as governors of Jersey: James Heane (1651–1654), Robert Gibbon (1655–9), John Mason (1659–60), and Carew Raleigh (1660). Interregnum governors of Guernsey were Colonel Alban Coxe (1649–50), Colonel John Bingham (1651–60), and Major Henry Wansey (1660). They governed as garrison commanders, using castle decrees and threats of martial law to impose their will. Parliament remained wary of the inhabitants of Jersey, suspicious of their possible disaffection. 'We dare not trust them; for we find that people to be as great dissemblers as the Scots, and seemingly compliers with the strongest party, let it be who it will,' wrote one military correspondent.[5]

Long-serving soldiers provided greater administrative continuity in the off-shore territories than in the turbulent world of 1650s Westminster. Regional refractoriness and ideological confusion undermined experiments in statecraft on the mainland, as office-holders rose and fell. Interregnum England experienced acute tension between the power of the capital and the concerns of the counties, that was echoed in the island fringe. These territories, not surprisingly, make few appearances in scholarly studies of this era.[6]

The Cromwellian Protectorate maintained its major island garrisons, as well as the force on Holy Island and 'the fort and island of Plymouth' (St Nicholas).[7] Several thousand soldiers had duty in these offshore outposts, familiarizing island residents with the voices and manners of the mainland. The military establishment on Guernsey cost £179 a month in 1655. The monthly cost for Jersey's two castles was £392. Garrisoning the Isle of Man cost £245 a month, the Scilly Isles £304, and the Isle of Wight more than £425. Garrison expenses at Beaumaris on Anglesey amounted to £142 a month in 1653. (For comparison, Dover Castle cost the state £148 a month, and the Tower of London £608.) The combined cost of castles and troops on these islands cost Cromwell's government more than £20,000 a year.[8] The state was hard-pressed to meet these expenditures, although they paled beside the cost of the navy, which consumed as much as a third of the state's revenue.[9]

Interregnum regimes continued the militarization of the Isle of Wight, expanding its garrisons, augmenting its firepower, and improving its coastal fortifications.[10] The islander Sir John Oglander lamented in 1650 'how willing were we to have soldiers brought us, and to have new forts built at Bembridge, Cowes, Nettlestone, etc., till now our island being all made a garrison, we now too late repent us'.[11] Some of the troops who had guarded Charles I were stood down, but waves of others replaced them. The military establishment on the Isle of Wight in 1651 was 500, more than at the naval base at Portsmouth.[12] The island continued to serve as a special prison, first holding high-level royalists, including the late king's younger children, and then Fifth Monarchists and other enemies of the Protectorate (see Chapter 13). Some of the religious disturbances in the Isle of Wight in the 1650s, especially involving anabaptists, may have been associated with radicalism in the army.

The Isles of Scilly never lost their importance to coastal and oceanic shipping. Parliament took possession of their harbours and fortifications, many of them in need of repair. A survey of the islands in 1652 found several structures ruined or damaged in the fighting of the previous year.[13] Scilly was garrisoned at first by Lieutenant Colonel Joseph Hunkin, with five companies of foot, mostly troops who took part in its capture.[14] Replacements and additions brought the military strength to over 600, outnumbering the island population, but few had adequate accommodation. Scilly was a hardship posting, remote, bleak, and ill-furnished. Supplies, medicine, and pay arrived late, delayed by wind and weather.[15] By May 1658, according to Colonel Hunkin, the island's store of ammunition was reduced to seventy-seven barrels of gunpowder, left over from the surrender of the royalists. Most of this powder was decayed and unfit for service. Shot was also in short supply, with only two balls apiece for all the sakers and minions on the islands. The guns too were past their prime, insufficient to defend the islands 'in case of any vicissitude of affairs'. The government agreed to restock Scilly's island armoury, but the ship carrying powder and shot was seriously delayed by storms.[16] Radical godliness made slight advance in Scilly's garrison, finding little but wind and loneliness on which to feed.[17]

Parliament's Isle of Man

Further north, the Isle of Man was a vital staging post for English operations in Ireland. Parliament, which previously had no role in Manx business, designated the former army general Lord Thomas Fairfax to be Lord of the Isle, and he was able to assume the powers and prerogatives of that position in October 1651 after the execution of the Earl of Derby. Fairfax ruled 'by authority of parliament . . . in as large and beneficial manner to all intents and purposes as the said James [Stanley] had', serving as Lord of Man until the Restoration without leaving his estates in Yorkshire.[18] Like most of the earls of Derby before him, he ruled through deputies and lieutenants, in cooperation with local elites.[19] The supplanting of Stanley power made island resources available to the English state, and allowed London to use Man for the first time as a prison for political dissidents (see Chapter 13).

As in other recently conquered islands, the soldiers who secured parliament's victory provided the Isle of Man's initial garrison. Their colonel, Robert Duckenfield, became the interim governor, with a military establishment funded by the English state rather than the feudal proprietor. Orders and reinforcements sometimes arrived months late, as troops faced 'the barrenness' of the island and the difficulty of securing supplies. In October 1653, there were over 220 English troops on the Isle of Man, comprising two companies of foot, each with a captain, a lieutenant, two sergeants, three corporals, two drummers, a marshal, a surgeon, and specialist artillerymen.[20]

The task of 'well-affected Englishmen' on the island was to promote the reformation of manners, as well as to provide security, though they were not unblemished by drunkenness, swearing, and fornication.[21] Soldiers complained of Man as 'a strange country far remote from the places of their nativity', though their presence hastened the anglicization of the island. Fewer troops were needed after the crushing of the royalists and the subjugation of Ireland, and gradually their numbers were reduced. With little else to occupy them, some enterprising soldiers busied themselves in farming, trading, and garrison provisioning.[22] Some took to Bible study and prayer. Fairfax promoted his kinsman and client the Presbyterian James Chaloner to be deputy governor in 1656, while Captain Samuel Rose took command of the soldiery.[23]

Manx civilians shared administrative responsibilities with English army opera-tives throughout the 1650s. Colonel Duckenfield was quick to praise William Christian, a former receiver for the Earl of Derby, as 'so useful in the garnering of the island'. Known locally as Illiam Dhône (brown-haired William), Christian gained higher office and a reputation for island patriotism under the Fairfax administration.[24]

The last years of the Protectorate were troubling for the Isle of Man, as they were for many parts of Britain, as soldiers and civilians, junior officers, army grandees, and adherents of competing religious factions jockeyed for advantage. Deputy governor Chaloner intrigued against the radicals and acquired the gover-norship in 1658. Royalist couriers and agents of the Stanleys stirred the mixture, as radical officers under lieutenant John Hathorne mounted a short-lived coup in November 1659. The fate of the island was decided by the fate of the Republic, and soon after the Restoration, by the summer of 1660, the eighth Earl of Derby regained control of his ancestral domain.[25]

Channel Islands under the Gun

The end of royalist resistance in the Channel Islands put parliamentary forces in control. The fruits of victory included such assets as the island castles and their equipment. Castle Elizabeth yielded fifty-three pieces of ordnance, plus stores of small arms, ammunition, food, and wine.[26] Even more valuable was a trunk of writings that exposed and incriminated diehards for the Stuart cause.[27] Colonel Heane garrisoned Jersey with sixty horsemen and six companies of foot, a military establishment close to 700 men.[28] Colonel Bingham on Guernsey commanded seven companies of foot with their captains, lieutenants, and lesser officers, and his complement exceeded 800 by the end of 1651.[29]

Such large numbers could not be housed in castle facilities, so most of the troops found billets in households whose language they did not understand, and some with families whose religion they did not share. Colonel Heane warned the Council that 'the generality of the islanders are undone by the constant quartering of the soldiers in their private houses', but his greater concern was that his men might be 'corrupted, or gained to [the] destructive principles' of Jersey's civil-ians.[30] Troop levels were reduced under the Protectorate, as the islands became less of a flashpoint, but the needs of the army remained paramount. When Colonel Robert Gibbon took over as governor of Jersey in 1655, he asked for supplies rather than manpower 'for the better safeguard of the said island'. His list of necessities included repairs to the castles, gun carriages for the ordnance, and beds and coverlets for his men.[31] A deputation of Guernseymen petitioned the Council in January 1656 'that Castle Cornet may be demolished, that the keeping of the island may be committed to the inhabitants thereof'. This represented a pitch for local autonomy rather than a reasoned military assessment, but it signalled that the glory days of Castle Cornet were past.[32] All three Channel Island castles could be used to hold royalist conspirators and others who threatened the regime.

The revolutionary government in London made efforts to understand the constitutional peculiarities of the Channel Islands, but generally attempted to conform them to the needs of the English state. There would be less toleration of insular peculiarities. The Council dispatched commissioners to Guernsey in August 1649 to examine grievances and complaints, so that parliament could settle the island in safety. In the absence of a king, the regime at Westminster constituted itself as arbiter and installed the exiled parliamentarian Peter de Beauvoir as bailiff.[33] After the regicide, the island government aligned itself with the English state and proposed the previously heretical notion that Guernsey should be 'joined to the English nation in the nearest way of union'. In November 1651, the States of Guernsey sent James de Haviland to London to request that their island be treated as 'a member of the English nation' and that all Acts of Parliament should 'comprehend the Island of Guernsey'.[34] There were even plans afoot for both Jersey and Guernsey to have 'a representor or two in parliament, to the end of a stronger union to this nation, and of a speedier expedition of necessaries from that superior power unto our people', so long as that did not intrude upon their 'freedom, liberties, and privileges'. Having forcibly taken Jersey 'out of the hands of a most cruel and tyrannous enemy', the Council of State proposed that the island 'be reconjoined to the Commonwealth of England'.[35] It was a stunning reversal after a century of constitutional distancing, which would have transformed the islands' future. Advocates of 'a stronger union' continued to press for integration, but the anomaly of the Norman isles proved irreducible.[36]

On Jersey there were scores to be settled between those who had stayed during the royalist ascendancy and those who had gone into exile, each group labelling the other as 'delinquents'. Bringing Jersey under parliamentary control, and absorbing it into the British state, would involve collisions with deeply cherished rights and customs that essentially sabotaged the project. Success for the Commonwealth would have required suppression of Jersey's affection for the crown, attachment to the prayer book, and its heritage of constitutional exceptionalism.

In the aftermath of the parliamentary conquest in 1651, some Jerseymen complained, the island was 'left without any form of civil government or settlement'. Customary arrangements were suspended or overthrown and 'many irregularities committed'. Rival petitioners appealed to the republican Council of State, as their predecessors had appealed to the king. One faction wanted parliamentary commissioners to protect people 'well-affected to the commonwealth' and 'to annul any corrupt laws and customs as have been introduced by kings or their interest'. Another wanted London to keep its distance, because 'our States have always had power to order and reform what was found amiss in the government of the people'. All were for the restoration of the island's 'ancient and rightful constitution', so long as they could be its interpreters and guardians. Most rejected as 'neither just nor equal' the military governor's proposal that law and justice should be in English, since 'the generality of the inhabitants cannot express themselves in the English tongue'. Petitioners deftly compared their situation in Francophone Jersey to 'the intolerable burden under which the people of England groaned during hundreds of years together, to have their laws in a language unknown to them', estimating that 'not one in forty' islanders knew English. Most agreed that English officers should be reminded of the islanders' rights to trade with France, and to customs-free transport of wheat, hops, wool, and other necessities, though whether they would sustain these privileges was uncertain.[37]

As their instrument of revolution in Jersey, commonwealth commanders reinstalled as bailiff Michael Lemprière, who had held that office briefly in 1643 before being removed by the Carteret royalists. Though a champion to some, Lemprière was demonized by others, and his body had been hanged in effigy. The new bailiff filled island offices with men like himself, appointing constables, centurions (deputy constables), and vingteniers (sub-officers) who had previously suffered for the Commonwealth. He set out to restructure the bench of jurats, disqualifying anyone guilty of 'extortions, pillages, and adherences to Captain Carteret, alias Sir George Carteret, in all his tyrannies and plunders'. Jersey's jurats had previously enjoyed secure tenure, but henceforth, it was proposed, all island offices were 'to be annually and freely elected by the inhabitants, and no longer to be of continuation during life'. Writing to Speaker Lenthall in February 1652, Lemprière promised that all delinquents (meaning former royalists) would be disbarred, all treacherous dealings would be investigated, and sufferings on behalf of the parliament would be rectified. Also excluded from meetings of the States were the ministers of Jersey's dozen parishes 'who by their turbulency and brouilleries have made themselves unworthy of that assembly'.[38]

Reacting to this disruption, which savoured of mainland interference as well as partisan absolutism, a collective of 'captains, constables, centurions, and others well-affected to the present government' protested 'that some persons have endeavoured to rent in pieces the frame of our politique government'. Fearing the loss of the island's 'ancient just rights and privileges', they petitioned the Council of State in June 1652, on behalf of 'the freeborn people of Jersey', to restore their traditional constitution. The petitioners were careful to praise Lemprière for his 'many rare abilities and virtues' and for 'his dexterity and wisdom' in managing differences, but they claimed that his government was arbitrary and disorderly. 'According to the ancient customs, the bailiff useth to take advice of justices [jurats] in suits of law', but none had been chosen 'since the parliament's forces came into this place', so 'the poor islanders suffer much', and crimes remained unpunished. Their 'earnest suit' was for 'justices to be chosen, and the jurisdiction re-established'. This would restore the island's privileges, put a check on Lemprière's authority, and perhaps also allow people like themselves to regain office.[39] Constitutional theory, as always, was shaded with ideological preference and laced with self-interest.

A further contribution appeared in a publication by Colonel James Stocall, who had served in parliament's occupying army and had taken notes from Lemprière. Entitled *Freedom. Or, the Description of the Excellent Civill Government of the Island of Jersey* (1652), Stocall's 'short epitome' of island government extolled Jersey's constitution as most excellent 'in respect of all other governments . . . since the commonwealth of Israel'. Relying heavily on earlier manuscripts, sometimes repeating phrases as well as information, this review of island offices, courts, and procedure reads like the description of a Greek polis, or an island utopia. It was, Stocall recommended, 'worthy the consideration of every good commonwealths man' and perhaps even a model for the reformation of England.[40]

In 1653, after Oliver Cromwell's coup that dissolved the Rump Parliament, the London government renewed attention to the Channel Islands. With Stocall's tract to hand, the Council decided that Jersey should be governed 'according to the ancient law and custom', until it could be 'otherwise settled and provided for'.[41] When Cromwell exercised his power to regrant 'the office of the bailiff of the Isle of Jersey' to Michael Lemprière, it was to hold 'during his highness's pleasure . . . with the powers, authorities, preeminences, profits, and emoluments thereunto incident, and of right accustomed'.[42] Thirty-seven Jerseymen were deemed 'notorious and capital enemies of the commonwealth' and were liable to lose their lands.[43]

As for Guernsey, the Council proposed that the office of bailiff should rotate among the jurats, each serving for a month at a time. Jurats customarily were appointed for life, but parliament now ordered that five of the twelve, disabled by age and infirmity (though also by political affiliation), should be replaced. This constituted another coup, reshaping island institutions in partisan English interests. Understanding that the choice of the jurats 'hath been by ancient privilege in the States of that island', the Council graciously allowed Guernseymen to appoint their own jurats, provided they proved 'fit'. Monthly rotations commenced in November 1653 and continued until the experiment ended in February 1656 with Peter de Beauvoir's reappointment.[44]

Island politics, as always, underlay constitutional issues and thwarted the intentions of London. Islanders who wanted their 'ancient privileges' protected were divided over principles and details and were reluctant to see an adversary prosper. Even more than usual, the island elites were riven by 'heats and clashings' and accusations of 'rancour and malignity'.[45]

Petitioners from Jersey reminded Protector Cromwell that the island had 'long been indulged with many privileges . . . for several hundreds of years' and should therefore be excused general compounding for their attachments under the royalists. But, considering 'the rebellion and delinquency of the greater part of the inhabitants of our said isle of Jersey', the government insisted in 1655 that delinquents should compound and conform. Commissioners for compounding would operate under Colonel Gibbon's supervision, so that islanders 'may live quietly and peaceably with the enjoyment of their estates under the government of this Commonwealth, in piety and honesty'.[46]

Guernsey's Commonwealth governor John Bingham reminded Oliver Cromwell in October 1655 that islanders had always been allowed to appeal from their courts 'to the kings and queens of England and their Councils'.[47] They continued to send appeals to London, with as much frustration and delay as ever.[48] The case of John Fautart v. Thomas Symon, concerning the descent of lands on Sark, dragged on for years, with unsuccessful appeals to the Protector and his Council.[49] Another dispute, between Andrew Monamy and William Dobree of Guernsey, began in 1656 but was still being litigated by their heirs and successors a quarter of a century later, with appeals and doléances on both sides.[50]

England and the Channel Islands remained legally entangled, even as most islanders valued the ways they stayed apart. Petitioners from both Jersey and Guernsey asserted their rights 'to victual, rig, and fit their ships' at the French port of St Malo 'and to transport all necessary provisions from thence, with many other privileges and immunities', after the government had sought to tighten maritime controls.[51] Customary privileges were further tested in 1656, when Captain Robert Sansum's officers from the frigate *Portsmouth* attempted to press forty Guernseymen for the English navy.[52] The islanders expressed their 'detestation' and resisted with billhooks and staves, but several men were shipped aboard. The bailiff and jurats asserted that it was 'contrary to the privileges of the island to press any men' and that 'they would take no notice of any order that was contrary to the privileges of the island'.[53]

Opponents of the parliamentary governor Colonel Robert Gibbon also invoked 'the ancient charters and privileges' of Jersey to attack him. Gibbon became governor in 1655 and ruled with a mixture of favouritism, peculation, and efficiency on behalf of the army and the English state. He and his lieutenant Captain Richard Yeardley were probably no more venial in their appetites, or more arbitrary in their administration, than many of their royalist counterparts. Yet, when the Protectorate collapsed and the Rump was restored in 1659, the governor's enemies charged him with 'high misdemeanours, abominations and oppressions' and presented 'articles of impeachment' to Westminster. The grievances against Gibbon were more economic than constitutional, although the one had implications for the other. Instead of making a fair distribution of the wool, leather, and other commodities allowed to the island, Gibbon allegedly granted licences to whom he pleased, reserving choice amounts 'for himself, allies, and particular friends' (which is what all governors did). Mariners were angry that he charged for a pass of limited duration to trade out of the island, and charged them for a new pass if their voyage was delayed by the weather. Farmers were upset when the governor's servants impounded animals that 'trespassed by entering the meadows of the state'. Market vendors complained that he manipulated trade in cattle and fish 'to advance his particular gain and profit'. Other grievances related to imports of tanned leather, and exports of boots and shoes, where the governor's 'avarice and covetousness' were again displayed. Gibbon's further 'tyrannical proceedings' included excessive demand for forced labour at the castle, abuse of impressment, searching for letters bound for England, and arbitrary imprisonment of opponents. Captain Yeardley's apparent crime, besides abetting the governor, was to spend too much time drinking in company with 'notorious cavaliers'. Better was hoped of the next nominee as governor, Colonel John Mason, who was reputed 'a professed enemy of tyranny'.[54]

Colonel Mason was a radical anabaptist who encouraged the army to rebel against the parliament. Within days of his arrival in July 1659 he imprisoned officers of the previous regime, gave positions to 'creature[s] of his own judgement', and promoted divisive designs. His allies were said to be 'dissembling hypocrites' who only followed their appetites, and his control of intelligence was so tight that 'if a man did but break wind backward the governor should know of it for fear of a plot'. These accusations came from Thomas Ashton, an army chaplain of more moderate inclinations, who denounced Mason in print as 'Satan in Samuel's mantle', guilty of 'arbitrary, bloody, and tyrannical proceedings'. Ashton claimed to have witnessed 'greater abominations than ever I have heard or known acted in so short a time and so small a place as the island of Jersey'.[55] Before autumn was out, Mason was recalled to England, amid the wreckage of the Protectorate, and in April 1660, a month before the Restoration, was arrested as 'a person dangerous to the public peace'.[56] Colonel Carew Raleigh, who succeeded Mason on Jersey, was only a caretaker governor, until more traditional rule could be restored.

With no more campaigns to conduct in England's offshore territories, and no major crises to confront there, Interregnum governments treated the island perimeter as a backwater. Jersey, Guernsey, the Isles of Scilly, the Isle of Wight, and the Isle of Man faced intermittent attention from London, mostly for defensive purposes, and their indigenous cultures survived. Insular identities were to varying degrees modified, but by no means extinguished. Local constitutional arrangements were only superficially adjusted under the pressures of military rule, and, if there was grumbling, it was barely registered in London.

10

Restoration Responsibilities

The Restoration of the Stuart monarchy, and with it the Church of England, had the force of a counter-revolution. It put Charles II on his throne, brought his supporters to power, and crushed adherents of the Cromwellian 'good old cause'. As one of the crucial events of early modern history, this rearrangement of power has attracted a huge wealth of research. Very little of this scholarship makes mention of the islands or their role in the later-Stuart polity.[1]

Like other governments before it, the English Restoration regime balanced political and strategic needs against local customary rights and privileges. If there was a tilt to that balance, it generally favoured the crown. Most islanders were quick to acknowledge their allegiance to Charles II in 1660, and the government was happy to accept their submission. The king assured islanders that he recognized their traditions, immunities, liberties, and customs, but his own state interests were always paramount.[2] Over the previous decade the reach of central government had expanded, and its grip had tightened, and the restored monarchy would not see it relaxed. England's fiscal bureaucratic state grew more ambitious in the second half of the seventeenth century, as it sought revenue and duties from all dominions. The centre was newly ascendant, and the periphery was more and more brought into line. The constitutional status of the Isle of Man and the Channel Islands remained much as it had been before the revolution, but the world had changed, and so too had the ambitions of the English state.

The Restoration allowed legacy proprietors and previous appointees to retrieve their offices and possessions. Islanders, like other residents of the king's dominions, had to bow to royal authority, but learned both to invoke it and circumvent it. Aristocratic governors replaced the military administrators of the Interregnum. Sir Francis Godolphin regained the governorship of the Isles of Scilly (1660–7), and passed that title to his son Sidney Godolphin, who became an earl (1667–1700). Sir John Grenville (d. 1701), who had governed Scilly for the king from 1648 to 1651, recovered Lundy and became the Earl of Bath. The eighth Earl of Derby, Charles Stanley, reclaimed the Lordship of Man (1660–72), and was followed by his son the ninth earl, William Stanley (1672–1702). Jerome Weston, the second Earl of Portland, who had been ousted by parliament in 1642, was restored as governor of the Isle of Wight (1660–1). His more competent successors included Lord Thomas Culpeper (1661–7), Sir Robert Holmes (1668–92), and Lord John Cutts (1693–1707). Lord William Widdrington (d. 1675), the son

England's Islands in a Sea of Troubles. David Cressy, Oxford University Press (2020). © David Cressy 2020.
DOI: 10.1093/oso/9780198856603.001.0001

of a cavalier hero, became governor of Berwick and Holy Island, to be succeeded there by his son the third baron.

Regarding the Channel Islands, Sir Henry Jermyn, Earl of St Albans, resumed his governorship of Jersey after the interruption of the Interregnum (1660–5). Subsequent governors of Jersey were the baronet Sir Thomas Morgan (1665–79), Sir John Lanier (1679–84), and the earlier Jermyn's nephew Lord Thomas Jermyn (1684–1704). Guernsey was governed for the later Stuarts by Sir Hugh Pollard (1660–2), Lord Christopher Hatton (1662–5), Sir Jonathan Atkins (1665–70), and the second Lord Christopher Hatton (1670–1706). A consortium led by Edward and James de Carteret (the 'de' also restored) obtained the proprietorship of Alderney, which was later acquired by Sir Edmond Andros.[3] Lesser figures who had served the Stuarts came forward to claim their rewards, while stalwarts of the republican ascendancy were rounded up, and some sent into island detention (see Chapter 14).

Appointees from London clashed with island officials, as always, over matters of money, land, law, and jurisdiction. Administrators accrued profit from expanded maritime traffic and busied themselves in pursuit of perquisites. Living distant from their 'prince's eye', as Jersey's Sir Philip de Carteret complained in 1680, islanders were exposed 'to our enemies abroad, and often also to the oppression and covetousness of our governors at home'.[4]

Besides their salaries and fees, island governors gained reward from their command of castles and military equipment, and by rights of admiralty over maritime affairs. The Channel Island offices of procurer, controller, greffier, king's sergeant, and sometimes, contestably, the bailiff could be at the governor's disposal, as well as 'the right of patronage, and presenting to the deanery, and all rectories and schools in the island'. The governor and his family enjoyed the intangible benefit of local social pre-eminence, with myriad opportunities for patronage, nepotism, and graft. He issued licences, oversaw island shipping, and could requisition any horse he needed. The governor's position carried economic advantages, comparable to royal purveyance, that allowed him first pick and best price of market provisions. It was he who supervised the distribution of 'the wool allowed by act of parliament for the use of the island', with advantage to himself and his friends.[5] The post of governor also brought profits from manorial lands, church advowsons, tithes, and under-the-table perquisites.[6] Restoration governors, like their predecessors, greeted dignitaries, reviewed militias, attended ceremonies, guarded prisoners, and pocketed fees, or fulfilled these duties through surrogates.

Though honourable, and locally powerful, a position as island governor could constrict ambitions if it actually required relocation overseas. Aristocratic appointees were generally slow to take up their offshore duties, and quick to take leave, preferring to rule through deputies and lieutenants. Their careers in royal service continued while they reaped the rewards of island office. The first

Lord Christopher Hatton repeatedly delayed his passage to Guernsey, and spent barely a year in residence. His contemporary the Earl of St Albans was content to be governor and captain of Jersey from a distance, with 'all fees, rents, endowments, etc. appertaining to that office', so long as they did not limit his courtly, diplomatic, and propertied interests at home. London sometimes ordered absentee governors to their posts during periods of heightened international tension, or appointed military professionals as deputies. In July 1681, the Privy Council thought it necessary to order that no governor of Jersey or Guernsey should return to England without formal written permission from his majesty.[7] The second Lord Hatton sought permission to leave Guernsey in March 1684 to accompany his pregnant wife into England, 'this place affording her none[of] those helps and assistances which are requisite in that case'.[8] The observations of another English gentleman, Charles Trumbull, reflect the sense of remoteness shared by some in these circles. Returning to Oxford after visiting the 'foreign country' of the Channel Islands in 1677, he writes that he 'was received as from the dead'.[9]

Island Vulnerabilities

England's islands in the second half of the seventeenth century were as exposed as ever to the threat of foreign foes. The quality of intelligence varied, and the panic was sometimes overblown, but the danger could not be ignored. The foreign threat was enhanced and came from new directions. Though enmity with Spain had receded, the French and the Dutch were suspected of hostile designs. England's Dutch wars from 1665 to 1667, and 1672 to 1674, and war with France from 1688 to 1697, unnerved coastal communities everywhere, though especially along the Channel. It was part of a governor's job to prepare against such menaces.

Reports spread in December 1664 that 'the Zealanders are upon an enterprise to exploit at or about the Isle of Wight'.[10] The summer of 1666 saw similar fears that both the Dutch and the French were preparing to attack the island.[11] Another appearance of a Dutch fleet off the Isle of Wight in July 1667 led to the drumming-up of forces and the firing of emergency beacons.[12] A generation later, in September 1690, the French were feared to be menacing the island.[13]

The Isles of Scilly, too, faced Dutch incursions, including the landing of enemy troops on one of the outer islands in 1667.[14] French men-of-war were seen 'cruising towards Scilly' in September 1690, when Samuel Pepys registered 'the danger of...Scilly coming into the hands of the French'.[15] Reports spread in March 1696 of yet another French plan to surprise the Scillies.[16]

Even Anglesey was at risk, when Jacobites targeted the island for a possible invasion. In June 1689, 'the inhabitants of that island were under great apprehension that the Irish should land there, being not many hours sail from thence'. Lord

Bulkeley's agent registered the fear on Anglesey that, 'if an invasion should be made ... they could have little assistance from any of their neighbouring counties'.[17]

Naval and commercial competition with the Dutch made the North Sea a potential battleground and increased the strategic value of Holy Island. Fearing 'danger from sudden invasion' in June 1666, the government ordered fortifications to be readied and the garrison brought up to strength. Holy Island hosted a company of soldiers and in 1676 acquired eight extra cannons.[18] Recognizing the value of its castle and harbour, where enemy prizes were landed, the crown secured exclusive rights for 'enlarging and fortifying the same'. Private leases were repurchased, as the government took increasing responsibility for the island as a bulwark of the Restoration state.[19]

Further from England, the Channel Islands faced recurrent threats from abroad. Rumour in 1665 spoke of a French attempt on Guernsey that was happily repulsed.[20] Jersey too braced for a French assault and was fearful of Dutch intentions.[21] News broke in August 1666 of another treacherous plan to sell Jersey and Guernsey 'into the power of the French'. The French spy Jean François de Vaucourt was hanged for fomenting rebellion, but alarm persisted about French designs.[22] King Louis XIV warned England's Charles II in April 1668 that he had not forgotten his ancient title to the Channel Islands, 'but that in honour he was obliged not to attack them till he had given notice'.[23] The French king was known to be 'powerful in all things but in ports and conveniency for shipping' and so looked for opportunities to 'annoy the Channel and navigation of England'.[24]

Fears persisted of a surprise attack on the Channel Islands, even while England and France were at peace. 'Alarms of war' in 1678 brought more anxiety, fortunately ill-founded, that the French were about to attack. 'There is no part in his majesty's dominions in more danger than this island,' claimed the captain of Jersey's Castle Elizabeth, as he pressed for increased resources; being but six leagues from Normandy, he explained, 'the inhabitants apprehend themselves in great danger of surprisal by the French king'.[25] Sir John Lanier used similar arguments in December 1681 when three battalions of French and seven companies of Switzers were reported massing near Caen, with possible designs against Jersey.[26]

The skittishness of some islanders, and their fear of imminent invasion, were shown in 1685 when the deputy governor of Guernsey sailed to Alderney to proclaim the accession of James II. When he landed with a small entourage and a drummer, 'this did so affright the islanders that it was generally reported at least forty drummers were heard to beat, and at least 500 horse and 1200 foot were seen landed, and were marching in a body to take the town'.[27] Three years later, the revolution of 1688 was accompanied by the discovery on Jersey of 'a conspiracy for the betraying that island into the hands of the French', which led to the imprisonment of Catholic priests and Jacobite officers.[28]

The renewal of hostilities with France exposed the vulnerability of all English islands. Parliament warned William III in June 1689 of 'the great importance the isles of Wight, Guernsey, and Jersey are to your majesty's dominions', along with 'the isles of Man, Scilly, and Anglesey, and ... all other places that lie opposite to France and Ireland'. It was, they argued, 'of great importance to the safety of your majesty's person, government, and dominions' that these outposts should be supplied and defended, and that any papists there should be disarmed.[29] Island garrisons were rapidly reinforced.[30]

Responding the following year to new fears of a French invasion, the Church of England promoted 'a prayer of thanksgiving to God for his making us an island'. The naval administrator Samuel Pepys reflected that 'the more our country is an island, and by its particular position as such is looked upon and valued to have an advantage towards the rendering ourselves masters of trade, that does the more tempt others to expose us to the danger of invasion'.[31] If the 'island' of England was at risk, or even the English part of Britain, the lesser parts of the archipelago were especially vulnerable. They needed effective governors to quicken their defences, as well as the providence of divine protection.

The Isle of Wight

The imperious and grasping Lord Thomas Culpeper, who became 'captain for life' of the Isle of Wight in 1661, was more interested in profit than security or governance. He treated his island as a private bailiwick or satrapy, rather than as part of an English county, though his power depended on support from London. Culpeper's friction with local inhabitants grew to the point in 1666 when 'loyal subjects' petitioned for relief against his excesses and exhibited a copy of previous articles against an Elizabethan oppressor. Captain Culpeper, they complained, had assumed to himself 'the additional title of governor of the said isle, which doth no more belong to his lordship than it doth to your majesty's lieutenants of the several counties within this your kingdom'. Their grievance, however, was not just about Culpeper's title, which followed more than a century of precedent, but about his actions. Whether captain or governor, he 'doth exercise an arbitrary power in the said island, frequently intermeddling in the civil government ... to the great vexation and trouble of the inhabitants thereof, and hath sometimes proceeded so far as by his sole arbitrary power to imprison the persons of your majesty's good subjects in a noisome dungeon in Carisbrooke Castle'. Among other outrages, Culpeper had enclosed some of the common pasture in Parkhurst Forest, 'to the great dangerous impoverishment of many poor people', whose only redress was to appeal to the king.[32]

One of the islanders, Anthony Dowding of Godshill, a receiver for the Hearth Tax (which applied as much on the island as in other parts of England), was especially indignant that Culpeper refused to allow the assessors into Carisbrooke Castle, as if it were exempt, and committed him overnight to the dungeon. Other petitioners referred to Culpeper's overbearing behaviour, in which his greed exceeded any legitimate entitlement. When customs officers enquired of the governor's intentions regarding a cargo of Brazil tobacco, for example, he beat them and imprisoned them 'for daring to presume to ask his lordship such a question'.[33] When Joseph Bryers of West Cowes bought a boat that Culpeper coveted, the governor 'fell on [him] with his whip and gave him at least twenty blows', then put him in prison for three days to teach him a lesson.[34] When the sheriff complained that Culpeper had felled thirty-nine trees in the royal park for his own profit, the governor disowned the order and said 'his wife did it'.[35]

Charles II, however, was more indignant at the temerity of his subjects than the heavy-handedness of his official, saying that he 'neither likes the manner nor the matter of the petition'. The government in London saw no occasion to believe that 'the king's officer' had misbehaved toward the inhabitants of the island, and demanded that they accord him honour. The Earl of Clarendon understood that Culpeper 'was not respected by the gentry as became his government' but put the islanders at fault. The governor received £500 a year 'for his pay and entertainment', in addition to his fees and profits, and enjoyed royal commendations that would serve him well in his later posting as governor of Virginia (1677–83).[36]

Sir Robert Holmes, who became governor in 1668, was, by contrast, a naval hero, remembered for supporting 'the dignity of his office with great propriety, and by constantly residing in the island', where he acquired 'great popularity'. His residence on the Isle of Wight was not so constant as to prevent him also serving as a member of parliament and continuing in naval service. All three of the island's boroughs fell under his control. The social highlights of Holmes's tenure included the king's summer visits to Yarmouth in 1671 and 1675. His rewards of office included bounty from wrecks and two-thirds of the value of any prize that he might seize.[37] His share of the silver from the wreck of the St Anthony in 1691 would ensure that he died a wealthy man.[38]

Holmes was also responsible for improving the island's defences. Criticizing the negligence of his predecessor, he reversed plans made in 1661 to reduce the military footprint on the Isle of Wight and to slight some of the island fortifications. Instead he demanded more weaponry, men, and money for the garrisons at Carisbrooke, Sandham, Yarmouth, and Cowes.[39] The governor commanded 200 professional soldiers in 1668, but needed 200 more, he said, 'in case the war with France goes forward'. The island's volunteer militiamen were only of limited value. The island's forts had over a hundred pieces of ordnance, but many remained 'dismounted by decay of carriages'. 'Speedy repair' and infusions of money would be needed to guard against foreign threats.[40] Holmes helped to brace the island against the Dutch, oversaw further militarization under James II, and provided vital support for William III's war with the French. In July 1690, when the Isle of Wight became a staging post for continental campaigns, the 8,000 soldiers on the island were 'judged sufficient to prevent any descent that may be made upon them'.[41] How they engaged with the islanders is not recorded. An inventory in 1691 found 122 pieces of ordnance on the Isle of Wight, most presumably in operable condition.[42]

Tension between the islanders and their governor renewed when Lord John Cutts, another soldier–politician, was appointed in 1693. A governor in the Culpeper tradition, Cutts exercised his authority by interfering with Isle of Wight corporations, disenfranchising burgesses of Newtown, and imprisoning a clergyman for several weeks in Cowes Castle. He also manipulated elections to secure seats in parliament for himself and his brother. In addition to his customary wages, perquisites, and droits, Cutts augmented his income by claiming an allowance of 12d. a day 'for a company of archers, though not one archer had been known found there in the memory of man, but swallowed entirely by the governor'. Cutts's overbearing behaviour provoked a petition in 1697, in which local gentlemen protested against his greed and arbitrary excesses. The government at Westminster brokered a peace, whereby 'the ancient method of choosing members to serve in parliament' was restored, and the governor and his enemies pledged themselves to 'mutual and lasting friendship'. Fortunately for the islanders, Cutts spent much of his time on mainland business or with the army in Flanders, governing the Isle of Wight through his deputy, Joseph Dudley.[43] Strategic considerations weighed more with London than a few offended gentlemen, so successive regimes were allowed to ride roughshod over local sensibilities.

The Isles of Scilly

The Stuart Restoration not only brought the Godolphins back to power in the Isles of Scilly but allowed Sir Francis Godolphin to recover expenses incurred there on the late king's behalf in the civil wars.[44] Though never the centre of London's attention, these islands had strategic and commercial importance that grew with the expansion of European warfare and transatlantic ventures. The increasing use of the English language in the islands, rather than Cornish, may testify to their increased absorption into the cultural and economic spheres of the metropolis.[45]

An Italian visitor to the Isles of Scilly in 1669 remarked that 'the whole government is in the hands of the commandant of the fortress, who at present is Sir [Sidney] Godolphin; and as he has never been to take possession of it, it may be said he is unknown here; hence the whole authority is vested in ... his lieutenant governor'. Besides the absentee governor's stipend, reckoned to be 2,000 crowns (£500), his perquisites included anchorage fees of 3s. for every vessel that sheltered below the castle walls, plus the customary right of wrecks. The proprietor's steward collected rents and tithes, including the valuable tithe of fish.[46] Godolphin, who was ennobled in 1684, was too busy with his career as a courtier, diplomat, and treasury official to pay more than cursory heed to his offshore duties, so the proprietor's kinsmen, stewards, and lieutenants took care of the routine business and security of the Scillies and collected 'all wages, fees, profits, commodities, emoluments, and advantages thereof'.[47] Tapping into some of the commercial wealth that passed through the Scillies, the government established a customs station there in 1682, 'for the prevention of frauds by importing goods in and out of the islands'.[48]

The military establishment remained the anchor of Scilly's economy, costing the central government £4,400 a year for supplies, equipment, wages, and repairs, though payments were often in arrears.[49] It is not the case, as one historian of the islands asserts, that the end of the Dutch wars brought the military occupation of the islands to an end.[50] Garrison strength in the late 1660s was 200, down from the peak of 600 under the Protectorate, but still more than the castle could comfortably house. The Italian visitor commented on 'the increase of population produced by the marriages of the soldiers with the islanders' but noted that this was now 'remedied . . . by forbidding them to marry'.[51] That soldiers considered the Scillies an undesirable posting is suggested by the observation in September 1688, when a mainland regiment was required to send a company to Scilly, that the men 'cast lots for it'.[52] At the Restoration, St Mary's Castle had five culverins, eighteen demi-culverins, forty-one sakers, twenty-two minions, and two three-pounders, but time and weather had taken their toll, and many of their wooden carriages had rotted.[53] The level of fortification varied in later years, as some weaponry deteriorated and other pieces were replaced, and as wars and threats dictated. A civilian might be impressed by 'very beautiful iron culverins', but these were vulnerable to salt spray, rust, and mishandling.[54] Further strengthening by William III for his war against France brought Scilly's arsenal up to 106 heavy guns.[55]

The Isle of Man

The post-Restoration Isle of Man remained as unamenable as ever to English political influence, though not for want of trying. When Charles Stanley, the eighth Earl of Derby (d. 1672), regained his inheritance on the Isle of Man, he immediately retaliated against his family's former enemies. The charismatic William Christian, known on the island as Illiam Dhône, had returned from London, expecting protection under the 1660 Act of Indemnity and Oblivion, but Derby had him arrested for being 'captain of the insurrection'. Christian, Lord Stanley charged, had dishonoured the dowager countess, the present earl's mother, by leading islanders against her in 1651, and had committed 'treason' by violating his oaths and trusts. Significantly, framed by island law, Christian's treason was against the Earl of Derby, rather than the king of England.[56] Derby's revenge precipitated a constitutional conflict with the Restoration regime at Whitehall, which mostly went the earl's way.

Knowing that local power was against him, Christian appealed to Charles II, 'to be tried by your majesty's laws of England, where he many years lived and hath an estate'. Derby's proceedings, he argued, were 'without precedent, and contrary to the laws within the island', and in violation of the recent statute. He asked, as a subject, to be brought before the king and Council to have 'benefit of the laws of England'. The Council received Christian's petition on 9 January 1663 and ordered the earl to send his prisoner to London. They were not to know that William Christian had already been executed by a firing squad a week earlier at Hango Hill on the Isle of Man.[57]

Derby answered the Council by reciting the history of his family's rights to the Isle of Man. The Restoration, for him, was more about the Stanleys than the Stuarts. The late malefactor, Derby insisted, was condemned by the laws and justice of the island, which were in no way constrained by parliament's Act of Indemnity. Affairs on the Isle of Man were none of London's business. As far as he was concerned, the earl's authority on his island was absolute, so that Christian's death was a private 'concern of my own'.[58] Stanley's intransigence, compounding his overreach, stimulated challenges to the authority on which he acted. Though seventeenth-century charters extended 'the liberties and privileges of Englishmen' to colonies overseas, these rights of subjecthood could not be guaranteed on an island close to home.[59]

William Christian's sons Evan and George appealed to London for justice, protesting their father's 'untimely and innocent death'. Although Charles II had sent for Christian to be tried by the laws of England, he was instead 'condemned by the verdict of six ignorant and illiterate men, three of them being the earl's own soldiers'. Another of Christian's kinsmen protested that the earl's actions 'are beyond all that ever yet was put in practice'. Yet Derby maintained his contempt with impunity. As one observer explained, the earl 'stands on his power'.[60]

Charles II's Privy Council demanded that Isle of Man officials 'give an account of their proceedings in the execution of William Christian', but their warrant was ignored. The citing of island officers who 'have neglected to render obedience' to the royal mandate had no effect. London's orders to arrest them for 'their misdemeanours and contempts' went nowhere, as the Manxmen sheltered under Derby's power.[61] Councillors considered ways of 'seizing the franchises of the said Isle of Man, and reducing the same into his majesty's royal jurisdiction' but baulked at the task.[62]

The earl did all he could to obfuscate matters, even reminding King Charles that 'the Lords of the Isle of Man were sometimes homagers to the kings of Norway' and Scotland, before coming under English sway, and that 'all royalties, regalities, liberties, and franchises' there descended to the earls of Derby 'forever'. In a printed broadside, he acknowledged a feudal obligation to his majesty, but not to his laws, the Isle of Man 'not being taken anciently as a part of England', and no act of parliament making it so. Washing his hands of the Christian affair, the earl claimed to be ready at all times 'to do his utmost in humble obedience to his majesty's commands', which patently, adamantly, he was not.[63] Even while taunting the English, Derby reasserted his right to 'all royal mines found or to be found within the isle'.[64] Owing his lordship to the politics of the Wars of the Roses, the Restoration Earl of Derby became the last 'overmighty subject', with a fortified domain of quasi-independent power.

The constitutional conflict between the earls of Derby and the kings of England continued later in the seventeenth century on several fronts. The ninth earl William Stanley (d. 1702) was unyielding in his claims. When persecuted Quakers on Man asked 'the king of England to be real king and governor of this island', to relieve their suffering for religion, Derby acted 'as though the earl's power were above the king's', which seemed in practice to be true.[65] When islanders with grievances tried to take their case to the Privy Council, the earl declared himself 'most injuriously perplexed by complaints of several persons of the Isle of Man', and ruled their appeals out of order 'according to the laws of this island'. Any appeal to London was an 'injury' to his lordship, and an invasion of his 'property'. Religious radicals could be banished from the island, while Manx officials who wanted to travel to England had their requests denied.[66]

Efforts to crack down on smuggling across the Irish Sea foundered on the Isle of Man 'being not subject to the laws of any [of] the three kingdoms'. The island's jurisdictional independence thwarted efforts towards integration, giving constitutional cover to an economic advantage. There were no English customs commissioners on the Isle of Man before 1682, and when they arrived the earl instructed his officers to give them no obedience. Shipments of wine and other valuables through the Isle of Man were concealed, interfered with, or misrepresented, to his lordship's benefit and the English Treasury's loss. If curtailing the clandestine trade proved inconsistent with 'the constitutions and government of the place', observed Irish officials in 1683, 'there seems no other way but by act of parliament to annex it in this point of jurisdiction to the laws of England', a project that proved politically impossible. Charles II's revenuers encountered 'strange interruptions in the execution of their offices', and on at least one occasion Derby's men had them arrested. Resisting English customs searchers on the earl's behalf, Ferdinand Calcoll, the Isle of Man water bailiff (effectively the admiral), reported to his master in June 1683 'how much these kinds of practices do daily tend to the breach of your honour's prerogative and infringement of your honour's charter'.[67]

Derby's governor Roger Kenyon 'baffled' English customs officers in 1691 and told them that 'the king had nothing to do in the said island, the laws of England was nothing there'. William III, he declared, had no more rights in the Isle of Man than he did in Normandy or Gascony. When officer Benjamin Dewey attempted to perform the king's service, Kenyon reportedly asked, 'what king, what king?'

(a response with Jacobite as well as seditious connotations). The earl himself joined the fray a few days later, threatening Dewey, 'I will make you know yourself, I will lay you by the heels, get you gone out of the room,' but, when Dewey set out to leave for England, the earl put him in prison. The Privy Council received a full report of these outrages, but proved powerless to act on them.[68] Though *quo warranto* proceedings in other parts of England curtailed local privileges in favour of the crown, they made little headway against a remote proprietor who was rigidly protective of his prerogatives. Only after failure of the Stanley line in the eighteenth century, and the passing of the Lordship of Man to the Duke of Atholl, were major adjustments possible. The Revestment Act of 1765 reduced Manx independence, but the Isle of Man remained an anomaly, a self-governing dependency of the British crown (see Chapter 15).[69]

The Channel Islands: Guernsey

When the Restoration parliament debated the Act of Indemnity in August 1660, offering pardon to participants in recent 'troubles, discords, and wars', it originally omitted reference to the islands of Jersey and Guernsey. This was quite proper, in some regards, because the islands were 'ancient parts of the dukedom of Normandy', and 'the abrogating, altering, reforming, or new making' of their laws 'was never done by the parliament of England, but by the assemblies there'. Petitioners from Guernsey pointed out that 'they send no persons on their behalf to the parliament of England to take care of their interest, nor represent them therein ... there being no statute made in any parliament that do bind those islands'. Nonetheless, constitutional niceties aside, the islanders stood in great need in 1660 'of his majesty's gracious pardon' and requested parliament in this case 'to comprise the inhabitants of the said island in the general bill of oblivion now before them'. This had some urgency, since Guernsey had been staunch for the Commonwealth, and now feared retribution. Now subject to a king again, the islanders acknowledged 'their great guilt and unfeigned grief of heart, for having ... submitted to the usurping powers which lately tyrannized over his majesty's subjects' and sought pardon for 'their rebellious crimes'. Another petition from Jersey, Guernsey, Alderney, and Sark invoked their 'immediate relation to the crown only, as remains of the ancient dukedom of Normandy', and pleaded for the new king's 'pardon, clemency, and mercy'.[70] The resultant Act of Oblivion applied to his majesty's subjects everywhere, and specifically included the islands of Jersey and Guernsey.[71] This gave London political leverage a few years later when the crown reminded its subjects in Guernsey of his majesty's 'goodness and clemency ... particularly in passing by unpunished their miscarriages during the late troubles', when they stood against him.[72] Ordering the obliteration of the names of Oliver and Richard Cromwell from all island documents was relatively easy, though purging of the actual records was harder to accomplish.[73]

Royalists and Anglican conformists cemented their hold on power. The courtier Amice Andros, seigneur de Sausmarez, returned to Guernsey to become bailiff, but within a year had returned to England, leaving a kinsman as lieutenant to fulfil his functions.[74] The cleric John (or Jean) de Sausmarez, a canon of Windsor, was confirmed as dean of Guernsey by authority of the king and the bishop of Winchester, and spent the rest of his life attempting to bring the island's religious culture in line with the practices of the Church of England (see Chapter 6).[75]

As a former companion of Charles II in exile, Lord Christopher Hatton (1605–70), hoped for great preferment and fretted that he did not 'retain his majesty's wonted good opinion'. Instead of high office in London, Hatton was appointed governor of Guernsey in May 1662, though he did not establish residence there until April 1664. Shortly after his arrival at Castle Cornet, he wrote to the Duke of Ormonde, apologizing that 'my condition is in a remote sphere, and not so serviceable to your lordship as my pretensions and rights might have placed me'.[76] Never happy on Guernsey, Hatton wrote again a few months later that 'this place, as small and inconsiderable as it is, will require as much vigilance and activeness to govern as would some much bigger country'.[77] Hatton corresponded frequently with patrons and councillors in England, reporting his efforts, soliciting assistance, and nursing his grievances.[78]

That Hatton's regime as governor was predictably stormy was not entirely his fault. Relations between the castle and the island jurats severely worsened before he arrived, when the lieutenant governor Nathaniel Darrell tried to collect taxes, and threatened to suspend island officials. (This Nathaniel Darrell was the son of a previous lieutenant governor, also Nathaniel Darrell, originally from Kent, who married the islander Anne de Beauvoir.[79]) According to Darrell, the jurats gave 'great scandal of all the people ... for disobeying the king's command in so public a manner'. Islanders were in uproar when Darrell overstepped his authority and put the lieutenant bailiff, John de Quetteville, in the castle prison.[80] Religious disagreements raised the tension, as the newly installed dean tried to undo the legacy of island Presbyterianism.[81]

Dispatched from London in 1663 to report on conditions in Guernsey, Major Robert Walters found the island 'full of faction', with 'troublesome and unquiet spirits' spewing 'malice against the present government and religion'. Some of this division was a legacy of the civil war, but it was also energized by perennial disagreement between central and local government, between agents of the crown and officers of the island, and between soldiers and civilians. Deep-rooted jealousy among bailiffs, jurats, ministers, and governors was exacerbated by the novelty of a dean bent on uniformity, and the so-called 'sectarians' who resisted the new impositions of the Church of England. Jurats who had been recommended to Charles II at his restoration turned out to be some of 'the most bitter enemies to his majesty'. Major Walters named the jurats Peter Carey, James de Haviland, and James Merchant as abettors of 'the worst and most seditious people in the island' and recommended their dismissal.[82] Even more disturbing was the report that the brothers Eleazar and Thomas le Marchant were heard celebrating the 'bonnes nouvelles' (good news) they had recently heard, that the Princess Royal was dead. 'Ha, ha, ha', laughed Thomas, 'je voudrais que ce fust le dernier de la famillie' (I would wish that this was the last of that family). The news was old, or perhaps a seditious joke, for Charles II's sister Mary had died in December 1660.[83] Joke or not, the words had serious consequences, for Thomas le Marchant was banished from Guernsey and spent several years in the Tower of London.[84]

Matters only worsened when Hatton assumed direct command of the island. Finding that the bailiff and jurats challenged his actions as governor, he brandished his authority 'from a commission under the Great Seal'. He explained to the Earl of Clarendon that, pursuant to 'ancient authorized custom here', he had governed 'by Great Seal ... within the approved laws and customs of the island and the Acts of Parliament that name these islands in the enacting part'. This might impress London, but actions like imprisoning the jurats only seeded local resistance.[85] Hatton released de Quetteville from Castle Cornet but locked up the greffier and three jurats of Guernsey in his place.[86]

The grudges and grievances of the 1660s would reverberate for a generation. The new governor clashed with Dean de Sausmarez, over religious conformity, with lieutenant Darrell over appointments within the garrison, and with everybody else over privileges, justice, and finance. These controversies undercut Hatton's authority and weakened his standing in London. Writing to Clarendon, he sought repeatedly to justify himself against charges 'as injuriously as I believe unskilfully and maliciously imparted against me by Mr Darrell', and by the dean's 'spreading of lies throughout the island'.[87]

Hatton was no better at regulating his subordinates than governing his islanders. A bitter feud developed between the governor and his deputy, between the courtier and the veteran soldier. Their clashes over appointments, discipline, security, and arrangements for state prisoners were aggravated by 'the negligence, wilfulness, or ignorance' of island officials.[88] Councillors in London grew troubled, and Clarendon sought reassurance of the governor's unswerving loyalty to the crown and the church, especially in the light of 'the whispers I hear of my Lord Hatton's remissness'.[89] The last thing London needed was chaos in Guernsey in a time of domestic insecurity and increasing international tension.

Hatton had Darrell briefly imprisoned and managed to have the lieutenant governor recalled to England. But late in 1664 the Council also sought Hatton's removal from office. 'The clamour is great, and your friends can only urge the examination,' Clarendon warned him, but the governor was slow to comply. A royal command of 12 December 1664 had to be repeated on 10 February 1665 before Lord Hatton could be dislodged. He retained the titular office of governor, but never returned to the island. His son Christopher Hatton junior had the reversion (the right to succeed) and petitioned to serve as his deputy, but was effectively sidelined until Hatton senior's death in 1670.[90] Clarendon dryly described the first Lord Hatton as 'a person of great reputation ... which in a few years he found a way to diminish'.[91] The island States, its most senior legislative and deliberative assembly, seems not to have met at all during Hatton senior's time on Guernsey.[92]

Parliament had instructed in September 1660 that the Channel Islands, 'in respect of their fortification and walls, and numbers of men', should be restored to the condition they were in the year 1637, before the onset of England's troubles.[93] But this aim could not be accomplished, despite the pressure of foreign foes. Military readiness on Guernsey was compromised by 'perpetual resentments' between the governor and his deputy, conflict between troopers and civilians, and infighting among members of the garrison. Soldiers remained unpaid, veteran officers wanted to go home, and new recruits were hard to find. Some of the soldiers 'were barbarously wounded as the islanders found them passing up and down in their quarters singly', in the continuing bitterness between speakers of English and French.[94] For his own safety, in December 1663 lieutenant governor Nathaniel Darrell had padlocks put on the armoury at Castle Cornet.[95] By this time the castle was more useful as a prison than a fortress. The medieval pile was beginning to be considered redundant. Its peacetime complement still included a lieutenant, a marshal, a porter, a sutler, a master gunner, a smith, a carpenter, a boatman, a watchman, a chaplain, and fourteen soldiers, though the size of the garrison fluctuated.[96] A Treasury warrant in January 1663 reserved £944 10s. 8d. to pay eighty soldiers on Guernsey for eight months.[97] Restoration governors generally paid more attention to domestic comforts within the castle than to its defensive capabilities, and left military preparations to their under officers.

An order dated 30 June 1664 stripped Castle Cornet of most of its brass ordnance, sending two demi cannon and several smaller pieces to the Tower of London.[98] When Captain William Sheldon visited the island in December 1664, he found 'the castle altogether unprovided with provisions, not so much in it as will serve his company for one meal, nor any preparations to supply it'.[99] An island charter allowed imports 'yearly for the use of Castle Cornet' of a hundred hogshead of beer or malt and hops to make it, and specified amounts of beef, bacon, butter, cheese, fish, tallow, leather, wood, coal, and wool 'without payment of any duty for the same'.[100] But most of these comestibles had been misappropriated. A report in February 1665 concluded that the great sums annually spent on Castle Cornet 'signified very little to the security of the island'. No more should be spent than necessary 'for lodging of sixty soldiers, or the repairing the granges and storehouses'. The island would be better defended, the report suggested, by building breastworks at potential landing sites, and erecting a line or 'curtain' from shore to shore.[101]

To make sure that Guernsey was secure, amid much turmoil and uncertainty, the government dispatched Colonel Sir Jonathan Atkins as acting governor with full authority 'to redress all wrongs' (Hatton not having yielded his commission).[102] Soon after his arrival, the bailiffs, jurats, and inhabitants of Guernsey petitioned Charles II 'that they may enjoy their ancient charters and privileges...with all their law and customs'. This followed several years of friction, with the usual jockeying for advantage. It took another year for the king to respond to the Guernseymen, in the light of 'the great guilt that lay upon them for their activeness in the late rebellion against his father and himself', reminding them of the conditionality of post-civil-war oblivion and the bounty of the royal prerogative. Oblivion was evidently forgotten. Begrudgingly, the Council con-firmed the inhabitants of Guernsey in all 'liberties which they had lawfully enjoyed, saving their allegiance to the crown of England, and to the king, in right of the Duchy of Normandy, and saving appeals to the king as formerly'. These liberties, as of yore, included freedom 'from payment of all such tolls, customs, duties, taxes, payments, etc. in all the king's dominions, as they were exempted from by virtue of former grants and privileges', and in particular 'for any goods of the growth or manufacture of the island brought into England'. The government acknowledged the right of the islanders to 'free trade in all parts of England', and throughout the Stuart maritime realm, no different from inhabit-ants of Dover or Southampton. But, maintaining distinction from the mainland, where the fiscal demands of the crown were comprehensive, attempts to impose Hearth Tax on the Channel Islands were quietly set aside.[103]

The best informed of all island administrators was the younger Lord Christopher Hatton (the first viscount), who became governor of Guernsey in 1670. Islanders rushed to congratulate him, and to secure their positions, after he arrived on the island in June 1671. The States met frequently under his adminis-tration.[104] Hatton Jr had served as a garrison officer during his father's adminis-tration, and had watched that government falter. In his report on 'the state of Guernsey', the fruit of observations in the 1660s, Hatton recognized that 'the custom of Normandy has been the law by which the civil affairs there have been governed' for the last 600 years. He understood, much more than his father, that 'the people of that island, nor their estates, have never been under the jurisdiction of any of the courts of justice in England, nor has any writ out of any of those courts ever been in force there'.[105] A shrewd administrator would work with the islanders, not against them.

Despite these sensibilities, and his important recognition that Guernsey was not like Hampshire, the second governor Hatton also ran into difficulties. Writing from Castle Cornet in August 1672, he called it 'a great presumption in them, and...very unreasonable', that Guernseymen should resist his plans to quarter troops on the island. 'I cannot find that his majesty has given these gentlemen any power of making laws of this nature for themselves, more than all the rest of his subjects,' though the jurats of Guernsey considered their constituents exempt.[106] Hatton later reported 'little animosities' and 'some par-ticular piques' between his officers and the jurats, blaming the islanders for being 'more desirous to cavil than to receive a reasonable satisfaction'.[107]

The island administration was chronically short of money, and officials had difficulty paying the garrison and securing supplies. On one occasion the lieutenant governor threatened to let his men forage on the island, saying 'they could not eat stones in the castle'.[108] Hatton also endured criticism for his 'despotical power and government' when he presumed to advise on the nomination of a bailiff. Against Hatton's claim that 'the power of disposing of the office of bailiff... belongeth as a right to the governor', the Privy Council was forced to remind him 'that there is no right in the governor to name the bailiff' and repeatedly warned him not to 'intermeddle' in such affairs.[109]

Further miseries afflicted Guernsey in August 1672 when a violent fever struck the castle and garrison. Governor Hatton reported that 'more have died this year out of this place than died in twenty years before'.[110] Compounding the problem was island-wide poverty, caused by the slowing-down of trade during war.[111] But worse was to come. Castle Cornet was already past its prime when it was wrecked in a Christmas-tide lightning storm on 30 December 1672. Nothing prepared castle residents for one of 'the saddest disasters that the like was not seen since the creation'. The stronghold became a disaster zone.[112] Survivors reported 'a most terrible clap of thunder with lightning falling on that day between the hours of twelve and one in the morning, upon the magazine of powder in Castle Cornet', which 'blew up and destroyed the whole castle'. The blast shattered doors and walls, blew open 'locks and bolts and bars', and destroyed 'the great tower wherein was three stories: the lower a dungeon for prisoners, the middle the powder room, the uppermost another store room'. Governor Hatton and his children were spared, but his wife and mother were among the seven dead. Contemporary reports mention 'two blacks' among servants who assisted in the recovery. One of them, the negro James Chapple, was later rewarded with a pension. For many years the Hatton family followed a special form of prayer for use each 30 December, 'in commemoration of the fatal destruction' of some of them and 'the stupendous preservation' of others.[113]

Castle Cornet was barely habitable after 1672 and was no longer an administrative centre. An ordinance forbade the scavenging or purchasing of furnishings from the wreckage. The governor was forced to find lodgings in the town and was drawn increasingly to his estates in Northamptonshire, where he regularly received packets of island news.[114] Military discipline deteriorated during Hatton's absence, amid 'great contentions in our little commonwealth'. Ensign Ellis had to be imprisoned for a month for his 'opprobrious language', calling Captain Sheldon 'an old feeble cuckold and not fit to command'.[115]

When the Oxford scholar Charles Trumbull visited Guernsey in 1677, he found a depleted garrison, few men living in the castle, and most of the guns unmounted. Though the island was assigned two companies of soldiers, their captains kept them under strength to pocket their pay. Trumbull found the Guernsey militia 'all unexperienced in anything but training, and few of them skilful at that. This they do about once a year, but more for show and ceremony than any real improvement or advantage comes by that exercise.'[116] An official assessment of 'the present state of Guernsey' a few years later counted less than 1,600 islanders able to serve in the militia, 'not well disciplined and worse armed', with a motley of muskets, carbines, and blunderbuses.[117] The castle still had formidable armaments, including three demi-cannons, two culverins, and twenty-three demi-culverins, but few of them were combat-ready.[118] It was just as well that the French declined to invade.

Governor Hatton wanted control over comings and goings, for better security, but the islanders claimed that his requirement of passports violated their 'free liberty'. Tensions mounted in 1682, when the governor insisted that Guernseymen needed his 'leave or licence' to trade with any 'foreign ports or countries', and that no ship should enter or leave St Peter Port without a pass. This demand, the bailiff and jurats protested, was 'inconsistent' with their 'liberties and immunities'. The dispute echoed a similar crisis seventy-five years earlier when Governor Leighton forbade the islanders 'to go in foreign countries about their business without his leave, as if the said inhabitants were his domestical servants'. Hatton's demand that all vessels have a 'let pass' costing five sols was, they said, 'directly contrary to the privileges granted to the inhabitants of this island...and to the regulation thereof made by the royal commission...in 1607'. The confrontation turned violent in the autumn when the Guernsey mariner James Oliver tried to sail out without a pass and was turned back by musket fire from soldiers on the castle pier. While each side claimed the right, Hatton expressed frustration at the 'saucy and presumptuous' proceedings of the islanders and their agents, who 'watch all opportunities to promote their designs by what interest they can make at court'.[119]

Despite resistance from the periphery, the centralizing ambition of the crown became more dominant. Island resources, including their commercial traffic, became increasingly subject to London's control. Starting in 1687, the Treasury empowered customs officers in Guernsey and Jersey 'to go on board all vessels there, and take account of their lading'.[120] Answerable only to the Treasury and the Privy Council, these agents of the state subjected island trade to inspection and regulation. Pressures to end commercial neutrality signalled even more sharply the curtailment of ancient liberties and immunities.

The special Channel Island privilege that 'all merchants, as well enemies as friends, may come in in time of war as in time of peace' had survived the Dutch wars of the Protectorate, and had been confirmed by Charles II. It was tested whenever international conflict resumed, forcing island traders to stand on their rights or turn smugglers. Jersey petitioners to the king in 1679 cited their tradition of neutrality as 'a main privilege belonging to these islands...by which the subjects of other princes and states as well as your own, may securely come and trade with us, without trouble or molestation' in times of both peace and war. It was, however, a fragile privilege that was 'derided and slighted' and 'sundry ways

violated' by current and recent governors.[121] In principle, the commercial neutrality of the Channel Islands continued until the new wars with France in the
1690s. William III's temporary measure to curtail trade with France grew into a
permanent ban, but even that could not impede traffic between the islands and
St Malo.

Facing the France of Louis XIV, the government of William III decided that the
damaged and outmoded facilities at Guernsey's Castle Cornet should be repaired.
By 1691, the castle had forty heavy guns, most of them fit for service.[122] Increased
numbers of English soldiers were billeted in island garrisons, while the navy,
contrary to tradition, was recruiting Guernseymen and Jerseymen by impressment.[123] Adapting to changing times, Governor Hatton assured his masters in
London in 1696 that Channel Islanders 'have always lived happily under the
government of England'. But now, he warned, 'if in addition to the suspending
of free trade in time of war, their other privileges are needlessly invaded, the poor
island will be very miserable'.[124] Hatton demonstrated how a governor could be
both an advocate for his people and an instrument for their oppression.

The Channel Islands: Jersey

Similar frictions emerged in Charles II's Jersey, where the governor's principal
task was to secure the island against invasion from abroad. Recognizing the
constitutional distinctiveness of the island, and the prickliness of some of its
inhabitants, the Council in London specifically instructed the governor to assure
local magistrates of his care for their just rights and powers, and to assure the
inhabitants that he would uphold their customs and privileges.[125] It all looked
easier on paper than in practice.

Considering 'the present state and condition' of Jersey in March 1661, King
Charles II confirmed 'the present government thereof, for his majesty's service,
and the settlement of the minds and interests of his subjects there'. He also
declared his pleasure 'that the oaths of Allegiance and Supremacy be administered
in the said island of Jersey as the same are ordained to be taken in England by the
several Acts of Parliament for that purpose'. The islanders could choose their own
jurats, but only 'such persons ... as are of known loyalty and good affection to us
and our government, and of orthodox principles in matters relating to the
church'.[126] The *status quo ante* would resume, but only on London's terms.

Charles II had confirmed the special privilege of the Channel Islands that 'all
merchants, as well enemies as friends, may come in in time of war as in time of
peace ... and trade with us, without trouble or molestation'. Commercial neutrality was 'a main privilege belonging to these islands', but it was challenged in times
of conflict, had been 'derided and slighted' by governor Sir Thomas Morgan, and
was 'sundry ways violated by other governors'.[127] Morgan spent almost fourteen

years lording over Jersey, gaining a deserved reputation for high-handedness. He had been a parliamentary officer under Oliver Cromwell, but rode the Restoration under the patronage of the Duke of Albemarle. The Council instructed him to show his commission to Jersey's bailiff and jurats, 'requiring their obedience' while promising to 'protect their rights, and preserve then from invasion . . . according to the usual rules and customs' of the island.[128] Locked in conflict with his neighbours, Morgan sought permission to return to England in January 1678, ostensibly to obtain supplies but 'also having several things to acquaint his majesty, which I dare not commit to paper', relating to 'his majesty's interest in this island'.[129] Permission was denied, and Morgan died in post six months later.

Remonstrating against the 'usurped power of some late governors', who behaved as if their authority far exceeded that of the bailiff and jurats, petitioners greeted Morgan's successor, Sir John Lanier, in 1679 with a catalogue of grievances. Acting 'contrary to law and the charters and privileges of the island', they said, the late governor's officials had collected tunnage on imported wine, despite the authorizing act of parliament being 'only for the continent [sic] of England, wherein these islands were not named'; Morgan's men issued licences as acts of patronage, rather than to benefit to all islanders; and they encouraged the importation of Normandy cider and apples, to the detriment of Jersey producers, and to the inebriation of a corrupted garrison.[130]

These grievances went beyond matters of morality and money, and perhaps intersected Whig anxieties about unchecked power.[131] Like their Elizabethan and Jacobean predecessors, Jersey's petitioners in 1679 invoked fundamental features of the island's constitution. By right, they insisted, the bailiff and jurats had sole jurisdiction in civil and ecclesiastical matters, yet governors acted as though they were *solutus legibus*, above the law. If governors and bailiffs had equal power, they warned,

> what confusion would it be, to see two differing jurisdictions, one purely civil, the other civil and military; and so bench against bench, judge against judge, and officers against officers, to the ruin of your majesty's service . . . And as the decrees of this your Royal Court have been despised and broken by the said governor and his officers, so your majesty's own decrees, even under the Great Seal, have not been much better respected or observed.

Indeed, the remonstrators continued, the governor and his officers looked upon such decrees 'as if they came from Rouen or Paris', and regarded the islanders 'not as fellow subjects under the same laws with them, but as some new-conquered people, and not to be protected but suppressed and kept under'.[132] Jersey was never an English colony, but to some it began to feel like it.

The normal garrison strength on Jersey ranged from three companies in peacetime to five in wartime, mostly raised on the mainland. Companies were traditionally a hundred strong but by 1670 were reduced to fifty men apiece, with the governor pocketing some of the savings. Sir Thomas Morgan, Captain Thomas Jermyn, and Sir Herbert Lunsford were nominal commanders of companies in 1674.[133] The annual cost of the Jersey garrison around that time was a little over £3,000 (a reduction from the Interregnum peak). According to 'ancient regulations', the officers and soldiers in the castles should all be natives of England and Wales, but at the time of the report three out of five officers were 'natives of that island', including several cadets of the Carteret kindred.[134]

Jersey's militia was larger than Guernsey's, but no more competent. Governor Morgan thought it uncertain 'how they will stand before an enemy, except they have some of the king's standing forces to make way for them'.[135] Training in 1682 mustered 2,400 men, but discipline was compromised when captains having the name Carteret deemed themselves superior, and some companies 'were ready to mutiny for precedency'. It took every effort, Governor Lanier reported, 'to force them to their duty and prevent further sedition'.[136]

Differences between soldiers and civilians revived arguments about the balance of island and military law.[137] The Privy Council had to decide, after a murder committed by a soldier of the Jersey garrison in 1667, 'whether the punishment of that crime did properly belong to the Court Royal or the Court Martial of that island'. This was a technicality with both domestic and political consequences. The governor and the bailiff each claimed jurisdiction and addressed their constituencies in their respective languages. The Council instructed that, if the victim was an islander rather than a soldier, the civilian authorities should proceed 'according to the laws and constitutions of the said island'.[138] At the same time, the Council ordered the bailiff and jurats not to imprison any soldier of the garrison, except for breach of the peace, without permission of the military authorities.[139] These provisions were challenged again in 1679 when two English soldiers were arrested and taken to the island prison for stealing chickens, and were violently set free by 'four soldiers of the garrison'. After a stand-off with the governor, and intervention by the Privy Council, the thieves and those who had rescued them were handed over to civil magistrates.[140] This did not settle the matter, for Sir John Lanier secured an order a few months later prohibiting the bailiff and jurats from imprisoning any member of his garrison 'without leave of the governor first had and obtained', nor to 'intermeddle with any difference between soldier and soldier'.[141]

A much more important jurisdictional issue gained attention in 1679 in 'An Act for the better securing the Liberty of the Subject and for Prevention of Imprisonments beyond the Seas', better known as the Habeas Corpus Act. An achievement of the parliamentary Whigs, this Westminster statute specifically declared *habeas corpus* to apply in all 'privileged places', including 'the islands of Jersey or Guernsey, any law or usage to the contrary withstanding'. It did not necessarily end contention, however, since some still questioned whether an

English parliament could legislate for the Channel Islands, and enforcement depended on local actors. Arbitrary imprisonment did not end overnight. As the legal historian Paul Halliday has observed, it was the practical difficulty of serving the writ and the political obstacles of securing compliance that made *habeas corpus* ineffective, rather than the niceties of jurisdiction.[142] The new legislation did not necessarily settle the matter, though it may have offered relief to certain prisoners held in island detention (see Chapters 14 and 15).

Faced with a fractious and litigious population that generated a continuous flow of appeals, Charles II's government confirmed the right of island courts to hear and determine all cases, 'except such cases as by the laws and customs of these islands are referred to be examined by the king'.[143] Some of these disputes ran for years, accruing layers of grievance and complexity. The Council sought to limit the use of doléances—a distinctive and some said 'odious' Channel Island gambit that challenged the proceedings of a judge. Henceforth a fine would be laid against any complainant who 'shall not make good his doléance' by proving injustice or error.[144] The Channel Island gentry continued to be indefatigable litigants, for, as Sir Philip de Carteret warned in 1680, 'once a door be open for obtaining re-hearings the parties will never want pretexts, and will never cease till they be ruined'.[145] The Jerseymen, according to another contemporary observer, were 'generally ill-natured, obstinate, and given to wrangling'.[146]

This was well shown in the case of Dumaresq *v.* Lemprière, which gained traction in the 1650s, and continued through most of the 1660s, only to be continued intermittently by both parties' heirs and successors. The origins of the case in disputes about rents and the guardianship of children were somewhat lost amid the 'unseemly passions', 'incivilities and affronts', and 'false and horrible things' cast by one party upon the other.[147] Successive governors could well despair of governing a peaceable domain.

Sir John Lanier was a zealous royal officer, but his administration generated grievances similar to his predecessor's. Citing the expanding threat from France, Lanier repeatedly asked London for more money and munitions.[148] Sir Edward Carteret (not the bailiff, but another member of that powerful family) protested in 1682 against the governor's encroachment 'upon the privileges of this island . . . he not minding the king's interest but his own'. Similar complaints had been aired intermittently for more than a century. Charles II claimed to be satisfied by Lanier's service but recalled him in July 1684, to make way for the even more imperious Lord Thomas Jermyn.[149] The third member of his family to govern Jersey from a distance, Jermyn sponsored a series of lieutenant governors, including Sir Bevil Grenville from the family with Scilly and Lundy Island connections.

Mont Orgeuil Castle by this time was almost as dilapidated as Guernsey's Castle Cornet, despite Morgan's and Lanier's efforts to keep it in repair.[150] The Englishman Charles Trumbull, who visited Jersey in 1677, noted that 'the old castle called Mont Orgueil . . . is a huge pile of stones . . . and for aught I can hear from the best there, has no other use than that of a prison'. It cost the king some £1,500 a year in wages, supplies, and repairs, with little countervailing profit, 'therefore if it were well at the bottom of the sea, it were no great matter'. Outmatched by modern artillery, with only twenty ill-maintained guns, and poorly positioned to deter invaders, the medieval castle added little to the island's military posture. Mont Orgeuil 'makes a brave show at the distance', Trumbull remarked, but was 'not thought at present strong enough against the assault of any potent besieger'.[151] Assigned to garrison Mont Orgeuil in 1678, the officers of the Earl of Oxford's regiment distinguished themselves only by drinking, dining, and sports.[152]

Judging Mont Orgeuil 'of no use for the defence of the said island', the Privy Council issued a warrant in March 1679 for the demolition of the medieval relic, provided its lead, iron, and timbers were safeguarded from embezzlement.[153] The slighting was evidently not carried out, for the castle still stands, but it offered neither comfort nor security. Garrison and government would be concentrated henceforth in Castle Elizabeth, on its tidal islet 'a mile off shore at high water'. The newer fort had been 'much beautified and enlarged of late by Sir Thomas Morgan', but had been 'slenderly provided for here these several years'. It was, in Charles Trumbull's opinion, 'the fairest and strongest in the islands, perhaps the best at present in the king's dominions as it stands with all its fortifications and out-works'.[154] A survey in 1682 of this forward face of English power found the bastions, walls, ward, and lodgings of Castle Elizabeth in good repair, with seventy-nine pieces of ordnance fit for service. The companion offshore fort of St Aubin's, defending Jersey's main harbour, held fourteen guns and twenty-five soldiers.[155] This part of the king's dominions was well equipped to combat any aggressor.

William III's wars with Louis XIV brought the Channel Islands closer to the front line of international conflict and ended their tradition of commercial neutrality. A proclamation in May 1689 forbidding all traffic with France was specifically ordered to be observed in Jersey and Guernsey.[156] Despite the change of policy, island merchants found ways to maintain their profitable trade with St Malo. Jersey officials winked at the traffic, or even joined in, claiming it as their customary right. Castle Elizabeth in the 1690s was always provided with French wine, and people, papers, and goods went back and forth, notwithstanding the state of hostilities.[157] London was outraged to learn in March 1690 that Jerseymen met regularly with traders from Normandy on the French island of Chausey, and on Jersey's uninhabited islet of Écréhou, as they had always done, and that they even sold gunpowder and ammunition to the French in exchange for brandy. English smugglers collaborated with Channel Island traders to land French goods illicitly in remote coves in Dorset.[158] Even more scandalous were the slackness and corruption of lieutenant governor Edward Harris, holding the fort for the absentee Lord Jermyn. Harris maintained a secret night-time commerce with the French, allowed French prisoners to return home, and let it be known that, should the enemy attack Jersey, he would leave the islanders to fend for themselves. These dangerous dealings stirred fears that Channel Island officials might not just fill their purses but might aid the Jacobites and defect to Louis XIV.[159]

A key problem, which constitutional experts recognized, was that the Channel Islands were 'not represented in the House of Commons, and so have nobody there to take care to make exceptions for them'. Attempts to remedy this in the 1650s had come to nothing. Despite their protestations of loyalty, the islanders were not always 'treated as English natives, and the islands accounted as part of England'. Rather, they were still recognized as offshore and different, with dangerous foreign affinities. A report in 1691 rated the islands 'in greater danger of being betrayed than ever', with their attachment to the crown at risk.[160] The problem remained, as it had for many decades, that islanders wanted the benefits of English protection without cost to their historical privileges. They wanted to be treated as Englishmen for the purposes of homeland trade, yet with special exemptions when it came to dealing with France. Though the later seventeenth century saw a tightening of London's grip on the offshore periphery, island insularity limited the reach of the expanding state. The Channel Islanders' maintenance of their distinctive cultural identity, and their insistence upon their privilege, rights, and immunities, put them in perennial tension with the requirements of English governance. England and its islands remained legally entangled, even as most islanders valued the ways they stayed apart.

PART THREE
ISLAND CONFINEMENT

11

Puritan Martyrs in Island Prisons

Beginning in the reign of Charles I in the 1630s, and continuing for more than half a century, England's islands acquired a new utility as holding pens for political prisoners. The state made use of offshore facilities to isolate and punish its enemies—seditious libellers, malignant royalists, dangerous schismatics, and unconstructed republicans. The use of remote islands to confine such offenders was a novelty of the Caroline regime, although ancient and medieval precedents could be found. Metropolitan governments exercised their dominion over the island periphery by imposing celebrity offenders upon them. Island governors undertook new obligations of custody and security alongside their military duties, while the day-to-day care of state prisoners was entrusted to castle captains, who were supposed to keep their charges separate from the general population. Islanders and officials outside this chain of command had no control of this carceral imposition and no basis to challenge it by reference to island privileges. The liberties of English subjects had limited protection in offshore jurisdictions, and the secure facilities where prisoners were held were directly governed by appointees of the crown.[1]

It was an innovation in 1637 when the lawyer William Prynne, the clergyman Henry Burton, and the physician John Bastwick, puritan victims of Star Chamber prosecution, were sent respectively to castles in Jersey, Guernsey, and the Isles of Scilly, to remain there at the king's pleasure. Subsequent regimes discovered the convenience of shipping religious and political troublemakers to these and other island prisons. The revolutionary republic confined dangerous royalists to the Isle of Wight and the Channel Islands. The Protectorate of Oliver Cromwell sent religious and political dissidents to Jersey and Guernsey, the Isles of Scilly, the Isle of Wight, and the Isle of Man. Their detention was arbitrary and open-ended, and inaccessible to *habeas corpus*, even if island authorities could be persuaded to recognize such writs.

The Restoration regime found the practice of offshore incarceration too useful to abandon and made extensive use of island prisons. The physical remoteness and jurisdictional peculiarities of the islands made them especially suitable for the incarceration of surviving regicides and diehard republicans, who were usually left there until they died. These were men who had offended against the state rather than the law, and their treatment was governed more by political than judicial determination. Their fate was punitive oblivion, with little redress or appeal.

England's Islands in a Sea of Troubles. David Cressy, Oxford University Press (2020). © David Cressy 2020.
DOI: 10.1093/oso/9780198856603.001.0001

Few historians have commented on this use of England's islands as offshore prisons. Modern accounts of island penal facilities—from Napoleon's Elba and St Helena to the modern American cages of Guantanamo—generally omit precedents from early modern England. Yet the dispatch of men in chains to island prisons had domestic, legal, and administrative consequences, and the memorialization of offshore imprisonment by its victims imprinted the islands in the political culture of the seventeenth century. The isolation and natural boundedness of islands made them suitable sites for imprisonment, while the 'aura of extralegality' of some offshore outposts rendered them unreachable by conventional civilian law.[2]

This chapter examines the unprecedented island incarceration of three outspoken puritans between 1637 and 1640. Later chapters deal with the imprisonment of Charles I himself on the Isle of Wight, island imprisonment under the Commonwealth and Protectorate, and offshore political detention under the later Stuart kings.

A fresh analysis exposes this use of offshore facilities for penal purposes, expands discussion of law and politics in the seventeenth century, and contributes to the burgeoning field of prison studies. Embracing the local history of the islands and the national history of the state, it reveals the determination of both royal and revolutionary regimes to remove their enemies from the early modern public sphere. The dramas that brought state prisoners to remote prisons originated on the mainland and continued around the island periphery. Men of faith and principle endured as best they could, while their families and associates lobbied on their behalf. Supporters may have known little about the Channel Islands or the Isles of Scilly, except that was where their dear ones were held. Those who were sent there acquired an unwelcome intimacy with a previously unfamiliar environment.

Puritan Martyrs

The prosecution and punishment of Prynne, Burton, and Bastwick forms a notorious episode of the reign of Charles I, 'one of the *causes célèbres*...of seventeenth-century English history'. 'Puritan martyrs' or seditious libellers, according to one's point of view, they star in studies of early Stuart politics, religion, jurisprudence, and the press. Recent work attends to the anti-episcopal publications that got them into trouble, their trials in Star Chamber, the savagery or justice of their punishment, and their tumultuous homecoming on the threshold of the English revolution. Very little attention has been paid to the unusual nature of their imprisonment on England's remote islands and the ways in which they coped with banishment and exile.[3]

Custodial sentences were not normal features of early modern judicial practice. Prisons were primarily intended for suspects under examination, or plaintiffs awaiting trial. England's courts could order the disfigurement of a person's body, the mulcting of his purse, or the end of his or her life, but rarely deprived criminals of their liberty. Guilty felons faced corporeal or capital punishment, often within days of conviction. If they subsequently found mercy, they were normally released on bond. A small number of political offenders, suspected or found guilty of treason, were imprisoned in the Tower until the government ordered their release or execution. The royal prerogative enabled the king to incarcerate someone at his pleasure, until further notice, but political internment was used sparingly. Most of London's long-term prisoners were civil offenders, usually debtors, held in places such as Newgate, the Fleet, or the King's Bench prison until their obligations were discharged.

London's prisons were places of grim durance, with varying degrees of squalor and privation. But they were not cut off from the life of the metropolis. Social rank, money, good connections, and a pleasing manner could secure a range of privileges and comforts, including day release and almost unlimited discourse with visitors. Even behind bars, such prisoners could participate in the capital's public sphere.[4] Few mitigations of this sort prevailed on remote islands.

Until the Star Chamber trials of 1637 (leaving aside Mary Queen of Scots and Sir Walter Raleigh), England's most notable prisoners of conscience were the anti-episcopal agitator Alexander Leighton, the former prebendary of Durham Peter Smart, and Prynne himself, who had been in the Fleet and the Tower since 1634. Each spent years behind bars for offending against Charles I's state church. Arrested in 1630, Leighton went first to Newgate, 'a nasty dog-hole full of rats and mice', and then languished in the Fleet, for his reckless publication against bishops. Smart spent his prime as a prisoner of King's Bench, after refusing to pay a £500 fine in 1631 for his attack on Arminian ceremonies. Prynne suffered mutilation and imprisonment for his anti-theatrical treatise *Histriomastix*, which was construed as scandalous and seditious.[5] The worst that anyone might have anticipated for them in 1637 was further degradation, fines, and confinement, which, however miserable, would at least have allowed them contact with supporters.

The government of Charles I used the prerogative court of Star Chamber (rather than the common-law court of King's Bench and trial by jury) to silence and punish its critics. Prynne, despite confinement in the Tower, published agitational anti-episcopal pamphlets, including the scandalous *Newes from Ipswich*. Burton published his defiant Gunpowder Treason sermons *For God, and the King*, and his collection of providences against Sabbath-breakers, *A Divine Tragedie*. Bastwick published *Flagellum Pontificis*, *Apologeticus ad Praesules Anglicanos* and *The Letany of John Bastwick*, praying for delivery from the episcopal Antichrist and stirring discontent against the king's ecclesiastical government. The state retaliated vigorously against these celebrity offenders.[6]

The Star Chamber judges—Privy Councillors sitting with the chief justices—convicted Prynne, Burton, and Bastwick of seditious libel. They were deemed to be guilty *pro confesso*, as though they had confessed, after each plaintiff refused to plead. In addition to subjecting them to degrading, pillorying, physical disfigurement, and fines of £5,000 each, the court sentenced them to perpetual imprisonment in separate and remote bastions. Star Chamber fines of this magnitude were impossible to pay, but were normally mitigated, commuted, or forgiven; in this case, the convicts became perpetual debtors to the king. Burton was committed to the castle of Lancaster, Bastwick to Launceston Castle in Cornwall, and Prynne to Caernarvon Castle in Wales, there to remain close and isolated at his majesty's pleasure.[7] These were arbitrary exercises of royal power, but only the beginning.

Within a month of the trial the government had changed its mind, declaring the punishment insufficient and mainland prisons inadequate to the task. Instead, by Privy Council order of 27 August 1637 (rather than sentence in the court of Star Chamber), the libellers were reassigned to more remote places. Prynne would be removed to a castle on Jersey, 120 miles from England, Burton to the island of Guernsey, more than 90 miles offshore, and Bastwick 'to the castle or fort of the Isles of Scillies', some 28 miles out from Land's End.[8] These places, it was believed, were too distant for family or friends to follow, and lay beyond the reach of such instruments as the writ of *habeas corpus*. The Channel Islands, as relics of the Duchy of Normandy, claimed exemption from mainland jurisdiction, except under the authority of the king's Great Seal. The Scillies, as part of Cornwall, enjoyed no such historic privilege, but their rocky remoteness made effective appeals from London equally unlikely.[9]

The use of these islands as political prisons was a novel feature of the 1630s but would not be forgotten in later decades, when more state prisoners were sent there. Where the idea originated cannot be learned, but it is possible that Archbishop Laud's chaplain Peter Heylyn, who had visited Jersey and Guernsey a few years earlier, shared information about the Channel Islands. Prynne certainly counted Heylyn among his persecutors.[10] Heylyn's learning also reminded him that the fourth-century heretic Instantius, 'a very near kinsman of the English puritan', had been banished to the Isles of Scilly.[11] The Caroline regime acted similarly to prevent 'contagion' by consigning its enemies to island isolation.[12]

Marooned on their remote fastnesses, Prynne, Burton and Bastwick were ordered to be 'safely kept close prisoners in their chambers; and that to prevent the danger of spreading their schismatical and seditious opinions...none be admitted to have conference with them, or to have access unto them, but only such as being faithful and discreet persons shall be appointed by the governor or captains of those castles or their deputies for attendance upon them, to give them their daily sustenance and necessaries'. They would be allowed to read the Bible, the Book of Common Prayer, and other devotional books 'consonant to the doctrine and discipline established in the Church of England', but otherwise kept incommunicado. They would be forbidden the use of any pen, paper, or ink; no letters or writing would be permitted to be brought to them, and no written communications would be allowed from them 'to any person or place whatsoever'. The island prisons were intended to cut them off forever from the business of the world.[13] Archbishop Laud and his confederates had entombed him, William Prynne later wrote, 'as a dead man out of mind, whom they remember no more, reputing me among the number of those that go down into the pit, and as one quite cut off by their hands, never likely to rise up again till the general resurrection'.[14] Escape was not impossible, as a few earlier prisoners had proved, but it needed local knowledge, support, and a boat to leave an island.[15]

The 'puritan martyrs' used heightened biblical language to describe their island exile. Their vocabulary was infused by the Scriptures and histories of evangelism rather than stoicism or the consolations of philosophy. They harnessed the narrative of martyrdom to emphasize both their sufferings as prisoners and the cruelty of their opponents, with a compilation of miseries that lent itself to exaggeration. Perpetual imprisonment was a shocking sentence, outside the norms of law, but it was not necessarily the hell that its sufferers depicted. All three men drew on their spiritual resources, each of them maintained good health, and Prynne and Burton at least evaded the ban on reading and writing.

Island isolation meant the end of social and familial intimacy, which might have been maintained during imprisonment on the mainland. Prynne was unmarried, but Bastwick and Burton both had wives and children. Fearing that Susanna Bastwick and Sarah Burton would be 'evil instruments to disperse and scatter abroad these dangerous opinions and designs', the government prevented them from following their husbands, as they had on the mainland. In the very first weeks of the men's sentence, state intelligence revealed, 'the wives of the said Bastwick and Burton...have made some attempts to procure access to their said husbands, and to convey letters unto them'. It was therefore decreed that

> they shall not be permitted to land nor abide in any of the islands. And if contrary hereunto it should happen through the inadvertency of officers or otherwise that they or either of them should land in any of the said islands, that the same being discovered and made known...they or either of them so offending should be forthwith committed to prison.[16]

It was part of the cruelty of his oppressors, Burton later wrote, that his wife should be 'perpetually separated from him, so as if she shall dare to hazard her life in a far journey by sea, which she would do, to have but a sight of her husband's face, she must be sent prisoner back again'.[17] The women were not allowed to communicate with their husbands, but remained active on their behalf in puritan circles in London.

More than three years passed before a revolutionary parliament determined to undo the policies of Charles I's personal rule. Strong pressure built to reverse the sentence of the so-called puritan martyrs. Petitioning in November 1640 for Henry Burton's release, Sarah Burton described how her husband had been cruelly and unjustly censured in Star Chamber, and, after being sent to Lancaster, was transferred to Guernsey, 'by what order she knows not', where he was 'kept in strict durance of exile and imprisonment' for over three years, cut off from his wife, 'debarred of the access of friends', and denied 'the use of pen, ink, and paper ... to make known his just complaints'. Susannah Bastwick similarly stressed the irregularity of her husband's transfer to Scilly—'an island so barren and necessitated that it affords not ordinary necessaries'—and emphasized the 'great straits, want, and misery' that she and their children suffered in his absence. The House of Commons immediately agreed that all three prisoners should be sent for 'forthwith in safe custody', and that their keepers should 'certify this House by whose warrant and authority they are detained'.[18] All three returned to a rapturous homecoming and full vindication. The warrants and accounts of their transfers, petitions for relief and redress, and the writings they published in the 1640s reveal little-known aspects of their time in England's islands.

Prynne on Jersey

The English phase of Prynne's imprisonment was tumultuous and controversial, like much of that lawyer's life. Though disgraced and condemned, he was mobbed by well-wishers. Prynne's journey from London to North Wales in the summer of 1637 had some of the attributes of a defiant progress. Sir Kenelm Digby referred to it as a 'pilgrimage', attended by 'great flocking of the people'. At every halt along the way the prisoner was greeted with cries of 'God bless you' and 'God be with you', as supporters jostled to shake his hand. Adulation reached a pitch at Chester, where Prynne was cheered and feasted, and a local artist was commissioned to paint his portrait.[19] Incarceration in Caernarvon Castle, within spitting distance of the Isle of Anglesey, was more austere, though not as restricted as the government intended. The regime lost control of the narrative as their prisoner became a celebrity, but compensated by transferring him to Jersey, 'with all privacy and secrecy ... to prevent all concourse of people' in his passage.[20]

William Prynne's winter journey from North Wales began on 9 October 1637, but he did not reach Jersey until the following 18 January. It was one of the roughest of rough passages. Petitioning the House of Commons three years later, Prynne recalled how he was 'embarked among papists, in a bruised ship-wracked vessel, full of leaks, and after fourteen weeks voyage in the winter season, through dangerous storms and seas, which spoiled most of his stuff and bedding, and threatening often to shipwreck him, arrived at the said isle, and was conveyed close prisoner into Mont Orgeuil castle'. Isolation competed with discomfort, for throughout this time Prynne's conductors were charged 'not to admit any person whatsoever, but themselves only, to speak with [him] in his passage'.[21]

The man responsible for transporting Prynne, Robert Anwill, the son of the sheriff of Caernarvonshire, sent a detailed account of the voyage to the Privy Council to justify his expenses.[22] Daunting and distressing to professional mariners, the experience must have been terrifying for an untested landsman.

After casting off from Caernarvon on 9 October, the ill-equipped ship encountered 'very tempestuous' conditions and was forced to shelter for three weeks along a dangerous coast, the crew and passengers 'lying aboard the said barque in our clothes without bedding all that time'. They hoisted sail again on 1 November, but renewed bad weather drove them to 'a creek abutting on the coast of Merionith and Cardiganshire', near where they hove to for another six weeks. The crew used the time to trim the vessel and to take on cable and sail, 'all this while having no bedding'. How Prynne occupied himself is unknown, but he surely read his Bible and said his prayers, perhaps meditating on the perils of St Paul. Only four months earlier the Cambridge poet Edward King, John Milton's *Lycidas*, had been wrecked and drowned off the nearby North Wales coast.

Prynne's voyage resumed on 13 December, but 'extraordinary foul weather' blew them 'towards Sidwalls [St Tudwal's], a little island upon the coast of Caernarvonshire'. The next day they sailed as far as St David's Head, 'where such a terrible tempest arose (that place of all others being most dangerous) that we did all in a manner despair of our lives, expecting every minute to be devoured by the raging billows'. By this time the ship had sprung a leak, and only continuous pumping allowed them to approach Milford Haven, though not to enter the port. Anchored at night off Milford Castle, the ship was struck by 'such a storm of hail and wind' that she lost 'our best anchor and thirteen fathoms of our new cable'. This was a most unprosperous voyage, already two months at sea and they had not yet cleared Welsh waters.

Short of an anchor, and still leaking, the ship pressed on towards Land's End and, after 'much difficulty and exceeding danger', limped into Falmouth on 17 December. There they stopped the leak, took on stores, and enquired unsuccessfully for a pilot to conduct them to Jersey. They passed Christmas at Falmouth, still sleeping on board, and finally sailed into the Channel on 27 December, joining a convoy towards Plymouth. There they stayed for just over two weeks, eventually finding a pilot who knew the Channel Islands. They left England behind on 14 January, sailing day and night, and soon sighted land that could have been Alderney or Guernsey. These were difficult waters, with swirling currents and 'abundance of rocks', so proximity did not mean safety. After a night at anchor, they 'made towards a little island named Sark, but a great mist arising, after four or five hours sail, our pilot fearing some rocks', they stood out to sea for safety. Jersey was now within reach, but more frustrations were in store. 'A very high wind arising, and contrary to our course', the ship was blown back toward Sark, where they anchored 'one day and one night in very great peril and extremity'. At last, 'by God's mercy', they arrived at Jersey on 18 January 1638, after more than fourteen weeks of travel. Prynne's journey from Caernarvon Castle to his new island prison lasted longer than most emigrants took to cross the Atlantic and was probably more uncomfortable. Robert Anwill claimed expenses of £109 10s., including £40 for hire of the ship.[23] The total cost of moving Prynne to Jersey may have been twice that amount, but money well spent to those who wished Prynne to perdition.

The order for Prynne's transfer specified 'one of the two castles of the isle of Jersey, which by the governor of the same shall be thought fittest'.[24] Castle Elizabeth was by far more modern, better furnished, and better equipped, but Prynne's gaolors chose the medieval pile of Mont Orgeuil, surrounded by rocks and water. There Prynne remained until his liberation in November 1640. Castle accounts for 1637 include £10 12s. for 'iron bars for Mr Prynne's window, where there were none before', and £8 for a partition and door 'of the aforesaid chamber'.[25]

Like his fellow prisoners Burton and Bastwick, Prynne had no forgiveness for the Caroline regime, and no forgetting the privation and isolation of his imprisonment. But, unlike his married co-sufferers who were deprived of conjugal company, Prynne was accustomed to living alone. He had no relish for incarceration, but his spiritual and intellectual armour, and his unquenchable sense of righteousness, equipped him to endure it. As he said in the verse compendium he published soon after his release, 'where God is present, there no prison is'. 'Driven from country, lands, house, home', Prynne had Christ for company, and time abundant for prayer and reflection (see Figure 11).[26]

Mont Orgueil in Jersey was indeed a place of exile, a high-walled fortress with the sea on three sides, but Prynne found the prospect 'pleasant', the air 'healthy', and his accommodation 'ample'. It would have been a fair enough place to visit on a fine day. Prynne, however, was an exceptional prisoner, held by royal prerogative, and his gaoler, Sir Philip Carteret, lieutenant governor and bailiff of the island of Jersey, treated him honourably. Petitioning parliament in 1640, Prynne avowed that he would have 'certainly perished in his almost three years close imprisonment there, had not the extraordinary providence of God . . . and the noble charity of those under whose custody he did remain, furnished him with such diet and necessaries, as preserved him both in health and life'. Over three cycles of the seasons, Carteret allowed Prynne to share his leisure, to dine at his table, and to socialize with members of his family. Prisoner and keeper enjoyed each other's company. An affectionate letter of April 1639 from Captain George Carteret (Sir Philip's nephew), on naval service in England, to his betrothed Elizabeth at the

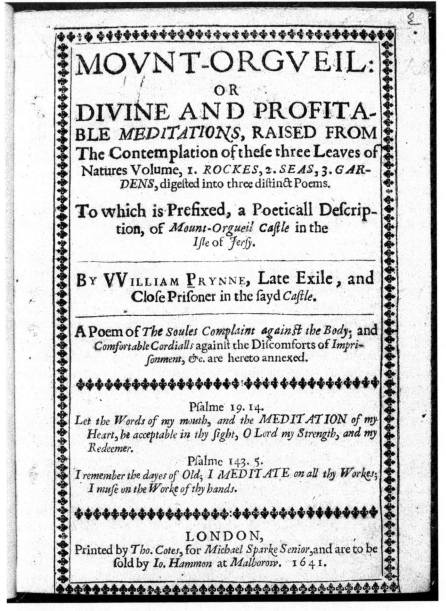

Figure 11. William Prynne, *Movnt-Orgveil*, 1641 (Huntington Library)

castle ends with the postscript, 'my services remembered to Mr Prynne'.[27] Prynne provided some wedding poetry, a godly verse, when the couple married at Mont Orgueil on 6 May 1640.[28]

It is not known how strictly the lieutenant governor enforced the ban on reading matter and writing materials, but little from Prynne's pen can be firmly dated to this period. His historical and polemical output was curtailed, he explained in 1641, because he was 'cloistered up so narrowly that I could neither have the use of pen, ink, paper, writings nor books to benefit myself or others', and because many of his manuscripts had been confiscated or hidden abroad.[29] Dedicating his poetic meditations on *Mount Orgueil* to his former hosts, Prynne thanked 'his ever honoured worthy friend, Sir Philip Carteret' for his 'great favour and humanity', and offered further thanks to Sir Philip's wife, 'the truly virtuous and religious Lady Anne Carteret', and the three Carteret daughters, Elizabeth, Margaret, and Mrs Douse, recognizing them as 'his honoured kind friends' who showed him 'love and courtesy'.[30] It seems that Prynne was free to move around the castle, though not to leave its limits. Visitors from across the island who had business at the castle may have gained permission from the Carterets to meet their interesting charge.

More details of Prynne's imprisonment on Jersey became available during the 1640s. Prynne described Sir Philip Carteret as 'a faithful, constant friend' and acknowledged yet again 'what extraordinary favours and respects' he received from Sir Philip and his lady. It was through Carteret's good graces, Prynne reported, that his fellow sufferer Henry Burton procured 'more liberty, respect, and better accommodations' during his imprisonment on nearby Guernsey.[31] Sir Philip's family, declared Prynne, 'was the most orderly, pious, religious... and best nurtured by far of any in the island'. Hours of discourse led Prynne to represent Carteret as 'an enemy to the bishops' tyranny and... innovations', who 'much joyed at the calling of this and the former parliament'.[32]

Carteret, however, had enemies, as perhaps would anyone who combined the offices of bailiff, lieutenant governor, and farmer of the king's revenues, and who also served as judge in the island court and captain of the militia. Jersey had more than a century of infighting among leading families and interests, and rivalry between governors and jurats, which became more acute as authority became concentrated. In 1642, a group of aggrieved inhabitants petitioned parliament against Carteret, charging him with arbitrary exercise of excessive power, 'being absolute in that island so far remote from the eyes of the state'. His listed offences were mostly fiscal and administrative, involving licences, imposts, and customs, but the petitioners also charged him with nepotism, awarding key positions to his son and nephew, and filling island offices with kindred of his faction.[33]

When civil war erupted between the king and parliament, Carteret, like many a moderate gentleman, attempted to 'adhere to both, without siding against either', desiring 'the parliament's friendship and [the] king's jointly'.[34] Such a neutralist position proved untenable, and in February 1643, while many of the islanders sided with parliament, Carteret promoted the king's commission of array, thereby earning the label 'malignant'. Sir Philip Carteret died in August 1643, but his defiance in holding the two Jersey castles for his majesty played a part in subsequent royalist successes. Parliamentary commissioners gained temporary ascendancy for a few months after Carteret's death, but the royalists soon regained control of a divided island and held it until 1651 (see Chapter 8).

Sir Philip Carteret's emergence as a royalist was deeply compromising for Prynne, who had publicly praised him as a friend. Prynne's enemies in England and Carteret's enemies on the island combined to besmirch both men's reputations, in a series of printed diatribes, to which Prynne responded with typically prolix vigour. Hostility between controversialists in civil-war London pitted the Independent John Lilburne against the Presbyterian William Prynne, each attacking the other in print. The failure of parliamentary efforts to retake Jersey stirred further antagonism against the island's 'malignants' and those who had taken their side. Critics charged Prynne with obstructing parliamentary plans to mount an expedition to Jersey in 1643, thereby ensuring the loss of the island. Prynne's 1645 counter-polemic *The Lyar Confounded* was answered at length in *Pseudo-Mastix: The Lyar's Whipp*, a full-scale assault on the administration of Sir Philip Carteret and his erstwhile puritan supporter, which may have circulated only in manuscript. Leading the assault was Michael Lemprière, a jurat of Jersey and a longtime foe of Carteret, who had been instrumental in preparing the anonymous *Articles* of 1642. Co-authors Henry Dumaresq and Abraham Hérault were also veterans of the anti-Carteret faction, linking island politics with the turmoils of the kingdom.[35]

The creators of *Pseudo-Mastix* charged in essence that Prynne had allowed himself to be seduced by Carteret's wiles, 'to maintain a particular man's pride and interest, against a whole and well affected commonwealth'. Prynne saw the island only from the castle's point of view and was oblivious to Carteret's 'oppressions' in Jersey's parishes. 'All he could know was only by Sir Philip's and his Lady's informations.' Indeed, they intimated, Prynne, the godly scourge of secular pastimes, had himself played cards into the night with the Carteret women, in an atmosphere of 'fiddling, dancing...drinking of healths, and lascivious and filthy discourse'. Prynne, by this account, was a dupe and a hypocrite, as well as an enabler of the royalist cause.[36] And his incarceration, although uncomfortable, was not the ordeal that Prynne the 'martyr' depicted, or that perhaps the state intended.

Prynne's troubles were not over, although he enjoyed periods of positions of responsibility and prolific pamphleteering during the Protectorate and the Restoration. Suspected of being a royalist spy, he was imprisoned in Dunster Castle, Somerset, in June 1650, then moved to Pendennis Castle, Cornwall, where he was confined from June 1651 to February 1653. Prynne had plenty of experience in comporting himself in prison, though never again on an island.[37] Prynne renewed his praise for 'the ancient family of the Carterets' in the changed circumstances of the Restoration, memorializing yet again 'their favour to me whiles a close prisoner in Mount Orgeuil Castle in Jersey'.[38]

Burton on Guernsey

Henry Burton had already spent three months in Lancaster Castle when orders came at the beginning of November 1640 for his further removal. He was taken to Liverpool and put on board a ship, and only then did his escort reveal that he was bound for 'the isle or castle of Guernsey', where his wife and family would not be allowed to join him. There followed a 'long, tedious, and perilous voyage' of six weeks' duration, another rough passage 'in the winter season, through dangerous seas', in which Burton was 'tumbled and tossed' by storms, and 'even nigh unto death' with sea-sickness. The leaking vessel made landfalls at Dublin, Milford Haven, and Dartmouth, before reaching Guernsey on 16 December, but the prisoner was 'not permitted to take the least refreshing on land'. It was a miserable and dangerous voyage, but mild compared to Prynne's harrowing experience. In his post-imprisonment *Narration*, burnishing his martyr's credentials, Burton explicitly compared himself to St Paul, who also suffered 'perils by sea' while bearing witness 'to the truth of the gospel'.[39]

'A true and perfect account of the money disbursed in and about the convoy of Mr Henry Burton from the castle of Lancaster...to the Castle Cornet within the isle of Guernsey', filed in the Exchequer, detailed the £115 6s. 7d. spent to move him between prisons. It included the £20 1s. 1d. charge for Burton's conveyance 40 miles from Lancaster to Liverpool, 'with the moneys necessarily expended before he went shipboard'; £48 5s. 6d. incurred in victualling the ship 'in regard of contrary winds occasioning delay in their journey'; and £15 to his conductor Brian Burton (no relation), who 'was absent by reason of storms and contrary winds from the 1st of November until the 21st of January...for his care and pains in all the same'.[40]

Occupying a similar position to Jersey's Mont Orgeuil, Guernsey's Castle Cornet was a towering medieval fortress on a rocky islet close to the harbour of St Peter Port. One of its deepest dungeons, so 'subterranean and humid' that prisoners' hair turned wet, had no more light than could be seen through the keyhole.[41] Burton found this facility an improvement on conditions at Lancaster, where he had been forced to share the gaol with papists and witches. Guernsey had a Presbyterian heritage, and Burton was not without local sympathizers. The governor, the Earl of Danby, resisted Laudian demands to conform Guernsey's church discipline to the Church of England, because 'it may well be thought dangerous to give a general discontent unto the inhabitants...by altering the form of their discipline so affected by them and long enjoyed' (see Chapter 6).[42] The castle lieutenant Nathaniel Darrell, 'a noble gentleman born in Kent', gave

Burton 'civil and courteous usage', and always provided him with 'good and wholesome diet...the best the island and sea afforded, which he sent me warm from his table'. On at least one occasion Darrell gave Burton a bottle of muscadine wine sent to Castle Cornet by Captain George Carteret.[43] Though not allowed to leave the castle, Burton was not necessarily hidden from visiting Guernseymen, bent on paying their respects to a distinguished if notorious and now unfortunate minister. The Guernsey Presbyterian Jean de la Marche was foremost among those rendering sympathy and assistance.[44]

Burton's initial accommodation was a bare cell with boarded windows, allowing glimpses of neither the sun by day nor the moon by night. But during his three years of island confinement he graduated to a room with a view, and a year and a half later to the highest chamber in the castle with a panoramic maritime prospect. Burton's social isolation was severe, but he occupied himself with useful chores and a strenuous programme of reading. 'God made everything a recreation; the making of mine own bed, and the sweeping of my chamber, was an exercise of my body, so a recreation of my mind.' Like his fellow prisoner Prynne, Burton engaged in 'meditations...to deceive the natural tedium of so horrid a solitariness'. And, like 'the birdman of Alcatraz', a much less salubrious island prisoner, he even fed pigeons at his windows.[45]

Burton spent much of his time with the Bible, studying Hebrew, Greek, Latin, French, and English editions. He also treasured a volume of ecclesiastical history in Greek. His keeper, Lieutenant Darrell, maintained the strict conditions of his imprisonment, denying him access to controversial texts and enforcing the ban on writing materials. Burton, however, discovered 'an art to make ink, and for pens I had goose wings, which were to sweep the dust off my windows, and for paper a private friend in Guernsey town supplied me'. (This was most likely the minister Jean de la Marche, who had himself endured imprisonment at Castle Cornet for seven months in 1633 and who shared Burton's enthusiasm for *Revelation*.[46]) Like many prisoners worldwide, Burton kept this contraband secret. He even managed to smuggle out controversial writings, 'some of which came to light, and some miscarried', including denunciations of Archbishop Laud. Burton's *Replie to a Relation of the Conference between William Laude and Mr Fisher the Jesuite*, printed surreptitiously in 1640, refers to the author as 'a late minister of the Gospel' who 'still suffereth both close imprisonment and punishment, with divorcement and separation from wife, children, and all friends whatsoever, as a man buried quick in a marble tomb of calamity, the very image of hell'. Exceeding 400 printed pages, this example of island prison writing would have required a dozen quires of smuggled paper. Other work attributed to Burton from the final year of his imprisonment includes *Englands Complaint to Iesvs Christ*, *Jesu-Worship Confuted*, and perhaps part of *Lord Bishops None of the Lord Bishops*, all printed in secret in the summer and autumn of 1640.[47]

Burton led an almost eremitic life on Guernsey and came to believe that he would have read and written less if his wife had been there to comfort him. The prisoner missed his family, and missed his pulpit and parish, but he was sustained, he later reported, by 'an infallible knowledge that the cause for which I thus suffered was a noble, holy, righteous, and innocent cause ... the cause of Christ, of his gospel, of his church, yea of the whole land, my native country'. The rainbow he saw on 25 April 1640—contemporary with the first parliament in England in eleven years—seemed to him to signify that 'God's church in England especially should have a miraculous deliverance through a sea of troubles'.[48] Clandestine correspondence from England, perhaps through the de la Marche connection, may have alerted him to political developments that would bring his ordeal to an end. Entries in de la Marche's diary, framed by references to *Joshua* and *Apocalypse*, suggest that they anticipated the end of Burton's exile 'plus de six moys paravat sa deliverance'.[49] Castle officials were also informed about quarrels in England, and the 'beginnings of bloodshed' in Scotland, and may have shared this news with their prisoner.[50]

Looking back in 1641, Burton compared his three and a half years of incarceration (including time in England) to the forty-two months foretold in *Revelation*, when 'the Beast out of the bottomless pit, that Antichrist, shall affront God's church'; and he saw his liberation in November 1640 as part of a general deliverance from 'the bonds and chains of a Babylonian and Antichristian captivity'. His suffering was worthwhile, he reflected, because now 'the Lord hath thus begun his great and glorious work of repairing his temple, and restoring religion'. His meditations on *Revelation*, 'digested ... during his banishment and close imprisonment in the Isle of Guernsey', indicated to Burton 'a prophecy of these last times'. Burton is usually considered a congregational Independent, but his study of John's work on Patmos seems to have made him a millenarian Sixth Trumpeter, if not an early Fifth Monarchist.[51]

The Guernsey minister Jean de la Marche applauded Burton as 'the faithful witness of Christ', who lay dead 'unburied in ... Castle Cornet', and drew parallels between the prisoner's suffering and the prophecies of St John of Patmos. After Burton's release, when Prynne joined him from Jersey, de la Marche hosted a celebratory farewell banquet for the two 'martyrs' before they set sail to England. They left Guernsey on 19 November 1640 and made landfall at Dartmouth on 22 November 1640 after an uneventful voyage. One week later they enjoyed a rapturous homecoming in London.[52]

Bastwick on Scilly

John Bastwick's isolation was especially severe. Unlike the Channel Islands, with their parishes and ports, and their active trade with England and France, which at least brought the world to their shores, the Isles of Scilly were a slenderly populated and lightly trafficked sprinkle of rocks, 28 miles beyond Land's End. They seemed like the end of the world. Bastwick had a shorter journey than his fellows, from one end of Cornwall to the other, followed by a day at sea, and by 16 October 1637 was ensconced in the island castle of St Mary's.[53] Facilities there were barely adequate for its military defenders, with no spare room for a seditious libeller. A survey in 1637 noted 'the want of conveniency' in St Mary's Castle, which was 'uncapable to lodge and accommodate a garrison of twenty soldiers, and so ill contrived in the fortification, that the least assault of an enemy could easily carry it'.[54] There would be scant welcome and little comfort for a controversial gentleman prisoner.

Details of Bastwick's confinement are hard to find. Susanna Bastwick's petition of November 1640 referred as much to her own suffering as her husband's. Bastwick's accompanying petition to the House of Commons, subsequently printed, echoed that of his wife, and dwelt more on the injustice of his sentence than the circumstances of his imprisonment. Further petitions from Susanna Bastwick in October 1644 and John Bastwick in March 1646, seeking reparations, add few details.[55]

The 1641 edition of Bastwick's Latin treatise *Flagellum Pontificis et Episcoporum Latialium* refers to the Isles of Scilly by their old name 'Sorlings', and describes them as stony and inhospitable, devoid of civility and culture. Bastwick describes his keeper, Thomas Bassett, as a man of disgraceful and degenerate life, which is what any puritan might say of any cavalier. Bassett was lieutenant governor of Scilly under his uncle Sir Francis Godolphin and had hoped to do more than command a fort. Susanna Bastwick in her 1644 petition says that Bassett 'carried himself most unworthily and inhumanely' towards her husband. There would be no cultivated evening conversation in St Mary's Castle, of the kind Prynne enjoyed at Mont Orgueil, and no supply of smuggled books and writing materials of the sort that sustained Burton at Castle Cornet. Instead, Bastwick complained in 1646, he 'was kept close prisoner two years and four months and for seven days and nights, never came into any bed, but lay in a dungeon, and endured unsufferable misery from inhumane gaolors'. One can imagine him marking the days on the wall. Susanna Bastwick had followed her husband to Launceston, and declared that she would 'undergo any difficulty or misery' to live with him, but after his removal to Scilly she was ordered, 'under pain of imprisonment, not to set her foot upon any part of the islands'. She was 'forced to live in a disconsolate condition', while Bastwick endured 'a living death and a dying life'.[56]

Though he never lost his knack for polemic, renewing his attack on popery, episcopacy, hierarchy, and ceremony as soon as he was released, Bastwick dwelt little on his personal history. Even when drawn into controversy between Presbyterians and Independents in the course of the civil war, he chose not to flout his credentials as a martyr or witness. *A Iust Defence of John Bastwick, Doctor in Phisicke, Against the Calumnies of John Lilburne* (1645) mentions his island 'banishment' only indirectly, as a time when his wife Susanna offered friendship and assistance to Lilburne, and Lilburne performed 'small favours . . . in the time of my imprisonment'.[57] In *The Utter Routing of the Whole Army of all the Independents and Sectaries* (1646), Bastwick recalled suffering 'such intolerable misery of all sorts, as would exceed belief to relate', but mentioned only the cruelty of separation from his wife and children: 'Paul found more favour from a heathen Roman Caesar, than I had from a Christian king', who 'would not then grant me that liberty in his kingdom, that he denied not to crows and kites and other vermin, that I might provide for my young ones'.[58]

Susanna Bastwick took up the struggle in *Innocency Cleared . . . in a Letter sent to Mr Henry Burton . . . in Defence of Dr Bastwick* (1645). She referred to Burton and Prynne as her husband's 'quondam fellow sufferers', but made little other mention of their time in prison.[59] After Bastwick's death in 1654, she reminded the high court of parliament of her late husband's 'long exile in the Isles of Scilly . . . his many years cruel close imprisonment', and the loss of his hearing, his practice, and his property. Though parliament had promised reparations, to be raised from the estates of delinquent royalists, the ordinance died when parliament was dissolved. Now, the distressed widow declared, 'the sufferings, afflictions, and miseries' of herself and her children were 'daily more and more increased', and John Bastwick's story demanded renewed public attention.[60]

Island Imprisonment

The 'puritan martyrs' and their supporters considered confinement to remote islands 'not only cruel and inhumane, but most unjust and unchristian'.[61] Their captivity was more burdensome than mainland incarceration because the offshore location created additional barriers between the prisoner and the world. The very experience of crossing by water marked a separation, as Prynne's and Burton's harrowing journeys to the Channel Islands attested. Each prisoner's experience was different, depending upon local social resources, the attitude of the garrison, and the personality and politics of island governors. Prynne enjoyed conversation with the Carterets, and Burton had the company of his books, but Bastwick could turn only to himself and his God, or the surly Thomas Bassett. Cut off from external streams of discourse, each found common reading in the Bible, especially the book of *Revelation*. All three returned to the fray in the 1640s, when some of John's prophecies seemed to be fulfilled.

Unsympathetic historians have suggested that Prynne, Burton, and Bastwick were lucky not to be treated as traitors for opposing the Caroline regime.[62] But the court of Star Chamber had no power to execute anyone, even if their offence so warranted, and the Council could not order their deaths. Instead, the government

kept its prisoners alive, at a distance, and even paid for their keep. Their supporters considered them 'martyrs', though their ordeal was not fatal, nor without
occasional compensations. In their tracts for public consumption, the prisoners
used the image of entombment, of living death, walled off from the world, to
describe their situation. They used the language of exile, as if they had been
banished abroad, although Jersey and Guernsey were English dominions, and
the Scillies part of an English county. Burton, Bastwick and Prynne adopted this
rhetoric, not only to make sense of their predicament, and to highlight the cruelty
of their persecutors, but to associate their suffering with the exiles of Scripture and
history. Recognition of these tropes by no means undermines their force or their
authenticity. The 'puritan martyrs' faced unprecedented perpetual confinement,
until the providential calling of a parliament brought them home.

Rebuking Charles I's Privy Council for presuming 'to determine of the estates
and liberties of the subject contrary to the law of the land', the parliament that
restored the 'puritan martyrs' to their liberty abolished the court of Star Chamber
in 1641. Reaffirming the principle of Magna Carta that none should suffer
arbitrary imprisonment, parliament specifically permitted anyone so 'restrained
of his liberty' to be granted the writ of *habeas corpus*, under the king's protection.
By implication, from parliament's perspective, this applied as well to the islands as
to the mainland. None henceforth should suffer 'heavier punishments than by any
law is warranted', though this was more a rhetorical than a substantive prohibition.[63] The 'puritan martyrs' were vindicated, and principles established for
future protection. But, like many of the good intentions of the early Long
Parliament, these salutary correctives were set aside in subsequent phases of the
revolution, when island prisons were needed again.

12

Charles I on the 'Ile of Wait'

The most famous and highest ranked of all island prisoners, King Charles I was held for thirteen months on the Isle of Wight in the period between his defeat and his execution. He arrived there on 13 November 1647, almost by accident, and spent most of the following year devising schemes to depart. Kings were supposed to be founts of power, justice, and mercy, but Charles himself became a petitioner to his subjects after losing his liberty. For a monarch accustomed to being called God's regent on earth, the reversal was extraordinary and galling. The persecutor of Burton, Bastwick, and Prynne himself became isolated and confined. King Charles's 'solitudes and sufferings' as an island prisoner were almost unbearable, from a royalist point of view, and marked him out for sainthood.[1] The king's imprisonment drew unprecedented attention to this generally quiet island, which for one crucial year lay at the centre of the kingdom's hopes and fears. The Isle of Wight's detached location served to protect and contain his majesty, and to frustrate any prospect of escape.

By the autumn of 1647, King Charles had already experienced eighteen months of captivity, following defeat in the English civil war. He had been held by the Scots at Newcastle, then by parliament in Northamptonshire, before being seized by agents of the New Model Army. In August, his captors moved him to the Thames-side palace of Hampton Court, where he stayed two and a half months before managing to escape. In a letter addressed to Lord Fairfax, he complained 'that kings less than any should endure captivity' and observed 'with what patience I have endured a tedious restraint'.[2]

Hampton Court was a somewhat run-down royal residence, barely serviceable for a court, and fit neither for a fortress nor for a gaol. Royalists looked back on the king's time there as 'halcyon days, and without clouds', compared to what came later.[3] It proved relatively easy for Charles to slip away, with three faithful companions, on the dark and rainy night of 11 November 1647. His accomplices claimed to be preserving the king from 'the resolution which a violent party in the army had to take away his life'—a rumoured assassination plot—and would have changed the course of history had they delivered him to safety.[4]

Sir John Berkeley, William Legg, and John Ashburnham, the cavaliers who engineered the king's escape, had no clear plan where to take him. Nor was King Charles firm of purpose or resolve. He needed a place of safety where he could regroup his forces, and from which further flight was possible. Every plausible destination carried political risks, besides the difficulties of logistics and security.

England's Islands in a Sea of Troubles. David Cressy, Oxford University Press (2020). © David Cressy 2020.
DOI: 10.1093/oso/9780198856603.001.0001

One possibility was for the king to dash to London, to rally his supporters and confound his enemies, though such a move could prove disastrous in a city filled with armed radicals. Another was to go west into the country, and thence to Ireland or France. Ashburnham asked Legg, 'whether the king had thought of any place to go to', and Legg replied that 'he inclined to go beyond the seas, and that he supposed Jersey a proper place for him'.[5] Authorities at Hampton Court had barely an inkling where he had gone: 'some think for Scotland, others for London, some for Jersey, others (which is more probable) to the Isle of Wight.'[6] Jersey remained a royalist stronghold, one of the king's dominions, yet close enough to the Continent for reinforcement or escape. His son the Prince of Wales had found refuge in Jersey, before crossing over to France and Holland, and the royalist Sir Edward Hyde spoke very highly of the island (see Chapter 8).

A strong case could be made for spiriting the king to France, where the queen was already resident, and a fledgling court in exile was forming. King Charles's life might be safer under French protection, and Bourbon resources might bolster his cause, but there would be a high cost to his reputation if the king deserted his kingdom and became dependent on a foreign power. Flight to Ireland posed comparable complications of over-reliance on Roman Catholics. According to Ashburnham, 'it rested then that his majesty was to make choice of a place where he might avoid the present danger, where he might give least offence to the interest of the parliament and army, where he might have frequent intercourse with both for settling peace, of which he then despaired not'.[7] Choices narrowed, however, as the king's 'coming into London was desperate, his hiding in England chimerical, and his escape to Jersey prevented'.[8] Trusting in God, the rescuers rode south towards the Channel, bickering most of the way.

Reaching the Hampshire coast, a day or two ahead of parliamentary pursuers, the group paused to refresh at the Earl of Southampton's house at Titchfield. The king was now 'in good hope' of finding transport to France, 'the wind serving, and the queen having sent a ship for that purpose'.[9] But no such ship materialized, and options shrank as the government closed the ports. In the panic aftermath of the king's escape, parliament ordered all ports, creeks, and passages to be blocked, all ships, barques, and boats to be searched, and every effort made 'to stop and seize the king and all that shall come with him'.[10] With barely an entourage and barely a plan, King Charles was a wanted man.

A Refuge for a King

The Isle of Wight lay just across the Solent from Titchfield and could serve as a short-term refuge or staging point for subsequent movements. Charles had visited the island in happier times and had hopes of sheltering at Sir John Oglander's house before sailing to a safer destination. He declared, however, that 'he would not go into the Isle until he knew how the governor would receive him'.[11] This was a wise precaution, since the governor, Robert Hammond, was a parliamentary colonel. But Hammond had withdrawn to the quietness of the Isle of Wight to distance himself from post-war political turmoil, and his loyalties were now uncertain.[12] For their part, with dangers pressing, the king and his companions had little choice but 'to put themselves upon Hammond', in the hope of being treated honourably. It was Charles himself, so his rescuers reported, who made 'election' of the Isle of Wight, because it was 'now too late to boggle'. The island, he now declared, was 'the best of any place he could make choice of' and 'most proper for his residence, especially if he could obtain honourable conditions from the governor of that place'.[13] It removed him, he hoped, from immediate oversight by parliament or the army. Hammond was reportedly 'very much discomposed' to learn of the king's presence and was hard-pressed to determine whether Charles would be his prisoner or his guest. Berkeley recalled that the governor 'fell into such a trembling . . . he would have fallen off his horse' when he heard that the king was nearby.[14]

With politeness and trepidation all round, King Charles and his attendants crossed over to Cowes on the night of 13 November 1647, accompanied by Governor Hammond. Sir John Oglander heard the news to his 'great astonishment' and 'could do nothing but sigh and weep for two nights and a day' on realizing that his majesty had sought a refuge but found a prison: 'I verily believe he could not come into a worse place for himself, and where he could be more securely kept.' On the next day, a Sunday, Hammond escorted King Charles through the town of Newport to Carisbrooke Castle, where the leading island gentry gathered to kiss his hand. There he entered a privileged kind of house arrest, with servants to attend him, and the best furnishings the castle could muster. Governor Hammond lamented that he lacked fowl and other provisions fit for a dinner for a king and had to rely on well-wishers for informal purveyance.[15] Some of Hammond's soldiers felt sympathy for the king, among them Captain John Urry, who 'privately amongst his friends made up a purse of gold and gave it to the king who was then in want'.[16]

Parliament knew within days that the king had arrived at Carisbrooke and was content for him to stay there under guard 'during the time the Houses shall think it fit to continue him in the Isle of Wight'.[17] Hammond assured his masters that 'the king stands engaged in his word not to stir', hopefully asking 'that if he be not thought safe here he may be removed'.[18]

Assigning responsibility for the king's sojourn on the Isle of Wight grew in significance as his situation deteriorated, and grew in subsequent retelling. Royalists understood that 'his majesty's design was not for that place when he left Hampton Court' but could not agree 'whether he were necessitated or betrayed thither'.[19] Ashburnham insisted that the decision was the king's alone, and all subsequent misfortunes the result of Hammond's duplicity. Others blamed

Ashburnham himself, and quoted King Charles saying to him at Titchfield, 'Oh, Jack, thou hast undone me.'[20] According to Henry Firebrace, a page of the bed-chamber who became a royal confidant, the king 'was unfortunately brought to the Isle of Wight, whither ... he did not intend to go'.[21] He was driven 'to such necessitous courses', according to another royalist source, 'to fly for fear of his life, in so obscure and mean a manner, to so remote (though strong) place of his dominions for shelter and refuge'.[22] The loyal courtier Sir Thomas Herbert felt sure that 'many that cordially loved the king did very much dislike his going to this place, it being so remote, and designed neither for his honour nor his safety'.[23] Some thought his going thither was part of an army 'design', to keep the king bottled up and under their control. Commissary General Ireton took the view that the king's coming to the Isle of Wight, 'though appearingly a choice', was 'really upon some emergent necessity, for the avoiding of a worse, when he someway found himself stopped, and unable to get clear away, according to his first intention'.[24] Charles himself told Hammond that the island was 'the place he first designed when he apprehended it not safe to continue longer at Hampton Court, and that if he were to choose any place within his three kingdoms he would not remove thence, except to London upon a personal treaty'.[25] Necessity drove the narrative as well as the action.

The king's arrival turned the Isle of Wight from a quiet frontier outpost to a centre of political attention. Governor Hammond acknowledged his responsibility for 'the security of his majesty's person', but thought the task impossible 'unless I should keep him close prisoner, which is a business of that nature that it is neither fit nor safe for me to do, especially of myself'. Writing to Westminster on 19 November, Hammond accepted the king's explanation

> that he came from Hampton Court for no other cause, but for the preservation of his person, which was (as he apprehended) in such danger, that he could not with safety continue longer there ... And that he chose this place rather than any other (when he was at liberty to have gone whither he pleased) that he might continue under the protection of the army (myself being a member thereof), and that he might have continuance of some intercourse between himself and the parliament, for the settling of a general peace.[26]

Though Charles was a prisoner, he was still king, and still prepared for kingly negotiations. Estranged from his kingdoms, he continued to engage in treaty-making, as he sought to recover his fortunes. Parliament ordered Hammond to 'take special care for securing of the king's person in the place where he now is'.[27]

Carisbrooke was a medieval fortress, commanding high ground near the centre of the island. The castle was moated and banked, double-ringed by stone walls, approached only by a crenellated gatehouse and drawbridge. Elizabethan bastions and earthworks had modernized its defences, and recent reinforcements had brought it up to date. The king was accommodated in the constable's lodging in the inner bailey, with garrison forces nearby. Hammond had orders to watch the king closely, but secret royal communications proved impossible to suppress.[28] The governor instructed that no boats should land 'neither persons nor goods in any part of this island, save only at Yarmouth Castle, Cowes Castle, and Ryde', where there were guards in place 'to detain and secure any that cannot give a very good account of themselves and their business',[29] but experienced smugglers knew alternative routes.

Despite his isolation, Charles was well supplied with news and maintained an active correspondence. He is estimated to have penned a thousand letters while on the Isle of Wight. He spent hours most evenings cyphering and decyphering messages, which were smuggled in and out of his bedchamber. Even under tight control, with guards at his doors, the king had access to trusted servants, and conversed with visitors through chinks in the wall. Hearing his informed discourse on 'the general affairs of this kingdom', observers wondered 'how such things should come to his majesty's knowledge'.[30] Papers passed in gloves, boots, bodices, and laundry baskets, and signals with handkerchiefs indicated when packages were ready. As the king's servant Henry Firebrace recalled, 'his majesty never wanted good intelligence from the queen, the prince, and many of his friends, even in the time when those cursed votes of no more addresses took place'. Maintaining secrecy relied on the use of cyphers, and sometimes on a courier who could neither read nor write.[31] The authorities knew, however, that 'the king had constant intelligence given him of all things', and intercepted many of his messages. Both Governor Hammond and the Committee at Derby House became privy to many of King Charles's 'plottings and contrivances', as informers among his servants passed information to parliament and the army.[32] On one occasion, parliament intercepted Henrietta Maria's letters to the king, but, 'not being able to decipher them, sent over to the Isle of Wight to have the king's cypher searched for'. A correspondent of Sir Richard Leveson reported that officers ransacked the king's cabinet, without success, because 'by chance the king had the cypher in his pocket, and with scorn to their incivility, burnt it before their faces'.[33]

Like other long-term island prisoners, Charles had to cope with separation from his family and friends, and the day-to-day exigencies of incarceration. He needed exercise for his body, ease for his mind, and news of the outside world. But the circumstances of a king under guard were extraordinary. Charles's experience since his capture by the Scots may have prepared him for privation, but it was a hard transition from a household of hundreds to a handful of servants and retainers. The king's diet, furnishings, and attendance at Carisbrooke far exceeded those of any gentleman prisoner but were lean and dishonourable by royal standards. The material conditions of Charles's detention retained barely a shadow of regality. The royal prerogative was in abeyance. It was only to put a brave face on a desperate situation that some royalists referred to 'his majesty's court in the Isle of Wight'.[34] Trapped on the island, his majesty was 'very strictly looked to, his lodging being locked every night, and the keys carried to the governor', so royalists learned in December 1647.[35] Spiritual conditions too were testing. Denied his choice of chaplains, King Charles steadfastly refused to join in the garrison's use of the puritan Directory of Public Worship. The king who had been most scrupulous in his religious observances maintained a regime of private devotions, but went many months without the sacrament of communion.[36] The conditions of the king's incarceration loosened over time as his captors had need of him, and tightened as they mistrusted his intentions. The number of servants allowed to attend him grew when the king was engaged on treaties and shrank when he returned to close confinement.

During his first few weeks at Carisbrooke, the king had 'liberty to ride and recreate himself anywhere within the isle, when or where he pleased'. He was seen 'taking his pleasure abroad in the island, both in hunting and other delightful sports'. Some of the gentry assured the king 'that the whole island was unanimously for him, except the garrisons of the castle and Colonel Hammond's captains', and nourished the notion that 'the king might choose his own time of quitting the island, having liberty to ride abroad daily'.[37] For a while the king believed this to be true. Local landowners paid their compliments, and Sir John Oglander offered hospitality at Nunwell House, near Brading. 'Any that were desirous to see his majesty might without opposal,' reported Sir Thomas Herbert, suggesting that within a limited compass, despite circumstances of constraint, King Charles was more accessible than ever.[38] He even had use of his coach, which parliament shipped over in December, along with furnishings and bedding from Hampton Court. He could write every evening, with works of devotional theology, poetry, and the plays of Shakespeare for company. There was never a shortage of books. Carisbrooke had no gallery, state room, or garden, where a king might find solace, but he could walk the castle perimeter, when his riding privileges were revoked, and, beginning in the spring, for 'solace and recreation', he enjoyed bowling on the green that Hammond constructed for his use. Weather permitting, he walked six or eight circuits of the castle wall each morning and afternoon.[39] Select visitors were permitted to be touched for the King's Evil, the royal laying-on of hands that was believed to have curative powers. Ashburnham, Berkeley, and Legg, who had conveyed the king to the island, were allowed to remain on their honour (until dismissed in February), and a few more servants and attendants arrived to provide royal courtesies and comforts. Parliament allocated an additional £200 to the governor of the Isle of Wight in January 1648, 'for the defraying of the extraordinary charge he hath been at, upon occasion of the king's being there', and 'for satisfaction of such soldiers appointed by him to be guards about the king', but Hammond asked for more, 'the condition of this place being not like others'.[40]

Plans to Escape

The period of King Charles's island imprisonment coincided with momentous developments in the three British kingdoms. His ability to conduct sensitive negotiations while under restraint demonstrated the apparent impossibility of settlement without him. The king hoped to profit from disagreements between the Scots and Westminster, between the army and parliament, and between Presbyterians and Independents, as disputes among the victors in the first civil war led to a second.[41] For the sake of the 'settling of the protestant religion, and the peace of the three kingdoms', King Charles was said, from time to time, to be willing 'to part with some of those jewels of his prerogative'.[42] But whether he was principled or perfidious in these negotiations has been argued ever since.

Among the king's visitors during his early months on the Isle of Wight were the Scottish Covenanter commissioners, the earls of Lauderdale, Loudoun, and Lanark, as well as representatives from Westminster. On 26 December 1647, Charles signed the 'Engagement', to advance Scottish interests and to safeguard English Presbyterianism, in exchange for military assistance against the Independents and the army.[43] This secret agreement was designed to re-establish Charles's kingship, but it set the stage for renewed civil war.

Under cover of the commissioners' comings and goings, Sir John Berkeley advised the king 'to meditate nothing but his immediate escape'. Ashburnham tried to find a boat to get the king off the island, but without success.[44] The Army Council in London had intelligence of some of these plans and urged 'great care to be taken'. Oliver Cromwell warned Hammond in late December that the royalist Sir George Carteret 'hath sent three boats from Jersey, and a barque for Cherbourg... to bring the king (if their plot can hold) from the Isle of Wight to Jersey'.[45] One such crew reached the Isle of Wight in January, under the guise of Normandy traders, but was able to do no more than exchange secret letters.[46] On 19 January 1648, the king counselled one of his go-betweens, 'let not cautiousness beget fear'.[47]

An ill-judged attempt by royalist officers to seize Carisbrooke Castle, 'to have either kept it for the king, or carried his majesty to Jersey island', was easily suppressed, with fatal consequence to the plotters. Captain John Burley, the leader of this 'irrational and impossible' rising (as Clarendon called it), was quickly caught and gruesomely executed.[48]

Reacting to news of these dangers, the militarily controlled parliament passed the Vote of No Addresses, banning further communication with the king. Oliver Cromwell declared Charles 'so great a dissembler, and so false a man, that he was not to be trusted'. Parliament sent Hammond new instructions 'for the security and safety of the king's person', and Cromwell urged him to discover the king's 'juggling'. Several of Charles's closest servants were dismissed, with further reductions to follow, and his liberty to leave the castle was curtailed. Not surprisingly, observers reported the king 'much discontented'. His household was capped at thirty, with everyone subject to army vetting. Among those dismissed was the royal barber, so after this time the king began to let his hair grow and started to sprout a beard.[49] He was now more a prisoner than ever, with greatly reduced prospects of gaining freedom through political accommodation. Parliament further fortified the Isle of Wight and augmented the garrison, adding a dozen brass ordnance in February, 200 more soldiers in March 1648, and a further 500 in June.[50] The island had become a fortress as well as a prison, impregnable to foreign attack and resistant to royalist uprising.

Unlike other long-term prisoners of state, who risked sinking into oblivion, King Charles was forever in the news. His whereabouts and circumstances were constant subjects of curiosity and commentary. Royalist propagandists compared the king's imprisonment to that of John the Baptist or the Apostle St Paul. The potent but pathetic image of *Carolus in vinculis*, King Charles in chains, invited outrage at his treatment and compassion for his plight. A famous woodcut showed King Charles, with crown and sceptre, peering through bars above the gatehouse of Carisbrooke Castle, saying, 'Behold your king' imprisoned on 'The Ile of Wait' (see Figure 12).[51] 'Never was any unfortunate ward held in greater bondage under an harsh guardian, than our sovereign hath been under his own subjects,' declared one royalist pamphlet.[52] He was 'the most unfortunate in the world', kept 'in worse

Figure 12. 'The Ile of Wait', *An Ould Ship Called an Exhortation*, 1648 (Alamy Images)

captivity than any subject ever was', complained others.[53] Supporters lamented the image of their sovereign immured 'in a small close room, under many bolts, bars, grates, locks and keys', bemoated and bereft.[54] The king was over the water, though still within his kingdom. He still commanded loyalty, though had no liberty of his own.

A principal aim of the royalists in 1648 was to free their sovereign from 'most barbarous restraint', to restore him to his 'lawful government' and to the embrace of 'his royal consort and children'. Otherwise, they feared, the kingdom faced the threat of 'slavery', and the king faced perpetual imprisonment, deposition, or assassination.[55] These were the grounds of the piecemeal and incoherent campaigns of the second civil war, which began in the spring of 1648. If Charles could appear at the head of his followers, or direct their efforts from freedom, his chances of regaining his kingdom would be transformed. Forces loyal to the king took Pembroke Castle on 8 March and had control of Berwick and Carlisle a month later. Kent was in revolt by the end of May, Essex royalists took up arms in June, and a Scottish army entered England in July. Fortune appeared to smile on his majesty when royalist forces led by 'persons of great quality' were reported gathering in Surrey, with intent to move towards the Isle of Wight. Several naval ships also declared for the king, with expectations 'they may bend their course to the Isle of Wight.' Their 'great design', it was widely believed, was 'for conveying his [majesty's] person from Carisbrooke castle'. A nervous parliament feared that mutinous sailors might attempt to put this design into practice and instructed Colonel Hammond to prevent their landing on the island. The renewed fighting altered the context of the king's imprisonment, with the king more than ever desiring to be free, and the Army all the more determined to keep him secure. Five hundred more soldiers augmented the island garrison that summer.[56]

If King Charles was to leave the Isle of Wight, it had to depend upon political negotiation, a royalist resurgence, or else his own local efforts. While hoping for a turn in the wheel of fortune, King Charles became an escapologist, though not a very good one. He designed to find ways to evade his captors, exit his chamber, escape from the castle, and find transport to freedom. Each of his efforts was thwarted. Schemes for the king's enlargement included breaking through to the roof of the room above his bedroom, crawling through a window and descending on a rope, filing through the bars or dissolving them with acid, bribing his guards, starting a fire in the castle and exiting amidst the confusion, leaving disguised in a porter's frock, switching clothes with a visitor coming to be touched for the King's Evil, and then taking a boat to Gosport, Jersey, or Holland. In almost every instance the authorities had word of these intentions before they could take effect.[57]

Plans were well advanced by March 1648 to spring the king from the island. He had escaped before, from Hampton Court, and was confident it could be done again. The plotters included the king's servant Henry Firebrace, Mr Edward

Worsley, Mr Richard Osborne, and Mr John Newland of Newport. Choosing a moonless night, they planned to befuddle the guards with wine, while his majesty escaped through a window. The king was supposed to descend on a cord, with a stick fastened across the end for him to sit on. The rope would then be used to help him over the counterscarp, where men with 'a good horse, saddle, and pistols, boots, etc. for the king' would be waiting, with 'a lusty boat' to take him to safety.[58]

When the plotters attempted to implement the plan on the night of 20 March, it all went awry. The king started to climb through his window, but 'too late found himself mistaken, he sticking fast between his breast and shoulders, and not able to get forwards or backwards'. Charles was not a large man, but he could not negotiate the opening. He had experimented by putting his head through, and assumed that the rest of his body would follow. He may have been insufficiently agile, or perhaps was over-dressed, with too many papers stuffed in his breast; in any case, the window was less negotiable than he imagined. He eventually hauled himself back in, with an audible groan, and set a candle in the window to inform his rescuers that 'the design was blown'.[59] It did not take long for army authorities to learn of this bungled attempt. It made the king appear foolish as well as deceitful, which may be why the Earl of Clarendon called the episode 'mere fiction'.[60]

According to the Firebrace letters, King Charles indicated to his assistants that 'the narrowness of the window was the only impediment for my escape, and therefore some instrument must be had to remove the bar'. He asked for a special tool—'I think it is called the endless screw, or the great force'—to clear the opening.[61] Resourceful as ever, Firebrace 'sent for files and *aqua fortis* [nitric acid] from London, to make the passage more easy, and to help in other designs'. The king was supposed to weaken the window bars to enlarge the opening in readiness for another attempt.[62] News of 'a new design in agitation to carry away the king' soon reached the Army Committee. By 15 April they knew that the king had acquired tools to attack the bars, and acid to eat the iron, and was expected to try again at the next dark night.[63] To thwart this attempt they moved him to a more secure bedroom, against the curtain wall, and the guard around the king was strengthened.

Charles's secret correspondence over the next six weeks shows him experimenting with files and acid on several sets of windows, learning to disguise the cuts with wax, clay, and scraps of glazing lead. He took into his confidence Colonel Silas Titus, a parliamentary officer with royalist inclinations, asking for technical advice on removing the bars. By one suggestion a conspirator was supposed to work on the metal while the king was at bowls. Then, late at night, when the signal was given, the bars would fall, the king would escape, and a boat would be ready to waft him away.[64]

Where the king would go if he escaped from the island was never made clear. One option that spring was to go into Kent, where a royalist revolt was brewing;

another was to join the court of exiles in France. Charles seems to have put himself in the hands of his escape team, asking one of them on 10 April, 'whither you intend that I should go, after I am over the water?' 'Concerning the place whither,' he wrote to Colonel Titus a few days later, 'I know you say true, that many of my friends thinks London the fittest place...but...I earnestly and particularly recommend the providing of a ship'. Titus arranged for horses at the water's edge near Titchfield on the mainland, in case the king escaped that way.[65] Options and opportunities shifted in the rapidly changing dynamics of the second civil war.

Meanwhile, alternative designs were hatching. The king himself asked, reasonably enough, if one or two of the castle's officers could be suborned, 'and may they not, more easily, help me out of the doors?' If he could find a way to pass by the guards, 'we need not stay for dark nights'.[66] Noting that people still came to the king to be touched for the King's Evil, and that Governor Hammond countenanced this activity, Firebrace suggested that Charles should switch clothes with one such visitor. The king could then walk out of the castle to waiting horses, disguised 'in a false beard and a periwig, and a white cap on, and a country grey or blue coat, over a pair of coloured fustian drawers to come over his breeches, and white cloth stockings, and great shoes, and an old brown coat'. The king told Firebrace on 13 April that he liked the plan, except for the false beard, 'upon which a clear judgement is easily made'. But to cover all bases, he still requested a file.[67]

Around this time observers noted that 'his majesty is in health, and merry, and sometimes very pleasant in his discourse', perhaps anticipating an end to his imprisonment. On 18 April, while taking his recreation, he 'spake in a rustical manner...saying, it will be hot bowling in May'. Some who followed the king's every utterance construed this reference to 'a hot game to be played in May' to allude to plans for a royal breakout.[68] The escape of Prince James, the Duke of York, from parliamentary custody on 20 April 1648 demonstrated that daring exploits could win success. The escape of the prince stripped parliament of a valuable asset, should they choose to depose King Charles in favour of his second son; the House of Stuart could regain the initiative if the king himself gained freedom.

Work on the Carisbrooke windows continued in secret, with continuing frustration. On 3 May, Charles informed Firebrace,

I have now made a perfect trial, and find it impossible to be done, for my body is much too thick for the breadth of the window; so that unless the middle bar be taken away I cannot get through. I have also looked upon the other two, and find the one much too little, and other so high that I know not how to reach it without a ladder; beside I do not believe it so much wider than the other, as that it will serve; wherefore it is absolutely impossible to do anything tomorrow at night.[69]

A ship was waiting, but the danger of discovery increased with every delay. Preparations for the king's escape continued but were hedged by caution and prevarication.

Eventually, on the night of 28 May, the team was ready. A few stones thrown at the king's window signalled that the operation should begin. The window bars had been weakened to allow the king's egress, and his guards were distracted by alcohol or bribes. A subsequent report to the army council revealed how the king had 'cut the top of a strong iron bar in his chamber, and was ready to descend on a rope' furnished by his servant, the clerk of the kitchen. The conspirators 'having corrupted the sentinels...had designed to convey the king over the castle wall at midnight', where horses would be waiting. This time there would be no sticking in the window, but the plan was never put to the test. As the army letter reports, 'it pleased God to move two of the three soldiers hearts [who had taken bribes to assist the king] to reveal it to the governor, who let the plot go as far as it would'. The writer (signed 'T. H.') expressed 'joy that so dangerous an attempt succeeded not according to the craft of those villains and the expectation of our enemies' and joy 'that God had vouchsafed us such a mercy'.[70] Hammond reportedly visited King Charles in his chamber and archly commented, 'I hear you are going away.'[71]

Royalists, of course, were disappointed. Henry Firebrace wrote that the attempt 'was unhappily discovered in the execution', and the cavaliers who organized it fled themselves in 'that boat that was to have carried away his majesty' to freedom.[72] Abraham Dowcett, another of the king's servants who was privy to the plan, who 'disbursed several sums of money amongst the soldiers for perfecting the same', spent years in a parliamentary prison for his part in the debacle.[73] A veteran of this episode on the other side, the parliamentarian major Edmund Rolph, later acknowledged that, if he king had come through the window, 'I had a gun ready charged to have dispatched him'. Rolph was also allegedly involved in 'a design to poison his majesty', or otherwise assassinate him, which would have been another way to solve the problem.[74] The royal attendant Richard Osborne spread the story that Rolph planned to kidnap or kill the king, and that his majesty's efforts with ropes and *aqua fortis* were to forestall that 'horrid design'.[75]

The king, however, had not given up hope of escaping. By July 1648 he was conspiring to foment an uprising to make royalists 'absolute masters of this island, and particularly of this castle'. He wrote to William Hopkins, the master of Newport grammar school, on 16 July, 'there must be a barque ready (and one will do it as well as a thousand)'. Ten days later King Charles was still adjusting plans to 'master this place' and 'make good the island' in order to escape.[76] But, as usual, there was too little action and too much delay, as time and advantage slipped away.

By this time many of the king's intimate servants had been dismissed, but a significant new figure had entered his circle. Mrs Jane Whorwood has been described as a royalist secret agent, the king's smuggler, and possibly his secret lover. She had intrigued on the king's behalf while he was at Holdenby House and was entrusted with movements of money.[77] She appears in King Charles's cyphered correspondence, represented by the number 715 or the letter N. On 27 April 1648, Charles confided in Firebrace, 'you may trust N, and I believe you will find her industrious in, and useful to, my service'.[78] She evidently had easy access to the castle, and cordial relations with the governor, as well as good contacts on the Isle of Wight and in the cavalier underground. She appears to have been privy to some of the king's escape plans and may have been instrumental in arranging shipping. She became especially close to the king in July, when Charles wrote of 'sweet Jane Whorwood' and his longing to 'embrace and nip' her. It is debatable whether erotic endearments led to sexual intimacy, but her presence distracted his majesty from the distresses of the kingdom. Charles is justly renowned for his uxorious probity, but his constancy may have waivered after years of separation and imprisonment.[79]

In the summer of 1648, Jane Whorwood became a comfort and an obsession to the king. If Sarah Poynting's reading of the royal cypher is correct, Charles could barely control himself when he invited her to his chamber on 26 July and promised to surprise her 'between jest and earnest' with 'a swyving' (a sexual encounter). The king described one letter to 'Sweet Jane' on 13 August as 'the best caudle I can send her; but if she would have a better, she must come to fetch it herself; and yet, to say truth, her Platonic way doth much spoil the taste, in my mind; and it she would leave me to my free cookery, I should think to make her confess so herself'.[80] Mrs Whorwood was an important link to the royalist resistance, though she may have resisted the king's amorous advances. The relationship would have been scandalous had it leaked out, but most of those privy to it maintained discretion. The anti-royalist press did its best to discredit King Charles in 1648 but could do no worse than to accuse him of fornication with laundry maids and pollution with the French pox, neither of which was true.[81]

Island Negotiations

Political pressures at Westminster that summer led parliament to reopen addresses to the island-bound king. Royalist and Scottish forces had been crushed in the second civil war, but cleavages remained between the army and the politicians, and between Presbyterians and Independents. Settlement of the nation's woes still seemed unimaginable without the monarch. Early in August parliament agreed to treat personally with the king, face to face, 'in such place as his majesty shall make choice of in the Isle of Wight ... with honour, freedom and safety to his majesty'.[82] It may have been the prospect of treaty negotiations, rather than the company of Mrs Whorwood, that induced the king to trim his beard, and to ask Governor Hammond 'if he saw not a new reformation in him'.[83]

The Isle of Wight grew even more in the nation's attention as fifteen parliamentary commissioners, with their retinues, were sent to treat directly with the king. They began to arrive on the island in mid-September 1648, for discussion that continued into November. Charles was released from the castle, to be lodged at William Hopkins's house in Newport, and was granted the use of his carriage and liveried servants. This gave him a taste of liberty, though few of the trappings of kingship. Once again the Isle of Wight became the centre of the Stuart political world, its hostelries bulging with aristocrats and officers. Reflecting on the season's storms, both meteorological and political, with King Charles in their midst, the islander Sir John Oglander characterized 1648 as 'a very strange year in all his three kingdoms, it we duly consider the heavens, men, and earth'.[84]

Among the many visitors drawn to the king's orbit was the royalist hack versifier John Taylor. Taylor came to see his 'suffering sovereign master' and stayed on the island from 21 October to 7 November. During this time he mingled with 'fine folks', kissed the king's hand, and took notes on sufferers of various ailments who had apparently been cured by the royal touch. Taylor was impressed that 'his majesty, with an heroic and unconquered patience, conquers his unmatchable afflictions, and with Christian constancy, expects a happy deliverance out of all his troubles'. Taylor hoped, as did no doubt most subjects, for 'speedy restoration of his majesty to his just rights, and a blessed peace for the church, people, and kingdom'.[85] However, the king himself had 'no great hopes that much good will come of it', observing 'what capacity a prisoner hath to treat, as yet I know not'.[86]

Sceptics feared that Charles could not be trusted and that 'all these packings and shufflings' were covers for deceit. 'We have justly cause to fear an escape', one correspondent at Carisbooke commented. Although his majesty 'hath passed his royal word not to depart within twenty days after the Treaty... methinks all true Englishmen should take heed of being lulled with this plot'.[87] Such distrust was justified, for the king was still working to outwit his captors. While publicly negotiating with parliament at Newport, he was secretly plotting to escape. On 7 October, he wrote secretly to his host William Hopkins: 'Where shall I take boat? Spare not my walking, in respect of security. Then, how the tide falls out? ... What winds are fair? ... Lastly, how soon all will be ready, and what impediments are which rest?' The king bared his thoughts in another extraordinarily candid letter to Hopkins, written late at night on 9 October:

Notwithstanding my too great concessions already made, I know that unless I shall make yet others, which will directly make me no king, I shall be, at best, a perpetual prisoner... The great concession I made this day was merely in order to my escape, of which, if I had not hope, I would not have done; for then I could have returned to my strait prison without reluctancy; but now I confess it would break my heart, having done that which only an escape can justify... My only hope is, that now they believe that I dare deny them nothing, and so be less careful of their guards. Wherefore, as you love my safety, let us dispatch this business as soon as we can, without expecting news from London. And let me tell you, that if I were once abroad, and under sail, I would willingly hazard the three pinnaces [parliamentary guard ships]. To conclude, I pray you to believe me, and not the common voice of mankind, that I am lost if I do not escape, which I will not be able to do if (as I have said) I stay for further demonstrations... I pray you be quick and diligent in freeing of me.[88]

This letter, if authentic, is extraordinary both for its content and for its mode of address, and would have been fatal had it been intercepted. Written to a humble subject, in a tone of pleading dependency, in the midst of the nation's most sensitive constitutional negotiations, it exposes the king's plight, his desperation, and his duplicity. Even a month later, when some members of parliament were sufficiently confident of a settlement to consider moving the king to London, Charles was asking about guards and tides that would favour his escape. 'If the ship came,' he wrote on 9 November, 'I like that way best; yet if she come not quickly, I must find some other way, for I daily find more and more reason to hasten'.[89]

In another letter from Newport in November, said by its copyist to be 'written by the king's own hand', Charles complained that his 'close imprisonment' was 'far different from what it was at Hampton Court', with 'the strict guards round about this island, and the troop of horse always attending, or rather watching me when I go abroad'. His mind was focused on escape, fully aware of its moral and political implications: 'I must either shipwreck my conscience or return to close prison; none that loves conscience or freedom, but must approve of my resolution of absenting myself.'[90]

Parliament gained intelligence of some of these intrigues, further fuelling their distrust of the king. The Committee of Both Houses warned Governor Hammond on 15 November that his prisoner 'intends to walk out on foot a mile or two as usually in the day time, and there horses are laid in the isle to carry him to a boat'. And, if this did not work, the king planned to exit 'at some private window in the night'.[91] The treaty negotiations provided unusual opportunities for escape, if only the king could evade his watchers. Parliament evidently expected some treacherous move, and later found evidence that its fears were well founded. A royalist captured after the regicide reported that 'some about [the king] advised him to escape; others of a higher rank, and those that were most near him, dissuaded it altogether; so that in diversity of opinions the counsel was quickly discovered, and made impossible'.[92]

Constitutional discussions at Newport stalled over episcopacy and control of the militia. Conciliatory delegates thought of continuing parlay with the king at

Westminster, but army radicals soon lost all patience. Their *Remonstrance* of exasperation, authored by Henry Ireton and adopted by the General Council on 18 November, demanded that 'King Charles, as the capital author of the late troubles, may be speedily brought to justice...for the treason, blood, and mischief he is...guilty of'.[93] Negotiations at Newport were quickly abandoned, with hopes for a treaty at an end. Governor Hammond was relieved of his command, replaced by the surly Colonel Isaac Ewers (a future regicide). Charles was plunged into despair. Not surprisingly, observers noted on 22 November, 'his majesty begins to grow exceeding discontented and melancholy, and feareth much the present overtures of the army, touching the seizing on his royal person'.[94] Such fears were apparently justified, for on 25 November the General Council issued orders 'that the person of the king be secured as formerly in Carisbrooke Castle', and two days later instructed Colonel Ewers to 'convey him over to Hurst Castle', a grim fortress along a shingle spit on the mainland. When crossing the narrow water between the two castles, the officers were warned to avoid 'any new ships come into the road', lest they threatened the security of the transfer.[95]

As late as 29 November 1648, with army reinforcements daily arriving on the island, the king's friends were considering his escape. Colonel Edward Cooke spent the evening with the Duke of Richmond and the Earl of Lindsey at Newport and heard 'that the army would that night seize upon the king's person'. 'The lords argued for the king's attempting an immediate escape', and Cooke mentioned 'horses ready at hand, and a vessel attending'. But the king would have none of it, 'first arguing the difficulties, if not the impossibility of accomplishing it; next the consequences...in case he should miscarry in the attempt'. The king insisted that he had given his word not to stir, and with that he bid his potential liberators 'good night'. Henry Firebrace confirmed the gist of this narrative, recording that King Charles spurned the escape initiative, avowing that 'there will be no danger'. He had pledged at Newport 'not go out of the island during the treaty, nor 28 days after', and in this he would be true to his word.[96] It may have been the king's final chance.

On 1 December, the army transferred King Charles from the Isle of Wight to Hurst Castle, a 'vile and unwholesome' facility, 'much unprovided with victual', with a garrison that one officer described as 'rotten'. The king's temporary quarters were cold and bare—'not that accommodate as might be desired'—but worse fates would be in store. The newspaper *The Moderate* reported an exchange in which the king told the officer in charge at Hurst Castle, Lieutenant Colonel Cobbett, that 'he had no desire to stay long in this place, yet he should be unwilling to be removed hence without sight of an order beforehand; to which was answered, that necessity was above order; he replied that it was true, but necessity was many times pretended when there was none'.[97] When orders came a few days later to move him to Windsor, one of his favourite places, Charles may have thought that his prospects were improving. If so, he was cruelly disappointed. Early in the new year his trial commenced at Westminster, and the axe on 30 January terminated his life and his reign. The king's island interlude was anything but idyllic, beginning in confusion, and ending in tragedy. The 'Ile of Wait' became again the Isle of Wight, a separate and sea-girt extension of Hampshire, with memories of the fate of 'sacred Charles'.[98]

13

Island Prisoners of the English Republic

Royalists still held important parts of the island periphery at the time of the regicide. The Isles of Scilly held out until 23 May 1651. The Isle of Man surrendered on 1 November. Jersey capitulated on 15 December, and the last hold-out at Castle Cornet on Guernsey yielded on 19 December 1651. Only when remaining offshore territories were in parliamentary hands could the government in London employ them for penal political purposes. The republic's conquest of island outposts increased its military and carceral assets.

Like the royal regime that they succeeded, the revolutionary governments of the Interregnum confined some of their most dangerous enemies to island prisons. Nervous of royalist revival and conspiracy, and troubled by religious radicals and protestors, the regimes of the Commonwealth and Protectorate exiled and incarcerated challengers to their authority. The dissidents included overzealous republicans and champions of liberty, and religious radicals of various sorts. Some had the benefit of formal trials, but others were dispatched arbitrarily. Legal historians of this period have noted 'a dramatic rise in the frequency of both executive and parliamentary imprisonment of political enemies without process of any kind'.[1] Most of these unfortunates went first to the Tower or the Fleet, but a score or more of high-profile opponents spent months and years behind bars on the Isle of Wight, the Channel Islands, the Isles of Scilly, or the Isle of Man. In many cases only recently subjected to the might of parliament, these islands now served to imprison opponents of the Whitehall–Westminster regime. This chapter tells their story.

Royals and Royalists on the Isle of Wight and Jersey

Looking to its security after the execution of the king, the regicide parliament named Charles Stuart, his brother James, and their principal supporters as 'enemies and traitors to the commonwealth'. Their estates were to be confiscated, and, if they were found 'within the limits of this nation', they were to 'die without mercy'. Royalist delinquents who escaped overseas, and any others who 'shall adhere to, or aid or assist Charles Stuart, son to the late king', were likewise deemed 'traitors and rebels'.[2] Stuart dynastic continuity was maintained in exile, as royalists dreamed of restoration. Though Prince Charles (now Charles II) and James, Duke of York, were safe overseas, their younger siblings Princess Elizabeth

England's Islands in a Sea of Troubles. David Cressy, Oxford University Press (2020). © David Cressy 2020.
DOI: 10.1093/oso/9780198856603.001.0001

(1635–50) and Prince Henry, Duke of Gloucester (1640–60), remained prisoners in England. Following the regicide, they were housed at Penshurst, Kent, the home of the Earl of Leicester. The government provided £3,000 for their maintenance, which allowed for their confinement in comfort.[3]

In July 1650, while civil war continued in Scotland, and the fate of the kingdom remained uncertain, the government decided that these two children 'shall be sent out of the limits of the commonwealth', to a secure offshore location. The Isle of Wight, the place of the late king's recent detention, lay well within 'the limits of the commonwealth', being part of England, but it was under military government, and the sea enhanced its security as a prison. 'The Ile of Wait' would again have royal residents. The Council authorized Anthony Mildmay and his wife to conduct the prince and princess from Penshurst to Portsmouth, and made Major General Thomas Harrison responsible for their conveyance across the water. They were allowed to bring eight servants, and such bedding, hangings, and plate as they thought would be useful. Colonel William Sydenham, the new governor at Carisbrooke Castle, had orders to make rooms ready for his royal guests, and to expel anyone from the island who 'may bring danger thereunto'.[4] The royalist islander Sir John Oglander noted on 13 August 1650 that 'two of the king's children, the Duke of Gloucester and the Lady Elizabeth, landed at Cowes to be kept at Carisbrooke Castle'.[5]

Carisbrooke, more suited as a residence than a fortress, and still shadowed by the memory of the late king, took on the quality of a superior boarding school. The idyll did not last. Princess Elizabeth, who suffered from rickets, caught a cold which became a fever, and died on 8 October 1650. She was buried in nearby Newport, a victim, supporters said, of 'Wight's fatal isle, and Carisbrooke's loathed den'. Royalists memorialized the incomparable piety and unparalleled virtues of the tragic Lady Elizabeth, in reproach to the cruelty of the republic.[6] Prince Henry continued his education, with Richard Lovell as his tutor, and at least once dined with Oglander at Nunwell House. But early in 1653, as the state felt more secure, he was allowed to join his mother in Paris. Oglander noted the prince's departure on 11 February 'in a small ship hired at Southampton', but the crew endured 'three nights watching and distemper at sea' as they battled contrary winds, and were forced to come ashore at Dover to relieve their distress.[7] Prince Henry remained an important figure for royalists, as second in line to the throne, until his unfortunate death from smallpox in September 1660.

Dangerous cavaliers who remained in England, or audaciously returned from abroad, also faced confinement in island prisons. Among them were Viscount Grandison and the Earl of Kellie, who were sent to the Isle of Wight; and John Ashburnham, Sir Thomas Armstrong, Henry Norwood, Sir Thomas Peyton, and John Weston imprisoned in the Channel Islands. The second Duke of Buckingham was also held for imprisonment on Jersey. The offshore detention of these supporters of the Stuart cause removed them from networks of conspiracy and helped to keep the Commonwealth secure.

Viscount Grandison (John Villiers, 1616–59) and the Earl of Kellie (Alexander Erskine, 1615–77) were among the royalist prisoners held by parliament following their defeat at Worcester in September 1651. Within two weeks of the battle, they were held in the Tower for bearing arms against the English republic. As noblemen of honour, Grandison and Kellie were permitted 'the liberty of the Tower' pending trial, and Grandison's wife was allowed to join him. Kellie was subsequently permitted to go within 10 miles of London, on bonds amounting to £10,000. They were named among forty-five state prisoners in the Tower in July 1654, when the government considered alternative arrangements for their restraint, including island confinement.[8]

Although no warrant can be found for their removal, Grandison and Kellie were both relocated to the Isle of Wight. Isolated from royalists on the mainland, they seem to have been well housed and fed, with liberty to hunt and ride, though no freedom to depart. In August 1655, they were offered release, with £50 each 'to discharge their debts since their restraint in the Isle of Wight, and the governor of that island to take their engagement' to do nothing 'contrary to the peace of the commonwealth'.[9] Vacation of their chambers at Carisbrooke would make room for radical millenarians, who apparently posed greater threats to the state than defeated royalists.

By November 1655, Grandison and Kellie had passes 'to go beyond seas' to join fellow royalists in exile, so long as they did 'nothing against his Highness and government'. They remained on the island until costs associated with their imprisonment and transport could be settled. Grandison wrote to his captors in December to say that their offer of £50 was not enough 'to be delivered from his long imprisonment', since 'that sum can scarce set him free from this place'. Kellie petitioned similarly, saying he was grateful for the grant of leave to go overseas, but not 'in the meanest capacity on what you have allowed me for it'. Still stuck on the Isle of Wight, he needed additional funds, 'as will enable me to leave your dominion, and seek my fortune in some other place in the world where providence may make me in a condition to live like a gentleman'.[10] After fifteen months of captivity on the island, the two ruined nobles were allowed to take passage for France, where Grandison died in exile.

The royalist John Ashburnham (1602–71), who had helped Charles I escape from Hampton Court and shared responsibility for bringing the king to the Isle of Wight, also spent years in island prisons. After being held in the Tower on charges of high treason, he was moved to Jersey in 1654.[11] In June 1655, the governor of Elizabeth Castle had orders to relocate Ashburnham to Deal Castle in Kent, noting that the prisoner was 'preparing to go by the next vessel'. Hopes were dashed, however, for in December 1655, when the authorities intercepted letters between Ashburnham and his wife, he was a 'prisoner in Guernsey Castle', meaning Castle

Cornet. He had only moved from one island to another. He was not cut off from the world, however, since local merchants and the garrison porter supplied him with newsbooks and correspondence. In one letter he sent his wife a lock of his hair; in another he remarked forlornly on the sight of ships 'drawing out of the port to go to England'. Lady Ashburnham wrote to Charles Waterhouse, the deputy governor of Guernsey, and actively petitioned Protector Cromwell on her husband's behalf. These efforts may have succeeded in returning Ashburnham to the mainland, though not to freedom, for his name appears in a list of royalist prisoners in England in September 1656.[12] He returned to offshore detention again in January 1658, when the Guernsey diarist Pierre le Roy noted 'three English lords were sent to this island, to Castle Cornet'.[13] These prisoners were John Ashburnham, by now a veteran of Channel crossings, his brother William Ashburnham, and fellow-royalist Sir Thomas Peyton. The Restoration brought them freedom, but Ashburnham could never shake off the suspicion that he had led Charles I to his doom (see Chapter 12).

Other royalists imprisoned on the island of Jersey included the conspirators Sir Thomas Armstrong, Major Henry Norwood, and John Weston. Norwood had gone to Virginia after the royalist defeat, but by April 1652 he was back in England, suspected of involvement in the murder of a parliamentary agent. Along with Armstrong and Weston, he became active in royalist plotting, sending arms to prospective insurgents under cover of supplying Virginia. Lax security among the plotters allowed the Protectorate to arrest them: Norwood in January, Weston in February, and Armstrong in March 1655.[14]

Offering 'the sad relation of my present condition', Henry Norwood wrote from the Tower of London in September 1656, that he would 'much rather be thrown away in exile', perhaps back to Virginia, 'than to languish here under so great prejudice and clamorous necessity'. He must have thought that such a move was possible, for he asked Secretary Thurloe for 'a little liberty upon bail to make some preparations necessary to so long a voyage'.[15] Instead of an Atlantic crossing, however, a shorter voyage was in the offing. Norwood, Armstrong, and Weston were among prisoners shipped to the Channel Islands, with instructions to the governor of Jersey to hold them 'under secure imprisonment at the castle at Jersey, until you shall receive further orders'. Norwood remained there behind bars until January 1659, Armstrong and Weston until the following June, when a change of fortune seemed at hand.[16]

Yet another royalist aristocrat to face imprisonment in the Channel Islands was George Villiers, the second duke of Buckingham. Buckingham had escaped to France in 1651 but returned to England from exile in 1657. In September that year he married the daughter of Lord Thomas Fairfax, who controlled most of Buckingham's confiscated estates. Still suspected of royalist intrigue, by October the duke was 'sought for to be committed to the island of Jersey'. Fairfax intervened on his behalf when the Council passed an order 'for the apprehending of the duke, and carrying him in custody to the isle of Jersey', where he was expected to undergo 'a sad restraint'. It is by no means certain that Buckingham served this penalty. The warrants to convey him are specific, but there is no record of his delivery. Buckingham had seen Jersey in 1650 as a courtier to Charles II and would not willingly return as a prisoner. By the spring of 1658, he was under house arrest in Yorkshire, and, after breaking the terms of this confinement, he was placed in the Tower of London and gained release at the Restoration.[17]

Island Prisoners of the Protectorate

Several radical and religious enthusiasts learned to their cost that the government of Oliver Cromwell could prove as harsh as its royal predecessor in dispatching its enemies to isolated island prisons. The establishing of the Protectorate in 1653, and its assumption of near-monarchical authority, drove erstwhile supporters of the Commonwealth into opposition.[18] Several were held without trial in the Tower, and then moved arbitrarily to offshore incarceration. Among them were the Leveller John Lilburne, who spent a year and a half at Mont Orgueil, Jersey; the anti-trinitarian John Biddle, who was held for almost three years on Scilly; the radical army officer Robert Overton, who was imprisoned for a year at Jersey's Castle Elizabeth; the radical millenarians Hugh Courtney, Christopher Feake, Thomas Harrison, John Rogers, and Sir Henry Vane, who served various terms on the Isle of Wight; and Arthur Squibb and Colonel Matthew Alured, who were confined on the Isle of Man. Most of these men had served parliament in England's civil wars and were supporters of the republican revolution. They locked horns with Cromwell over matters of law, religion, and the constitution, opposing the Protector's kinglike aggrandizement of power. The government attempted to separate them from their supporters by holding them in gaol, confining them in distant castles, and ultimately by incarceration in island prisons. Overuse of the small island of St Nicholas as a place of confinement and transshipment prompted the commander to request the Protector in April 1659 'to be as sparing as you can of sending prisoners to the island of Plymouth, in regard we have no place to imprison them in more than what is the soldier's quarters'.[19]

Men of principle sometimes protested that the protectorate was identical with the previous royal regime in its disregard for justice, and in this regard they may have been right. The gadfly lawyer William Prynne, still smarting from his treatment under Charles I, and a further falling out with the Council of State, raged in 1658 against 'these army reformers' who, 'contrary to the Great Charter, all other fundamental laws, statutes, the Petition of Right itself', subjected their enemies to arbitrary imprisonment. They had

close-imprisoned them in remote castles, under armed guards, and translated
them from one castle to another... without any legal examination, accusation,
hearing, or cause expressed; banished some, and imprisoned others (yea some of
their own military officers and greatest friends) in those foreign isles [and],
castles (whither the prelates and old Council-Table lords banished me and my
fellow brethren heretofore) without any legal sentence.[20]

England's islands were 'foreign' to Prynne in the sense of being alien, distant, and
outside one's own familiar land.

Lilburne on Jersey

Notorious for his agitation for the liberties of the subject, the Leveller John
Lilburne (1614–57) suffered repeated bouts of imprisonment, including a spell
on Jersey.[21] He had first been arrested under Charles I in January 1638, being
whipped and pilloried by order of Star Chamber, and held in the Fleet prison until
freed by parliament in November 1640. Lilburne fought energetically in the civil
war but was confined from November 1642 to May 1643 as a prisoner of the
royalists. He spent three more months in Newgate in 1645 as a prisoner of
the House of Commons and was locked up again by the House of Lords in 1646
for slandering the Earl of Manchester. On each occasion, his wife Elizabeth
petitioned for his release. He was held in Newgate, and then the Tower, for almost
a year and a half before being bailed, imprisoned again, and eventually freed in
1648. From March to November 1649, Lilburne was in the Tower again on charges
of treason, but was triumphantly acquitted by a jury. He was banished by the
Rump in 1652, relocating to the Netherlands, but was put in the Tower again after
his return, and was retried in June 1653. Once again, a jury found him 'not guilty',
but the government kept him imprisoned for nine more months 'for the peace of
this nation'. Newsbooks speculated that Lilburne would be 'sent to the islands of
Man, Guernsey, or Sorlings [Scilly], there to evaporate his turbulent humours'.
Dutch reports had him 'carried... to the Isle of Wight, or some other island
belonging to this commonwealth', though he was more likely to be confined in
the Tower or Newgate prison.[22]

Prolonged and repeated imprisonment did not stop Lilburne from pamphleteering and enhanced his role and reputation as the victim and scourge of tyranny.
His writings upheld the rights of freeborn Englishmen, including fair trial and due
process 'according to the known and declared laws of the land'; but the lieutenant
of the Tower was specifically instructed in November 1653 to disregard any writ of
habeas corpus on Lilburne's behalf 'until the parliament take further order'. His
enemies deemed him 'of so great violence and rashness, as not to be trusted with
his own liberty'.[23]

Arbitrary regimes could impede the granting of *habeas corpus*, and its application was even more questionable in the Channel Islands, which considered
themselves beyond the reach of English law. This may have been a compelling
reason for the Protectorate to remove Lilburne to Jersey in March 1654, where
English writs were not likely to relieve him. He was taken, via Portsmouth, to be
'secured and kept in safe custody' in the castle of Mont Orgeuil, in Prynne's old
prison quarters, with 'a strict eye upon him . . . not to be suffered to stir out of the
compass thereof'. The military governor, Colonel James Heane, had strict instructions not to release him without special authorization.[24] The state paid £13 8s. 7d.
for 'the conducting of Lieutenant Colonel John Lilburne to the island of Jersey
upon the Council's warrant' (a fraction of the cost of moving Prynne to Jersey in
more tempestuous conditions), and paid £19 5s. 4d. for his quarterly keep there as
a prisoner.[25]

Exiled royalists in Paris soon heard that Cromwell 'hath sent Lilburne to the
island of Jersey to be close prisoner, and kept from pen, ink and paper', but gave
little credit to rumours that 'Lilburne is put to death' on the island.[26] Captain
Robert Clarke of the frigate *Bristol*, who had transported Lilburne to Jersey,
reported in June 1654 that 'all things are very well in the island, there being left
Colonel John Lilburne, who is in very good health, and much freedom to walk
about the castle'.[27]

Despite this good start, Lilburne's health and spirits deteriorated in Mont
Orgeuil, and his pen fell silent during almost a year and a half on Jersey. Little
can be learned about his material conditions, day-to-day circumstances, and
interactions with islanders. He may have been moved from time to time between
Mont Orgeuil and Elizabeth Castle across the island. During this period, he
became acquainted with Quaker writings, if not actual Quakers, and undertook
'serious reading therein'. He was nursed in his sickness by Elizabeth Crome, an
old Jersey woman, whom he thanked in one of his pamphlets.[28] The final months
of Lilburne's imprisonment may have been softened by a pension of 40s. a week,
his due as a parliamentary lieutenant colonel, approved by the government in
April 1655.[29]

Family members petitioned on his behalf and tried to reconcile him with
the regime. Lilburne's father-in-law met him in June 1655, in company with the
governor of Elizabeth Castle, and discussed the prospect of moving him to the Isle
of Wight. The governor also wanted him removed, 'for he is more trouble than
ten such as Ashburnham', but Lilburne insisted 'he will own none for his liberty,
but by the way of the law'.[30] Elizabeth Lilburne appealed movingly to the
Protector for relief from her 'many grievous afflictions' during her husband's
'most severe' restraint. She told Cromwell that Lilburne's 'senses, health, and
life' were endangered, and that he was 'tired and wearied out with long and sore
affliction'. If Lilburne could have his liberty, she promised, he would do nothing
to the prejudice of the regime, 'nor to the disturbance of the state'.[31] Cromwell

seems to have been persuaded that the troublemaker was broken, for he told Mrs Lilburne in September 1655 'that by the first ship that came over from Jersey her husband should be brought over to England'.[32] Lilburne was finally repatriated in October, returning in a ship laden with Guernsey cider. He was confined to Dover Castle, where he embraced a Quaker quietism, and died on parole in 1657.[33]

Biddle on Scilly

The radical anti-trinitarian John Biddle (1615–62) served repeated stretches in prison for views that the authorities deemed heretical. On the key question of the Trinity, Biddle preached 'that Jesus Christ was not the Almighty or most high God', a position anathema to orthodox Christians.[34] He was first arrested at Gloucester in 1644, was held again briefly in 1645, and spent extended periods in London's Gatehouse prison between 1646 and 1655. By the summer of 1655, he was incarcerated at Newgate, while supporters petitioned for his release, and enemies brayed for his execution.[35] Biddle continued to publish the most challenging tracts while behind bars, and in July 1655 wrote two letters to Cromwell asserting his own righteousness. Biddle argued that Cromwell's Instrument of Government 'did maintain liberty of conscience', to which the Protector responded 'that the Instrument was never intended to maintain and protect blasphemers from the punishment of the laws in force against them, neither would he'. Biddle petitioned from Newgate 'for discharge from his imprisonment', but without success.[36]

Faced with mounting clamour for the heretic to be executed, Protector Cromwell intervened to remove this troublesome prisoner to the security of a remote island. On 5 October 1655, the Council approved a warrant for 'removing of the body of Mr John Biddle, now a prisoner in Newgate, to the island of Scilly', and four days later arranged for 'a fit vessel to be at Portsmouth, and to receive aboard Mr John Biddle, and transport him to the Island of Scilly in order to his securing there'.[37] Biddle's religious enemies were horrified that the Protector should extend his tolerance to 'blasphemers and heretics', and denounced as dangerous 'the sending John Biddle to the Isle of Scilly'.[38] Cromwell responded in January 1656 by granting a pension of 10s. a week 'to satisfy and pay to John Biddle, now prisoner at the island of Scilly...for his maintenance', payable from the first of the year. Since prisoners were expected to pay fees to their keepers, this meagre grant would help to alleviate his discomforts.[39] The island was both refuge and prison for Biddle, and a resource in the armoury of power.

Scilly under the Protectorate was as primitive as it had been a decade and a half earlier, when John Bastwick knew its castle walls. The garrison had been enlarged, but facilities were still sparse and spartan. Biddle would remain a prisoner in

St Mary's Castle for almost three years. The *Oxford Dictionary of National Biography* describes Biddle's internment on Scilly as 'beyond the courts and the reach of *habeas corpus*', but the islands remained subject to English law. It was just more difficult, at such a distance, for writs to be served and honoured. It bears repeating that the effectiveness of *habeas corpus*, like decisions for confinement or enlargement, were matters of politics more than law. In May 1658, Biddle's friends in London did secure *habeas corpus* on his behalf, and it proved effective in freeing him from the island. He was brought before the Upper Bench at Westminster and released when no case was presented for his continuing imprisonment.[40] Like many prisoners of faith, Biddle used his time on the island to write, studying the Revelation that St John composed in prison on Patmos, and comparing the visionary's circumstances with his own. After the Restoration, he was arrested once more in June 1662 and died later that year in Newgate.[41]

Fifth Monarchists on England's Patmos

It was common for ideological and religious prisoners to find mirrors of their plight in the Bible. Burton, Bastwick and Prynne had compared their suffering to that of saints Peter, Paul, and John the theologian. Reflecting on a second bout of imprisonment in Somerset and Cornwall in the early 1650s, Prynne thought it worse than John's confinement on Patmos, where at least the saint could write and send letters 'without any perusal or restraint by his heathen guardians'.[42] The prophetic books of Scripture, especially the Old Testament book of Daniel and the New Testament Revelation, provided inspiration and guidance to Cromwellian-era radicals. An influential cluster of preachers and army officers became convinced that the 'Fifth Monarchy'—the predicted reign of Christ and his saints on earth—was about to dawn, and that John's meditations on Patmos explained the direction of the times. Though the government of Oliver Cromwell looked sympathetically on their theology, it came to view their agitations as disruptive and seditious. The Fifth Monarchists Major General Thomas Harrison, Quartermaster General Hugh Courtney, the clerics Christopher Feake and John Rogers, and the agitator Sir Henry Vane all suffered imprisonment on the Isle of Wight, an outlier of Hampshire that became their Isle of Patmos.

Harrison

The Regicide Thomas Harrison (1606–60) was an important politician and military leader in the opening year of the Protectorate, whose growing religious radicalism turned him from an ally to an enemy of Oliver Cromwell. Harrison's support within the army made him a greater danger than radical civilian preachers, who were backed mainly by their congregations.

In February 1654, Harrison was forced to retire to his father's house in Staffordshire, where he was supposed to live 'peaceably' away from controversy. This worked for a while, and by May of that year he was thought to be 'already forgotten, and totally laid aside'.[43] Summoned by the Holy Spirit, however, Harrison re-entered the fray, and was arrested in September 1654. He was held in the Tower for several months, but in February 1655 the government decided that Harrison and other troublemakers should be removed to more remote locations, where isolation would negate their influence. News circulated on 24 February that 'Major General Harrison, Quartermaster General Courtney, and Mr John Carey are sent away prisoners in a coach and four horses westward, it is conceived to Pendennis Castle' in Cornwall. By evening the news was revised and corrected, 'that Mr Carey is sent to the Mount [St Michael] in Cornwall, Major General Harrison to Portland Castle [on the coast of Dorset], and Mr Courtney to Cowes Castle in the Isle of Wight'.[44] Harrison was soon moved offshore from Portland to Carisbrooke Castle in the Isle of Wight, which he had visited in 1650 as the escort for the Stuart princelings. Courtney too was relocated to Carisbrooke Castle, where other Fifth Monarchists soon joined them. Custodial charges for 'Colonel Thomas Harrison and other prisoners in the Isle of Wight' in the first quarter of 1656 amounted to £30.[45] Harrison was the most senior of these imprisoned radicals, both in age and rank, and was their natural leader. In February 1656, the government decided to 'enlarge' him from Carisbrooke, 'under pretence of the very desperate danger of death of his father', and return him to house arrest in London. When Harrison was transferred in March, the other Fifth Monarchists grieved at his departure.[46]

In April 1657, Harrison was arrested again for suspected Fifth Monarchist plotting and spent several more months in prison. Along with Feake, Rogers, and other dangerous radicals, he was observed at meetings in London in June 1657, 'where they profess themselves ready for an insurrection'. Further intelligence in February 1658 implicated Harrison in more conspiracy against the Protectorate, but he managed to stay out of gaol.[47] The Restoration, however, proved lethal, and Harrison was among the first of the Regicides to die a traitor's gruesome death (see Chapter 14).

Feake

The Fifth Monarchist Christopher Feake (1611–83) briefly shared imprisonment with Harrison on the Isle of Wight. He was first arrested in 1653, and then spent 'near ten months of days', from January 1654 to September 1655, as a prisoner in Windsor Castle. 'For no other crime...but for preaching the gospel,' he relates,

'I was apprehended, taken from my dearest relations, snatched from my wife and eight children', and clapped into prison. Was this not proof that England had become Babylon, and that the current power and the old monarchy 'are one and the same'? Feake described his experienc, in *The Oppressed Close Prisoner in Windsor-Castle* (1655), written 'in his prison watch tower', and in later addresses to supporters in London.[48]

Feake's published letters show that, at least for the first few months, his 'yoke-fellow' Jane Feake kept him company in prison. Then from April to September 1655 he shared quarters at Windsor with his fellow Fifth Monarchist John Rogers, where they prayed and preached together, making as much noise as possible for the Lord. Friends from London sent letters and visited with solidarity and prayer. When their keepers tried to silence them, they preached all the more loudly, proclaiming the Lord's work through the windows and doors. On one occasion Feake commandeered the castle chapel before being forcibly removed. His punishment was to be 'shut up in a very narrow compass from the common air and, which is worse, from the sweet society of the saints'. It served only to remind him of 'the prisoners and martyrs of the New Testament', who were also persecuted for 'truth's and righteousness sake'.[49]

'Because of their clamourous inveighings against his Highness and government', and to remove them beyond the orbit of their co-religionists, the Council decided late in September 1655 to transfer Feake and Rogers offshore to the Isle of Wight.[50] They travelled under guard in miserable October weather, while Feake used the opportunity to preach to his escort of soldiers. Their transport cost the government £10. Arrived on the island, they were lodged at first at Sandham Castle, which Feake described as 'a most miserable cold disconsolate place, the sea on one side, and a most nasty marsh on the other'. No provision had been made for them, 'not so much as a bed to lie on', so they hunkered down on bare boards. After a brief stay at Sandham they were moved to other lodgings 'meet for accommodation of their health, and with respect to their security and privacy', which allowed some contact with islanders.[51]

Feake's wife Jane had remained in London and used every opportunity to agitate about her husband's condition. Feake would not say that she 'petitioned' Oliver Cromwell, for that would indicate compliance with the regime of Babylon, but she did effectively make the case for his relief. An 'unexpected' order reached the Isle of Wight early in November to transport Feake 'back over the sea' to house arrest in Hampshire. Two troopers were assigned to guard him, but, when they reached their destination, Feake 'ran away directly for London, saying he would obey no order, but forthwith into France'. Although the order signed 'Oliver P' (for Protector) enjoined him 'to continue in that place, and not to stir from thence', Feake reasoned that it no more constrained him than did the orders of Caiaphas and Ananias to the apostles Peter and John. He was quickly recaptured in London but was not sent back to prison. On 10 November 1655, the Council ordered his release, though he remained under scrutiny, with a soldier assigned to watch over him. He continued to preach against 'Babylon', a government informer describing one of his addresses in January 1657 as 'his three hours ranting discourse'. He was arrested again in April 1658 and spent more time in the Tower.[52] After the Restoration he was arrested one more time in 1663 but spent his later years as a tolerated nonconformist.

Rogers

John Rogers (1627–70?) spent a year imprisoned on the Isle of Wight and wrote extensively about his experience. The son of the formidable puritan Nehemiah Rogers, John Rogers became a Presbyterian minister at the age of 20, and then moved rapidly through congregational independency to a radically engaged millenarianism. Expecting the imminent return of King Jesus, he preached and wrote about the Fifth Monarchy. His activism cost him more than three years in prison in the 1650s, including a long spell of island detention. He argued publicly with Oliver Cromwell and came to see the Protectorate as symptomatic of the 'hypocrisies, blasphemies, persecutions, and cruelties of this serpent power now up in England'.[53] His treatise *Jegar-Sahadutha. An Oyled Pillar. Set up for Posterity* (1657) not only expounds 'the cause and testimony of Jesus', but also dwells on the ordeal of island incarceration.[54]

When Christopher Feake and other Fifth Monarchists were first arrested, Rogers joined a delegation that demanded 'that the prisoners of the Lord might be set at liberty'. Protector Cromwell responded that 'there was nobody in prison in England' for the sake of the Lord or the Gospel, and that the Fifth Monarchists were 'evil doers...for railing, reviling, telling untruths, stirring up the people to arms, etc.'. If they were imprisoned, it was for the crime of sedition, not for the sake of religion.[55] They were enemies of the state for spreading false information.

Arrested himself in July 1654, but never tried, Rogers spent three-quarters of a year in confinement at Lambeth House before being moved in April 1655 to join Feake at Windsor Castle. They spent almost half a year together, baiting the authorities and proclaiming the Lord, until orders came for their removal to the Isle of Wight. Rogers was accompanied by his wife and children, whose hardships were intensified by the October rains. The Fifth Monarchists were first housed at Sandham Castle, where facilities were completely inadequate, and then at Arten House, 'an isle within an isle' in the Freshwater marshes, before taking up residence at Carisbrooke Castle.[56]

During his captivity on the mainland, Rogers had complained of being 'hurried about from post to pillar'. But coming to the Isle of Wight was a more traumatic rupture, 'out of our native country into exile'. He referred over and again to himself as an exile, 'a poor pilgrim, prisoner, and forsaken banished man'. 'I am bound thus, beaten, banished, and so barbarously handled... in this iron grave of exile', he wrote. 'I am bound with this double chain, or double honour of imprisonment and banishment.' Although the Isle of Wight was part of Hampshire, barely half a dozen miles from Portsmouth, Rogers wrote as if he had been transported out of his 'native country', abroad. Island isolation reduced his effectiveness as a London prophet, but the experience strengthened his dedication to the Lord: 'it is a most teaching dispensation to be beaten and buffeted for Christ, which hath made this prison so precious as school to me.' Rogers believed that he gained 'a very clear perspective... from these prisons, exiles, and pilgrimages, in this mine isle of Patmos'.[57] A green island off the English Solent was reimagined as John the Theologian's prison in the Aegean.

John and Elizabeth Rogers and their children arrived at Carisbrooke on 5 December 1655, with no 'earthly home but a prison now'. To their delight they were reunited with their 'dear con-captives', the fellow Fifth Monarchists Thomas Harrison and Hugh Courtney, 'who were a long time kept up in this close gaol'. The reunion compensated for the loss of Christopher Feake, who had been ordered back to the mainland. Together they engaged in prayer and praise, thanking 'sweet providence which had brought us together in one gaol, as well as one exile'. As at Windsor, they preached to the garrison and to visitors, resisting all efforts to silence them. Rogers gave repeated thanks for 'the help of my honoured con-captivated co-exiles', who eased both his spiritual and his material condition. Carisbrooke took on the complexion of a Fifth Monarchist conclave, much to the annoyance of the castle authorities.[58] Although the Protectorate had exiled its most troublesome religious opponents, it inadvertently strengthened the movement by bringing its principals together.

The material circumstances of Rogers's imprisonment varied during his time on the island. At Carisbrooke, his family was promised 'two rooms, two beds, and better accommodation' than the miseries of Sandham and Arten, but the promise was not fulfilled. On arrival early in December, they were assigned a 'little inward lodging room, where there was no chimney', which Rogers described as a 'merciless hole' from which he doubted he would emerge alive; it was 'a very little, poor, smoking, cold garret... worse than Bonner's coal house', referring to the place of confinement of some of the Marian martyrs. After a few weeks, however, they were moved to better rooms, with sticks of furniture and a window overlooking the castle yard. Some of the soldiers murmured that the prisoner's accommodation was better than their own. Rogers and his family obtained bedding from supporters in Newport, but the governor sometimes ordered this removed, forcing them 'to lie in pads of straw'. One set of sheets, pillow, and bolster that Rogers acquired was confiscated for the use of the garrison lieutenant. Mrs Rogers suffered chronic illness during her stay on the island, and her children were often sick. One child died, and another was a 'poor prison-born babe'. Carisbrooke at this time experienced an outbreak of swine pox, which some feared might be smallpox, so control of the bedding might have had sanitary as well as punitive purposes.[59]

The allocation of rooms within the castle was used as an instrument of discipline. When the authorities sought to punish Rogers, they would keep him 'close prisoner', confined to his cell. If this was not enough, they moved him to 'a little hole, or the dark chamber... some three steps long and three steps broad', from which all bedding was removed. His family likewise suffered serial privations, sometime being confined to a room too small for the beds, and sometimes having all bedding and curtains removed. Rogers described most of these rooms as small, dark, cold, and smoky, affected by 'unwholesome vapours... and filthy damp mists.'[60] The worse the conditions, the more Rogers relished the sanctity of his suffering.

Rogers was outraged that his gaolers at Carisbrooke, like those at Windsor, demanded fees of 'somewhat more than £6 a week, which I was not able to do', since 'those that imprisoned me must pay'. Parliament contributed 10s. a day towards the prisoner's maintenance, but candles, fires, and chamber fees cost extra.[61] Prisoners were normally allowed to send out for 'necessities', within the limits of their financial resources, but this privilege could be withdrawn at the will of the prison keeper. Late in January 1656, after Rogers had infuriated the authorities by his relentless preaching, they suffered 'none, man, woman, nor child to come to us, nor our victuals or necessaries to come to us, or any of our families to fetch it in for us... but when we would have sent out for our provisions the servant was stayed by the captain of the guard'. Rogers remonstrated that his keepers treated them 'worse than the veriest rogues in Newgate... for they if they have money can send for meat to eat, or be ministered to, or receive letters and necessaries; but you hinder us most tyrannically and unjustly by your ungodly swords'. They were, he said, 'in perils of life, sickness, fevers, storms, cold, snow, and tempests, without bed, without bread, in sore travails'. But these privations were temporary. The castle captain 'sent word... that we might send out for things', though all of the provisions brought in for Rogers and his family were thoroughly searched. Indeed, Rogers remarked, the very butter was dirtied and mishandled, and the very bones of the meat were examined for hidden letters.[62]

Surveillance was always tight and intrusive. Visitors were watched, and conversations monitored, though the prisoners found ways to talk and write. Rogers complained that he was so closely guarded that his keepers would 'dog me much immodestly, when I eased nature'. But at other times they allowed him to walk within the walls of the castle, and even 'liberty to take the air a mile or two on the downs, a soldier or two attending me'.[63]

Rogers sometimes writes as if he was isolated, but in fact he had company not only with his wife and children but with fellow men of faith. He had shared imprisonment at Windsor and transfer to the island with Christopher Feake, and he became very close to Hugh Courtney and Thomas Harrison. So close was their community that when orders came to Carisbrooke on 20 March 1656 to repatriate Harrison to house arrest in Highgate, the remaining Fifth Monarchists were 'much troubled about his going'.[64] Harrison's place was taken later in the year by Sir Henry Vane, an even more prominent Fifth Monarchist, who was imprisoned at Carisbrooke from early September to New Year's Eve. In October 1656, the government ordered 'that Mr Hugh Courtney who is now a prisoner in the Isle of Wight be forthwith discharged from his imprisonment', and by the end of December Rogers was free too, after a year confined to the castle.[65]

Though isolated on the island, the Fifth Monarchists were not cut off from the world. In addition to his company of 'con-captives', Rogers had an intermittent stream of admirers and well-wishers. Friends from London made 'long and chargeable journeys out of England', sometimes to be admitted but just as likely to be 'sent away without seeing us'. The prisoners were used to receiving visitors, but this privilege depended on the whim of the governor and could be arbitrarily withdrawn. Curious islanders were allowed to enter the castle so long as they were orderly and respectable. Rogers claimed that 'poor people came in a pace many miles to hear me', and gathered outside his window, or even outside the walls, while he preached. The castle authorities often disrupted these exercises, 'setting sentinels upon my door, driving away the people who came to hear the Gospel'.[66]

Like privileged captives before him, Rogers was inseparable from his Bible, had access to paper, and was determined to memorialize his suffering. Behind bars at Carisbrooke, he wrote secretly but prolifically, and worked on the study of biblical languages. After his release he remarked: 'I have not been idle in the prison . . . I have prepared, I think, above 300 sheets upon several subjects.' He referred to these writings as 'prison-born morning beams', 'prison threnodies' (lamentations), and 'the vison of the prison Patmos' (referring again to the island of Revelation). Like other prisoners (including Charles I at Carisbrooke and Henry Burton at Castle Cornet), Rogers was quick to learn such tricks as to hide 'a few of my papers into the bottom of my stockings at the soles of my feet, to preserve them'; to carry 'my papers in my clothes, and other ways, as the martyr Tyndale did his'; and to hide them 'in holes and walls, and pots and pans, to preserve them from the enemy'. At one point he feared that his writings might never reach their audience, 'my papers lying hid underground where I fear they will rot'. He sent and received correspondence, though the traffic was hazardous and irregular. Captain Richard Bull, acting as lieutenant governor, instructed the island's carriers to bring all letters to him first, coming or going, and many never reached their intended recipient.[67]

Unlike some detainees, who developed cordial relations with their keepers, Rogers and his gaolers were continually at loggerheads. Carisbrooke for him was a place of 'cruelty and tyranny', 'a kennel of unclean creatures', made worse by the hostility of the 'raging' Captain Bull. Rogers called his captors the worst sort of men, like cavaliers who would sit, swear, and swill. The garrison guards were given over to 'drinking and drabbing, whoring and rogueing', not least on the Lord's day, when Bull and his company would be 'feasting, ranting, gaming, making merry, and bowling in a green they have for that purpose'.[68] (This, of course, was the bowling green made at Carisbrooke for Charles I. Rogers avoids all reference to the royal prisoner who preceded him.) If Rogers attempted to reprove the roisterers, they responded with verbal and physical abuse, which only confirmed his sense of his righteousness. Efforts to spread Fifth Monarchist ideas within the garrison fell mainly on deaf ears.[69] When Rogers attempted to preach through the bars of his cell, or to address auditors outside the castle walls, the soldiers responded with laughter and noise. Rogers thanked 'the Lord who teacheth me to preach in tumults' for a voice that rose above the murmuring and mockery of his detractors.[70]

Like Burton, Bastwick, and Prynne under Charles I, Rogers referred repeatedly to the injustice of his imprisonment. He was, he wrote, 'imprisoned and banished against all law, but the arbitrary lawless sword'. It was 'the beast's law', the law of 'lust and will', that raged against him. Though by his own lights he had done nothing wrong, he was 'very wickedly and irrationally imprisoned, exiled, hardly handled, and almost hindered to breath the air'. Like the 'puritan martyrs' of the 1630s, the Fifth Monarchists of the 1650s were punished 'as if we were felons or fearful villains and miscreants', rather than people of the Lord. It was outrageous that these men of God were exiled and imprisoned 'without any law condemning, any crime charged formally upon us', or any accuser, witness, or trial, when 'cavaliers...Newgate thieves, and whores are not so cruelly handled at this day'.[71]

As a prisoner of conscience, a self-proclaimed witness for the Lord, Rogers was convinced that the Cromwellian regime punished him more harshly than any previous tyranny treated its enemies. He construed his experience of 'bonds and banishment' to be 'worse than Roman tyranny', and worse than the 'prelatick arbitrariness' of Archbishop Laud, with 'worse usage...than the worst malefactors, cavaliers, plotters, ranters, blasphemers or offenders'.[72] He took comfort, however, in suffering for 'Christ and his kingdom', like John of Patmos, the prophet Daniel, and the evangelist Paul: 'in such company we must needs run this race of ours with sweet contentment, serenity, calmness of spirit, whatever our enemies maliciously report of us.' The verse from Deuteronomy, 'let the blessing come upon the head of...him that was separated from his brethren', offered reassurance, since it seemingly applied to his case. Like Burton earlier on Guernsey, Rogers became fascinated by the numerology of his confinement, counting forty-two months as the period of the power of the Beast.[73] 'Behold the present apostasy of spirit, principles, and persons...death and darkness is upon us,' he wrote. But the events foretold in Revelation were about to unfold. 'Great things' were impending: 'the great tent and trumpet...the great bonfire and flame...and the great sun or light' of 'the Fifth Kingdom', the reign of Christ and his saints on earth.[74]

On 11 December 1656, the Council ordered Rogers released. By 21 January 1657 he was back in London, bringing his manuscripts with him. These included work on 'Daniel, the Apocalypse, and the prophets concerning the kingdom', though not all led to publication. Rogers estimated that 'above an hundred sheets' he had prepared for the press while at Carisbrooke had been 'plundered', 'stifled', or otherwise lost.[75] Most of what survived went into *Jegar-Sahadutha. An Oyled Pillar. Set up for Posterity*, published in July 1657 with a postscript apologizing that, owing to 'the forced absence of the author, in banishment, the press lets many mistakes in printing pass uncontrolled'.[76] Passionate, repetitive, and sometimes incoherent, *Jegar-Sahadutha* is a classic Fifth Monarchist diatribe, the fruit of a year in an island prison.

Free to preach, though not free from suspicion, Rogers resumed his life in London. He was arrested again in February 1658 for raising 'seditions and commotions' and was held in the Tower for almost two months.[77] At the Restoration, Rogers withdrew to the Netherlands, where he studied medicine. He eventually returned to London and spent his last years in obscurity on the outskirts of the metropolis.

Vane

Another who fell foul of Oliver Cromwell in the vortex of Protectorate politics, and suffered island imprisonment as a result, was the veteran religious and constitutional agitator Sir Henry Vane (1613–1662). Sharing many of the beliefs of the Fifth Monarchists, Vane considered himself a champion of 'God and true freedom' against an 'apostatizing and backsliding' regime. His publication of 1656, *A Healing Question*, struck at the foundation of the Protectorate, and threatened to 'involve the nation into blood again'. He was arrested in August 1656 as an enemy to 'his Highness and present government', and early in September he was sent to the Isle of Wight. Confined to Carisbrooke Castle, he was forbidden 'to speak with any person during his abode there, but in the presence of some officer'. Though he shared the castle with John Rogers, the prisoners were not supposed to communicate. Vane spent almost four months on the island, before being released at the end of December.[78] His troubles were not over, however, for he was arrested again in April 1657 for involvement in a Fifth Monarchist plot.[79] Vane's fortunes improved towards the end of the Protectorate, but the Restoration brought him further imprisonment, and ultimately execution (see Chapter 14).

Overton on Jersey

Like Sir Henry Vane, the parliamentary colonel Robert Overton (1609–1679) offended both the Cromwellian Protectorate and the restored monarchy of

Charles II, and suffered island imprisonment twice.[80] He was a man of humane disposition with a distinguished military career, but in 1654 Overton was relieved of his command, and summoned to London. Incriminating verses found among his papers, perhaps in his own hand, derided the Protector as 'a counterfeit piece.... but the ape of a king'.[81] Though never tried, Overton was deemed an enemy of the state, guilty of sedition, and in January 1655 he was taken to the Tower of London. He was still a prisoner three years later when an unnamed supporter at Hull petitioned Cromwell on his behalf: 'Colonel Overton hath many pretty children, and pity it is he should want the comfort of them. And if it might please your highness to give him his liberty I will engage both my life and little estate I have to be a true and diligent watchman over him.'[82]

This intervention may have precipitated a change in Overton's circumstances, though not necessarily for the better. In January 1658 he was shipped to the Channel Islands, in company with the imprisoned royalists Norwood, Armstrong and Weston.[83] Arriving at Jersey after 'one of the most dangerous winter voyages', Overton was lodged in Elizabeth Castle in 'such an old rotten windy room, that he could not ... be kept warm in his bed, but continually cried out, and complained in the night of aches in his limbs and wounds'. His physical distress was exacerbated by separation 'from his concernments and relations' and 'his family of small children'. Overton's wife Ann had previously obtained permission 'to abide with her husband in the Tower'. Hearing of his sickness on Jersey she left her children to tend him. Overton's sister Grizell Williamson also appealed to the Protector, having heard that her brother's health 'doth daily decay', and that if he remained in that 'consumptive confinement' he was likely to die.[84] Overton languished on Jersey for year, removed from the clamour of London, and beyond the reach of *habeus corpus*, until England's political climate changed again as the Protectorate began to disintegrate.

Springtime 1659 was a season of release for Robert Overton. His sister's petitions gained attention, and several publications addressed 'the present deplorable case of that most generous, noble, constant sufferer for his country Major General Overton'. Some compared his 'illegal imprisonment and banishment' to that of Burton, Bastwick, and Prynne under Charles I. Especially egregious, declared *The Plain Case of the Common-Weal Neer the Desperate Gulf of the Common-Woe*, was the denial of *habeas corpus*, which 'ought to be granted to every man that is committed', yet 'could not be allowed to the prerogative prisoners or exiles of these times'. *The Sad and Suffering Case of Major-General Rob. Overton, Prisoner in the Isle of Jersey*, presented Overton's arbitrary imprisonment as betrayal of 'the good old cause'.[85] The government summoned him to appear at Westminster, and sent a frigate to Jersey to fetch him. By the second week of March Overton was back in England.[86]

One observer likened Overton's homecoming to that of 'the puritan martyrs', when the streets of the metropolis were thronged with well-wishers. Supporters lined the roads from Brentford to Westminster, 'some in coaches, some on horseback, some of them with their wives, and others on foot. The colonel was in a coach with the captain of the castle from whence he came, with one servant for his guard...As he passed by the people...he kept off his hat, and bowed to them.' The returned prisoner was supposed to make his way to Lambeth, but the crowds were too thick, so soldiers from the Tilt Yard took him to a house near St James. 'After candlelight he was permitted to go to the George in King Street, where his wife and friends had made provision for him.'[87]

Allowed to address parliament on 16 March 1659, Overton described his sufferings. 'I had better have been torn in pieces by wild horses, than to have endured this great torment. That had been but for a moment', but island incarceration was seemingly without end. Members were concerned 'to know the reason of his imprisonment', and argued that the Protector's warrant in Overton's case, 'wherein there is no cause expressed, is illegal and unjust'. To hold him arbitrarily, without charge and trial, and beyond the reach of *habeas corpus*, they declared, was 'a great breach of the liberty of the subject, so long and so much fought and contended for, and so dearly purchased'. The prisoner's fate became wrapped up with the fundamental issues of the English revolution. It also illuminated yet again the constitutional anomalies of the Channel Islands, with members arguing whether or not '*habeas corpus* lies to Jersey', and whether it could operate at a distance. Understanding 'that divers commoners of England had, by illegal warrants, been committed to prison into the islands of Jersey and other islands belong to this commonwealth, out of reach of an *habeas corpus*', parliament also examined the cases of imprisoned royalists, and set Overton free 'without paying any fees'. He was reunited with his family, restored to his military rank, and resumed his public career. By June 1659 he had command of a regiment.[88] This recovery of fortune was brief, however, for Overton's anti-monarchical views proved incompatible with the Restoration. He spent much of the rest of his life in prison, including seven more years in Jersey (see Chapter 14).

Alured and Squibb on the Isle of Man

Spreading their special prisoners around the island periphery, the regime of Oliver Cromwell also dispatched the radical Colonel Matthew Alured and the Fifth Monarchist politician Arthur Squibb to 'confinement in the Isle of Man'. Only under Lord Fairfax's government, after the ouster of the Stanleys, was that island available to the English state. After Alured's arrest in August 1656 the Council's Sergeant at Arms had instructions for his passage, England's Major Generals were required to lend assistance, and the deputy governor of the Isle of Man had orders to 'receive...the body of Colonel Matthew Alured...to keep and detain in safe and sure custody, in the most convenient place of security within the island'.

Alured and Squibb appear to have spent more than two years on the Isle of Man, but whether they engaged with radicals in the parliamentary garrison is unknown; details of their confinement are wanting. Both men gained release after the reassembly of the Rump Parliament in May 1659. Alured was quickly rehabilitated, becoming captain of parliament's Life Guard with a colonel's pay. By February 1660 he was a commissioner for the army. He sided with General Lambert in that officer's campaign for the republic, and fell from grace when that operation failed.[89] Alured and Squibb both continued service after the Restoration, putting the revolution, and their island episode, behind them. The Republican regime had dealt with some of its most difficult opponents by confining them to offshore prisons, but it could not save itself from its own contradictions, or the appeal of resurgent royalism.

The revolution unraveled amidst the irreconcilable complexities of liberty, autocracy, and godly freedom. Experimental regimes from the Rump to the Cromwells sought to deal with their difficulties by political and military means, and found in the island castles a remedy for some awkward embarrassments. England's offshore facilities provided a ready-made solution to the problem of diehard royalists, godly extremists, and republican purists, who could be silenced, or at least muted, by island exile. The succeeding regime of Restoration royalists expanded this practice, until new demands for 'liberty' brought it to an end.

14

The Restoration Prison Archipelago

As the Cromwellian Protectorate collapsed in 1659 and 1660, partisans of 'the good old cause' struggled to maintain a republic, while savvy opportunists negotiated with the exiled Stuarts. The army was divided, and the republicans were outmaneuvered by General George Monck, who became the Duke of Albemarle. Pre-emptive arrests isolated important potential troublemakers in advance of the return of the king, and many of them remained in prison. Beginning in May 1660, Charles II's regime undertook a selective settling of scores. The regicides, who had signed the late king's death warrant, would face execution as traitors, and other named leaders of the commonwealth were excepted from acts of indemnity and oblivion. Successful pleas for mercy might result in commutation of death sentences to lifetime incarceration. Some enemies of the state faced imprisonment in the Tower, allowing connections to the life of the capital, but others were scattered to the periphery and beyond.

The device of dispatching troublemakers to offshore prisons—pioneered by Charles I and developed under the Protectorate—proved too useful for the restored Stuart monarchy to abandon. Rather, the Restoration regime expanded the practice, consigning some two dozen political offenders to long-term overseas detention. With royal appointees in charge as governors of castles, and London controlling the purse strings, the assets of the archipelago could be mobilized in a network of confinement and control. This chapter examines the deployment of island prisons in the perilous politics of the Restoration.

Faced with continuing sedition, and recurrent threats of republican resurgence, the government moved several Interregnum grandees into island isolation. Among men on the wrong side of the Restoration were Major General John Lambert, Lieutenant Colonel Edward Salmon, and Major Richard Creed, sent to imprisonment in Guernsey; Colonel Ralph Cobbett, Major General Robert Overton, and the regicides Gilbert Millington, Henry Smith, James Temple, Thomas Waite, and Sir Hardress Waller, held on Jersey; and Sir Henry Vane, Sir John Ireton, and Colonel John Wildman, sent to the Isles of Scilly.

With so many 'delinquents' to dispose of, every available fortress was pressed into service. While the castles of Guernsey and Jersey were heavily used for high-level internment, facilities on other islands also housed diehards and dissidents. Even the Isle of Man was considered, despite being barely subject to royal authority. It was a recurrent threat against post-Restoration dissenters 'that they should be sent beyond seas, or carried to some island, where they should be kept

England's Islands in a Sea of Troubles. David Cressy, Oxford University Press (2020). © David Cressy 2020.
DOI: 10.1093/oso/9780198856603.001.0001

close prisoners', a far more severe threat than incarceration on the mainland.[1] Colonel John Hutchinson was 'designed for the Isle of Man', but was sent instead to a castle in Kent. James Harrington and Robert Lilburne were confined to St Nicholas Island in Plymouth Sound, and John Lambert spent his last years there. The regicides Robert Tichborne and Henry Marten were held successively on Holy Island in the North Sea.

A cluster of republican grandees were thought too guilty or too threatening to keep alive, even in chains on islands. One of the first to die was the regicide Thomas Harrison, the Fifth Monarchist major general who had earlier experienced imprisonment on the Isle of Wight. Harrison was 'secured' again in April 1660, in company with other agitators, and remained a prisoner of the Restoration. Parliament excepted him from indemnity, a hostile court found him guilty, and he was condemned as a traitor. On the morning of 13 October 1660, Samuel Pepys joined the crowd at Charing Cross 'to see Major General Harrison hanged, drawn, and quartered...he looking as cheerfully as any man could do in that condition'. On his way to execution Harrison was asked derisively what had become of 'the good old cause', and he replied with a smile, clapping his hand on his breast, saying 'here it is, and I go to seal it with my blood'. Another vaunt attributed to him was that he would rise from the dead within three days, and sit with God to sentence his judges.[2] Ten more men met similar deaths in the week that followed, a warning for others who might refuse accommodation with the crown.

Sir Henry Vane, another veteran of the Isle of Wight prison, was not a regicide, but he was a millenarian closely identified with radical republicanism and was considered too dangerous to live at liberty. Vane was arrested soon after the Restoration and was held in the Tower from July 1660 to October 1661. He was then shipped in irons to the Isles of Scilly aboard the frigate *Firefight* and was expected to remain there in isolation.[3] Confinement in the Scillies, however, was not punishment enough, nor were Vane's offences forgotten. In June 1662, the Cavalier Parliament recalled Vane to London, to face trial at the King's Bench. Despite (or perhaps because of) his spirited defence, Vane was found guilty, and was condemned to die as a traitor. He was beheaded at Tower Hill on 14 June, impressing witnesses with the nobility of his death, which some supporters construed as martyrdom.[4] The fate of Vane, Harrison, and others alerted similarly targeted republicans to consider the choice between a principled death and ignominious exile.

Several of those arrested in 1660 experienced long-term incarceration as state prisoners. At least eight of the signers of the late king's death warrant were held on the Channel Islands until they died. The regicide Sir Hardress Waller had the chance of exile in France, but surrendered to Restoration authorities and pleaded for mercy. He was attainted with treason in October 1660 for involvement in the 'Presbyterian Plot' but was remanded to life imprisonment after pleading guilty.

Edmund Ludlow described him as 'one who would say anything to save his life'. Waller, who had previously commanded forces in the Channel Islands, was now sent there as a prisoner, and remained confined in Jersey until his death in 1666.[5]

The regicides Gilbert Millington, Henry Smith, James Temple, and Thomas Waite bargained for mercy, and spent the rest of their lives in prison on Jersey. William Heveningham may have joined them, for his name was included in transit orders in April 1664. For several years in the 1660s, Jersey housed as many as eight former Commonwealth grandees, though nothing is known of their interactions under internment. We may imagine a fellowship of disgruntlement and despair. When Sir Thomas Morgan arrived as governor in 1666, he found Waller and Millington in 'the old castle' (Mont Orgeuil), and Waite, Temple, and Smith, 'three of the king's pretended judges', along with Major General Overton and Colonel Cobbett, in Elizabeth Castle. All was not well, Morgan reported to the Earl of Clarendon in September, for 'Mr Gilbert Millington, a prisoner in Mont Orgueil Castle, died some weeks since, and was interred in unhallowed ground. Sir Hardress Waller, we all suppose, hastens after him, having been near death these two month; but to say the truth, my lord, he is the most penitent of all the prisoners here.' A 'certificate of prisoners in the isle of Jersey' in February 1668 listed the survivors.[6]

Temple was still on Jersey in July 1674, when he was transferred 'from the old castle to the new castle, within that island, for his better health'.[7] Visiting Jersey in 1677, Charles Trumbull observed that

at present there be three prisoners kept and secured, who were committed since the king's return, I suppose for the crime and villainous design of the last king's murder ... They have been condemned to death, and sent hither by the clemency of the present king, to expiate by a long repentance that great and notorious wickedness, for the continuance of whose life they may as heartily pray as ever they did for his father's death ... it being very uncertain whether their condition will be so well after his decease. Their names are Colonel Temple and Colonel Smith, kept in Elizabeth Castle, and one Mr. Waite at the old castle.

The world had mostly forgotten them, though a visitor from the mainland could briefly reflect on their plight.[8]

Lambert on Guernsey

The most important political prisoner of the Restoration, and the one whose life is best documented, was the former army grandee John Lambert (1619–84). Lambert was dashing, cultivated, and highly regarded for his political acumen. As a leading military commander, a significant constitutional thinker, and the architect of the Protectorate and the Instrument of Government, he might well have become the successor to Oliver Cromwell. As the Interregnum experiment disintegrated, he could have become the agent of the Restoration. Instead, his attempt to direct the army failed, and he spent the remainder of his life as a prisoner of state. Lambert's experience of eight years on Guernsey, followed by fourteen more on the island of St Nicholas, shows how the experience of island confinement was affected by changing political conditions.[9] Jonathan Duncan's classic *History of Guernsey* (1841) misrepresents Lambert's confinement by saying that 'the celebrated republican obtained permission to retire to the island at the king's return' and wrongly reports that he 'died in exile in Guernsey'.[10]

Contemporary records refer to Lambert variously as General, Major General, Colonel, or Mr Lambert. Exiled royalists in 1659 considered him essential for 'settling the king's business', to achieve the Restoration, and established secret communications with Lambert that they hoped would lead to them power. Intimate advisers to Charles II—Lord Christopher Hatton, Chancellor Sir Edward Hyde, and Secretary Sir Edward Nicholas—went so far in October 1659 as to propose, in utmost secrecy, 'that the king should marry the Lord Lambert's daughter'. Hatton assured Hyde that Lambert came from 'a very good gentleman's family, and kings have condescended to gentlemen and subjects. The lady is very pretty, of an extraordinary sweetness of disposition, and very virtuously and ingeniously disposed. The father is a person—set aside his unhappy engagement—of great parts, and very noble inclinations.'[11] November 1659 saw more royalist talk of 'treating with Lambert', this time considering Prince James, the Duke of York, as a possible match to his daughter. Hyde told Hatton that 'I do verily believe that Lambert hath much in his power to contribute to the king's restoration ... and if he shall act his part, he will deserve as great a reward both in honour and fortune, as a prince can give, and a subject expect'.[12] Lambert could have been a duke, a royal counsellor, even a royal kinsman, but he chose instead a path of independent republican resistance that led to imprisonment and exile.

Even before the Restoration, Lambert clashed with General Monck and the returned Rump Parliament, who sent him to the Tower on 5 March 1660. After less than a month in captivity he escaped on the evening of 10 April, with the help of a chamber maid who wore his nightcap and impersonated him in bed. When the warder bid him 'Good night, my lord', the maid grunted a convincing acknowledgement, while Lambert dropped down to the Tower ditch, roped over a wall, and slipped away on a waiting barge.[13] He was nearly captured in a riverside house in Westminster, but escaped again in woman's clothes by breaking through a wall. Of such stories were legends made.[14]

Once free, Lambert set out to rally soldiers for 'the good old cause'. It was widely believed that he had gone 'to head some party of the discontented soldiers and fanatics', that 'he would draw a considerable body of the army together speedily', and that many in London were ready to take up arms. At York 'the townsmen that were discovered were all Lambertonians and sectaries'. The Council of State accused Lambert of endeavouring 'to raise a new war, and to embroil the nation in blood and distractions, and to hinder the members from meeting in the next parliament'. He was captured without a fight near Daventry, Northamptonshire, on 22 April, and was brought back to London, where he was made to stand below the gallows at Tyburn before being returned to confinement.[15] The danger he posed was made manifest in a Londoner's remark, 'that my Lord Lambert deserved the crown and to be a king better than Charles II'.[16]

Lambert remained in the Tower during Charles II's May homecoming and came close to being executed, after parliament excepted him from the 1660 Act of Indemnity. Though he had been named in December 1648 to the court to judge Charles I, Lambert had taken no part in the proceedings, and was therefore not strictly a Regicide. Seeking to survive in the new dispensation, he petitioned the king for mercy and pardon, promising to spend 'the remainder of his life in loyalty and obedience' to the Stuart regime. His wife, Frances Lambert, submitted a similar humble request, evoking the sadness of her condition, with her ten children, and seeking permission 'to take a little house in the Tower that we may all live together there', the prisoner 'giving good security for his safe imprisonment'. Lambert is known to have consulted astrologers at this time concerning his prospects for freedom, and rumour circulated that a second escape attempt had been foiled. The prisoner still had powerful friends, and valuable advocates, but none so vigorous and persuasive as his wife. She not only followed her husband to successive places of confinement but used all her skills of petitioning and law to preserve the remnants of his estate.[17]

The government permitted Lambert to live, but only in distant isolation. Samuel Pepys thought he would be sent to Scilly along with Sir Henry Vane, though Vane's destination was kept secret for as long as possible.[18] In October 1661, an official warrant entrusted custody of Colonel John Lambert to Captain Hugh Hide of the ship *Adventure* to take him to Castle Cornet, Guernsey. He shared the voyage with other prisoners of state, Colonel Ralph Cobbett and Sir Hardress Waller, who were bound respectively for Elizabeth Castle and Mont Orgueil in Jersey.[19] All now lay beyond the effective reach of *habeas corpus*, in jurisdictions exempt from English law. The Guernsey schoolmaster Pierre le Roy recorded (in French) in his diary for 17 November: 'arrived at Castle Cornet, John Lambert, general of the sectarian rebels in England, enemy to the king, and prisoner for life.'[20] Every islander would know who was held behind the castle walls.

In February 1662, Frances Lambert petitioned again to join her husband, asking the king to allow them to take a house 'in the island he is now a prisoner', so that she and her children and family 'may all live there together with him'. This appeal was successful, and Frances was permitted to move to Guernsey with three of her children and three maidservants. The governor, Sir Hugh Pollard, was said to have promised her that 'Honest John (meaning her husband) should have all the comfort that place could afford him, which is much rejoiced at by divers of that family'.[21] The Lamberts had hardly begun arrangements to take up residence in the Channel Islands when changing political circumstances returned them to greater dangers in London.

A hardening of the Royalist position led the so-called Cavalier Parliament to recall republican prisoners to put them on trial. Vengeance would substitute for mercy. As grandees of the Protectorate, John Lambert and Sir Henry Vane were particular targets for retribution, not just for their past misdeeds but also for threats they still posed. Reports of republican insurgency continued to surface in the early years of the Restoration, including 'a brave design on foot' with Lambert the rebels' champion. Intelligence of meetings between Lambert's servants and former Cromwellian officers heightened suspicion. Leading politicians thought the crown would be safer if its most dangerous opponents were dead. Monck's humbly born wife Anne, now Duchess of Albemarle, was among those most eager for Vane and Lambert to be hanged.[22]

Warrants went out accordingly on 1 April 1662 to fetch Lambert from Guernsey and to return Vane from the Isles of Scilly. By 22 April they were back in the Tower, where the indefatigable Frances Lambert again won permission 'to have access to Mr Lambert...to converse with him in the presence of his keeper'.[23] Dutch intelligence claimed that Frances Lambert intended 'to throw herself at the king's feet to ask for her husband's pardon, and leave to follow him to Portugal', but the details could not be substantiated. Charles II was sometimes amenable to appeals from attractive women, so the idea is not implausible.[24]

Lambert and Vane faced trial together at King's Bench in June 1662, charged with 'compassing, imagining, and intending to levy and stir up war, rebellion, and insurrection against the king within his kingdom'. Expressions of support from the radical community underscored the danger these republicans posed to the Restoration regime. Reports circulated that 'all the Independents, Anabaptists, Socinians, and Fifth Kingdom Men' held 'private meetings to pray for them', and that veteran soldiers of the Commonwealth threatened violent retribution if Lambert should suffer.[25] Both men were found guilty of high treason, and were condemned to death. Vane was beheaded at Tower Hill on 14 June, but Lambert's sentence was commuted to life imprisonment. Frances Lambert and her royalist kin played a vital role behind the scenes.[26] According to the exiled regicide Edmund Ludlow, Sir Henry Vane 'pleaded for the life of his country, and the liberties thereof', whereas Lambert pleaded 'for his own' and appealed successfully for mercy.[27]

Lambert was returned to Castle Cornet, to be joined again by members of his family. When he arrived on Guernsey in the autumn of 1662, he was 'very ill in the disease of the scurvy...by reason of his long being at sea', but with his wife Frances to attend him he began to recover.[28] He would remain there for the next eight years.

Lambert arrived on an island beset by poverty, in a castle short of money, with a garrison reduced by lack of pay and low morale. Friction between the governor and his deputy created administrative tensions, exacerbated by the usual disagreements between the castle and the island. Major Robert Walters, visiting Guernsey in April 1663, remarked that 'troublesome and unquiet spirits' disturbed both the civilian and military communities, and 'the people's hatred to one another fills the place full of faction' (see Chapter 10).[29]

Lambert was not always a 'close' prisoner, isolated and confined, but was often free to move within the castle walls. From time to time the authorities permitted him to visit other parts of the island, always with watchful guards. The conditions of his internment altered with the state of his health, the efforts of his wife and friends, the strictness of his keepers, and perceptions of the threat he still posed to national security. For most of the time he had company and conversation, letters from England, and a few items of his own domestic furniture for his comfort and convenience. His library included works of history, theology, and military science, all carefully inventoried.[30] Though given access to paper and ink, he did not write about his ideas or conditions. Nor do we know whether his reading was more recreational, religious, or philosophic, nor what went on in his mind. If he wrote his reflections, they have not survived. The danger Lambert posed to the Restoration state was more symbolic than discursive, more a matter of history than of agitation on the prisoner's part. He enjoyed a suite of rooms in Castle Cornet, rather than a cell. He was able to cultivate a walled garden, with seeds and plantings from his property at Wimbledon, and is credited with introducing the exotic Guernsey Lily, *nerine sarniensis*, to the island. The artist Baptist Gaspars, employed by the Hatton family, gave him lessons in drawing.[31] As a prisoner of state, he was constantly under guard, but such circumstances were endurable for someone who had come close to execution. The garrison at Castle Cornet included men who had served under the Protectorate, as 'followers of Cromwell and Lambert', who may have accorded him respect. The civilian inhabitants of Guernsey also included 'notorious' republicans who were inclined to show sympathy for the imprisoned colonel, so one royalist officer warned.[32]

Sir Christopher (Lord) Hatton (1605–70), who became governor of Guernsey in 1662 but did not take up formal residence until 1664, enjoyed cordial relations with the Lambert family. They may sometimes have dined together, like the Carterets and William Prynne. Though political and ideological antagonists, on opposite sides of the wheel of fortune, the prisoner and his keeper had prior dealings. Back in September 1656, when Lambert was at the peak of his power, and Hatton was an exile in Paris, they exchanged friendly letters, saluting each other as 'your very humble servant'. Both men were horticultural enthusiasts, touched by the craze for 'rare and unknown' plants, and shared catalogues of anemones, irises, and tulips. Hatton, on the Continent, served briefly as Lambert's bulb agent, entrusted 'for the setting up of a young garden...to make a better choice for me', and 'to order them as you judge best'.[33] The connection was renewed in the final year of the Protectorate, when a Stuart restoration seemed likely. Hatton commended Lambert strongly to Hyde and the king in 1659, avowing that he knew the family from top to bottom, and recommending Lambert's daughter for royal marriage.[34] Now, in November 1662, it was Governor Hatton's responsibility to follow orders to 'give such liberty...to Colonel John Lambert...as will consist with the security of his person, and as your discretion shall think fit'. This flexibility would continue so long as the prisoner maintained good behaviour and entertained no correspondence to the prejudice of the king's service.[35]

Hardliners, however, thought that Lambert was over-privileged, and that the traitor enjoyed too many favours. Lieutenant Governor Nathaniel Darrell, in charge at Castle Cornet until the new governor arrived, was hostile to Hatton, and used the matter of Lambert's imprisonment to undermine him. 'I...cannot help it', Darrell wrote to the Secretary of State in November 1662, 'if Mrs Lambert gives not her letters to my Lord Hatton, which must be the care had in England'. Darrell was at pains to point out that, at least on in his watch, Lambert 'has not had liberty as is reported to walk about the castle, his freedom having extended no farther than to walk upon the platform before his lodging, with a guard upon him, and to exercise himself in a little garden in the corner of the castle'. Security was tight, Darrell insisted, with Lambert and his family locked up in one chamber, and 'their cook and maid is locked in a room apart and comes not near them'.[36]

As to secret correspondence between Lambert and 'the ill affected party in England', Darrell asserted that he had used his 'best endeavours to find out any such commerce, but cannot, with all the strictness I can use, trace any footsteps'. The only exception involved Mrs Lambert's letters, which were purportedly of a private and familial nature. Any communications he found, Darrell boasted, 'I send them to my Lord Hatton, though I never had orders for it'.[37] Deep antagonism between the governor and lieutenant governor frustrated Christopher Hatton's desire to treat his celebrity prisoner like a gentleman. Taking a harder line was one way for authorities at the castle to demonstrate their dutifulness.

Lambert sought to be a model prisoner, but he remained at the mercy of other people's actions and perceptions. Reports of resurgence of 'the good old cause' only jeopardized his condition. London was awash with rumours of designs for Lambert's freedom, imagining him leading an insurrection. One report circulating in December 1662 was 'that if his majesty should send to Guernsey, the place where Lambert is prisoner, for the execution of him, the governor would not only refuse it but oppose it, and that if insurrection went on, Guernsey and England was but a little distance'.[38] Another in July 1663 quoted a Northamptonshire minister, Samuel Bagley, who reportedly said that he 'looks for a turn', and hoped to see Lambert 'rise and take down the cavaliers'. Even more frighteningly, Bagley was heard to say of Charles II that 'we will serve him as we did his father', meaning 'we will cut off his head'.[39] More reports circulated from time to time of 'a great desire for Lambert's liberty' among the discontented, though Lambert himself was 'probably ignorant or averse to such things'.[40] Seditious murmurings on the island and in England only worsened his situation.

Major Robert Walters, who had been sent to check on conditions on Guernsey, reported to Sir Henry Bennett on 3 April 1663 that

> the prisoner in the castle is very melancholy, troubled at many things he hears. [He] saith some scandalous tongues have traduced him to his majesty as guilty of some new thoughts of sedition, which he utterly disavows, giving great protestations of his innocence, and says he can never be so wicked to act nor think the least thing that might be prejudicial to such a prince who so mercifully had bestowed life upon him, who so little deserved it; he lays the fault of his close confinement upon the Lord Hatton, and seems to wonder much at his severity. My lord has given him the liberty of the castle, having the porter of the place for his guard, a person so odious (I know not upon what occasion) to the prisoner, as he refuseth all stirrings abroad rather than to have his keeper for a companion, nor do his children stir abroad, though they have liberty granted to them to come into the island. I would sometimes invite them to me, if I had encouragement so to do. I pity their restraint.[41]

Walters found Guernsey politically disordered, with jurats against jurats, the island against the castle, and the administration at odds with itself. Early in 1664, by Lieutenant Governor Darrell's instruction, the lieutenant bailiff, John de Quetteville, joined Lambert in the castle prison. Later that year, by authority of Governor Hatton, three more leading islanders were imprisoned: Peter Carey, William de Beauvoir, and James de Haviland. These Guernsey gentlemen would have been interesting company for any long-term prisoner, though they were held for less than a fortnight. Even Darrell himself was briefly held 'close prisoner' in Castle Cornet, before being sent back to England.[42]

Lambert's friends and his enemies both ensured that he was not forgotten. As a traitor to the crown he needed to be punished, and as a danger to the state he had to be monitored and kept secure; his sentence of death was only suspended. But Lambert was still a gentleman, a man of great honour and talent, with influential family connections. The prisoner's royalist kinsmen lobbied to ameliorate his condition and to safeguard the remains of his estate, as he had done for them in the 1650s when their situations were reversed. Writing to the younger Christopher Hatton in 1664, Sir Charles Lyttleton described Colonel Lambert as 'one...I would take a great deal of pains to serve...being the person in the world my wife has frequently owned to me she and her [former] husband has received the greatest obligation or support from'. In another letter Lyttleton ventured, 'I will use all my interest for Colonel Lambert', in the matter of a contested annuity, 'as if it were my own'.[43] Lambert's relations, especially the Belasyse family of Viscount Fauconberg, provided similar networks of support for his wife and children. Lyttleton told the younger Hatton that some of Lambert's friends 'have complained to me that my lord your father has treated him very severely under his government of Guernsey; though it may be that I cannot possibly credit, or that it is rather so given out to hide his kind usage'.[44]

The authorities' 'usage' of their prisoner of state oscillated between strictness and remission. Having earlier allowed 'liberty and indulgence to Col. John Lambert' to range 'within the precincts' of the island, the government subsequently 'found reason since to abridge' those provisions and confine him to the castle. Sometimes, as Major Walters noted, he seemed to isolate himself. By March 1664, Lambert was once again a 'close' prisoner and could no longer enjoy 'the liberty of the island'. This prompted Frances Lambert to petition again on her husband's behalf, seeking relief for 'his present sad state of health, by reason of his close restraint, which renders him in a dangerous and almost a desperate condition'. She asked the king to order Governor Hatton 'for leave that one of her daughters may have permission personally to attend on her said father during his present distemper and weakness of health'. Once again, her intervention appears to have been effective. On 12 March 1664, the Council ordered Hatton again to allow Lambert 'the full benefit of our gracious favour and indulgence as it was signified to you', subject to the governor's 'discretion'.[45]

Hatton was able to oversee these arrangements in person after he took over the reins of government on Guernsey in April. Lambert himself acknowledged the change in his treatment, in a deferential letter to the Earl of Clarendon dated 27 April 1664, thanking him for

> what your lordship has been so industrious to procure . . . My Lord Hatton, since his arrival, has been pleased to give a great allay to my afflictions, by assuring me that I still live under those gracious reflections his majesty was once pleased to cast upon me . . . My lord has not only poured this oil onto my bones, but has confirmed and improved it by a most friendly and candid deportment towards me.

In this masterfully flattering epistle, a unique example of Lambert's prison writing, he emphasized his dependence on King Charles's 'clemency and royal generosity'.[46]

Maintaining and securing a prisoner of state were by no means the greatest of Hatton's problems. In an island riven by political and religious faction, he may have found some relief in conversation with his esteemed former correspondent and fellow horticulturist, a gentleman of many parts. Hatton's 'friendly and candid deportment' towards Lambert was not matched by the governor's dealings with his enemies, especially the lieutenant governor and the island's dean, bailiff, and jurats.

Fending off complaints about his administration, Hatton wrote to Clarendon on 7 May 1664, saying of Lambert:

> I account him my friend... He is as wary and fearful to commit any error by his liberty, as I should be to afford it were I not permitted; and hath only been once in the island [i.e. outside the castle] since [the return of his wife from England], and that not without me, by his own desires. He will not quit the castle, and I have enlarged his quarters. Yet my lady [Frances Lambert] hath taken a house in the island, and intends with some of her children to live much there, it is so near us.[47]

These domestic arrangements became momentous for both families when Lambert's daughter Mary, who was supposed to nurse her father, entered into a courtship relationship with the governor's second son, Charles. Links between the royalist governor and his republican prisoner became unexpectedly complicated when this unauthorized dalliance proceeded to a clandestine marriage. Adding to Hatton's troubles, it prompted backbiters to fault him for the 'misfortune... of his son's marriage with a prisoner's daughter... being to a person whose father was attainted, and who had no portion'. Writing a year or two later, after his recall from Guernsey, Hatton was eager to explain to the king that as soon as he learned of the 'pretended marriage... he turned his son out of doors, and hath never given him a penny'. And as to the prisoner, 'the thing had no ill effect', for he 'remained in safe custody, and... in that safety he remains'[48] The date of this family catastrophe is undetermined, but it may lie behind two extraordinary letters Charles Hatton wrote to his father and brother on 1 August 1665. Charles complained that he had been expelled and denied the blessing of a father who 'hath a natural aversion to me, and is fully resolved never to regard or provide for me as his child'. The occasion for this falling-out, according to the letters, was a scandal involving an uncle, but the writer may have cited this to deflect attention from his unfortunate marriage.[49] Despite this inauspicious beginning, Charles Hatton and his wife Mary (née Lambert) eventually prospered, setting up a distinguished gentle establishment in London's Pall Mall. When Charles wrote to his elder brother, now Lord Hatton, in 1670 and 1671, he closed with variants of 'my wife gives her humble service to you'.[50]

The first Lord Hatton's governorship of Guernsey effectively ended in December 1664, though several more months would pass before he left the island, and he retained his office in principle until his death. London's disfavour fell on the prisoner as well as his erstwhile keeper. Lambert became, once again, a close prisoner in Castle Cornet, with a diminished register of conversation. Until further notice, by royal order, he was now 'to be restrained from that liberty of the island and castle, which we were graciously willing should for some time past be indulged to him, which we find reason to believe he hath not made so good use of, as in gratitude to our royal clemency he ought to have done'.[51]

Lambert was closely constrained by the caretaker administration that followed the departure of the Hattons. But many of his supporters still hoped for his liberation. The government in London received intelligence in 1665 'that Lambert intended to escape', as well as false reports that he had already succeeded. So-called fanatics in Yorkshire were said in February 1665 to be 'much taken with a report that General Lambert hath made an escape, and got into Holland'. Lambert in fact had made no such escape but became implicated in the 'malicious hopes and bloody intentions' of anti-monarchical plotters. More extravagant and unfounded 'fancies' in March 1665 claimed that 'Lambert with the governor of the isle are gone to the Dutch, and that . . . six ships came to receive them'.[52]

One of London's first instructions to the acting governor Jonathan Atkins was 'to secure Colonel Lambert, yet treating him with all fair courtesy, and informing yourself particularly whether he has given any grounds during his imprisonment there to make himself less worthy of our grace to him'.[53]

In 1666, it was the French, rather than the Dutch, with designs on Guernsey. The French had long coveted the Channel Islands, and their current 'treacherous' and 'perfidious' plot allegedly included plans to rescue Lambert. Jean François de Vaucourt, governor of the small French island of Chausey, between Jersey and St Malo, was arrested on Guernsey, charged with planning 'the escape of John Lambert, prisoner in that island, for debauching our good subjects there from their duty and allegiance . . . and for raising and fomenting a rebellion'. Vaucourt and the master of the ship that transported him were 'without further form of process hanged as spies', and Lambert's close imprisonment was made more secure.[54] The government in London instructed that,

> if at any time hereafter an enemy shall chance to appear before that our island with an appearance of invading it, our will and pleasure is, and we do hereby sufficiently authorize and require you immediately to cause the said John Lambert to be shot to death (he being already a condemned person by the law), for having contrary to his allegiance, and the eminent obligations he hath to our royal clemency, held correspondency with our enemies.[55]

Once again, Lambert suffered from events beyond his control.

Dramatic political developments in England had potential to alter the prisoner's circumstances. Edward Hyde, the Earl of Clarendon, Charles II's Lord Chancellor, a statesman with rare knowledge of the Channel Islands, who had consigned a series of troublemakers thither, fell precipitously from power in the autumn of 1667. Among the articles of impeachment, overshadowed by more treasonous charges, was that 'he hath advised and procured divers of his majesty's subjects to be imprisoned against law, in remote islands, garrisons, and other places, thereby to prevent them from the benefit of law'.[56] Perhaps a reconsideration of that practice was in order.

According to a report by Colonel Jonathan Atkins in October 1667, Lambert was the only prisoner of state on the island of Guernsey. Tellingly, the acting governor could find 'no warrant nor record of his commitment, his straight confinement was by order from his majesty...He remains still close till I shall receive further orders; and I cannot say otherwise than that he hath carried himself ever since with modesty and discretion conformed to his majesty's commands.'[57]

No doubt prompted by Frances Lambert, Lambert's friends in England seized the moment to make 'humble suit' on his behalf. By royal warrant of 3 December 1667, the government was 'graciously pleased to condescend to' the request by Thomas Viscount Fauconberg, John Lord Belasyse, and Chancellor of the Exchequer Sir Thomas Ingram, that 'Colonel John Lambert, now a prisoner on our isle of Guernsey' be granted 'the liberty of the said island, and to take a house therein for himself and his family to live in, he passing the word or giving security to remain a true prisoner in our said island'. After several iterations of 'indulgence' and 'abridgement', the crown again allowed Lambert 'the full benefit of our former gracious favour', to have liberty within the precincts of the island, though no further enlargement.[58] This grant of 'liberty' may have been short-lived, for just two months later, in February 1668, another royal warrant authorized Frances Lambert and Mary Hatton to remain with 'John Lambert, close prisoner...on account of his present distemper'. Mary Hatton, of course, was Lambert's daughter, married to the son of the absent governor, who had tended him during previous illness.[59]

The younger Lord Christopher Hatton, who must have known Lambert well, was formally made governor of Guernsey in July 1670. In handing over power, the acting governor Colonel Atkins was ordered 'to deliver up the person of Colonel John Lambert' to Hatton.[60] But Lambert's time on Guernsey was coming to an end. Frances Lambert's kindred may have been influential in moving him closer to home. In September 1670, Captain Charles Honey of the ketch Merlin 'received from the hands of my Lord Hatton the body of John Lambert, commonly called Major General Lambert', and landed him at Plymouth.[61] Castle Cornet's prison quarters were empty, though not for long.

Though close to the mainland, within sight of a bustling international port, Lambert was again confined to an island. Rooms were found for him on the garrison island of St Nicholas, sometimes known as Drake's Island, in Plymouth Sound, where other political prisoners had been held. St Nicholas was a fortified islet of six and a half acres, 300 yards long, little more than 1,000 yards offshore. Lambert spent the rest of his life there, cultivating yet another garden and receiving a stream of visitors. He also kept his mind alert through correspondence with members of the Royal Society, and by exchanging algebraic problems with Thomas Baker, the vicar of Bishop's Nympton, north Devon.[62] One historian of the Restoration, Ronald Hutton, claims that the burden of Lambert's imprisonment 'may have been eased latterly by the fact that his mind gave way', a 'fact' for which there is no basis.[63]

Determined to be close to her husband, Frances Lambert followed Lambert from Guernsey to the mainland, and arrived with her family at Portsmouth on 16 October, sharing transport with Sir Jonathan Atkins, the late governor of Guernsey, and his household. 'They were in that great storm the Friday night, and very like to be cast away,' in the ever-turbulent Channel.[64] As soon as they were settled, the Lamberts rented a house at Plymouth, and resumed their much-interrupted domestic intimacy until Frances died in 1676.

As the island was so close to the mainland, anyone with a boat could row to St Nicholas, and seek permission from the garrison to see its famous prisoner. King Charles II and his brother the Duke of York were among visitors to St Nicholas Island in July 1671, and again in August 1677, while reviewing the navy. There is no record of direct contact between these royal Stuarts and the man whose daughter one of them might once have married, but several courtiers conversed with the ageing republican.[65] Among less exalted visitors was John Blackwell, one of Lambert's creditors and kinsmen, who sought permission to confer with the prisoner about an outstanding bond.[66]

The Quaker Miles Halhead visited St Nicholas Island in 1673 and discussed with Lambert the recent history and politics of persecution and toleration. Halhead recalled that, while staying with a Friend in Plymouth, 'the word of the Lord came to me saying, arise and go thy way, and speak to John Lambert the words that I shall give thee'. Thus commanded, he procured a boat, 'and passed to the island the same day; and there we found a strong guard of soldiers. A lieutenant asked me, what was my business to the island? I said, I desire to speak to John Lambert; and then he asked me if I was ever a captain under his command, and I said, no.' Assured that this was no military reunion, but rather an affair of the spirit, the officers brought Halhead face to face with their prisoner: 'I said, Friend, is thy name John Lambert, and he said, yea; then I said unto him, Friend, I pray thee hear what the servant of the Lord hath to say to thee.' According to Halhead, God had given the parliamentary commander the opportunity to do good 'for the deliverance of his people'; but, alas, 'John Lambert, you soon forgot your promises . . . and turned the edge of your sword against the Lord's servants and hand-maids, whom he sent forth to declare his eternal truth'. Lambert's sufferings since 1660, by these lights, were recompense for the Protectorate's persecution of Quakers, rather than his failure to support the Restoration. After delivering this message, Halhead continues, Lambert 'desired me to sit down, and so I did, and he called for some beer, and gave me to drink . . . So he and his wife, and two of his daughters, and myself and a Friend of Plymouth, discoursed two hours or more, in love and plainness of my heart.'[67] It would be interesting to have Lambert's account of this challenging but convivial conversation.

Lambert in old age was still considered a security risk, but also a historical curiosity. The Plymouth burgess James Yonge referred to him as 'the arch rebel' and 'that old rebel'.[68] In 1678, at the height of the Popish Plot scare, the fantasist Titus Oates claimed that Lambert was involved in a conspiracy to kill King Charles II, and that the pope intended him to be Adjutant-General of a Roman Catholic England. The government sent Sir Hugh Piper and Sir Thomas Carew to St Nicholas to interview Lambert in November 1678, to investigate his engagement in 'this wicked design', and to determine whether he had a papal commission. They were to expressly warn him 'that there is already so much proved against him that, if his majesty finds he does not deal ingenuously in his confession, he can expect nothing but the immediate execution of the sentence depending against him'. Carew was eager to undertake this task, he told Secretary Williamson, 'because it has been common discourse in our parts at least this fortnight that [Lambert] is involved in the horrible conspiracy'. Nothing incriminating could be discovered, but Lambert was once again troubled by events beyond his control. It was preposterous to imagine that Cromwell's understudy had gone over to Rome, though the historian David Hume asserted that Lambert died a Catholic.[69] One of his last visitors of note was the naval commissioner Samuel Pepys, who called at St Nicholas in 1683, on his way to Tangier, to converse with 'my Lord Lambert'.[70]

Local records report an exceptionally cold winter in 1683–4, which may have contributed to the prisoner's death. Plymouth weather was 'very severe, east wind, frost and snow continued three months, so that ships were starved in the mouth of the channel, and almost all the cattle famished. The fish left the coast almost five months. All provision excessive dear.'[71] Dr George Clarke, who visited St Nicholas Island in 1684, a few months after Lambert's death, was told that

> he always loved gardening, and took a delight, during his confinement, to work in a little one that he had there. One day, as he was at work, some gentlemen came in a boat to see the island, and the Major-General went in to change his night gown, that he might wait upon the company in a more decent dress, and catched a cold that brought him to his grave.[72]

The prisoner on the island passed into local folk memory, which sometimes became confused. When the traveller Celia Fiennes visited Plymouth in 1695 she noted 'part of the main ocean, in which are some islands. There is St Nicholas Island with a fort in it; there it was Harry Martin, one of the king's judges, was banished during life.'[73] She, or her guide, confused John Lambert with the regicide Henry Marten (1602–80), who was imprisoned at Windsor, Holy Island, and

Chepstow. Daniel Defoe was better informed, when he saw St Nicholas Island in 1703: 'In this island the famous General Lambert, one of Cromwell's great agents and officers in the rebellion, was imprisoned for life, and lived many years there.'[74]

Other Island Prisoners

Lambert was the most distinguished of long-term prisoners but was not the only dissident republican to suffer offshore confinement. Remaining regicides, trouble-makers, and suspected traitors were rounded up at the Restoration and, if not executed, faced perpetual imprisonment. While the castles of Guernsey and Jersey were heavily used for high-level internment, the fortresses on other islands also housed diehard and dissident republicans. Like Frances Lambert, their wives and loved ones petitioned where possible for their relief, and sometimes had limited success.

Among civilian detainees, the radical Londoner Sir John Ireton (Henry Ireton's brother) was considered a threat to the monarchy and was excepted from the general pardon. Ireton had served as alderman, mayor, and sheriff of London, and accepted a knighthood from Oliver Cromwell. He was taken to the Tower of London in April 1660, on suspicion of involvement in Lambert's rising, and was held there again in November 1661 on further suspicion of conspiracy. Samuel Pepys remarked in his diary on 'the great clapping up of some old statesmen, such as Ireton ... and others ... they say upon a great plot, but I believe no such thing'. The arrests were precautionary and punitive, to bring potential opponents under control. Ireton's wife gained permission in February 1662 to visit her husband in the Tower with a doctor and a nurse, during his 'indisposition'. In April that year he was moved to the Isles of Scilly, much to his discomfort and disgruntlement, where he spent three more years as a prisoner. In August 1665, he was briefly in the Tower again, for alleged seditious practices, and was then released.[75]

The cramped facilities at St Mary's on Scilly also held the former Leveller Colonel John Wildman, who was taken to the Tower in November 1661 before being sent offshore. Wildman's enemies described him as 'inclined to antimonar-chy, as subtle a person as any of his quality in England'.[76] His wife, Lucy, petitioned actively on his behalf, gaining permission to visit him in the Tower, to gain access to Wildman's papers, and to secure a doctor to treat his illness.[77] When after eight months she sought a writ of habeas corpus to bring her husband to trial, the authorities responded by removing him abruptly to a remote location. Wildman was transferred to St Mary's Castle, where he shared his imprisonment with the republican John Ireton. The governor Sir Francis Godolphin visited the island in August 1662, and found Wildman and Ireton 'very sensible of their change from the Tower to that desolate place to be much for the worse ... Sir Anthony Bassett [the garrison commander, perhaps the son of the civil-war commander Thomas Bassett] is civil to them, but keeps them strictly guarded'. The Scillies were remote and primitive, in contrast to the Tower of London, and friends and family members had difficulty reaching them. Lucy Wildman described the islands as 'a place very destitute of all conveniences for a sickly person...without any provision of necessaries'. Conditions there endangered her husband's life, while 'the distance of that place' threatened 'the ruin and final destruction of his estate'. Lucy petitioned again that John Wildman might be released 'upon reasonable bail', with liberty either to 'move to some more mild and favourable restraint in the city of London or Westminster', or else have licence to travel beyond the seas to 'some kingdom in amity with your majesty', but neither request was granted.[78]

The Restoration government still considered Wildman a threat and held him in the castle of St Mary's for three and a half years. His isolation may not have been entirely complete, having Ireton for company, and occasional letters from the mainland. One of Wildman's former servants was suspected of 'holding correspondence with his majesty's prisoners in the isle of Jersey', raising fears of an inter-island conspiracy of republicans.[79] In January 1666, the Council issued a warrant to remove Wildman from the Scillies to Pendennis Castle on the mainland, to be held there indefinitely for his 'treasonable and seditious practices'. Lucy Wildman continued to petition, and her efforts bore fruit the following March, when the government allowed the prisoner 'the comfort of his son's company, and use of a servant'. In April they gave him liberty to stroll outside the walls of Pendennis Castle, in company with a keeper, provided he did not go too far. Eventually in October 1667, as the Earl of Clarendon fell from power, Wildman was permitted to repair to London, provided he engaged to keep the peace and attempted nothing against the government. This allowed him to live again as a country gentleman, and in July 1670 he gained permission to travel abroad for his health with his wife and son. The former Leveller even returned to politics, becoming a Whig member of parliament in 1681, and suffering imprisonment again in 1683 for his part in the Rye House Plot.[80]

Major General Robert Overton, who had already suffered imprisonment on Jersey under the Protectorate, was among dozens more republicans arrested in December 1660 for his opposition to 'arbitrary or kingly innovation', and for allegedly stockpiling weapons.[81] He spent eleven months in the Tower before being moved to Chepstow Castle, and was imprisoned again without trial in May 1663 after a brief period of freedom. In January 1664, the Council decided to send him to Jersey, this time to Mont Orgeuil, where he remained for almost eight years. His wife Ann Overton was permitted to visit him, but they were apart when she died in 1665.[82] Little would be known of Overton's time in Jersey, in the company of languishing regicides, had he not spent his years compiling 'Gospel observations and religious manifestations' in his late wife's memory, a manuscript that has attracted the attention of literary scholars. It is apparent that he had access to papers and books, though their titles can only be inferred. Heavy with biblical references and reworkings of metaphysical poetry, Overton's prison writings were melancholy and contemplative, with none of the vaunting certitude of some earlier godly prisoners. His political maxims counselled patience and submission, for 'they that pursue perfection on earth leave nothing for saints to find in heaven'. Men like himself, 'ground to powder in this mill of vicissitudes', should accept their situation rather than 'obstinately glory in the repute of suffering as state martyrs'.[83] A writ of *habeas corpus* on Overton's behalf in 1669 had no immediate effect, but in December 1672 his island confinement ended. He died in obscurity in England in 1679 and was all but forgotten for 300 years.[84]

Major Richard Creed, another Cromwellian veteran and a long-term political prisoner, was moved to Guernsey in 1670 after Lambert had vacated Castle Cornet, and stayed there almost ten years. He is not to be confused with the Richard Creed who served the Protectorate as a Commissioner for the Navy and secretary to the Generals of the Fleet. This Major Creed had a dutiful but unspectacular career in military disbursements, and was associated with the Fifth Monarchists, one of whom thanked him in 1653 for sharing 'the melody of experienced saints'. No friend of the Stuart monarchy, Creed was arrested on the eve of the Restoration, and was held successively in the Tower and in Cornwall and Devon. He sailed to the Channel Islands late in 1670 as a prisoner on board the *Merlin*, which had earlier transported Lambert to Plymouth.[85]

Creed's experience on Guernsey is illuminated by the Hatton family correspondence. Writing in September 1670 to Lord Christopher Hatton, who had succeeded his father as governor but had not yet moved to the island, the Earl of Bath remarked that Major Creed 'hath comported himself very civilly, and in nothing abused the liberty that hath been afforded him'. Sir Gilbert Talbot, who commanded the *Merlin*, added his opinion that 'there is so much justice due to his modest and civil behaviour that such a bare certificate could not be denied him'. Creed's wife, like so many others, followed him from prison to prison, and obtained permission from the captain to sail with him to Guernsey with their children and servants. Although she had doubts whether Hatton would admit her to the island, 'she not being within the order for her husband', Talbot assured her of the governor's 'great civility to all people'. Seasonal impediments of wind and weather kept the Creeds in England a little longer, delaying their arrival in Guernsey until October.[86]

Preparing accommodation for a new state prisoner required some rudimentary housekeeping at Castle Cornet, and this too generated correspondence. On 5 December 1670, Captain William Sheldon reported to Governor Hatton that, 'according to your lordship's order, I shall remove Major Creed into Colonel Lambert's lodgings, which is the most convenient place in the castle; but I doubt prejudicial enough to your lordship's concerns when you return'. On hearing from Sheldon 'that Major Creed was to be removed prisoner into the castle', the steward Thomas Richardson informed Hatton that

I was forced to remove bedding and other things that I had put in Mr Anly's lodgings the better to preserve them, to make rooms ready for his reception. Mr Green the next day came to the castle and showed me the order; upon the Wednesday after Major Creed with his family came to the castle, where they remain.[87]

The Creeds, like the Lamberts, maintained a semblance of domestic intimacy in challenging and unusual circumstances. The monotony of their life at Castle Cornet was interrupted on the night of 30 December 1672 when a freak lightning strike ignited the gunpowder store, destroyed the keep, and killed seven people, including the governor's wife and mother (see Chapter 10). Among the survivors, 'very much hurt, but all safe alive', were 'Mr Creed (a prisoner) with his wife and children and servants, and other attendants of the family'.[88]

Languishing on Guernsey, in a broken fortress, Creed considered himself as someone 'laid by and forgotten, who did see no other, but that I must end my days in this condition'.[89] But, after nine years of confinement, his circumstances were about to change. Parliament's Habeas Corpus Act came into force in June 1679 and removed all doubts that the writ applied in England's 'island territories or dominions'. Promoted by the Whigs, and specifically encompassing Jersey and Guernsey, this statute was intended 'for the better securing the liberty of the subject', and forbade further imprisonment in 'garrisons, islands or places beyond the seas'.[90]

Responding to the changing political climate, Governor Hatton obtained an order in Council whereby Creed would be released on bond, with two securities of £500 apiece for his 'peaceable living under the king and his government, and not to take up arms'. Further writs from King's Bench secured his freedom, even though that court had no formal jurisdiction in Guernsey. Thanking the governor for the 'unexpected favour bestowed upon me in procuring my liberty', Creed promised to do nothing that would stain Lord Hatton's honour.[91] No longer a danger to the state, he returned to die in England.

Information about other Restoration detainees is much more fragmentary. Lieutenant Colonel Edward Salmon, who had served under Ireton, Overton, and Lambert, was arrested in 1660 after the collapse of Lambert's rising. He remained a prisoner throughout the 1660s, first on Guernsey and then on Jersey. By 1668 he was granted 'the liberty of the island, to follow a mean calling for [his family's] daily subsistence', provided he was accompanied by a guard and returned to the castle each night. Early in 1670, the court of King's Bench granted a *habeas corpus*, 'with the advice that he submit to the Council for his delivery', but Salmon's keepers responded by moving the prisoner from one island castle to another. In

October 1670, hearing that Lord Christopher Hatton was about to take up his post in the Channel Islands, a former associate of the republican officer begged the favour that his lordship might deliver a letter 'in a business wherein Colonel Salmon is concerned'. Whether it arrived is unknown. Still protesting his innocence, Salmon petitioned in September 1671 to be freed. 'After nine years restraint', he found himself once more 'enclosed in Castle Cornet without any relief'. At the very least he asked permission to work on the island, 'that he may be in a capacity to get his own bread'.[92]

Colonel Ralph Cobbett, the former custodian of Charles I at Hurst Castle, was another of the republican officers 'confined to their several houses furthest off from London' in January 1660. In April, he was committed close prisoner to the Tower, where he stayed for a year and half before being shipped to Jersey. There he stayed for more than a dozen years, before being summoned to London 'to be further disposed of'. By 1676 he was in the Tower again, when his daughter gained permission to visit him. He was finally released in May of that year on a £1,000 bond, 'much impaired in his health...he paying the usual fees'.[93] Jersey was also most likely the destination of the radical Alderman Downes, who was moved from the Tower 'to one of the islands' early in 1664.[94]

A few more men of 'dangerous principles' were imprisoned on the Isle of Wight. One of those held at Carisbrooke Castle from 1663 to at least 1666 was Major Edmund Rolph, who had previously served there as an officer guarding Charles I. The irony was not lost that Rolph, who once threatened he 'would have murdered' King Charles, was now 'secured in the same place where he would have pistolled the king'. The Act of Oblivion did not forgive his offence. Rolph, however, was a skilled surveyor, and in 1667 he was released to work for the island governor Lord Culpeper, on promise to return to prison.[95]

Others sent to the Isle of Wight included the insurrectionist Robert Danvers in 1664,[96] and the former parliamentary grandee Colonel Robert Duckenfield in 1665, for plotting against the king. Duckenfield, who had commanded troops on the Isle of Man, spent three years in the Isle of Wight prison, 'to the great hinderance of his health', suffering 'great diseases...which he never had before'. He was eventually released on good behaviour to his home in Cheshire.[97]

Some sources erroneously place the parliamentary Colonel John Hutchinson in prison on the Isle of Wight, mistaking that island's Sandham Castle for Sandown Castle in Kent. Hutchinson had been arrested for treason in November 1663, and early in 1664 he was designated for transfer to the Isle of Man, though not sent there. Lucy Hutchinson's loving memoir confirms that he was sent to 'a far prison, not much different from exile', but, instead of crossing the Irish sea, he was held at Sandown, which for its bleakness and unwholesomeness matched any island dungeon.[98]

Also arrested 'for treasonable designs and practices' was the political philosopher James Harrington, author of Oceana (1656). He was taken to the Tower in October 1661, and later transferred to St Nicholas Island. Harrington's sisters, the well-connected Lady Elizabeth Assheton and Anne Evelyn, used all their influence on his behalf. On one occasion they softened the Lieutenant of the Tower 'into more humanity with a present of fifty pounds under the notion of fees'. Harrington petitioned 'the favour of a public trial, or a more easy confinement', but without avail. After he had spent six months in prison, his sisters obtained a writ of *habeas corpus* on his behalf. But, before the writ could be served, his captors spirited him out of the Tower in the pre-dawn darkness, the same trick they played with Wildman. According to his biographer John Toland, Harrington was 'put on board a ship to be transported he knew not whither, without any time given him either to see his friends or make provision of money, linen, or other necessaries'. He was bound, he discovered, to 'a kind of rock opposite to Plymouth, called St Nicholas's Island'. Eventually, on bond of £5,000, he was moved to the fort on the mainland, and, after his health had collapsed, was allowed to return to London.[99] Also imprisoned on tiny St Nicholas was the regicide Colonel Robert Lilburne, the famous Leveller's younger brother, who had sided with Lambert in the last months of the Protectorate. Robert Lilburne's sentence of death in October 1660 was reprieved to life imprisonment, after he had pleaded that he acted in ignorance, and he sat on his rock across from Plymouth until he died in August 1665.[100]

Yet another regicide, Robert Tichborne, a London alderman and member of Cromwell's House of Lords, was imprisoned in the fortress on Holy Island. 'Unable to perform those things that are necessary to his subsistence', he was allowed a servant to attend him. By October 1663 he was suffering 'a sharp fit of sickness', and his wife feared he might not last the winter. Anne Tichbourne submitted a series of petitions to the king's secretary, detailing her husband's 'much weakness and distemper of body', and the hardships of separation 'through the distance of the place, and great difficulty of sending to him'. By March 1664 her efforts had borne fruit, and Tichbourne was brought south to the balmier confines of Dover Castle.[101] His place on Holy Island was taken by his fellow regicide Henry Marten, who seems to have been moved frequently from prison to prison.[102] Other prisoners of the Restoration regime included the Fifth Monarchist Hugh Courtney, a veteran of Isle of Wight prisons, who was gaoled again from 1661 to 1663, and the Unitarian John Biddle, previously held on Scilly, who was imprisoned again in 1662 and died that year in Newgate.[103] Island imprisonment was not necessarily the first recourse, but the regime understood the utility and availability of its offshore penal resources.

Last Gasps

The dying-off of the Commonweath generation, the apparent passing of the republican threat, and the final eclipse of 'the good old cause' reduced the compulsion to put political prisoners on islands. Greater respect for *habeas corpus*, associated with the legislation of 1679, limited the likelihood of perpetual incarceration, and the island prisons gradually reverted to their original function as castles. By 1680 most of the island prisoners of state had died or been released.

In 1682, however, Star Castle in the Isle of Scilly was pressed into service again to house another batch of prisoners, this time William Marshall and six other Roman Catholic priests condemned for high treason.[104] The Privy Council ordered their keepers at Newgate to hand over the priests 'to be conveyed into the island of Scilly', and instructed the governor of St Mary's 'to reserve them and keep them in safe custody'. The matter came to public notice, and was challenged at law, when Thomas Pilkington and Samuel Sute, the sheriffs of London and Middlesex, questioned the sufficiency of the Privy Council warrant. If they allowed their prisoners to depart as demanded, they claimed, 'it would be at least very doubtful whether the same may not in strictness of law be called an escape'. Leading Whigs insisted that all delivery of prisoners be done 'in due and legal manner', which would avoid arbitrary transfers to remote islands.[105] This did not prevent the priests from being sent to Scilly, but the state's use of offshore detention was almost at an end. A London newsletter reported that, on being told to prepare for their banishment to the islands, two of the priests asked 'to let them suffer according to their [death] sentence rather than send them thither'. Others people wondered if the priests were being kept 'to be living witnesses of the intended popish massacre of England' that some feared was forthcoming.[106]

The regime of James II made occasional use of island detention. In April 1686, it sent the Rye House plotter Colonel John Rumsey to the prison recently occupied by John Lambert on St Nicholas, 'till we think fit to dispose of him otherwise'. The island commander Sir Hugh Piper reported Rumsey's arrival 'under a strong guard', and ingratiated himself with the court by remarking: 'I hope in good time that he and all others of his principles will receive a just reward according to their deserts.'[107]

In June 1686, the government sent the Whig traitor Richard Goodenough to Jersey to be confined in Castle Elizabeth until further notice. *Habeas corpus*, apparently, had only limited effect. Goodenough had been sheriff of London, had fled abroad after the Rye House Plot, and was captured and condemned for his involvement in Monmouth's rebellion. He remained a prisoner on Jersey until May 1687, when the governor received instructions 'to discharge and set Richard Goodenough at liberty'. Other political prisoners were sent as far away as Jamaica, to labour until they died.[108]

The wheel of fortune turned again with the so-called Glorious Revolution, when William and Mary supplanted James II. The Jacobite Theophilus Hastings, the seventh Earl of Huntington, cancelled his intended visit to St Nicholas Island in November 1688 for fear that he might be detained there as a prisoner. Instead he spent a month in gaol at Plymouth before being released.[109] Other supporters of the runaway Stuart were not so lucky, being sent as prisoners to St Mary's in the Scillies, despite the inadequacy of the castle's facilities.[110] A scattering of fleeing Irish Catholics reached Anglesey, where they 'were generally seized upon, and imprisoned, and kept prisoners till they were discharged'. The Irish took affront at this, according to the diarist Roger Morrice, 'and have ever since meditated and threatened revenge upon the inhabitants of this island'.[111]

For half a century the Stuart state had flexed its muscles and enhanced its security by isolating offenders offshore. By the end of the seventeenth century, the practice of confining state prisoners to island facilities had passed. Political offenders were more likely to be held in the Tower than shipped overseas, though common criminals faced transportation to America and later to Australia. The arrival in England in 1709 of destitute German protestants known as the 'poor Palatines' posed moral and logistical problems that some thought could be solved by shipping them to the Isles of Scilly, though fortunately this did not come to pass.[112]

Little more was heard of dumping troublemakers on island outposts, though later regimes elsewhere have found the practice persuasive. One thinks of the confinement of Napoleon on Elba and St Helena, France's Devil's Island, South Africa's Robben Island, and America's Guantanamo Bay, all places of abandoned hope, remote from metropolitan scrutiny. When the nineteenth-century United States used island outposts to confine civil-war secessionists to Alcatraz Island in San Francisco Bay, and imprisoned conspirators in the assassination of Abraham Lincoln on the islet of Dry Tortugas off the Florida Keys, they followed a practice pioneered in Stuart England. So too have the keepers of Changu island, Zanzibar, Coiba island, Panama, and Goli Otok in former Yugoslavia, all places of confinement and isolation for political prisoners. As in seventeenth-century England, such facilities gave regimes a measure of security at the expense of the liberty of the subject.[113] Island outposts had proved their efficacy against enemies domestic as well as foreign.

15

Islands in an Island Empire[1]

England's islands faced the eighteenth century with more ships in their road-steads, more soldiers in their castles, and more guns on their walls than ever before. As forward bases of the fiscal–military state, they were resources as well as responsibilities in a growing global struggle. Royal officials at their quaysides as well as in their castles attended to the ligaments and sinews of power. Recurrent war with France put the islands in peril, but also made them indispensable for sheltering warships and staging troops. London needed them to be loyal, and firmly under control, with no prospect of falling into enemy hands. Tensions between local authority and imperial oversight continued unresolved, so managing the heritage of difference required patience and understanding.[1]

As commercial nodes and military assets, the islands commanded continuing attention at Whitehall and Westminster. Their importance was unabated as maritime havens and outposts of power. Oceanic traffic brought the merchants and merchantmen of the Americas and the orient to island harbours, while local commerce quickened their connections to domestic and nearby hinterlands. Channel Island mariners in particular were active in the Newfoundland fisheries, and in the carrying trade with England's plantations. Customs officers kept busy in the Isles of Scilly, the Isle of Wight, Guernsey, and Jersey. Even the Earl of Derby's Isle of Man felt pressure to allow agents of the crown to scrutinize its trade. The invigoration of imperial commerce energized the entire archipelagic perimeter, enriching its participants but also drawing the attention of boards, councils, and commissions based in London.

From 1689 to 1815, with varying intervals of peace, England's islands were threatened by war with France. The international situation, wrote John Shebbeare in 1771, 'renders them the peculiar objects of British vigilance', as England's enemies commanded greater resources.[2] The central government assumed a greater role in island affairs, as fortifications were hardened and garrisons expanded to guard against attack. Militarization and anglicization were among the cultural consequences of this strategic shift. Increasing numbers of British troops saw service in England's islands, where some of them subsequently settled. The Guernsey garrison, rarely more than 500 strong before the seventeenth century, comprised as many as 4,000 infantrymen and a company of artillery by 1805.[3] Other islands saw comparable infusions of British military force.

Though foreign foes had long menaced English shores, they made few landings in the early modern era. Guns, ships, and perilous coastlines kept the enemy at bay.

England's Islands in a Sea of Troubles. David Cressy, Oxford University Press (2020). © David Cressy 2020.
DOI: 10.1093/oso/9780198856603.001.0001

The level of threat escalated later in the eighteenth century, especially in the era of the French and American wars. A French force of more than 5,000 men attempted to land in Jersey in May 1779 but was repulsed by the island militia. A more successful attempt in January 1781 took advantage of a lapse of military attention and allowed a French war party to advance as far as St Helier, where they occupied the market square. In extraordinary circumstances, the French commander Baron de Rullecourt declared himself governor of Jersey and persuaded the English lieutenant governor Major Moses Corbet to surrender. Corbet's officers, however, refused to capitulate, ignoring their commander's orders. Urban fighting ensued, and the invaders were routed after Rullecourt had been killed. Jersey remained English, with all the more reason to fear the French. Major Corbet was relieved of his post, and faced court martial, but was allowed to retire with a pension.[4]

Shocked by the ease of the French incursion, military planners looked again to their defences. Governor Henry Seymour Conway of Jersey expanded a series of loophole towers, to be manned by the island militia. More sophisticated Martello towers were erected on Guernsey and Jersey after 1804 to deter the ambitions of Napoleon. Some of these installations were still usable, though completely outmatched, when German forces occupied the Channel Islands from June 1940 to May 1945. The cultural character of Jersey and Guernsey changed as large numbers of garrisoned troops were followed by settlers from Victorian Britain, but this was to some degree offset by the arrival of refugees from political turmoil in France. The exiled French novelist Victor Hugo found refuge in Jersey from 1852 to 1855, and lived on Guernsey from 1855 to 1870, describing local maritime culture in Les Travailleurs de la Mer (1866). Increasing numbers spoke English, though the Francophone ascendancy persisted until the start of the twentieth century.

Like other inhabitants of the expanding British empire, England's islanders mostly cherished their relationship to the crown. A benign monarch offered them military protection, and also membership in a community of rights and privileges. Quite apart from their historical insular particularities, which they still guarded and valued, islanders enjoyed the benefits of Magna Carta, Habeas Corpus, and the Declaration of Rights. In common with subjects throughout the king's dominions, they exercised their rights to hold and inherit property, to sue for justice, and to petition the crown. The 'liberties of the subject' that followed settlers overseas applied as much in the Channel Islands or the Isle of Wight as Barbados, Grenada, or New England, though subject to local interpretation. Modern scholars have followed eighteenth-century lawyers in tracing these constitutional commonalities and claims across mainlands and oceans, where a sense of connection to the monarchy did not necessarily soften resistance to the demands of the state. Sophisticated modern analysis of legal pluralism and jurisdictional anomalies underscores strains across the British Atlantic world but has little to say so far about comparable tensions closer to home.[5] Settler and plantation islands acquired by imperial Britain had different racial, demographic, and economic histories, but shared some legal complexities with islands offshore from England. Several even had governors and officers experienced in domestic island postings.[6]

Despite developments that tended to integrate offshore territories into the greater British domain, the islands of Jersey, Guernsey, and the Isle of Man in particular retained their legal distinctiveness, with institutions and exemptions that others of their majesties' subjects found strange. They had no representation at Westminster, and parliamentary legislation touched them only if appropriately drafted. Channel Islanders especially made fulsome protestations of loyalty, while shielding their privileges from encroachments by the crown. Generations of Guernseymen spoke of their 'unalterable attachment to their sovereign', while asserting traditions of peculiarity, difference, and independence.[7] The eighteenth-century historian of Guernsey Thomas Dicey remarked that the islanders were unquestionably loyal to King George III, and thought themselves 'happy under the mild auspices of his reign, enjoying fully, as they do, their own privileges and immunities'.[8] Protected by the British state, yet free from demanding obligations towards it, they seemingly enjoyed the best of all worlds.

The late-Georgian historian of Jersey Edward Durell took similar pride in his observation that the Channel Islands 'have under British protection retained their nationality, together with their constitution, their language, their usage and customs', over many hundred years. He was especially grateful, to God and the crown, for being long preserved 'from that despotism and anarchy which would have been the result of our incorporation' into France.[9] Dicey and Durell contributed to a tradition, which still continues, of Channel Islanders celebrating their 'special constitutional rights and privileges' along with their attachment to the crown, as if each depended on the other.[10]

Political and constitutional tussles continued unabated in the eighteenth-century Channel Islands, as bailiffs and jurats argued about their respective jurisdictions, and both clashed with governors and their deputies. The British official John Harrison complained in exasperation in 1753 that Guernsey merchants claimed 'privileges and immunities, which at present exist nowhere but in their minds and practice', and that the island's Royal Court played such 'a fine game' of 'abusive delay' that 'his majesty's right [was] no longer considered in its true light'.[11] Strains reached crisis on Jersey in the 1760s when the concentration of power in the hands of the Lemprière faction led to rioting against their arbitrary actions.[12] Peace was restored by judicious pardons, and London's token recitation of the island's laws, but this did not prevent the prolonged political contest between the radical Magots (later the Rose party) and the establishment Charlots (who became the Laurels), which raged into the nineteenth century.[13]

It long remained contentious whether British parliamentary statutes had effect in the Channel Islands, and whether the writ of *habeas corpus* applied there.

Despite the apparent resolution of this matter by the 1679 Habeas Corpus Act, which specifically included offshore territories, 'any law or usage to the contrary notwithstanding', island lawyers persisted in claims of autonomy and exemption. During the reign of William IV, when the Privy Council asked Channel Island authorities to register legislation relating to *habeas corpus* (the statutes of 31 Charles II and 56 George III), the bailiffs of Jersey and Guernsey vigorously refused, citing their charters and privileges. The imposition of such legislation on the islands, they contended, would have been 'an infringement of the privileges of the island' and 'a direct violation of the rights and immunities of the inhabitants'. Westminster legislation had never been registered or enforced in the Channel Islands, and so could be regarded as 'a dead letter'. Nineteenth-century islanders thought it necessary to remind London that 'not only the laws and customs, but the forms, and the whole course of proceedings in the islands, differ materially from those in England'. Their recitation of orders and charters from the thirteenth to the seventeenth centuries set forth an abbreviated history of 'the difference of the laws, custom, practice, and language'. Their remonstrance of August 1832 formed a fierce defence of insular independence, which the British government, in its wisdom, chose to ignore.[14] When I asked a leading constitutional authority on Guernsey whether *habeas corpus* applied today on his island, he stroked his chin and answered, 'that is a very interesting question'.[15]

Oversight by London of their commercial and financial dealings was never welcome in the Channel Islands. Local and central governments locked horns in the early eighteenth century over plans to establish customs houses. The bailiffs and jurats of Guernsey and Jersey vigorously opposed such moves and won concessions in 1709 by petitioning Queen Anne.[16] The Treasury renewed its demands in the reign of George III, and eventually prevailed. In 1767, the Channel Islands submitted to the establishment of a customs registry office and inspectors, not by agreement but by arbitrary imposition, which, the Guernsey patriot historian Jonathan Duncan thought, 'completely subverted the ancient commercial privileges' of the island.[17] British representatives in the 1780s registered 'unfortunate differences' between themselves and island leaders, while bailiffs and jurats complained to London that their charters and privileges were 'questioned and disputed by the officers of your majesty's forces sent hither for . . . the protection of the inhabitants'.[18] Constitutional tensions remained unresolved, though not to the point of compromising allegiance.

Smuggling continued with impunity, in times of peace and war, protected by local interests. When, in 1805, in the course of the Napoleonic wars, the British parliament passed a bill 'for the more effectual prevention of smuggling', the Royal Court in Guernsey stood on its privileges and refused to register the act. Islanders were by no means persuaded that laws of the imperial legislature applied to them.[19] It remained contentious in Jersey too whether registration of Orders in Council was 'procedural' or 'substantive'. The degree to which parliamentary or Home Office authority extended to the Channel Islands remained controversial throughout the nineteenth century, and still occasions disagreement today.[20] A minor but telling episode at the beginning of the twentieth century involved British medical commissioners complaining about 'obstruction' by island officials. Recognizing Jersey and Guernsey as 'two distinct and separate commonwealths...each with their own lunacy laws, which are entirely different both from English lunacy law and from each other', they attributed 'the rather peculiar nature' of island social and medical services to their 'ancient constitutions and privileges'.[21]

The Bailiwicks of Jersey and Guernsey, like the Isle of Man, thrive today as self-governing dependencies of the British crown. They are technically not part of the United Kingdom, nor of the European Union, but operate separate legal, fiscal, and administrative systems. They have no representation in the UK parliament, and are not normally covered by its legislation, though most of their residents are British citizens. Often-repeated histories explain their continuing autonomy by reference to medieval charters granted to the Channel Islands, and to medieval feudal arrangements on the Isle of Man.[22]

The retention of legal and constitutional privileges facilitated the modern emergence of these islands as centres of offshore financial services that are sometimes associated with tax avoidance and money laundering. Their legacy of medieval separateness continues to pay dividends, as island bankers provide confidential services to clients from across the world. Visitors may marvel at the presence of high-performance exotic cars on islands with limited room for driving, and luxury yachts in harbours formerly frequented by fishing smacks and sailing frigates. Jersey, Guernsey and the Isle of Man today host tens of thousands of companies and handle funds of hundreds of billions of pounds, entirely disproportionate to their meagre populations.[23]

The Isle of Man remained especially resistant to British domination. It long continued as an autonomous domain, defiant of the regulatory ambitions of London. After the Stanley line failed in 1736, with the death of the tenth Earl of Derby, all rights to the Lordship passed to his kinsman James Murray, the second Duke of Atholl. The new lord made energetic use of his privileges, especially encouraging 'the trade', or smuggling, that bypassed his majesty's customs inspectors. One English official called the island the 'warehouse of frauds'.[24] When Murray died in 1764, the British government put pressure on his heir, the third Duke of Atholl, to surrender control over Isle of Man trade. 'The clear revenue of the customs for imports' by this time exceeded £6,000 a year, more than four times the lord's revenue from land, and well worth attaching to London. Parliament drafted an act 'for more effectually preventing the mischiefs arising to the revenue and commerce of Great Britain and Ireland from the illicit and clandestine trade to and from the Isle of Man'. Hard bargaining, and £70,000 in compensation, persuaded Atholl to yield his rights in this regard. The Revestment Act or Isle of Man Purchase Act of 1765 (5 George III c. 26) effectively revested sovereignty in the crown. It allowed the British state to establish customs houses on the island, to appoint revenue officers to suppress smuggling, and to integrate the Isle of Man into Treasury fiscal administration.[25]

The value of the Isle of Man trade grew substantially in the final third of the eighteenth century, and, eyeing this, the fourth Duke of Atholl, John Murray, sought to undermine the revestment arrangements and restore his family's revenue and power. Murray's moves towards a feudal reaction angered Manxmen as well as the government in London, prompting the speaker of the House of Keys to complain of 'the unconstitutional interference of his grace in obstructing all acts of our insular legislation'. The duke still exercised his manorial rights as Lord of Man, and was generously rewarded when these too passed to the crown by purchase in 1828. Further changes in the 1860s modernized the island's governance without relinquishing its residual independence.[26]

The Isle of Man retained, and still retains, its peculiar laws and Manx administrative structure. Late Hanoverian proposals to annexe the island to the county of Cumberland came to nothing.[27] In two world wars in the twentieth century the British government established internment camps for enemy aliens on the Isle of Man, subordinating insular interests to the needs of the nation. Distance and isolation again provided secure confinement, this time for thousands of foreign prisoners.[28] More recently the island has exploited the fiscal privileges attendant on its legacy of autonomy, which has fostered the development of offshore financial services, including the registration of companies and ships. Today's Isle of Man is a major international centre of online gaming, as well as private wealth management. Like Jersey and Guernsey, it thrives on its peculiar status as a 'British island' that is free of British and European laws.[29] British governments and bankers seem content with these arrangements.

While constitutional conflicts still troubled the Channel Islands and the Isle of Man, the residual distinctiveness of other islands faded as those places sank towards provincial quietude. Most communities grew and prospered in the eighteenth and nineteenth centuries, although the Isles of Scilly shared little in the benefits of commercial expansion. Correspondence about Scilly in the 1790s referred to 'the distress and poverty that too generally prevail'.[30] A petition to parliament in 1826 attributed the economic misfortune of the Scillies to 'the very peculiar circumstances under which the islands are held from the crown' and cited 'the evils to public morals' occasioned by want of civil government. The anomalies of insularity, in this case, had unfortunate social consequences.[31]

The late-Hanoverian Isles of Scilly experienced change in their seigneurial lordship, amid pressure for more regularized arrangements. Generation after generation of Godolphins had succeeded as proprietors and governors, until their male line failed in 1785. Francis Osborne (1751–99), Marquess of Carmarthen and later fifth Duke of Leeds, whose mother was a Godolphin, became lord proprietor and governor of the Isles of Scilly in 1785 but gave them little attention. Like his predecessors, the new proprietor ruled through deputies and agents. All island residents, except members of the garrison, were his tenants, and owed him rents and service. The traditional twelve-man council dealt informally with civil disputes, notwithstanding calls for it to become 'a sure and permanent establishment'. A capital crime, if such occurred, would normally be referred to Penzance or Bodmin. Mainland authorities impinged occasionally on this outlier of Cornwall, especially when garrison commanders or customs officials claimed authority that clashed with that of the governor or proprietor.[32] But few army officers wanted the posting. The veteran Henry Bowen, captain of Star Castle, wrote plaintively in 1795 of 'the extreme hardship' of his 'irksome situation' and begged 'the favour of a removal to England'.[33] St Mary's, of course, was an English village, but it felt like the edge of the world.

Though connected by shipping to the commerce of the nation and empire, the Isles of Scilly remained politically as isolated as ever. According to John Troutbeck, chaplain for the Duke of Leeds at St Mary's from 1780 to 1796, the islanders paid more heed to their lord's council than to any act of parliament. Sheriffs of Cornwall had minimal clout, while 'the commanding officer's warrant is more terrible to them than a writ from any of the courts of Westminster'. Residents of the Isles of Scilly had no charters of liberties and privileges, of the sort that distinguished Jersey and Guernsey, and their isolation from the mainland heightened dependency on the proprietor. Troutbeck despaired of 'such a lawless place as Scilly is, where the honest industrious cannot protect themselves and their property', and thought the island would remain poor 'till the civil power is more firmly established there'.[34] Though answerable to the Duke of Leeds, Troutbeck claimed to act as surrogate for the archdeacon of Cornwall, an ecclesiastical authority with no established standing in the archipelago.[35] Activists from the Society for Promoting Christian Knowledge attempted to upgrade spiritual conditions in the islands, but their 'overseas' mission to the Scillies, according to its historian, 'was perhaps more isolated than if it had been in Canada'.[36]

Philanthropic enquiries after the end of the Napoleonic wars found extreme poverty in the Isles of Scilly. Barred from their traditional offering of pilotage to incoming shipping, punished for smuggling or wrecking, unable to profit from fishing, and barely scraping subsistence from the land, some inhabitants of the outer-islands were reduced to eating limpets. Public subscription and parliamentary outrage drew attention to the islands but did little to relieve their hardship.[37]

The Leeds lease expired in 1831, at which time all property in the Isles of Scilly reverted to the crown, and thence to the Duchy of Cornwall. The Oxford-educated landowner Augustus Smith (1804–72) acquired a ninety-nine-year lease of the islands in 1834, and began a programme of philanthropic investment and reform. Referred to locally as 'the governor' or 'the emperor', Smith built roads and quays, churches and schools, and tried to bring the Scillies into the nineteenth century.[38] The Bishop Rock lighthouse was completed in 1857 during Smith's regime, while

Her Majesty's Customs and Excise expanded their presence in the islands. Taking advantage of Scilly's benign climate, and Smith's interest in horticulture, the commercial shipping of flowers to the mainland began in the 1860s. Late Victorian steamship navigation facilitated this trade and opened the islands to recreational visitors.[39]

The material and demographic circumstances of England's islands changed in the eighteenth and nineteenth centuries, as most of them grew in prosperity and population. Most saw investment in infrastructure, land reclamation, harbour improvements, and new roads, as well as improvements in dairying and fruit farming. Beginning in the eighteenth century, the islands attracted gentlemen with a 'taste for the beauties and sublimities of nature'.[40] Later they became destinations for family holidays. Though not yet recommending the Scillies for vacations, a late Georgian survey found them 'very picturesque', and 'the mountainous water dashing over the rocks' to be 'beautifully terrible'.[41] Victorian steam packets transformed connections with the mainland.[42] All islands participated in the twentieth-century boom in leisure, before Jersey, Guernsey, and the Isle of Man developed unique niches as tax havens. The Isle of Man proved especially attractive to holidaymakers from England's industrial north, until cheap air travel opened up the Mediterranean.[43]

Guernsey's population grew from around 10,000 in the mid-seventeenth century to 14,000 a century later. By 1821, it had passed 20,000, and would expand in the following decades to 29,757 in 1851. Jersey was always more populous, with perhaps 12,000 inhabitants under the early Stuarts, and 20,000 under the mid-Georgians. Jersey had 28,000 inhabitants by the 1820s, more than doubling to 57,020 in 1851. By the early twenty-first century there were approximately 105,000 people on Jersey, and 65,000 on Guernsey and its dependencies.[44]

Similar expansion affected other islands. The Isle of Man, with perhaps 10,000 inhabitants in the seventeenth century, had some 14,000 people by the 1720s, 20,000 by the 1750s. The census recorded more than 40,000 in 1821, almost 47,000 in 1841, and 52,344 in 1851. Its population in the twenty-first century exceeds 85,000. The population of the Isle of Wight, barely 9,000 at the end of the sixteenth century, doubled to 18,000 by the mid-eighteenth century and more than doubled again in the nineteenth century. The census of 1821 recorded 31,618 people on the Isle of Wight, a figure that grew to 50, 324 by 1851. The early twenty-first-century population of the Ise of Wight exceeds 139,000.[45] The population of the Welsh island of Anglesey grew just as fast, from less than 10,000 in the late sixteenth century, to over 22,000 people by 1700, and almost 27,000 in 1750. The census recorded 48,325 on Anglesey in 1831, 57,318 in 1851, growing to approximately 70,000 by the early twenty-first century.[46] Even the impoverished Isles of Scilly added people, though numbers remained low. With barely 300 residents in the Elizabethan era, and more than 800 under the later Stuarts, the population of the Scillies approached 1,500 by the mid-eighteenth century, and over 2,000 by the early nineteenth.[47] The census of 1831 found 2,465 people in the Isles of Scilly, slightly more than the twenty-first century count of barely 2,300 year-round residents.[48]

*

From the sixteenth century to the nineteenth, while acknowledging the distinctiveness of offshore traditions, metropolitan authorities increasingly sought to conform the islands to the needs of the centralizing state. Channel Islanders and Manxmen, ever protective of their privileges, and wary of encroachment, were forced to acknowledge the growing role of London in their lives, and sometimes to request it. Even Scillionians were affected by the demands of the mainland. Official dealings with island populations were shaped by legal, cultural, and constitutional considerations that stretched back hundreds of years. The heritage of insularity had deep roots and continuing ramifications. But military planners, privy councillors, diocesan officials, and customs and excisemen were among those subjecting the islands to scrutiny. Many of the flashpoints and areas of contention have already been discussed.

Every island was the centre of its own world, and the fringe of someone else's. Every island was different, conditioned by its unique history and perspective. Strategic, legal, commercial, and religious concerns varied according to viewpoints at the core or along the edge. Insular perspectives also affected local relationships, so that interests in the parish of St Samson might vary from those of St Peter Port, those of St Ouen from St Helier, and those of the islands in general from communities in Hampshire or Devon. The view from Castletown on the Isle of Man could be different from the castle at Peel, just as perceptions and concerns varied from St Mary's to St Agnes in the Scillies, and from Carisbrooke to Cowes on the Isle of Wight. Nuances of social and geographical position, cultural and economic advantage, and mutualities of interest affected participation in both island and national stories.

Centuries of engagement between England's metropolitan centre and its scattered offshore periphery produced a history of asserted authority and fractured communication. The centralizing tendencies of London officialdom were neither consistent nor inexorable, as they dealt with insular traditions. Shrewd administrators recognized the variety and vitality of island experiences, even if they did not fully comprehend the islanders' attachment to their privileges. Islanders everywhere could be agitated by aspirations or resentments, riven by faction, and constrained by local limits. From London's point of view, the islands could appear as liabilities as much as assets, resources as well as responsibilities, costs as much as benefits.

Statesmen with a wider strategic viewpoint understood the importance of England's islands as patrimonies, properties, and dominions of the British crown. Imperial honour as well as national security were implicated in their safe-keeping. Island communities prospered with naval, military, and commercial investment, and developed as desirable places to live or visit. National attention varied with the changing international situation, with the measure, direction, and intensity of perceived foreign threats, as England braced against real or potential enemies, and guarded its posture in Europe and the world. Island insularity continues to flourish within the integrated complexity of the modern British realm. Though modernized and better connected, the islands remain, to varying degrees, as they always were, strange, separate, and perversely independent.

Endnotes

Introduction

1. H. E. Marshall, *Our Island Story: A Child's History of England* (1905); Henry Newbolt, *The Island Race* (1898); Winston S. Churchill, *The Island Race* (1964); http://www. telegraph.co.uk/culture/books/booknews/8094333/Revealed-David-Camerons-favourite-childhood-book-is-Our-Island-Story.html (accessed April 2018); Kathleen Wilson, *The Island Race: Englishness, Empire and Gender in the Eighteenth Century* (2003), 54–5.

2. William Shakespeare, *Richard II*, Act 2, scene 1; William Cuningham, *The Cosmographical Glasse, Conteinyng the Pleasant Principles of Cosmographie, Geographie, Hydrography, or Navigation* (1559), 172–3; Francis Hastings, *A Watch-Word to all Religious, and True-Hearted English-Men* (1598), 7, 53; Slingsby Bethel, *The Interest of Princes and States* (1680), 52; Edward Chamberlayne, *The Present State of England... An Account of the Riches, Strength, Magnificence, Natural Production, Manufactures of this Island* (1683), title page.

3. Kate Chedgzoy, 'This Pleasant and Sceptred Isle: Insular Fantasies of National Identity in Anne Dowriche's *The French Historie* and William Shakespeare's *Richard II*', in Philip Schwyzer and Simon Mealor (eds), *Archipelagic Identities: Literature and Identity in the Atlantic Archipelago, 1550–1800* (Aldershot and Burlington, VT, 2004), 25–42.

4. Edward Chamberlayne, *The Fourth Part of the Present State of England* (1683), 49.

5. Peter Heylyn, *A Full Relation of Two Journeys: The One to the Main-Land of France. The Other into some of the Adjacent Islands* (1656), 280, 300.

6. Lord Byron to the Earl of Ormonde, 12 October 1649, in S. Elliott Hoskins, *Charles the Second in the Channel Islands*, 2 vols (1854), ii. 332

7. *The Remonstrance of the Inhabitants of the Three Isles of Wight, Garnsey, and Jersey* (1647), 6.

8. William Harrison, 'Description of Britaine', in Raphael Holinshed, *The First and Second Volumes of Chronicles* (1587), 30–2, 44.

9. William Lambard, *The Perambulation of Kent... Corrected and Enlarged* (1656), 96, 268.

10. William Camden, *Britain, or A Chorographical Description* (1637), 211.

11. William Shakespeare, *Hamlet*, Act 3, scene 1; William Painter, *The Palace of Pleasure Beautified* (1566), fo. 115ᵛ; John Foxe, *Actes and Monuments of Matters Most Speciall and Memorable* (1583), 961; William Perkins, *The Combat between Christ and the Divell Displayed* (1606), sig. A4. See also Henry Smith, *The Sermons of Maister Henrie Smith* (1593), 486, on the righteous who 'must go through a sea of troubles' before coming to 'a haven of rest'.

12. Henry Burton, *A Narration of the Life of Mr Henry Burton* (1643), 28, 32.

Chapter 1

1. Tim Thornton, *The Channel Islands, 1370–1640: Between England and Normandy* (Woodbridge, 2012), 129; Lauren Benton, *A Search for Sovereignty: Law and Geography in European Empires, 1400–1900* (Cambridge, 2010), pp. xiii, 35. See also Tim Thornton, 'Nationhood at the Margin: Identity, Regionality and the English Crown in the Seventeenth Century', in Len Scales and Oliver Zimmer (eds), *Power and the Nation in European History* (Cambridge, 2005), 232–47.

2. Philip Bailhache (ed.), *A Celebration of Autonomy 1204–2004: 800 Years of Channel Islands' Law* (St Helier, 2005); Darryl Ogier, *The Government and Law of Guernsey* (St Peter Port, 2005). See also, more whimsically, David Le Feuvre, *Jersey: Not Quite British. The Rural History of a Singular People* (St Helier, 1993).

3. J. G. A. Pocock, *The Discovery of Islands: Essays in British History* (Cambridge, 2005), 55.

4. J. G. A. Pocock, 'British History: A Plea for a New Subject' [1974], and 'The Atlantic Archipelago and the War of the Three Kingdoms' [1996], in Pocock, *Discovery of Islands*, 28–43, 77–91; John Kerrigan, *Archipelagic English: Literature, History, and Politics 1603–1707* (Oxford, 2008), 2, 24.

5. Brendan Bradshaw and John Morrill (eds), *The British Problem, c.1534–1707: State Formation in the Atlantic Archipelago* (New York, 1996); Philip Schwyzer, 'Archipelagic History', in Paulina Kewes, Ian W. Archer, and Felicity Heal (eds), *The Oxford Handbook of Holinshed's Chronicles* (Oxford, 20123), 593–607.

6. Norman Davies, *The Isles: A History* (Oxford, 1999), 243, 252, 448, 719.

7. Hugh Kearney, *The British Isles: A History of Four Nations*, 2nd edn (Cambridge, 2006), 303. See also Richard S. Tompson, *The Atlantic Archipelago: A Political History of the British Isles* (Lewiston, NY, and Queenstown, Canada, 1986); Jeremy Black, *A History of the British Isles* (New York, 1996, and subsequent editions); Steven G. Ellis and Christopher Maginn, *The Making of the British Isles: The State of Britain and Ireland, 1450–1660* (Harlow, 2007); and Kenneth L. Campbell, *A History of the British Isles: Prehistory to the Present* (2017), none of which attends to the lesser parts of the archipelago.

8. Pocock, *Discovery of Islands*, 4.

9. Jack P. Greene, *Peripheries and Center: Constitutional Development in the Extended Polities of the British Empire and the United States, 1607–1788* (New York, 1990), 7–9. See also Michael Hechter, *Internal Colonialism: The Celtic Fringe in British National Development*, 2nd edn (New York, 2017), 3–28.

10. Contrast Norman Jones, *Governing by Virtue: Lord Burghley and the Management of Elizabethan England* (Oxford, 2015), and Christopher Durston, *Cromwell's Major Generals: Godly Government during the English Revolution* (Manchester and New York, 2001).

11. K. M. E. Murray, *The Constitutional History of the Cinque Ports* (Manchester, 1935); W. J. Jones, 'Palatine Performance in the Seventeenth Century', in Peter Clark, Alan G. R. Smith, and Nicholas Tyacke (eds), *The English Commonwealth 1547–1640* (New York, 1979), 189–204; Brodie Waddell, 'Governing England though the Manor Courts, 1550–1850', *Historical Journal*, 55 (2012), 279–15.

12. M. B. Hooker, *Legal Pluralism: An Introduction to Colonial and Neo-Colonial Laws* (Oxford, 1975); John Griffiths, 'What is Legal Pluralism?', *Journal of Legal Pluralism and Unofficial Law*, 18 (1986), 1–55; Sally Engle Merry, 'Legal Pluralism', *Law and Society Review*, 22 (1988), 869–96; Lauren Benton and Richard J. Ross, 'Empires and Legal Pluralism: Jurisdiction, Sovereignty, and Political Imagination in the Early Modern World', in Benton and Ross (eds), *Legal Pluralism and Empires, 1500–1850* (New York, 2013), 1–17. See also Philip Loft, 'A Tapestry of Laws: Legal Pluralism in Eighteenth-Century Britain', *Journal of Modern History*, 91 (2019), 276–310.

13. Joan Thirsk (ed.), *The Agrarian History of England and Wales. Volume IV 1500–1640* (Cambridge, 1967), 4,128; Joan Thirsk (ed.), *The Agrarian History of England and Wales. Volume V 1640–1750* (Cambridge, 1984), p. xx. See also Joan Thirsk (ed.), *The English Rural Landscape* (Oxford, 2000) for pointillist historicized accounts of rural diversity.

14. Margaret Spufford, *Contrasting Communities: English Villagers in the Sixteenth and Seventeenth Centuries* (Cambridge, 1974); David Underdown, *Revel, Riot and Rebellion: Popular Politics and Culture in England 1603–1660* (Oxford, 1985).

15. Underdown, *Revel, Riot and Rebellion*, 40; John Morrill, 'The Ecology of Allegiance in the English Civil Wars', *Journal of British Studies*, 26 (1987), 451–67; David Underdown, 'A Reply to John Morrill', *Journal of British Studies*, 26 (1987), 468–79.

16. Alan Everitt, *Change in the Provinces: The Seventeenth Century* (Leicester, 1972), 8, 25.

17. John Morrill, *The Revolt in the Provinces: The People of England and the Tragedies of War 1630–1648* (1999), 35, 42, 93.

18. Ann Hughes, 'Local History and the Origins of the Civil War', in Richard Cust and Ann Hughes (eds), *Conflict in Early Stuart England: Studies in Religion and Politics 1603–1642* (New York, 1989), 225, 227.

19. Michael J. Braddick, *State Formation in Early Modern England c.1550–1700* (Cambridge, 2000), 4, 9, 90, 94, 179, 420–24.

20. Steve Hindle, *The State and Social Change in Early Modern England, 1550–1640* (Basingstoke and New York, 2002), pp. ix–x, 3, 232, 236.

21. Hughes, 'Local History and the Origins of the Civil War', 228, 236.

22. Stephen A. Royle, *A Geography of Islands: Small Island Insularity* (2001); Rod Edmond and Vanessa Smith (eds), *Islands in History and Representation* (2003); John Gillis, *Islands of the Mind: How the Human Imagination Created the Atlantic World* (Basingstoke and New York, 2004); Godfrey Baldacchino, 'Islands, Island Studies, Islands Studies Journal', *Island Studies Journal*, 1 (2006), 3–18; Pete Hay, 'A Phenomenology of Islands', *Island Studies Journal*, 1 (2006), 19–42; Godfrey Baldacchino, *Island Enclaves: Offshoring Strategies, Creative Governance, and Subnational Island Jurisdictions* (Montreal and London, 2010), pp. xxiv, 4, 6; Adam Grydehøj, ' A Future of Island Studies', *Island Studies Journal*, 12 (2017), 3–16; 'Insularities Connected: Bridging Seascapes, from the Mediterranean to the Indian Ocean and Beyond', report of a conference held in Crete, June 2016, https://medins.ims.foreth.gr/ conference.php (accessed April 2019).

23. Gillis, *Islands of the Mind*, 118; Maeve McCusker and Anthony Soares (eds), *Islanded Identities: Constructions of Postcolonial Cultural Insularity* (Amsterdam and New York, 2011), pp. xiv, xvi. See also Anna Kouremenos (ed.), *Insularity and Identity in the Roman Mediterranean* (Oxford and Philadelphia, 2018).

24. David Worthington (ed.), *The New Coastal History: Cultural and Environmental Perspectives from Scotland and Beyond* (Cham, Switzerland, 2017).

25. 'Le Procés entre les États et le Gouvereur Lanier: La Rémonstrance des États', *Société Jersiaise Bulletin Annuel*, 13 (1888), 258; 'The Journal of Charles Trumbull', ed. Richard Hocart, *La Société Guernesiaise Report and Transactions* (1985 for 1984), 567.

26. D. H. Lawrence, 'The Man Who Loved Islands', in *The Tales of D. H. Lawrence* (1934), 917–39; J. H. Ingram, *The Islands of England: A Survey of the Islands around England and Wales and the Channel Islands* (1952); John Fowles, *Islands* (1978); Gillis, *Islands of the Mind*; David W. Moore, *The Other British Isles: A History of Shetland, Orkney, the Hebrides, Isle of Man, Anglesey, Scilly, Isle of Wight and the Channel Islands* (Jefferson, NC, and London, 2005); Mathew Clayton and Anthony Atkinson, *Lundy, Rockall, Dogger, Fair Isle: A Celebration of the Islands around Britain* (2015), 2.

27. Thomas Blenerhasset, *The Seconde Part of the Mirrour for Magistrates* (1578), sig. *iiii; Harriet Archer, *Unperfect Histories: The* Mirror for Magistrates, *1559–1610* (Oxford, 2017), 73–85.

28. See Chapter 11 for Burton and Prynne, Chapter 13 for Rogers, Chapter 8 for Hyde, Chapter 12 for Charles I, Chapter 2 for Saye and Sele, and Chapter 14 for Overton.

29. Modern island programmes for creative writers range from Jura, Scotland, to Sanibel, Florida, from Whidbey Island, Washington, to Martha's Vineyard, Massachusetts, each offering a distinctive offshore experience.

30. Roland Greene, 'Island Logic', in Peter Hulme and William H. Sherman (eds), *'The Tempest' and its Travels* (Philadelphia, 2000), 138–45; Steven Mentz, 'Toward a Blue Cultural Studies: The Sea, Maritime Culture, and Early Modern English Literature', *Literature Compass*, 6 (2009), 997; John R. Gillis, 'The Blue Humanities', *Humanities*, 34 (2013), 10–13; John Steve Mentz, *Shipwreck Modernity: Ecologies of Globalization, 1550–1719* (Minneapolis, 2015); Elizabeth McMahon, *Islands, Identity and the Literary Imagination* (London and New York, 2016), 3, 5. See also Fowles, *Islands*, a poetic meditation on the mystery and allure of the Isles of Scilly.

31. William Shakespeare, *Richard II*, Act 2, scene 1; *Henry V*, Act 3, scene 5; *Tempest*, Act 3, scene 2.

32. William Harrison, 'Description of Britaine', in Raphael Holinshed, *The First and Second Volumes of Chronicles* (1587), 29,

33. BL, Lansdowne MS 657, fo. 1ᵛ. Greenvile Collins, *Great Britain's Coasting Pilot: The First Part. Being a New and Exact Survey of the Sea-Coast of England* (1693), preface, acknowledged that some rocks and shelves remained unknown, while sandbanks often changed their 'situation'.

34. Iacob Columne, *The Fierie Sea-Columne, Wherein are Shewed the Seas, and Sea-Coasts of the Northern, Eastern, and Western Navigation* (Amsterdam, 1640), pt 2, 18–19; Thomas Dicey, *An Historical Account of Guernsey* (1798), 8–9; HMC, *Report on the Manuscripts of F. W. Leyborne-Popham* (1899), 30, 42; Henry D. Inglis, *The Channel Islands: Jersey, Guernsey, Alderney, etc. (The Result of a Two Years' Residence)*, 2nd edn (1835), 265–6.

35. SP 15/42, fo. 80.

36. SP 16/526, fo. 112.

37. SP 16/529, fo. 65; *Actes des États de L'Île de Guernsey.1605 à 1651* (St Peter Port, 1851), 134–35.

38. Peter Heylyn, *A Full Relation of Two Journeys: The One into the Main-Land of France. The Other into some of the Adjacent Islands* (1656), 287. 423.
39. SP 16/330, fo. 77; 'Jean de la Marche...The Diary', ed. W. Rolleston and T. W. M. de Guerir, *Report and Transactions Société Guernesiase,* 11 (1930–2), 200.
40. BL, Add. MS 72,608, fo. 1.
41. SP 16/385, fos 87–9.
42. Henry Burton, *A Narration of the Life of Mr Henry Burton* (1643), 17–19, 34; SP 16/537, fo. 90; David Cressy, 'Puritan Martyrs in Island Prisons', *Journal of British Studies,* 57 (2018), 736–54.
43. Bod., MS Clarendon 28/2211; BL, Add. MS 11,315, fos 11, 17; SP 18/188, fo. 66.
44. HMC, *Leyborne-Popham*, 31.
45. SP 18/188, fo. 119. For the 'Little Ice Age', see Geoffrey Parker, *Global Crisis: War, Climate Change and Catastrophe in the Seventeenth Century* (London and New Haven, 2013).
46. SP 47/1, fo. 78.
47. Harrison, 'Description of Britaine', 33.
48. John Troutbeck, *A Survey of the Ancient and Present State of the Scilly Islands* (1794), 175.
49. BL, MS Egerton 2533, fo. 474.
50. SP 25/96, fo. 599.
51. *CSPD May 1658–June 1659*, 48, 512.
52. Simon Harris, *Sir Cloudesley Shovell: Stuart Admiral* (Staplehurst, 2001), 333–58; Richard Larn (ed.), *'Poor England has lost so many men': The Loss of Queen Anne's Man o'War* Association (St Mary's, Isles of Scilly, 2006).
53. HMC, *The Manuscripts of the Earl Cowper,* 2 vols (1888–9), i. 437.
54. Heylyn, *Full Relation of Two Journeys,* 284.
55. SP 16/385, fo. 43; *A Royalist's Notebook: The Commonplace Book of Sir John Oglander,* ed. Francis Bamford (1936), 46–47.
56. SP 18/33, fo. 96; SP 18/133, fo. 93; SP 18/156, fo. 124.
57. *A Full and True Account of a Most Dreadful and Terrible Accident* (1706).
58. Thomas Denton, *A Perambulation of Cumberland 1687–1688 Including...the Isle of Man,* Surtees Society, 207 (2003), 497.
59. SP 16/263, fo. 40, 111; Barry Coward, *The Stanleys. Lords Stanley and Earls of Derby 1385-72: The Origins, Wealth and Power of a Landowning Family,* Chetham Society, 3rd ser., 30 (Manchester, 1983), 99; J. R. Dickinson, *The Lordship of Man under the Stanleys: Government and Economy in the Isle of Man, 1580-1704,* Chetham Society, 3rd ser., 41 (Manchester, 1996), 324–25.
60. SP 18/100, fo. 309
61. SP 18/158, fo. 1; 'The Diary of Bulkeley of Dronwey, Anglesey, 1630–1638', ed. Hugh Owen (*Anglesey Antiquarian Society and Field Club Transactions,* 1936), 135; Royal Commission on Ancient and Historical Monuments in Wales and Monmouthshire, *An Inventory of the Ancient Monuments in Anglesey* (1937, repr. 1960), p. clxxvi; *Calendar of Wynn (of Gwydir) Papers 1515-1690* (Aberystwyth, 1926), 154.
62. PC 2/23, fo. 14.
63. J. Karl Franson, 'The Fatal Voyage of Edward King, Milton's Lycidas', *Milton Studies,* 25 (1989), 43–67.

Chapter 2

1. Guy Miege, *The New State of England under Their Majesties K. William and Q. Mary* (1691), 65; William Brereton, *Travels in Holland, the United Provinces, England, Scotland, and Ireland, MDCXXXIV–MDCXXV*, ed. Edward Hawkins, Chetham Society, 1 (1844), 167.

2. William Harrison, 'Description of Britaine', in Raphael Holinshed, *The First and Second Volumes of Chronicles* (1587), 35.

3. Tristram Risdon, *The Chorographical Description or Survey of the County of Devon* [c.1630] (1811), 239.

4. Michael Drayton, *Poly-Olbion* (1612), 55.

5. Risdon, *Chorographical Description*, 240.

6. TNA, E 367/1422, claiming a yearly value of 34s. 4d.

7. John R. Chanter, *Lundy Island: A Monograph, Descriptive and Historical* (1877), 57–74; Myrtle Ternstrom, 'Lundy's Legal and Parochial Status', *Devonshire Association Report and Transactions*, 134 (2002), 145–56; John Thomas, 'A History of Lundy from 1390 to 1775', *Devonshire Association Report and Transactions*, 110 (1976), 113–54.

8. Myrtle Ternstrom, 'The Ownership of Lundy by Sir Richard Grenville and his Descendants, 1577–1775', *Devonshire Association Report and Transactions*, 130 (1998), 65–80; Alan Rowland, Michael Williams, André Coutanche, and Roger Chapple, 'A Particular of Lundy Island: The Clayton Manuscript', *Journal of the Lundy Field Society*, 6 (2018), 15.

9. TNA, C 3/208/37; Albert J. Loomie, 'An Armada Pilot's Survey of the English Coastline, October 1597', *Mariner's Mirror*, 49 (1962), 293; Thomas, 'History of Lundy', 140–41.

10. HMC, *Calendar of the Manuscripts of . . . the Marquis of Salisbury*, 24 vols (1883–1976), ix. 111.

11. TNA, PC 2/26, fos 295, 429; SP 12/274, fo. 31; SP 78/50, fo. 13; Myrtle Sylvia Ternstrom, 'Lundy: An Analysis and Comparative Study of Factors Affecting the Development of the Island from 1577 to 1869, with a Gazetteer of Sites and Monuments' (Cheltenham and Gloucester College of Higher Education, Ph.D. thesis, 1999), 145–46; P. W. Hasler, 'Bassett, Robert (1574–1641 of Umberleigh, Devon', www.historyofparliamantonline.org/volume/1558–16–3/member/bassett-robert-1574-1641 (accessed January 2019).

12. Thomas, 'History of Lundy', 117.

13. C. G. Harfield, 'In the Shadow of the Black Ensign: Lundy's Part in Piracy', *Report of the Lundy Field Society*, 47 (1996), 60–71; C. G. Harfield, 'A Gazetteer with Notes: References to Pirates and Lundy', *Report of the Lundy Field Society*, 48 (1997), 37–55.

14. Thomas, 'History of Lundy', 117–19; *Letters and Papers, Foreign and Domestic, Henry VIII*, ed. J. S. Brewer et al. 23 vols. (1862–1932), vii. 148.

15. Cecil Papers, Hatfield House, vol. 30, fo. 59.

16. Cecil Papers, vol. 174, fo. 136.

17. SP 63/178, fo. 50; SP 12/274, fo. 31; *APC* 1595–6, 379, HMC, *Salisbury*, vi. 34, viii. 58; Ternstrom, 'Ownership of Lundy', 65–6; John C. Appleby, 'Jacobean Piracy: English

Maritime Depredation in Transition, 1603–1625', in Cheryl A. Fury (ed.), *The Social History of English Seamen, 1485–1659* (2012), 295–6.

18. SP 14/53, fo. 148; *A Calendar of Material Relating to Ireland from the High Court of Admiralty Examinations 1536–1641*, ed. J. C. Appleby (Dublin, 1992), 296; HMC, *Salisbury*, xxi. 209–15; HMC, *Report of the Manuscripts of the Marquis of Downshire*, 3 vols (1924–40), ii. 279; Thomas, 'History of Lundy', 118–22; *Calendar of State Papers Relating to Ireland . . . 1603–1625*, ed. Charles William Russell et al., 5 vols (1872–88), iii. 480, 495.

19. *Proceedings in Parliament 1625*, ed. Maija Jansson and William B. Bidwell (New Haven and London, 1987), 723–4; SP 16/5, fos 109, 143; SP 16/169/67; *CSPD 1625–6*, 78; *CSPD 1628–9*, 89, 99; Thomas, 'History of Lundy', 122.

20. TNA, C 2/Jas I/S16/46; Thomas, 'History of Lundy', 122.

21. Thomas, 'History of Lundy', 123–4; Ternstrom, 'Ownership of Lundy', 66–9; Ternstrom, 'Lundy: An Analysis and Comparative Study', 148; Rowland et al., 'Particular of Lundy Island', 31–2.

22. SP 16/220/11 and 39; SP 16/221/52; SP 16/222/20; SP 16/223/5; Thomas, 'History of Lundy', 123–4.

23. SP 16/241, fo. 4; SP 16/243, fos 70–2; SP 16/244, fo. 96; SP 16/260, fo. 206; SP 16/270, fo. 95; SP 16/288, fo. 82; SP 63/253, fo. 95; SP 63/254, fo. 181; Thomas, 'History of Lundy', 123,

24. Brereton, *Travels in Holland*, 166–7; SP 16/259/52; SP 16/269/19; Thomas, 'History of Lundy', 124.

25. Ternstrom, 'Lundy: An Analysis and Comparative Study', 148, 152–3.

26. Nathaniel Fiennes, *Colonell Fiennes his Reply to a Pamphlet Entitled An Answer to Colonell Nathaniel Fiennes Relation . . . by Clem. Walker* (1643), 15. See also Clement Walker's claim in parliament that 'it was a rumour in the country, that some goods were carried into the Isle of Lundy, by Colonel Fiennes' (*Lords Journal*, vi. 240).

27. Thomas, 'History of Lundy', 125, 145; J. W. Gough, *The Superlative Prodigall: A Life of Thomas Bushell* (Bristol, 1932), 68–75; Wyndham S. Boundy, *Bushell and Harman of Lundy* (Bideford, 1961), 12–13. For scepticism about Bushell's 'mint', see Ternstrom, 'Lundy: An Analysis and Comparative Study', 158.

28. Amos C. Miller, *Sir Richard Grenville of the Civil War* (1979), 140.

29. Thomas, 'History of Lundy', 124–9; Thomas Bushell, *A Brief Declaration of the Severall Passages in the Treaty Concerning the Surrender of the Garrison of Lundy* (1648), 3, 7, 11, 22.

30. SP 21/13, fo. 91; Bushell, *Brief Declaration*, 1–3.

31. Bushell, *Brief Declaration*, 2–8; Thomas, 'History of Lundy', 126; Chanter, *Lundy Island*, 83–6.

32. Parliamentary Archives, HL/PO/JO/10/1/206.

33. *Commons Journal*, v. 239; Bushell, *Brief Declaration*, title page.

34. Parliamentary Archives, HL/PO/JO/10/1/264 and 265; Bushell, *Brief Declaration*, 21–4; Thomas Bushell, *The Apologie of Thomas Bushell* (1650), 1–3; Thomas, 'History of Lundy', 124–30.

35. Thomas, 'History of Lundy', 130–1; *A Calendar of Material Relating to Ireland from the High Court of Admiralty 1641–1660*, ed. Elaine Murphy (Dublin, 2011), 85–6, 91, 214, 254, 263.

36. *The Letters of Robert Blake*, ed. J. R. Powell, *Navy Records Society*, 76 (1937), 72.
37. John Musgrave, *A True and Exact Relation of the Great and Heavy Pressures and Grievances* (1650), 23. Lampit graduated BA from Oxford in 1626 and was ejected from the rectory of Aikton, Cumberland, in 1650.
38. Ternstrom, 'Ownership of Lundy', 66–7.
39. *The Letters of Dorothy Osborne to William Temple*, ed. G. C. Moore Smith (1928), 91; J. S. A. Adamson, 'The *Vindiciae Veritatis* and the Political Creed of Viscount Saye and Sele', *Historical Research*, 60 (1987), 54–63.
40. *Letters of Robert Blake*, 262–3; *A Perfect Diurnall*, 2–9 January 1654; SP 18/207, fo. 100.
41. Parliamentary Archives, HL/PO/JO/10/1/283; Thomas Bushell, *An Extract by Mr Bushell of his Late Abridgement* (1660); Thomas Bushell, *The Case of Thomas Bushell Esq.* (1660?).
42. SP 29/206, fo. 144.
43. Samuel Lewis, *A Topographical Dictionary of England*, 4 vols (1831), iii. 183.
44. 'The Journals of Jeremy Roch', in *Three Sea Journals of Stuart Times*, ed. Bruce S. Ingram (1936), 215.
45. SP 44/100, fo. 385.
46. Chanter, *Lundy Island*, 93; Thomas, 'History of Lundy', 135–7.
47. Edward Carson, *The Ancient and Rightful Customs: A Brief History of the English Customs Service* (1972), 75.
48. *The Times*, 30 October 1786.
49. *The Times*, 31 August 1840, 26 September 1906, 8 August 1911, 17 April 1930, 7 December 1959; Ternstrom, 'Lundy: An Analysis and Comparative Study', 54–5, 306.

Chapter 3

1. H. G. Keene, 'The Channel Islands', *English Historical Review*, 2 (1887), 21, 30; A. J. Eagleston, *The Channel Islands under Tudor Government, 1485–1642* (Cambridge, 1949); Tim Thornton, *The Channel Islands, 1370–1640: Between England and Normandy* (Woodbridge, 2012); Richard Morieux, *The Channel: England, France and the Construction of a Maritime Border in the Eighteenth Century* (Cambridge, 2016), 68–9, 76–7; Richard Hocart, *The Country People of Guernsey and their Agriculture, 1640–1840* (St Peter Port, 2016), 7–9, 17; J. K. Oudendijk, *Status and Extent of Adjacent Waters: A Historical Orientation* (Leyden, 1970). Guernsey's populated minor islands included Herm, Jethou, Lihou, and Brecou.
2. William Harrison, 'Description of Britaine', in Raphael Holinshed, *The First and Second Volumes of Chronicles* (1587), 32
3. HCA 13/55/495, cited in G. G. Harris, *List of Witnesses in the High Court of Admiralty, 1619–49*, List and Index Society, 335 (2010), 123.
4. 'A Briefe State of Guernsey by the Right Honourable Christopher Lord Hatton', Bod., MS Eng. Hist. b.134, fo. 4. The author was the son of the Restoration governor Lord Hatton and himself governed Guernsey from 1670 to 1706.
5. John Foxe, *Actes and Monuments of Matters Most Speciall and Memorable* (1583), 1947.

6. In 1635, the Public Orator of the University of Oxford praised Charles I for supporting fellowships for students from the Channel Islands, '*ut munificenta aspergines in transmarinas imperii tui micase Jersiam Gernersiamque*' (for the benefit of Jersey and Guernsey, those tiny outlying sprinklings of your dominions) (SP 16/294, fo. 145^v).

7. S. Elliott Hoskins, *Charles the Second in the Channel Islands*, 2 vols (1854), ii. 330–2, 347.

8. Philip Falle, *An Account of the Island of Jersey*, with notes by Edward Durell (St Helier, 1837), pp. xv–xvi, xxix.

9. Victor Hugo, *The Toilers of the Sea* [1866] (New York, 2000), 20.

10. Philippe Dumaresq, 'A Survey of ye Island of Jersey... 1685', *Société Jersiaise Bulletin Annuel*, 12 (1932–5), 441.

11. Falle, *Account of the Island of Jersey*, 90, 357.

12. *Ile de Jersey. Ordres du Conseil et Pièces Analogues Enregistrés a Jersey. Vol. 1. 1536–1678* (St Helier, 1897), 62–7.

13. *Actes des États de L'Île de Guernsey.1605 á 1651* (St Peter Port, 1851), 273; 'The Journal of Charles Trumbull', ed. Richard Hocart, *La Société Guernesiaise Report and Transactions* (1985 for 1984), 567, 568, 574.

14. SP 16/528, fo. 15; BL, Add. MS 72,608, fo. 4^v; John Speed, *The Theatre of the Empire of Great Britaine* (1632), 94; Peter Heylyn, *A Full Relation of Two Journeys: The One into the Main-Land of France. The Other into some of the Adjacent Islands* (1656), 303; Keene, 'Channel Islands', 37.

15. Huntington Library, MS EL 1904, fo. 46.

16. SP 16/528, fo. 85; Heylyn, *Full Relation of Two Journeys*, 295.

17. Heylyn, *Full Relation of Two Journeys*, 295; Falle, *Account of the Island of Jersey*, 66; Marie Axton and Richard Axton (eds), *Calendar and Catalogue of Sark Seigneurie Archive 1526-1927*, List and Index Society, Special Series, 26 (1991).

18. *The Charters of Guernsey*, ed. Tim Thornton (Bognor Regis, 2004), 171.

19. BL, MS Lansdowne 53, fo. 13; 'Briefe State of Guernsey', Bod., MS Eng. Hist. b.134, fo. 7; Hoskins, *Charles the Second in the Channel Islands*, i. 24; Jonathan Duncan, *The History of Guernsey; with Occasional Notices of Jersey, Alderney, and Sark* (1841), 228; A. C. Saunders, *Jersey in the 15th and 16th Centuries* (St Helier, 1933), 13–23; Thornton, *Channel Islands*, 9–55; Tim Thornton, 'The English King's French Islands: Jersey and Guernsey in English Politics and Administration, 1485–1642', in George W. Bernard and Steven J. Gunn (eds), *Authority and Consent in Tudor England: Essays Presented to C. S. L. Davies* (Aldershot, 2002), 197–217.

20. Heylyn, *Full Relation of Two Journeys*; 'Briefe State of Guernsey', Bod., MS Eng. Hist. b.134; James Stocall, *Freedom. Or, the Description of the Excellent Civill Government of the Island of Jersey* (1652); Jean Poingdestre, *Caesarea, Or a Discourse of the Island of Jersey* [c.1682] (St Helier, 1889); Jean Poingdestre, *Les Lois et coûtumes de l'Isle de Jersey* (St Helier, 1928).

21. *Charters of Guernsey*, ed. Thornton, 83, 89, 96, 102; Keene, 'Channel Islands', 24–76; A. J. Eagleston, 'Guernsey under Sir Thomas Leighton (1570–1610), *Report and Transactions of the Société Guernesiase*, 13 (1937–45), 72–108.

22. Duncan, *History of Guernsey*, 35.

23. HMC, *Tenth Report* (1906), 113; J. C. Appleby, 'Neutrality, Trade and Privateering 1500–1689', in A. G. Jamieson (ed.), *A People of the Sea: The Maritime History of the Channel Islands* (London and New York, 1986), 61–2.

24. Laurent Carey, *Essai sur les institutions, lois et coûtumes de l'Ile de Guernesey* (St Peter Port, 1889), 2–3.

25. Thomas Egerton, *The Speech of the Lord Chancellor... Touching the Post-Nati* (1609), 65; *Robert Paynell's Exchequer Reports (1627-1631)*, ed. W. H. Bryson (Tempe, AZ, 2009), 7; Richard Warner (ed.), *Collections for the History of Hampshire*, 6 vols (1795), iv. 137.

26. Edward Coke, *The Fourth Part of the Institutes of the Laws of England: Concerning the Jurisdiction of Courts* (1644), 286; Darryl Ogier, *The Government and Law of Guernsey* (St Peter Port, 2005), 109–13. See also John Pym, *The Declaration of John Pym Esquire upon the whole matter of the Charge of High Treason against Thomas Earle of Strafford* (1641), 62–3: 'Guernsey or Jersey are under the king's subjection, but are not parcels of the crown of England, but of the Duchy of Normandy; they are not governed by the laws of England, as Ireland is; and yet parliaments in England have usually held plea of, and determined all causes concerning lands or goods.' The first part of this was correct, but not the claim of parliamentary competence.

27. *Ile de Jersey. Ordres du Conseil... 1536-1678*, 327–30, 367.

28. *Ceremonies of Charles I: The Note Books of John Finet 1628-1641*, ed. Albert J. Loomie (New York, 1987), 218–19; Hugh Lenfestey, 'Homage and Suit-of-Court in the Channel Islands Denoting Allegiance to the English Crown', *La Société Guernesiaise Report and Transactions*, 25 (2004), 674–88; Richard Cust, *Charles I and the Aristocracy, 1625-1642* (Cambridge, 2013), 104; Hocart, *Country People of Guernsey and their Agriculture*, 22–8. Amice Andros was Bailiff of Guernsey 1661–74, succeeded by his son Sir Edmond Andros (1637–1714), who later served as governor of New York, Virginia, and New England.

29. John Kelleher, 'The Mysterious Case of the Ship Abandoned off Sark in 1608: The Customary Law Relating to *choses gaives*', in Gordon Dawes (ed.), *Commise 1204: Studies in the History and Law of Continental and Insular Normandy* (St Peter Port, 2005), 171–90.

30. *Sir Matthew Hale's The Prerogatives of the King*, ed. D. E. C. Yale, Selden Society, 92 (1976), 41. As a judge in the king's central courts, Hale argued that the Channel Islands 'were rendered in some kind of subordination to the English jurisdiction', and cited precedents from the reigns of Edward II and Edward III to show 'the power of King's Bench extending thither', a view not shared on Jersey or Guernsey.

31. English courts also reported their business in 'Law French' until the late seventeenth century: Sir Edward Coke, *Le Tierce Parts des reportes* (1602), sig. Ei.

32. Heylyn, *Full Relation of Two Journeys*, 280, 294; 'Journal of Charles Trumbull', 572.

33. Egerton, *Speech of the Lord Chancellor*, 65; Warner (ed.), *Collections for the History of Hampshire*, iv. 137.

34. John Selden, *Mare Clausum; The Right and Dominion of the Sea* (1663), 335–43; Philip Morant, 'Remarks on the 19th Chapter of the 2nd Book of Mr. Selden's *Mare Clausum*' (1733), in Falle, *Account of the Island of Jersey*, 266–73.

35. Poingdestre, *Caesarea, Or a Discourse of the Island of Jersey*, 42.

36. Falle, *Account of the Island of Jersey*, 40, 42, 166. See also *Les Manuscrits de Philippe le Geyt, Ecuyer, Lieutenant-Bailli de l'Isle de Jersey, sur la constitution, les lois, et les usages de cette ile*, 4 vols (St Helier, 1846–9). Le Geyt (d. 1716) was a long-serving jurat of Jersey.

37. BL, MS Lansdowne 53, fo. 8.

38. Duncan, *History of Guernsey*, 37, 40–1, 229.

39. SP 15/30, fo. 55; SP 29/224, fo. 204; Heylyn, *Full Relation of Two Journeys*, 30; 'Briefe State of Guernsey', Bod., MS Eng. Hist. b.134, 7ᵛ; Poingdestre, *Caesarea, Or a Discourse of the Island of Jersey*, 52–60; Ferdinand Brock Tupper, *The Chronicles of Castle Cornet, Guernsey* (1851), 25–6.

40. Duncan, *History of Guernsey*, 226–7.

41. SP 29/224, fo. 204; 'Briefe State of Guernsey', Bod., MS Eng. Hist. b.134, 7ᵛ; Carey, *Essai sur les institutions, lois et coûtumes de l'Ile de Guernesey*, 13.

42. SP 16/526, fos 146, 163; SP 16/528, fos 72, 80, 82; Tupper, *Chronicles of Castle Cornet*, 321; J. C. Appleby, 'A Memorandum on the Defence of the Channel Islands, 1627', *Société Jersiaise Bulletin Annuel*, 23 (1984), 506–9

43. SP 16/527, fo. 125; SP 16/528, fo. 85.

44. *A Calendar of Material Relating to Ireland from the High Court of Admiralty Examinations 1536–1641*, ed. J. C. Appleby (Dublin, 1992), 167, 175–6.

45. SP 16/528, fo. 201; Duncan, *History of Guernsey*, 126, 227–9.

46. Tupper, *Chronicles of Castle Cornet*, 20.

47. Stephen Saunders Webb, *The Governors General: The English Army and the Definition of Empire, 1569–1681* (Chapel Hill, NC, 1979).

48. SP 16/75, fo. 100; SP 16/526, fo. 2.

49. *CSPD 1640–1*, 56, 67, 82, 315. The seigneur D'Anneville was among those who saw Lord Danby when 'he came to this isle' in 1629: Greffe, St Peter Port, 'Notebooks of George Fouachin', 45.

50. SP 16/533, fo. 127.

51. Heylyn, *Full Relation of Two Journeys*, 322; Hocart, *Country People of Guernsey and their Agriculture*, 29. The Guernsey seigneur George Fouachin helpfully described 'a duty called the champart which is the twelfth sheaf of every villain tenant's corn': Greffe, St Peter Port, 'Notebooks of George Fouachin', 5.

52. Duncan, *History of Guernsey*, 409.

53. *Ile de Jersey. Ordres du Conseil... 1536–1678*, 460; SP 44/55, fo. 124; Carey, *Essai sur les institutions, lois et coûtumes de l'Ile de Guernesey*, 14–15.

54. *Ile de Jersey. Ordres du Conseil... 1536–1678*, 35–41; Falle, *Account of the Island of Jersey*, 139; Duncan, *History of Guernsey*, 21.

55. Poingdestre, *Lois et coûtumes de l'Isle de Jersey*, 5, 7, 8.

56. SP 15/42/45; Poingdestre, *Caesarea, Or a Discourse of the Island of Jersey*, 34; Havilland de Sausmarez, 'Guernsey's *Précept d'Assise* of 1441: Translation and Notes', *Jersey and Guernsey Law Review*, 12 (2008), 211–12.

57. Falle, *Account, of the Island of Jersey*, 148; Carey, *Essai sur les institutions, lois et coûtumes de l'Ile de Guernesey*, 29–30.

58. Duncan, *History of Guernsey*, 434–6; Thomas Dicey, *An Historical Account of Guernsey* (1798), 59–60.

59. Bod., MS Rawlinson B 385, fos 666–7; Poingdestre, *Caesarea, Or a Discourse of the Island of Jersey*, 34; Ogier, *Government and Law of Guernsey*, 69–71; de Sausmarez, 'Guernsey's *Précept d'Assise* of 1441', 212–13.

60. Stocall, *Freedom. Or, the Description of the Excellent Civill Government of the Island of Jersey*, sigs A2ᵛ, A3ᵛ, 1–9; Poingdestre, *Caesarea, Or a Discourse of the Island of Jersey*, 36–41; Carey, *Essai sur les institutions, lois et coûtumes de l'Ile de Guernesey*, 197–9; Falle, *Account of the Island of Jersey*, 10, 151–5, 286; Dicey, *Historical Account of Guernsey*, 22–6; Warner (ed.), *Collections for the History of Hampshire*, iv. 125–8, v. 22–5; *Recueil D'Ordonnances de la Cour Royale de l'Isle de Guernsey . . . 1533–1800*, ed. Robert MacCulloch (St Peter Port, 1852), *passim*; Charles Le Quesne, *A Constitutional History of Jersey* (1856), 38–9; 'Clameur de Haro!', *Société Jersiaise Bulletin Annuel*, 17 (1960), 339–41.

61. Duncan, *History of Guernsey*, 409.

62. Hoskins, *Charles the Second in the Channel Islands*, i. 21.

63. Poingdestre, *Lois et coutumes de l'Ile de Jersey*, 5–9; Poingdestre, *Caesarea, Or a Discourse of the Island of Jersey*, 49, 61, 65–7; Duncan, *History of Guernsey*, 13–14, 17, 18, 82.

64. SP 47/1, fo. 134; 'Le Procés entre les États et le Gouverneur Lanier. La Rémonstrance des États', *Société Jersiaise Bulletin Annuel*, 13 (1888), 254–80; *Ile de Jersey. Ordres du Conseil . . . 1536–1678*, 73.

65. Bod., MS Eng. Hist. c. 343, fo. 173; Bod., MS. Rawlinson A270, fos 19, 23, 35; de Sausmarez, 'Guernsey's *Précept d'Assise* of 1441', 207–19. Edward III's Precept of Assize of 1331 was confirmed in 1441,

66. SP 47/1, fo. 120; Eagleston, 'Guernsey under Sir Thomas Leighton', 72–108.

67. BL, MS Lansdowne 53, fo. 8.

68. BL, MS Egerton 2812, fos 5, 21ᵛ, 24, 31, 39, 46, 48ᵛ.

69. A. C. Saunders, *Jersey in the 17th Century* (St Helier, 1931), 15–43; Thornton, *Channel Islands*, 132–50.

70. Huntington Library, MS HM 72020, fo. 28. The complaints and grievances presented to the 1607 commission on Guernsey are set down in detail in fos 1–152.

71. *CSPD Addenda, James I*, 463; Bod., MS Gough Islands 3; *Ile de Jersey. Ordres du Conseil . . . 1536–1678*, 37, 55.

72. HMC, *Calendar of the Manuscripts of . . . the Marquis of Salisbury*, 24 vols (1883–1976), xx. 23, 26.

73. HMC, *Salisbury*, xxi. 227.

74. PC 2/31, fo. 53, PC 2/32, fo. 423; *APC 1615–1616*, 144, 178–9, 287; SP 15/41, fo. 1; *CSPD Addenda 1580–1625*, 553; *Ile de Jersey. Ordres du Conseil . . . 1536–1678*, 90–7; Huntington Library, MSS EL 1907, 1908, 1909, 1910; Falle, *Account of the Island of Jersey*, 409–11; Warner (ed.), *Collections for the History of Hampshire*, iv. 185–6; Saunders, *Jersey in the 17th Century*, 52–6; Thornton, *Channel Islands* 138–9.

75. SP 15/41; HMC, *The Manuscripts of the Earl Cowper*, 2 vols (1888–9), i. 84; 'The Report of the Royal Commissioners sent to Jersey in 1617', *Société Jersiaise Bulletin Annuel*, 30 (1905), 386–96.

76. SP 16/524, fo. 199; SP 16/526, fo. 37.

77. SP 16/527, fo. 97.
78. SP 16/529, fo. 77; SP 16/531, fos 69–72, 76–78ᵛ, 84–84ᵛ.
79. SP 16/218, fo. 83.
80. 'Briefe State of Guernsey', Bod., MS Eng. Hist. b.134, fo. 9ᵛ; SP 44/28, fos 155, 203; D. M. Ogier, *Reformation and Society in Guernsey* (Woodbridge, 1996), 12–14.
81. W. J. Jones, *The Elizabethan Court of Chancery* (Oxford, 1967), 372–7. Huntington Library, MS HM 72020, fo. 61, discusses the distance and danger of appealing to London.
82. *The Letter-Books of Sir Amias Poulet*, ed. John Morris (1874), 133.
83. SP 130/62, fos 143, 145, 146, 154, 165, and *passim*; SP 16/390, fo. 220; SP 16/437, fo. 128; SP 16/439, fo. 5; SP 16/538, fo. 86; *APC 1618–1618*, 51, 326; *APC 1619–1621*, 12, 296; 'Briefe State of Guernsey', Bod., MS Eng. Hist. b.134, fos 4–5; Poingdestre, *Caesarea, Or a Discourse of the Island of Jersey*, 44; Joseph Henry Smith, *Appeals to the Privy Council from the American Plantations* (New York, 1950, repr. 1965), 5–39, 63–99; Ogier, *Government and Law of Guernsey*, 79.
84. *Ile de Jersey. Ordres du Conseil… 1536–1678*, 60, 456–9; *CSPD 1676–7*, 387, 528; Poingdestre, *Lois et coutumes de l'Isle de Jersey*, 235; Duncan, *History of Guernsey*, 477; Smith, *Appeals to the Privy Council*, 27–8; Lucy Marsh-Smith, 'A Very Particular Remedy; Doleance in the Crown Dependencies', *Jersey and Guernsey Law Review*, 15/2 (2011), https://www.jerseylaw.je/publications/jglr/Pages/JLR1106_Marsh-Smith.aspx (accessed July 2019).
85. 'Journal of Charles Trumbull', 578.
86. BL, Add. MS 72,608, fo. 5ᵛ.
87. See the many cases in *Ile de Jersey. Ordres du Conseil… 1536–1678*, *passim*.
88. *CSPD 1639–40*, 250.
89. *Ile de Jersey. Ordres du Conseil… 1536–1678*, 383.
90. BL, MS Lansdowne 57, fo. 59; SP 15/29, fo. 218.
91. SP 15/30, fos 166–176; BL, MS Lansdowne 57, fos 61–2.
92. SP 15/41/50; PC 2/29, fo. 119.
93. A ruling 'by the king's majesty's commissioners at St Peter Port the 30th of November 1607' only added to complexities in a suit of George Fouachin, which was still in dispute half a dozen years later: Greffe, St Peter Port, 'Notebooks of George Fouachin', 18–19.
94. PC 2/3, fos 509, 603; PC 2/32, fo. 101; SP 15/43/118; SP 16/538, fo. 102; *Actes des États de L'Île de Guernsey.1605 á 1651*, 180–2; *Ile de Jersey. Ordres du Conseil… 1536–1678*, 447–9. See also *Charters of Guernsey*, ed. Thornton, *passim*.
95. 'Briefe State of Guernsey', Bod., MS Eng. Hist. b.134, fo. 12ᵛ.
96. SP 16/31, fo. 1; SP 16/523, fo. 238; SP 16/525, fo. 114; SP 16/531, fo. 130; SP 16/533, fos 60, 69, 120, and more.
97. SP 16/439, fo. 5; SP 16/450, fo. 120; SP 16/536, fo. 79; SP 16/538, fo. 102; *Actes des États de L'Île de Guernsey.1605 á 1651*, 179–80.
98. Parliamentary Archives, HL/PO/JO/10/1/44 and 45.
99. SP 16/437, fo. 128; SP 16/536, fo. 41; SP 16/538, fo. 86.
100. Parliamentary Archives, HL/PO/JO/10/1/26, nos 259, 266, 271, 275, 277.

Chapter 4

1. John Speed, *The Theatre of the Empire of Great Britaine* (1632), 91; J. R. Dickinson, *The Lordship of Man under the Stanleys: Government and Economy in the Isle of Man, 1580–1704*, Chetham Society, 3rd ser., 41 (Manchester, 1996), 10; James Sharpe, 'Towards a Legal Anthropology of the Early Modern Isle of Man', in Richard McMahon (ed.), *Crime, Law, and Popular Culture in Europe 1500–1900* (2008), 130. Manx belongs to the Goidelic of northern branch of Gaelic.

2. Bod., MS Rawlinson D 977, fos 48–48ᵛ.

3. Guy Miege, *The New State of England under Their Majesties K. William and Q. Mary* (1691), 51.

4. William Sacheverell, *An Account of the Isle of Man* (1702), 7.

5. Edward Coke, *The Fourth Part of the Institutes of the Laws of England: Concerning the Jurisdiction of Courts* (1644), 283–4; *The Ancient Ordinances and Statute Laws of the Isle of Man*, ed. Mark Anthony Mills (Douglas, 1821); R. H. Kinvig, *History of the Isle of Man* (Douglas, 1944); Sybil Sharpe, 'The Isle of Man—in the British Isles but not Ruled by Britain: A Modern Peculiarity from Ancient Occurrences', in Peter Davey and Peter Finlayson (eds), *Mannin Revisited: Twelve Essays on Manx Culture and Environment* (Edinburgh, 2002), 161–72.

6. 'Deemster John Parr's Abstract of Manx Laws', Dedication to Governor Heywood, 2, transcribed by Peter Edge from Manx Museum MS 03176C, https://radar.brokes/ac.uk/radar/items/a1e352c0-f1ed-45a0-b7d5-3434669ed078/1 (accessed April 2019). The island's constitutional peculiarity is also reviewed in Peter W. Edge and C. C. Augur Pearce, 'The Development of the Lord Bishop's Role in the Manx Tynwald', *Journal of Ecclesiastical History*, 57 (2006), 494–14.

7. William Blundell, *A History of the Isle of Man*, ed. William Harrison, 2 vols (Manx Society, Douglas, 1876–7), ii. 30. Jersey and Guernsey used heraldic seals with three lions, said to have been approved by Edward I.

8. Sacheverell, *Account of the Isle of Man*, Sig B.

9. William Harrison, 'Description of Britaine', in Raphael Holinshed, *The First and Second Volumes of Chronicles* (1587), 38; Barry Coward, *The Stanleys. Lords Stanley and Earls of Derby 1385–1672: The Origins, Wealth and Power of a Landowning Family*, Chetham Society, 3rd ser., 30 (Manchester. 1983), 101; Dickinson, *Lordship of Man*, 13–74; J. R. Dickinson and J. A. Sharpe, 'Courts, Crime and Litigation in the Isle of Man, 1580–1700', *Historical Research*, 27 (1999), 140–59, esp. 142.

10. Peter Heylyn, *A Help to English History* (1675), 60–1.

11. Thomas Denton, *A Perambulation of Cumberland 1687–1688 Including . . . the Isle of Man*, Surtees Society, 207 (2003), 499.

12. Miege, *New State of England*, 53.

13. *Sir Matthew Hale's The Prerogatives of the King*, ed. D. E. C. Yale, Selden Society, 92 (1976), 41; Coward, *Stanleys*, 99.

14. Huntington Library, MS EL 782, 'A Breviat for the Title of the Isle of Manne'; Dickinson, *Lordship of Man*, 15–16.

15. Francis Peck, *Desiderata Curiosa: Or, a Collection of Divers Scarce and Curious Pieces*, 2 vols (1732–5), ii, bk 11, 26; Coward, *Stanleys*, 101; Dickinson, *Lordship of Man*, 16.

16. Huntington Library, MS EL 777; Dickinson, *Lordship of Man*, 18–19, 24, 40; Coward, *Stanleys*, 48.

17. Huntington Library, MSS EL 774, 962, 963, 974, 975, 7470; John Parr, *An Abstract of the Laws, Customs, and Ordinances of the Isle of Man*, ed. James Gell (Douglas, 1867), 36–40; Dickinson, *Lordship of Man*, 24, 40.

18. Parr, *Abstract of the Laws, Customs, and Ordinances of the Isle of Man*, 36; Coward, *Stanleys*, 103–4.

19. SP 14/27, fos 122–7; HMC, *Calendar of the Manuscripts of . . . the Marquis of Salisbury*, 24 vols (1883–1976), xxiv. 98

20. SP 14/27, fos 120–4; SP 29/159, fo. 144.

21. James Chaloner, 'A Description of the Isle of Man', in Daniel King, *The Vale-Royall of England. Or, The County Palatine of Chester* (1656), separate pagination, 16; Sacheverell, *Account of the Isle of Man*, sig. B3v, 89–91, 93–4; Dickinson and Sharpe, 'Courts, Crime and Litigation', 140–59; Sharpe, 'Towards a Legal Anthropology of the Early Modern Isle of Man', 122–9.

22. Coward, *Stanleys*, 58–61; Dickinson, *Lordship of Man*, 31–2, 326; Edge and Pearce, 'Development of the Lord Bishop's Role in the Manx Tynwald', 498.

23. Huntington Library, MS EL 966, 971, 973, 7479.

24. SP 16/539, fo. 212; HMC, *The Manuscripts of the Earl Cowper*, 2 vols (1888–9), ii. 29, 31–2; Sara Goodwins, *A Brief History of the Isle of Man* (Sutton, 2011), 77–78.

25. Bod., MS Rawlinson C 441, fos 47, 57; SP 16/126, fo. 61; Huntington Library, MS EL 782.

26. PC 2/32, fo. 463; SP 14/173, fos 35, 68, 152; SP 16/126, fo. 61.

27. Dickinson and Sharpe, 'Courts, Crime and Litigation', 148.

28. J. R. Dickinson, 'The Earl of Derby and the Isle of Man, 1643–1651', *Transactions of the Historic Society of Lancashire and Cheshire*, 141 (1991–2), 45–8.

29. SP 12/122, fo. 37; William Borlase, *Observations on the Ancient and Present State of the Islands of Scilly* (1756), 106; A. L. Rowse, *Tudor Cornwall* (1941, 1969 edn), 221, 384.

30. *Calendar of Treasury Books, 1679–1680*, ed. William A. Shaw (1913), 665.

31. Daniel Defore, *A Tour thro' the Whole Island of Great Britain* [1724–6], 2 vols (1968), i. 244; Cambridge University Library, MS Add. 6458, 'A Geographical and Nautical Description of Scilly', fo. 9.

32. *Acts of the Privy Council 1542–1631*, ed. J. R. Dasent et al., 46 vols (1890–1964), vii. 33; Rowse, *Tudor Cornwall*, 384,

33. SP 16/323, fo. 14.

34. Bod., MS Bankes 38/6; SP 12/122, fo. 37; Robert Heath, *A Natural and Historical Account of the Islands of Scilly* (1750), 15, 201, 203; John Troutbeck, *A Survey of the Ancient and Present State of the Scilly Islands* (1794), 177–9.

35. HMC, *Tenth Report* (1906), 389.

36. Heath, *Natural and Historical Account of the Islands of Scilly*, 24, 43–50; Martyn F. Wakelin, *Language and History in Cornwall* (Leicester, 1975), 28–9, 100, 203; Matthew Spriggs, 'Where Cornish was Spoken and when: A Provisional Synthesis', *Cornish Studies*, ser. 2, 11 (2003), 228–69, esp. 241–44.

37. SP 18/26, fos 141 ff; 'The Parliamentary Survey of the Duchy of Cornwall, part II', ed. Norman J. G. Pounds, *Devon and Cornwall Record Society*, NS 27 (1984), 131–51.

38. TNA, C 213/464.
39. G. Forrester Matthews, *The Isles of Scilly: A Constitutional, Economic and Social Survey of the Development of an Island People from Early Times to 1900* (1960), 19, 41.
40. Richard Carew, *The Survey of Cornwall* (1602), 85; HMC, *Salisbury*, iv. 294.
41. SP 44/51, fo. 392; Bod., MS Bankes 55, fo. 53.
42. Bod., MS Jones 27*, fo. 17; HMC, *The Manuscripts of S. H. Le Fleming* (1890), 46.
43. HMC, *Salisbury*, v. 160.
44. Bod., MS Bankes 55, fo. 53; 'Parliamentary Survey of the Duchy of Cornwall, part II', 149–51.
45. BL, Add. MS 33,124, fos 102, 105^v; Cambridge University Library, MS Add. 6458, 'A Geographical and Nautical Description of Scilly', fo. 9; Heath, *Natural and Historical Account of the Islands of Scilly*, 107–8, 183, 185; Borlase, *Observations on the Ancient and Present State of the Islands of Scilly*, 133; Troutbeck, *Survey of the Ancient and Present State of the Scilly Islands*, 177–9; Davies Gilbert, *The Parochial History of Cornwall*, 4 vols (1838), iv. 175; Matthews, *Isles of Scilly*, 35–7.
46. Troutbeck, *Survey of the Ancient and Present State of the Scilly Islands*, 43, 52–3, 199.
47. BL, Add. MS 45,501, fo. 28; Richard Worsley, *The History of the Isle of Wight* (1781), preface; Richard Warner (ed.), *Collections for the History of Hampshire*, 6 vols (1795), iii. 32.
48. Henry Jones, *Vectis. The Isle of Wight: A Poem in Three Cantos* (1766), 2.
49. Andrew M. Coleby, *Central Government and the Localities: Hampshire 1649–1689* (Cambridge, 1987), 4.
50. Harrison, 'Description of Britaine', 31; Miege, *New State of England*, 98; John Selden, *Mare Clausum; The Right and Dominion of the Sea* (1663), 341; Coke, *Fourth Part of the Institutes*, 287; Heylyn, *Help to English History*, 63; John Sturch, *A View of the Isle of Wight*, 4th edn (1791), 49.
51. HMC, *Report on the Manuscripts of Mrs Frankland-Russell-Astley* (1900), 75–6; APC 1626, 201; Worsley, *History of the Isle of Wight*, 81–5, 91, 108.
52. BL, MS Lansdowne 8, fo. 131.
53. BL, Add. MS 48,101, fo. 138; Worsley, *History of the Isle of Wight*, 9–19, appendix 14.
54. SP 16/44, fo. 111; David W. Moore, *The Other British Isles: A History of Shetland, Orkney, the Hebrides, Isle of Man, Anglesey, Scilly, Isle of Wight and the Channel Islands* (Jefferson, NC, and London, 2005), 251. The eighteenth-century population of the Isle of Wight was said to be 18,024: Worsley, *History of the Isle of Wight*, 9–19, appendix 6.
55. Coleby, *Central Government and the Localities*, 4. Eighteen gentlemen attended the governor's tribunal, the Knighten Court. Sir John Oglander (1585–1655) recalled seeing 'thirty or forty knights and gentlemen at bowls with Lord Southampton on St George's Down' (Worsley, *History of the Isle of Wight*, 83, 109). Twenty-two Isle of Wight gentlemen subscribed 'The Declaration to the King and Parliament' in August 1642, in *Three Declarations* (1642), 6.
56. BL, MS Lansdowne 8, fo. 131; SP 16/22, fo. 139; Coleby, *Central Government and the Localities*, 5.

57. HMC, *Salisbury*, xxi. 69.
58. SP 16/3, fo. 117.
59. SP 16/3, fo. 117; SP 16/34, fo. 27; SP 16/521, fo. 282; *CSPD 1627–8*, 346.
60. SP 16/41, fo. 100; SP 16/44, fo. 113; *CSPD 1637*, 323; Coleby, *Central Government and the Localities*, 121–2.
61. BL, MS Lansdowne 8, fo. 131; HMC, *Frankland-Russell-Astley*, 75; Worsley, *History of the Isle of Wight*, 37
62. HMC, *Cowper*, i. 203.
63. HMC, *Sixth Report* (1877), 499; HMC, *Salisbury*, xxi. 179; *CSPD 1611–18*, 69; *A Royalist's Notebook: The Commonplace Book of Sir John Oglander*, ed. Francis Bamford (1936), 15, 19–21, 43–4.
64. SP 29/291, fo. 143; SP 29/372, fos 266, 280, 287; *Royalist's Notebook*, 19–21, 43, 44, 46, 49.
65. HMC, *Report on the Manuscripts of the Late Reginald Rawdon Hastings*, 3 vols (1928–47), ii. 329.
66. SP 16/58/14; Lindsay Boynton, 'Billeting: The Example of the Isle of Wight', *English Historical Review*, 74 (1959), 35.
67. SP 16/88/54; SP 16/103/78; *Royalist's Notebook*, 46; Boynton, 'Billeting: The Example of the Isle of Wight', 25–9, 32, 36; Coleby, *Central Government and the Localities*, 5.
68. *Royalist's Notebook*, 19–21, 43, 44, 46, 49.
69. Worsley, *History of the Isle of Wight*, 39.
70. BL, Add. MS 46,501, fo. 14; Worsley, *History of the Isle of Wight*, 96–107.
71. Worsley, *History of the Isle of Wight*, 108–14; *Royalist's Notebook*, 9.
72. Harrison, 'Description of Britaine', 36.
73. David A. Pretty, *Anglesey: The Concise History* (Cardiff, 2002), 35.
74. 'Anglia Wallia' [the perambulation of Thomas Phaer], *Archaeologia Cambrensis*, 6th ser., 11 (1911), 431; Speed, *Theatre of the Empire of Great Britaine*, 125.
75. 'The Diary of Bulkeley of Dronwey, Anglesey, 1630–1638', ed. Hugh Owen (*Anglesey Antiquarian Society and Field Club Transactions*, 1936), 135; Royal Commission on Ancient and Historical Monuments in Wales and Monmouthshire, *An Inventory of the Ancient Monuments in Anglesey* (1937, repr. 1960), p. clxxvi; Pretty, *Anglesey: The Concise History*, 42.
76. Speed, *Theatre of the Empire of Great Britaine*, 125; Pretty, *Anglesey: The Concise History*, 41, 55, citing estimates of 9,770 in 1563 and 16,456 in 1670.
77. Pretty, *Anglesey: The Concise History*, 44, 56. According to modern estimates, as many as 99% of the early modern Anglesey population spoke Welsh: personal communication, Jerry Hunter, Bangor University, November 2018.
78. G. Nesta Evans, *Social Life in Mid-Eighteenth Century Anglesey*, (Cardiff, 1936), 16.
79. *Calendar of Wynn (of Gwydir) Papers 1515–1690* (Aberystwyth, 1926), 30, 203.
80. SP 14/175, fos 67–8.
81. PC 2/34, fo. 1.
82. HMC, *Fifth Report* (1876), 420–1.
83. *Calendar of Wynn (of Gwydir) Papers*, 161, 230–1.
84. SP 29/23, fo. 198.

Chapter 5

1. William Harrison, 'Description of Britaine', in Raphael Holinshed, *The First and Second Volumes of Chronicles* (1587), 29.
2. Anna Kouremenos (ed.), *Insularity and Identity in the Roman Mediterranean* (Oxford and Philadelphia, 2018), 1–3.
3. Harrison, 'Description of Britaine', 31.
4. John Speed, *The Theatre of the Empire of Great Britaine* (1632), 15.
5. Joan Thirsk (ed.), *The Agrarian History of England and Wales. Volume V 1640–1750* (Cambridge, 1984), 346. The Isle of Wight is unaccountably omitted from the key map of farming regions in Joan Thirsk (ed.), *The Agrarian History of England and Wales. Volume IV 1500–1640* (Cambridge, 1967), 4, but is mentioned by Jose Bettey, 'Downlands', in Joan Thirsk (ed.), *The English Rural Landscape* (Oxford, 2000), 37–8, 49.
6. Guy Miege, *The New State of England under Their Majesties K. William and Q. Mary* (1691), 97; Richard Worsley, *The History of the Isle of Wight* (1781), 2–3; Richard Warner (ed.), *Collections for the History of Hampshire*, 6 vols (1795), iii. 33, 42.
7. SP 16/44, fo. 111. The eighteenth-century population of the Isle of Wight was said to be 18,024, Worsley, *History of the Isle of Wight*, 9–19, appendix 6.
8. 'Anglia Wallia' [the perambulation of Thomas Phaer], *Archaeologia Cambrensis*, 6th ser., 11 (1911), 431; Harrison, 'Description of Britaine', 36; Speed, *Theatre of the Empire of Great Britaine*, 125; George Kay, *General View of the Agriculture and Rural Economy of Anglesey* (1794), 7–8; Thirsk (ed.), *Agrarian History of England and Wales. Volume IV*, 116, 129–31, 143; Thirsk (ed.), *Agrarian History of England and Wales. Volume V*, 394, 404, 417.
9. Harrison, 'Description of Britaine', 29, 33–4; Robert Heath, *A Natural and Historical Account of the Islands of Scilly* (1750), 24, 43–50.
10. SP 18/26, fos 141 ff; 'The Parliamentary Survey of the Duchy of Cornwall, part II', ed. Norman J. G. Pounds, *Devon and Cornwall Record Society*, ns 27 (1984), 131–51.
11. James Sharpe, 'Towards a Legal Anthropology of the Early Modern Isle of Man', in Richard McMahon (ed.), *Crime, Law, and Popular Culture in Europe 1500–1900* (2008), 120. See also J. R. Dickinson, *The Lordship of Man under the Stanleys: Government and Economy in the Isle of Man, 1580–1704*, Chetham Society, 3rd ser., 41 (Manchester, 1996), 80 ff. for the economy of the island.
12. SP 16/539, fos 212–13; Bod., MS Rawlinson D 977, fo. 42ᵛ; James Chaloner, 'A Description of the Isle of Man', in Daniel King, *The Vale-Royall of England. Or, The County Palatine of Chester* (1656), second pagination, 2–3, 30; William Sacheverell, *An Account of the Isle of Man* (1702), Sig Bᵛ; Thomas Denton, *A Perambulation of Cumberland 1687–1688 including... the Isle of Man*, Surtees Society, 207 (2003), 494–98.
13. Harrison, 'Description of Britaine', 38; Miege, *New State of England*, 52; Thirsk (ed.), *Agrarian History of England and Wales. Volume IV*, 26; Thirsk (ed.), *Agrarian History of England and Wales. Volume V*, 63.
14. Richard Rolt, *The History of the Island of Man: From the Earliest Accounts to the Present Time* (1773), 101.

15. Speed, *Theatre of the Empire of Great Britaine*, 94.

16. SP 15/39, fo. 58^v.

17. Philip Falle, *An Account of the Island of Jersey*, with notes by Edward Durell (St Helier, 1837), 98; Jean Poingdestre, *Caesarea, Or a Discourse of the Island of Jersey* [c.1682], (St Helier, 1889), 13–15.

18. Philippe Dumaresq, 'A Survey of ye Island of Jersey . . . 1685', *Société Jersiaise Bulletin Annuel*, 12 (1932–5), 417–19.

19. Peter Heylyn, *A Full Relation of Two Journeys: The One into the Main-Land of France. The Other into some of the Adjacent Islands* (1656), 280, 300, 301.

20. 'Notebooks of Elie Brevint', http://societe-jersiaise.org/digital-publications/brevint? file=../bulletin-pdfs/Brevint, 260 (accessed June 2018).

21. Heylyn, *Full Relation of Two Journeys*, 302–3.

22. 'The Journal of Charles Trumbull', ed. Richard Hocart, *La Société Guernesiaise Raport and Transactions* (1985 for 1984), 568, 576; *The Channel Island Journals of Charles and William Trumbull 1677*, ed. Joan Stevens, Jean Arthur, and Collette Stevens (St Helier, 2004), 9–10.

23. Christopher Duncan, *The History of Guernsey; with Occasional Notices of Jersey, Alderney, and Sark* (1841), 284.

24. Richard Hocart, *The Country People of Guernsey and their Agriculture, 1640–1840* (St Peter Port, 2016), 81, 98.

25. SP 44/235, fo. 161; SP 44/341, fo. 143.

26. Bod., MS Clarendon 82, fo. 124; Hocart, *Country People of Guernsey and their Agriculture*, 68–70, 240.

27. John D. Kelleher, *The Triumph of the Country: The Rural Community in Nineteenth-Century Jersey* (St Helier, 1995).

28. Poingdestre, *Caesarea, Or a Discourse of the Island of Jersey*, 17–19; Falle, *Account of the Island of Jersey*, 103; Duncan, *History of Guernsey*, 289–92; Hocart, *Country People of Guernsey and their Agriculture*, 94–5; Jeannette Mary Neeson, 'Coastal Commons: Custom and the Use of Seaweed in the British Isles *c*.1700–1900', in Simonetta Cavaicocchi (ed.), *Ricchezza del Mar: secc. XII–XVIII* (Florence, 2006), 343–67; Renaud Morieux, *The Channel: England, France and the Construction of a Maritime Border in the Eighteenth Century* (Cambridge, 2016), 186–87.

29. SP 16/117, fo. 16; *Stuart Royal Proclamations, Volume I. Royal Proclamations of King James I 1603–1625*, ed. James F. Larkin and Paul L. Hughes (Oxford, 1973), 457–60.

30. *Stuart Royal Proclamations, Volume I*, 11–12, 162–5.

31. HMC, *The Manuscripts of the Earl Cowper*, 2 vols (1888–9), i. 316.

32. *Stuart Royal Proclamations. Volume II. Royal Proclamations of King Charles I 1625–1646*, ed. James F. Larkin (Oxford, 1983), 600–4;Joan Thirsk, 'New Crops and their Diffusion: Tobacco-Growing in 17th Century England', in C. W. Chalkin and M. A. Havinden (eds), *Rural Change and Urban Growth, 1500–1800* (Woodbridge, 1974), 76–103.

33. Dickinson, *Lordship of Man*, 78–92, 279–80, 299, 303, 315.

34. Joan Thirsk, 'The Fantastical Folly of Fashion: The English Stocking Knitting Industry, 1500–1700', in N. B. Harte and Kenneth G. Pointing (eds), *Textile History and*

Economic History (Manchester, 1973), 52; Hocart, *Country People of Guernsey and their Agriculture,* 59–68.

35. F. Wearis, *News from the Channel, or The Discovery and Perfect Description of the Isle of Serke* (1673), 6.
36. 'Journal of Charles Trumbull', 580; *Channel Island Journals of Charles and William Trumbull,* 16.
37. Heylyn, *Full Relation of Two Journeys,* 299; 'Journal of Charles Trumbull', 571; *Channel Island Journals of Charles and William Trumbull,* 14; Thirsk, 'Fantastical Folly of Fashion', 55–8; T. F. Priaulx, 'The Guernsey Stocking Export Trade in the Seventeenth Century', *Report and Transactions. Société Guernesiase,* 17 (1961), 210–22.
38. Speed, *Theatre of the Empire of Great Britaine,* 94.
39. PC 2/31, fo. 297.
40. Ferdinand Brock Tupper, *The Chronicles of Castle Cornet, Guernsey* (1851), 321.
41. SP 16/497, fo. 221.
42. Parliamentary Archives, BRY/45B/51.
43. SP 25/29, fo. 75; SP 25/30, fo. 53.
44. Bod., MS Clarendon 28/2320, 23121, 2359; S. Elliott Hoskins, *Charles the Second in the Channel Islands,* 2 vols (1854), ii. 73–4.
45. 'Lettres Inédités du Roi Charles II', *Société Jersiaise Bulletin Annuel,* 3 (1890–5), 6.
46. SP 18/73, fo. 165; SP 25/75, fo. 537.
47. J. C. Appleby, 'Neutrality, Trade and Privateering 1500–1689', in A. G. Jamieson (ed.), *A People of the Sea: The Maritime History of the Channel Islands* (London and New York, 1986), 72.
48. SP 29/16, fo. 6.
49. SP 44/3, fo. 73; Parliamentary Archives, HL/PO/JO/10/1/302; *Statutes of the Realm,* 12 Car II, c. 32; 14 Car II, c. 18.
50. SP 29/152, fo. 87; SP 44/23, fo. 71; SP 44/46, fo. 197.
51. Thirsk, 'Fantastical Folly of Fashion', 67.
52. SP 29/450, fo. 56.
53. BL, Add. MS 72,608, fo. 4ᵛ; BL, Add. MS 29,557, fos 197, 199; Hocart, *Country People of Guernsey and their Agriculture,* 14.
54. *Channel Island Journals of Charles and William Trumbull,* 17, 32.
55. *Ile de Jersey. Ordres du Conseil et Pièces Analogues Enregistrés a Jersey. Vol. 2. 1678–1724* (St Helier, 1898), 21.
56. SP 44/55, fo. 124.
57. SP 47/1, fo. 124.
58. SP 32/3, fo. 260.
59. Poingdestre, *Caesarea, Or a Discourse of the Island of Jersey,* 5, 51; David le Feuvre, *Jersey: Not Quite British. The Rural History of a Singular People* (St Helier, 1994), 83–91.
60. SP 47/1, fo. 82.
61. Dumaresq, 'Survey of ye Island of Jersey', 418–19.
62. *Calendar of Treasury Books, 1685–1689,* ed. William A. Shaw (1923), 1449.
63. HMC, *Report on the Manuscripts of the Marquis of Downshire,* 3 vols (1924–40), i. 685.
64. HMC, *Downshire,* i. 745–6.

65. Hocart, *Country People of Guernsey and their Agriculture*, 151, 242.
66. Morieux, *Channel*, 18.
67. Henry Parker, *Of a Free Trade. A Discourse* (1648), 1.
68. *Calendar of Treasury Books, 1672–1675*, ed. William A. Shaw (1909), 335; *Calendar of Treasury Books, 1676–1679*, ed. William A. Shaw (1911), 647–8, 1376; *Calendar of Treasury Books, 1685–1689*, 1035.
69. SP 12/122, fo. 37; SP 16/520, fo. 43; Davies Gilbert, *The Parochial History of Cornwall*, 4 vols (1838), vol. 4, 173–75.
70. Earl of Torrington to Earl of Nottingham, 14 June 1690, HMC, *Report on the Manuscripts of Allan George Finch*, 2 vols (1913–22), ii. 296.
71. SP 16/281, fos 168, 170.
72. *Calendar of Treasury Papers 1556/7–1696*, ed. Joseph Redington (1868), 33, 78.
73. Harrison, 'Description of Britaine', 36.
74. 'The Diary of Bulkeley of Dronwey, Anglesey, 1630–1638', ed. Hugh Owen (*Anglesey Antiquarian Society and Field Club Transactions*, 1936), 28, 33, 35. See also *Calendar of Wynn (of Gwydir) Papers 1515–1690* (Aberystwyth, 1926), 209, 225 for consumption of wine and Malmsey.
75. Bod., MS Rawlinson D 977, fo. 42^v; Chaloner, 'Description of the Isle of Man', second pagination, 2–3, 30; Sacheverell, *Account of the Isle of Man*, sig B^v; Dickinson, *Lordship of Man*, 221–42; C. W. Gawne, *The Isle of Man and Britain Controversy 1651–1895: From Smuggling to the Common Purse* (Douglas, 2009), 13–20.
76. *Calendar of Treasury Books, 1685–1689*, 985.
77. SP 16/526, fo. 18.
78. 'A Jerseyman in New England', *Société Jersiaise Bulletin Annuel*, 13 (1936–9), 399–404.
79. *Ile de Jersey. Ordres du Conseil… 1678–1724*, 20. See also Patience Ward et al., *A Scheme of the Trade, as it is at Present Carried on Between England and France* (1674), which tabulates exports and imports through customs houses at London and Dover.
80. *Channel Island Journals of Charles and William Trumbull*, 14,
81. Poingdestre, *Caesarea, Or a Discourse of the Island of Jersey*, 50–1.
82. *Ile de Jersey. Ordres du Conseil et Pièces Analogues Enregistrés a Jersey. Vol. 1. 1536–1678* (St Helier, 1897), 406–11.
83. *Ile de Jersey. Ordres du Conseil… 1678–1724*, 19, 23–4, 29–34, 90.
84. HMC, *Finch*, ii. 421–2; Appleby, 'Neutrality, Trade and Privateering', 59–105.
85. *CSPD Addenda 1625–49*, 264; SP 29/445, fos 48, 49; Appleby, 'Neutrality, Trade and Privateering', 72–3.
86. SP 29/450, fo. 11; *Ile de Jersey. Ordres du Conseil… 1678–1724*, 178.
87. SP 47/1, fo. 71.
88. Bod., MS Clarendon 82, fo. 233.
89. *Ile de Jersey. Ordres du Conseil… 1678–1724*, 20.
90. Edward Carson, *The Ancient and Rightful Customs: A Brief History of the English Customs Service* (1972), 43–45.
91. *Ile de Jersey. Ordres du Conseil… 1678–1724*, 143, 148; *Calendar of Treasury Books, 1685–1689*, 1638.

92. Morieux, *Channel*, 255. See also Robert C. Nash, 'The English and Scottish Tobacco Trades in the Seventeenth and Eighteenth Centuries: Legal and Illicit Trade', *Economic History Review*, NS 35 (1982), 354–72; Paul Monod, 'Dangerous Merchandize: Smuggling, Jacobitism, and Commercial Culture in Southeast England, 1690–1760', *Journal of British Studies*, 30 (1991), 150–87; Richard Platt, *Smuggling in the British Isles: A History* (Stroud, 2007); Gavin Daly, 'English Smugglers, the Channel, and the Napoleonic Wars, 18001814', *Journal of British Studies*, 46 (2007), 30–46.

93. Duncan, *History of Guernsey*, 232; Christian Fleury and Henry Johnson, 'The Minquiers and Écréhous in Spatial Context: Contemporary Issues and Cross Perspectives on Border Islands, Reefs, and Rocks', *Island Studies Journal*, 10 (2015), 163–80.

94. Bod., MS Carte 68, fo. 330^{v}.

95. Bod., MS Clarendon 92, fos 238–45, MS Carte 68, fos 330–330^{v}; *Calendar of Treasury Papers 1556/7–1696*, 189–90; *Calendar of Treasury Books, 1689–1692*, ed. William A. Shaw (1931), 1961; Nash, 'English and Scottish Tobacco Trades', 361.

96. Denton, *Perambulation*, 498.

97. Platt, *Smuggling in the British Isles*; W. A. Cole, 'Trends in Eighteenth-Century Smuggling', *Economic History Review*, NS 10 (1958), 395–10; Rupert C. Jarvis, 'Illicit Trade with the Isle of Man 1671–1765', *Transactions of the Lancashire and Cheshire Antiquarian Society*, 58 (1945–6), 245–67; Gawne, *The Isle of Man and Britain Controversy*, 17–35.

98. Richard Carew, *The Survey of Cornwall* (1602), 151.

99. John Leland, *The Itinerary of John Leland the Antiquary*, 9 vols (Oxford, 1769), iii. 19.

100. [De Selve]. *Correspondence politique de Odet de Selve Ambassadeur de France en Angleterre (1546–1549)* (Paris, 1888), 130, 135.

101. HMC, *Calendar of the Manuscripts of . . . the Marquis of Salisbury*, 24 vols (1883–1976), i. 299.

102. SP15/13, fo. 90; Huntington Library, MS HM 72020, fos 352–61; Duncan, *History of Guernsey*, 44–6; Tupper, *Chronicles of Castle Cornet*, 29–30.

103. BL, MS. Lansdowne 33, fos 185–6.

104. SP 15/43/90; PC 2/31, fo. 357; Clive Senior, *A Nation of Pirates: English Piracy in its Heyday* (Newton Abbot, 1976); John C. Appleby, 'Jacobean Piracy: English Maritime Depredation in Transition, 1603-1625', in Cheryl A. Fury (ed.), *The Social History of English Seamen, 1485–1659* (2012), 277–300.

105. Cecil Papers, vol. 125, fo. 14; vol. 195, fo. 224.

106. Appleby, 'Jacobean Piracy', 289, 295; *CSPD 1611–18*, 55. For Salkeld, see Chapter 2.

107. PC 2/31, fo. 359; SP 15/43/65.

108. PC 2/33, fo. 59.

109. PC 2/33 fo. 59; SP 14/171, fo. 101; SP 16/3, fo. 8; SP 16/5, fos 109, 143.

110. Anthony Ersfield to Sir John Coke, 12 June 1625, HMC, *Cowper*, i. 203; SP 16/27, fo. 58.

111. *Proceedings in Parliament 1625*, ed. Maija Jansson and William B. Bidwell (New Haven and London, 1987), 724.

112. SP 16/74, fo. 148.

113. SP 16/523, fo. 51; PC 2/33, fo. 126.

114. SP 16/98, fo. 116^v; SP 16/101, fo. 72; SP 16/104, fo. 29; SP 16/528, fos 96, 159, 159; SP 16/529, fo. 190; PC 2/28, fos 61, 63. Carteret is still 'de Carteret" in some of these records.

115. *Calendar of State Papers... Venice, 1628–9*, 49.

116. SP 16/142, fos 87–87^v.

117. SP 16/169, fo. 117.

118. SP 16/162, fo. 39; SP 16/218. fo. 170; SP 16/531, fos 26, 61, 68, 69.

119. 'Notebooks of Elie Brevint', 182, 242.

120. SP 16/534, fos 45–45^v.

121. SP 16/196, fo. 2; SP 63/254, fo. 136.

122. J. R. Dickinson, 'The Earl of Derby and the Isle of Man, 1643–1651', *Transactions of the Historic Society of Lancashire and Cheshire*, 141 (1991–2), 43.

123. *A Calendar of Material Relating to Ireland from the High Court of Admiralty Examinations 1536–1641*, ed. J. C. Appleby (Dublin, 1992), 226.

124. SP 16/182, fo. 33; SP 16/193, fo. 35.

125. SP 16/266, fo. 5; John Taylor, *John Taylors Wandering, to see the Wonders of the West* (1649); Mary Coate, *Cornwall in the Great Civil War and Interregnum 1642–1660* (Oxford, 1933; 2nd edn, Truro, 1963), 253.

126. *Commons Journal*, v. 130.

127. SP 25/94, fos 115, 521; SP 25/87, fo. 101; SP 25/63/2, fo. 179.

128. *A Collection of the State Papers of John Thurloe*, ed. Thomas Birch, 7 vols (1742), iii. 637.

129. 'The Hartlib Papers', 55/14/1/1A, https://www.dhi.ac.uk/hartlib/view?shelf=55% 2F14%2F1 (accessed August 2019).

130. Bod., MS Rawlinson D 1481, fo. 365.

131. *Collection of the State Papers of John Thurloe*, ii. 288.

132. SP 18/8/126, fo. 199; SP 18/147, fo. 42; SP 47/1, fo. 118.

133. HMC, *Report on the Manuscripts of F. W. Leyborne-Popham* (1899), 78.

134. *The Entring Book of Roger Morrice 1677–1691*, ed. Mark Goldie et al., 6 vols (Woodbridge, 2007), iv. 96.

135. BL, MS Harley 1510, fos 575, 682; SP 47/1, fos 18, 40, 54, 63.

136. *CSPD 1675–6*, 467; SP 29/379, fo. 42.

137. SP 47/1, fos 63–4.

138. SP 47/1, fo. 133; HMC, *Downshire*, i. 468.

139. Ralph Davis, *The Rise of the English Shipping Industry in the Seventeenth and Eighteenth Centuries* (1962), 7, 10, 15; Richard W. Unger, 'The Tonnage of Europe's Merchant Fleet, 1300–1800', in Richard W. Unger (ed.), *Ships and Shipping in the North Sea and Atlantic, 1400–1800* (Aldershot and Brookfield, VT, 1997), 260–1.

140. William J. McCarthy, 'Gambling on Empire: The Economic Role of Shipwreck in the Age of Discovery', *International Journal of Maritime History*, 23 (2011), 69–84; Cathryn J. Pearce, *Cornish Wrecking, 1700–1860: Reality and Popular Myth* (Woodbridge, 2010), 20–1.

141. Sir Matthew Hale, 'Concerning the Prerogative and Franchise of Wreck', in Stuart A. Moore, *A History of the Foreshore and the Law Relating Thereto*, 3rd edn (1888),

408; Laurent Carey, *Essai sur les institutions, lois et coûtumes de l'Ile de Guernesey* (St Peter Port, 1889), 99–102; Rose Melikan, 'Shippers, Salvors, and Sovereigns: Competing Interests in the Medieval Law of Shipwreck', *Journal of Legal History*, 11 (1990), 174; Sir Graham Dorey, 'Rights to Wreck in Norman Customary Law', *Guernsey Law Journal*, 15 (1993), 63–6; John Kelleher, 'The Mysterious Case of the Ship Abandoned off Sark in 1608: The Customary Law Relating to *choses gaives*', in Gordon Dawes (ed.), *Commise 1204: Studies in the History and Law of Continental and Insular Normandy* (St Peter Port, 2005), 171–90.

142. 3 Edward I (1275), *Statutes of the Realm*, ed. T. E. Tomlins et al., 11 vols (1810–28), i. 28.

143. *Statutes of the Realm*, 27 Edward III stat. 2, c. 13.

144. Thomas Fuller, *The Historie of the Holy Warre* (1639), 120; John Rastell, *The Exposicions of the Termes of the Lawes of England* (1563), fos 115ᵛ–116; John Cowell and Thomas Manley, *The Interpreter of Words and Terms, Used either in the Common Statute Laws of this Realm* (1701), sub 'Wrecke'; William Blackstone, *Commentaries on the Laws of England*, 11th edn, 4 vols (1791), i. 291–4, iii. 106; Hale, 'Concerning the Prerogative and Franchise of Wreck', 406–9; John Talbot, 'Observations Touching the King's Prerogative to Wreck of Sea', in Moore, *History of the Foreshore*, 243–7. Modern studies include John Rule, 'Wrecking and Coastal Plunder', in Douglas Hay, Peter Linebaugh, John Rule, et al. (eds), *Albion's Fatal Tree: Crime and Society in Eighteenth-Century England* (1975), 167–88; Melikan, 'Shippers, Salvors, and Sovereigns', 163–82; George F. Steckley, 'The Seventeenth-Century Origins of Modern Salvage Law', *Journal of Legal History*, 35 (2014), 209–30; Tom Johnson, 'Medieval Law and Materiality: Shipwrecks, Finders, and Property on the Suffolk Coast, ca. 1380–1410', *American Historical Review*, 120 (2015), 407–32.

145. *Select Pleas in the Court of Admiralty, Vol. II*, ed. Reginald G. Marsden, Selden Society, 11 (1897), xxxiv; Huntington Library, MS EL 1904, fos 37ᵛ, 63.

146. SP 15/42/17, 22; *Samuel Pepys's Naval Minutes*, ed. J. R. Tanner, Navy Records Society, 60 (1926), 437; 'Seigneurial Rights of Wreckage Disputed', *Société Jersiaise Bulletin Annuel*, 11 (1928–31), 417–18.

147. Jersey Archives, D/AL/A/1/2, 5.

148. SP 25/112, fo. 11; Steckley, 'Seventeenth-Century Origins of Modern Salvage Law', 20, 224.

149. SP 29/182, fo. 142; *Ile de Jersey. Ordres du Conseil ... 1536–1678*, 314–16, 331–6, 359–61; BL, Add. MS 29,552, fos 430–6, 465

150. BL, Add. MS 29,552, fo. 54,

151. William Blundell, *A History of the Isle of Man*, ed. William Harrison, 2 vols (Manx Society, Douglas, 1876–7), ii. 74;'Deemster John Parr's Abstract of Manx Laws', Dedication to Governor Heywood, 2, transcribed by Peter Edge from Manx Museum MS 03176C, section 101, <https://radar.brokes/ac.uk/radar/items/a1e352c0-f1ed-45a0-b7d5-3434669ed078/1> (accessed April 2019); Barry Coward, *The Stanleys. Lords Stanley and Earls of Derby 1385–1672: The Origins, Wealth and Power of a Landowning Family*, Chetham Society, 3rd ser., 30 (Manchester, 1983), 60.

152. APC 1619–1621, 96; SP 84/162, fo. 221,

153. 'Diary of Bulkeley of Dronwey', 54.

154. SP 16/311, fo. 41; SP 16/364, fo. 105.

155. SP 16/244, fo. 36.

156. BL, Add MS 46,501l, fos 221–2; SP 16/303, fo. 268; SP 16/305, fo. 221; SP 16/349, fo. 38; SP 16/350, fo. 22; SP 16/364, fos 57, 75; *High Court of Admiralty Examinations (MS Volume 53) 1637–1638*, ed. Dorothy O. Shilton and Richard Holworthy (New York and London, 1932), 124–5.

157. SP 16/311, fo. 41; SP 16/364, fo. 105.

158. HCA 13/71, fos 246ᵛ–247ᵛ, in *A Calendar of Material Relating to Ireland from the High Court of Admiralty 1641–1660*, ed. Elaine Murphy (Dublin, 2011), 144.

159. SP 29/332, fo. 129; SP 29/362, fo. 334; SP 44/68, fo. 197.

160. Bod., MS Jones 27*, fo. 17.

161. SP 12/122, fo. 37; Juliet du Boulay, 'Wrecks in the Isles of Scilly', *Mariner's Mirror*, 46 (1960), 89; G. Forrester Matthews, *The Isles of Scilly: A Constitutional, Economic and Social Survey of the Development of an Island People from Early Times to 1900* (1960), 239.

162. *Samuel Pepys's Naval Minutes*, 202, 221, 367; Matthews, *Isles of Scilly*, 8, 24; SP 44/164, fo. 347.

163. *Calendar of Treasury Books, 1685–1689*, 544; *Calendar of Treasury Books, 1689–1692*, 835; 'Parliamentary Survey of the Duchy of Cornwall, part II', 148.

164. *High Court of Admiralty Examinations*, 4.

165. Heath, *A Natural and Historical Account of the Islands of Scilly*, 86; John Troutbeck, *A Survey of the Ancient and Present State of the Scilly Islands* (1794), 31; Du Boulay, 'Wrecks in the Isles of Scilly', 92–4.

166. 'The Travels of Cosmo III, Grand Duke of Tuscany, through England', in Alan Gibson and R. Pearse Chope (eds), *Early Tours in Devon and Cornwall* (Newton Abbot, 1967), 93; Richard Larn, *Cornish Shipwrecks. Volume 3, The Isles of Scilly* (New York, 1971).

167. SP 29/225, fo. 159. More Scilly shipwrecks are related in SP 29/359, fo. 106; Bod., MS Rawlinson A 195, fos 180–180ᵛ; *Diary of The Samuel* Pepys, ed. Robert Latham and William Matthews, 11 vols (Berkeley and Los Angeles, 1970–83), vi. 3; Dutch East India Company Shipping 1595–1795, www.resources.huygens.knaw.nl/das/detailVoyage/92573 (accessed November 2018); and Todd Stevens, 'Wreck of the *Princess (Prinses) Maria*, Scilly, 1686'; http://scillypedia.co.uk/WreckPrinsesMaria.htm (accessed November 2018).

168. Daniel Defoe, *A Tour thro' the Whole Island of Great Britain* [1724–6], 2 vols (1968), ii. 245.

169. Abel Boyer, *The History of the Reign of Queen Anne... Year the Sixth* (1708), 241–2; Huntington Library, MS JR 3 (Sir Cloudesely Shovel Papers); James Herbert Cooke, *The Shipwreck of Sir Cloudesley Shovell, on the Scilly Island in 1707* (Society of Antiquaries, 1883); J. G. Pickwell, 'Improbable Legends Surrounding the Shipwreck of Sir Clowdisley Shovell', *Mariners Mirror*, 59 (1973), 221–3; Simon Harris, *Sir Cloudesley Shovell: Stuart Admiral* (Staplehurst, 2001), 333–58; Richard Larn (ed.), *'Poor England has lost so many men': The Loss of Queen Anne's Man o' War Association* (St Mary's, Isles of Scilly, 2006), 21–3.

Chapter 6

1. The huge bibliography on the early modern English church may be sampled in Patrick Collinson, *The Religion of Protestants: The Church in English Society 1559–1625*

(Oxford, 1992); David Cressy, 'Conflict, Consensus and the Willingness to Wink: The Erosion of Community in Charles I's England', *Huntington Library Quarterly*, 6 (2000), 131–49; John Spurr, *The Restoration Church of England, 1646–1689* (New Haven and London, 1991); Grant Tapsell (ed.), *The Later Stuart Church, 1660–1714* (Manchester, 2012).

2. William Harrison, 'Description of Britaine', in Raphael Holinshed, *The First and Second Volumes of Chronicles* (1587), 31. The 1577 edition of Holinshed mistakenly linked the Isle of Wight to the Diocese of Chichester.

3. Richard Worsley, *The History of the Isle of Wight* (1781), 8–9, appendix 6. John Speed, *The Theatre of the Empire of Great Britaine* (1632), 15.

4. Worsley, *History of the Isle of Wight*, 110; *Commons Journal*, ii. 142–3, 155, 173; *Commons Journal*, iv. 30–1.

5. *Proceedings in the Opening Session of the Long Parliament*, ed. Maija Jansson, 7 vols (Rochester, NY, 2000–7), vi. 215; *The Orders for Ecclesiasticall Discipline According to that which Hath Been Practiced since the Reformation of the Church in ... the Iles of Garnsey, Gersey, Spark, and Alderny* (1642).

6. *Commons Journal*, iii. 536; A. G. Matthews, *Walker Revised* (Oxford, 1948, 1988 edn), 180–9.

7. Parliamentary Archives, HL/PO/JO/10/1/232.

8. Parliamentary Archives, HL/PO/JO/10/1/237.

9. Robert Dingley, *The Deputation of Angels* (1653), epistle dedicatory.

10. Daniel Baker, *With the Light is Fifteen Priests of the Isle of Wight Reproved* (1658). See also Joseph Besse, *A Collection of the Sufferings of the People called Quakers*, 2 vols (1753), i. 228–30.

11. Percy Goddard Stone, *The Architectural Antiquities of the Isle of Wight From the XIth to the XVIIIth Centuries* (1891), pt 2, 20.

12. Andrew M. Coleby, *Central Government and the Localities: Hampshire 1649–1689* (Cambridge, 1987), 147.

13. Coleby, *Central Government and the Localities*, 139.

14. SP 29/82, fo. 97; SP 29/83, fo. 62; SP 29/331, fos 76, 78, 130, 204; Coleby, *Central Government and the Localities*, 133, 137.

15. *Psallmyr neu Psalmae' Dauid* (1567); *Y Beibl Cyssegr-lan. Sef yr Hen Destament, a'r Newydd* (1588); *Llyfr gweddi gyffredin, a gwenidogaeth y sacramentau, ac eraill gynneddfau a ceremoniau yn Eglwys Loegrl* (1599);
David A. Pretty, *Anglesey: The Concise History* (Cardiff, 2005), 44, 56.

16. Pretty, *Anglesey: The Concise History*, 39, 46, 50, 52; Robin Grove-White, 'Hugh Hughes and Late Sixteenth-Century Anglesey', *Transactions of the Anglesey Antiquarian Society and Field Club* (2013), 35–50; Thomas Richards, 'The Puritan Movement in Anglesey: A Re-Assessment', *Transactions of the Anglesey Antiquarian Society and Field Club* (1954), 34–58, quotes at 34, 36; Sarah Ward Clavier, '"Horrid Rebellion" and "Holie Cheate": Royalist Gentry Responses to Interregnum Government in North-East Wales, 1646–1660', *Welsh Historical Review*, 29 (2018), 51–72; Anglesey Declaration, 14 July 1648, in Richard Llwyd, *The Poetical Works of Richard Llwyd, The Bard of Snowden* (1837), 60–1. See also Christopher Hill, 'Puritans and "The Dark Corners of the Land"', *Transactions of the Royal Historical Society*, 5th

ser., 13 (1963), 77–102; Daniel MacCannell, '"Dark Corners of the Land"? A New Approach to Regional Factors in the Civil Wars of England and Wales', *Cultural and Social History*, 7 (2010), 171–89.

17. SP 16/493, fo. 104; John Troutbeck, *A Survey of the Ancient and Present State of the Scilly Islands* (1794), 175–7.

18. HMC, *Report on Franciscan Manuscripts* (1906), 220–21.

19. *Lords Journal*, ix. 91.

20. *Joyful Newes for England* (1648), 5–6; *A Great Victory Obtained by the Kings Forces in the West of England at the Island of Silley* (1648), 2–3.

21. Bod., MS Tanner 57, fo. 324. Cf. Ann Hughes, *Gangraena and the Struggle for the English Revolution* (Oxford, 2004).

22. *A Letter Intercepted (at Sea) by Captaine Moulton . . . Written from Parson Wolby* (1649), 2, 5. Wolley was in France by the end of 1649, but returned to England as a schoolmaster in the 1660s. He received preferments after the Restoration and ended his life as an Irish bishop.

23. Christopher Salter, *Sal Scylla: Or, A Letter Written from Scilly to Mr John Goodwin, Minister of the Gospel in London* (1653), 5–7.

24. 'The Travels of Cosmo III, Grand Duke of Tuscany, through England', in Alan Gibson and R. Pearse Chope (eds), *Early Tours in Devon and Cornwall* (Newton Abbot, 1967), 95; Troutbeck, *Survey of the Ancient and Present State of the Scilly Islands*, 21, 61, 64, 173; G. Forrester Matthews, *The Isles of Scilly: A Constitutional, Economic and Social Survey of the Development of an Island People from Early Times to 1900* (1960), 77.

25. Nicholas Phillips, *The Holy Choice: Or, Faith's Triumph over all Worldly Pomp and Glory* (1679).

26. Troutbeck, *Survey of the Ancient and Present State of the Scilly Islands*, 175.

27. Bob Tennant, 'Managing Overseas Missions: The SPCK in the Scilly Isles, 1796-1819', in Brett C. McInelly and Paul E. Kerry (eds), *New Approaches to Religion and the Enlightenment* (Madison, PA, and Vancouver, 2018), 345–64; Cambridge University Library, SPCK MSS.

28. William Sacheverell, *An Account of the Isle of Man* (1702), 2, 104.

29. SP 16/265, fo. 89.

30. Harrison, 'Description of Britaine', 38; Anne Ashley, 'The Spiritual Courts of the Isle of Man, Especially in the Seventeenth and Eighteenth Centuries', *English Historical Review*, 72 (1957), 35–6; J. R. Dickinson, 'The Earl of Derby and the Isle of Man, 1643-1651', *Transactions of the Historic Society of Lancashire and Cheshire*, 141 (1991–2), 59.

31. Guy Miege, *The New State of England under Their Majesties K. William and Q. Mary* (1691), 53; Peter W. Edge and C. C. Augur Pearce, 'The Development of the Lord Bishop's Role in the Manx Tynwald', *Journal of Ecclesiastical History*, 57 (2006), 494–14.

32. SP 14/55/1; Sacheverell, *Account of the Isle of Man*, 117.

33. SP 16/265, fo. 89; Ashley, 'Spiritual Courts of the Isle of Man', 38.

34. Harrison, 'Description of Britaine', 37–8.

35. James Sharpe, 'Witchcraft in the Early Modern Isle of Man', *Cultural and Social History*, 4 (2007), 11–28.

36. SP 18/33, fo. 17; A. W. Moore, *A History of the Isle Man*, 2 vols (1900), i. 356–69.
37. John Callow, '"In so Shifting a Scene": Thomas Fairfax as Lord of the Isle of Man, 1651–60', in Andrew Hopper and Philip Major (eds), *England's Fortress: New Perspectives on Thomas, 3rd Lord Fairfax* (Farnham and Burlington, VT, 2014), 37, 39–40, 51; Philip Major, 'Thomas Fairfax, Lord of Man', *Notes and Queries*, 54/1 (2007), 45.
38. Callow, '"In so Shifting a Scene"', 46–8; John Callow, 'The Limits of Indemnity: The Earl of Derby, Sovereignty and Retribution at the Trial of William Christian, 1660–63', *Seventeenth Century*, 15 (2013), 206.
39. SP 29/372, fo. 124; *Calendar of Treasury Books, 1660–1667*, ed. William A. Shaw (1904), 211; *Calendar of Treasury Books, 1672–1675*, ed. William A. Shaw (1909), 721.
40. SP 29/225, fo. 323; SP 29/239, fo. 81; Sara Goodwins, *A Brief History of the Isle of Man* (Sutton, 2011), 83.
41. Thomas Denton, *A Perambulation of Cumberland 1687–1688 Including . . . the Isle of Man*, Surtees Society, 207 (2003), 497–8.
42. Sacheverell, *Account of the Isle of Man*, sig. B2, 122.
43. S. Elliott Hoskins, *Charles the Second in the Channel Islands*, 2 vols (1854), i. 24.
44. *Le Livre des prieres communes, de l'administration des sacremens et autres ceremonies en l'eglise d'Angleterre* (1553); BL, MS Lansdowne 116, fo. 59.
45. BL, MS Harley 260, fo. 103^v.
46. SP 44/6, fo. 49; *Instruction que l'on doit faire lire et apprendre aux enfants . . . en l'Isle de Iersey* (St Helier?, 1649); John Durel (trans.), *La Liturgie. C'est à dire, le formulaire des prieres publiques, de l'administration des sacramens; et des autres ceremonies & coûtumes de l'eglise, selon l'usage de l'eglise anglicane* (1667).
47. Jonathan Duncan, *The History of Guernsey; with Occasional Notices of Jersey, Alderney, and Sark* (1841), 423; Tim Thornton, *The Channel Islands, 1370–1640: Between England and Normandy* (Woodbridge, 2012); 57; Darryl Ogier, *The Government and Law of Guernsey* (St Peter Port, 2005), 11–12.
48. *Visitation Articles and Injunctions . . . Vol. 3 (1559–1575)*, eds. W. H. Frere and W. P. M. Kennedy, (1910), 219–22.
49. A. J. Eagleston, *The Channel Islands under Tudor Government, 1485–1642* (Cambridge, 1949); 38–43, 55, 56, 58; HMC, *Report on the Pepys Manuscripts* (1911), 80.
50. *The Zurich Letters (Second Series)*, ed. Hastings Robinson, Parker Society, 51 (Cambridge, 1845), 264–68.
51. John Foxe, *Actes and Monuments of Matters Most Speciall and Memorable* (1583), 1943–49; Peter Heylyn, *A Full Relation of Two Journeys: The One into the Main-Land of France. The Other into some of the Adjacent Islands* (1656), 323; Eagleston, *Channel Islands under Tudor Government*, 36–7; D. M. Ogier, *Reformation and Society in Guernsey* (Woodbridge, 1996), 55–61.
52. Ogier, *Reformation and Society in Guernsey*, 67–68.
53. Eagleston, *Channel Islands under Tudor Government*, 38–43, 55; HMC, *Pepys*, 80.
54. SP 15/13, fo. 228.
55. *Recueil D'Ordonnances de la Cour Royale de l'Isle de Guernsey . . . 1533–1800*, ed. Robert MacCulloch (St Peter Port, 1852), 19, 24, 28, 40, 52.
56. Ogier, *Reformation and Society in Guernsey*, 88.
57. Thornton, *Channel Islands*, 113.

58. Huntington Library, MS EL1897, 'Ecclesiasticall Discipline...of the Isles of Guerneze, Jerze, Serch and Alderny'; Ferdinand de Schickler, *Les Églises du refuge en Angleterre*, 3 vols (Paris, 1892), iii. 311–55; Heylyn, *Full Relation of Two Journeys*, 335, 338–63; A. J. Eagleston, 'Guernsey under Sir Thomas Leighton (1570–1610)', *Report and Transactions of the Société Guernesiase*, 13 (1937–45), 74.

59. Duncan, *History of Guernsey*, 42.

60. Huntington Library, MS EL 1897; Patrick Collinson, *The Elizabethan Puritan Movement* (1967), 408–15, 441; Ogier, *Reformation and Society in Guernsey*, 89.

61. BL, MS Lansdowne 116, fos 59^v–60.

62. Lucy Hutchinson, *Memoirs of the Life of Colonel Hutchinson*, ed. Julius Hutchinson and C. H. Firth (1906), 9.

63. Darryl Ogier, 'Night Revels and Werewolfery in Calvinist Guernsey', *Folklore*, 109 (1998), 53–62.

64. 'Notebooks of Elie Brevint,' http://societe-jersiaise.org/digital-publications/brevint?file=../bulletin-pdfs/Brevint (accessed June 2018).

65. 'Notebooks of Elie Brevint'.

66. Heylyn, *Full Relation of Two Journeys*, epistle dedicatory, to the reader, sigs a3^v–a4, cv.

67. Heylyn, *Full Relation of Two Journeys*, sig. cv, 'to the reader', 334–5, 415; Anthony Milton, *Laudian and Royalist Polemic in Seventeenth-Century England: The Career and Writings of Peter Heylyn* (Manchester, 2007), 23–25.

68. Margo Todd, *The Culture of Protestantism in Early Modern Scotland* (New Haven and London, 2002).

69. Heylyn, *Full Relation of Two Journeys*, 339, 362; 'Notebooks of Elie Brevint', 442.

70. Cambridge University Library, MS Dd. XI 43; S. W. Bisson, 'The Minute Book of the Jersey Colloquy, 1577–1614', *Société Jersiaise Bulletin Annuel*, 22 (1979), 310–17; Eagleston, *Channel Islands under Tudor Government*, 59–60; Priaulx Library, Guernsey, MS *Papier ou livre des Colloques des Eglises de Guernezy* (1585–1619), cited in Ogier, 'Night Revels', 60 and *passim*.

71. Eagleston, *Channel Islands under Tudor Government*, 57; Ogier, *Reformation and Society in Guernsey*, 81.

72. PC 2/27, fo. 92; Heylyn, *Full Relation of Two Journeys*, 378–80; 'A Briefe State of Guernsey by the Right Honourable Christopher Lord Hatton', Bod., MS Eng. Hist. b.134, fo. 4; Thornton, *Channel Islands*, 138; Ogier, *Reformation and Society in Guernsey*, 92–3; Eagleston, *Channel Islands under Tudor Government*, 128.

73. Cambridge University Library, MS Dd. XI 43, fo. 156^v.

74. PC 2/27, fos 93–5, 167; BL, MS Lansdowne 116, fos 60–60^v; Eagleston, *Channel Islands under Tudor Government*, 129–31; Ogier, *Reformation and Society in Guernsey*, 92–3.

75. PC 2/27, fos 92–5; *Actes des États de L'Île de Guernsey.1605 à 1651* (St Peter Port, 1851), 35–6; Philip Falle, *An Account of the Isle of Jersey*, with notes by Edward Durell (St Helier, 1837), 246; Eagleston, *Channel Islands under Tudor Government*, 131–2; Ogier, *Reformation and Society in Guernsey*, 92.

76. SP 14/90, fo. 210; SP 15/41, fos 8, 91, 208, 212; SP 16/526, fo. 18.

77. SP 15/41, fos 212, 216; PC 2/30, fo. 525; Eagleston, *Channel Islands under Tudor Government*, 136–8.

78. Heylyn, *Full Relation of Two Journeys*, 399–401; Greffe, St Peter Port, Métevier Collection, no. 11; Hoskins, *Charles the Second in the Channel Islands*, i. 30.

79. Falle, *Account of the Island of Jersey*, 251–4.

80. Heylyn, *Full Relation of Two Journeys*, 390–410; Jean Poingdestre, *Caesarea, Or a Discourse of the Island of Jersey* [c.1682] (St Helier, 1889), 32; Eagleston, *Channel Islands under Tudor Government*, 138–9; Ogier, *Reformation and Society in Guernsey*, 93.

81. SP 15/43/15; 1623 canons in Falle, *Account of the Isle of Jersey*, 245–62.

82. Cambridge University Library, MS Dd. XI 43; Bisson, 'Minute Book of the Jersey Colloquy, 1577–1614', 310–17.

83. 'Jean de la Marche...The Diary', ed. W. Rolleston and T. W. M. de Guerir, *Report and Transactions Société Guernesiase*, 11 (1930–2), 204.

84. PC 2/31, fo. 53.

85. SP 16/524, fo. 81; SP 16/527, fos 12, 13; SP 16/529, fo. 188; SP 16/534, fos 14, 23.

86. SP 16/527, fo. 11.

87. SP 16/219, fo. 107; SP 16/296, fo. 145; SP 16/537, fo. 24; Falle, *Account of the Isle of Jersey*, 215. The fellowships were at Exeter, Jesus, and Pembroke colleges.

88. SP 16/536, fo. 101.

89. *Ile de Jersey: Ordres du Conseil et Pièces Analogues Enregistrés a Jersey. Vol. 1. 1536–1678* (St Helier, 1897), 181–6; Falle, *Account of the Island of Jersey*, 334–6.

90. *Journal de Jean Chevalier* (St Helier, 1914), 316–17.

91. HMC, *Calendar of the Manuscripts of...the Marquis of Salisbury*, 24 vols (1883–1976), xxi. 227; SP 15/41, fo. 208; Eagleston, *Channel Islands under Tudor Government*, 140.

92. *Recueil D'Ordonnances de la Cour Royale de l'Isle de Guernsey...1533–1800*, 81–6.

93. Eagleston, *Channel Islands under Tudor Government*, 141; Ogier, *Reformation and Society in Guernsey*, 92; Conrad Russell, *The Causes of the English Civil War* (Oxford, 1990), 51. Island born and Cambridge educated, Jean de la Marche (1585–1651) had theological training at the Huguenot University of Saumur and served as rector in a series of Guernsey parishes.

94. *Actes des États de L'Île de Guernsey. 1605 à 1651*, 44–5, 46, 48.

95. Heylyn, *Full Relation of Two Journeys*, 421.

96. *Actes des États de L'Île de Guernsey. 1605 à 1651*, 383; Jean de la Marche, *A Complaint of the False Prophets Mariners upon the Drying up of their Hierarchicall Euphrates* (1641), title page, sigs. a–a2ᵛ.

97. SP 16/536, fo. 101. See also Thornton, *Channel Islands*, 147; Ogier, *Reformation and Society in Guernsey*, 93.

98. SP 16/537, fo. 27–27ᵛ.

99. 'Notebooks of Elie Brevint', 447; 'Jean de la Marche...The Diary', 202–4.

100. *Proceedings in the Opening Session of the Long Parliament*, iv. 4, 413, vi. 624–5; de la Marche, *Complaint of the False Prophets Mariners*, sigs a, aᵛ; *The Orders for Ecclesiasticall Discipline...the Iles of Garnsey, Gersey, Spark, and Alderny*; Ogier, *Reformation and Society in Guernsey*, 96.

101. Parliamentary Archives, HL/PO/JO/10/1/123.

102. *Commons Journal*, iii. 332.

103. Greffe, Guernsey, Métevier Collection, no. 11, 1 December 1644; Ferdinand Brock Tupper, *The Chronicles of Castle Cornet, Guernsey* (1851), 94.

104. Thomas Edwards, *The Third Part of Gangraena. Or, A New and Higher Discovery of the Errors, Heresies, Blasphemies, and Insolent Proceedings of the Sectaries of These Times* (1646), 29–30, 40; 'Notebooks of Elie Brevint,' 411.

105. BL, Add. MS 34,262, fo. 20.

106. G. R. Balleine, *All for the King: The Story of Sir George Carteret* (St Helier, 1976), 89.

107. Bod., MS Clarendon 29/2378.

108. Parliamentary Archives, HL/PO/JO/10/1/230.

109. BL, Add. MS 29,554, fo. 62.

110. SP 16/490, fo. 18.

111. Balleine, *All for the King*, 66.

112. SP 16/497, fo. 221.

113. HMC, *Ninth Report* (1884), pt 1, 264–5, for an *agnus dei* brought in by Irish mariners.

114. Thomas Ashton, *Satan in Samuels Mantle, Or the Cruelty of Germany Acted in Jersey* (1659), 25.

115. BL, Add. MS 11,315, fo. 5.

116. Bod., MS Tanner 59, fo. 636^v; Lemprière to Lenthall, 2 February 1652, in Henry Cary (ed.), *Memorials of the Great Civil War in England from 1646 to 1652*, 2 vols (1842), ii. 411; 'Notebooks of Elie Brevint', 445.

117. BL, Add. MS 34,262, fos 44^v, 48^v.

118. R. G. Warton, 'St Ouen's Church', *Bulletin of the Société Jersiaise*, 7 (1914), 439.

119. Ashton, *Satan in Samuels Mantle*, title page, 3–32.

120. 'The Autobiography of Increase Mather', ed. M. G. Hall, *Proceedings of the American Antiquarian Society*, 71 (1962), 271–360, quotes from 283–5; E. F. Carey, 'Increase Mather: A Sidelight on Guernsey in the Seventeenth Century', *Société Guernesiase Transactions*, 9 (1923), 256–66.

121. SP 44/6, fo. 25.

122. Richard Hocart, *The Country People of Guernsey and their Agriculture, 1640–1840* (St Peter Port, 2016), 13.

123. Spurr, *Restoration Church of England*; Tapsell (ed.), *Later Stuart Church*.

124. *CSPD 1660–70 Addenda*, 661; SP 44/6, fo. 25; *Note-Book of Pierre le Roy*, ed. G. E. Lee (St Peter Port, 1893), 33; 'Autobiography of Increase Mather', 285.

125. BL, Add. MS 29,550, fos 14, 442, 447; SP 44/53, fo. 167; Bod., MS Clarendon 80, fo. 331^v–332; Huntington Library, MS HM 72020, fos 374–5; Duncan, *History of Guernsey*, 342–3.

126. 'A Briefe State of Guernsey by the Right Honourable Christopher Lord Hatton', Bod., MS Eng. Hist. b.134, fo.4.

127. Bod., MS Clarendon 82, fo. 123.

128. Bod., MS Clarendon 80, fos 329–30. Guernsey parish clergy still declined to wear the surplice in the early nineteenth century: Duncan, *History of Guernsey*, 350.

129. Bod., MS Clarendon 77, fo. 118.

130. Bod., MS Clarendon 77, fos 73–73^v, Clarendon 92, fo. 158^v.

131. *Note-Book of Pierre le Roy*, 33–4.

132. Bod., MS Clarendon 80, fos 330^v–331.

133. SP 29/448, fo. 110; Bod., MS Clarendon 80, fos 331–3.

134. Bod., MS Clarendon 80, fo. 332^{v}.

135. SP 29/270, fo. 37; Bod., MS Clarendon 81, fos 234–234^{v}.

136. Bod., MS Clarendon 82, fos 55^{v}, 57, 91, 119.

137. Bod., MS Rawlinson D 1481, fos 350–5.

138. Bod., MS Clarendon 82, fo. 251, MS Clarendon 81, fo. 3.

139. William Sheldon to Viscount Fitzharding, 31 December 1664, HMC, *Seventh Report* (1879), 260.

140. SP 29/449, fo. 117.

141. Bod., MS Rawlinson D 1481, fo. 356.

142. SP 44/17, fo. 122.

143. SP 44/6, fo. 49.

144. BL, Add. MS 29,553, fo. 299; Duncan, *History of Guernsey*, 344, 452.

145. 'The Journal of Charles Trumbull', ed. Richard Hocart, *La Société Guernesiaise Report and Transactions* (1985 for 1984), 579, 581; *The Channel Island Journals of Charles and William Trumbull 1677*, ed. Joan Stevens, Jean Arthur, and Collette Stevens (St Helier, 2004), 41

146. 'Journal of Charles Trumbull', 579, 581; *Channel Island Journals of Charles and William Trumbull*, 41.

147. BL, Add. MS 29,571, fo. 196.

148. Bod., MS Rawlinson D 1481, fo. 356.

149. BL, Add. MS 29,554, fos 7, 62, and fos 153–6 and 354–6 on nonconformist assemblies.

150. SP 47/1/50.

151. SP 44/47, fo. 47.

152. HMC, *First Report* (1870), 16.

153. SP 47/1, fo. 102; SP 44/43, fos 82, 87.

154. SP 29/397, fos 20, 101; SP 47/1, fos 103, 104.

155. 'Journal of Charles Trumbull', 578.

156. Duncan, *History of Guernsey*, 347.

157. *Actes des États de L'Île de Guernsey. Vol. II. 1651 à 1780* (St Peter Port, 1907), 66–106, quote at 86. See also the petition from the parishioners of Torteval, and letters from their minister Thomas Picot, objecting to the new canons: Lambeth Palace Library MS 929, nos 19, 22, 23, 27, 29, 33.

158. Thomas Dicey, *An Historical Account of Guernsey* (1798), 50–1.

159. SP 47/1, fo. 69.

160. BL, Add MS 72,608, fo. 7; *Channel Island Journals of Charles and William Trumbull*, 41.

161. Bod., MS Tanner 37, fo. 132.

162. SP 47/1, fo. 7.

163. 'Holograph Document' (Falle to Archbishop Tenison), *Société Jersiaise Bulletin Annuel*, 12 (1887), 192–3; Falle, *Account of the Isle of Jersey*, pp. xii–xiii, 221.

164. SP 47/1, fos 108, 118; HMC, *Report on the Manuscripts of the Marquis of Downshire*, 3 vols (1924–40), i. 217.

165. Falle, *Account of the Island of Jersey*, 87.

166. Bod., MS Tanner 38, fo. 20.

167. M. G. Smith, 'Bishop Trelawny and the Church in the Channel Islands 1680–1730', *Société Jersiaise Annual Bulletin*, 23 (1983), 320–30.

168. Bod., MS Rawlinson B 383, fos 672–5; PC 1/1/275; SP 44/350, fo. 383.

Chapter 7

1. Henry Jones, *Vectis. The Isle of Wight: A Poem in Three Cantos* (1766), 22; Baptista Boazio, *The True Description or Drafte of That Famous Ile of Wighte* (1591); Guy Miege, *The New State of England under Their Majesties K. William and Q. Mary* (1691), 97.

2. John Speed, *The Theatre of the Empire of Great Britaine* (1632), 94.

3. Slingsby Bethel, *The Interest of Princes and States* (1680), 1.

4. Sir Francis Godolphin to Robert Cecil, 17 May 1599, HMC, *Calendar of the Manuscripts of... the Marquis of Salisbury*, 24 vols (1883–1976), ix. 171.

5. SP 16/526, fos 2^v–3.

6. Robert Norton, *The Gunner: Shewing the Whole Practice of Artillerie* (1629), 51–3; Nathaniel Nye, *The Art of Gunnery* (1647), 71–8.

7. William Bourne, *The Arte of Shooting in Great Ordnaunce* (1587), 45–6, 62.

8. BL, MS Egerton 2812, fo. 6.

9. PC 2/31, fo. 145.

10. William Harrison, 'Description of Britaine', in Raphael Holinshed, *The First and Second Volumes of Chronicles* (1587), 33.

11. Jean Poingdestre, *Caesarea, Or a Discourse of the Island of Jersey* [c.1682] (St Helier, 1889), 84; Philip Falle, *An Account of the Island of Jersey*, with notes by Edward Durell (St Helier, 1837), 64; Jonathan Duncan, *The History of Guernsey; with Occasional Notices of Jersey, Alderney, and Sark* (1841), 38; Tim Thornton, *The Channel Islands 1370–1640: Between England and Normandy* (Woodbridge, 2012), 83–88.

12. SP 15/9/1, fos 51, 80.

13. HMC, *Salisbury*, i. 277.

14. *A Royalist's Notebook: The Commonplace Book of Sir John Oglander*, ed. Francis Bamford (1936), 4.

15. John Stow, *The Annales, or a Generall Chronicle of England* (1615), 589; Richard Worsley, *The History of the Isle of Wight* (1781), 34, 94.

16. 'Documents Illustrating the History of the Spanish Armada', ed. George P. B. Naish, *The Naval Miscellany*, vol. IV, ed. Christopher Lloyd, Navy Records Society, 92 (1952), 19–20.

17. SP 78/24, fo. 92^v.

18. John Parr, *An Abstract of the Laws, Customs, and Ordinances of the Isle of Man*, ed. James Gell (Douglas, 1867), 36; J. R. Dickinson, *The Lordship of Man under the Stanleys: Government and Economy in the Isle of Man, 1580–1704*, Chetham Society, 3rd ser., 41 (Manchester, 1996), 40.

19. HMC, *Salisbury*, v. 164.

20. HMC, *Salisbury*, iv. 294, v. 164, 274.

21. David A. Pretty, *Anglesey: The Concise History* (Cardiff, 2002), 39.

22. HMC, Salisbury, xxiv. 178.

23. BL, MS Cotton, Caligula E.X, fo. 267.
24. SP 15/42/62.
25. *APC 1621–1623*, 74.
26. HMC, *Report on the Manuscripts of the Late Reginald Rawdon Hastings*, 3 vols (1928–47), ii. 64.
27. *Royalist's Notebook*, 7–8
28. *Royalist's Notebook*, 17, 21
29. *Royalist's Notebook*, 56.
30. Bod., MS Clarendon 16/1246.
31. SP 16/524, fos 143, 149; SP 16/526, fo. 112.
32. J. C. Appleby, 'A Memorandum on the Defence of the Channel Islands, 1627', *Société Jersiaise, Bulletin Annuel*, 23 (1984), 506.
33. SP 16/528, fos 71, 201.
34. SP 16/74, fo. 128; SP 16/524, fos 149, 151; SP 16/525, fo. 114; SP 16/527, fos 23, 97; SP 16/528, fos 1, 5, 14; *Actes des États de L'Île de Guernsey. Vol. II. 1605 à 1651* (St Peter Port, 1851), 133.
35. HMC, *The Manuscripts of the Earl Cowper*, 2 vols (1888–9), i. 400.
36. SP 16/262, fo. 39.
37. HMC, *Salisbury*, ix. 9, 171, 293, 412; HMC, *Report on Franciscan Manuscripts* (1906), 221; SP 16/126, fo. 62.
38. SP 16/368, fo. 190; William Borlase, *Observations on the Ancient and Present State of the Islands of Scilly* (1756), 129.
39. Harrison, 'Description of Britaine', 33.
40. SP 16/323, fo. 14.
41. A. L. Rowse, *Tudor Cornwall* (1941, 1969 edn), 384; Killigrew accounts, in Mark Stoyle, '"Fullye Bente to Fighte Oute the Matter": Reconsidering Cornwall's Role in the Western Rebellion of 1549', *English Historical Review*,129 (2014), 561.
42. HMC, *Salisbury*, iv. 294; Rowse, *Tudor Cornwall*, 385, 401.
43. Richard Carew, *The Svrvey of Cornwall* (1602), fo. 85; HMC, *Salisbury*, ix. 273. A sketch of the almost-finished Star Castle is in Cecil Papers, Maps, vol. 2.
44. SP 16/368, fo. 190.
45. 'The Parliamentary Survey of the Duchy of Cornwall, part II', ed. Norman J. G. Pounds, *Devon and Cornwall Record Society*, NS 27 (1984), 146.
46. Rowse, *Tudor Cornwall*, 416.
47. SP 16/323, fo. 14; SP 16/368, fo. 190.
48. Robert Heath, *A Natural and Historical Account of the Islands of Scilly* (1750), 201; Borlase, *Observations on the Ancient and Present State of the Islands of Scilly*, 10–11; Allan Brodie, 'The Garrison Defences on St Mary's in the Isles of Scilly in the 17th and 18th Centuries', *English Heritage Historical Review*, 7 (2012), 36–65.
49. SP 16/65, fo. 54; SP 16/90, fo. 76; SP 16/91, fo. 149; SP 16/108, fo. 9.
50. SP 16/266, fo. 54.
51. SP 16/368, fo. 190; SP16/377, fo. 282.
52. SP 16/493, fo. 104. The royal ship *Assurance*, carrying Peter Heylyn to the Channel Islands in 1629, carried forty-two pieces of ordnance.
53. Bod., MS Clarendon 84, fo. 97; SP 29/234, fo. 151.

54. *APC 1626*, 202.
55. Bod., MS Carte 75, fo. 251, MS Rawlinson D 924, fo. 65; SP 16/524, fo. 178.
56. Miege, *New State of England*, 98.
57. SP 12/97, fo. 41.
58. Worsley, *History of the Isle of Wight*, 41–5; Christopher Young, *Carisbrooke Castle* (2010); SP 16/279, fo. 74.
59. SP 16/44, fo. 111; SP 16/58, fo. 138; SP 16/89, fo. 73; SP 16/521, fos 125, 190; SP 16/524, fo. 131; *APC 1626*, 201; Worsley, *History of the Isle of Wight*, 46–7.
60. *Royalist's Notebook*, 21; repairs to Sandham Castle costing £1,200 were completed in 1635: SP 16/291, fo. 143; SP 16/304, fo. 90.
61. *Royalist's Notebook*, 52–3
62. SP 16/325, fo. 147.
63. SP 16/448, fo. 17; SP 16/467, fo. 4.
64. *APC 1626*, 201.
65. Worsley, *History of the Isle of Wight*, 40, appendix 14.
66. SP16/44, fo. 111.
67. SP 16/34, fo. 37; SP 16/64, fo. 36, 88; SP 16/88, fo. 102; SP 16/100, fo. 42; SP 16/103, fo. 149; HMC, *Cowper*, i. 360; *Royalist's Notebook*, 30, 46. 48.
68. SP 16/64, fos 36, 88; SP 16/88, fo. 192; SP 16/103, fo. 148; *Royalist's Notebook*, 46; Lindsay Boynton, 'Billeting: The Example of the Isle of Wight,' *English Historical Review*, 74 (1959), 25–9, 32, 36.
69. *CSPD 1627–8*, 346.
70. SP 15/9/2, fo. 78; SP 12/254, fo. 51; SP 12/262, fo. 81; SP 16/73, fo. 81; SP 16/404, fo. 272; HMC, *Ninth Report* (1884), pt i, 280.
71. Speed, *Theatre of the Empire of Great Britaine*, 93
72. SP 16/467, fo. 203; SP 16/470, fo. 144.
73. SP 16/11, fo. 83.
74. James Chaloner, 'A Description of the Isle of Man', in Daniel King, *The Vale-Royall of England. Or, The County Palatine of Chester* (1656), second pagination, 31; Thomas Denton, *A Perambulation of Cumberland 1687–1688 Including…the Isle of Man*, Surtees Society, 207 (2003), 495–9.
75. SP 47/1, fo. 98.
76. 'Memorial of the State of the Militia and Forts in the Island of Jersey' (1642), in S. Elliott Hoskins, *Charles the Second in the Channel Islands*, 2 vols (1854), i. 19.
77. SP 15/13, fo. 228.
78. SP 15/30, fo. 55; SP 78/24, fo. 92^v; SP 15/39, fo. 58.
79. BL, MS Kings 48, fo. 2; Heylyn, *Full Relation of Two Journeys*, 299.
80. Dr Henry Janson to Sir Edward Hyde, November 1645, Bod, MS Clarendon 26/2027.
81. Governor Danvers to Secretary Conway, June 1624, SP 15/43/65.
82. SP 15/13, fos 155, 228.
83. SP 15/20, fo. 149.
84. SP 15/33, fo. 128; PC 2/31, fo. 145; HMC, *Salisbury*, vi. 556; Bod., MS Eng. Hist. b. 134, fos 9–9v; Bod., MS Eng. Hist. c. 34, fo. 183.
85. SP 15/42/62, 84; SP 15/43/65, 77.

86. SP 16/537, fo. 27.

87. PC 2/36, fos 71, 76; SP 16/71, fo. 134; HMC, *Third Report* (1872), 70; *Actes des États de L'Île de Guernsey. 1605 à 1651* (St Peter Port, 1851), 102–10.

88. *Actes des États de L'Île de Guernsey. 1605 à 1651*, 107, 109, 114–17; Huntington Library, MS HM 72020, fo. 404. See also John M. Collins, *Martial Law and English Laws, c.1500–c.1700* (Cambridge, 2016), esp. 137–8 for anxieties and confusions in 1628.

89. BL, Add. MS 27,873, fo. 87. See also accounts for work on Castle Cornet, 1603–1634: TNA, E 351/3564, 3565, 3573.

90. Parliamentary Archives, HL/PO/JO/10/1/27; HMC, *Third Report*, 35.

91. *Actes des États de L'Île de Guernsey. 1605 à 1651*, 103; Peter Heylyn, *A Full Relation of Two Journeys: The One into the Main-Land of France. The Other into some Adjacent Islands* (1656), 299.

92. Huntington Library, MS EL 1904, fo. 48.

93. PC 2/38, fo. 83.

94. SP 16/528, fo. 3; SP 16/537, fo. 131; SP 46/78, fo. 4.

95. *Ile de Jersey. Ordres du Conseil et Pièces Analogues Enregistrés a Jersey. Vol. 1. 1536–1678* (St Helier, 1897), 81; SP 15/42/60.

96. BL, Add. MS 72,608, fo. 1; *CSPD Addenda James I*, 503.

97. *Ile de Jersey. Ordres du Conseil... 1536–1678*, 431–2.

98. Hoskins, *Charles the Second in the Channel Islands*, ii. 341.

99. SP 16/528, fo. 15.

100. SP 78/24, fo. 92^v; Philippe Dumaresq, 'A Survey of ye Island of Jersey... 1685', *Société Jersiaise Bulletin Annuel*,12 (1932–5), 423; Colin Platt and Neil Rushton, *Tudor Mont Orgueil and its Guns* (St Helier, 2012).

101. William Prynne, *Movnt-Orgveil: Or Divine and Profitable Meditations* (1641), sig. A; SP 16/528, fo. 15; Parliamentary Archives, HL/PO/JO/10/1/117.

102. SP 15/41, fo. 8; SP 16/528, fo. 15; Poingdestre, *Caesarea, Or a Discourse of the Island of Jersey*, 29.

103. 'Memorial of the State of the Militia and Forts in the Island of Jersey', in Hoskins, *Charles the Second in the Channel Islands*, i. 9, 23.

104. Sir Amias Paulet to Sir Francis Walsingham, 27 December 1585, in *The Letter-Books of Sir Amias Poulet*, ed. John Morris (1874), 121.

105. SP 15/39, fo. 60; HMC, *Salisbury*, xxi. 219.

106. PC 2/28, fos 231–3.

107. SP 15/41, fo. 16.

108. PC 2/36, fos 71, 76; SP 16/71, fo. 134.

109. 'Reparations for His Majesties Castles of Mont Orgeuil and Elizabeth', *Société Jersiaise Bulletin Annuel*, 7 (1910–14), 147–56.

110. SP 16/536, fos 64–66^v; PC 2/31, fo. 145.

111. Prynne, *Movnt-Orgveil*, sig A.

112. PC 2/31, fo. 145; SP 15/41, fos 16–20; SP 16/ 524, fo. 161; 'The Report of the Royal Commissioners sent to Jersey in 1617', *Société Jersiaise Bulletin Annuel*, 30 (1905), 389–93.

113. Falle, *Account of the Island of Jersey*, 400.

114. SP 15/42, fo. 116; PC 2/31, fo. 77.
115. SP 16/529, fo. 185.
116. SP 16/148, fo. 145; PC 2/39, fo. 81.

Chapter 8

1. Useful accounts include Charles Carlton, *Going to the Wars: The Experience of the British Civil Wars, 1638–1651* (1992); Martyn Bennett, *The Civil Wars in Britain and Ireland 1638–1651* (Oxford, 1997); John Kenyon and Jane Ohlmeyer (eds), *The Civil Wars: A Military History of England, Scotland, and Ireland 1638–1660* (Oxford, 1998); Diane Purkiss, *The English Civil War: A People's History* (2006); Michael Braddick, *God's Fury, England's Fire: A New History of the English Civil Wars* (2008). Neither Ronald Hutton, *The Royalist War Effort, 1642–1646*, 2nd edn (1999) nor Barry Robertson, *Royalists at War in Scotland and Ireland, 1638–1650* (Abingdon and New York, 2016), discusses royalist positions in the Channel Islands, the Isles of Scilly, or the Isle of Man.

2. Jonathan Duncan, *The History of Guernsey; with Occasional Notices of Jersey, Alderney, and Sark* (1841), 84.

3. Geoffrey Smith, *The Cavaliers in Exile 1640–1660* (Basingstoke and New York, 2003).

4. *A Calendar of Material Relating to Ireland from the High Court of Admiralty 1641–1660*, ed. Elaine Murphy (Dublin, 2011), 22, 219, 213, 225.

5. *Note-Book of Pierre le Roy*, ed. G. E. Lee (St Peter Port, 1893). The content ranges from 1615 to 1665.

6. Jean Chevalier, *Journal de Jean Chevalier* (St Helier, 1914). Chevalier's journal covers the years 1643 to 1651. An English translation is in preparation.

7. 'Notebooks of Elie Brevint', http://societe-jersiaise.org/digital-publications/brevint?file=../bulletin-pdfs/Brevint (accessed June 2018). Born on Sark around 1587, the second son of a refugee Huguenot cleric, Elie Brevint was ordained in 1611, succeeded his father as pastor in 1612, and served his island parish until his death in 1674. For most of these years he recorded observations in archaic French on life of his community, and on the affairs of the wider world. Brevint's notebooks were discovered in the nineteenth century and were transcribed by an island antiquary in 1900. Though occasionally cited by Channel Island historians, they have not yet been printed.

8. Bod., MS Ashmole 830, fo. 285; HMC, *Fifth Report* (1876), 162; *Three Declarations* (1642), 5–6; *Ioyfull News from Portsmouth and the Isle of Wight* (1642).

9. HMC, *Manuscripts of . . . the Duke of Portland*, 2 vols (1891–7), i. 54–5; *Documents Relating to the Civil War 1642–1648*, ed. J. R. Powell and W. K. Timings, Navy Records Society, 195 (1963), 39–40.

10. *A True and Brief Relation How, and by what Means, the Isle of Wight was Secured, in August, 1642* (1642), 4–5; *Commons Journal*, ii., 321, 702, 708; Richard Worsley, *The History of the Isle of Wight* (1781), 108–116.

11. *Commons Journal*, ii. 460, 702, 708, 870, 880, 891.

12. *Commons Journal*, ii. 870, 880, 891, iii. 31, 196, 255, 338, 608; *Lords Journal*, vi. 242.

13. SP 21/8, fos 205, 247, 249; SP 21/20, fos 147, 367.

14. HMC, *Fifth Report*, 420.

15. HMC, *Report on the Manuscripts of the Earl of Egmont*, 2 vols (1905–9), i. 184.
16. Bod., MS Clarendon 26/2046; Clarendon, *The History of the Rebellion and Civil War in England*, ed. W. Dunn Macray, 6 vols (Oxford, 1888), iv. 116; John Roland Phillips, *Memoirs of the Civil War in Wales and the Marches 1642–1649*, 2 vols (1874), ii. 264–5.
17. Bod., MS Clarendon 25/1936; Clarendon, *History of the Rebellion*, iv. 78; Phillips, *Memoirs of the Civil War in Wales*, i. 315.
18. Clarendon, *History of the Rebellion*, iv. 116–17; Phillips, *Memoirs of the Civil War in Wales*, i. 332.
19. Bod., MS Clarendon 26/2046; Clarendon, *History of the Rebellion*, iv. 112.
20. John Hacket, *Scrinia Reserta: A Memorial Offer'd to the Great Deservings of John Williams* (1693), 208–9.
21. HMC, *Egmont*, i. 296; *Calendar of Wynn (of Gwydir) Papers 1515–1690* (Aberystwyth, 1926), 291–5; Norman Tucker, *North Wales in the Civil War* (Wrexham, 1992), 99–100.
22. HMC, *Fifth Report*, 421.
23. Anglesey Declaration, 14 July 1648, in Richard Llwyd, *The Poetical Works of Richard Llwyd, The Bard of Snowden* (1837), 60–1; *Calendar of the Proceedings of the Committee for Advance of Money, 1642–1656*, ed. Mary Anne Everett Green (1888), 1163.
24. *CSPD 1648–9*, 211, 251–, 288; *Calendar of Wynn (of Gwydir) Papers*, 316; Phillips, *Memoirs of the Civil War in Wales*, ii. 399–400; Tucker, *North Wales in the Civil War*, 147–50.
25. SP 21/24, fos 259, 311, 335; SP 21/25, fo. 47, SP 46/95, fo. 128: Bod., MS Clarendon 31/2883.
26. *Calendar of the Proceedings of the Committee for Compounding*, ed. Mary Anne Everett Green, 5 vols (1892), iv. 3131.
27. Bod., MS Clarendon 31/2887, MS Tanner 57, fo. 343; HMC, *Report on the Manuscripts of F. W. Leyborne-Popham* (1899), 14; Tucker, *North Wales in the Civil War*, 150–7.
28. SP 16/412, fo. 184; SP 16/467, fo. 6.
29. SP 16/488, fo. 26; SP16/ 491, fo. 237.
30. SP 16/514, fo. 27.
31. HMC, *Portland*, i. 487.
32. SP 16/514/2, fo. 63, SP 18/94, fo. 194, SP 21/9, fo. 65; SP 21/10, fo. 135; SP 46/95, fo. 66; John Rushworth, *Historical Collections of Private Passages of State*, 8 vols (1721), iv. 1236.
33. *A Petition from the Island of Silley* (1642).
34. Bod., MS Bankes 38/6, MS Bankes 55, fo. 53.
35. HMC, *Second Report* (1974), 99.
36. *Calendar of Materials Relating to Ireland from the High Court of Admiralty 1641–1660*, 22.
37. Bod. Library, MS Clarendon 25/1937.
38. Mary Coate, *Cornwall in the Great Civil War and Interregnum 1642–1660* (Oxford, 1933; 2nd edn, Truro, 1963), 214; Bod., MS Clarendon 28/2201. Royalists around the queen wanted Hamilton rehabilitated, and recommended in May 1646 that he be bought to Jersey or Scilly. Instead he gravitated to the king in Scotland.
39. *A Collection of Original Letters and Papers... Found among the Duke of Ormonde's Papers*, ed. Thomas Carte, 2 vols (Dublin, 1759), i. 107; Roger Granville, *The King's*

General in the West: The Life of Sir Richard Granville, Bart., 1600–1659 (1908), 162; Amos C. Miller, *Sir Richard Grenville of the Civil War* (1979), 140; Mark Stoyle, *West Britons: Cornish Identities and the Early Modern British State* (Exeter, 2002), 169–70. Grenville later wrote a 'defence against all aspersions ... of malignant persons', reciting his service to the crown: Bod., MS Clarendon 47, fos 310–14.

40. Bod., MS Clarendon 26/2072.
41. Coate, *Cornwall in the Great Civil War*, 190, 205–10; S. Elliott Hoskins, *Charles the Second in the Channel Islands*, 2 vols (1854), i. 299.
42. Clarendon, *History of the Rebellion*, iv. 140, 151; Jane H. Ohlmeyer, *Civil War and Restoration in the Three Stuart Kingdoms: The Career of Randall MacDonnell, Marquis of Antrim, 1609–1683* (Cambridge, 1993), 162–3.
43. *The Memoirs of Ann Lady Fanshawe*, ed. Beatrice Marshall (London and New York, 1907), 40.
44. Bod., MS Clarendon 27/2152, 2153, 2372.
45. Bod., MS Clarendon 27/2199.
46. *Memoirs of Ann Lady Fanshawe*, 41.
47. Bod., MS Clarendon 27/2152, 2153, 2211, 2372.
48. Coate, *Cornwall in the Great Civil War*, 208.
49. Clarendon, *History of the Rebellion*, iv. 140.
50. Bod., MS Clarendon 27/2140; *Calendar of the Clarendon State Papers Preserved in the Bodleian Library. Volume 1: to January 1649*, ed. O. Ogle and W. H. Bliss (Oxford, 1872), 306; Clarendon, *The Life of Edward Earl of Clarendon*, 2 vols (Oxford, 1760), i. 152; Richard Ollard, *Clarendon and his Friends* (New York, 1988), 104, 118.
51. Greffe, Guernsey, Métevier Collection, no. 11, 18/28 March 1646; Ferdinand Brock Tupper, *The Chronicles of Castle Cornet, Guernsey* (1851), 144; HMC, *Seventh Report* (1879), 453.
52. *Documents Relating to the Civil War*, 249.
53. Sir Thomas Fanshawe to Sir Peter Osborne, 25 March 1646, *Actes des États de L'Île de Guernsey. 1605 à 1651* (St Peter Port, 1851), 270–2.
54. Bod., MS Clarendon 27/ 2169, 2170.
55. Parliamentary Archives, HL/PO/JO/10/1/204, 205; Bod., MS Clarendon 28/2211; Coate, *Cornwall in the Great Civil War*, 170.
56. Coate, *Cornwall in the Great Civil War*, 213–14; Bod., MS Clarendon 28/2211.
57. *Memoirs of Ann Lady Fanshawe*, 41–2; J. D. Davies, *Kings of the Sea: Charles II, James II and the Royal Navy* (Barnsley, 2017), 38.
58. Bod., MS Clarendon 28/2211; Coate, *Cornwall in the Great Civil War*, 213–14; Hoskins, *Charles the Second in the Channel Islands*, i. 351–2, 400–1.
59. Bod., MS Clarendon 28/2209; HMC, *Egmont*, i. 285, 290.
60. Parliamentary Archives, HL/PO/JO/10/1/228; *Lords Journal*, ix. 91; John Haslock, *A True and Perfect Relation of the Surrender of the Strong and Impregnable Garrison of the Island of Scillie* (1646); Coate, *Cornwall in the Great Civil War*, 241
61. Sir George Ayscue to Committee of Both Kingdoms, 12 September 1646, HMC, *Portland*, i. 392.
62. Parliamentary Archives, HL/PO/JO/10/1/233, 235.

63. SP 21/25, fos 29–31; *Joyful Newes for England* (1648), 5–6; *A Great Victory Obtained by the Kings Forces in the West of England at the Island of Silley* (1648), 2–3. Royalist letters taken after the battle of Worcester included one dated 27 August 1648 regarding the seizure of Scilly: HMC, *Report on the Pepys Manuscripts* (1911), 274.
64. John Noy to parliamentary officers, 30 September 1648, Bod., MS Tanner 57, fo. 324.
65. SP 21/25, fos 25, 29, 31, 65; Hoskins, *Charles the Second in the Channel Islands*, ii. 243; Coate, *Cornwall in the Great Civil War*, 241.
66. *Journal de Jean Chevalier*, 589–90, 593–4, 595–6, 601–2, 604–6; *Memoirs of Prince Rupert and the Cavaliers*, ed. Eliot Warburton, 3 vols (1849), iii. 290, 295.
67. SP 21/25, fo. 25; SP 21/10, fos 57, 65, 71; *Calendar of Materials Relating to Ireland from the High Court of Admiralty 1641–1660*, 219–22.
68. BL, MS Egerton 2533, fos 474–474ᵛ; *Collection of Original Letters and Papers ... Found among the Duke of Ormonde's Papers*, i. 213,
69. BL, MS Egerton 2533, fo. 474; SP 18/15, fos 115–17.
70. Granville, *King's General in the West*, 179–80, 147; Miller, *Sir Richard Grenville*, 147.
71. *A Letter Intercepted (at Sea) by Captaine Moulton ... Written from Parson Wolby* (1649), 2, 4–5.
72. SP 25/94, fos 31, 147, 163; SP 25/63, fo. 119; Bod., MS Clarendon 37, fo. 54; HMC, *Leyborne-Popham*, 16, 23.
73. SP 25/63/2, fos 179, 261, 269; *A Great Sea Fight near Pendennis Castle in Cornwall* (1640), 2; HMC, *Portland*, i. 583.
74. HMC, *Portland*, i. 393; John Taylor, *John Taylors Wandering, to See the Wonders of the West* (1649), 13; Coate, *Cornwall in the Great Civil War*, 253.
75. SP 25/118, fo. 123; SP 25/120, fo. 15; Bod., MS Clarendon 37, fos 121–2, MS Clarendon 38, fo. 121ᵛ; MS Clarendon 39, fo. 89ᵛ; HMC, *Leyborne-Popham*, 98; Hoskins, *Charles the Second in the Channel Islands*, ii. 380; Joseph Henry Smith, *Appeals to the Privy Council from the American Plantations* (New York, 1950, repr. 1965), 38.
76. Parliamentary Archives, WIL/1/23.
77. SP 25/65, fo. 167.
78. *Letter Intercepted (at Sea)*, 2.
79. *Collection of Original Letters and Papers ... Found among the Duke of Ormonde's Papers*, i. 377; Bod., MS Clarendon 39, fo. 152ᵛ.
80. *A Message Sent from the Lord Hopton, and Sire Richard Greenvill to the Prince* (1650), 4.
81. *The Letters of Robert Blake*, ed. J. R. Powell, Navy Records Society, 76 (1937), 112–17.
82. HMC, *Leyborne-Popham*, 99.
83. SP 25/96, fos 93, 95, 131; *Collection of Original Letters and Papers ... Found among the Duke of Ormonde's Papers*, i. 477.
84. *A Collection of the State Papers of John Thurloe*, ed. Thomas Birch, 7 vols (1742), i. 177.
85. BL, MS Egerton 2542, fos 73–4; Joseph Leveck, *A True Accompt of the Late Reducement of the Isles of Scilly* (1651), 4–9; J. R. Powell, 'Blake's Reduction of the Scilly Isles in 1651', *Mariner's Mirror*, 17 (1931), 205–22.
86. SP 18/15, fo. 115; SP 25/20, fo. 15; *Letters of Robert Blake*, 99–105, 113–17, 119–36; Bernard Capp, *Cromwell's Navy: The Fleet and the English Revolution 1643–1660* (Oxford, 1989), 67.

87. SP 25/23, fo. 73; SP 29/39, fo. 9.

88. Worcester College, Oxford, William Clarke Papers, MS vol. 19, fos 18–18^V.

89. James Waynwright to Mr Bradshaw, 6 June 1651, HMC, *Sixth Report* (1877), 435.

90. Barry Coward, *The Stanleys. Lords Stanley and Earls of Derby 1385–1672: The Origins, Wealth and Power of a Landowning Family*, Chetham Society, 3rd ser., 30 (Manchester, 1983), 173–6; J. R. Dickinson, 'The Earl of Derby and the Isle of Man, 1643–1651', *Transactions of the Historic Society of Lancashire and Cheshire*, 141 (1991–2), 39–76.

91. Dickinson, 'Earl of Derby and the Isle of Man', 51–3, 67; Jennifer Kewley Draskau, *Illiam Dhone: Patriot or Traitor? The Life, Death and Legacy of William Christian* (2012), 31–6.

92. *Calendar of the Proceedings of the Committee for Advance of Money*, 1295.

93. Bod., MS Clarendon 26/2046; Clarendon, *History of the Rebellion*, iv. 112.

94. Smith, *Cavaliers in Exile*, 16

95. William Sacheverell, *An Account of the Isle of Man* (1702), sig. B2^V.

96. HMC, *Pepys*, 266.

97. Digby to Sir Edward Hyde, January 1646, in Rushworth, *Historical Collections of Private Passages of State*, vi. 129; Bod., MS Clarendon 26/2083.

98. SP 25/94, fo. 115; Captain Robert Clarke to William Lenthall, 12 August 1646, HMC, *Portland*, i. 388; William Blundell, *A History of the Isle of Man*, ed. William Harrison, 2 vols (Manx Society, Douglas, 1876–7), i, p. xxiii; Elaine Murphy, *Ireland and the War at Sea, 1641–1653* (Woodbridge, 2012), 83, 113.

99. James Stanley, *A Declaration of the Right Honourable, James, Earle of Darby* (1649), 3–5; Marmaduke Langdale and Lewis Dives, *A Declaration of the Noble Knights... to Keep the Isle of Man, Against all Opposition, for His Majesties Service* (1649), 2–3; Dickinson, 'Earl of Derby and the Isle of Man', 65.

100. SP 25/65, fo. 289; SP 25/96, fo. 45.

101. SP 25/96, fo. 325.

102. SP 18/16, fo. 117; SP 46/96, fo. 96; *A Perfect Diurnall*, 20–7 October 1651, 3–10 November 1651; A. W. Moore, *A History of the Isle Man*, 2 vols (1900), i. 279–90; Dickinson, 'Earl of Derby and the Isle of Man, 45, 48, 68–9. Sara Goodwins, *A Brief History of the Isle of Man* (Sutton, 2011), 80, dates the fall of Castle Rushen to 3 November 1651 and wrongly describes the countess as 'the last person to surrender to parliamentary forces during the English civil war'. Royalists in the Channel Islands held out until mid- December,

103. SP 16/497, fo. 221.

104. Parliamentary Archives, BRY/45B/50. The petitioners to parliament were led by Peter de Beauvoir, John Bonamy, and Jaques Guille.

105. BL, MS Stowe 184, fo. 115^V; Tupper, *Chronicles of Castle Cornet*, 82.

106. Greffe, Guernsey, Métevier Collection, no. 11, 30 August 1643, 18 September 1643; Tupper, *Chronicles of Castle Cornet*, 52–77.

107. *Actes des États de L'Île de Guernsey. 1605 à 1651*, 192–201.

108. *Private Journals of the Long Parliament 3 January to 5 March 1642*, eds. Willson H. Coates, Anne Steele Young, and Vernon F. Snow (New Haven and London, 1982), 478; Parliamentary Archives, HL/PO/JO/10/1/117.

109. *Actes des États de L'Île de Guernsey. 1605 à 1651*, 317.

110. Parliamentary Archives, BRY/45B/48, 50.

111. Huntington Library, MS HM 72020, 284.

112. 'Jean de la Marche...The Diary', ed. W. Rolleston and T. W. M. de Guerir, *Report and Transactions Société Guernesiase*, 11 (1930–32), 215–16, 219; Tupper, *Chronicles of Castle Cornet*, 163.

113. *Note-Book of Pierre le Roy*, 15.

114. Parliamentary Archives, HL/PO/JO/10/1/264; *Actes des États de L'Île de Guernsey. 1605 á 1651*, 221–5, 255–7, 316; HMC, *Eighth Report* (1881), 7; Greffe, Guernsey, Métevier Collection, no. 11, 11 October 1648; Tupper, *Chronicles of Castle Cornet*, 221.

115. Tupper, *Chronicles of Castle Cornet*, 101–11, 122, 129, 155, 157–60, 171, 189, 203.

116. 'Jean de la Marche...The Diary', 215–16, 219; Duncan, *History of Guernsey*, 62–71; Tupper, *Chronicles of Castle Cornet*, 56–8; Peter Carey, 'Account of the Captivity of Messrs. de Beauvoir des Granges, de Havilland, Pierre Carey', ed. R. W. J. Payne, *Report and Transactions of Société Guernesiase*, 19 (1973), 307–13. Huntington Library, MS HM 72020, fos 572–86, has the story in French.

117. Parliamentary Archives, HL/PO/JO/10/1/175.

118. Parliamentary Archives, BRY/45B/48.

119. BL, MS Stowe 184; Tupper, *Chronicles of Castle Cornet*, 138–41, 161–2.

120. Bod., MS Clarendon 27/2197; Tupper, *Chronicles of Castle Cornet*, 99; Hoskins, *Charles the Second in the Channel Islands*, ii. 51–5; G. R. Balleine, *All for the King: The Story of Sir George Carteret* (St Helier, 1976), 32–3.

121. Bod., MS Tanner 59, fos 19, 21; Murphy, *Ireland and the War at Sea*, 63–4.

122. *Commons Journal*, iv. 711.

123. Bod., MS Clarendon 31/2860; Ollard, *Clarendon and his Friends*, 123.

124. *Actes des États de L'Île de Guernsey. 1605 à 1651*, 311–22, 336–42.

125. Richard Hocart, *The Country People of Guernsey and their Agriculture, 1640–1840* (St Peter Port, 2016), 81, 148–9.

126. SP 25/96, fo. 99.

127. Greffe, Guernsey, Métevier Collection, no. 11, 26 January 1647; Tupper, *Chronicles of Castle Cornet*, 146–8, 231–2.

128. Bod., MS Clarendon 29/2423, 2494; Tupper, *Chronicles of Castle Cornet*, 212, 218; Hoskins, *Charles the Second in the Channel Islands*, ii. 92.

129. Bod., MS Clarendon 31/2885, Greffe, Guernsey, Métevier Collection, no. 11.

130. HMC, *Pepys*, 276.

131. SP 25/94, fo. 381; SP 25/123, fo. 53; *Actes des États de L'Île de Guernsey. 1605 à 1651*, 306–8.

132. BL, Add. MS 11,315, fos 2, 7; HMC, *Leyborne-Popham*, 50.

133. *Note-Book of Pierre le Roy*, 15; Tupper, *Chronicles of Castle Cornet*, 254, 259, 304; Hoskins, *Charles the Second in the Channel Islands*, ii. 310, 391.

134. Parliamentary Archives, HL/PO/JO/10/1/117; SP 16/490, fo. 18.

135. Parliamentary Archives, HL/PO/JO/10/1/117, 118; SP 16/490, fo. 18; *Articles Exhibited against Sir Philipp Carteret, Governour of the Isle of Jersy* (1642); *To the Right Honovrable the Lords Assembled in Parliament. The Humble Remonstrance of... Jerzey* (1642); Hoskins, *Charles the Second in the Channel Islands*, i. 50–8.

136. *Acts and Ordinances of the Interregnum, 1642–1660*, ed. C. H. Firth and R. S. Rait, 3 vols (1911), i. 772–4; Parliamentary Archives, HL/PO/JO/10/1/192; SP 16/497, fo. 64; SP 16/510, fo. 197.
137. A detailed account of this period, mostly from the Carteret perspective, is in *Journal de Jean Chevalier*, 2–58.
138. SP 16/497, fo. 64; Parliamentary Archives, BRY/45B/48, 50; Greffe, Guernsey, Métevier Collection, no. 11, 13 March 1643; William Prynne, *The Lyar Confounded or A Brief Refutation of John Lilburnes Miserably-Mistated Case* (1645), 39; Tupper, *Chronicles of Castle Cornet*, 67; Hoskins, *Charles the Second in the Channel Islands*, i. 23.
139. *Commons Journal*, iii. 562.
140. Prynne, *Lyar Confounded*, 39.
141. Michael Lemprière, Henry Dumaresq, and Abraham Hérault, *Pseudo-Mastix: The Lyar's Whipp*, in *Société Jersiaise Bulletin Annuel*, 13 (1888), 344.
142. SP 16/510, fo. 246; SP 130/672, fo. 166; 'Ordre de Faire Recherche des Biens Appartenant aux Parlementaires, le 25 Octobre 1645', *Société Jersiaise Bulletin Annuel*, 3 (1890–5), 424–8.
143. Hoskins, *Charles the Second in the Channel Islands*, i. 51–175; HMC, *Second Report*, 158–68; *Stuart Royal Proclamations. Volume II. Royal Proclamations of King Charles I 1625–1646*, ed. James F. Larkin (Oxford, 1983), 937–9; Philip Falle, *An Account of the Island of Jersey*, with notes by Edward Durell (St Helier, 1837), 334–6; Balleine, *All for the King*, 33–5. Those excepted from the royal pardon were Benjamin Bisson, Francis Carteret, Henry Dumaresq, and David and John (i.e. Jacques) Bandinell.
144. *Journal de Jean Chevalier*, 15–17, 94; *Stuart Royal Proclamations. Volume II*, 937–9.
145. 'Lettre émanant du Comité du Parlement nommant Michael Lemprière, Bailli de Jersey', *Société Jersiaise Bulletin Annuel*, 30 (1905), 399–400.
146. *Journal de Jean Chevalier*, 107.
147. *Journal de Jean Chevalier*, 83. The States had ordered a similar fast in April 1642: SP 16/490, fo. 18.
148. *Isle de Jersey. Ordres du Conseil et Pièces Analogues Enregistrés a Jersey. Vol. 1, 1536–1678* (St Helier, 1897), 185–6.
149. *Journal de Jean Chevalier*, 103–5, 109.
150. *Journal de Jean Chevalier*, 106, 117, 152–5, 266; Falle, *Account of the Island of Jersey*, 334–6.
151. *Journal de Jean Chevalier*, 117–36, 127, 265, 270, 274.
152. BL, Add. MS 34,262, fos 6–23; *Journal de Jean Chevalier*, 255–63; *Manifeste declarant la Resolution des Etats et habitants de l'Isle de Jersey du 5–15 Mars, 1645-6, Fac-simile de la copie signée par les habitants de la paroisse de St-Laurent* (St Helier, 1886).
153. Bod., MS Clarendon 26/2027.
154. *A Declaration of the Lords and Commons Assembled in Parliament, Concerning Prisoners in the Island of Iersey* (1645); *An Ordinance...for the Making Void all Commissions and Warrants, or other Writings issued forth in His Majesties Name to Sir George Carteret, Governour of Jersey. And that the said Carteret and his Adherents shall be called to a Just Account for his and their illegall Proceedings against the Well-Affected Persons of that Island* (1645).

155. SP 16/497, fo. 221; Hoskins, *Charles the Second in the Channel Islands*, i. 187–9; *Journal de Jean Chevalier*, 268, 272; A. C. Saunders, *Jean Chevalier and his Times: A Story of Sir George Carteret, Baronet, and The Great Rebellion* (St Helier, 1937); *Calendar of Materials Relating to Ireland from the High Court of Admiralty 1641–1660*, 122, 225.

156. Bod., MS Clarendon 37, fo. 54; Clarendon, *History of the Rebellion*, v. 105.

157. Smith, *Cavaliers in Exile*, 16.

158. *The Kings Cabinet Opened* (1645), 16.

159. Balleine, *All for the King*, 50–7; *Journal de Jean Chevalier*, 140, 164, 251, 276–7, 282–3.

160. Bod., MS Clarendon 28/2354; 'Lettres Inédités du Roi Charles II', *Société Jersiaise Bulletin Annuel*, 3 (1890–5), 2; Philip Ahier, 'The Money Problems of Charles Prince of Wales', *Société Jersiaise Bulletin Annuel*, 21 (1973), 192–3.

161. *Journal de Jean Chevalier*, 286–9, 292–7; Greffe, Guernsey, Métevier Collection, no. 11, 24 April 1646; *Commons Journal*, iv. 571; Hoskins, *Charles the Second in the Channel Islands*, i. 354–9, 367. Robert Russell, the Earl of Warwick's deputy governor of Guernsey, estimated the royalist presence on Jersey after the arrival of the prince as 'six hundred men, together with those there before' (*Actes des États de L'Île de Guernsey. 1605 à 1651*, 276).

162. *Memoirs of Ann Lady Fanshawe*, 42; Smith, *Cavaliers in Exile*, 26.

163. 'Lettres Inédités du Roi Charles II', 4.

164. *The Works of Abraham Cowley*, ed. J. Aikin, 3 vols (1805), i. 63: 'An Answer to a Copy of Verses Sent me to Jersey'.

165. *Journal de Jean Chevalier*, 291–1, 304, 320, 322.

166. Greffe, Guernsey, Métevier Collection, no. 11, 24 April 1646; *Journal de Jean Chevalier*, 291, 316–17, 321–2; *Commons Journal*, iv. 571; Hoskins, *Charles the Second in the Channel Islands*, i. 354–9, 367.

167. Bod., MS Clarendon 27/ 2167–2170, 2174, 2197–2199, 2222; *Collection of Original Letters and Papers . . . Found among the Duke of Ormonde's Papers*, i. 187.

168. Bod., MS Clarendon 28/2209.

169. Bod., MS Clarendon 28/ 2209, 2210, 2227.

170. Bod., MS Clarendon 28/2211.

171. Bod., MS Clarendon 28/2222, 2227; T. H. Lister, *Life and Administration of Edward, First Earl of Clarendon*, 3 vols (1838), i. 282–5. Report that Charles fathered a child in Jersey appears in Saunders, *Jean Chevalier and his Times*, 113–4.

172. *Journal de Jean Chevalier*, 334–6; Bod., MS Clarendon 28/2249. Among those meeting Sir Edward Hyde were Sir William Davenant, Sir Marmaduke Langdale, and Lords Capel, Culpeper, Digby, Jermyn, Wentworth, and Withrington.

173. Bod., MS Clarendon 28/2249.

174. *Journal de Jean Chevalier*, 338–40; Bod., MS Clarendon 28/2249; Clarendon, *Life*, i. 154–5; 'Lettres Inédités du Roi Charles II', 3.

175. Clarendon, *History of the Rebellion*, iv. 215–16; *Journal de Jean Chevalier*, 370–2; Coate, *Cornwall in the Great Civil War*, 220; Hoskins, *Charles the Second in the Channel Islands*, ii. 27–31.

176. *Journal de Jean Chevalier*, 357, 366, 375.

177. PC 1/1, fo. 4; Bod., MS Clarendon 298/2339, 2359; Greffe, Guernsey, Métevier Collection, no. 11, October 1646; 'Articles of Association entered into between the Lords Capel & Hopton, and Sir Edward Hyde, & Sir Geo: Carteret', *Société Jersiaise Bulletin Annuel*, 3 (1890–5), 342–7; Tupper, *Chronicles of Castle Cornet*, 201; Hoskins, *Charles the Second in the Channel Islands*, ii. 55–6; Balleine, *All for the King*, 59–60.

178. Bod., MS Clarendon 29/2347, 2370, 2372, 2394; Hoskins, *Charles the Second in the Channel Islands*, ii. 59–60.

179. Bod., MS Clarendon 28/2354, 2359, 2372, MS Clarendon 30/2561, 2577.

180. Bod., MS Clarendon 28/2227, 2255, 2258, 2354, MS Clarendon 29/2371, 2394, MS Clarendon 31,2740; Clarendon, *Life*, i. 157, 159; Hoskins, *Charles the Second in the Channel Islands*, ii. 7.

181. Philip Major, *Writings of Exile in the English Revolution and Restoration* (Farnham and Burlington, VT, 2013), 3, 29.

182. Edward Hyde, 'Contemplations and Reflections upon the Psalms of David: Applying those Devotions to the Troubles of the Time, Jersey. Dec 26. 1647', in Earl of Clarendon, *A Collection of Several Tracts* (1727), 370, 384–95.

183. Bod., MS Clarendon 27/2140; Ollard, *Clarendon and his Friends*, 114, 118.

184. *Journal de Jean Chevalier*, 342.

185. Parliamentary Archives, HL/PO/JO/10/1/230; *Commons Journal*, iv. 522, 535; SP 16/515, fo. 97; SP 21/9, fo. 31; SP 25/94, fo. 205; Bod., MS Clarendon 29/2459, 2462, 2467, 2487.

186. Bod., MS Clarendon 29/2515, 2561; MS Clarendon 93, fo. 74 (foliated not numbered).

187. Bod., MS Clarendon 30/2670, 2667.

188. Clarendon, *Life*, i. 162–8; *Journal de Jean Chevalier*, 560; Tupper, *Chronicles of Castle Cornet*, 245; Hoskins, *Charles the Second in the Channel Islands*, ii. 197–8, 202; Ollard, *Clarendon and his Friends*, 122. For the military events of 1648, see Robert Ashton, *Counter-Revolution: The Second Civil War and its Origins, 1646–8* (New Haven and London, 1994).

189. *Collection of Original Letters and Papers…Found among the Duke of Ormonde's Papers*, i. 187; Hoskins, *Charles the Second in the Channel Islands*, ii. 212, 237, 263–4; Eva Scott, *The King in Exile: The Wanderings of Charles II from June 1646 to July 1654* (1905), 48–9.

190. *Journal de Jean Chevalier*, 611–4, 620; Balleine, *All for the King*, 70–1.

191. Hoskins, *Charles the Second in the Channel Islands*, ii. 254–6, 298; *A Great Sea Fight near Pendennis Castle in Cornwall*, 4.

192. Bod., MS Clarendon 37, fo. 54; Clarendon, *History of the Rebellion*, v. 105.

193. Jersey Archives, L/F/08/H/37.

194. BL, MS Egerton 2542, fo. 16; Bod., MS Clarendon 38, fo. 121; *Journal de Jean Chevalier*, 608–714.

195. SP 25/64, fo. 339; SP 25/87, fos 9–11.

196. *A Declaration of the Proceedings of the Prince of Wales, and his Coming to the Isle of Jersey* (1642), 1–2; *Prince Charles Proclaimed King, and Landed in Jersey* (1642), 1–2; 'Lettres Inédités du Roi Charles II', 8; *Journal de Jean Chevalier*, 705–8; Clarendon, *History of the Rebellion*, v. 65.

197. HMC, *Leyborne-Popham*, 36, 39, 40, 44, 52; *Collection of Original Letters and Papers...Found among the Duke of Ormonde's Papers*, i. 314.

198. HMC, *Tenth Report* (1906), 147; *Journal de Jean Chevalier*, 708–13; Tupper, *Chronicles of Castle Cornet*, 251–2.

199. 'Notebooks of Elie Brevint', 425.

200. *Instruction que l'on doit faire lire et apprendre aux enfants... en l'Isle de Iersey* (St Helier? 1649); *Journal de Jean Chevalier*, 717–8.

201. SP 18/3, fo. 2; SP 25/94, fos 431, 433, 495; BL, MS Egerton 2542, fo. 26; Bod., MS Clarendon 37, fo. 22; *Journal de Jean Chevalier*, 729; *His Majesties Declaration to all his Loving Subjects* (1649); *Several Occurrences, Touching the Further Proceedings of the Scots with their Declared King* (1650), 3; HMC, *Leyborne-Popham*, 30, 36–7, 52; Hoskins, *Charles the Second in the Channel Islands*, ii. 328; Balleine, *All for the King*, 75–9.

202. Hoskins, *Charles the Second in the Channel Islands*, ii. 330–2, 347.

203. BL, MS Egerton 2542, fos 37–9; Bod., MS Clarendon 38, fos 122, 142, MS Clarendon 39, fos 22, 88; Tupper, *Chronicles of Castle Cornet*, 255–6; Hoskins, *Charles the Second in the Channel Islands*, ii. 359, 364, 368, 375–7, 385; Balleine, *All for the King*, 81–2.

204. *Journal de Jean Chevalier*, 766, 799; Saunders, *Jean Chevalier and his Times*, 168–9.

205. *Journal de Jean Chevalier*, 766–71.

206. George Granville, *The Genuine Works in Verse and Prose, of the Right Honourable George Granville, Lord Lansdown*, 3 vols (1736), ii. 226–8.

207. *Collection of Original Letters and Papers...Found among the Duke of Ormonde's Papers*, i. 366.

208. HMC, *Leyborne-Popham*, 58, 98.

209. 'Instructions Made by Sr. George Carteret 25 July 1651', *Société Jersiaise Bulletin Annuel*, 3 (1890–5), 284–7; Balleine, *All for the King*, 85–9.

210. *Journal de Jean Chevalier*, 939.

211. SP 25/23, fo. 73, SP 25/96, fos 543, 551; *A Perfect Diurnall*, 20–27 October 1651, 27 October–5 November 1651.

212. SP 25/66, fo. 617; *Commons Journal*, vii. 37, 63; Bod., MS Clarendon 42, fo. 179; *Journal de Jean Chevalier*, 945–69; 'A Letter from Aboard the *Entrance*, Riding off Mount Orgueil Castle in Jersey, 27 Octob. 1651', in *A List of all the Victories and Successefull Atchievements of the Parliaments Fleet* (1651), broadside; Kimpton Hilliard to William Clarke, 30 October 1651, in *The Clarke Papers: Selections from the Papers of William Clarke*, ed. C. H. Firth, 3 vols (1891–9), ii. 228–31; 'La Prise de Jersey par le Parlement en 1655. Récit Contemporain', *Société Jersiaise Bulletin Annuel*, 10 (1885), 16–29; Thomas Wright, *A Perfect Narrative of the Particular Service Performed by Thomas Wright, Firemaster, with a Morter-Piece of Fifteen Inches and a Half Diameter, against the Castle of Elizabeth in the Isle of Jersey* (1652), 2–3; Hoskins, *Charles the Second in the Channel Islands*, ii. 391; Balleine, *All for the King*, 91–8; J. R. Powell, 'Blake's Reduction of Jersey in 1651', *Mariner's Mirror*, 18 (1932), 64–80; *Letters of Robert Blake*, 111, 136–41; Richard E. Blakemore and Elaine Murphy, *The British Civil Wars at Sea, 1638–1653* (Woodbridge, 2018).

213. Kimpton Hilliard to William Clarke, 30 October 1651, in *Clarke Papers*, ii. 232.

214. *The Articles of the Rendition of Elizabeth Castle in the Ile of Jersey* (1651), 8; *A Perfect Diurnall*, no. 102 (17–24 November 1651).

215. Huntington Library, MS HM 72020, fo. 560.

216. *Articles of the Rendition of Elizabeth Castle in the Ile of Jersey; Commons Journal*, vii. 63; Falle, *Account of the Island of Jersey*, 353–4; Duncan, *History of Guernsey*, 47–8; Lemprière to Lenthall, 2 February 1652, in Henry Cary, *Memorials of the Great Civil War in England from 1646 to 1652*, 2 vols (1842), ii. 408.

217. *Commons Journal*, vii. 63, 318; Bod., MS Clarendon 43, fos 151, 337; *Actes des États de L'Île de Guernsey.1605 à 1651*, 397–400; *Calendar of the Proceedings of the Committee for Compounding*, iii. 2329.

218. BL, Add. MS 11,315, fo. 19.

219. SP 18/9, fo. 175; SP 25/123, fo. 198.

220. SP 25/96, fo. 99.

221. Tupper, *Chronicles of Castle Cornet*, 259.

222. SP 29/39, fo. 9.

223. SP 29/6, fo. 72; SP 29/5, fo. 61.

Chapter 9

1. John Morrill, 'Three Kingdoms and One Commonwealth? The Enigma of Mid-Seventeenth-Century Britain and Ireland', in Alexander Grant and K. J. Stringer (eds.), *Uniting the Kingdom? The Making of British History* (1995), 170–92.

2. *A Collection of the State Papers of John Thurloe*, ed. Thomas Birch, 7 vols (1742), i. 214; BL, Add. MS 34,262, fo. 51.

3. *CSPD 1649–50*, 267.

4. SP 25/77, fo. 43; John Callow, 'The Limits of Indemnity: The Earl of Derby, Sovereignty and Retribution at the Trial of William Christian, 1660–63', *Seventeenth Century*, 15 (2013), 200, 210.

5. *A Perfect Diurnall*, 24 November–1 December 1651.

6. David Underdown, 'Settlement in the Counties, 1653–1658', in G. E. Aylmer (ed.), *The Interregnum: The Quest for Settlement 1646–1660* (1972), 165–82; Austin Woolrych, *Commonwealth to Protectorate* (Oxford, 1982); Christopher Durston, *Cromwell's Major Generals: Godly Government during the English Revolution* (Manchester and New York, 2001); Bernard Capp, *England's Culture Wars: Puritan Reformation and its Enemies in the Interregnum 1649–1660* (Oxford, 2013); Caroline Boswell, *Disaffection and Everyday Life in Interregnum England* (Woodbridge, 2017).

7. *Collection of the State Papers of John Thurloe*, ii. 713–14.

8. SP 25/76A, fos 40ff.; Llwyd Angharad, *A History of the Island of Mona, or Anglesey* (Ruthin, 1833), 138.

9. Interregnum public finance may be approached through H. J. Habakkuk, 'Public Finance and the Sale of Confiscated Property during the Interregnum', *Economic History Review*, ns 15 (1962), 70–88; and J. S. Wheeler, 'Navy Finance, 1649–1660', *Historical Journal*, 39 (1996), 457–66.

10. Parliamentary Archives, HL/PO/JO/10/1/280; *Commons Journal*, vii. 341.

11. *A Royalist's Notebook: The Commonplace Book of Sir John Oglander*, ed. Francis Bamford (1936), 132.

12. Andrew M. Coleby, *Central Government and the Localities: Hampshire 1649–1689* (Cambridge, 1987), 23.

13. SP 18/26, fos 141ff; 'The Parliamentary Survey of the Duchy of Cornwall, part II', ed. Norman J. G. Pounds, *Devon and Cornwall Record Society*, NS 27 (1984), 131–51; Allan Brodie, 'The Garrison Defences on St Mary's in the Isles of Scilly in the 17th and 18th Centuries', *English Heritage Historical Review*, 7 (2012), 39.

14. *Commons Journal*, vii. 19; SP 25/96, fos 289, 599.

15. *Commons Journal*, vii. 19; SP 18/100, fo. 309; SP 25/96, fo. 599; *CSPD May 1658–June 1659*, 48, 512.

16. SP 18/181, fo. 2; *CSPD May 1658–June 1659*, 1, 125, 512.

17. Christopher Salter, *Sal Scylla: Or, A Letter Written from Scilly to Mr John Goodwin, Minister of the Gospel in London* (1653), 5–7.

18. James Chaloner, 'A Description of the Isle of Man', in Daniel King, *The Vale-Royall of England. Or, The County Palatine of Chester* (1656), separate pagination, 16.

19. SP 18/100, fo. 309; John Callow, '"In so Shifting a Scene": Thomas Fairfax as Lord of the Isle of Man, 1651–60', in Andrew Hopper and Philip Major (eds), *England's Fortress: New Perspectives on Thomas, 3rd Lord Fairfax* (Farnham and Burlington, VT, 2014), 21–52, esp. 23, 26–7, 43; Philip Major, 'Thomas Fairfax, Lord of Man', *Notes and Queries*, 54/1 (2007), 43–5.

20. SP 25/97, fo. 121; SP 18/100, fo. 309.

21. SP 18/33, fo. 17.

22. SP18/100 fo. 309; Callow, '"In so Shifting a Scene"', 43–4.

23. SP 25/77, fo. 439; Callow, '"In so Shifting a Scene"', 37, 39–40, 51.

24. *Calendar of the Proceedings of the Committee for Advance of Money, 1642–1656*, ed. Mary Anne Everett Green (1888), 1432; Callow, '"In so Shifting a Scene"', 28–29, 40–1.

25. Callow, '"In so Shifting a Scene"', 30–4, 39, 41, 46–47, 50; John Callow, '"The Force of Angry Heaven's Flame": Lieutenant John Hathorne and Garrison Government on the Isle of Man, 1651–1660', *Isle of Man Studies*, 14 (2016), 90–108.

26. *The Articles of the Rendition of Elizabeth Castle in the Ile of Jersey* (1651), 8.

27. SP 25/60, fo. 617.

28. SP 25/97, fo. 99.

29. *Note-Book of Pierre le Roy*, ed. G. E. Lee (St Peter Port, 1893), 17–18.

30. BL, Add. MS 34,262, fos 36, 54^v.

31. Bod., MS Rawlinson A 24, fos 217–20; *Collection of the State Papers of John Thurloe*, iii. 213, 231.

32. SP 25/76, fo. 488.

33. SP 25/94, fo. 381; SP 26/123, fo. 53.

34. *Actes des États de L'Île de Guernsey. Vol. II. 1651 à 1780* (St Peter Port, 1907), 4

35. Bod., MS Rawlinson D 1481, fo. 365; James Stocall, *Freedom. Or, the Description of the Excellent Civill Government of the Island of Jersey* (1652), 7.

36. Bod., MS Rawlinson D1481, fo. 365; Stocall, *Freedom. Or, the Description of the Excellent Civill Government of the Island of Jersey*, 7.

37. Bod., MS Rawlinson D 1481, fo. 365; BL, Add. MS 34,262, fos 34–42; SP 46/101, fo. 53.

38. Lemprière to Lenthall, 2 February 1652, in Henry Cary (ed.), *Memorials of the Great Civil War in England from 1646 to 1652*, 2 vols (1842), ii. 403–14; Bod., MS Rawlinson D 1481, fo. 365.

39. Bod., MS Tanner 53, fos 57–57^v.

40. Stocall, *Freedom. Or, the Description of the Excellent Civill Government of the Island of Jersey*, sigs A2^v, A3^v, 1–9.

41. BL, Add. MS 34,262, fos 40–8; SP 25/96, fo. 117; *Ordres du Conseil et Pièces Analogues Enregistrés a Jersey. Vol. 1. 1536–1678* (St Helier, 1897), 480–2.

42. *Collection of the State Papers of John Thurloe*, iii. 688; *Ile de Jersey: Ordres du Conseil et Pièces Analogues Enregistrés a Jersey. Vol. 1. 1536–1678* (St Helier, 1897), 491–3.

43. *Commons Journal*, vii. 318.

44. SP 25/70, fo. 239; *Actes des États de L'Île de Guernsey. Vol. II. 1651 à 1780*, 5–6; *Note-Book of Pierre le Roy*, 3–4, 14; *Commons Journal*, vii. 309.

45. *Actes des États de L'Île de Guernsey. Vol. II. 1651 à 1780*, 8–9.

46. SP 18/100, fo. 149; *Ile de Jersey. Ordres du Conseil... 1536–1678*, 483–90.

47. SP 18/101, fo. 1.

48. SP 25/93, fo. 3; SP 25/78, fo. 731.

49. *CSPD 1655–6*, 81, 188; *CSPD 1656–7*, 286; *CSPD 1657–8*, 107; *The Diary of Bulstrode Whitelocke, 1605–1675*, ed. Ruth Spalding (1990), 415.

50. SP 47/1, fos 113–15; *Diary of Bulstrode Whitelocke*, 489, 507.

51. SP 46/101, fo. 53.

52. *Note-Book of Pierre le Roy*, 12–13.

53. SP 18/124, fo. 77; SP 18/132, fo. 298; *Ile de Jersey. Ordres du Conseil... 1536–1678*, 483–93; Bernard Capp, *Cromwell's Navy: The Fleet and the English Revolution 1643–1660* (Oxford, 1989), 267–68.

54. *Articles of Impeachment Exhibited against Col. Robert Gibbons and Cap. Richard Yeardley, Late Governors of the Isle of Jersey* (1659), 1–16.

55. Thomas Ashton, *Satan in Samuels Mantle, Or the Cruelty of Germany Acted in Jersey* (1659), title page, 3, 6–7, 14, 23–25.

56. SP 25/79, fo. 117; SP 25/115, fo. 1.

Chapter 10

1. Among major studies, see especially Godfrey Davies, *The Restoration of Charles II, 1658–1660* (San Marino, CA, 1955); Ronald Hutton, *The Restoration: A Political and Religious History of England and Wales 1658–1667* (Oxford, 1985); N. H. Keeble, *The Restoration: England in the 1660s* (Oxford, and Malden, MA, 2002); Tim Harris, *Restoration: Charles II and his Kingdoms, 1660–1685* (2006); George Southcombe and Grant Tapsell, *Restoration Politics, Religion and Culture: Britain and Ireland, 1660–1714* (Basingstoke, 2010).

2. *Actes des États de L'Île de Guernsey. Vol. II. 1651 à 1780* (St Peter Port, 1907), 20–3; SP 29/449, fo. 146.

3. *Calendar of Treasury Books, 1681–1685*, ed. William A. Shaw (1916), 698, 753.

4. *CSPD 1679–80*, 468.

5. 'A Briefe State of Guernsey by the Right Honourable Christopher Lord Hatton', Bod., MS Eng. Hist. b.134, fos 8–9ᵛ; SP 44/55, fos. 124, 468.
6. *CSPD 1673–5*, 560.
7. *CSPD 1680–1*, fo. 380.
8. SP 47/1, fo. 133.
9. 'The Journal of Charles Trumbull', ed. Richard Hocart, *La Société Guernesiaise Report and Transactions* (1985 for 1984), 567, 581,
10. Bod., MS Carte 75, fo. 285.
11. SP 29/162, fo. 140; SP 29/162, fo. 81; SP 29/168, fo. 84; SP 29/170, fo. 36.
12. SP 29/210, fo. 113.
13. SP 8/7, fo. 205; *The Entring Book of Roger Morrice 1671–1691*, ed. Mark Goldie, 6 vols (Woodbridge, 2007), v. 465; *Samuel Pepys's Naval Minutes*, ed. J. R. Tanner, Navy Records Society, 60 (1926), 140.
14. SP 29/212, fo. 145.
15. SP 8/7, fo. 205; *Entring Book of Roger Morrice*, v. 465; *Samuel Pepys's Naval Minutes*, 140.
16. HMC, *The Manuscripts of S. H. Le Fleming* (1890), 297; SP 44/99, fo. 271.
17. *Entring Book of Roger Morrice*, v. 121.
18. SP 44/14, fo. 19; SP 44/44, fo. 25; *Calendar of Treasury Books, 1669–1672*, ed. William A. Shaw (1908), 1305, 1333.
19. *Calendar of Treasury Books, 1669–1672*, 477, 682, 783, 980, 1183, 1223.
20. HMC, *First Report* (1870), 17.
21. Bod., MS Clarendon 84, fo. 236.
22. *CSP Venetian 1666–1668*, 55; SP 44/17, fo. 194; SP 29/450, fos 30, 74, 76.
23. HMC, *Tenth Report* (1906), 113; J. C. Appleby, 'Neutrality, Trade and Privateering 1500–1689', in A. G. Jamieson (ed.), *A People of the Sea: The Maritime History of the Channel Islands* (London and New York, 1986), 61–2.
24. Jean Poingdestre, *Caesarea, Or a Discourse of the Island of Jersey* [c.1682] (St Helier, 1889), 70.
25. SP 47/1, fo. 75; BL, Add. MS 29,557, fos 21, 106; *CSPD 1679–80*, 635.
26. SP 47/1, fo. 105.
27. BL, Add. MS 41,763, fo. 5.
28. *Entring Book of Roger Morrice*, iv. 466.
29. *Commons Journal*, x. 183.
30. TNA, ADM 106/385.
31. *Samuel Pepys's Naval Minutes*, 300.
32. SP 29/153, fo. 154; Bod., MS Clarendon 84, fos 96–7; Richard Worsley, *The History of the Isle of Wight* (1781), 136–8.
33. Bod., MS Clarendon 84, fos 98–104. For Hearth Tax on the Isle of Wight, see *Calendar of Treasury Books, 1667–1668*, ed. William A. Shaw (1905), 27, 175. Charles II's marriage contract with Catherine of Braganza brought the English trading privileges in Brazil.
34. Bod., MS Clarendon 84, fo. 105.
35. *Calendar of Treasury Books 1667–1668*, 480–1, 501, 629.
36. SP 29/153, fo. 155; SP 29/370, fo. 35; Worsley, *History of the Isle of Wight*, 138–9.

37. SP 29/250, fo. 241; SP 29/291, fo. 254; SP 29/338, fo. 158; SP 29/371, fos 266, 280; HMC, *Le Fleming*, 59; Worsley, *History of the Isle of Wight*, 140–1; Andrew M. Coleby, *Central Government and the Localities: Hampshire 1649–1689* (Cambridge, 1987), 102, 151, 177, 218, 223.
38. SP 44/99, fo. 69.
39. SP 29/29, fo. 140; SP 29/47, fo. 50; SP 29/450, fo. 16.
40. SP 29/234, fo. 151; SP 29/257, fo. 199; SP 29/275, fo. 61; Coleby, *Central Government and the* Localities, 112.
41. HMC, *Le Fleming*, 279. There were ten regiments of foot camped on the Isle of Wight in July 1695: *Calendar of Treasury Books, 1693–1696*, ed. William A. Shaw (1935), 1153.
42. SP 8/10, fo. 255.
43. BL, Add MS 46,501, fos 27–9; SP 44/341, fos 541, 545; SP 44/167, fo. 198; *Samuel Pepys's Naval Minutes*, 323; Worsley, *History of the Isle of Wight*, 141, appendix 45.
44. *Calendar of Treasury Books, 1660–1667*, ed. William A. Shaw (1904), 231, 240.
45. Charles Thomas, 'A Glossary of Spoken English in the Isles of Scilly', *Journal of the Royal Institution of Cornwall*, NS 8 (1979), 109–47.
46. 'The Travels of Cosmo III, Grand Duke of Tuscany, through England', in Alan Gibson and R. Pearse Chope (eds), *Early Tours in Devon and Cornwall* (Newton Abbot, 1967), 94–5.
47. SP 44/51, fo. 392; *Calendar of Treasury Books, 1679–1680*, ed. William A. Shaw (1913), 665.
48. G. Forrester Matthews, *The Isles of Scilly: A Constitutional, Economic and Social Survey of the Development of an Island People from Early Times to 1900* (1960), 17.
49. *CSPD 1664–5*, 121; 'Travels of Cosmo III', 93–4; *Calendar of Treasury Books, 1660–1667*, 474, 534, 571.
50. Matthews, *Isles of Scilly*, 14–15.
51. 'Travels of Cosmo III', 93–4.
52. HMC, *Report on the Manuscripts of the Late Reginald Rawdon Hastings*, 3 vols (1928–47), ii. 186.
53. Allan Brodie, 'The Garrison Defences on St Mary's in the Isles of Scilly in the 17th and 18th Centuries', *English Heritage Historical Review*, 7 (2012), 41.
54. *Commons Journal*, vii. 19; 'Travels of Cosmo III', 95. Robert Heath counted sixty-four pieces on St Mary's during his service there in the 1740s: Robert Heath, *A Natural and Historical Account of the Islands of Scilly* (1750), 69.
55. SP 8/10, fo. 255.
56. HMC, *The Manuscripts of Lord Kenyon* (1894), 73–4; John Callow, 'The Limits of Indemnity: The Earl of Derby, Sovereignty and Retribution at the Trial of William Christian, 1660–63', *Seventeenth Century*, 15 (2013), 199–216; G. D. Kinley, 'Illiam Dhone's Petition to the King in Council and its Aftermath: Some New Light', *Isle of Man Natural History and Antiquarian Society Proceedings*, 7 (1974), 576–601. The story is also told in Jennifer Kewley Draskau, *Illiam Dhone: Patriot or Traitor? The Life, Death and Legacy of William Christian* (2012).
57. SP 29/67, fo. 75; SP 44/9, fo. 228.
58. SP 29/67, fo. 174; HMC, *Kenyon*, 73–5; Callow, 'Limits of Indemnity', 209.
59. Dan Hulsebosch, 'English Liberties Outside England: Floors, Doors, Windows, and Ceilings in the Legal Architecture of Empire', in Lorna Hutson (ed.), *The Oxford Handbook of English Law and Literature, 1500–1700* (Oxford, 2017), 747–72.

60. SP 29/67, fo. 304; SP 29/68, fo. 232; SP 29/69, fo. 6; HMC, *Kenyon*, 71–2.
61. SP 29/73, fo. 179; SP 29/75, fo. 180; HMC, *Kenyon*, 70; Draskau, *Illiam Dhone*, 150–66.
62. Kinley, 'Illiam Dhone's Petition', 589.
63. SP 29/448; HMC, Kenyon, 73–5; *The Earl of Derby's Case Stated for the Vindication of the Proceedings at Law in the Isle of Man* (1663), broadside. See also Sir Philip Musgrove's justification of proceeding against Christian: SP 29/80, fo. 139.
64. SP 29/159, fo. 144; SP 44/23, fo. 232.
65. SP 29/23, fo. 163; SP 29/239, fo. 81; HMC, *The Manuscripts of the Marquis of Ormonde*, 7 vols (1895–1912), iv. 9.
66. HMC, *Kenyon*, 85, 135–6.
67. Bod., MS Carte 68, fo. 330^v; HMC, *Kenyon*, 135–6, 259–62, 265; HMC, *Ormonde*, vii. 44. 49, 148, 158; *Calendar of Treasury Books, 1681–1685*, 449, 452, 568, 716, 734, 876.
68. Lancashire Archives, DDKE/acc. 7840 HMC/782.
69. R. H. Kinvig, *History of the Isle of Man* (Douglas, 1944), 152–54; C. W. Gawne, *The Isle of Man and Britain Controversy 1651–1895: From Smuggling to the Common Purse* (Douglas, 2009), 13–28; Sara Goodwins, *A Brief History of the Isle of Man* (Sutton, 2011), 90–2, 97–100.
70. Parliamentary Archives, HL/PO/JO/10/1/286, 302; Huntington Library, MS HM 72020, fos 542–3.
71. *Statutes of the Realm*, 12 Car II. c. 11.
72. Jonathan Duncan, *The History of Guernsey; with Occasional Notices of Jersey, Alderney, and Sark* (1841), 342.
73. *Recueil D'Ordonnances de la Cour Royale de l'Isle de Guernsey . . . 1533–1800*, ed. Robert MacCulloch (St Peter Port, 1852), 192; *Ile de Jersey: Ordres du Conseil et Pièces Analogues Enregistrés a Jersey. Vol. 1. 1536–1678* (St Helier, 1897), 480–92.
74. *Note-Book of Pierre le Roy*, ed. G. E. Lee (St Peter Port, 1893), 4, 19, 27, 31.
75. *Note-Book of Pierre le Roy*, 32–3.
76. Bod., MS Carte 33, fo. 578; Ferdinand Brock Tupper, *The Chronicles of Castle Cornet, Guernsey* (1851), 306.
77. Bod., MS Clarendon 82, fo. 237^v.
78. For Hatton's correspondence, see BL, Add. MSS 29,550–29,552; Bod., MS Clarendon 81–4.
79. Tupper, *Chronicles of Castle Cornet*, 239.
80. BL, Add. MS. 29,551, fo. 77; *Note-Book of Pierre le Roy*, 35; Ferdinand Brock Tupper, *The History of Guernsey, and its Bailiwick; with Occasional Notices of Jersey*, 2nd edn (St Peter Port, 1876), 361–2.
81. SP 29/270, fo. 37; Bod., MS Clarendon 81, fos 234–234^v.
82. SP 29/448, fos 110, 141.
83. SP 29/448, fo. 144.
84. Huntington Library, MS HM 72020, fo. 401; SP 29/448, fo. 178; SP 29/449, fo. 87.
85. Bod., MS Clarendon 81, fos 3–3^v; Tupper, *History of Guernsey*, 361–2.
86. *Note-Book of Pierre le Roy*, 36.
87. SP 29/449, fo. 33; SP 29/450, fo. 79; Bod., MS Clarendon 82, fos 55^v, 119.
88. SP 29/449, fo. 82; 'Briefe State of Guernsey', Bod., Eng. Hist. b.134, c. 34, fo. 5.
89. SP 29/449, fo. 33; SP 29/450, fo. 79; Bod., MS Clarendon 82, fos 55^v, 119.

90. SP 29/449, fo. 87; Bod., MS Clarendon 82, fos 251–2.
91. Tupper, *Chronicles of Castle Cornet*, 276.
92. *Actes des États de L'Île de Guernsey. Vol. II. 1651 à 1780*, p. xix.
93. *Commons Journal*, viii. 167.
94. SP 29/448, fos 141–3.
95. SP 29/448, fo. 141; BL, Add. MS 29,550, fos 434, 443; BL, Add. MS 29,551, fos 45, 47, 71, 73.
96. 'Briefe State of Guernsey', Bod., Eng. Hist. b.134, c. 34, fos 9–9^v; SP 29/38, fo. 75; SP 44/29, fo. 345.
97. *Calendar of Treasury Books, 1660–1667*, 494.
98. SP 44/16, fo. 162^v.
99. William Sheldon to Viscount Fitzharding, 31 December 1664, in HMC, *Seventh Report* (1879), 260.
100. 'Briefe State of Guernsey, Bod., Eng. Hist. b.134, c. 34. fo. 7^v; *The Charters of Guernsey*, ed. Tim Thornton (Bognor Regis, 2004), 154, 167.
101. SP 29/112, fos 76–76^v; Bod., MS Carte 75, fo. 267.
102. *CSPD Charles II Addenda 1660–85*, 132.
103. SP 29/224, fo. 204; 'Briefe State of Guernsey', Bod., Eng. Hist. b.134, c. 34, 7^v; *Charters of Guernsey*, 144–70; *Calendar of Treasury Books, 1667–1668*, 81.
104. BL, Add MSS 29,552–7; *Actes des États de L'Île de Guernsey. Vol. II. 1651 à 1780*, pp. xix–xx; H. D. Turner, 'Viscount Hatton and the Government of Guernsey 1670–1706', *Report and Transactions. Société Guernesiase*, 18 (1970 for 1969), 415–26.
105. 'Briefe State of Guernsey', Bod., Eng. Hist. b.134, c. 34, fo. 4.
106. SP 47/1, fo. 18.
107. SP 29/380, fo. 244.
108. BL, Add. MS 29,553, fo. 44.
109. BL, Add MS 29,554, fos 358–9; Huntington Library, MS HM 72020, fos 259–61, 443–4.
110. SP 47/1, fo. 18.
111. *Actes des États de L'Île de Guernsey. Vol. II. 1651 à 1780*, 34.
112. SP 47/1, fo. 19; HMC, *Le Fleming*, 99.
113. Bod., MS Rawlinson D 1481, fos 366–7, MS Rawlinson D 1298, fos 93–6; Duncan, *History of Guernsey*, 111–13; Tupper, *Chronicles of Castle Cornet*, 280–3; Christine Ozanne, 'Contemporary Accounts of the Explosion at Castle Cornet, December 1672', *Reports and Transactions of Société Guernesiase* (1930), 41–55.
114. BL, Add MS 29,554, fos 259–99, 354–8, 363–77, 472–4; *Recueil D'Ordonnances de la Cour Royale de l'Isle de Guernsey... 1533–1800*, 202; *CSPD 1682*, 515.
115. BL, Add. MS 29,555, fos 35, 52, 56, 123, 146.
116. 'Journal of Charles Trumbull', 569, 573. For expectations in December 1677 that the number of troops in the Channel Islands would be doubled, see *Entring Book of Roger Morrice*, ii. 39.
117. BL, Kings MS 48, fo. 2.
118. BL, Kings MS 48, fos 35, 55.
119. SP 47/1, fos 24, 28, 34, 45, 119–21, 127.
120. *Calendar of Treasury Books, 1685–1689*, ed. William A. Shaw (1923), 1475, 1638.

121. 'Le Procés entre les États et le Gouverneur Lanier: La Rémonstrance des États', *Société Jersiaise Bulletin Annuel*, 13 (1888), 278–9.
122. SP 8/10, fo. 255; SP 32/5, fo. 91; SP 44/205, fo. 103.
123. SP 32/5, fo. 91; SP 44/205, fo. 103; SP 47/2, fo. 17; HMC, *Hastings*, ii. 344; HMC, *Report on the Manuscripts of the Marquis of Downshire*, 3 vols (1924–40), i. 343, 685.
124. HMC, *Downshire*, i. 685.
125. SP 44/164, fo. 9.
126. SP 47/1, fo. 69; *Ile de Jersey: Ordres du Conseil . . . 1536–1678*, 187–9, 228.
127. 'Le Procés entre les États et le Gouverneur Lanier', 278–9; Thornton (ed.), *Charters of Guernsey*, 146, 159–60.
128. SP 29/449, fo. 146–8.
129. SP 47/1, fo. 74.
130. 'Le Procés entre les États et le Gouverneur Lanier', 254–80.
131. Harris, *Restoration*, 138–46.
132. 'Le Procés entre les États et le Gouverneur Lanier', 264–9.
133. SP 29/363, fo. 208.
134. *Calendar of Treasury Books, 1660–1667*, 86, 362, 393, 420; BL, Add. MS. 72,608, fo. 4.
135. SP 47/1, fo. 78.
136. SP 47/1, fo. 160.
137. SP 32/14, fo. 41.
138. SP 29/450, fo. 117; *Ile de Jersey: Ordres du Conseil . . . 1536–1678*, 290.
139. *CSPD 1679–80*, 313. In a similar case in Guernsey, the jurats claimed an interest if a soldier murdered an islander, but declared 'it did not belong to them' if one member of the garrison killed another: BL Add. MS 29,556, fo. 46.
140. *Ile de Jersey: Ordres du Conseil et Pièces Analogues Enregistrés a Jersey. Vol. 2. 1678–1724* (St Helier, 1898), 8–13.
141. *Ile de Jersey: Ordres du Conseil . . . 1678–1724*, 37; see also the orders of James II establishing martial law on the island, pp. 106–30; John M. Collins, *Martial Law and English Laws, c.1500–c.1700* (Cambridge, 2016).
142. *Statutes of the Realm*, 31 Charles II c. 2; Paul D. Halliday, *Habeas Corpus: From England to Empire* (Cambridge, MA, 2010), 81–85, 204, 227–9, 437; Paul D. Halliday, '11,000 Prisoners: Habeas Corpus, 1500–1800', in Paul Brand and Joshua Getzler (eds), *Judges and Judging in the History of the Common Law and Civil Law: From Antiquity to Modern Times* (Cambridge, 2012), 259–76.
143. SP 29/224, fo. 204.
144. SP 47/1, Orders in Council 19 May 1671, amending orders of April 1668. Dozens of cases are reported in *Ile de Jersey: Ordres du Conseil . . . 1536–1678*, 190–417.
145. *CSPD 1680–1*, 57; SP 47/1 fo. 41.
146. *The Channel Island Journals of Charles and William Trumbull 1677*, ed. Joan Stevens, Jean Arthur, and Collette Stevens (St Helier, 2004), 324.
147. *Ile de Jersey: Ordres du Conseil . . . 1536–1678*, 204–5, 229–30, 260–4. Dozens of cases are reported in this and the succeeding volume, under successive administrations.
148. SP 47/1, fos 105–7; SP 44/164, fo. 39.
149. 'A Relation of Sir Edward Carteret Knt. Complaint against Sr John Lanier', *Société Jersiaise Bulletin Annuel*, 4 (1897–1901), 71–4, 386.

150. Jersey Archives, L/F/08/A/1 and D/AP/AE/19 for expenditures in 1665–6.
151. BL, Add. MS 72,608, fo. 1; BL, Kings MS 48, fo. 69; *Channel Island Journals of Charles and William Trumbull*, 11, 32–3, 37.
152. HMC, *Report on the Manuscripts of Lord Montagu* (1900), 173.
153. SP 44/42, fo. 21; SP 44/164, fos 7, 9; SP 44/48, fo. 123.
154. SP 47/1, fos 74, 105; BL, Add. MS 72,608, fo. 1; Bod., MS Clarendon 84, fos 236, 296; BL, Kings MS 48, fo. 69; *Channel Island Journals of Charles and William Trumbull*, 10.
155. Bod., MS Tanner 46, fo. 48; *Channel Island Journals of Charles and William Trumbull*, 11.
156. *Ile de Jersey: Ordres du Conseil . . . 1678–1724*, 157–61; *Calendar of Treasury Books, 1689–1692*, ed. William A. Shaw (1931), 146, 324.
157. SP 32/3, fos 260–262, SP 32/14, fo. 94; *Calendar of Treasury Books, 1689–1692*, 1285, 1297.
158. SP 44/97, fo. 295; Huntington Library, MS. EL 1891, 'Considerations Relating to the Affairs of Jersey', 1691; *Calendar of Treasury Books, 1693–1696*, 878.
159. SP 32/3, fo. 260; *CSPD 1689–1702*, iv. 446.
160. Bod., MS Rawlinson D 1481, fo. 365; James Stocall, *Freedom. Or, the Description of the Excellent Civill Government of the Island of Jersey* (1652), 7; Huntington Library, MS EL 1891, 1897.

Chapter 11

1. An earlier version of this chapter appeared as David Cressy, 'Puritan Martyrs in Island Prisons', *Journal of British Studies*, 57 (2018), 736–54.
2. Lauren Benton, *A Search for Sovereignty: Law and Geography in European Empires, 1400–1900* (Cambridge, 2010), 163, 220.
3. Reports of the Star Chamber proceedings survive in manuscript, most accessible, though not complete, in *Cobbett's Complete Collection of State Trials*, 34 vols (1809–28), iii. 711–70. Recent historiography includes Kevin Sharpe, *The Personal Rule of Charles I* (New Haven and London, 1992), 758–65; David Cressy, 'The Portraiture of Prynne's Pictures: Performance on the Public Stage', in David Cressy, *Travesties and Transgressions in Tudor and Stuart England* (Oxford, 2000), 213–33; Mark Kishlansky, 'Martyrs' Tales,' *Journal of British Studies*, 53 (2014), 334–55; Cressy, 'Puritan Martyrs in Island Prisons', 736–54.
4. Peter Lake and Michael Questier, 'Prisons, Priests and People', in Nicholas Tyacke (ed.), *England's Long Reformation 1500–1800* (1998), 195–33. See also 'Early Modern Prisons: Exploring Gaols, Bridewells and other Forms of Detention, 1500–1800', https://earlymodernprisons.org/ a blog hosted by Richard Bell and Rachel Weil (accessed June 2018).
5. *ODNB*, sub. 'Alexander Leighton', 'Peter Smart', and William Prynne'.
6. SP 16/354, fos 379ff; *Documents Relating to the Proceedings against William Prynne, in 1634 and 1637*, ed. Samuel Rawson Gardiner, Camden Society, NS 18 (1877), 63–4.
7. SP 16/362, fos 141, 208.
8. SP 16/367, fos 192–95; *Documents Relating to the Proceedings against William Prynne*, 63–6.

9. Paul D. Halliday, *Habeas Corpus: From England to Empire* (Cambridge, MA., 2010), 81–5, 204, 227–9, 437. The peculiarity of island jurisdiction is discussed in A. J. Eagleston, *The Channel Islands under Tudor Government 1485-1642* (Cambridge, 1949); Darryl Ogier, *Reformation and Society in Guernsey* (Woodbridge, 1996); Tim Thornton, *The Channel Islands 1370-1640: Between England and Normandy* (Woodbridge, 2012), also Chapters 3 and 4. See also Amanda L. Tyler, *Habeas Corpus in Wartime: From the Tower of London to Guantanamo Bay* (New York, 2017).

10. Peter Heylyn, *A Full Relation of Two Journeys: The One into the Main-Land of France. The Other into some of the Adjacent Islands* (1656), 279–89; *The Severall Humble Petitions of D. Bastwicke, M Burton, M. Prynne* (1641), 9.

11. *Severall Humble Petitions of D. Bastwicke, M Burton, M. Prynne*, 9; Peter Heylyn, *Cyprianus Anglicus: Or, the History of the Life and Death of the Most Reverend and Renowned Prelate William, by Divine Providence Lord Archbishop of Canterbury* (1668), 334–5. For Instantius, banished 'in Sylinancim insulam, quae utltra Britannia sita est', see Daniel Washburn, *Banishment in the Later Roman Empire, 284-476* CE (2012), 31.

12. Heylyn, *Cyprianus Anglicus*, 334; Clarendon, *The History of the Rebellion and Civil War in England*, ed. W. Dunn Macray, 6 vols (Oxford, 1888), i. 267.

13. *Documents Relating to the Proceedings against William Prynne*, 65; Thomas May, *The History of the Parliament of England, which began November the Third, MDCXL* (1647), 79–80; Andrew McRae, *Literature, Satire and the Early Modern State* (2004), 189; Andrew McRae, 'Stigmatizing Prynne: Seditious Libel, Political Satire and the Construction of Opposition', in Ian Atherton and Julie Sanders (eds), *The 1630s: Interdisciplinary Essays* (Manchester, 2006), 171–88.

14. William Prynne, *Romes Master-Peece, or, The Grand Conspiracy of the Pope and his Iesuited Instruments* (1644), epistle dedicatory.

15. An imprisoned debtor escaped from Mont Orgeuil, Jersey, in 1631, after two years' confinement, and fled to France: SP 16/533, fos 105, 186. A Flemish pirate made a similar escape in 1677: *CSPD 1677-8*, 500. The failed attempt of the Bandinells in 1645 points to some of the difficulties: Philip Falle, *An Account of the Island of Jersey*, with notes by Edward Durell (St Helier, 1837), 334–6.

16. *Documents Relating to the Proceedings against William Prynne*, 65–6.

17. Henry Burton, *Englands Complaint to Iesvs Christ, Against the Bishops Canons* (1640), sig. B2^v. Burton's authorship is established in David Como, *Radical Parliamentarians and the English Civil War* (Oxford, 2018), 67–72.

18. SP 16/471, fos 65–8; *Severall Humble Petitions of D. Bastwicke, M Burton, M. Prynne*, 9–20; *Proceedings in the Opening Session of the Long Parliament*, ed. Maija Jansson, 7 vols (Rochester, NY, 2000–7), i. 28–9, 48–50.

19. *CSPD 1637*, 332, 403, 433, 434, 492; Cressy, 'Portraiture of Prynne's Pictures', 226–9.

20. SP 16/385, fo. 87; *Documents Relating to the Proceedings against William Prynne*, 64–5.

21. *Severall Humble Petitions of D. Bastwicke, M Burton, M. Prynne*, 8–9.

22. The following description is derived from SP 16/385, fos 87–9.

23. SP 16/385, fo. 87.

24. *Documents Relating to the Proceedings against William Prynne*, 64–5, 68.

25. 'Reparations for His Majesties Castles of Mont Orgeuil and Elizabeth', *Société Jersiaise Bulletin Annuel*, 7 (1910–14), 170–3.

26. William Prynne, *Movnt-Orgveil: Or Divine and Profitable Meditations* (1641), 7, 28. See also William Prynne, *Comfortable Cordials against Discomfortable Feares of Imprisonment* (1641), sig. B2.

27. *Severall Humble Petitions of D. Bastwicke, M Burton, M. Prynne*, 9; SP 16/418, fo. 198. George Carteret was nephew to Sir Philip Carteret and followed his uncle as bailiff and lieutenant governor.

28. G. R. Balleine, *All for the King: The Life Story of Sir George Carteret* (St Helier, 1976), 18.

29. William Prynne, *The Antipathie of the English Lordly Prelacie* (1641), epistle dedicatory.

30. Prynne, *Movnt-Orgveil*, sigs ¶3, A^v, A4, 55, 113.

31. William Prynne, *The Lyar Confounded or A Brief Refutation of John Lilburnes Miserably-Mistated Case* (1645), 33, 42.

32. Prynne, *Lyar Confounded*, 42.

33. *Articles Exhibited against Sir Philipp Carteret, Governour of the Isle of Jersy* (1642).

34. Prynne, *Lyar Confounded*, 38, 39.

35. Michael Lemprière, Henry Dumaresq, and Abraham Hérault, *Pseudo-Mastix: The Lyar's Whipp*, in *Société Jersiaise Bulletin Annuel*, 13 (1888), 309–55. No seventeenth-century edition of *Pseudo-Mastix* is known to survive. The nineteenth-century scribal copy is in the Lord Coutanche Library, Jersey.

36. *Pseudo-Mastix*, 314–15, 345, 348, 352.

37. William M. Lamont, *Marginal Prynne 1600–1669* (1963), 188.

38. William Prynne, *Brief Animadversions on, and Additional Explanatory Amendments of ... the Fourth Part of the Institutes* (1669), 207.

39. *Severall Humble Petitions of D. Bastwicke, M Burton, M. Prynne*, 12 (i.e. 20); Henry Burton, *A Narration of the Life of Mr Henry Burton* (1643), 17–19, 34; SP 16/537, fo. 90.

40. TNA, E 178/540; SP 16/378, fo. 132; SP 16/537, fo. 132.

41. Ferdinand Brock Tupper, *The Chronicles of Castle Cornet, Guernsey* (1851), 59, account of Peter Carey, prisoner in 1643.

42. SP 16/537, fo. 27–27^v.

43. Burton, *Narration*, 20–1; SP 16/458, fo. 77.

44. 'Jean de la Marche ... The Diary', ed. W. Rolleston and T. W. M. de Guerir, *Report and Transactions Société Guernesiase*, 11 (1930–2), 201.

45. 'Jean de la Marche ... The Diary', 201; Burton, *Narration*, 20–1, 37; Henry Burton, *The Sovnding of the Two Last Trvmpets* (1641), sig. A3. *The Birdman of Alacatraz* was an award-winning film of 1962 on the life of inmate Robert Stroud.

46. Jean de la Marche, *A Complaint of the False Prophets Mariners upon the Drying up of their Hierarchicall Euphrates* (1641), title page, sigs a–a2^v, 1; 'Jean de la Marche ... The Diary', 198. An admirer of Burton, de la Marche was later a member of the Westminster Assembly, and may have been responsible for recommending *The Orders for Ecclesiastical Discipline According to that which Hath Been Practiced since the Reformation of the Church in ... the Iles of Garnsey, Gersey, Spark and Alderny* (1642) as an alternative to episcopal government.

47. Burton, *Narration*, 22; Henry Burton, *A Replie to a Relation of the Conference Between William Laude and Mr Fisher the Jesuite* (Amsterdam, i.e. London?, 1640), sigs C2^v–C3. The final page is dated 26 June 1639. For the printing history of *Replie to a Relation*

and other works attributed to Burton, see Como, *Radical Parliamentarians and the English Civil War*, 67–72.

48. Burton, *Narration*, 28, 32.
49. 'Jean de la Marche... The Diary', 204.
50. Nathaniel Darrell to George Carteret, 27 June 1640, SP 16/458, fo. 77.
51. Burton, *Sovnding of the Two Last Trvmpets*, title page, sig. A4, 33, 41. Cf. Henry Burton, *The Seven Vials or A Brief and Plain Exposition upon the 15: and 16: Chapters of the Revelation* (1628), which is concerned more with the Beast and the Antichrist than the end of days.
52. de la Marche, *Complaint of the False Prophets Mariners*, sigs a–a2; 'Jean de la Marche ... The Diary', 204; Cressy, *Travesties*, 230.
53. SP 16/369, fo. 242.
54. SP 16/368, fo. 190.
55. *Severall Humble Petitions of D. Bastwicke, M Burton, M. Prynne*, 11–15; SP 16/471, fo. 68; SP 16/473, fo. 148; Parliamentary Archives, HL/PO/JO/101/174, 202.
56. Parliamentary Archives, HL/PO/JO/101/174, 202; SP 16/448, fo. 50; John Bastwick, *Flagellum Pontificis et Episcoporum Latialium* (1641), 8; John Bastwick, *The Utter Routing of the Whole Army of all the Independents and Sectaries* (1646), 4. Bastwick's phrase echoes that of St Augustine: 'a dying life, shall I call it, or a living death' (*Saint Augustines Confessions Translated ... by William Watts* (1631), 12).
57. John Bastwick, *A Iust Defence of John Bastwick* (1645), 14, 37. Neither John Bastwick, *The Confession of the Faithfull Witnesse of Christ* (1641), nor John Bastwick, *A Declaration Demonstrating and Infallibly Proving that all Malignants, whether they be Prelates, Popish-cavaliers, with All Other Ill-Affected Persons, Are enemies to God and the King* (1643), mentions his imprisonment in Scilly.
58. Bastwick, *Utter Routing of the Whole Army*, 4.
59. Susanna Bastwick, *Innocency Cleared, True Worth Predicated, against False Aspertions: in a Letter sent to Mr Henry Burton. From a Christian Friend; In Defence of Dr Bastwick, one of his Quondam Fellow Sufferers* (1645), title page, 3.
60. Susanna Bastwick, *To the High Court of Parliament ... The Remonstrance and Humble Petition of Susanna Bastwick* (1654).
61. William Prynne, *A New Discovery of the Prelates Tyranny* (1641), 2nd pagination, 179.
62. Kishlansky, 'Martyrs' Tales', 342.
63. Statutes of the Realm, 16 Car. I. c. 10.

Chapter 12

1. *Eikon Basilike. The Povrtaictvre of His Sacred Maiestie in His Solitvdes and Svfferings* (1648).
2. *A New Declaration of the Kings Majesties Going to the Isle of Weight* (1647), 1.
3. Sir Thomas Herbert, 'Threnodia Carolina', Bod., MS Ashmole 1141, fo. 9ᵛ.
4. John Ashburnham, *The True Copie of a Letter from Mr Ashburnham to a Friend* (1648), 2.
5. *A Narrative by John Ashburnham*, 2 vols (1830), ii. 102.
6. Edward Whalley, *Joyfull Newes of the Kings Majesties Safe Arrivall in the Isle of Wheight* (1647), 2.

7. Ashburnham, *True Copie of a Letter*, 3.
8. *Memoirs of Sir John Berkeley* (1702), 47, 51.
9. *Narrative by John Ashburnham*, ii. 118; *Memoirs of Sir John Berkeley*, 76–8.
10. *Commons Journal*, v. 356; *Documents Relating to the Civil War 1642–1648*, ed. J. R. Powell and W. K. Timings, Navy Records Society, 195 (1963), 296,
11. *Narrative by John Ashburnham*, ii. 112.
12. Cromwell later reminded Hammond of the time in 1647 when he 'desired retirement from the army, or thought of quiet in the Isle of Wight' (*The Writings and Speeches of Oliver Cromwell*, ed. Wilbur Cortez Abbott, 4 vols (Cambridge, MA., 1937–47, repr. Oxford, 1988), i. 696.
13. *Memoirs of Sir John Berkeley*, 54, 65; Ashburnham, *True Copie of a Letter*, 3–4.
14. *Narrative by John Ashburnham*, ii. 114; *Memoirs of Sir John Berkeley*, 57. A similar story is told in *The Memoirs of Edmund Ludlow*, ed. C. H. Firth, 2 vols (Oxford, 1864), i. 167–70.
15. *A Royalist's Notebook: The Commonplace Book of Sir John Oglander*, ed. Francis Bamford (1936), 112–15.
16. *CSPD 1702–3*, 350. The story was told half a century later to intercede for the life of Captain Urry, who was condemned by court martial.
17. *Commons Journal*, v. 360.
18. *The Clarke Papers: Selections from the Papers of William Clarke*, ed. C. H. Firth, 3 vols (1891–9), i. 420.
19. Bod., MS Clarendon 30/2667, London intelligence, 6 and 9 December 1647.
20. Ashburnham, *True Copie of a Letter*, 4–5; Clarendon, *The History of the Rebellion and Civil War in England*, ed. W. Dunn Macray, 6 vols (Oxford, 1888), iv. 265–7.
21. C. W. Firebrace, *Honest Harry: Being the Biography of Sir Henry Firebrace, Knight (1619–1691)* (1932), 254.
22. *The Remonstrance of the Inhabitants of the Three Isles of Wight, Garnsey, and Jersey* (1647), 5.
23. Sir Thomas Herbert, *Memoirs of the Last Two Years of the Reign of that Unparallell'd Prince, of Ever Blessed Memory, King Charles I* (1711), 38.
24. Ireton to Hammond, 21 November 1647, in *Letters between Col. Robert Hammond, Governor of the Isle of Wight, and the Committee of Lords and Commons at Derby-House*, ed. Thomas Birch (1764), 21.
25. Hammond to Fairfax, 19 December 1647, in *Clarke Papers*, i. 420.
26. Parliamentary Archives, HL/PO/JO/10/1/245.
27. *Commons Journal*, v. 413–14.
28. George Hillier, *A Narrative of the Attempted Escapes of Charles the First from Carisbrook Castle* (1852); Jack D. Jones, *The Royal Prisoner: Charles I at Carisbrooke* (1965).
29. Parliamentary Archives, HL/PO/JO/10/1/245; *Royalist's Notebook*, 114.
30. *The Kings Maiesties Last Speeche in the Isle of Weight* (1648), 2.
31. Firebrace, *Honest Harry*, 255, 265, 32; Jones, *Royal Prisoner*, 62–3, 141–42; Clarendon, *History of the Rebellion*, iv. 457; HMC, *Manuscripts of . . . the Duke of Portland*, 2 vols (1891–7), i. 601, 603.
32. *Letters between Col. Robert Hammond . . . and the Committee . . . at Derby-House*, 27, 33, 36; *Royalist's Notebook*, 117.

33. William Smith to Sir Richard Leveson, 20 February 1648, in HMC, *Fifth Report* (1876), 173.

34. Edward Baynton, *The Kings Majesties Remonstrance to His Subjects of England* (1647), 1.

35. Bod., MS Clarendon 30/2667.

36. Herbert, *Memoirs of the Last Two Years*, 40.

37. Baynton, *The Kings Majesties Remonstrance*, 1; *Memoirs of Edmund Ludlow*, i. 171.

38. Herbert, *Memoirs of the Last Two Years*, 39–40; Jones, *Royal Prisoner*, 46. For general discussion of the king's accessibility, see David Cressy, *Charles I and the People of England* (Oxford, 2015), 151–76.

39. HMC, *Report on the Pepys Manuscripts* (1911), 224; Herbert, *Memoirs of the Last Two Years*, 42; *CSPD January 1648–January 1649*, 13, 37 (from *Perfect Occurrences*, nos 58, 64); Richard Worsley, *The History of the Isle of Wight* (1781), 118–19.

40. *Commons Journal*, v. 413–14; HMC, *Ninth Report* (1884), pt ii, 439; HMC, *Pepys*, 222.

41. Robert Ashton, *Counter-Revolution: The Second Civil War and its Origins, 1646–8* (New Haven and London, 1994).

42. *Remonstrance of the Inhabitants of the Three Isles of Wight, Garnsey, and Jersey*, 4.

43. *Constitutional Documents of the Puritan Revolution 1625–1660*, ed. Samuel Rawson Gardiner, (Oxford, 1906), 347–53.

44. *Memoirs of Sir John Berkeley*, 75; *Narrative by John Ashburnham*, ii. 125.

45. *Writings and Speeches of Oliver Cromwell*, i. 574. Sir Edward Hyde was also privy to plans to bring the king to Jersey: Bod., MS Clarendon 30.2/2670.

46. S. Elliott Hoskins, *Charles the Second in the Channel Islands*, 2 vols (1854), ii. 193.

47. Bod., MS Rawlinson B 225, fo. 1^v (eighteenth-century transcript of Dowcett letters).

48. *Commons Journal*, v. 413–14; *A Designe by Captain Barley, and Others, to Surprize Carisbrook Castle* (1648), 1; John Rushworth, *Historical Collections the Fourth and Last Part*, 2 vols (1701), ii. 955; Clarendon, *History of the Rebellion*, iv. 279–80. For the quartering of Burley's body, see *CSPD 1648–9*, 13–14, citing *Perfect Occurrences*, NS 58.

49. *Writings and Speeches of Oliver Cromwell*, i. 574–7; *Letters between Col. Robert Hammond . . . and the Committee . . . at Derby-House*, 24, 32; *Designe by Captain Barley, and Others*, 6; Rushworth, *Historical Collections the Fourth and Last Part*, ii. 955; Jones, *Royal Prisoner*, 73.

50. *Letters between Col. Robert Hammond . . . and the Committee . . . at Derby-House*, 34, 37, 68.

51. The image appears on the title page of *An Ould Ship Called an Exhortation to Continue All Subjects in their Due Obedience* (1648), *New Articles for Peace, Delivered by the Kings Majesty* (1648), and *A Most Gracious Message sent by the Kings Majesty* (1648).

52. *Remonstrance of the Inhabitants of the Three Isles of Wight, Garnsey, and Jersey*, 5.

53. *The Declaration of Col. Poyer, and Col. Powel* (1648), 3; *A Speedy Cvre to Open the Eyes of the Blinde, and the Eares of the Deafe Citizens of London* (1648), 7.

54. John Taylor, *Tailors Travels, from London, to the Isle of Wight* (1648), 13.

55. *The Declaration, Together with the Petition and Remonstrance of . . . Hampshire* (1648), sig. A3^v; *The Remonstrance and Declaration of the Knights, Esquires, Gentlemen, and Freeholders, in Colchester* (1648), 4, 7, 8. See also *The Wisedome Patience and Constancie of our Most Gracious Soveraigne Lord, King Charles* (1648), title page, 5. The newspaper *Mercurius Pragmaticus*, 4–7 January 1648, remarked similarly on the

unchristian cruelty of the king's captors, who 'debar him of the society of wife, children, and friends, which is never denied to the veriest rogue in Newgate'.

56. SP 21/24, fos 129, 141, 153, 187, 229, 253, 275; HMC, *Portland*, i. 487, 589; *His Maiesties Demands to Collonel Hammond* (1648), 1–2; *His Majesties Declaration In the Isle of Wight* (1648), 3.

57. *Letters between Col. Robert Hammond . . . and the Committee . . . at Derby-House*, 33, 41, 43, 45, 48, 86, 90.

58. Firebrace, *Honest Harry*, 256.

59. Firebrace, *Honest Harry*, 257. For sanitized and contradictory accounts of this episode, see *Narrative by John Ashburnham*, ii. 124–6.

60. *Writings and Speeches of Oliver Cromwell*, i. 594; Clarendon, *History of the Rebellion*, iv. 459.

61. Firebrace, *Honest Harry*, 271; Jones, *Royal Prisoner*, 84, plate 6.

62. Firebrace, *Honest Harry*, 267.

63. Rushworth, *Historical Collections the Fourth and Last Part*, ii. 1038; *Narrative by John Ashburnham*, ii. 126; *Writings and Speeches of Oliver Cromwell*, i. 594; *Letters between Col. Robert Hammond . . . and the Committee . . . at Derby-House*, 40–5.

64. Firebrace, *Honest Harry*, 276–83, 305–7.

65. HMC, *Portland*, i. 589; Firebrace, *Honest Harry*, 306, 308.

66. Firebrace, *Honest Harry*, 307–8.

67. Firebrace, *Honest Harry*, 273–5.

68. *The Kings Maiesties Last Speeche in the Isle of Weight*, 1, title page.

69. Firebrace, *Honest Harry*, 285.

70. *Clarke Papers*, ii. 23; *A Letter from His Maiesties Court in the Isle of Wight* (1648), 1–2; Firebrace, *Honest Harry*, 315–17.

71. *His Maiesties Demands to Collonel Hammond*, 3; Jones, *Royal Prisoner*, 95–7.

72. Firebrace, *Honest Harry*, 258, 287, 288.

73. SP 29/2, fo. 39. Petitioning for a place at the Restoration, Dowcett claimed that he 'to the utmost endeavoured his majesty's escape', risked trial for treason during the Commonwealth, and eventually found refuge in Holland.

74. SP 29/88, fo. 98; *His Majesties Declaration in the Isle of Wight*, 1–2; Clarendon, *History of the Rebellion*, iv. 458.

75. Richard Osborne, *Two Letters Sent by Mr Richard Osburn* (1648); Richard Osborne, *The Charge of High-Treason Delivered Into the House of Lords* (1648); Richard Osborne, *The Independent's Loyalty. Or, The Most Barbarous Plot (to Murther His Sacred Majestie)* (1648). After the Restoration, Rolph suffered for his part in this episode and was himself imprisoned at Carisbrooke Castle.

76. Firebrace, *Honest Harry*, 323–7. Transcriptions of the king's letters to Hopkins also appear in Thomas Wagstaffe, *A Vindication of K. Charles the Martyr*, 3rd edn (1711), 141–63. At the Restoration, George Hopkins petitioned for a position, because he and his father, attending King Charles on the Isle of Wight, 'found a way of corresponding with his majesty by letter', and spent money on the king's behalf when he stayed with them in Newport: SP 63/305, fo. 173. Other later petitioners who claimed to have served Charles I 'in his closest restraint in the Isle of Wight' included Mabella Cole, the wife of John Cole of Odiham, SP 29/224, fo. 114, and the widow of Sir John Weems,

who allegedly advanced money 'toward rescuing King Charles from captivity in the Isle of Wight' (*CSPD 1703–4*, 419). Thomas Bishop, the butcher who supplied meat to King Charles in the Isle of Wight, was still petitioning for his payment in 1670: *Calendar of Treasury Books, 1669–1672*, ed. William A. Shaw (1908), 356, 411, 560.

77. Sarah Poynting, 'Deciphering the King: Charles I's Letters to Jane Whorwood, *Seventeenth Century*, 21 (2006), 128–40; Nadine Akkerman, *Invisible Agents: Women and Espionage in Seventeenth-Century Britain* (Oxford, 2018), 34–5, 42, 45–59. See also John Fox, *The King's Smuggler: Jane Whorwood, Secret Agent to Charles I* (2011).

78. Firebrace, *Honest Harry*, 283.

79. Firebrace, *Honest Harry*, 291–3; Poynting, 'Deciphering the King', 134; Akkerman, *Invisible Agents*, 56–8.

80. Firebrace, *Honest Harry*, 333; Poynting, 'Deciphering the King', 134–7.

81. *Mercurius Militaris* (10–17 October 1648); *Making the News: An Anthology of the Newsbooks of Revolutionary England 1641–1660*, ed. Joad Raymond (Moreton-in-Marsh, 1993), 178–79.

82. *Commons Journal*, v. 658.

83. HMC, *Pepys*, 224.

84. *Royalist's Notebook*, 121.

85. Taylor, *Tailors Travels, from London, to the Isle of Wight*, 1, 8, 10–12.

86. Wagstaffe, *Vindication*, 150; Hillier, *Narrative*, 258–72.

87. *A Copy of a Letter Sent from a Gentleman in Carisbrooke-Castle* (1648), 2–4.

88. Firebrace, *Honest Harry*, 343–4.

89. Firebrace, *Honest Harry*, 346–7; Wagstaffe, *Vindication*, 162–3.

90. Bod., MS Ashmole 800, fos 208ᵛ–209.

91. SP 21/25, fo. 97.

92. Examination of Thomas Coke, in HMC, *Portland*, i. 593.

93. *A Remonstrance or Declaration of the Army: Presented to the House of Commons on Munday Novemb. 20. 1648* (1648), title page, 1; *Writings and Speeches of Oliver Cromwell*, i. 685–8.

94. *A Declaration Concerning the King from the Citizens of London* (1648), 6.

95. *Clarke Papers*, ii. 55, 59–60.

96. Edward Cooke, *Certain Passages which Happened at Newport in the Isle of Wight* (1690), 1–2, 12–18; Firebrace, *Honest Harry*, 259, 345–7; Rushworth, *Historical Collections the Fourth and Last Part*, ii. 1236, 1346; Jones, *Royal Prisoner*, 130–67.

97. *Clarke Papers*, ii. 66; *The Moderate*, 12–19 December 1648; Clarendon, *History of the Rebellion*, iv. 463. Cobbett would end his life as a prisoner on the island of Guernsey (see Chapter 14).

98. Henry Jones, *Vectis. The Isle of Wight: A Poem in Three Cantos* (1766), 16, 35–6.

Chapter 13

1. Amanda L. Tyler, *Habeas Corpus in Wartime: From the Tower of London to Guantanamo Bay* (New York, 2017), 22.

2. Resolutions of 14 March, 24 August, and 31 August 1649, in a compilation of 'Ordinances of the Parliament', *Die Veneris, 24 Augusti* (1649), Huntington Library, RB 481390 (80).
3. SP 18/11, fo. 132; SP 25/9, fo. 13; SP 25/87, fo. 45.
4. SP 18/11, fo. 132; SP 25/8, fo. 26; *A Collection of the State Papers of John Thurloe*, ed. Thomas Birch, 7 vols (1742), i. 158. Mildmay had been a gentleman usher to Charles I during his island captivity.
5. *A Royalist's Notebook: The Commonplace Book of Sir John Oglander*, ed. Francis Bamford (1936), 131.
6. *An Elegy Upon the Decease of . . . the Princesse Elizabeth* (1650); 'An Elegy on the Death of the Princesse Elizabeth in Carisbrooke Castle', BL, Thomason E. 850 [23].
7. *Royalist's Notebook*, 133; SP 18/11, fos 16, 33, 132; SP 18/26, fo. 108; SP 18/33, fo. 96
8. SP 25/22, fo. 53; SP 25/23, fo. 39; SP 18/73, fos 166, 170; SP 25/66, fo. 110.
9. SP 25/76, fo. 259.
10. SP 18/102, fos 99–100.
11. SP 18/73, fo. 170.
12. *Collection of the State Papers of John Thurloe*, iii. 512, iv. 339.
13. SP 18/188, fo. 66; *Note-Book of Pierre le Roy*, ed. G. E. Lee (St Peter Port, 1893), 11.
14. David Underdown, *Royalist Conspiracy in England 1649–1660* (New Haven, 1960), 14, 130, 131, 143, 160; P. H. Hardacre, 'The Further Adventures of Henry Norwood', *Virginia Magazine of History and Biography*, 67 (1959), 271–83.
15. *Collection of the State Papers of John Thurloe*, v. 427–8.
16. SP 18/188, fo. 66; *Diary of Thomas Burton Esq, Member in the Parliament of Oliver and Richard Cromwell, from 1656 to 1659*, ed. J. T. Rutt, 4 vols (1828), iv. 151; Underdown, *Royalist Conspiracy*, 234.
17. SP 18/157A, fo. 23; SP 25/78, fo. 209; SP 25/114, fo. 1011; *Collection of the State Papers of John Thurloe*, vi. 580, 617; HMC, *Fifth Report* (1876), 177; Underdown, *Royalist Conspiracy*, 224.
18. Austin Woolrych, *Commonwealth to Protectorate* (Oxford, 1982), 325–64.
19. SP 18/211, fo. 24.
20. William Prynne, *Demophilos, or, The Assertor of the Peoples Liberty* (1658), 54–5.
21. Pauline Gregg, *Free-Born John: A Biography of John Lilburne* (1961); Michael Braddick, *The Common Freedom of the People: John Lilburne & the English Revolution* (Oxford, 2018).
22. *Collection of the State Papers of John Thurloe*, i. 451; ii. 582.
23. *Commons Journal*, vii. 358; SP 18/99, fo. 235.
24. SP 18/71, fo. 153; SP 18/81, fo. 31; SP 25/75, fos 183, 263, 275; SP 25/112, fos 17–19. On Lilburne and *habeas corpus*, see Paul D. Halliday, *Habeas Corpus: From England to Empire* (Cambridge, MA, 2010), 193–7, 227–8.
25. SP 25/75, fos 263, 435, 539; SP 25/112 fos 17, 19; SP 25/105, fo. 108.
26. Bod., MS Clarendon 48, fos 186, 251ᵛ.
27. SP 46/116, fo. 194.
28. John Lilburne, *The Resurrection of John Lilburne, Now a Prisoner in Dover-Castle* (1656), 6–8.

29. SP 25/76, fos 29, 183.
30. *Collection of the State Papers of John Thurloe*, iii. 512.
31. SP 18/99, fo. 235, petition of 31 July 1655.
32. *The Clarke Papers: Selections from the Papers of William Clarke*, ed. C. H. Firth, 3 vols (1891–9), iii. 53.
33. SP18/115, fo. 155; Lilburne, *Resurrection of John Lilburne*, 6–8.
34. SP 25/76, fo. 155; *Two Letters from Mr John Biddle, Late Prisoner in Newgate* (1655), 4.
35. SP 25/76, fo. 155; *A Short Account of the Life of John Biddle* (1691).
36. SP 25/76, fo. 208; *Clarke Papers*, iii. 53.
37. SP 18/101, fo. 39; SP 18/115, fo. 143; SP 25/76, fo. 326.
38. SP 18 101, fo. 133: 'Petition of Thomas Underhill and Nathaniel Webb, Stationers of London', 24 October 1655.
39. SP 25/76, fos 499–500; Sarah Mortimer, *Reason and Religion in the English Revolution: The Challenge of Socinianism* (Cambridge, 2010), 224–25.
40. *ODNB*, sub. Biddle, John; *CSPD May 1658–June 1659*, 40.
41. SP 29/56, fo. 57; Joshua Toulmin, *A Review of the Life, Character and Writings of the Rev. John Biddle, who was Banished to the Isle of Scilly in the Protectorate of Oliver Cromwell* (1789), 140–41.
42. William Prynne, *A New Discovery of Free-State Tyranny* (1655), 2nd pagination, 14.
43. B. S. Capp, *The Fifth Monarchy Men: A Study in Seventeenth-Century English Millenarianism* (1972), 100.
44. *Clarke Papers*, iii. 23, 24; *Collection of the State Papers of John Thurloe*, v. 407.
45. SP 25/77, fo. 13.
46. SP 25/76, fo. 552; John Rogers, *Jegar-Sahadutha: An Oyled Pillar. Set up for Posterity* (1657), 113–14.
47. *Clarke Papers*, iii. 106, 113; *Collection of the State Papers of John Thurloe*, vi. 349; *The Diary of Bulstrode Whitelock 1605–1675*, ed. Ruth Spalding (Oxford, 1990), 485.
48. Christopher Feake, *The Oppressed Close Prisoner in Windsor-Castle, His Defiance to the Father of Lyes, in the Strength of the God of Truth* (1655), sig. A2, 119; John Rogers, *Jegar-Sahadutha*, 2–18.
49. Christopher Feake, *The New Non-Conformist* (1654), 5, 24; *Collection of the State Papers of John Thurloe*, v. 755–6.
50. SP 25/76, fo. 314; *Clarke Papers*, iii. 3, 53.
51. SP 25/76, fo. 328; *Collection of the State Papers of John Thurloe*, v. 75; Rogers, *Jegar-Sahadutha*, 23.
52. *Collection of the State Papers of John Thurloe*, v. 757–9; *Clarke Papers*, iii. 61, 146; Richard L Greaves and Robert Zaller (eds), *Biographical Dictionary of British Radicals in the Seventeenth Century*, 3 vols (Brighton, 1982), i. 270–1.
53. Rogers, *Jegar-Sahadutha*, title page. See also John Rogers, *Sagir. Or Doomes-Day Drawing Nigh* (1654); John Rogers, *Mene, Tekel, Perez, or, a Little Appearance of the Hand-Writing...By a Letter Written to, and Lamenting over Oliver Lord Cromwell* (1654); *The Faithfull Narrative of the Late Testimony and Demand Made to Oliver Cromwel* (1654).
54. Rogers, *Jegar-Sahadutha*; Edward Rogers, *Some Account of the Life and Opinions of a Fifth-Monarchy-Man* (1867); Capp, *Fifth Monarchy Men*.

55. *Clarke Papers*, ii. 242–3; Capp, *Fifth Monarchy Men*, 107

56. SP 18101, fo. 357; SP 25/76, fo. 328; *Collection of the State Papers of John Thurloe*, v. 75; Rogers, *Jegar-Sahadutha*, 24. 'Arten' is Afton, Isle of Wight.

57. Rogers, *Jegar-Sahadutha*, title page, 1, 20, 53, 61, 63, 72.

58. Rogers, *Jegar-Sahadutha*, 23–4, 26, 33, 61, 137.

59. Rogers, *Jegar-Sahadutha*, introduction, 5, 18, 19, 24, 33, 34, 122, 130.

60. Rogers, *Jegar-Sahadutha*, 122, 124, 125, 128.

61. Rogers, *Jegar-Sahadutha*, introduction.

62. Rogers, *Jegar-Sahadutha*, 42, 47, 54, 62.

63. Rogers, *Jegar-Sahadutha*, 25, 26.

64. Rogers, *Jegar-Sahadutha*, 23, 56, 113–14.

65. SP 25/77, fo. 435.

66. Rogers, *Jegar-Sahadutha*, 25, 34–36, 38–40, 116, 120.

67. Rogers, *Jegar-Sahadutha*, 'To the reader', introduction, 1, 19, 24, 67, 133.

68. Rogers, *Jegar-Sahadutha*, 28 59, 129, 137.

69. Rogers, *Jegar-Sahadutha*, 'To the reader', 33, 120.

70. Rogers, *Jegar-Sahadutha*, introduction, 117.

71. Rogers, *Jegar-Sahadutha*, 'To the reader', introduction, 4, 23, 57.

72. Rogers, *Jegar-Sahadutha*, 'To the reader', introduction, 48.

73. Rogers, *Jegar-Sahadutha*, 'To the reader', introduction, 13, 72, 133, 148; Deuteronomy 33:16; Revelation 11:2, 13:5.

74. Rogers, *Jegar-Sahadutha*, introduction, 1, 2, 65–6, 72.

75. Rogers, *Jegar-Sahadutha*, introduction, 67.

76. Rogers, *Jegar-Sahadutha*, 152.

77. *Collection of the State Papers of John Thurloe*, vi. 775, 796.

78. *Clarke Papers*, iii. 68, 71; *Collection of the State Papers of John Thurloe*, v. 407.

79. *Clarke Papers*, iii. 106.

80. David Norbrook, '"This blushing tribute of a borrowed muse"; Robert Overton and his Overturning of the Poetic Canon', *English Manuscript Studies, 1100–1700*, 4 (1993), 220–66; Andrew Shifflett, '"A Most Humane Foe": Colonel Robert Overton's War with the Muses', in Claude J. Summers et al. (eds), *The English Civil Wars in the Literary Imagination* (Columbia, MO, 1999), 159–73; Barbara Taft, '"They that pursew perfection on earth…": The Political Progress of Robert Overton', in Ian Gentles et al. (eds), *Soldiers, Writers and Statesmen of the English Revolution* (Cambridge, 1998), 286–303; *ODNB*, sub 'Overton, Robert'.

81. Shifflett, 'Most Humane Foe', 162.

82. 'Two Letters Addressed to Cromwell', ed. C. H. Firth, *English Historical Review*, 22 (1907), 313.

83. SP18/188, fo. 66.

84. Shifflett, 'Most Humane Foe', 171; *The Sad Suffering Case of Major-General Rob. Overton, Prisoner in the Isle of Jersey* (1658, i.e. 1659), 7–8; SP 18/200, fo. 102.

85. *The Plain Case of the Common-Weal Neer the Desperate Gulf of the Common-Woe* (1658, i.e. 1659), 15–16; *Sad Suffering Case*, 1–10. Both pamphlets appeared on the London bookstalls on 3 March 1659, while Overton was still in transit from Jersey.

86. Bod., MS Clarendon 60, fo. 83.

87. *Clarke Papers*, iii. 184–5.
88. *Commons Journal*, vii. 614–15; *Diary of Thomas Burton*, iii. 45–6, iv. 150–62; SP 25/128, fo. 17.
89. SP 25/77, fo. 329; SP 25/114, fo.27; SP 25/128, fo. 17; Henry Vane, *The Proceeds of the Protector (so called) and his Councill against Sir Henry Vane* (1656), preface, 2–6; *Clarke Papers*, iii. 70; *Diary of Bulstrode Whitelocke*, 569; Ronald Hutton, *The Restoration: A Political and Religious History of England and Wales 1658–1667* (Oxford, 1985), 51, 57, 98, 116; Capp, *Fifth Monarchy Men*, 128, 263.

Chapter 14

1. Theodosia Allein, *The Life & Death of that Excellent Minister of Christ Mr Joseph Allein* (1677), 71.
2. *The Diary of Bulstrode Whitelock 1605–1675*, ed. Ruth Spalding (Oxford, 1990), 582, 598; Edmund Ludlow, *The Voyce from the Watch Tower*, ed. A. B. Worden, Camden Society, 4th ser., 21 (1978), 209–16; *Diary of Samuel Pepys*, ed. Robert Latham and William Matthews, 11 vols (Berkeley and Los Angeles, 1970–83), i. 265, 270.
3. SP 44/5, fos 25, 27; Richard L. Greaves, *Deliver Us from Evil: The Radical Underground in Britain, 1660–1663* (Oxford and New York, 1986), 32.
4. Ludlow, *Voyce from the Watch Tower*, 311; *Diary of Bulstrode Whitelocke*, 610; Pepys, *Diary*, iii, 103–4, 108–9, 112, 117; John Coffey, 'The Martyrdom of Sir Henry Vane the Younger: From Apocalyptic Witness to Heroic Whig', in Thomas S. Freeman and Thomas F. Mayer (eds), *Martyrs and Martyrdom in England c.1400–1700* (Woodbridge, 2007), 221–39.
5. *Diary of Bulstrode Whitelocke*, 607; Ludlow, *Voyce from the Watch Tower*, 209; Greaves, *Deliver Us*, 71.
6. Paul D. Halliday, *Habeas Corpus: From England to Empire* (Cambridge, MA., 2010), 230, 423; Bod., MS Clarendon 84, fos 296–296ᵛ; SP 29/96, fo. 38, SP 29/234, fo. 293; SP 130/63, fo. 119.
7. SP 44/40, fo. 227.
8. *The Channel Island Journals of Charles and William Trumbull 1677*, ed. Joan Stevens, Jean Arthur, and Collette Stevens (St Helier, 2004), 18.
9. William Harbutt Dawson, *Cromwell's Understudy: The Life and Times of General John Lambert* (1938); David Farr, 'New Information with Regard to the Imprisonment of Major General John Lambert, 1662-1684', *Cromwelliana: The Journal of the Cromwell Association 1998* (1998), 44–57; David Farr, *John Lambert, Parliamentary Soldier and Cromwellian Major-General, 1619–1684* (Woodbridge, 2003).
10. Jonathan Duncan, *The History of Guernsey; with Occasional Notices of Jersey, Alderney, and Sark* (1841), 110, 566.
11. Bod., MS Clarendon 66, fos 100–100ᵛ; *The Letter-Book of John Viscount Mordaunt 1658–1660*, ed. Mary Coate, Camden Society, 3rd ser., 69 (1945), 55, 112.
12. Bod., MS Clarendon 66, fos 184, 291.
13. *The Diurnal of Thomas Rugg 1659–1661*, ed. William L. Sachse, Camden Society, 3rd ser., 91 (1961), 69–71; Ludlow, *Voyce from the Watch Tower*, 111; Pepys, *Diary*, vol. 1, 81, 108.

14. HMC, *Fifth Report* (1876), 146; HMC, *Report on the Manuscripts of F. W. Leybourne-Popham.* (1899), 203, 228.
15. Bod., MS Clarendon 71, fo. 225; *Diary of Bulstrode Whitelocke*, 579, 580, 581; Pepys, *Diary*, i. 81, 108, 117; Ludlow, *Voyce from the Watch Tower*, 111; Farr, *John Lambert*, 212; *By the Council of State. A Proclamation* (21 April 1660).; Greaves, *Deliver Us*, 27–8.
16. John Cordy Jeaffreson (ed.), *Middlesex County Records. Vol. III . . . 1 Charles I to 18 Charles II* (Clerkenwell, 1888), 304.
17. SP 25/116, fo. 2; SP 29/1, fo. 160; SP 29/10, fo. 17; SP 29/48, fo. 29; *Commons Journal*, viii. 65, 126, 143; Farr, *John Lambert*, 215–16. For Frances Lambert's dealings regarding her family's properties and bonds, see SP 29/59, fo. 15; SP 29/75, fos 65, 225.
18. Pepys, *Diary*, ii. 204; HMC, *Eleventh Report* (1888), appendix VII, 3–4.
19. SP 44/5, fo. 27; Ludlow, *Voyce from the Watch Tower*, 291.
20. *Note-Book of Pierre le Roy*, ed. G. E. Lee (St Peter Port, 1893), 32; Ferdinand Brock Tupper, *The History of Guernsey and its Bailiwick; with Occasional Notices of Jersey*, 2nd edn (St Peter Port, 1876), 353; Jean le Pelley, 'The Knight of the Golden Tulip: John Lambert at Castle Cornet 1660/70', *Report and Transaction of Société Guernesiase*, 18 (1969), 409–15.
21. SP 29/50, fo. 108; SP 29/51, fo. 59; SP 44/5, fo. 165.
22. *Commons Journal*, viii. 368; Ludlow, *Voyce from the Watch Tower*, 165; SP 29/51, fo. 59.
23. SP 44/5, fo. 239; SP 44.7, fo. 17.
24. *CSPD 1661–2*, 372; Farr, *John Lambert*, 217.
25. Farr, *John Lambert*, 217; SP 29/56, fos 16, 80.
26. Ludlow, *Voyce from the Watch Tower*, 311; *The Journals of William Schellink's Travels in England 1661–1663*, ed. Maurice Exwood and H. L. Lehmann, Camden Society, 5th ser., 1 (1993), 92–3.
27. Ludlow, *Voyce from the Watch Tower*, 311; *Diary of Bulstrode Whitelocke*, 610; Pepys, *Diary*, iii. 103–4, 108–9, 112, 117; Coffey, 'Martyrdom of Sir Henry Vane', 221–39.
28. SP 29/448, fo. 57.
29. SP 29/448, fo. 110; BL, Add. MS 29,550, fos 435, 442, 443, 444; Add. MS 29,551, fos 41, 45, 57, 71, 73.
30. Dawson, *Cromwell's Understudy*, 425.
31. Tupper, *History of Guernsey*, 354; Margaret Willes, *The Making of the English Gardener* (New Haven and London, 2011), 264–5. Lambert's enthusiasm for gardening had been satirized in playing cards of the 1650s that depicted him as 'The Knight of the Golden Tulip'. Gaspars had earlier worked for Lambert as a tutor and art adviser.
32. SP 29/448, fo. 141.
33. BL, Add. MS 29,569, fos 212–212^v. Lambert instructed Hatton to look out especially for half a dozen named plants 'which I found not either in the Duke of Orleans' or M. Morin's catalogues'.
34. Bod., MS Clarendon 66, fo. 101; Farr, *John Lambert*, 210, 221.
35. SP 44/9, fo. 61.
36. SP 29/448, fo. 57.
37. SP 29/448, fo. 57.
38. SP 29/65, fo. 71

39. SP 29/88, fo. 58. Bagley was rector of Hazelbeach, Northamptonshire, from 1660.

40. *CSPD 1664–5*, 140 (from SP 29/109, fo. 24).

41. SP 29/448, fo. 110, partially transcribed in Tupper, *History of Guernsey*, 354. See also SP 29/448, fo. 141 for more of Walters's comments.

42. Tupper, *History of Guernsey*, 361–2; SP 29/449, fo. 82.

43. *Correspondence of the Family of Hatton*, ed. Edward Maunde Thompson, Camden Society, NS 22 (1878), 34–5, 38.

44. *Correspondence of the Family of Hatton*, 35.

45. SP 29/94, fo. 58; SP 46/16, fo. 67; Bod., MS Clarendon 81, fo. 232.

46. Bod., MS Clarendon 74, fo. 347.

47. Bod., MS Clarendon 74, 347, MS Clarendon 81, fo. 232.

48. SP 29/270, fo. 37.

49. BL, Add. MS 29571, fos 30–3.

50. H. D. Turner, 'Charles Hatton: A Younger Son', *Northamptonshire Past and Present*, 3 (1965–6), 255–61; BL, Add. MS 29,571, *passim*.

51. SP 29/449, fo. 87; Bod., MS Clarendon 82, fos 251–2.

52. SP 29/110, fo. 133; SP 29/112, fo. 180; SP 29/113, fo. 92; SP 29/114, fo. 45.

53. *CSPD Charles II Addenda 1660–85*, 132.

54. SP 44/17, fo. 194; *CSP Venice 1666–8*, 54.

55. SP 44/17, fo. 194; SP 29/450, fo. 30; SP 130/63, fo. 39.

56. *Cobbett's Complete Collection of State Trials*, 34 vols (1809–26), vi. 330; Amanda L. Tyler, *Habeas Corpus in Wartime: From the Tower of London to Guantanamo Bay* (New York, 2017), 22–23.

57. SP 29/450, fo. 142.

58. SP 44/28, fo. 10; SP 29/251, fo. 174.

59. *CSPD 1667–8*, 234; Dawson, *Cromwell's Understudy*, 440.

60. BL, Add. MS 29,552, fos 376–80; SP 44/31, fo. 56.

61. SP 29/278, fos 243, 275–6.

62. *Correspondence of Scientific Men of the Seventeenth Century*, ed. Stephen Peter Rigaud, 2 vols (Oxford, 1841), ii. 32; Farr, *John Lambert*, 4. See also *A Catalogue of the Mathematical Works of the Learned Mr. Thomas Baker, Rector of Bishop Nympton in Devonshire* (1683).

63. Ronald Hutton, *The Restoration: A Political and Religious History of England and Wales 1658–1667* (Oxford, 198), 163–64.

64. SP 29/279, fo. 196.

65. Dawson, *Cromwell's Understudy*, 436, 439, 441.

66. SP 29/39, fo. 254; Farr, *John Lambert*, 224–7. Blackwell had married one of Lambert's daughters in 1672, after the prisoner's relocation to St Nicholas Island.

67. Myles Halhead, *A Book of Some of the Sufferings and Passages of Myles Halhead* (1690), 24–7; Farr, *John Lambert*, 176.

68. *Plymouth Memoirs. A Manuscript by Dr James Yonge, F.R.S. Mayor of Plymouth 1694–95, who Died in the Year 1721*, ed. John J. Beckerlegge (Plymouth Institution and Devon and Cornwall Natural History Society, Plymouth, 1951), 35, 42.

69. SP 44/43, fo. 117; SP 29/366, fo. 313; *CSPD 1678*, 511–12, 517; David Hume, *The History of England, by Hume and Smollett*, continued by T. S. Hughes, 21 vols (1834–6), viii. 27.

70. Dawson, *Cromwell's Understudy*, 441–2.
71. *Plymouth Memoirs*, 41.
72. HMC, *Leybourne-Popham*, 263.
73. Celia Fiennes, 'Through England on a Side Saddle', in Alan Gibson and R. Pearse Chope (eds), *Early Tours in Devon and Cornwall* (Newton Abbot, 1967), 121.
74. Daniel Defoe, 'A Tour through Great Britain', in Gibson and Chope (eds.), *Early Tours in Devon and Cornwall*, 153–4.
75. *Commons Journal*, viii. 63; Pepys, *Diary*, ii. 225; SP 29/50, fo. 35; SP 29/58, fo. 79; SP 44/5, fo. 153; SP 44/22, fo. 125; Greaves, *Deliver Us*, 78–9.
76. SP 29/40, fo. 13; Maurice Ashley, *John Wildman: Plotter and Postmaster* (New Haven, 1947), 72–85; Greaves, *Deliver Us*, 78–80.
77. SP 29/49, fo. 173; SP 44/1, fo. 39.
78. SP 29/46, fo. 64; SP 29/49, fo. 73; SP 29/58, fos 75, 79; SP 29/66, fo. 247.
79. SP 29/81, fo. 204.
80. SP 29/81, fo. 204; SP 44/23, fo. 5; SP 44/14, fo. 74; SP 44/25, fo. 171, SP 44/28, fo. 4; *Diary of Bulstrode Whitelocke*, 707, 744; Ashley, *John Wildman*, 206–9, 227.
81. *Diary of Bulstrode Whitelocke*, 575; Greaves, *Deliver Us*, 36; *ODND*, sub 'Overton, Robert'.
82. SP 29/91, fo. 125; SP 29/96, fo. 38; SP 44/34, fo. 129.
83. David Norbrook, '"This blushing tribute of a borrowed muse"; Robert Overton and his Overturning of the Poetic Canon', *English Manuscript Studies, 1100–1700*, 4 (1993), 220–66; Andrew Shifflett, '"A Most Humane Foe": Colonel Robert Overton's War with the Muses', in Claude J. Summers et al. (eds), *The English Civil Wars in the Literary Imagination* (Columbia, MO., 1999), 159–73; Barbara Taft, '"They that pursew perfection on earth...": The Political Progress of Robert Overton', in Ian Gentles et al. (eds), *Soldiers, Writers and Statesmen of the English Revolution* (Cambridge, 1998), 286–303.
84. Ludlow, *Voyce from the Watch Tower*, 275; *The English Reports. Volume LXXXIV King's Bench Division XI* (Edinburgh and London, 1908), 1173; Richard L. Greaves, *Enemies under his Feet: Radicals and Nonconformists in Britain, 1664–1677* (Stanford, 1990), 222, notes the warrant for Overton's release in December 1672 as part of an amnesty, but speculates that he may not have survived the trip back to England.
85. SP 18/35, fo. 321; SP 18/95, fo. 102; SP 25/98, fo. 115; SP 28/136, fo. 84; SP 29/9, fo. 224; SP 29/269, fo. 41; SP 46/102, fo. 37; SP 46/114, fo. 81; *Diary of Bulstrode Whitelocke*, 560, 581–2; BL, Add. MS 29,552, fos 392–4; Ashley, *John Wildman*, 215.
86. BL, Add. MS 29,552, fos 392–4.
87. BL, Add. MS 29,552, fos 430, 454.
88. Christine Ozanne, 'Contemporary Accounts of the Explosion at Castle Cornet, December 1672', *Reports and Transactions of Société Guernesiase* (1930), 48.
89. BL, Add. MS 29,557, fo. 167.
90. *The History and Proceedings of the House of Commons from the Restoration to the Present Time*, 14 vols (1742), i. 201, 237, 572, 584, 590; *Statutes of the Realm*, 31 Charles II c. 2. Section 11; Halliday, *Habeas Corpus*, 240, 268, 426.
91. BL, Add. MS 29,557, fos 167, 174, 177, 205. William Neale, imprisoned for civil debt, turned down a writ of *habeas corpus* and preferred to remain on Guernsey.

92. SP 29/234, fo. 293; SP 29/293, fo. 57; SP 44/34, fo. 8; BL, Add. MS 29,552, fo. 406; *The English Reports. Volume LXXXIV King's Bench Division XIII* (Edinburgh and London, 1908), 282; Richard L. Greaves and Robert Zaller (eds), *Biographical Dictionary of British Radicals in the Seventeenth Century*, 3 vols (Brighton, 1982), iii. 113–14; Greaves, *Deliver Us*, 80.

93. SP 25/99, fo. 7; SP 44/28, fo. 154; SP 44/40, fo. 187; *Diary of Bulstrode Whitelocke*, 560, 581–2; Greaves and Zaller (eds), *Biographical Dictionary*, i. 155.

94. SP 29/91, fo. 125; Greaves and Zaller (eds), *Biographical Dictionary*, ii. 121.

95. SP 29/47, fo. 97; SP 29/81, fo. 193; SP 29/88, fo. 98; SP 29/168, fo. 77; SP 29/210, fo. 113; SP 29/230, fo. 139.

96. SP 29/91, fo. 125; Greaves and Zaller (eds), *Biographical Dictionary*, ii. 121.

97. SP 29/251, fo. 136.

98. SP 29/91, fo. 125; Lucy Hutchinson, *Memoirs of the Life of Colonel Hutchinson*, ed. Julius Hutchinson and C. H. Firth (1906), 368–70; Greaves and Zaller (eds), *Biographical Dictionary*, ii. 121.

99. James Harrington, *The Oceana ... with an Account of his Life Prefix'd by John Toland* (1700), pp. xxx–xxxvii; Ashley, *John Wildman*, 183–4; Ludlow, *Voyce from the Watch Tower*, 291; Greaves, *Deliver Us*, 80.

100. SP 44/5, fo. 27; *Diary of Bulstrode Whitelocke*, 615; Greaves and Zaller (eds), *Biographical Dictionary*, ii. 190.

101. SP 29/67, fo. 196; SP 44/10, fo. 31; SP 29/81, fo. 56; SP 29/94, fos 28, 73; SP 44/16, fo. 63; SP 44/22, fo. 70.

102. SP 44/22, fo. 70; SP 29.57, fo. 199; SP 29/217, fo. 42.

103. B. S. Capp, *The Fifth Monarchy Men: A Study in Seventeenth-Century English Millenarianism* (1972), 247.

104. *Cobbett's Complete Collection of State Trials*, vii. 830, 848, 873.

105. SP 44/54, fos 121–2; *CSPD January–December 1682*, 20; HMC, *The Manuscripts of S. H. Le Fleming* (1890), 184.

106. *CSPD September 1680–December 1681*, 591; SP 29/421/2, fo. 242; *An Account of the Tryals of Several Notorious Malefactors* (1682), 3.

107. SP 44/337, fo. 1; SP 31/3, fo. 299.

108. SP 44/337, fos 65, 281; *The Entring Book of Roger Morrice 1671–1691*, ed. Mark Goldie, 6 vols (Woodbridge, 2007), iii. 170.

109. HMC, *Report on the Manuscripts of the Late Reginald Rawson Hastings*, 3 vols (1928–47), ii. 196.

110. SP 44/97, fo. 203.

111. *Entring Book of Roger Morrice*, v. 121.

112. HMC, *Eighth Report* (1881), 47.

113. Stephen I. Vladeck with Gregory F. Jacob, 'Detention Policies,' in Harvey Rishikof, Stewart Baker, and Bernard Horowitz (eds), *Patriots Debate: Contemporary Issues in National Security Law* (Chicago, 2012), 205–23; Tyler, *Habeas Corpus in Wartime*, 178, 263, 366.

Chapter 15

1. John Brewer, *The Sinews of Power: War, Money, and the English State, 1688–1783* (Cambridge, MA., 1990); Lauren Benton, *A Search for Sovereignty: Law and Geography in European Empires, 1400–1900* (Cambridge, 2010), 35.

2. John Shebbeare, *An Authentic Narrative of the Oppressions of the Islanders of Jersey*, 2 vols (1771), i. 318.

3. Allan Brodie, 'The Garrison Defences on St Mary's in the Isles of Scilly in the 17th and 18th Centuries', *English Heritage Historical Review*, 7 (2012), 36–65; Jonathan Duncan, *The History of Guernsey; with Occasional Notices of Jersey, Alderney, and Sark* (1841), 176, 213–14.

4. Philip Falle, *An Account of the Island of Jersey*, with notes by Edward Durell (St Helier, 1837), 469–73; Duncan, *History of Guernsey*, 151–6.

5. Jack P. Greene, *Peripheries and Center: Constitutional Development in the Extended Polities of the British Empire and the United States, 1607–1788* (New York, 1990); Christine Daniels and Michael V. Kennedy (eds), *Negotiated Empires: Centers and Peripheries in the Americas, 1500–1820* (New York, 2002); Paul D. Halliday, *Habeas Corpus: From England to Empire* (Cambridge, MA, 2010); Hannah Weiss Muller, *Subjects and Sovereign: Bonds of Belonging in the Eighteenth-Century British Empire* (Oxford and New York, 2017); Dan Hulsebosch, 'English Liberties outside England: Floors, Doors, Windows, and Ceilings in the Legal Architecture of Empire', in Lorna Hutson (ed.), *The Oxford Handbook of English Law and Literature, 1500–1700* (Oxford, 2017), 747–73. See also Lauren Benton and Richard J. Ross (eds), *Legal Pluralism and Empires, 1500–1850* (New York, 2013); and Philip Loft, 'A Tapestry of Laws: Legal Pluralism in Eighteenth-Century Britain', *Journal of Modern History*, 91 (2019), 276–310.

6. Early modern island acquisitions included Newfoundland 1497, Bermuda 1609, Grenada 1609, St Kitts 1623, Barbados 1625, St Vincent 1627, Nevis 1628, Bahamas 1629, Antigua 1632, Montserrat 1632, Anguilla 1650, Jamaica 1655, St Helena 1658, the Virgin Islands 1666, the Cayman Islands 1670, and the Turks and Caicos 1678. The North American colonies included Rhode Island (1636), Manhattan (1674), and the myriad islands of the Chesapeake and New England. Later acquisitions included islands in the Atlantic and Pacific oceans.

7. Duncan, *History of Guernsey*, 133–5, 215.

8. Thomas Dicey, *An Historical Account of Guernsey* (1797), 50.

9. Notes by Durell in Falle, *Account of the Island of Jersey*, 288.

10. Philip Bailhache (ed.), *A Celebration of Autonomy 1204–2004: 800 Years of Channel Islands' Law* (St Helier. 2005).

11. BL, Lansdowne MS 657, fos 28, 40; Duncan, *History of Guernsey*, 130–2, 146–8, 157–60.

12. Shebbeare, *Authentic Narrative*, ii.

13. Edmund Toulmin Nicole, 'Some Account of the Jersey Revolution of 1769 and of the Political Parties in Jersey at the End of the 18th Century', *Société Jersiaise Bulletin Annuel*, 9 (1922), 318–19,

14. Bailiffs, deputies, and officers of Jersey and Guernsey to Lord Melbourne, 13 August 1832, in Duncan, *History of Guernsey*, 215–18; TNA, HO 45/2834. I am grateful to Paul Halliday for discussion of this dispute.

15. For some clarification, see Daryl Ogier, *The Government and Law of Guernsey* (St Peter Port, 2005).

16. Charles Le Quesne, *A Constitutional History of Jersey* (1856), 403–4.

17. Duncan, *History of Guernsey*, 234–6.

18. TNA, HO 98/1, HO 98/23.

19. TNA, ADM 1/4293; Ferdinand Brock Tupper, *The History of Guernsey, and its Bailiwick; with Occasional Notices of Jersey*, 2nd edn (St Peter Port, 1876), 440; Gavin

Daly, 'English Smugglers, the Channel, and the Napoleonic Wars, 1800–1814', *Journal of British Studies*, 46 (2007), 37–8.

20. D. B. Swinfen, 'The Daniel and Jersey Prison Board Case of 1890 and 1894', *Société Jersiaise Bulletin Annuel*, 21 (1975), 363–80, esp. 363–4.

21. 'A Report on Guernsey Lunacy Administration', *British Medical Journal*, 2 June 1906, 1289–92; David Hirst, 'Lunacy and the "Islands in the British Seas"', *History of Psychiatry*, 18 (2007), 411–33.

22. George Drower, *Britain's Dependent Territories: A Fistful of Islands* (Aldershot, 1992); Charles Cawley, *Colonies in Conflict: The History of the British Overseas Territories* (Newcastle upon Tyne, 2015); Ministry of Justice, *Fact Sheet on the UK's Relationship with the Crown Dependencies* (2014).

23. John Belcham, 'The Onset of Modernity', in John Belcham (ed.), *A New History of the Isle of Man, Volume 5* (Liverpool, 2001), 18–93; Hilton McCann, *Offshore Finance* (Cambridge, 2006), 380–2; Andrew P. Morris (ed.), *Offshore Financial Centers and Regulatory Competition* (Washington, 2010), 93, 97.

24. Edward Carson, *The Ancient and Rightful Customs: A Brief History of the English Customs Service* (1972), 70; C. W. Gawne, *The Isle of Man and Britain Controversy 1651–1895: From Smuggling to the Common Purse* (Douglas, 2009), 13–36.

25. Richard Rolt, *The History of the Island of Man: From the Earliest Accounts to the Present Time* (1773), 107, 120–4; H. Kinvig, *History of the Isle of Man* (Douglas, 1944), 152–4, 182; Sara Goodwins, *A Brief History of the Isle of Man* (Sutton, 2011), 90–2, 97–100; Belcham, 'The Onset of Modernity', 18–93; Gawne, *Isle of Man and Britain Controversy*, 37–56.

26. TNA, HO 98/63; Gawne, *Isle of Man and Britain Controversy*, 57–80, 165–72, 201, 212.

27. Goodwins, *Brief History*, 90–1.

28. Goodwins, *Brief History*, 117–18, 122–3.

29. Goodwins, *Brief History*, 128–30.

30. BL, Egerton MS 3505, fo. 147.

31. *Hansard House of Commons*, 7 April 1826.

32. Cambridge University Library, MS Add. 6458, fo. 9; John Troutbeck, *A Survey of the Ancient and Present State of the Scilly Islands* (1794), 177–82; G. Forrester Matthews, *The Isles of Scilly: A Constitutional, Economic and Social Survey of the Development of an Island People from Early Times to 1900* (1960), 43–6, 239.

33. BL, Egerton MS 3505, fos 161, 170.

34. Troutbeck, *Survey of the Ancient and Present State of the Scilly Islands*, 187–8.

35. Matthews, *Isles of Scilly*, 107–8. Troutbeck resigned his curacy in 1796.

36. Bob Tennant, 'Managing Overseas Missions: The SPCK in the Scilly Isles, 1796–1819', in Brett C. McInelly and Paul E. Kerry (eds), *New Approaches to Religion and the Enlightenment* (Madison, PA, and Vancouver, 2018), 345–64, quote at 360.

37. *The Times*, 3 March 1819, 8 April 1826; *Hansard House of Commons*, 7 April 1826.

38. Amanda Martin, *The Isles of Scilly Museum: Inside the Archipelago* (St Mary's, 2011), 19, 25.

39. Matthew, *Isles of Scilly*, 17, 159–67.

40. John Sturch, *A View of the Isle of Wight*, 4th edn (1791), 4.

41. Cambridge University Library, MS Add. 6458, fo. 3.

42. Tupper, *History of Guernsey*, 450; J. Bertrand Payne, *The Gossiping Guide to Jersey* (1865), xii. 87–9.
43. Goodwins, *Brief History*, 107–10.
44. Duncan, *History of Guernsey*, 177–8, 191–2; Le Quesne, *Constitutional History of Jersey*, 1; Bod., MS Top. Jersey e.1; See also Philippe Dumaresq, 'A Survey of ye Island of Jersey . . . 1685', *Société Jersiaise Bulletin Annuel*, 12 (1932–5), 418; Jason St John Nicolle, 'New Evidence for the Population of Jersey in the Seventeenth and Eighteenth Centuries', *Société Jersiaise Bulletin Annuel*, 25 (1990), 463–67; David W. Moore, *The Other British Isles: A History of Shetland, Orkney, the Hebrides, Isle of Man, Anglesey, Scilly, Isle of Wight and the Channel Islands* (Jefferson, NC, and London, 2005), 251, 463–7; Richard Hocart, *The Country People of Guernsey and their Agriculture, 1640–1840* (St Peter Port, 2016), 5; Edward Cheshire, 'The Results of the Census of Great Britain in 1851', *Journal of the Statistical Society of London*, 17 (1854), 50.
45. Richard Worsley, *The History of the Isle of Wight* (1781), appendix 6; Cheshire, 'Results of the Census', 50; Moore, *Other British Isles*, 251.
46. Llwyd Angharad, *A History of the Island of Mona, or Anglesey* (Ruthin, 1833), 30; G. Nesta Evans, *Social Life in Mid-Eighteenth Century Anglesey* (Cardiff, 1936); David A. Pretty, *Anglesey: The Concise History* (Cardiff, 2005), 41, 56.
47. Cambridge University Library, MS Add. 6458, 'A Geographical and Nautical Description of Scilly'; Matthews, *Isles of Scilly*, 19, 41; Moore, *Other British Isles*, 251.
48. Davies Gilbert, *The Parochial History of Cornwall*, 4 vols (1838), v. 4, 175; Martin, *Isles of Scilly Museum*, 18. The following table offers rough population figures for the principal islands, based on historical estimates and the modern census:

Island	Early 17th C	Mid 18th C	Early 19th C	1851	Early 21st C
Guernsey	10,000	14,000	21,000	29,757	63,000
Jersey	12,000	20,000	28,000	57,020	105,000
Isle of Man	10,000	20,000	40,000	52,344	85,000
Isle of Wight	10,000	18,000	32,000	50,324	139,000
Isles of Scilly	500	1,500	2,000	2,610	2,300
Anglesey	10,000	25,000	48,000	57,318	70,000
Total:	52,500	98,500	171,000	199,049	464,300

Bibliography

Manuscript Sources

Bodleian Library, Oxford
Ashmole 800, 830, 1141
Bankes 36–55
Carte 33, 68,75
Clarendon 16–92
Eng. Hist. b. 134, c. 34
Gough Islands 2, 3
Jones 27*
Rawlinson A 14, A 24, A 195A, A 270, A 290, B 225, B 383, B 515, C 441, D 924,
    D 977, D 1298, D 1481
Tanner 37, 38, 46, 53, 57, 59
Top. Jersey e.1

British Library, London
Additional 11,315, 27,873, 29,550–71, 33,124, 34,262, 41,763, 46,501, 60,393, 61,649,
    72,608.
Cotton Augustus I. ii, Caligula E. x
Egerton 2533, 2542, 2812, 3505
Harley 36, 260, 1510
Kings 45, 48
Lansdowne 8, 33, 40, 53, 57, 58, 116, 145, 657
Sloane 2446
Stowe 184, 885
Thomason E. 850 [23]

Cambridge University Library, Cambridge
Additional 6458, 2766
Dd. XI. 43
SPCK Papers

Folger Shakespeare Library, Washington, DC
X. d. 675

Greffe, St Peter Port, Guernsey
Métevier Collection
'Notebooks of George Fouachin'

Hatfield House, Hertfordshire
Cecil Papers

Huntington Library, San Marino, California
Ellesmere 774, 777, 782, 962, 963, 966, 973, 974, 975, 1897, 1904, 1907, 1908, 1909, 1910, 7470, 7479
HM 72020
JR 3

Jersey Archives, St Helier, Jersey
D/AL/A/1/2 and 5
D/AP/AE/19
L/F/08/A/1
L/F/08/H/37

Lambeth Palace Library, London
MS 929

Lancashire Archives, Preston
DDKE/acc. 7840 HMC/782

Lord Coutanche Library, St Helier, Jersey
Chevalier Journal
Messervy Papers
'Pseudo-Mastix: The Lyar's Whipp'
Trumbull Journal

Parliamentary Archives, Westminster
BRY/45B/48, 50, 51
HL/PO/JO/10/1/26–302.
WIL/1/23

The National Archives, Kew
Navy Board ADM 1/4293, ADM 106/385
Chancery C 2/Jas I/S16/46, C 3/208/37, C 213/464
Exchequer E 178, E 351, E 367
High Court of Admiralty HCA 13
Home Office HO 45/2834, HO 98/1, 23, 63.
Privy Council PC 1, 2
State Papers SP 8, 12, 14, 15, 16, 18, 21, 29, 32, 44, 47, 63, 78, 130

Worcester College, Oxford
William Clarke Papers.

Printed Primary Sources

An Account of the Tryals of Several Notorious Malefactors (1682).

Acts and Ordinances of the Interregnum, 1642–1660, ed. C. H. Firth and R. S. Rait, 3 vols (1911).

Acts of the Privy Council 1542–1631, ed. J. R. Dasent et al., 46 vols (1890–1964).

Actes des États de L'Île de Guernsey. 1605 à 1651 (St Peter Port, 1851).

Actes des États de L'Île de Guernsey. Vol. II. 1651 à 1780 (St Peter Port, 1907).

Allein, Theodosia, *The Life & Death of that Excellent Minister of Christ Mr Joseph Allein* (1677).

The Ancient Ordinances and Statute Laws of the Isle of Man, ed. Mark Anthony Mills (Douglas, 1821).

Articles Exhibited against Sir Philipp Carteret, Governour of the Isle of Jersy (1642).

Articles of Impeachment Exhibited against Col. Robert Gibbons and Cap. Richard Yeardley, Late Governors of the Isle of Jersey (1659).

The Articles of the Rendition of Elizabeth Castle in the Ile of Jersey (1651).

'Articles of Association entered into between the Lords Capel & Hopton, and Sir Edward Hyde, & Sir Geo: Carteret', *Société Jersiaise Bulletin Annuel*, 3 (1890–5), 342–7.

Ashburnham, John, *The True Copie of a Letter from Mr Ashburnham to a Friend* (1648).

Ashburnham. *A Narrative by John Ashburnham*, 2 vols (1830).

Ashton, Thomas, *Satan in Samuels Mantle, Or the Cruelty of Germany Acted in Jersey* (1659).

Augustine. *Saint Augustines Confessions Translated...by William Watts* (1631).

Baker, Daniel, *With the Light is Fifteen Priests of the Isle of Wight Reproved* (1658).

Baker. *A Catalogue of the Mathematical Works of the Learned Mr Thomas Baker, Rector of Bishop Nympton in Devonshire* (1683).

Bastwick, John, *Flagellum Pontificis et Episcoporum Latialium* (1641).

Bastwick, John, *The Confession of the Faithfull Witnesse of Christ* (1641).

Bastwick, John, *A Declaration Demonstrating and Infallibly Proving that all Malignants, whether they be Prelates, Popish-cavaliers, with All Other Ill-Affected Persons, Are Enemies to God and the King* (1643).

Bastwick, John, *A Iust Defence of John Bastwick* (1645).

Bastwick, John, *The Utter Routing of the Whole Army of all the Independents and Sectaries* (1646).

Bastwick, Susanna, *Innocency Cleared, True Worth Predicated, against False Aspertions: in a Letter sent to Mr Henry Burton. From a Christian Friend; In Defence of Dr Bastwick, one of his Quondam Fellow Sufferers* (1645).

Bastwick, Susanna, *To the High Court of Parliament... The Remonstrance and Humble Petition of Susanna Bastwick* (1654).

Baynton, Edward, *The Kings Majesties Remonstrance to His Subjects of England* (1647).

Berkeley. *Memoirs of Sir John Berkeley* (1702).

Besse, Joseph, *A Collection of the Sufferings of the People called Quakers*, 2 vols (1753).

Bethel, Slingsby, *The Interest of Princes and States* (1680).

Biddle. *Two Letters from Mr John Biddle, Late Prisoner in Newgate* (1655).

Blackstone, William, *Commentaries on the Laws of England*, 11th edn, 4 vols (1791).

Blake. *The Letters of Robert Blake*, ed. J. R. Powell, *Navy Records Society*, 76 (1937).

Blakhal, Gilbert, *A Brieffe Narration of the Services Done to Three Noble Ladies* (Spalding Club, Aberdeen, 1844).

Blenerhasset, Thomas, *The Seconde Part of the Mirrour for Magistrates* (1578).

Blundell, William, *A History of the Isle of Man*, ed. William Harrison, 2 vols (Manx Society, Douglas, 1876–7).

Boazio, Baptista, *The True Description or Drafte of that Famous Ile of Wighte* (1591).

Borlase, William, *Observations on the Ancient and Present State of the Islands of Scilly* (1756).

Bourne, William, *The Arte of Shooting in Great Ordnaunce* (1587).

Boyer, Abel, *The History of the Reign of Queen Anne . . . Year the Sixth* (1708).

Brereton, William, *Travels in Holland, the United Provinces, England, Scotland, and Ireland, MDCXXXIV–MDCXXXV*, ed. Edward Hawkins, Chetham Society, 1 (1844).

Bulkeley. 'The Diary of Bulkeley of Dronwey, Anglesey, 1630–1638', ed. Hugh Owen (*Anglesey Antiquarian Society and Field Club Transactions*, 1936).

Brevint, 'Notebooks of Elie Brevint', http://societe-jersiaise.org/digital-publications/brevint?file=../bulletin-pdfs/Brevint (accessed June 2018).

Burton, Henry, *The Seven Vials or A Brief and Plain Exposition upon the 15: and 16: Chapters of the Revelation* (1628).

Burton, Henry, *Englands Complaint to Iesvs Christ, Against the Bishops Canons* (1640).

Burton, Henry, *A Replie to a Relation of the Conference between William Laude and Mr Fisher the Jesuite* (Amsterdam, i.e. London?, 1640).

Burton, Henry, *The Sovnding of the Two Last Trvmpets* (1641).

Burton, Henry, *A Narration of the Life of Mr Henry Burton* (1643).

Burton. *Diary of Thomas Burton Esq, Member in the Parliaments of Oliver and Richard Cromwell, from 1656 to 1659*, ed. J. T. Rutt, 4 vols (1828).

Bushell, Thomas, *A Brief Declaration of the Severall Passages in the Treaty Concerning the Surrender of the Garrison of Lundy* (1648).

Bushell, Thomas, *The Apologie of Thomas Bushell* (1650).

Bushell, Thomas, *The Case of Thomas Bushell Esq.* (1660?).

Bushell, Thomas, *An Extract by Mr Bushell of his Late Abridgement* (1660).

By the Council of State. A Proclamation (21 April 1660).

A Calendar of Material Relating to Ireland from the High Court of Admiralty Examinations 1536–1641, ed. J. C. Appleby (Dublin, 1992).

A Calendar of Material Relating to Ireland from the High Court of Admiralty 1641–1660, ed. Elaine Murphy (Dublin, 2011).

Calendar of the Proceedings of the Committee for Advance of Money, 1642–1656, ed. Mary Anne Everett Green (1888).

Calendar of the Proceedings of the Committee for Compounding, ed. Mary Anne Everett Green, 5 vols (1892).

Calendar of State Papers, Domestic, ed. Mary Anne Everett Green et al., 84 vols (1856–2006).

Calendar of State Papers Relating to Ireland . . . 1603–1625, ed. Charles William Russell et al., 5 vols (1872–88).

Calendar of State Papers . . . Venice, ed. Rawdon Brown et al., 38 vols (1864–1947).

Calendar of Treasury Books, 1660–1667, ed. William A. Shaw (1904).

Calendar of Treasury Books, 1667–1668, ed. William A. Shaw (1905).

Calendar of Treasury Books, 1669–1672, ed. William A. Shaw (1908),

Calendar of Treasury Books, 1672–1675, ed. William A. Shaw (1909).

Calendar of Treasury Books, 1676–1679, ed. William A. Shaw (1911).

Calendar of Treasury Books, 1679–1680, ed. William A. Shaw (1913).

Calendar of Treasury Books, 1681–1685, ed. William A. Shaw (1916).

Calendar of Treasury Books, 1685–1689, ed. William A. Shaw (1923).

Calendar of Treasury Books, 1689–1692, ed. William A. Shaw (1931).

Calendar of Treasury Books, 1693–1696, ed. William A. Shaw (1935).

Calendar of Treasury Papers 1556/7–1696, ed. Joseph Redington (1868).

Camden, William, *Britain, or A Chorographical Description* (1637).

Camden, William, *Camden's Britannia, Newly Translated into English: With Large Additions and Improvements* (1695).

Carew, Richard, *The Survey of Cornwall* (1602).

Carey, Laurent, *Essai sur les institutions, lois et coûtumes de l'Ile de Guernesey* (St Peter Port, 1889).

Carey, Peter, 'Account of the Captivity of Messrs de Beauvoir des Granges, de Havilland, Pierre Carey', ed. R. W. J. Payne, *Report and Transactions of Société Guernesiase*, 19 (1973), 307–13.

Chaloner, James, 'A Description of the Isle of Man', in Daniel King, *The Vale-Royall of England. Or, The County Palatine of Chester* (1656).

Chamberlayne, Edward, *The Fourth Part of the Present State of England* (1683).

Chamberlayne, Edward, *The Present State of England . . . An Account of the Riches, Strength, Magnificence, Natural Production, Manufactures of this Island* (1683).

The Charters of Guernsey, ed. Tim Thornton (Bognor Regis, 2004).

Chevalier, Jean, *Journal de Jean Chevalier* (St Helier, 1914).

Clarendon, *The Life of Edward Earl of Clarendon*, 2 vols (Oxford, 1760).

Clarendon, Earl of, *A Collection of Several Tracts* (1727).

Clarendon. *Calendar of the Clarendon State Papers Preserved in the Bodleian Library. Volume 1: to January 1649*, ed. O. Ogle and W. H. Bliss (Oxford, 1872).

Clarendon, *The History of the Rebellion and Civil Wars in England*, ed. W. Dunn Macray, 6 vols (Oxford, 1888).

The Clarke Papers: Selections from the Papers of William Clarke, ed. C. H. Firth, 3 vols. (1891–9).

Cobbett's Complete Collection of State Trials, 34 vols (1809–28).

Coke, Sir Edward, *Le Tierce Parts des reportes* (1602).

Coke, Sir Edward, *The Fourth Part of the Institutes of the Laws of England: Concerning the Jurisdiction of Courts* (1644).

Collins, Greenvile, *Great Britain's Coasting Pilot: The First Part. Being a New and Exact Survey of the Sea-Coast of England* (1693).

Columne, Iacob, *The Fierie Sea-Columne, Wherein are Shewed the Seas, and Sea-Coasts of the Northern, Eastern, and Western Navigation* (Amsterdam, 1640).

Constitutional Documents of the Puritan Revolution 1625–1660, ed. Samuel Rawson Gardiner (Oxford, 1906).

Cooke, Edward, *Certain Passages which Happened at Newport in the Isle of Wight* (1690).

A Copy of a Letter Sent from a Gentleman in Carisbrooke-Castle (1648).

Correspondence of Scientific Men of the Seventeenth Century, ed. Stephen Peter Rigaud, 2 vols (Oxford, 1841).

Cosmo III. 'The Travels of Cosmo III, Grand Duke of Tuscany, through England', in Alan Gibson and R. Pearse Chope (eds), *Early Tours in Devon and Cornwall* (Newton Abbot, 1967), 92–111.

Cowley. *The Works of Abraham Cowley*, ed. J. Aikin, 3 vols (1805).

Cowell, John, and Thomas Manley, *The Interpreter of Words and Terms, Used either in the Common Statute Laws of this Realm* (1701).

Cromwell. *The Writings and Speeches of Oliver Cromwell*, ed. Wilbur Cortez Abbott, 4 vols (Cambridge, MA, 1937–47, repr. Oxford, 1988).

Cuningham William, *The Cosmographical Glasse, Conteinyng the Pleasant Principles of Cosmographie, Geographie, Hydrography, or Navigation* (1559).

The Declaration of Col. Poyer, and Col. Powel (1648).

A Declaration Concerning the King from the Citizens of London (1648).

A Declaration of the Lords and Commons Assembled in Parliament, Concerning Prisoners in the Island of Iersey (1645).

A Declaration of the Proceedings of the Prince of Wales, and his Coming to the Isle of Jersey (1642).

The Declaration, Together with the Petition and Remonstrance of ... Hampshire (1648).

Defoe, Daniel, *A Tour thro' the Whole Island of Great Britain* [1724–6], 2 vols (1968).

Defoe, Daniel, 'A Tour through Great Britain', in Alan Gibson and R. Pearse Chope (eds), *Early Tours in Devon and Cornwall* (Newton Abbot, 1967), 145–78.

Denton, Thomas, *A Perambulation of Cumberland 1687–1688 Including ... the Isle of Man*, Surtees Society, 207 (2003).

A Designe by Captain Barley, and Others, to Surprize Carisbrook Castle (1648).

Dicey, Thomas, *An Historical Account of Guernsey* (1798).

Die Veneris, 24 Augusti (1649).

Dingley, Robert, *The Deputation of Angels* (1653).

'Documents Illustrating the History of the Spanish Armada', ed. George P. B. Naish, *The Naval Miscellany*, vol. IV, ed Christopher Lloyd, Navy Records Society, 92 (1952), 19–20.

Documents Relating to the Civil War 1642–1648, ed. J. R. Powell and W. K. Timings, Navy Records Society, 195 (1963).

Documents Relating to the Proceedings against William Prynne, in 1634 and 1637, ed. Samuel Rawson Gardiner, Camden Society, NS 18 (1877).

Drayton, Michael, *Poly-Olbion* (1612).

Dumaresq, Philippe, 'A Survey of ye Island of Jersey ... 1685', *Société Jersiaise Bulletin Annuel*, 12 (1932–5), 415–41.

Durel, John (trans.), *La Liturgie. C'est à dire, le formulaire des prieres publiques, de l'administration des sacramens; et des autres ceremonies & coûtumes de l'eglise, selon l'usage de l'eglise anglicane* (1667).

The Earl of Derby's Case Stated for the Vindication of the Proceedings at Law in the Isle of Man (1663).

Edwards, Thomas, *The Third Part of Gangraena. Or, A New and Higher Discovery of the Errors, Heresies, Blasphemies, and Insolent Proceedings of the Sectaries of These Times* (1646).

Egerton, Thomas, *The Speech of the Lord Chancellor ... Touching the Post-Nati* (1609).

Eikon Basilike. The Povrtraictvre of His Sacred Maiestie in His Solitvdes and Svfferings (1648).

An Elegy upon the Decease of ... the Princesse Elizabeth (1650).

The English Reports. Volume LXXXIV King's Bench Division XI (Edinburgh and London, 1908),

The English Reports. Volume LXXXIV King's Bench Division XIII (Edinburgh and London, 1908).

An Exact Relation of the Whole Proceedings of Galland Col. Mitton in North-Wales (1646).

The Faithfull Narrative of the Late Testimony and Demand Made to Oliver Cromwel (1654).

Falle, Philip, *An Account of the Island of Jersey*, with notes by Edward Durell (St Helier, 1837).

Falle. 'Holograph Document' (Falle to Archbishop Tenison), *Société Jersiaise Bulletin Annuel*, 12 (1887), 192–203.

Fanshawe. *The Memoirs of Ann Lady Fanshawe*, ed. Beatrice Marshall (London and New York, 1907).

Feake, Christopher, *The New Non-Conformist* (1654).

Feake, Christopher, *The Oppressed Close Prisoner in Windsor-Castle, His Defiance to the Father of Lyes, in the Strength of the God of Truth* (1655).

Fiennes, Celia, 'Through England on a Side Saddle', in Alan Gibson and R. Pearse Chope (eds), *Early Tours in Devon and Cornwall* (Newton Abbot, 1967), 111–37.

Fiennes, Nathaniel, *Colonell Fiennes his Reply to a Pamphlet Entitled An Answer to Colonell Nathaniel Fiennes Relation . . . by Clem. Walker* (1643).

Finet. *Ceremonies of Charles I: The Note Books of John Finet 1628–1641*, ed. Albert J. Loomie (New York, 1987).

Foxe, John, *Actes and Monuments of Matters Most Speciall and Memorable* (1583).

A Full and True Account of a Most Dreadful and Terrible Accident (1706).

Fuller, Thomas, *The Historie of the Holy Warre* (1639).

Le Geyt. *Les Manuscrits de Philippe le Geyt, Ecuyer, Lieutenant-Bailli de l'Ile de Jersey, sur la constitution, les lois, et les usages de cette ile*, 4 vols (St Helier, 1846–9).

Granville, George, *The Genuine Works in Verse and Prose, of the Right Honourable George Granville, Lord Lansdown*, 3 vols (1736).

A Great Fight near Pendennis Castle in Cornwall (1649).

A Great Sea Fight near Pendennis Castle in Cornwall (1640).

A Great Victory Obtained by the Kings Forces in the West of England at the Island of Silley (1648).

Hacket, John, *Scrinia Reserta: A Memorial Offer'd to the Great Deservings of John Williams* (1693).

Hale. *Sir Matthew Hale's The Prerogatives of the King*, ed. D. E. C. Yale, Selden Society, 92 (1976).

Hale, Sir Matthew, 'Concerning the Prerogative and Franchise of Wreck', in Stuart A. Moore, *A History of the Foreshore and the Law Relating Thereto*, 3rd edn (1888), 406–9.

Halhead, Myles, *A Book of Some of the Sufferings and Passages of Myles Halhead* (1690).

Hansard, *House of Commons Debates*.

Harrington, James, *The Oceana . . . with an Account of his Life Prefix'd by John Toland* (1700).

Harrison, William, 'Description of Britaine', in Raphael Holinshed, *The First and Second Volumes of Chronicles* (1587).

The Hartlib Papers', https://www.dhi.ac.uk/hartlib/ (accessed August 2019).

Haslock, John, *A True and Perfect Relation of the Surrender of the Strong and Impregnable Garrison of the Island of Scillie* (1646).

Hastings, Francis, *A Watch-Word to all Religious, and True-Hearted English-Men* (1598).

Hatton. *Correspondence of the Family of Hatton*, ed. Edward Maunde Thompson, Camden Society, NS 22 (1878).

Heath, Robert, *A Natural and Historical Account of the Islands of Scilly* (1750).

Herbert, Sir Thomas, *Memoirs of the Last Two Years of the Reign of that Unparallell'd Prince, of Ever Blessed Memory, King Charles I* (1711).

Heylyn, Peter, *A Full Relation of Two Journeys: The One into the Main-Land of France. The Other into some of the Adjacent Islands* (1656).

Heylyn, Peter, *Cyprianus Anglicus: Or, the History of the Life and Death of the Most Reverend and Renowned Prelate William, by Divine Providence Lord Archbishop of Canterbury* (1668).

Heylyn, Peter, *A Help to English History* (1675).

High Court of Admiralty Examinations (MS Volume 53) 1637–1638, ed. Dorothy O. Shilton and Richard Holworthy (New York and London, 1932).

His Majesties Declaration in the Isle of Wight (1648).

His Majesties Declaration to all his Loving Subjects (1649).

His Maiesties Demands to Collonel Hammond (1648).

The History and Proceedings of the House of Commons from the Restoration to the Present Time, 14 vols (1742).

Holinshed, Raphael, *The First and Second Volumes of Chronicles* (1587).

HMC, *First Report* (1870).

HMC, *Second Report* (1874).

HMC, *Third Report* (1872).

HMC, *Fourth Report* (1874).

HMC, *Fifth Report* (1876).

HMC, *Sixth Report* (1877).

HMC, *Seventh Report* (1879).

HMC, *Eighth Report* (1881).

HMC, *Ninth Report* (1884).

HMC, *Tenth Report* (1906).

HMC, *Eleventh Report* (1888).

HMC, *Calendar of the Manuscripts of... the Marquis of Salisbury*, 24 vols (1883–1976).

HMC, *The Manuscripts of the Marquis of Ormonde*, 7 vols (1885–1912).

HMC, *The Manuscripts of the Earl Cowper*, 2 vols (1888–9).

HMC, *The Manuscripts of S. H. Le Fleming* (1890).

HMC, *Manuscripts of... the Duke of Portland*, 2 vols (1891–7).

HMC, *The Manuscripts of Lord Kenyon* (1894).

HMC, *Report on the Manuscripts of F. W. Leyborne-Popham* (1899).

HMC, *Report on the Manuscripts of Mrs Frankland-Russell-Astley* (1900).

HMC, *Report on the Manuscripts of Lord Montagu* (1900).

HMC, *Report on the Manuscripts of the Earl of Egmont*, 2 vols (1905–9).

HMC, *Report on Franciscan Manuscripts* (1906).

HMC, *Report on the Pepys Manuscripts* (1911).

HMC, *Report on the Manuscripts of Allan George Finch*, 2 vols (1913–22).

HMC, *Report on the Manuscripts of the Marquis of Downshire*, 3 vols (1924–40).

HMC, *Report on the Manuscripts of the Late Reginald Rawdon Hastings*, 3 vols (1928–47).

Hugo, Victor, *Les Travailleurs de la mer* (Paris, 1866).

Hugo, Victor, *The Toilers of the Sea* (New York, 2000).

Hume, David, *The History of England, by Hume and Smollett*, continued by T. S. Hughes, 21 vols (1834–6).

Hutchinson, Lucy, *Memoirs of the Life of Colonel Hutchinson*, ed. Julius Hutchinson and C. H. Firth (1906).

Ile de Jersey: Ordres du Conseil et Pièces Analogues Enregistrés a Jersey. Vol. 1. 1536–1678 (St Helier, 1897).

Ile de Jersey: Ordres du Conseil et Pièces Analogues Enregistrés a Jersey. Vol. 2. 1678–1724 (St Helier, 1898).

Inglis, Henry D., *The Channel Islands: Jersey, Guernsey, Alderney, etc. (The Result of a Two Years' Residence)*, 2nd edn (1835).

Instruction que l'on doit faire lire et apprendre aux enfants... en l'Isle de Iersey (St Helier?, 1649).

'Instructions Made by Sr. George Carteret 25 July 1651', *Société Jersiaise Bulletin Annuel*, 3 (1890–5), 284–7.

Jeaffreson, John Cordy (ed.), *Middlesex County Records. Vol. III . . . 1 Charles I to 18 Charles II* (Clerkenwell, 1888).

Jones, Henry, *Vectis: The Isle of Wight: A Poem in Three Cantos* (1766).

Journal of the House of Commons, 10 vols (1802).

Journal of the House of Lords, 10 vols (1802).

Joyfull Newes for England (1648).

Ioyfull News from Portsmouth and the Jsle of Wight (1642).

Kay, George, *General View of the Agriculture and Rural Economy of Anglesey* (1794).

King, Daniel, *The Vale-Royall of England. Or, The County Palatine of Chester* (1656).

The Kings Cabinet Opened (1645).

The Kings Maiesties Last Speeche in the Isle of Weight (1648).

Lambard, William, *The Perambulation of Kent . . . Corrected and Enlarged* (1656).

Langdale, Marmaduke, and Lewis Dives, *A Declaration of the Noble Knights . . . to Keep the Isle of Man, against all Opposition, for His Majesties Service* (1649).

Leland, John, *The Itinerary of John Leland the Antiquary*, 9 vols (Oxford, 1769).

Lemprière, Michael, Henry Dumaresq, and Abraham Hérault, *Pseudo-Mastix: The Lyar's Whipp*, in *Société Jersiaise Bulletin Annuel*, 13 (1888), 309–55.

'A Letter from Aboard the *Entrance*, Riding off Mount Orgueil Castle in Jersey, 27 Octob. 1651', in *A List of all the Victories and Successefull Atchievements of the Parliaments Fleet* (1651).

A Letter from His Majesties Court in the Isle of Wight (1648).

A Letter Intercepted (at Sea) by Captaine Moulton . . . Written from Parson Wolby (1649).

Letters and Papers, Foreign and Domestic, Henry VIII, ed. J. S. Brewer et al., 23 vols (1862–1932).

Letters between Col. Robert Hammond, Governor of the Isle of Wight, and the Committee of Lords and Commons at Derby-House, ed. Thomas Birch (1764).

'Lettre émanant du Comité du Parlement nommant Michael Lemprière, Bailli de Jersey', *Société Jersiaise Bulletin Annuel*, 30 (1905), 399–400.

'Lettres Inédités du Roi Charles II', *Société Jersiaise Bulletin Annuel*, 3 (1890–5), 1–8.

Leveck, Joseph, *A True Accompt of the Late Reducement of the Isles of Scilly* (1651).

Lewis, Samuel, *A Topographical Dictionary of England*, 4 vols (1831).

Lilburne, John, *The Just Defence of John Lilburn* (1653).

Lilburne, John, *The Resurrection of John Lilburne, Now a Prisoner in Dover-Castle* (1656).

A List of all the Victories, and Successefull Atchievements of the Parliaments Fleet (1651).

Le Livre des prieres communes, de l'administration des sacremens et autres ceremonies en l'eglise d'Angleterre (1553).

Llwyd, Richard, *The Poetical Works of Richard Llwyd, The Bard of Snowden* (1837).

Llyfr Gweddi Gyffredin, a gwenidogaeth y sacramentau, ac eraill gynneddfau a ceremoniau yn Eglwys Loegr (1599).

Ludlow. *The Memoirs of Edmund Ludlow*, ed. C. H. Firth, 2 vols (Oxford, 1864).

Ludlow, Edmund, *The Voyce from the Watch Tower*, ed. A. B. Worden, Camden Society, 4th ser., 21 (1978).

Making the News: An Anthology of the Newsbooks of Revolutionary England 1641–1660, ed. Joad Raymond (Moreton-in-Marsh, 1993).

Manifeste declarant la Resolution des Etats et habitants de l'Isle de Jersey du 5–15 Mars, 1645–6: Fac-simile de la copie signée par les habitants de la paroisse de St-Laurent (St Helier, 1886).

Marche, Jean de la, *A Complaint of the False Prophets Mariners upon the Drying up of their Hierarchicall Euphrates* (1641).

Marche, de la. 'Jean de la Marche... The Diary', ed. W. Rolleston and T. W. M. de Guerir, *Report and Transactions Société Guernesiase*, 11 (1930–2), 193–220.

Mather. 'The Autobiography of Increase Mather', ed. M. G. Hall, *Proceedings of the American Antiquarian Society*, 71 (1962), 271–360.

May, Thomas, *The History of the Parliament of England, which began November the Third, MDCXL* (1647).

Mercurius Militaris (10–17 October 1648).

Mercurius Pragmaticus (4–7 January 1648).

A Message Sent from the Lord Hopton, and Sire Richard Greenvill to the Prince (1650).

Miege, Guy, *The New State of England under Their Majesties K. William and Q. Mary* (1691).

The Moderate (12–19 December 1648).

Moll, Herman, *A Set of Fifty New and Complete Maps* (1739).

Morant, Philip, 'Remarks on the 19th Chapter of the 2nd Book of Mr. Selden's *Mare Clausum*' (1733), in Philip Falle, *An Account of the Island of Jersey*, with notes by Edward Durell (St Helier, 1837), 266–73.

Mordaunt. *The Letter-Book of John Viscount Mordaunt 1658–1660*, ed. Mary Coate, Camden Society, 3rd ser., 69 (1945).

Morrice. *The Entring Book of Roger Morrice 1677–1691*, ed. Mark Goldie et al., 6 vols (Woodbridge, 2007).

A Most Gracious Message sent by the Kings Majesty (1648).

Musgrave, John, *A True and Exact Relation of the Great and Heavy Pressures and Grievances* (1650).

New Articles for Peace, Delivered by the Kings Majesty (1648).

A New Declaration of the Kings Majesties Going to the Isle of Weight (1647).

Norton, Robert, *The Gunner: Shewing the Whole Practice of Artillerie* (1629).

Nye, Nathaniel, *The Art of Gunnery* (1647).

Oglander. *A Royalist's Notebook: The Commonplace Book of Sir John Oglander*, ed. Francis Bamford (1936).

The Orders for Ecclesiasticall Discipline According to that which Hath Been Practiced since the Reformation of the Church in... the Iles of Garnsey, Gersey, Spark and Alderny (1642).

An Ordinance of the Lords and Commons... for the Making Void all Commissions and Warrants, or other Writings Issued forth in His Majesties Name to Sir George Carteret, Governour of Jersey. And that the said Carteret and his Adherents shall be called to a Just Account for his and their illegall Proceedings against the Well-Affected Persons of that Island (1645).

'Ordre de Faire Recherche des Biens Appartenant aux Parlementaires, le 25 Octobre 1645', *Société Jersiaise Bulletin Annuel*, 3 (1890–5), 424–8.

Ormonde. *A Collection of Original Letters and Papers... Found among the Duke of Ormonde's Papers*, ed. Thomas Carte, 2 vols (Dublin, 1759).

Osborne. *The Letters of Dorothy Osborne to William Temple*, ed. G. C. Moore Smith (1928).

Osborne, Richard, *The Charge of High-Treason Delivered into the House of Lords* (1648).

Osborne, Richard, *The Independent's Loyalty. Or, The Most Barbarous Plot (to Murther His Sacred Majestie)* (1648).

Osborne, Richard, *Two Letters Sent by Mr Richard Osburn* (1648).

An Ould Ship Called an Exhortation to Continue All Subjects in their Due Obedience (1648).

Painter, William, *The Palace of Pleasure Beautified* (1566).

Parker, Henry, *Of a Free Trade: A Discourse* (1648).

'The Parliamentary Survey of the Duchy of Cornwall, part II', ed. Norman J. G. Pounds, *Devon and Cornwall Record Society*, NS 27 (1984), 131–51.

Parr, John, *An Abstract of the Laws, Customs, and Ordinances of the Isle of Man*, ed. James Gell (Douglas, 1867).

Parr. 'Deemster John Parr's Abstract of Manx Laws', Dedication to Governor Heywood, 2, transcribed by Peter Edge from Manx Museum MS 03176C, https://radar.brokes/ac.uk/radar/items/a1e352c0-f1ed-45a0-b7d5-3434669ed078/1 (accessed April 2019).

Paynell. *Robert Paynell's Exchequer Reports (1627–1631)*, ed. W. H. Bryson (Tempe, AZ, 2009).

Peck, Francis, *Desiderata Curiosa: Or, a Collection of Divers Scarce and Curious Pieces*, 2 vols (1732–5).

Pepys. *Samuel Pepys's Naval Minutes*, ed. J. R. Tanner, *Navy Records Society*, 60 (1926).

Pepys. *Diary of The Samuel Pepys*, ed. Robert Latham and William Matthews, 11 vols (Berkeley and Los Angeles, 1970–83).

A Perfect Diurnall (20 October–1 December 1653; 2–9 January 1654).

Perkins, William, *The Combat between Christ and the Divell Displayed* (1606).

A Petition from the Island of Silley (1642).

Phaer. 'Anglia Wallia' [the perambulation of Thomas Phaer], *Archaeologia Cambrensis*, 6th ser., 11 (1911), 421–31.

Phillips, Nicholas, *The Holy Choice: Or, Faith's Triumph over all Worldly Pomp and Glory* (1679).

The Plain Case of the Common-Weal Neer the Desperate Gulf of the Common-Woe (1658, i.e. 1659).

Poingdestre, Jean, *Caesarea, Or a Discourse of the Island of Jersey* [c.1682] (St Helier, 1889).

Poingdestre, Jean, *Les Lois et coûtumes de l'Ile de Jersey* (St Helier, 1928).

Poulet. *The Letter-Books of Sir Amias Poulet*, ed. John Morris (1874).

Prince Charles Proclaimed King, and Landed in Jersey (1642).

'La Prise de Jersey par le Parlement en 1655: Récit Contemporain', *Société Jersiaise Bulletin Annuel*, 10 (1885), 16–29.

Private Journals of the Long Parliament 3 January to 5 March 1642, ed. Willson H. Coates, Anne Steele Young, and Vernon F. Snow (New Haven and London, 1982).

Proceedings in Parliament 1625, ed. Maija Jansson and William B. Bidwell (New Haven and London, 1987).

Proceedings in the Opening Session of the Long Parliament, ed. Maija Jansson, 7 vols (Rochester, NY, 2000–7).

'Le Procés entre les États et le Gouverneur Lanier: La Rémonstrance des États', *Société Jersiaise Bulletin Annuel*, 13 (1888), 254–80.

Prynne, William, *Movnt-Orgveil: Or Divine and Profitable Meditations* (1641).

Prynne, William, *Comfortable Cordials against Discomfortable Feares of Imprisonment* (1641).

Prynne, William, *The Antipathie of the English Lordly Prelacie* (1641).

Prynne, William, *A New Discovery of the Prelates Tyranny* (1641).

Prynne, William, *Romes Master-Peece, or, The Grand Conspiracy of the Pope and his Iesuited Instruments* (1644).

Prynne, William, *The Lyar Confounded or A Brief Refutation of John Lilburnes Miserably-Mistated Case* (1645).

Prynne, William, *A New Discovery of Free-State Tyranny* (1655).

Prynne, William, *Demophilos, or, The Assertor of the Peoples Liberty* (1658).

Prynne, William, *Brief Animadversions on, and Additional Explanatory Amendments of...* *the Fourth Part of the Institutes* (1669).

Psallmyr neu Psalmae' Dauid (1567).

Pym, John, *The Declaration of John Pym Esquire upon the whole matter of the Charge of High Treason against Thomas Earle of Strafford* (1641).

R., J., *The Sad Suffering Case of Major-General Rob. Overton, Prisoner in the Isle of Jersey* (1658, i.e. 1659).

Rastell, John, *The Exposicions of the Termes of the Lawes of England* (1563).

Recueil D'Ordonnances de la Cour Royale de l'Isle de Guernsey... 1533–1800, ed. Robert MacCulloch (St Peter Port, 1852).

'A Relation of Sir Edward Carteret Knt. Complaint against Sr John Lanier', *Société Jersiaise Bulletin Annuel*, 4 (1897–1901), 71–4.

The Remonstrance and Declaration of the Knights, Esquires, Gentlemen, and Freeholders, in Colchester (1648).

A Remonstrance or Declaration of the Army: Presented to the House of Commons on Munday Novemb. 20. 1648 (1648).

The Remonstrance of the Inhabitants of the Three Isles of Wight, Garnsey, and Jersey (1647).

'Reparations for His Majesties Castles of Mont Orgeuil and Elizabeth', *Société Jersiaise Bulletin Annuel*, 7 (1910–14), 147–75.

'The Report of the Royal Commissioners sent to Jersey in 1617', *Société Jersiaise Bulletin Annuel*, 30 (1905), 386–96.

'Report of the Council of State 31 August 1653', *Société Jersiaise Bulletin Annuel*, 5 (1902–05), 156–57.

Risdon, Tristram, *The Chorographical Description or Survey of the County of Devon* [*c.*1630] (1811).

Roch. 'The Journals of Jeremy Roch', in *Three Sea Journals of Stuart Times*, ed. Bruce S. Ingram (1936).

Rogers, John, *Mene, Tekel, Perez, or, a Little Appearance of the Hand-Writing... by a Letter Written to, and Lamenting over Oliver Lord Cromwell* (1654).

Rogers, John, *Sagrir. Or Doomes-Day Drawing Nigh* (1654).

Rogers, John, *Jegar-Sahadutha: An Oyled Pillar. Set up for Posterity* (1657).

Rolt, Richard, *The History of the Island of Man: From the Earliest Accounts to the Present Time* (1773).

Le Roy. *Note-Book of Pierre le Roy*, ed. G. E. Lee (St Peter Port, 1893).

Rugg. *The Diurnal of Thomas Rugg 1659–1661*, ed. William L. Sachse, Camden Society, 3rd ser., 91 (1961).

Rupert. *Memoirs of Prince Rupert and the Cavaliers*, ed. Eliot Warburton, 3 vols (1849).

Rushworth, John, *Historical Collections of Private Passages of State*, 8 vols (1721).

Rushworth, John, *Historical Collections the Fourth and Last Part*, 2 vols (1701).

Sacheverell, William, *An Account of the Isle of Man* (1702).

Salter, Christopher, *Sal Scylla: Or, A Letter Written from Scilly to Mr John Goodwin, Minister of the Gospel in London* (1653).

Selden, John, *Of the Dominion and Ownership of the Sea* (1652).

Selden, John, *Mare Clausum; The Right and Dominion of the Sea* (1663).

Select Pleas in the Court of Admiralty, Vol. II, ed. Reginald G. Marsden, Selden Society, 11 (1897).

De Selve. *Correspondence politique de Odet de Selve Ambassadeur de France en Angleterre (1546–1549)* (Paris, 1888).

Several Occurrences, Touching the Further Proceedings of the Scots with their Declared King (1650).

The Severall Humble Petitions of D. Bastwicke, M Burton, M. Prynne (1641).

Shakespeare, William, *Hamlet*.

Shakespeare, William, *Henry V*.

Shakespeare, William, *Richard II*.

Shakespeare, William, *The Tempest*.

Shebbeare, John, *An Authentic Narrative of the Oppressions of the Islanders of Jersey*, 2 vols (1771).

Schellink. *The Journals of William Schellink's Travels in England 1661–1663*, ed. Maurice Exwood and H. L. Lehmann, Camden Society, 5th ser., 1 (1993).

A Short Account of the Life of John Biddle (1691).

Smith, George Charles, *A Report Detailing the Extreme Miseries of the Off-Islands of Scilly* (1818).

Smith, Henry, *The Sermons of Maister Henrie Smith* (1593).

Speed, John, *The Theatre of the Empire of Great Britaine* (1632).

Speed, John, *The Theatre of the Empire of Great-Britain* (1676).

A Speedy Cvre to Open the Eyes of the Blinde, and the Eares of the Deafe Citizens of London (1648).

Stanley, James, *A Declaration of the Right Honourable, James, Earle of Darby* (1649).

Statutes of the Realm, ed. T. E. Tomlins et al., 11 vols (1810–28).

Stocall, James, *Freedom. Or, the Description of the Excellent Civill Government of the Island of Jersey* (1652).

Stow, John, *The Annales, or a Generall Chronicle of England* (1615).

Stuart Royal Proclamations, Volume I. Royal Proclamations of King James I 1603–1625, ed. James F. Larkin and Paul L. Hughes (Oxford, 1973).

Stuart Royal Proclamations. Volume II. Royal Proclamations of King Charles I 1625–1646, ed. James F. Larkin (Oxford, 1983).

Sturch, John, *A View of the Isle of Wight*, 4th edn (1791).

Talbot, John, 'Observations Touching the King's Prerogative to Wreck of Sea', in Stuart A. Moore, *A History of the Foreshore and the Law Relating Thereto*, 3rd edn (1888), 243–7.

Taylor, John, *Tailors Travels, from London, to the Isle of Wight* (1648).

Taylor, John, *John Taylors Wandering, to see the Wonders of the West* (1649).

Three Declarations (1642).

Thurloe. *A Collection of the State Papers of John Thurloe*, ed. Thomas Birch, 7 vols (1742).

The Times, 1786–1959.

To the Right Honovrable the Lords Assembled in Parliament. The Humble Remonstrance of The Iustices, Gentry, Ministers, and Constables assembled in the State and Common Councell of the Island of Jerzey (1642).

Toulmin, Joshua, *A Review of the Life, Character and Writings of the Rev. John Biddle, who was Banished to the Isle of Scilly, in the Protectorate of Oliver Cromwell* (1789).

Troutbeck, John, *A Survey of the Ancient and Present State of the Scilly Islands* (1794).

A True and Brief Relation How, and by what Means, the Isle of Wight was Secured, in August, 1642 (1642).

Trumbull. 'The Journal of Charles Trumbull', ed. Richard Hocart, *La Société Guernesiaise Report and Transactions* (1985 for 1984), 566–85.

Trumbull. *The Channel Island Journals of Charles and William Trumbull 1677*, ed. Joan Stevens, Jean Arthur, and Collette Stevens (St Helier, 2004).

The Tryal of Sir Henry Vane (1662).

'Two Letters Addressed to Cromwell', ed. C. H. Firth, *English Historical Review*, 22 (1907), 308–15.

Vane, Henry, *The Proceeds of the Protector (so called) and his Councill against Sir Henry Vane* (1656).

Visitation Articles and Injunctions... Vol. 3 (1559–1575), ed. W. H. Frere and W. P. M. Kennedy (1910).

Wagstaffe, Thomas, *A Vindication of K. Charles the Martyr*, 3rd edn (1711).

Ward, Patience, et al., *A Scheme of the Trade, as it is at Present Carried on between England and France* (1674).

Warner, Richard (ed.), *Collections for the History of Hampshire*, 6 vols (1795).

Wearis, F., *News from the Channel, or The Discovery and Perfect Description of the Isle of Serke* (1673).

Whalley, Edward, *Joyfull Newes of the Kings Majesties Safe Arrivall in the Isle of Wheight* (1647).

Whitelock, Bulstrode, *Memorials of the English Affairs*, 4 vols (Oxford, 1853).

Whitelock. *The Diary of Bulstrode Whitelocke, 1605–1675*, ed. Ruth Spalding (Oxford, 1990).

The Wisedome Patience and Constancie of our Most Gracious Soveraigne Lord, King Charles (1648).

Worsley, Richard, *The History of the Isle of Wight* (1781).

Wright, Thomas, *A Perfect Narrative of the Particular Service Performed by Thomas Wright, Firemaster, with a Morter-Piece of Fifteen Inches and a Half Diameter, against the Castle of Elizabeth in the Isle of Jersey* (1652).

Wynn. *Calendar of Wynn (of Gwydir) Papers 1515–1690* (Aberystwyth, 1926), 154.

Y Beibl Cyssegr-lan. Sef yr Hen Destament, a'r Newydd (1588).

Yonge. *Plymouth Memoirs. A Manuscript by Dr James Yonge, F.R.S. Mayor of Plymouth 1694–95, who Died in the Year 1721*, ed. John J. Beckerlegge (Plymouth Institution and Devon and Cornwall Natural History Society, Plymouth, 1951).

The Zurich Letters (Second Series), ed. Hastings Robinson, Parker Society, 51 (Cambridge, 1845).

Modern Sources

Adamson, J. S. A., 'The *Vindiciae Veritatis* and the Political Creed of Viscount Saye and Sele', *Historical Research*, 60 (1987), 54–63.

Ahier, Philip, 'The Money Problems of Charles Prince of Wales', *Société Jersiaise Bulletin Annuel*, 21 (1973), 192–3.

Akkerman, Nadine, *Invisible Agents: Women and Espionage in Seventeenth-Century Britain* (Oxford, 2018).

Angharad, Llwyd, *A History of the Island of Mona, or Anglesey* (Ruthin, 1833).

Appleby, J. C., 'A Memorandum on the Defence of the Channel Islands, 1627', *Société Jersiaise Bulletin Annuel*, 23 (1984), 506–9.

Appleby, J. C., 'Neutrality, Trade and Privateering 1500–1689', in A. G. Jamieson (ed.), *A People of the Sea: The Maritime History of the Channel Islands* (London and New York, 1986), 59–105.

Appleby, John C., 'Jacobean Piracy: English Maritime Depredation in Transition, 1603–1625', in Cheryl A. Fury (ed.), *The Social History of English Seamen, 1485–1659* (2012), 277–300.

Archer, Harriet, *Unperfect Histories: The* Mirror for Magistrates, *1559–1610* (Oxford, 2017).

Ashley, Anne, 'The Spiritual Courts of the Isle of Man, Especially in the Seventeenth and Eighteenth Centuries', *English Historical Review*, 72 (1957), 31–59.

Ashley, Maurice, *John Wildman: Plotter and Postmaster* (New Haven, 1947).

Ashton, Robert, *Counter-Revolution: The Second Civil War and its Origins, 1646–8* (New Haven and London, 1994).

Axton, Marie, and Richard Axton (eds), *Calendar and Catalogue of Sark Seigneurie Archive 1526–1927*, List and Index Society, Special Series, 26 (1991).

Bailhache, Philip (ed.), *A Celebration of Autonomy 1204–2004: 800 Years of Channel Islands' Law* (St Helier, 2005).

Baldacchino, Godfrey, 'Islands, Island Studies, Islands Studies Journal', *Island Studies Journal*, 1 (2006), 3–18.

Baldacchino, Godfrey, *Island Enclaves: Offshoring Strategies, Creative Governance, and Subnational Island Jurisdictions* (Montreal and London, 2010).

Balleine, G. R., *All for the King: The Story of Sir George Carteret* (St Helier, 1976).

Belcham, John, 'The Onset of Modernity', in John Belcham (ed.), *A New History of the Isle of Man, Volume 5* (Liverpool, 2001), 18–93.

Bennett, Martyn, *The Civil Wars in Britain and Ireland 1638–1651* (Oxford, 1997).

Benton, Lauren, *A Search for Sovereignty: Law and Geography in European Empires, 1400–1900* (Cambridge, 2010).

Benton, Lauren, and Richard J. Ross, 'Empires and Legal Pluralism: Jurisdiction, Sovereignty, and Political Imagination in the Early Modern World', in Benton and Ross (eds), *Legal Pluralism and Empires, 1500–1850* (New York, 2013), 1–17.

Benton, Lauren, and Richard J. Ross, *Legal Pluralism and Empires, 1500–1850* (New York, 2013).

Bettey, Joseph, 'Downlands', in Joan Thirsk (ed.), *The English Rural Landscape* (Oxford, 2000), 27–49.

Bisson, S. W., 'The Minute Book of the Jersey Colloquy, 1577–1614', *Société Jersiaise Bulletin Annuel*, 22 (1979), 310–17.

Black, Jeremy, *A History of the British Isles* (New York, 1996).

Blakemore, Richard E., and Elaine Murphy, *The British Civil Wars at Sea, 1638–1653* (Woodbridge, 2018).

Boswell, Caroline, *Disaffection and Everyday Life in Interregnum England* (Woodbridge, 2017).

Boulay, Juliet du, 'Wrecks in the Isles of Scilly', *Mariner's Mirror*, 46 (1960), 88–112.

Boundy, Wyndham S., *Bushell and Harman of Lundy* (Bideford, 1961).

Boynton, Lindsay, 'Billeting: The Example of the Isle of Wight', *English Historical Review*, 74 (1959), 23–40.

Braddick, Michael J., *State Formation in Early Modern England c.1550–1700* (Cambridge, 2000).

Braddick, Michael, *God's Fury, England's Fire: A New History of the English Civil Wars* (2008).

Braddick, Michael, *The Common Freedom of the People: John Lilburne & the English Revolution* (Oxford, 2018).

Bradshaw, Brendan, and John Morrill (eds), *The British Problem, c.1534–1707: State Formation in the Atlantic Archipelago* (New York, 1996).

Brewer, John, *The Sinews of Power: War, Money, and the English State, 1688–1783* (Cambridge, MA, 1990).

Brodie, Allan, 'The Garrison Defences on St Mary's in the Isles of Scilly in the 17th and 18th Centuries', *English Heritage Historical Review*, 7 (2012), 36–65.

Callow, John, 'The Limits of Indemnity: The Earl of Derby, Sovereignty and Retribution at the Trial of William Christian, 1660–63', *Seventeenth Century*, 15 (2013), 199–216.

Callow, John, '"In so Shifting a Scene": Thomas Fairfax as Lord of the Isle of Man, 1651–60', in Andrew Hopper and Philip Major (eds), *England's Fortress: New Perspectives on Thomas, 3rd Lord Fairfax* (Farnham and Burlington, VT, 2014), 21–52.

Callow, John, '"The Force of Angry Heaven's Flame": Lieutenant John Hathorne and Garrison Government on the Isle of Man, 1651–1660', *Isle of Man Studies*, 14 (2016), 90–108.

Campbell, Kenneth L., *A History of the British Isles: Prehistory to the Present* (2017).

Capp, B. S., *The Fifth Monarchy Men: A Study in Seventeenth-Century English Millenarianism* (1972).

Capp, Bernard, *Cromwell's Navy: The Fleet and the English Revolution 1643–1660* (Oxford, 1989).

Capp, Bernard, *England's Culture Wars: Puritan Reformation and its Enemies in the Interregnum 1649–1660* (Oxford, 2013).

Carey, E. F., 'Increase Mather: A Sidelight on Guernsey in the Seventeenth Century', *Société Guernesiase Transactions*, 9 (1923), 256–66.

Carlton, Charles, *Going to the Wars: The Experience of the British Civil Wars, 1638–1651* (1992).

Carson, Edward, *The Ancient and Rightful Customs: A Brief History of the English Customs Service* (1972).

Cary, Henry (ed.), *Memorials of the Great Civil War in England from 1646 to 1652*, 2 vols (1842).

Cawley, Charles, *Colonies in Conflict: The History of the British Overseas Territories* (Newcastle upon Tyne, 2015).

Chanter, John R., *Lundy Island: A Monograph, Descriptive and Historical* (1877).

Chedgzoy, Kate, 'This Pleasant and Sceptred Isle: Insular Fantasies of National Identity in Anne Dowriche's *The French Historie* and William Shakespeare's *Richard II*', in Philip Schwyzer and Simon Mealor (eds), *Archipelagic Identities: Literature and Identity in the Atlantic Archipelago, 1550–1800* (Aldershot and Burlington, VT, 2004), 25–42.

Cheshire, Edward, 'The Results of the Census of Great Britain in 1851', *Journal of the Statistical Society of London*, 17 (1854), 45–72.

Churchill, Winston S., *The Island Race* (1964).

'Clameur de Haro!', *Société Jersiaise Bulletin Annuel*, 17 (1960), 339–41.

Clavier, Sarah Ward, '"Horrid Rebellion" and "Holie Cheate": Royalist Gentry Responses to Interregnum Government in North-East Wales, 1646–1660', *Welsh Historical Review*, 29 (2018), 51–72.

Clayton, Mathew, and Anthony Atkinson, *Lundy, Rockall, Dogger, Fair Isle: A Celebration of the Islands around Britain* (2015).

Coate, Mary, *Cornwall in the Great Civil War and Interregnum 1642–1660* (Oxford, 1933; 2nd edn, Truro, 1963).

Coffey, John, 'The Martyrdom of Sir Henry Vane the Younger: From Apocalyptic Witness to Heroic Whig', in Thomas S. Freeman and Thomas F. Mayer (eds), *Martyrs and Martyrdom in England c.1400–1700* (Woodbridge, 2007), 221–39.

Cole, W. A., 'Trends in Eighteenth-Century Smuggling', *Economic History Review*, NS 10 (1958), 395–10.

Coleby, Andrew M., *Central Government and the Localities: Hampshire 1649–1689* (Cambridge, 1987).

Collins, John M., *Martial Law and English Laws, c.1500–c.1700* (Cambridge, 2016).

Collinson, Patrick, *The Elizabethan Puritan Movement* (1967).

Collinson, Patrick, *The Religion of Protestants: The Church in English Society 1559–1625* (Oxford, 1992).

Como, David, *Radical Parliamentarians and the English Civil War* (Oxford, 2018).

Cooke, James Herbert, *The Shipwreck of Sir Cloudesley Shovell, on the Scilly Island in 1707* (Society of Antiquaries, 1883).

Coward, Barry, *The Stanleys. Lords Stanley and Earls of Derby 1385–1672: The Origins, Wealth and Power of a Landowning Family*, Chetham Society, 3rd ser., 30 (Manchester, 1983).

Cressy, David, 'Conflict, Consensus and the Willingness to Wink: The Erosion of Community in Charles I's England,' *Huntington Library Quarterly*, 6 (2000), 131–49.

Cressy, David, 'The Portraiture of Prynne's Pictures: Performance on the Public Stage', in David Cressy, *Travesties and Transgressions in Tudor and Stuart England* (Oxford, 2000), 213–33.

Cressy, David, *Travesties and Transgressions in Tudor and Stuart England* (Oxford, 2000),

Cressy, David, *Charles I and the People of England* (Oxford, 2015).

Cressy, David, 'Puritan Martyrs in Island Prisons', *Journal of British Studies*, 57 (2018), 736–54.

Cust, Richard, *Charles I and the Aristocracy, 1625–1642* (Cambridge, 2013).

Daly, Gavin, 'English Smugglers, the Channel, and the Napoleonic Wars, 1800–1814', *Journal of British Studies*, 46 (2007), 30–46.

Daniels, Christine, and Michael V. Kennedy (eds), *Negotiated Empires: Centers and Peripheries in the Americas, 1500–1820* (New York, 2002).

Davies, Godfrey, *The Restoration of Charles II, 1658–1660* (San Marino, CA, 1955).

Davies, J. D., *Kings of the Sea: Charles II, James II and the Royal Navy* (Barnsley, 2017).

Davies, Norman, *The Isles: A History* (Oxford, 1999).

Davis, Ralph, *The Rise of the English Shipping Industry in the Seventeenth and Eighteenth Centuries* (1962).

Dawson, William Harbutt, *Cromwell's Understudy: The Life and Times of General John Lambert* (1938).

Dickinson, J. R., 'The Earl of Derby and the Isle of Man, 1643–1651', *Transactions of the Historic Society of Lancashire and Cheshire*, 141 (1991–2), 39–76.

Dickinson, J. R., *The Lordship of Man under the Stanleys: Government and Economy in the Isle of Man, 1580–1704*, Chetham Society, 3rd ser., 41 (Manchester, 1996).

Dickinson, J. R., and J. A. Sharpe, 'Courts, Crime and Litigation in the Isle of Man, 1580–1700', *Historical Research*, 27 (1999), 140–59.

Dorey, Sir Graham, 'Rights to Wreck in Norman Customary Law', *Guernsey Law Journal*, 15 (1993), 63–6.

Draskau, Jennifer Kewley, *Illiam Dhone: Patriot or Traitor? The Life, Death and Legacy of William Christian* (2012).

Drower, George, *Britain's Dependent Territories: A Fistful of Islands* (Aldershot, 1992).

Duncan, Jonathan, *The History of Guernsey; with Occasional Notices of Jersey, Alderney, and Sark* (1841).

Durston, Christopher, *Cromwell's Major-Generals: Godly Government during the English Revolution* (Manchester and New York, 2001).

'Dutch East India Company Shipping 1595–1795', www.resources.huygens.knaw.nl/das/detailVoyage/92573 (accessed November 2018).

Eagleston, A. J., 'Guernsey under Sir Thomas Leighton (1570–1610)', *Report and Transactions of the Société Guernesiaise*, 13 (1937–45), 72–108.

Eagleston, A. J., *The Channel Islands under Tudor Government, 1485–1642* (Cambridge, 1949).

'Early Modern Prisons: Exploring Gaols, Bridewells and other Forms of Detention, 1500–1800', https://earlymodernprisons.org/ (accessed July 2019).

Edge, Peter W., and C. C. Augur Pearce, 'The Development of the Lord Bishop's Role in the Manx Tynwald', *Journal of Ecclesiastical History*, 57 (2006), 494–14.

Edmond, Rod, and Vanessa Smith (eds), *Islands in History and Representation* (2003).

Ellis, Steven G., and Christopher Maginn, *The Making of the British Isles: The State of Britain and Ireland, 1450–1660* (Harlow, 2007).

Evans, G. Nesta, *Social Life in Mid-Eighteenth Century Anglesey* (Cardiff, 1936).

Everitt, Alan, *Change in the Provinces: The Seventeenth Century* (Leicester, 1972).

Farr, David, 'New Information with Regard to the Imprisonment of Major General John Lambert, 1662–1684', *Cromwelliana: The Journal of the Cromwell Association 1998* (1998), 44–57.

Farr, David, *John Lambert, Parliamentary Soldier and Cromwellian Major-General, 1619–1684* (Woodbridge, 2003).

Feuvre, David Le, *Jersey: Not Quite British. The Rural History of a Singular People* (St Helier, 1993).

Firebrace, C. W., *Honest Harry: Being the Biography of Sir Henry Firebrace, Knight (1619–1691)* (1932).

Fleury, Christian, and Henry Johnson, 'The Minquiers and Écréhous in Spatial Context: Contemporary Issues and Cross Perspectives on Border Islands, Reefs, and Rocks', *Island Studies Journal*, 10 (2015), 163–80.

Fowles, John, *Islands* (1978).

Fox, John, *The King's Smuggler: Jane Whorwood, Secret Agent to Charles I* (2011).

Franson, J. Karl, 'The Fatal Voyage of Edward King, Milton's Lycidas', *Milton Studies*, 25 (1989), 43–67.

Freeman, Thomas S., '*Imitatio Christi* with a Vengeance: The Politicisation of Martyrdom in Early Modern England', in Thomas S. Freeman and Thomas F. Mayer (eds), *Martyrs and Martyrdom in England c.1400–1700* (Woodbridge, 2007), 35–69.

Fury, Cheryl A. (ed.), *The Social History of English Seamen, 1485–1659* (2012).

Gawne, C. W., *The Isle of Man and Britain Controversy 1651–1895: From Smuggling to the Common Purse* (Douglas, 2009).

Gilbert, Davies, *The Parochial History of Cornwall*, 4 vols (1838).

Gillis, John, *Islands of the Mind: How the Human Imagination Created the Atlantic World* (Basingstoke and New York, 2004).

Gillis, John R., 'The Blue Humanities', *Humanities*, 34 (2013), 10–13.

Goodwins, Sara, *A Brief History of the Isle of Man* (Sutton, 2011).

Gough, J. W., *The Superlative Prodigall: A Life of Thomas Bushell* (Bristol, 1932).

Granville, Roger, *The King's General in the West: The Life of Sir Richard Granville, Bart., 1600–1659* (1908).

Greaves, Richard L., *Deliver Us from Evil: The Radical Underground in Britain, 1660–1663* (Oxford and New York, 1986).

Greaves, Richard L., *Enemies under His Feet: Radicals and Nonconformists in Britain, 1664–1677* (Stanford, 1990).

Greaves, Richard L., and Robert Zaller (eds), *Biographical Dictionary of British Radicals in the Seventeenth Century*, 3 vols (Brighton, 1982).

Greene, Jack P., *Peripheries and Center: Constitutional Development in the Extended Polities of the British Empire and the United States, 1607–1788* (New York, 1990).

Greene, Roland, 'Island Logic', in Peter Hulme and William H. Sherman (eds), '*The Tempest' and its Travels* (Philadelphia, 2000), 138–45.

Gregg, Pauline, *Free-Born John: A Biography of John Lilburne* (1961).

Griffiths, John, 'What is Legal Pluralism?', *Journal of Legal Pluralism and Unofficial Law*, 18 (1986), 1–55.

Grove-White, Robin, 'Hugh Hughes and Late Sixteenth-Century Anglesey: The Public Life of an Elizabethan Welshman', *Transactions of the Anglesey Antiquarian Society and Field Club* (2013), 35–50.

Grydehøj, Adam, 'A Future of Island Studies', *Island Studies Journal*, 12 (2017), 3–16.

Habakkuk, H. J., 'Public Finance and the Sale of Confiscated Property during the Interregnum', *Economic History Review*, NS 15 (1962), 70–88.

Halliday, Paul D., *Habeas Corpus: From England to Empire* (Cambridge, MA, 2010).

Halliday, Paul D., '11,000 Prisoners: Habeas Corpus, 1500–1800', in Paul Brand and Joshua Getzler (eds), *Judges and Judging in the History of the Common Law and Civil Law: From Antiquity to Modern Times* (Cambridge, 2012), 259–76.

Hardacre. P. H., 'The Further Adventures of Henry Norwood', *Virginia Magazine of History and Biography*, 67 (1959), 271–83.

Harfield, C. G., 'In the Shadow of the Black Ensign: Lundy's Part in Piracy', *Report of the Lundy Field Society*, 47 (1996), 60–71.

Harfield, C. G., 'A Gazetteer with Notes: References to Pirates and Lundy', *Report of the Lundy Field Society*, 48 (1997), 37–55.

Harris, G. G., *List of Witnesses in the High Court of Admiralty, 1619–49*, List and Index Society, 335 (2010).

Harris, Simon, *Sir Cloudesley Shovell: Stuart Admiral* (Staplehurst, 2001).

Harris, Tim, *Restoration: Charles II and his Kingdoms, 1660–1685* (2006).

Hasler, P. W., 'Bassett, Robert (1574–1641 of Umberleigh, Devon', www. historyofparliamantonline.org/volume/1558–16–3/member/bassett–robert–1574–1641, (accessed January 2019).

Hay, Pete, 'A Phenomenology of Islands', *Island Studies Journal*, 1 (2006), 19–42.

Hechter, Michael, *Internal Colonialism: The Celtic Fringe in British National Development*, 2nd edn (New York, 2017).

Hill, Christopher, 'Puritans and "The Dark Corners of the Land"', *Transactions of the Royal Historical Society*, 5th ser., 13 (1963), 77–102.

Hillier, George, *A Narrative of the Attempted Escapes of Charles the First from Carisbrook Castle* (1852).

Hindle, Steve, *The State and Social Change in Early Modern England, 1550–1640* (Basingstoke and New York, 2002).

Hirst, David, 'Lunacy and the "Islands in the British Seas"', *History of Psychiatry*, 18 (2007), 411–33.

Hocart, Richard, *The Country People of Guernsey and their Agriculture, 1640–1840* (St Peter Port, 2016).

Hooker, M. B., *Legal Pluralism: An Introduction to Colonial and Neo-Colonial Laws* (Oxford, 1975).

Hoskins, S. Elliott, *Charles the Second in the Channel Islands*, 2 vols (1854).

Hughes, Ann, 'Local History and the Origins of the Civil War', in Richard Cust and Ann Hughes (eds), *Conflict in Early Stuart England: Studies in Religion and Politics 1603–1642* (New York, 1989), 224–33.

Hughes, Ann, *Gangraena and the Struggle for the English Revolution* (Oxford, 2004).

Hulsebosch, Dan, 'English Liberties outside England: Floors, Doors, Windows, and Ceilings in the Legal Architecture of Empire', in Lorna Hutson (ed.), *The Oxford Handbook of English Law and Literature, 1500–1700* (Oxford, 2017), 747–73.

Hutton, Ronald, *The Restoration: A Political and Religious History of England and Wales 1658–1667* (Oxford, 1985).

Hutton, Ronald, *The Royalist War Effort, 1642–1646*, 2nd edn (1999).

Ingram, J. H., *The Islands of England: A Survey of the Islands around England and Wales and the Channel Islands* (1952).

'Insularities Connected: Bridging Seascapes, from the Mediterranean to the Indian Ocean and Beyond', report of a conference held in Crete, June 2016, https://medins.ims.foreth.gr/ conference.php (accessed April 2019).

Jarvis, Rupert C., 'Illicit Trade with the Isle of Man 1671–1765', *Transactions of the Lancashire and Cheshire Antiquarian Society*, 58 (1945–6), 245–67.

'A Jerseyman in New England', *Société Jersiaise Bulletin Annuel*, 13 (1936–9), 399–404.

Johnson, Tom, 'Medieval Law and Materiality: Shipwrecks, Finders, and Property on the Suffolk Coast, ca. 1380–1410', *American Historical Review*, 120 (2015), 407–32.

Jones, Jack D., *The Royal Prisoner: Charles I at Carisbrooke* (1965).

Jones, Norman, *Governing by Virtue: Lord Burghley and the Management of Elizabethan England* (Oxford, 2015).

Jones, W. J., *The Elizabethan Court of Chancery* (Oxford, 1967).

Jones, W. J., 'Palatine Performance in the Seventeenth Century', in Peter Clark, Alan G. R. Smith and Nicholas Tyacke (eds), *The English Commonwealth 1547–1640* (New York, 1979), 189–204.

Kearney, Hugh, *The British Isles: A History of Four Nations*, 2nd edn (Cambridge, 2006).

Keeble, N. H., *The Restoration: England in the 1660s* (Oxford, and Malden, MA, 2002).

Keene, H. G., 'The Channel Islands', *English Historical Review*, 2 (1887), 21–39.

Kelleher, John, 'The Mysterious Case of the Ship Abandoned off Sark in 1608: The Customary Law Relating to *choses gaives*', in Gordon Dawes (ed.), *Commise 1204: Studies in the History and Law of Continental and Insular Normandy* (St Peter Port, 2005), 171–90.

Kelleher, John D., *The Triumph of the Country: The Rural Community in Nineteenth-Century Jersey* (St Helier, 1995).

Kenyon, John, and Jane Ohlmeyer (eds), *The Civil Wars: A Military History of England, Scotland, and Ireland 1638–1660* (Oxford, 1998).

Kerrigan, John, *Archipelagic English: Literature, History, and Politics 1603–1707* (Oxford, 2008).

King, David J. Cathcart, *Castellarium Anglicanum: An Index and Bibliography of the Castles of England, Wales and the Islands*, 2 vols (New York and London, 1983).

Kinley, G. D., 'Illiam Dhone's Petition to the King in Council and its Aftermath: Some New Light', *Isle of Man Natural History and Antiquarian Society Proceedings*, 7 (1974), 576–601.

Kinvig, R. H., *History of the Isle of Man* (Douglas, 1944).

Kishlansky, Mark, 'Martyrs' Tales', *Journal of British Studies*, 53 (2014), 334–55.

Knott, John R., *Discourses of Martyrdom in English Literature, 1563–1694* (Cambridge, 1993).

Koster, Patricia, 'Revelations of a Reluctant Jersey-Dweller: Roger Manley in Jersey, 1666–72', *Société Jersiaise Bulletin Annuel*, 23 (1984), 458–69.

Kouremenos, Anna (ed.), *Insularity and Identity in the Roman Mediterranean* (Oxford and Philadelphia, 2018).

Lake, Peter, and Michael Questier, 'Prisons, Priests and People', in Nicholas Tyacke (ed.), *England's Long Reformation 1500–1800* (1998), 195–33.

Lamont, William M., *Marginal Prynne 1600–1669* (1963).

Larn, Richard, *Cornish Shipwrecks. Volume 3, The Isles of Scilly* (New York, 1971).

Larn, Richard (ed.), *'Poor England has lost so many men': The Loss of Queen Anne's Man o' War* Association (St Mary's, Isles of Scilly, 2006).

Lawrence, D. H., 'The Man Who Loved Islands', in *The Tales of D. H. Lawrence* (1934), 917–39.

Lenfestey, Hugh, 'Homage and Suit-of-Court in the Channel Islands Denoting Allegiance to the English Crown', *La Société Guernesiaise Report and Transactions*, 25 (2004), 674–88.

Le Quesne, Charles, *A Constitutional History of Jersey* (1856).

Lister, T. H., *Life and Administration of Edward, First Earl of Clarendon*, 3 vols (1838).

Loft, Philip, 'A Tapestry of Laws: Legal Pluralism in Eighteenth-Century Britain', *Journal of Modern History*, 91 (2019), 276–310.

Loomie, Albert J., 'An Armada Pilot's Survey of the English Coastline, October 1597', *Mariner's Mirror*, 49 (1962), 288–300.

McCann, Hilton, *Offshore Finance* (Cambridge, 2006).

MacCannell, Daniel, ' "Dark Corners of the Land"? A New Approach to Regional Factors in the Civil Wars of England and Wales', *Cultural and Social History*, 7 (2010), 171–89.

McCarthy, William J., 'Gambling on Empire: The Economic Role of Shipwreck in the Age of Discovery', *International Journal of Maritime History*, 23 (2011), 69–84.

McCusker, Maeve, and Anthony Soares (eds), *Islanded Identities: Constructions of Postcolonial Cultural Insularity* (Amsterdam and New York, 2011).

McMahon, Elizabeth, *Islands, Identity and the Literary Imagination* (London and New York, 2016).

McRae, Andrew, *Literature, Satire and the Early Modern State* (2004).

McRae, Andrew, 'Stigmatizing Prynne: Seditious Libel, Political Satire and the Construction of Opposition', in Ian Atherton and Julie Sanders (eds), *The 1630s: Interdisciplinary Essays* (Manchester, 2006), 171–88.

Major, Philip, 'Thomas Fairfax, Lord of Man', *Notes and Queries*, 54/1 (2007), 43–45.

Major, Philip, *Writings of Exile in the English Revolution and Restoration* (Farnham and Burlington, VT, 2013).

Marsh-Smith, Lucy, 'A Very Particular Remedy; Doleance in the Crown Dependencies', *Jersey and Guernsey Law Review*, 15/2 (2011), https://www.jerseylaw.je/publications/jglr/Pages/JLR1106_Marsh-Smith.aspx (accessed July 2019).

Marshall, H. E., *Our Island Story: A Child's History of England* (1905).

Martin, Amanda, *The Isles of Scilly Museum: Inside the Archipelago* (St Mary's, 2011).

Matthews, A. G., *Walker Revised* (Oxford, 1948, 1988 edn).

Matthews, G. Forrester, *The Isles of Scilly: A Constitutional, Economic and Social Survey of the Development of an Island People from Early Times to 1900* (1960).

Melikan, Rose, 'Shippers, Salvors, and Sovereigns: Competing Interests in the Medieval Law of Shipwreck', *Journal of Legal History*, 11 (1990), 163–82.

Mentz, Steven, 'Toward a Blue Cultural Studies: The Sea, Maritime Culture, and Early Modern English Literature', *Literature Compass*, 6 (2009), 997–1013.

Mentz, Steve, *Shipwreck Modernity: Ecologies of Globalization, 1550–1719* (Minneapolis, 2015).

Merry, Sally Engle, 'Legal Pluralism', *Law and Society Review*, 22 (1988), 869–96.

Miller, Amos C., *Sir Richard Grenville of the Civil War* (1979).

Milton, Anthony, *Laudian and Royalist Polemic in Seventeenth-Century England: The Career and Writings of Peter Heylyn* (Manchester, 2007).

Ministry of Justice, *Fact Sheet on the UK's Relationship with the Crown Dependencies* (2014).

Monod, Paul, 'Dangerous Merchandize: Smuggling, Jacobitism, and Commercial Culture in Southeast England, 1690–1760', *Journal of British Studies*, 30 (1991), 150–87.

Moore, A. W., *A History of the Isle Man*, 2 vols (1900).

Moore, David W., *The Other British Isles: A History of Shetland, Orkney, the Hebrides, Isle of Man, Anglesey, Scilly, Isle of Wight and the Channel Islands* (Jefferson, NC, and London, 2005).

Morieux, Renaud, *The Channel: England, France and the Construction of a Maritime Border in the Eighteenth Century* (Cambridge, 2016).

Morrill, John, 'The Ecology of Allegiance in the English Civil Wars', *Journal of British Studies*, 26 (1987), 451–67.

Morrill, John, 'Three Kingdoms and One Commonwealth? The Enigma of Mid-Seventeenth-Century Britain and Ireland', in Alexander Grant and K. J. Stringer (eds), *Uniting the Kingdom? The Making of British History* (1995), 170–92.

Morrill, John, *The Revolt in the Provinces: The People of England and the Tragedies of War 1630–1648* (1999).

Morriss, Andrew P. (ed.), *Offshore Financial Centers and Regulatory Competition* (Washington, 2010).

Mortimer, Sarah, *Reason and Religion in the English Revolution: The Challenge of Socinianism* (Cambridge, 2010).

Muller, Hannah Weiss, *Subjects and Sovereign: Bonds of Belonging in the Eighteenth-Century British Empire* (Oxford and New York, 2017).

Murphy, Elaine, *Ireland and the War at Sea, 1641–1653* (Woodbridge, 2012).

Murray, K. M. E., *The Constitutional History of the Cinque Ports* (Manchester, 1935).

Nash, Robert C., 'The English and Scottish Tobacco Trades in the Seventeenth and Eighteenth Centuries: Legal and Illicit Trade', *Economic History Review*, NS 35 (1982), 354–72.

Neeson, Jeannette Mary, 'Coastal Commons: Custom and the Use of Seaweed in the British Isles *c*.1700–1900', in Simonetta Cavaicocchi (ed.), *Ricchezza del Mar: secc. XII–XVIII* (Florence, 2006), 343–67.

Newbolt, Henry, *The Island Race* (1898).

Nicole, Edmund Toulmin, 'Some Account of the Jersey Revolution of 1769 and of the Political Parties in Jersey at the End of the 18th Century', *Société Jersiaise Bulletin Annuel*, 9 (1922), 311–22.

Nicolle, Jason St John, 'New Evidence for the Population of Jersey in the Seventeenth and Eighteenth Centuries', *Société Jersiaise Bulletin Annuel*, 25 (1990), 463–67.

Norbrook, David, '"This blushing tribute of a borrowed muse"; Robert Overton and his Overturning of the Poetic Canon', *English Manuscript Studies, 1100–1700*, 4 (1993), 220–66.

Ogier, D. M., *Reformation and Society in Guernsey* (Woodbridge, 1996).

Ogier, Darryl, 'Night Revels and Werewolfery in Calvinist Guernsey', *Folklore*, 109 (1998), 53–62.

Ogier, Darryl, *The Government and Law of Guernsey* (St Peter Port, 2005).

Ohlmeyer, Jane H., *Civil War and Restoration in the Three Stuart Kingdoms: The Career of Randall MacDonnell, Marquis of Antrim, 1609–1683* (Cambridge, 1993).

Ollard, Richard, *Clarendon and his Friends* (New York, 1988).

Oudendijk, J. K., *Status and Extent of Adjacent Waters: A Historical Orientation* (Leyden, 1970).

'Our Island Story', http://www.telegraph.co.uk/culture/books/booknews/8094333/Revealed-, David-Camerons-favourite-childhood-book-is-Our-Island-Story.html, accessed April 2018.

Oxford Dictionary of National Biography.

Ozanne, Christine, 'Contemporary Accounts of the Explosion at Castle Cornet, December 1672', *Reports and Transactions of Société Guernesiase* (1930), 41–55.

Parker, Geoffrey, *Global Crisis: War, Climate Change and Catastrophe in the Seventeenth Century* (London and New Haven, 2013).

Payne, J. Bertrand, *The Gossiping Guide to Jersey* (1865).

Pearce, Cathryn J., *Cornish Wrecking, 1700–1860: Reality and Popular Myth* (Woodbridge, 2010).

Pelley, Jean Le, 'The Knight of the Golden Tulip: John Lambert at Castle Cornet 1660/70', *Report and Transaction of Société Guernesiase* 18 (1969), 409–15.

Phillips, John Roland, *Memoirs of the Civil War in Wales and the Marches 1642–1649*, 2 vols (1874).

Pickwell, J. G., 'Improbable Legends Surrounding the Shipwreck of Sir Clowdisley Shovell', *Mariner's Mirror*, 59 (1973), 221–3.

Platt, Colin, and Neil Rushton, *Tudor Mont Orgueil and its Guns* (St Helier, 2012).

Platt, Richard, *Smuggling in the British Isles: A History* (Stroud, 2007).

Pocock, J. G. A., *The Discovery of Islands: Essays in British History* (Cambridge, 2005).

Pocock, J. G. A., 'British History: A Plea for a New Subject' [1974] in Pocock, *The Discovery of Islands: Essays in British History* (Cambridge, 2005), 28–43.

Pocock, J. G. A., 'The Atlantic Archipelago and the War of the Three Kingdoms' [1996], in Pocock, *The Discovery of Islands: Essays in British History* (Cambridge, 2005), 77–91.

Powell, J. R., 'Blake's Reduction of the Scilly Isles in 1651', *Mariner's Mirror*, 17 (1931), 205–22.

Powell, J. R., 'Blake's Reduction of Jersey in 1651', *Mariner's Mirror*, 18 (1932), 64–80.

Poynting, Sarah, 'Deciphering the King: Charles I's Letters to Jane Whorwood', *Seventeenth Century*, 21 (2006), 128–40.

Pretty, David A., *Anglesey: The Concise History* (Cardiff, 2002).

Priaulx, T. F., 'The Guernsey Stocking Export Trade in the Seventeenth Century', *Report and Transactions. Société Guernesiase*, 17 (1961), 210–22.

Purkiss, Diane, *The English Civil War: A People's History* (2006).

'A Report on Guernsey Lunacy Administration', *British Medical Journal*, 2 June 1906, 1289–92.

Richards, Thomas, 'The Puritan Movement in Anglesey: A Re-Assessment', *Transactions of the Anglesey Antiquarian Society and Field Club* (1954), 34–58.

Robertson, Barry, *Royalists at War in Scotland and Ireland, 1638–1650* (Abingdon and New York, 2016).

Rogers, Edward, *Some Account of the Life and Opinions of a Fifth-Monarchy-Man* (1867).

Rowland, Alan, Michael Williams, André Coutanche, and Roger Chapple, 'A Particular of Lundy Island: The Clayton Manuscript', *Journal of the Lundy Field Society*, 6 (2018), 7–34.

Rowse, A. L., *Tudor Cornwall* (1941, 1969 edn).

Royal Commission on Ancient and Historical Monuments in Wales and Monmouthshire, *An Inventory of the Ancient Monuments in Anglesey* (1937, repr. 1960).

Royle, Stephen A., *A Geography of Islands: Small Island Insularity* (2001).

Rule, John, 'Wrecking and Coastal Plunder', in Douglas Hay, Peter Linebaugh, John Rule, et al. (eds), *Albion's Fatal Tree: Crime and Society in Eighteenth-Century England* (1975), 167–88.

Russell, Conrad, *The Causes of the English Civil War* (Oxford, 1990).

Saunders, A. C., *Jersey in the 17th Century* (St Helier, 1931).

Saunders, A. C., *Jersey in the 15th and 16th Centuries* (St Helier, 1933).

Saunders, A. C., *Jean Chevalier and his Times: A Story of Sir George Carteret, Baronet, and The Great Rebellion* (St Helier, 1937).

Sausmarez, Havilland de, 'Guernsey's *Précept d'Assise* of 1441: Translation and Notes', *Jersey and Guernsey Law Review*, 12 (2008), 207–19.

Schickler, Fernand de, *Les Églises du refuge en Angleterre*, 3 vols (Paris, 1892).

Schwyzer, Philip, and Simon Mealor (eds), *Archipelagic Identities: Literature and Identity in the Atlantic Archipelago, 1550–1800* (Aldershot and Burlington, 2004).

Schwyzer, Philip, 'Archipelagic History', in Paulina Kewes, Ian W. Archer, and Felicity Heal (eds), *The Oxford Handbook of Holinshed's Chronicles* (Oxford, 2013), 593–607.

Scott, Eva, *The King in Exile: The Wanderings of Charles II from June 1646 to July 1654* (1905).

'Seigneurial Rights of Wreckage Disputed', *Société Jersiaise Bulletin Annuel*, 11 (1928–31), 417–18.

Senior, Clive, *A Nation of Pirates: English Piracy in its Heyday* (Newton Abbot, 1976).

Sharpe, James, 'Towards a Legal Anthropology of the Early Modern Isle of Man', in Richard McMahon (ed.), *Crime, Law, and Popular Culture in Europe 1500–1900* (2008), 118–37.

Sharpe, James, 'Witchcraft in the Early Modern Isle of Man', *Cultural and Social History*, 4 (2007), 11–28.

Sharpe, Kevin, *The Personal Rule of Charles I* (New Haven and London, 1992).

Sharpe, Sybil, 'The Isle of Man—in the British Isles but not Ruled by Britain: A Modern Peculiarity from Ancient Occurrences', in Peter Davey and Peter Finlayson (eds), *Mannin Revisited: Twelve Essays on Manx Culture and Environment* (Edinburgh, 2002), 161–72.

Shifflett, Andrew, '"A Most Humane Foe": Colonel Robert Overton's War with the Muses', in Claude J. Summers et al. (eds), *The English Civil Wars in the Literary Imagination* (Columbia, MO, 1999), 159–73.

'Shipwreck', http://www.hmssurprise.org/shipwreck-sir-cloudesley-shovell (accessed April 2018).

Smith, Geoffrey, *The Cavaliers in Exile 1640–1660* (Basingstoke and New York, 2003).

Smith, Joseph Henry, *Appeals to the Privy Council from the American Plantations* (New York, 1950, repr. 1965).

Smith, M. G., 'Bishop Trelawny and the Church in the Channel Islands 1680–1730', *Société Jersiaise Bulletin Annuel*, 23 (1983), 320–30.

Southcombe, George, and Grant Tapsell, *Restoration Politics, Religion and Culture: Britain and Ireland, 1660–1714* (Basingstoke, 2010).

Spriggs, Matthew, 'Where Cornish was Spoken and when: A Provisional Synthesis', *Cornish Studies*, ser.2, 11 (2003), 228–69.

Spufford, Margaret, *Contrasting Communities: English Villagers in the Sixteenth and Seventeenth Centuries* (Cambridge, 1974).

Spurr, John, *The Restoration Church of England, 1646–1689* (New Haven and London, 1991).

Steckley, George F., 'The Seventeenth-Century Origins of Modern Salvage Law', *Journal of Legal History*, 35 (2014), 209–30.

Stevens, Todd, 'Wreck of the *Princess (Prinses) Maria*, Scilly, 1686', http://scillypedia.co.uk/WreckPrinsesMaria.htm (accessed November 2018).

Stone, Percy Goddard, *The Architectural Antiquities of the Isle of Wight from the XIth to the XVIIIth Centuries* (1891).

Stoyle, Mark, *West Britons: Cornish Identities and the Early Modern British State* (Exeter, 2002).

Stoyle, Mark, '"Fullye Bente to Fighte Oute the Matter": Reconsidering Cornwall's Role in the Western Rebellion of 1549', *English Historical Review*, 129 (2014), 549–77.

Swinfen, D. B., 'The Daniel and Jersey Prison Board Cases of 1890 and 1894', *Société Jersiaise Bulletin Annuel*, 21 (1975), 363–80.

Taft, Barbara, '"They that pursew perfection on earth . . . ": The Political Progress of Robert Overton', in Ian Gentles et al. (eds), *Soldiers, Writers and Statesmen of the English Revolution* (Cambridge, 1998), 286–303.

Tapsell, Grant (ed.), *The Later Stuart Church, 1660–1714* (Manchester, 2012).

Tennant, Bob, 'Managing Overseas Missions: The SPCK in the Scilly Isles, 1796–1819', in Brett C. McInelly and Paul E. Kerry (eds), *New Approaches to Religion and the Enlightenment* (Madison, PA, and Vancouver, 2018), 345–64.

Ternstrom, Myrtle, 'The Ownership of Lundy by Sir Richard Grenville and his Descendants, 1577–1775', *Devonshire Association Report and Transactions*, 130 (1998), 65–80.

Ternstrom, Myrtle, 'Lundy's Legal and Parochial Status', *Devonshire Association Report and Transactions*, 134 (2002), 145–56.

Ternstrom, Myrtle Sylvia, 'Lundy: An Analysis and Comparative Study of Factors Affecting the Development of the Island from 1577 to 1869, with a Gazetteer of Sites and Monuments' (Cheltenham and Gloucester College of Higher Education, Ph.D. thesis, 1999).

Thirsk, Joan (ed.), *The Agrarian History of England and Wales. Volume IV 1500–1640* (Cambridge, 1967).

Thirsk, Joan, 'The Fantastical Folly of Fashion: The English Stocking Knitting Industry, 1500–1700', in N. B. Harte and Kenneth G. Pointing (eds), *Textile History and Economic History* (Manchester, 1973), 50–73.

Thirsk, Joan, 'New Crops and their Diffusion: Tobacco-Growing in 17th Century England', in C. W. Chalkin and M. A. Havinden (eds), *Rural Change and Urban Growth, 1500–1800* (Woodbridge, 1974), 76–103.

Thirsk, Joan (ed.), *The Agrarian History of England and Wales. Volume V 1640–1750* (Cambridge, 1984).

Thirsk, Joan (ed.), *The English Rural Landscape* (Oxford, 2000).

Thomas, Charles, 'A Glossary of Spoken English in the Isles of Scilly', *Journal of the Royal Institution of Cornwall*, NS 8 (1979), 109–47.

Thomas, John, 'A History of Lundy from 1390 to 1775', *Devonshire Association Report and Transactions*, 110 (1976), 113–54.

Thornton, Tim, 'The English King's French Islands: Jersey and Guernsey in English Politics and Administration, 1485–1642', in George W. Bernard and Steven J. Gunn (eds), *Authority and Consent in Tudor England: Essays Presented to C. S. L. Davies* (Aldershot, 2002), 197–217.

Thornton, Tim, 'Nationhood at the Margin: Identity, Regionality and the English Crown in the Seventeenth Century', in Len Scales and Oliver Zimmer (eds), *Power and the Nation in European History* (Cambridge, 2005), 232–47.

Thornton, Tim, *The Channel Islands, 1370–1640: Between England and Normandy* (Woodbridge, 2012).

Todd, Margo, *The Culture of Protestantism in Early Modern Scotland* (New Haven and London, 2002).

Tompson, Richard S., *The Atlantic Archipelago: A Political History of the British Isles* (Lewiston, NY and Queenstown, Canada, 1986).

Tucker, Norman, *North Wales in the Civil War* (Wrexham, 1992).

Tupper, Ferdinand Brock, *The Chronicles of Castle Cornet, Guernsey* (1851).

Tupper, Ferdinand Brock, *The History of Guernsey, and its Bailiwick; with Occasional Notices of Jersey*, 2nd edn (St Peter Port, 1876).

Turner, H. D., 'Charles Hatton: A Younger Son', *Northamptonshire Past and Present*, 3 (1965–6), 255–61.

Turner, H. D., 'Viscount Hatton and the Government of Guernsey 1670–1706', *Report and Transactions. Société Guernesiase*, 18 (1970 for 1969), 415–26.

Tyler, Amanda L., *Habeas Corpus in Wartime: From the Tower of London to Guantanamo Bay* (New York, 2017).

Underdown, David, *Royalist Conspiracy in England 1649–1660* (New Haven, 1960).

Underdown, David, 'Settlement in the Counties, 1653–1658', in G. E. Aylmer (ed.), *The Interregnum: The Quest for Settlement 1646–1660* (1972), 165–82.

Underdown, David, *Revel, Riot and Rebellion: Popular Politics and Culture in England 1603–1660* (Oxford, 1985).

Underdown, David, 'A Reply to John Morrill', *Journal of British Studies*, 26 (1987), 468–79.

Unger, Richard W., 'The Tonnage of Europe's Merchant Fleets, 1300–1800', in Richard W. Unger (ed.), *Ships and Shipping in the North Sea and Atlantic, 1400–1800* (Aldershot and Brookfield, VT, 1997), pp. xvi, 247–61.

Vladeck, Stephen I., with Gregory F. Jacob, 'Detention Policies, ' in Harvey Rishikof, Stewart Baker, and Bernard Horowitz (eds), *Patriots Debate: Contemporary Issues in National Security Law* (Chicago, 2012), 205–23.

Waddell, Brodie, 'Governing England though the Manor Courts, 1550–1850', *Historical Journal*, 55 (2012), 279–15.

Wakelin, Martyn F., *Language and History in Cornwall* (Leicester, 1975).

Warton, R. G., 'St Ouen's Church', *Bulletin of the Societe Jersiaise*, 7 (1914), 433–40.

Washburn, Daniel, *Banishment in the Later Roman Empire, 284–476* CE (2012).

Webb, Stephen Saunders, *The Governors General: The English Army and the Definition of Empire, 1569–1681* (Chapel Hill, NC, 1979).

Wheeler, J. S., 'Navy Finance, 1649–1660', *Historical Journal*, 39 (1996), 457–66.

Willes, Margaret, *The Making of the English Gardener* (New Haven and London, 2011).

Wilson, Kathleen, *The Island Race: Englishness, Empire and Gender in the Eighteenth Century* (2003).

Woolrych, Austin, *Commonwealth to Protectorate* (Oxford, 1982).

Worthington, David (ed.), *The New Coastal History: Cultural and Environmental Perspectives from Scotland and Beyond* (Cham, Switzerland, 2017).

Young, Christopher, *Carisbrooke Castle* (2010).

Index